Choosing And Using Your Home Computer

Choosing And Using Your Home Computer

Edited by
Jonathan Hilton

Guild Publishing·London

This edition published 1984 by
Book Club Associates by arrangement with
Orbis Publishing Limited, London

© Orbis Publishing Limited 1984

The material in this book was designed and
produced by Bunch Partworks Limited and
previously appeared in *The Home
Computer Course*

All rights reserved. No part of this
publication may be reproduced, stored in a
retrieval system, or transmitted in any form
or by any means, electronic, mechanical,
photocopying, recording or otherwise,
without the prior permission of the
publishers. Such permission, if granted, is
subject to a fee depending on the nature of
the use.

Printed in Spain by Grijelmo S.A., Bilbao

Contents

Understanding The Computer

So much is written and spoken about the computer these days, but all too often the most fundamental questions go unanswered: what is a computer, and what does it do?

What Is A Computer?

How do computers 'think' and how much do they 'know'? The answers are vital to understanding computers

THE FUTURE
STARTS HERE!

The question "What is a computer?" is not as easily answered as "What is a television?" or "What is a washing machine?" because the computer, unlike these other appliances, has no single purpose. Digital computers, including those you can buy for £50 in your local high street, are a new breed of machine that can perform an almost infinite variety of jobs, according to the program their owners give them.

The idea of programmability is not altogether unfamiliar to the modern home; after all, many devices such as washing machines and cookers now have a number of different programs built into them so that you can use them in different ways. With a computer, though, the whole function of the machine can be changed by putting in a new program: from a word processor, to an arcade game, to a machine that looks after your accounts, in a matter of minutes.

How does a computer perform so many different tasks? We shall be learning more about that as this book progresses, but first of all let's take a

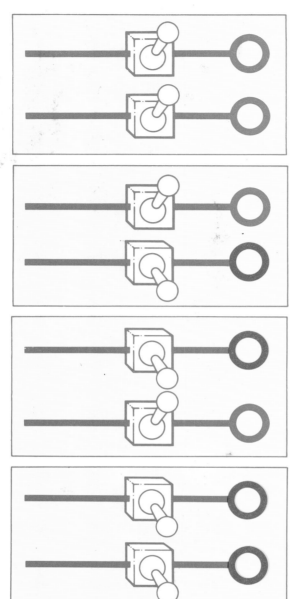

Switching Into Numbers
Computers use electrical circuits to represent numbers. The circuits consist largely of switches. A switch may be in either of two states; on or off. Two switches together can make four combinations of on and off. Computers use a system like this to represent numbers. Off/off is zero, off/on is one, on/off is two and on/on is three. Using groups of more than two allows larger numbers to be represented. Computers can process large numbers and complicated mathematical operations very quickly using thousands of microscopic switches

quick look at some of the principles involved.

On one level, a computer is nothing but a box full of tiny electric switches that can be connected together in different ways. This, however, is not the best place to start if you want to understand what computers can *do*; only the men and women who design and build them really need to understand this level, but the rest of us don't. For one thing a modern computer is an exceedingly complex machine; thanks to the astonishing developments in microelectronics (the famous silicon chip) it is possible for even a small home computer to contain some 250,000 of these little switches. All of these switches can be either 'on' or 'off'. Any pools punter will tell you that the number of combinations of 'on' or 'off' is staggeringly large. For another thing the computer you buy will have a program permanently built into it that disguises this mind-boggling complexity, and allows you to 'talk' to the machine using a few shortened but

easily recognisable English words.

Many people are surprised when they first use a computer because when they switch it on, they discover that it knows nothing useful at all. Oddly enough, the notion is not yet dead that the computer is an 'electronic brain' that is supposed to know everything. Surely it must know what the capital of Afghanistan is called? Or the height of Mt Kilimanjaro? In fact, far from knowing all these things, the silicon chip that forms the 'brain' of a microcomputer doesn't even know the alphabet or any arithmetic. All it understands are several hundred number combinations, and everything else that it can be taught has eventually to be translated into these numbers. The little switches already mentioned can remember numbers; a pattern of ON and OFF switches represents a number (in the binary number system which only uses '0's and '1's). The fact that the computer can remember, in other words, *store,* information, is vital to the way it works; the electronic memory in a Sinclair Spectrum holds information equivalent to six pages of words in this book (it could store much, much more again on tape, but that is all it can hold on its own).

As well as storing numbers in its memory, a computer can do things *to* these numbers: it can add and subtract them, compare them with each other and move them about inside its memory. Everything that the machine can do is built up from these simple acts. Suppose we want to store text in the computer. Let's invent a code, so that each letter of the alphabet is given a number: then the computer can store words as numbers and shuffle them around. We want to play Frogger? Let's take a picture of a frog and draw it in the squares of a grid so that each little square can be given a number . . . It isn't, of course, necessary to invent these codes yourself because all this work has already been done by the manufacturers and designers and put together in the shape of computer programs.

What is a program? It's a list of instructions to the computer to perform those simple actions (add, compare, etc.) in a particular order, just as a knitting pattern tells the knitter how to perform a sequence of simple stitches in a certain order to produce a garment. But what are these instructions, and how do they get to the computer? Actually they are just more numbers and they are also stored in the computer's memory! This seems to present us with a chicken-and-egg paradox. The computer can do nothing without a program to tell it what to do; every time you press the letter 'A' on the keyboard a program inside the computer must scan the keyboard, find out what key you pressed and then tell the computer the number code for that letter. But at some point, when the computer was first designed, this keyboard-scanning program did not exist. Painstakingly, someone had to put the right numbers directly into the keyboard's memory, using special instruments, just to enable it to understand letters typed on its keyboard and to let it show those letters on a television screen.

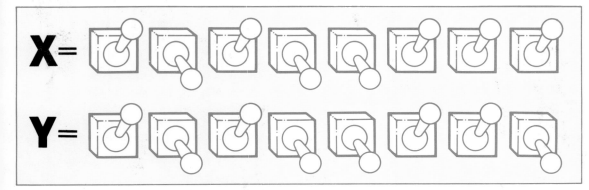

A group of eight switches allows 256 unique combinations of on and off. This is more than enough for an individual code (using nothing more than ones and zeros) for each of the letters, numerals and special signs on a computer's typewriter-like keyboard. The illustration shows how the letters X and Y are represented inside the computer using the ASCII code

But once those first essential programs are made, everything becomes easier. You can now put new numbers into the computer's memory by typing them in. This process is called machine code programming and we'll be talking more about it in the future. But machine code programming is rather difficult and tedious and so some ingenious programmers have written programs (in machine code) that will translate English words like PRINT, BEEP, LOAD and LIST into machine code instructions that the computer can use. All but the most sophisticated home micro-computers have such a program built into them; as a result you can program them in a simple computer language called BASIC, rather than in streams of numbers. But every time you use BASIC (even if it is only the word LOAD to load up Missile Command) remember that the product of hours of programmers' work is already there inside the computer working for you.

With computer languages like BASIC it is quite easy to write programs to do useful or amusing things, and to be blissfully unaware of all the frantic and complex activity that goes on inside the machine merely to detect that you've typed the letter 'A'. For instance, it is a simple matter to write a program that will store away the names of the capitals in the world and produce to someone's query "What is the capital of Afghanistan?", the answer "Kabul". In other words the electronic brain knows only what you tell it in the first place; it can't discover things for itself.

If this is the case, why are computers so useful? Because they can store vast quantities of information, and they can manipulate it much better than people can. And, of course, putting the information there in the first place needn't always be done by *you*. You might buy a program, written by someone else, with all the world's capitals stored on it; in this case the computer is acting like an electronic reference book. Alternatively, you might buy a program that works upon information that you have typed into it: a 'word processor' that lets you type, correct and redraft documents and letters for instance, or a 'database' program that will let you catalogue a huge library of books and find out answers to questions like "What books do I have by George Bernard Shaw published in London before 1926?" in a few seconds.

The fact that the poor dumb computer under-stands only numbers is in practice a strength rather than a weakness. If computers actually dealt with the objects that interest us, say words or colours, they would be many times more complex even than they are now, and you would need a different sort of computer to handle each kind of job. How exactly would you store GREEN in a computer's memory anyway? But once the principle is grasped that the computer does not need to 'undertand' what it is dealing with, in the way that a person does, then one kind of computer can deal with almost anything. All that is necessary is that a programmer should be able to describe the problem in a way that can ultimately be reduced to

WHY SOFTWARE?

The micro is a natural teacher

Useful for letters and accounts

Computers were invented for science

Games and entertainment

A computer is a versatile machine and can assume many roles. Software focuses its power. The same machine can be used by the businessman with business software, the technologist using statistics software, or for entertainment by supplying the computer with games software. It is the software that determines what the computer does

TONY LODGE

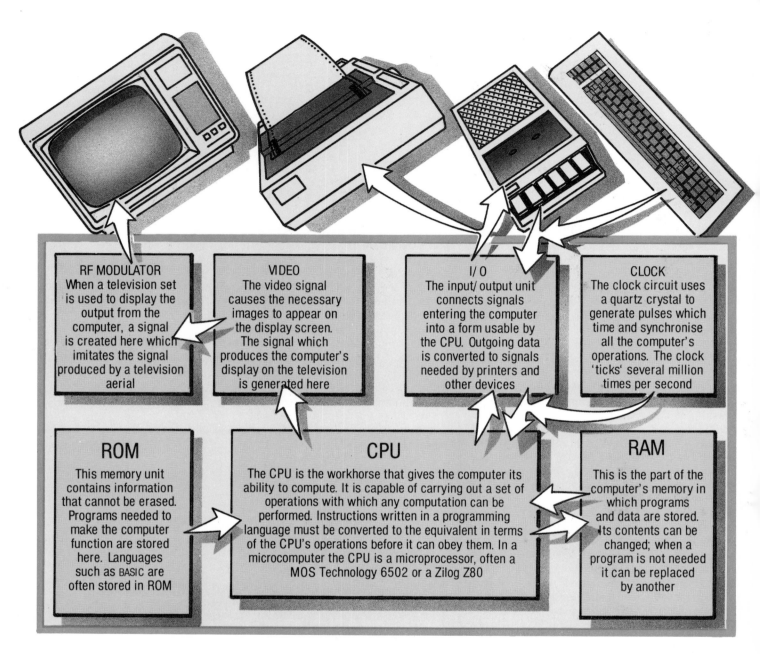

RF MODULATOR
When a television set is used to display the output from the computer, a signal is created here which imitates the signal produced by a television aerial

VIDEO
The video signal causes the necessary images to appear on the display screen. The signal which produces the computer's display on the television is generated here

I/O
The input/output unit connects signals entering the computer into a form usable by the CPU. Outgoing data is converted to signals needed by printers and other devices

CLOCK
The clock circuit uses a quartz crystal to generate pulses which time and synchronise all the computer's operations. The clock 'ticks' several million times per second

ROM
This memory unit contains information that cannot be erased. Programs needed to make the computer function are stored here. Languages such as BASIC are often stored in ROM

CPU
The CPU is the workhorse that gives the computer its ability to compute. It is capable of carrying out a set of operations with which any computation can be performed. Instructions written in a programming language must be converted to the equivalent in terms of the CPU's operations before it can obey them. In a microcomputer the CPU is a microprocessor, often a MOS Technology 6502 or a Zilog Z80

RAM
This is the part of the computer's memory in which programs and data are stored. Its contents can be changed; when a program is not needed it can be replaced by another

What Goes On Inside

To set up a complete computer system and make it ready for use, it is necessary to connect several units together. The silicon chips that make the home computer possible are packed inside the case, usually under the keyboard. Take the lid off and these are the main components you'll find

numbers. For instance, if we want to make a computer produce music, then we certainly wouldn't expect to have real sounds floating inside it; instead we would describe each note of the scale by a number that is proportional to its pitch or frequency. We can arrange for the computer to send the electrical signals that it uses to represent numbers to a loudspeaker instead of a television screen so that we can hear the results. How do we make a missile shoot across the screen towards the oncoming Space Invaders? Merely move some numbers, which represent a missile shape, from one place to another in the part of the computer's memory that acts as a 'map' of the television screen. Pictures, movement, colour, sound can all be given a suitable number code so that the computer can manipulate them, and a suitable 'transmitter', like a television or a loudspeaker, to turn them back into signals that have meaning for us.

So the final answer to the original question "What is a computer?" must go something like this. It is a machine that stores electronic signals that represent numbers. Some of these numbers are instructions that tell the computer what to do with the other numbers. It will follow these instructions, exactly, without tiring, without making mistakes (though it will faithfully reproduce our own programming mistakes) at the rate of many thousands of operations per second. The end result of these tireless manipulations is yet more numbers. These are 'translated' into the information we want, in a form we can understand. It is the activity of human programmers that makes the computer useful, by exploiting its dexterity with numbers to perform tasks that are meaningful to us; taking in information in various forms and transforming it in ways that would otherwise be too tedious, time consuming or complex.

The Micro Buyer's Survival Kit

Set out to buy a computer and you'll be reeling at the range on offer. Here's how to emerge unscathed

Video recorders, television sets and hi-fi systems all have one thing in common — each performs a specific task. The degree of sophistication between different models may vary. But a stereo system can only reproduce sound, a washing machine washes clothes, and a television set just receives and displays broadcast signals.

A computer is different. A hundred people can buy the same computer and each will find a unique task for the machine to carry out. This is why purchasing a home computer is so different from any other item you have bought before.

When you set out to buy a home computer, several factors require careful consideration. The very first thing to do is to write out a check list of the things you want the computer to do. For instance, you may want to learn the fundamentals of BASIC programming — in which case a Sinclair Spectrum or an Atmos may be the machine for you. Alternatively, you may wish to use your home computer to play games, act as a word processor or handle the home accounts — so a BBC or Commodore 64 might be a better choice. Factors such as price and reliability will probably come high on your list.

Your check list should be exhaustive, so that you don't end up with a computer that simply will not do what you want it to.

The home computer of your choice may be only the heart of a system. To exploit its full potential you will also require a means of saving programs for future use. A cassette recorder or disk system are typical methods. You will need a television set so that you can see programs and react to games. Often this will involve buying a second set, particularly if you have a family — they won't take kindly to missing their favourite programmes while you are busy with your micro! For anything other than games you may require printed copies of programs or of results produced by the computer, and for this you will need a printer.

If the computer is to be used purely for games, your main consideration will probably be the amount of software that is available. Here micros such as the Sinclair Spectrum, Vic 20 and BBC score highly, as there is a vast and varied number of programs available for them on cassette.

How much memory will you need? This will depend on the complexity of the programs you want to use. The more complex programs will often be larger in size and will therefore require more memory to hold them. Word processors need large amounts of memory to store text. Generally 32K of RAM should satisfy most needs, although 16K will probably be sufficient to run entertaining games software with good graphics. As a rule, go for a machine with as much memory as you can afford.

Some of the more expensive home computers (such as the BBC, Commodore 64, and Atari 800) can be considered suitable for office use. All three have the facilities for adding disk drives, printers, and modems, which link to other computers via the telephone.

So do make sure that you've thought of everything when you've made out your check list. You should be absolutely clear in your own mind what you want from your home computer before parting with your money.

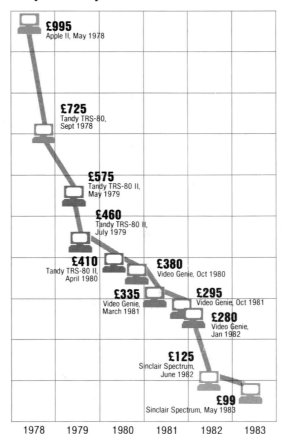

£995
Apple II, May 1978

£725
Tandy TRS-80, Sept 1978

£575
Tandy TRS-80 II, May 1979

£460
Tandy TRS-80 II, July 1979

£410
Tandy TRS-80 II, April 1980

£380
Video Genie, Oct 1980

£335
Video Genie, March 1981

£295
Video Genie, Oct 1981

£280
Video Genie, Jan 1982

£125
Sinclair Spectrum, June 1982

£99
Sinclair Spectrum, May 1983

1978 1979 1980 1981 1982 1983

The Fall In Price Of The Micro

These are selling prices from dealers for the most competitively priced computers with at least 16K of RAM. (Prices do not include an add-on RAM pack)

Setting Up Your System

You need extra hardware for two-way communication with your computer, to store programs — and for some games

Printer

A printer is required when paper copies of programs or printed results from the computer are needed. There are several different types of printer; the price reflects the speed and quality of printing

Disk Drives

Like cassettes, disk drives store programs. Instead of a cassette, a 'floppy disk' is used. Disk drives are much more expensive than cassette recorders but they store more information and work much faster. Generally, disk drives are necessary for business computing

Cassette Recorder

The domestic audio cassette recorder provides a low-cost way of saving programs. The program is stored in the computer's memory while the computer is using it. When the power is switched off the contents of this memory disappear. Before this the program can be recorded on audio cassette tape, and played back into the computer when it is needed again

Television

An ordinary television set allows the computer to display messages. And when you are writing programs, anything you type at the keyboard will also appear on the screen. The monitor shown behind the television is designed to give better-quality pictures with more detail

Joystick

These are similar to the controls found on some arcade games. Their actual use depends on the game being played with them. They might control a spaceship or a character in a maze, for example. Some joysticks have a 'pad' of 10 or more buttons (set out like a calculator); how these are used again depends on the game being played

Track Ball Controller

This is used to play games. By rolling the ball in its holder a game piece can be moved around the screen. It provides much finer, faster, more accurate positioning than joysticks and is more comfortable to use. Buttons are provided for firing 'lasers' and so on

The Computer

The computer is the heart of the computer system, though it needs 'extras' to help it communicate with the user. It has a keyboard similar to that on a typewriter, but with some extra keys. Several sockets are provided (usually on the back of the computer) to connect it to other machines such as the cassette recorder or disk drive and the television set

Controlling Computers

Your computer 'hardware' won't run without the aid of appropriate 'software'. We explain this crucial term — and how to assess the software you find in the shops

Software is the invisible half of a computer system. Without software, the computer is no more than an inert mass of electronic machinery. Without software, the computer can do literally nothing.

Peek inside the silicon chips of a computer and you will find they consist of thousands, perhaps millions, of microscopic electronic switches. Just as a light switch cannot turn a light on or off by itself, the switches in a computer need to be made to turn on or off. They don't all turn on or off together, however. Each individual switch needs to be specifically turned on (or off) and in exactly the right sequence in relation to all the other thousands of switches. Software is how that is done.

Software is the name given to the instructions which make the computer work. These instructions are in the form of numbers which, when presented to the CPU (the heart of the computer; see page 10), set and reset the internal switches to cause specific things to happen. These numbers are only 'understood' by the computer when they are in so-called binary form (converted into ones and zeros as explained on page 43).

These ones and zeros which the computer understands (in the sense that they make it perform specified tasks) are the end product of a long chain of events that started as ideas in the mind of the program writer. A computer program ('program' is the word for any particular single piece of software) can exist in many different forms. The only definite thing we can say about any program is that it must end up in the form the computer understands. Let's take a specific example. Suppose a traffic engineer wants to control a set of traffic lights using a computer. To do this the controlling computer will need a program to make it instigate the correct sequence of events (it's no good having all the lights on green at the same time!). But before this software can be written, the engineer has to think carefully about what exactly it is he wants the computer to do. Usually, these

ROM

ROM (Read Only Memory) is one of the main kinds of computer memory devices. A product of the silicon chip revolution, it allows computer programs to be stored permanently. Most home computers are supplied with a ROM chip containing the BASIC programming language. Other ROMs can be bought for some computers to upgrade their performance by adding another language. Word processor ROMs, which turn the computer into an 'intelligent typewriter', are also available

CASSETTE

Software is often supplied on cassette tape identical to that used in recording sound. Games programs usually come in this form. A program is fed from the tape into the computer by connecting the machine to an ordinary cassette recorder and 'playing' the program cassette. The tape is stopped when the program has been loaded and the computer normally does not need to 'look' at it again

FLOPPY DISK

Software (programs) can be stored by recording it on a disk of magnetic film. The recording is made in 'tracks' on the surface, like the bands on an ordinary LP, by a magnetic 'read/write' head, which also 'reads' (plays back) the program when required. Disks offer a large capacity and a high speed of operation, which have to be paid for: they need sophisticated 'disk drives' (see page 12), which are expensive

CARTRIDGE

A cartridge is essentially a ROM packaged in a convenient housing. Some home computers have readily accessible sockets into which these cartridges can be plugged. The software that comes on cartridges tends to be either a programming language (such as BASIC) or sophisticated arcade-style games

To make your computer work, it needs to be 'fed' with software (a set of electronic instructions). The devices pictured here are the 'media' on which those instructions can be stored. They represent the four commonest ways in which software is supplied. Each has its own special advantages. Software is tailored for each make of computer — a program written for one make will not necessarily work on another.

would be written down using ordinary English sentences (e.g.: At this point I want signal number one to turn on the orange light whilst keeping on the red light. Then I want both the red and orange lights to go off and the green light to come on). Clearly, these sentences are not in a form any computer could understand so they need to be converted into a program. He uses a programming language such as BASIC. A language of this kind allows logically arranged thoughts (in English) to be rewritten in a way that the BASIC interpreter can understand. The BASIC interpreter is itself a program which converts the original program (written in BASIC) into the form understood by the computer's central processing unit (CPU). Software in this form is called 'machine language' or 'machine code'.

The software you actually buy to use with your computer will always be in machine language and it is stored in a form readily accessible to the computer. Sometimes the software is stored in ROM memory inside the computer. More commonly it is supplied on cassette or on floppy disk. These objects are not the software itself, simply the 'media' in which the software is supplied. To be used by the computer, the software has to be transferred from the cassette (or floppy disk or ROM) into the computer. Once these instructions have been loaded (as the process of transferring the software is called) the program can start to operate.

Buying Software

With a couple of thousand pounds in the bank, you might possibly say to yourself "I think I'll buy a car". It's most unlikely anyone would say "I think I'll buy a machine" because the obvious question would be "What kind of machine? What's it supposed to do?"

It's the same with software. A computer by itself is inert, but the software you buy to use with the computer is capable of turning it into a home arcade game, an automated typewriter or an in-house accountant. So the first thing to decide is what you want your computer to do for you.

Start with the problem and then find the software that provides the solutions. In the search for the right piece of software, there will naturally be a refining process as you analyse your actual needs. If the starting point is how to entertain the kids on a Sunday afternoon, the next stage is to find out what kind of programs are likely to provide that entertainment. Computer games range from arcade-style slaughter of aliens to complex and challenging fantasy simulations (see page 106). If an arcade-style game is what you want the computer to provide, the next question is whether or not it's available for your machine.

Since the differences between computers are more than skin deep (each computer has its own electronics inside and requires individually written software) there is virtually no compatibility between models. A program that works on the

FIRMWARE

The origin of the term 'hardware' is obvious: it's the physical and electronic part of the computer — the power supply connections, keyboard, silicon chips and so on. In contrast, software takes its name from its intangible nature, since it consists simply of a set of instructions. Computer experts also talk about 'firmware'. In the early days of computing, 20 to 30 years ago, software was coded and stored on punched paper tape of the kind familiar to telex operators. Then cassettes and magnetic disks took the place of paper tape. In the 1970s a new technique for storing software in ROMs (purpose-designed chips — see page 10) was invented. ROM chips have the software instructions built into them during the manufacturing stage. It is this combination of 'intangible' software and 'concrete' hardware that is called firmware

Being basically a 'blank' machine means that the home computer is uniquely versatile. After being 'fed' with the appropriate software, the same computer is just as happy handling words as an 'intelligent' typewriter, balancing your books, filing information in a database, making cash forecasts in a constantly changing financial environment, or simply playing one of the multitude of games presently available

Handle Words

Word Processing

With word processing software, your computer takes you one stage beyond the typewriter. Even good typists make mistakes, but with a word processor you can have perfectly printed letters every time and increased productivity too.

The computer keyboard takes the place of the keys on the typewriter; the television screen substitutes for the paper in the typewriter. The words you type appear instantly on the screen, just as they do on the paper in a typewriter. But there the similarities end, and the power of the computer takes over.

Mistakes can be corrected instantly — on the screen. Words can be retyped or made to disappear. Even whole paragraphs can be deleted. Word processors do more than just delete words, though. If your thoughts could be expressed better by rearranging sentences, you can do exactly that, right there on the screen. The words or sentences you want to move around the 'page' are temporarily deleted (the word processor program takes them off the screen and stores them inside the computer's memory). They can then be inserted exactly where you want them.

When the document has been written exactly the way you want, it can be printed using the computer printer, or it can be stored on cassette or floppy disk for later use

WHAT DO I WANT MY COMPUTER TO DO?

Balance The Books

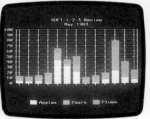

Accounts Package

Since computers can handle mathematical operations, it is hardly surprising that many programs are available to help the businessman. The range of accounting software is impressive, from automated bookkeeping to full accounting. Programs like these usually have to handle large amounts of information and need to store large numbers of records. Consequently they usually require at least one floppy disk drive to cope with the large storage requirements.

Accounting programs generally work through a system of questions (displayed on the computer screen) and answers (supplied by the computer operator). The information typed in by the operator is manipulated by the computer program, all the necessary calculations are done and the results are stored on the floppy disk or printed on the printer as appropriate.

Such programs include the automatic issuing of invoices, reordering of stock, keeping ledgers and keeping track of work in progress. Prices of software range from about £50 to well over £1000 per program. Such expensive software may be a good investment for a business as it saves on labour costs and gives quicker results

Filing

Databases

Computers can search through files of information far quicker than people can; the more massive the amount of information you need to search through, the more a computer can help. At its simplest (and cheapest) a database may be little more than a computerised address book that can look up names, addresses and telephone numbers. More sophisticated and expensive database programs can perform far more complex operations.

To give an idea of the power of a database, consider a botanist who is compiling information for a book on exotic and poisonous mushrooms. He will have built up extensive files on various species and their habitats. He may also have notes on a wide variety of reference books, and an endless list of individual specialists.

Before the days of an affordable computer, this information would have been written out on cards and filed in a card index system. With a database program and a computer, the information can all be stored in the computer's memory. Using the power of the database, the botanist can get instant answers to his problems. If he needs to have a list of all the fungi ever recorded in Sussex, the database can give it to him. If he needs a list in alphabetical order of all the books containing the word 'poison' or 'poisonous' and 'mushroom', 'mushrooms' or 'fungi', the database can give him that too.

Databases need to handle massive amounts of information and are usually available only on floppy disks. They tend to be expensive, with prices ranging from £50 to over £500 per program

Handle Numbers

Spreadsheets

The spreadsheet is the computer's answer to all those 'what if' questions that used to be tackled with a calculator and reams of paper. Any business with a product to sell has many variables. Changing any one of them will generally affect most of the others.

Consider the questions a cinema proprietor might ask. "If all the seats were sold, how cheap could we make the seat price?" or "Would we get more revenue by reducing the price of ice cream with the same number of usherettes, or should we increase the price and employ two more people?". Each decision is likely to affect the entire business — lower prices may mean increased sales but lower profits. A spreadsheet is a special program that can give instant results to questions like these.

All the essential numbers to be manipulated are arranged in a grid of rows and columns and the relationship between each row and column is specified (for example, the numbers in each row of column C is the result of subtracting the number in column A from the number in column B). Once all the real and hypothetical data is assembled, any single figure can be altered and the 'impact' on all the other numbers can be seen instantly.

The people who use spreadsheets are usually businessmen working out costings or engineers and scientists with very variable numerical data to manipulate. Spreadsheets range in price from £30 to over £500 and usually require both disk drives and a printer

Entertain

Play Games

Computers are not only good for processing numbers and words. They can also provide many hours of entertainment if used with one of the many games programs available. These cover a wide range from chess and backgammon to arcade style games and simulations (such as 'lunar lander' and flight simulators). There are also extraordinarily complex adventure games that can take days or weeks to play (see page 106). Many computer games are not only fun, but have considerable educational value too.

Computer games are highly interactive. In other words, they require constant attention and input from the player. This input is usually via the keyboard; a key might be used to fire a 'laser' or a 'missile' or to control the movement of something on the screen. The number of keys used will vary, depending on the game being played, and how much control the program requires.

A popular alternative to keyboard input is the joystick. These are plugged into the computer and operate somewhat like aircraft joysticks. They give greater control, and make playing computer games even more fun

Ready-To-Wear Software

Most off-the-shelf software is sold as a disk or cassette with a manual describing how to use and get the most from the program. Apple Writer is a typical word processor program, costing £120. It comprises a single floppy disk and a comprehensive manual explaining how to use the program. The manual includes a quick tutorial so that beginners can start to use it right away. Standards of documentation vary enormously. Some software comes with manuals so incomplete and badly written that the software may be difficult or impossible to use. It's an important point to watch out for when shopping for software

Atari 800 will not work on the Spectrum (unless a special Spectrum version has been produced), so you have to buy software that has been produced specifically for your machine.

Even now you're not ready to make a purchase. The next considerations are the physical limitations of your machine. Check how much memory your computer has. If it has 16K of ROM see if the game you want needs extra memory to be added. As a rule, the more interesting and sophisticated games require longer programs, so you will need more memory in the computer. And don't forget that software comes in a number of different physical forms (see previous page). If a program is supplied only on floppy disk, but all you possess is a cassette player, you will not be able to use it without first buying a costly disk drive. Some software (particularly games) requires other extras such as joysticks. You are not likely to need a printer for your games, but business software frequently requires one in order to print results.

Finally, there's how much you can afford. Games on cassette start at under £5, but prices can rise rapidly after that. Some business packages on disk cost hundreds of pounds.

Types of Software

In some ways, games are a class apart. The function of a game, after all, is to entertain. Most other software is designed to make a particular job easier and quicker. The ways in which writers of software have managed to increase profitability and efficiency are legion. Consider the poor copytypist whose ability doesn't satisfy the boss. With a microcomputer and a piece of software called a word processor, the computer takes the place of the typewriter and the corrections are all made on screen. Once all the words are seen to be correct, the whole page can be printed out on paper, automatically and at the touch of a switch. The savings in time and frustration are enormous.

Another tiresome task that lends itself to computerisation is financial administration. Many of the activities that used to keep armies of clerks busy — working out salaries and balancing the company books — can now be performed by specially written software. The programs themselves are quite specialised, so it's unlikely that a single piece of software will answer all of a business's needs. Categories include 'payroll' programs to calculate wages and print pay slips, 'stock control' programs to keep tabs on what goods have been sold or used (sometimes the program can order new stocks automatically) and there are even programs to help work out the most economical sizes and qualities of paper on which to print books and magazines.

Another task computers can do spectacularly well is to file and sort information. This type of program is called a 'database'. Databases can replace whole filing cabinets and can do all the arranging and cross-referencing for you.

The final broad category of software is that known as the 'spreadsheet'. A spreadsheet program allows complicated budgets or financial forecasts to be laid out and endlessly tinkered with, replacing reams of paper and the familiar calculator.

All the types of software we have been talking about are sold 'off the peg'. They are ready-made in the sense that the original writer had a specific set of solutions in mind for the problems as he or she envisaged them. There may come a time, however, when no piece of commercially available software will make your computer do exactly what's needed — and then what do you do? One solution, albeit an expensive one, is to hire a computer programmer to write a program exactly tailored to your needs. The other way is to learn how to write programs yourself. Armed with a language such as BASIC it is possible to generate programs that make your computer do all kinds of amazing things. And the only expense is the time it takes you to write the program.

FAUSTO DORELLI

Selecting A Computer

Having made the decision to buy a computer,
the choice available in the high street stores can
be bewildering. The trick is knowing what
questions to ask.

The Small Print

You can't judge a book by its cover — but you can tell a lot about a micro by its technical specification

Keyboard

The keyboard is specially designed to be easy and pleasant to use. Its keys have the standard typewriter-style layout. The character on any key can be displayed repeatedly by keeping the key depressed. Capitals and ordinary letters can be displayed and a separate group of keys (numeric keypad) is provided for entering numbers

Display

The ASCII (American Standard Code for Information Interchange) character set is a standard set of letters, numbers and symbols used by many computers. On some computers the screen displays these characters in 80 columns and 25 rows. The picture can be shown on a television or a special monitor

Memory

The numbers give memory capacity in kilobytes, or thousands of bytes. ROM (Read Only Memory) contains the facilities needed for the fundamental operation of the computer, usually including a language such as BASIC. RAM (Random Access Memory) is for storing the user's programs and data

Interfaces

There are special sockets through which a printer, communications equipment, a cassette recorder and cartridges can connect to the computer. A cartridge is a special ROM which can contain a program, a language or even a new O/S (operating system)

CPU

The CPU is the Central Processing Unit — the silicon chip that is the heart of the computer. This one, a Zilog Z80 microprocessor, is one of the most common. The clock that times all its operations can measure as accurately as 2.2 million times a second

BASIC

The computer's resident language provides commands for using the sound and graphics facilities. It checks instructions given to it to ensure that they are correct: if they are wrong it produces an error message. Screen dump reproduces the screen on the printer. Extra BASIC commands are provided to ensure that programs are written with good 'structure' —meaning that they are easy to read and correct

Sound

Individual notes or chords can be played over a range of five octaves, and the sound signal can be played through a hi-fi system

Graphics

The displays created by Teletext and Viewdata can be shown on the screen which has 256 rows each containing 640 dots for displaying graphics. Perspective views of three dimensional objects can be created and shown

Peripherals Available .

The units that can be attached to the computer include a cassette recorder, floppy disk drive and a hard disk drive. All three store programs and data. A dot matrix or a letter quality printer, a plotter and a digitiser for graphical output and input, can be used for producing words and pictures, and joysticks can be attached for games. A modem is a device for allowing computers to communicate by telephone

Languages Available

These computer languages can be used instead of BASIC; each is well suited to a particular kind of application. ASSEMBLER is a kind of programming language that is more difficult to learn (than BASIC for example) but it makes programs 'run' much faster

Features of "TYPICAL" Computer

Memory	16 Kbytes ROM, 32 Kbytes RAM, capable of addressing 48 Kbytes RAM
Display	Can display ASCII character set 25 rows each with 80 character positions, outputs to domestic TV & monitor
CPU	Z80 running at 2.2 MHz
Keyboard	Ergonomic design, QWERTY keyboard, repeat facility, upper & lower case numeric keypad
Interfaces	Printer interface, communications interface, cassette port, cartridge slot
BASIC	Sound and graphics commands, syntax checking, error messages, screen dump, structured features
Graphics	Teletext and viewdata compatible, max. resolution of 640 x 256, 3-d effect
Sound	Music synthesiser, 5 octaves, hi-fi output
Peripherals available	Cassette unit, floppy disk drives, hard disk drive, printers, plotter, digitiser, joystick, modem, speech synthesiser
Languages available	FORTH, PASCAL, LOGO, LISP, PROLOG, ASSEMBLER

Sinclair Spectrum

Superb colour graphics and the unique Microdrive storage system at an amazingly low price are the star features of the Spectrum — but beware the keyboard

The Sinclair Spectrum is a small personal computer with colour graphics, the ability to produce sounds and a large memory. The main reason for its success is that it is cheap — the 16K version of the Spectrum was the first colour computer to be sold for under £100. The low cost of the Spectrum has resulted in high volume sales which, in turn, have led to the existence of companies producing programs to be run on the Spectrum and extras that can be added to it.

The Spectrum offers a large amount of memory to its users, up to 48K in fact, so that it can act as a vehicle for long programs written in the machine's own BASIC computer language. These programs can be ready-written (stored on cassette, or disks), or they can be written by the Spectrum's users. The Spectrum's version of BASIC, like that of almost any other personal computer, has its own distinctive features, but it is sufficiently close to the generally accepted standard version of BASIC to be familiar to any BASIC programmer.

The facilities of the Spectrum for producing sounds and for creating graphics can both be controlled from BASIC. The Spectrum's control of sound is fairly primitive, using the appropriately named BEEP command. With some ingenuity it can be made to produce a small repertoire of sound effects. In contrast, the colour graphics capabilities are very impressive. They permit the creation of displays with features ranging from the cleverly named PAPER and INK commands for the control of background and foreground colours to commands for drawing circles and causing areas of the screen to flash on and off.

The ready-written programs that are available for the Spectrum include a tremendous variety of games. These range from the ever-popular Space Invaders and Pac-Man types to adventure games and flight simulators, and can display startling originality in their conception.

The Spectrum's capability for expansion has been satisfied to some extent by Sinclair itself with the provision of a supporting printer and storage system, the ZX Printer and ZX Microdrive. However, many other manufacturers provide add-ons for it, and these include joysticks, interfaces with which it can control or communicate with other equipment, typewriter-style keyboards, and sound and speech synthesisers.

The Sinclair Keyboard

The Spectrum has a low cost keyboard with limited movement in the keys. Sinclair opted for an improvement over the flat keyboard of the ZX81 but without incurring the extra costs of a full moving keyboard.

The Spectrum's keyboard uses a single moulded piece of rubber incorporating the keytops, which protrude through the casing. When a key is pressed it closes a contact underneath. The computer then recognises that a key has been pressed and operates the appropriate character. The means to pop the key up again is provided by the elasticity of the rubber sheet, which is stretched when the key is depressed.

This design technique has cut down the cost of the keyboard and has helped make the Spectrum the low cost computer it is

The ZX Microdrive

The ZX Microdrive connects to the Spectrum via an interface attached to the rear of the base of the machine. It provides 100 Kbytes of storage and the average time needed to access stored material is 3.5 seconds

The ZX Printer

The ZX Printer plugs directly into the Spectrum. It prints nine lines of text to the inch. The printer also produces graphics by printing the graphics characters. The contents of the screen can be copied out on the printer using the COPY command

Clock

This electronic clock beats 3.5 million times a second to provide the timing reference for the operations carried out within the Spectrum

Video Chip

The integrated circuit produces the colour signal that is sent to the modulator to produce the display on a televison screen

16K RAM

This is the memory of the Spectrum. The 16K size is made up from 2K memory chips arranged in a row of 8

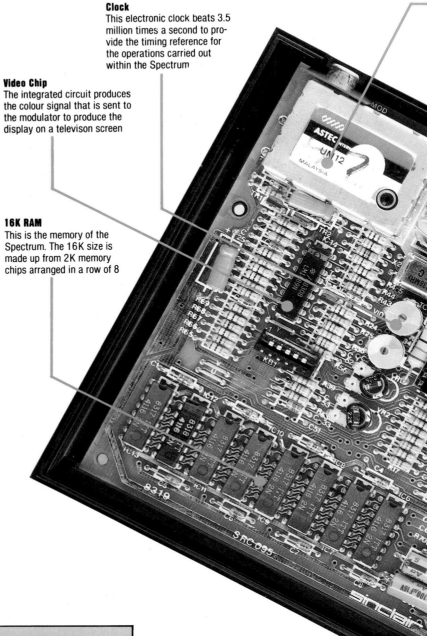

Sir Clive Sinclair

Sir Clive Sinclair founded his first company, Sinclair Radionics, in 1962. The introduction of the first pocket calculator, the Executive, in 1972 confirmed his flair for miniaturising and styling popular products, as well as that for selling them in huge numbers. In 1979 Sir Clive left Sinclair Radionics and founded Sinclair Research. In 1980 he developed the ZX80, followed a year later by a modified and improved version, the ZX81. These were both monochrome computers, but 1982 saw the arrival of the ZX Spectrum. In 1983 Sinclair established his own research centre in Cambridge.

User Memory

This is the memory which is provided with the computer for the programmer to store programs and data. The smaller of the standard allocations is 16 Kbytes, the larger is 48 Kbytes

Heatsink

This large aluminium plate dissipates any unwanted power as heat. The Spectrum will become hot after being left on for a long time, which means that this plate is doing its job

Keyboard Socket

This is where the keyboard plugs into the main computer

Modulator
This takes the colour signal from the video chip and converts it to a signal of the same type as that broadcast to the aerial of a television set to produce its display

Ear and Microphone Sockets
These sockets are for use with a cassette recorder to transfer information to the computer from a cassette and vice versa

Power Socket
This is where the nine volt power supply from the Spectrum's power supply unit is connected to the computer

Input/Output Chip
This converts inputs from the keyboard and cassette unit to a form suitable for use by the computer, and changes information from the computer to the appropriate form when it is to be displayed on the screen

Edge Connector
This is where peripherals such as the ZX Printer are attached to the Spectrum

Microprocessor
This is the computing engine at the heart of the Spectrum. It is a Zilog Z80A microprocessor

Basic Chip
This chip provides the Spectrum's BASIC programming language. It is a 16 Kbyte ROM. The chip examines the program instructions given to the Spectrum and translates them into a suitable form for the microprocessor to carry them out

Voltage regulator
This accepts the nine volt supply from the power socket and converts it to the levels needed by the various electronic components in the Spectrum

Speaker
This small electric buzzer generates the sounds which the Spectrum can produce

SINCLAIR SPECTRUM

PRICE
£99.95 for 16K model (approx)

SIZE
232 x 144 x 30mm

WEIGHT
552g

CPU
Z80A

CLOCK SPEED
3.5MHz

MEMORY
16 Kbytes of RAM expandable to 48 Kbytes. 16 Kbyte ROM containing BASIC

VIDEO DISPLAY
24 lines with 32 character positions, or 192 x 256 dots for high resolution graphics. Both modes have 8 colours

INTERFACES
TV connector, cassette connector (no remote control), 28-pin edge connector for connecting peripherals

LANGUAGE SUPPLIED
BASIC

OTHER LANGUAGES AVAILABLE
FORTH, PASCAL, LISP, LOGO, PROLOG

COMES WITH
Power supply unit (but no plug), aerial lead, cassette leads, demonstration cassette, 2 manuals

KEYBOARD
40 moving keys all on a single rubber sheet

DOCUMENTATION
The Spectrum comes with a thin introductory manual on setting up the machine and a more substantial manual on BASIC programming. The latter begins with a tour of the keyboard that really needs to be more detailed to describe to the beginner how the various shift keys are used. The chapters on BASIC programming demonstrate the Spectrum's capabilities with numerous examples of individual commands and a number of short programs.

A series of appendices provides a fairly complete reference guide to the Spectrum and its BASIC. The manuals are well produced and give a complete coverage, respectively, of how to set up the Spectrum and of the machine's capabilities

Tandy MC-10

Although clearly designed to be low in price this computer offers good colour, and many features of more expensive machines

Reset Button
Because it's large and bright red, the reset button is much easier to find than on some other machines. When using the MC-10, take care not to bump the back of the machine too hard here

Cassette Interface
Remote control is provided through this five-pin DIN plug on pins 1 and 3. Signal input is on pin 4, output on 5, and the signal ground is on pin 2

System Bus
This is not explained in the manual, though it is obviously intended to be used with some unspecified expansion units. There are, however, enough lines to handle some complex devices

ROM
This is soldered firmly onto the board, and so is not likely to be replaced with upgrades or alternatives. The Microsoft BASIC is stored on the 8 Kbytes of ROM

Tandy MC-10 Keyboard
The keyboard is a button-type, but it's better than many. The keys are hard plastic with engraved legends that take longer to wear off, and there's a real space bar. Unfortunately, there's only one SHIFT key, which is placed on the right-hand side, and the large button on the left is the more conveniently positioned CONTROL key. The feel of the keys is comfortable, but they are not suitable for speed-typing

RS232 Interface
This is also a DIN plug, but is constructed of four pins. Carrier detect is on pin 1, receive data on pin 2, ground is on pin 3 and transmit data on pin 4

CPU
Unusually, the Tandy MC-10 uses a 6803 processor, rather than one of the more popular types. This processor is a member of one of the older families, and isn't as well-known as the 6502 or Z80. However, it's a useful 8-bit chip with a reasonable instruction set

Static RAM
The nominal 4 Kbytes of user RAM is held on these two 2 Kbytes x 8-bit static RAM chips, as are the screen RAM and some system variables

6847 VDP
In common with many other machines, the screen is controlled by a special chip, which in this case is the MC 6847 Video Display Processor. This chip is the same as that used in the Dragon 32, and (in theory at least) can be programmed for different screen formats. In practice, however, this is seldom done

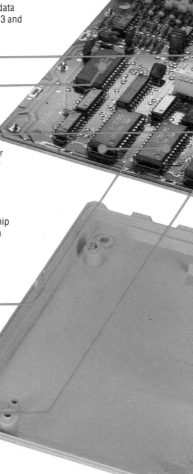

The Tandy MC-10 is a compact little machine that achieves a lot using a few sophisticated chips. The keyboard is a button-type, though slightly larger than others of that kind, and possesses a proper space bar. Other features make the machine quite easy to use. Single-key BASIC keyword entry, for example, is achieved by holding the CONTROL key down while pressing the desired function key. The machine also defaults to 'all capitals' mode when it's switched on, and the lower case mode is a toggle — activated by pressing SHIFT 0, and de-activated by pressing the same keys again.

The screen display is smaller than that of most other home computers. There are only 16 lines of 32 characters, and only fairly low resolution graphics can be achieved. The display has other shortcomings as well, including rather limited colour facilities, although the quality of the colour is very good. Most surprisingly, it will not display lower case characters, which are recognised but shown as inverse upper case letters instead. Text can only be green on black or vice versa, and though the block-graphic symbols may be in any one of nine colours, either the letter or the

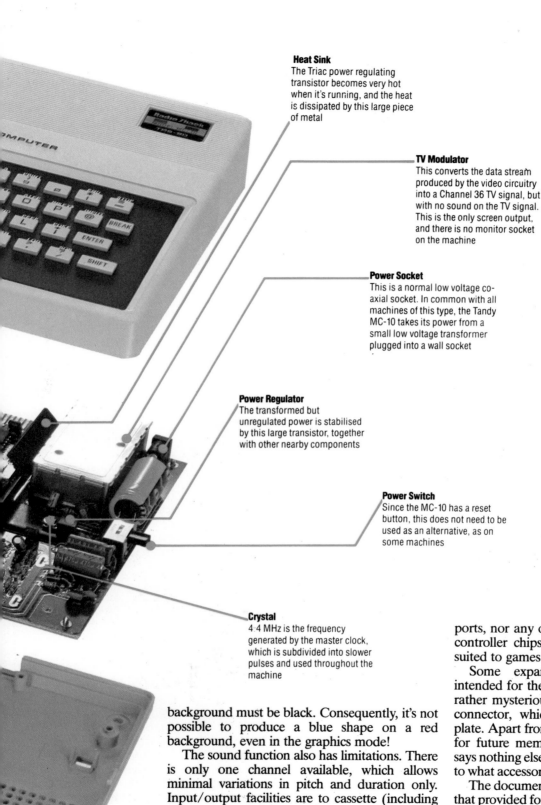

Heat Sink
The Triac power regulating transistor becomes very hot when it's running, and the heat is dissipated by this large piece of metal

TV Modulator
This converts the data stream produced by the video circuitry into a Channel 36 TV signal, but with no sound on the TV signal. This is the only screen output, and there is no monitor socket on the machine

Power Socket
This is a normal low voltage co-axial socket. In common with all machines of this type, the Tandy MC-10 takes its power from a small low voltage transformer plugged into a wall socket

Power Regulator
The transformed but unregulated power is stabilised by this large transistor, together with other nearby components

Power Switch
Since the MC-10 has a reset button, this does not need to be used as an alternative, as on some machines

Crystal
4·4 MHz is the frequency generated by the master clock, which is subdivided into slower pulses and used throughout the machine

CHRIS STEVENS

TANDY MC-10

PRICE	
£99.95 (approx)	
SIZE	
210 x 178 x 51mm	
CPU	
6803	
CLOCK SPEED	
4.4 MHz	
MEMORY	
8 Kbytes ROM 4 Kbytes RAM	
VIDEO DISPLAY	
16 lines of 32 characters, 9 colours with only background settable. 75 pre-defined characters	
INTERFACES	
RS232 serial, cassette	
LANGUAGES SUPPLIED	
BASIC	
OTHER LANGUAGES AVAILABLE	
NONE	
COMES WITH	
Operation and BASIC reference manuals, TV lead	
KEYBOARD	
48 button-style keys	
DOCUMENTATION	
Clear, competent and well-designed but rather lacking in technical information. The only major failing is the absence of an index. A quick-reference card is included, which gives enough details about the BASIC for an experienced person to start working the machine without delay	

background must be black. Consequently, it's not possible to produce a blue shape on a red background, even in the graphics mode!

The sound function also has limitations. There is only one channel available, which allows minimal variations in pitch and duration only. Input/output facilities are to cassette (including remote control), television and an RS232 serial port. The serial port can be used as a data transfer line to and from other computers or, alternatively, to drive a printer. It can also be used to create a network with other Tandy MC-10s.

Games do not seem to have been a high priority with the machine's designers, who provided nothing in the way of paddle or joystick ports, nor any of the special graphics and sound controller chips found in other machines more suited to games playing.

Some expansion possibilities are clearly intended for the future, however, since there is a rather mysterious system-bus ending in an edge connector, which is covered by a screwed-on plate. Apart from stating that 'this slot is reserved for future memory expansion kits', the manual says nothing else about it, and provides no clues as to what accessories will be available to plug into it.

The documentation for the MC-10 is typical of that provided for Tandy's other machines: a rather aloof style of writing with few breaks in a fairly solid text.

As a low-cost machine, it is worth considering, but when reading the specifications remember that while it may have a nominal four Kbytes of RAM, only 3,142 bytes are available to the user, since the screen-RAM and some system variables have to come out of this allocation.

Questions And Answers

Questions about computing that often spring to mind but are rarely answered in the manuals and magazines

What can a home computer be used for, apart from playing games?
Home computers are used to run small businesses, handle accounts, do word processing, and can even keep records of golf club members and their handicaps, or help in designing interiors. These are fairly typical of the uses to which home computers are put. More generally, the uses can be classified as handling numbers, handling words, storing information and displaying information in a way that suits the user.

Computers seem to be getting smaller and cheaper. When and where is this process likely to stop?
Computers are getting smaller as technology continues to advance. The electronic components inside are getting smaller, but the keyboard cannot drastically change its size. It must remain large enough to be used by our fingers. For this reason, computers are unlikely to become much smaller until the traditional keyboard is replaced by other ways of communicating with the computer. With several computers costing less than £100, it is unlikely that prices can drop much below this level.

Is BASIC a difficult language to learn?
BASIC itself is not at all difficult to learn. By comparison with English, which after all is a language that we have all learnt, BASIC is a small language with rigid rules. This makes it much easier to learn than a foreign language.
Although the elements of BASIC are easy to learn, it is not so easy to write very long and complicated programs.

When should I start learning BASIC?
The best time to start is when you need to. It may be that the computer can be made to do exactly what you want by running a program that you can buy. In that case, you don't need to learn BASIC at all. Unfortunately, programs you can buy do not always do exactly what you want. By learning a little BASIC you can sometimes adapt them to your needs. In the end, though, to make the computer do all the things you want, so that it really is a personal computer, you need to start learning BASIC as soon as possible.

A monitor seems to be more expensive than a television. What extra do I get for the money?
You get a much clearer and crisper display on its screen. If you expect to spend any length of time using your computer, a lot of it will be spent looking at the screen, and you will be less likely to get a headache if it is clear and easy to read. Besides this, any graphic images you create with the computer will look better on a monitor (see page 90).

How much electricity does a home computer use?
Less than a 60 watt light bulb.

The advertisements seem to tell me that I can use my computer to help with my children's education. Is this really true?
Yes. They can also help educate adults. The Department of Education and Science has done its best to ensure that every school in the country has a computer, so they are bound to play an increasingly bigger role in education. The key to using them as a learning aid lies in having suitable software. There are many drill programs to teach multiplication tables and spelling, for example. This is not a particularly stimulating way to use the computer, however. A more imaginative educational use is through the LOGO language. LOGO allows children to learn by exploring a so-called microworld and by carrying out experiments to see what happens. Here, the child learns by actually programming the computer. For more on computing for children, see page 108.

Some computers, like the Spectrum, have rubber 'calculator-style' keyboards; others, like the Dragon, have 'typewriter-style' keyboards. What difference does this make?
Very little, unless you are a trained typist, in which case you can type in your BASIC programs at great speed on a 'typewriter-style' keyboard, but not so rapidly on the other kind.

Commodore 64

Commodore's latest home computer offers lively 'sprite' moving graphics, and uses your TV or hi-fi speakers to generate high-quality sound

The Commodore 64 is really the first of a new generation of home computers equally suitable for playing games, or assisting in the running of a small business.

Sixty-four Kbytes of memory as standard is enough to cope with sophisticated graphic displays, or business programs such as spreadsheets, word processors, and databases. Some compatability with the Commodore VIC-20 and PET business systems, has increased the range of available software further.

The 64's range of interfaces means that it will operate with most types of peripherals including the VIC disk drive and printers. A complete system, consisting of the computer, disk drive and a printer can thus be purchased for around £700.

Two of the 64's strongest features are: sprite graphics (see page 128) and full music synthesis. Sprites are visual objects created on the screen using high resolution graphics, which can then be moved around using simple commands — ideal for space invaders, aircraft, explosions etc. Such effects are possible without sprite graphics, but require far more programming. On the 64, sprites can be made to move, grow in size, shrink or change colour, or can be made to pass in front of or behind other sprites or stationary graphic objects such as background scenery — giving depth to a picture. It is even possible to detect when two sprites have collided — the cue for an explosion!

The sound synthesis is equally sophisticated, by contrast with the simple 'beeps' and 'squawks' of cheaper machines. In addition to having three separate voices (allowing chords and harmonies instead of just simple notes), the 64 permits full control over the various parameters that govern the sound or timbre of the note being played. In other words, the 64 can simulate a whole variety of musical instruments, and more abstract noises.

The weakness of the 64 is its BASIC language — which is virtually the same version as Commodore were using on their very first computers. Instead of a nice range of user-friendly commands to take advantage of the 64's otherwise superb features, most sophisticated operations require the unfriendly POKE command. Fortunately it is now possible to buy cartridge add-ons (such as Simon's BASIC — about £50) to rectify this deficiency.

Commodore 64 Keyboard

The Commodore 64 has an excellent keyboard with 'sculptured' keys (contoured for easy typing). Besides the normal characters there is a wide range of block graphic characters. A multi-purpose key marked with the Commodore company logo shifts between the various sets of characters. Colours are changed using the CONTROL (CTRL) key and one of the top row of keys.

The four function keys to the right of the keyboard can be assigned special functions within a program, thereby providing shorthand entry of special commands.

1530 C2N Cassette Deck
This is Commodore's own standard and reliable cassette unit and is designed to plug directly into the 64's cassette port. It draws its power from the computer which can also turn the cassette motor on and off

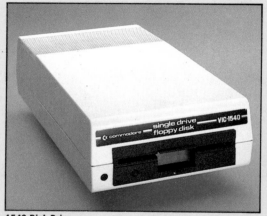

1540 Disk Drive
This single disk drive connects to the 64 via the serial port. One 5¼-inch disk provides 170 Kbytes of storage and the maximum time taken to access any stored information is 2 seconds

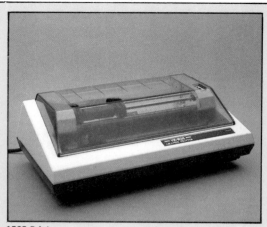

1525 Printer
This dot matrix printer can print all the characters that the 64 can display, including graphics characters. It is connected via the serial port, and prints at 30 characters per second

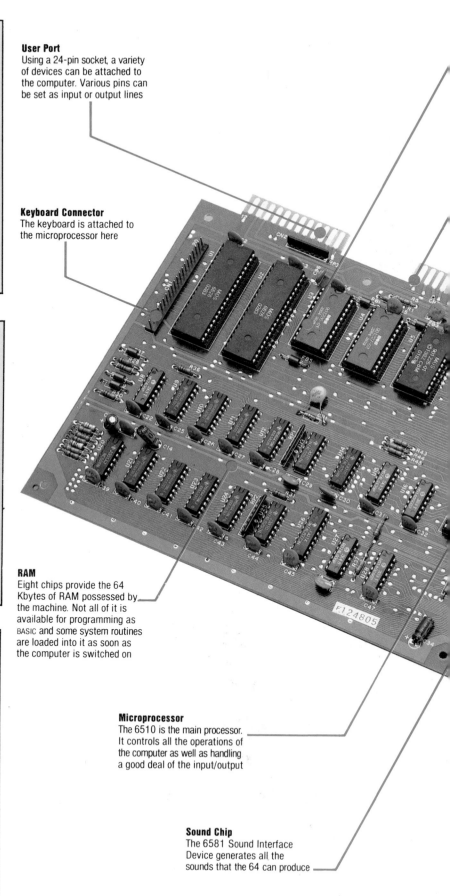

User Port
Using a 24-pin socket, a variety of devices can be attached to the computer. Various pins can be set as input or output lines

Keyboard Connector
The keyboard is attached to the microprocessor here

RAM
Eight chips provide the 64 Kbytes of RAM possessed by the machine. Not all of it is available for programming as BASIC and some system routines are loaded into it as soon as the computer is switched on

Microprocessor
The 6510 is the main processor. It controls all the operations of the computer as well as handling a good deal of the input/output

Sound Chip
The 6581 Sound Interface Device generates all the sounds that the 64 can produce

BASIC ROMs
These three chips contain the computer's BASIC language

Cassette Port
A special port for connecting Commodore's standard cassette deck to the computer. It will not accept other makes of recorder without special modifications

Serial Port
This is a socket for 'serial' communication with additional devices. In serial communication binary digits are sent one after the other

Audio/Video connector
The computer can be connected to a hi-fi system or a monitor via this socket

Cartridge Slot
Cartridges containing languages or programs for games can be plugged in here

Power Socket
This is where the power supply unit is connected to the computer

On/off switch

Video Chip
The 6566 Video Interface Chip generates the high resolution colour graphics and handles sprites. It is covered by a heat protection unit

Games Ports
These two ports allow light pens, joysticks and paddles to be plugged into the computer

COMMODORE 64

PRICE
£200 (approx)

SIZE
404 x 216 x 75mm

WEIGHT
1820g

CLOCK SPEED
1 MHz

MEMORY
A total of 64 Kbytes. 20 Kbytes of ROM supply the operating system and BASIC. A maximum of 54 Kbytes of RAM is available to the user if the BASIC interpreter is not used

VIDEO DISPLAY
25 rows with 40 character positions. High resolution with 320 x 200 dots. 16 colours

INTERFACES
Cassette port, TV connector, cartridge slot, monitor connector. RS232 interface, user port

LANGUAGE SUPPLIED
BASIC

OTHER LANGUAGES AVAILABLE
FORTH, COMAL, PILOT, LOGO, UCSD, PASCAL, and other versions of BASIC

COMES WITH
Power supply unit, aerial lead, manual

KEYBOARD
Typewriter-style keys, QWERTY layout with 62 keys and four function keys

DOCUMENTATION:
The User's Guide is of the low standard associated with Commodore's manuals. The machine, its operation and language are described but not at a level that is entirely appropriate for beginners. It does not provide a comprehensive guide to the addresses of the special registers. This is particularly unfortunate since the sound and graphics of the 64 are programmed using these special registers.

For all but the complete beginner it might be better to ingnore the User's Guide and acquire a copy of Commodore 64 Programmer's Reference Guide', published by Commodore Business Machines Inc and Howard W Sams

Dragon 32

A Welsh computer boasting a new chip and a set of sophisticated graphics

Dragon Data, as the name and logo suggest, is a Welsh company, backed by investors such as the Welsh Development Agency and the Prudential Group but originally founded by toymakers Mettoy.

The Dragon 32 was introduced for Christmas 1982 and achieved instant success because of its full 32 Kbytes of RAM and its Microsoft BASIC interpreter.

The Dragon 32 is highly compatible with the Tandy Color Computer: it is possible to use Tandy add-ons and some game cartridges, but not the cassettes. The two machines use the same microprocessor, the Motorola 6809E (see box), where most home computers favour the 6502 or Z80.

A set of sophisticated graphics commands gives greater control than that offered by many machines with better maximum resolution. Examples of such commands are: DRAW, CIRCLE, PAINT, COLOUR and MOVE.

The Dragon can only play one note at a time, as distinct from computers with more than one 'voice', which can generate chords. But the BASIC commands available make it far easier than on most machines to produce a recognisable tune.

Though well-endowed with interfaces, there are few expansion devices for the Dragon 32 apart from joysticks.

Plans to introduce an upgrade board giving the machine 64 Kbytes of memory are well underway. The recent introduction of the Dragon 64 has greatly increased the company's challenge to the more established manufacturers.

Dragon Disk Drive
This unit comes in two parts: a disk controller card that plugs into the Dragon's cartridge slot, and the main box, which contains one disk drive and costs approximately £275.

CHRIS STEVENS

Keyboard
The Dragon 32 has a typewriter-style keyboard.
The cursor movement keys for up/down and left/right are inconveniently situated at opposite ends of the keyboard. The BREAK key interrupts the operation of a program and CLEAR wipes the screen.
Although the design suggests that a small television might be placed on top of the casing, this is not recommended.

Reset Button
Pressing this has the same effect as switching the computer off and on again but results in less wear on the power supply

Cassette Port
An ordinary cassette recorder can be plugged in here, and Dragon 32 BASIC allows control of the cassette's motor

Joystick Ports
The Dragon 32 can cope with two joysticks for playing games

Printer Port
A standard eight-bit parallel interface allows the Dragon 32 to work with most makes of printer

Video Controller
This chip generates the video signals required by a television or monitor screen from the characters and graphic symbols stored in memory

RF Modulator
Converts the video signals to a form suitable for input to the aerial socket of a television set

Video Interface
Separate red, green and blue signals are provided here for driving the appropriate monitor. This system yields the best quality results

On/Off Power Switch

Interface Chips
Two 6821 Peripheral Interface Adaptors (PIAs) handle all the necessary conversion of signals from the CPU to the keyboard, cassette recorder and external devices such as the printer

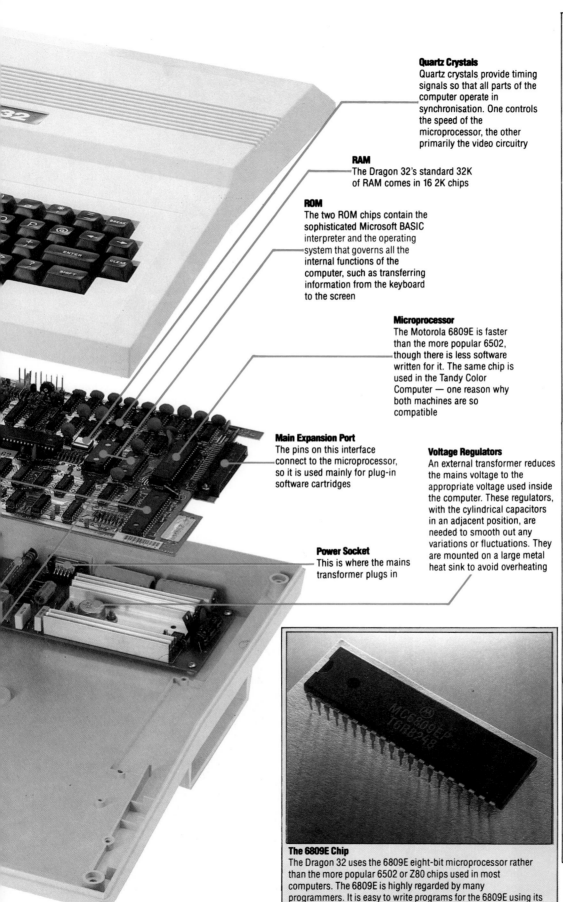

Quartz Crystals
Quartz crystals provide timing signals so that all parts of the computer operate in synchronisation. One controls the speed of the microprocessor, the other primarily the video circuitry

RAM
The Dragon 32's standard 32K of RAM comes in 16 2K chips

ROM
The two ROM chips contain the sophisticated Microsoft BASIC interpreter and the operating system that governs all the internal functions of the computer, such as transferring information from the keyboard to the screen

Microprocessor
The Motorola 6809E is faster than the more popular 6502, though there is less software written for it. The same chip is used in the Tandy Color Computer — one reason why both machines are so compatible

Main Expansion Port
The pins on this interface connect to the microprocessor, so it is used mainly for plug-in software cartridges

Voltage Regulators
An external transformer reduces the mains voltage to the appropriate voltage used inside the computer. These regulators, with the cylindrical capacitors in an adjacent position, are needed to smooth out any variations or fluctuations. They are mounted on a large metal heat sink to avoid overheating

Power Socket
This is where the mains transformer plugs in

The 6809E Chip
The Dragon 32 uses the 6809E eight-bit microprocessor rather than the more popular 6502 or Z80 chips used in most computers. The 6809E is highly regarded by many programmers. It is easy to write programs for the 6809E using its own machine language

DRAGON 32

PRICE
£175 (approx)

SIZE
380 × 325 × 97mm

WEIGHT
2.1 kg

CLOCK SPEED

MEMORY
The 32K of RAM in the Dragon 32 represents quite a substantial amount of memory power, complemented by 16K of ROM containing the Microsoft BASIC interpreter and operating system

VIDEO DISPLAY
The screen can hold 16 lines of 32 character positions. A total of eight colours is available, reducing to two colours at the maximum graphics resolution of 256 × 192 dots

INTERFACES
Cassette, joysticks (two ports), television monitor, cartridge slot, parallel interface for printer, etc.

LANGUAGE SUPPLIED
BASIC

OTHER LANGUAGES AVAILABLE
None

COMES WITH
Power supply unit, aerial lead, instruction manual

KEYBOARD
Typewriter-style layout with 53 moving keys

DOCUMENTATION
The user's manual, written by the computer's designer, Richard Wadman, has been produced to a high standard.
All responses from the computer are printed in a different colour, and there are plenty of helpful hints and tips.
Dragon 32 BASIC is taught from an elementary level to the level of comprehensive graphics and sound. This is followed by a set of appendices including helpful screen layout grids. These are used to create graphic designs before programming.
There is a good choice of books available about the Dragon 32, both instructional courses on programming and listings of programs

Questions And Answers

Could computers have emotions?

Computers do not and could not have emotions at the moment. The really interesting question is: Why not? The computers of today are not intelligent — they cannot think for themselves. How long it will take to produce thinking computers is not known, but probably it will be within the lifetimes of people living today. Some researchers hold the view that creative thought processes are inseparable from emotions. Computers that can think will, according to this view, be computers with emotions.

What is the difference between a computer and a robot?

Robots are mechanical extensions of computers; the arms and eyes do what the 'brain' of the computer tells them. The robots helping to build today's cars and stereo systems all incorporate microcomputers, but they are still fairly 'dumb'. Confronted with an unexpected situation, they simply don't know what to do. The robots of tomorrow will incorporate more sophisticated computers and robots with limited

intelligence are just around the corner.

Why is some software so expensive? Many games programs cost only a few pounds, but business programs often cost hundreds.

Writing large programs, especially thoroughly tested business software, takes teams of highly paid programmers months or years of work. To recoup the huge financial investment and to make a profit, software companies have to sell their products at prices guaranteed to cover costs. A computer game may sell hundreds or even thousands of copies, so a retail price of a few pounds may ensure a profit. If the potential market is strictly limited, the retail price will have to be far higher. Many programs are highly specialised; a printer's estimating package (allowing estimates for printing jobs to be made quickly and accurately) has a potential market limited to the total number of printers in the country. An investment of hundreds of thousands of pounds will have to be recouped whether sales are measured in tens or in thousands.

They say the silicon chip will throw millions out of work. How could a microcomputer make me redundant?

The long-term social effects of the microcomputer are hard to predict, but what seems very clear is that we are witnessing the start of the second industrial revolution. Computers, particularly miniaturised and low-cost micro-computers, when linked to mechanical robots, can easily be adapted to replace expensive manual labour. Even skilled jobs are not safe. Bookkeeping and accounting can now be handled by computer programs, and newspaper typesetters' jobs are threatened now that journalists' word processors can be directly linked to electronic typesetting equipment. Computers can do complex arithmetical processes so quickly, and robots can perform complex mechanical operations so well, that fewer workers are needed to get a job done.

Can computers be used to rob a bank or start a Third World War?

Since computers can communicate with each other using ordinary

telephone lines, it would be possible in theory to tap in to a bank's central computer and issue orders to transfer funds to your account. In practice things are not so simple. The banks use advanced data protection methods to ensure there is no unauthorised access to confidential information. The techniques used involve secret methods of encoding all the information. These codes are almost impossible to break and in many cases are not even available to the bank employees. One of the codes used for highly confidential information is so difficult to crack it has been estimated that the world's most powerful computer would take billions of years to do it.

Breaking into a military

DAVID HIGHAM

computer system would be even more difficult. Military computers generally do not use public telephone lines for this very reason. The microwave and satellite links used are not readily accessible to ordinary people — even dedicated computer buffs. Even if one were able to intercept a microwave link carrying computer information, the problem of cracking the codes would still remain.

BBC Model B

A fine technical specification backed by the marketing and programming resources of the BBC has made this micro popular in both schools and homes

The BBC Model B is manufactured by Acorn Computers in Cambridge and marketed by the BBC. There were originally two models, but the cheaper and less sophisticated Model A is now being phased out.

The Model B has sold very well to schools and is on the official Government approval list for this purpose. A considerable amount of educational software has been developed for this machine — from programming languages to Computer Aided Learning packages.

The technical specification of the Model B is still considered to be extremely fine, despite the number of new machines that have been launched since its introduction. In particular, the programming language BBC BASIC is very well equipped with commands to cope with the special functions. It also makes the task of developing and editing programs easier.

There are eight distinct graphics modes. This means that the user has a choice of low, medium or high resolution, though in the latter case the number of colours available is limited. The maximum resolution obtainable is 640 × 256. Most users opt for a domestic television set, but a dedicated monitor is recommended to get the very best results from the Model B's graphics. Commands exist to draw lines, circles and construct a variety of images on the screen.

Having the power supply unit inside the casing makes the physical design very neat and self-contained, but the interfaces on the back and underside of the case are more numerous than on most machines. This has meant that a large number of devices suitable for expanding the standard computer are available, including several makes of disk drive other than that manufactured specially for the BBC.

In addition to interfaces for disk drive, printer, and an analogue device such as a piece of laboratory equipment or measurement device, there is a facility for networking. This is ideal for classroom use because several users can share one disk drive or printer.

Finally there is 'The Tube' — a sophisticated interface for connecting an alternative micro-processor, either to achieve faster computing, or to run software written for other machines. However, few users seem to have taken advantage of this feature.

Join The Network
If you have a Ceefax Adaptor for your television (or a slightly modified Ceefax set with an extra output), you will be able to receive programs to be broadcast by the BBC.

These will range from games to business programs, and will be periodically updated and upgraded.

Most of the programs will be in BASIC, but programs in machine-code or other languages may also be broadcast.

BBC Model B Keyboard
The keyboard is a strong point of the BBC Model B, in terms of layout, facilities and quality of construction. The keys are properly sculptured, which means that even a touch typist would feel at home.

The four arrow keys on the left hand side are for moving the cursor around the screen for editing text or programs.

The top row of 10 red programmable function keys are particularly useful for educational programs as the user simply has to pick the right answer from up to 10 possibilities.

A pleasing feature is the inclusion of three LEDs (Light Emitting Diodes) to indicate whether the cassette motor is running, and whether the Shift Lock and Capitals Lock Keys have been activated

The Disk Drive
The single disk drive for the BBC micro is a very attractive 'extra' but costs around £260 and stores only 100 Kbytes, making it a rather expensive peripheral. However, cheaper drives are available from other sources and should be considered

Foreign Chips
If you look carefully at the chips, you will see that the manufacture of microprocessors is a very international affair. The BBC Model B contains chips made in Malaysia, Japan, Portugal, Scotland, and the USA

Interface Chip
Versatile interface adaptors such as this MOS Technology 6522 look after the interfacing to external devices. Although they are not processors, these chips are as sophisticated as the microprocessor itself

Analogue Input
This enables the computer to read a voltage from a non-digital piece of equipment such as a heat sensing device. It is mostly used in the laboratory or for experimentation work

Video Controller
This chip takes information from the user memory and converts it into a video signal for display

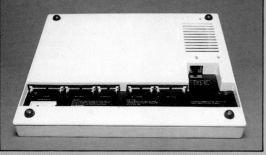

Peripheral Sockets
A view of the underside of the BBC Model B, showing the sockets where the peripherals may be connected

Printer Port
This is where any printer using a parallel signal, is plugged in

User Port
For experimentation with digital devices and home-built logic

IAN McKINNELL

Cassette Interface
Programs can be saved on a domestic cassette recorder in two ways: one giving maximum speed: the other increasing recording reliability

RGB Output
Provides separate signals for the red, green and blue components of the colour video signal. This drives a high-quality colour monitor

Television Output
This is joined to the aerial socket on a television set

Video Output
For use with a monochrome monitor

RS232 Port
A high speed serial interface for use with a number of peripherals

Modulator
This takes the colour signal from the video controller and converts it to an output suitable for a television set

Quartz Crystal
A pulsating crystal that forms the heart of the clock, synchronising all operations

Microprocessor
The MOS Technology 6502 carries out all the processing

User Memory
The BBC Model B contains 32K of RAM for storing programs, data, and graphic displays

ULA
This specially-designed Uncommitted Logic Array does the work of dozens of individual components found in other computers. The piece of metal mounted on top acts as a heatsink to prevent the chip from overheating

ROM
These two ROM chips provide the BASIC programming language and the operating system, which is the set of programs needed by the computer to manage all its internal functions

The Tube
A special interface designed by Acorn to enable the BBC Model B to work with alternative microprocessors

BBC MODEL B

PRICE
£399 (approx)

SIZE
409 × 358 × 78mm

WEIGHT
3700g

CPU
6502A

CLOCK SPEED
2 MHz

MEMORY
32 Kbytes of RAM
32 Kbytes of ROM including BASIC and sophisticated operating system

VIDEO DISPLAY
8 different graphics modes give a wide choice of displays. Largest text area: 32 lines of 80 characters. Highest resolution graphics: 640×256 pixels. Up to 16 colours at a lower resolution

INTERFACES
Television, monochrome and colour monitors, disk, printer, analogue input, user port, the Tube (for connecting additional microprocessors)

LANGUAGE SUPPLIED
BASIC

OTHER LANGUAGES AVAILABLE
LISP, FORTH, LOGO

COMES WITH
Leads for cassette deck and television. User Guide. 'Welcome' demonstration cassette and brochure

KEYBOARD
Typewriter-style with 74 moving keys, including 10 programmable function keys

DOCUMENTATION
The BBC Microcomputer User Guide shows all the signs of being written by highly trained minds, who seem to assume that their readers have already mastered computers.

Several large chapters are devoted to specialised usage of the system programs, which control the sophisticated graphics, sound and Input/Output features of the machine.

A detailed and very complete explanation of the operation and programming of the 6502 microprocessor is included, and unlike many such sections in other manuals, is not merely a copy of the original Rockwell documentation

33

Sinclair QL

The Quantum Leap offers the most advanced microprocessor on any home computer, and the potential for half a megabyte of memory

All Sir Clive Sinclair's innovations in the field of home computers have represented quantum leaps both in terms of technology and value for money, but his latest microcomputer is the first of his machines to take that description as its name: the Sinclair Quantum Leap (QL). At £399, it is aimed at a growing number of users who are either serious computer enthusiasts or have business as well as home applications in mind. As such, it represents very serious competition for machines like the Commodore 64 and BBC Model B, though in terms of technical specification it is dramatically superior.

It is quite apparent that the QL has been designed by stringing together all the components and features that currently represent the height of computer fashion. Making a break from the usual choice of Z80 or 6502, the CPU is a member of the Motorola 68000 family, which is currently the most sophisticated microprocessor found in any microcomputer and used in business machines like Apple's Lisa. However, the CPU is a

Expansion Interface
Peripherals, and up to 0.5 Megabytes of RAM can be coupled on here

ROM Cartridge Slot
Up to 32K of additional ROM can be plugged in here

Joystick Ports

68008 Microprocessor
This processor features internal 16- and 32-bit registers, with an 8-bit external data bus

Custom Chips
An increasing number of new computers feature a custom-designed chip. The QL has two, to handle the display and various interfaces

QL Software

QL Quill is a word processing package that displays the text on the screen in the same format as it will be printed

QL Abacus is a spreadsheet with the unusual feature that cells can be referred to by name instead of just co-ordinates

QL Archive is a database package. Record layouts can be designed by the user, with the aid of a screen editor

QL Easel is a graphics utility designed for producing graphs and charts, handling aspects of design like scaling automatically

68008, which means that though its internal registers are 16-bit (and it can perform many functions across a full 32 bits), its external data bus is only eight bits wide. This will slow the operation of the CPU very slightly, because the loading and storing of the registers will have to be done in halves. But this also means that the cost of the memory chips is kept down, and economics is often a prime consideration in Sinclair's choice of components.

The QL comes with 128 Kbytes of RAM as standard, but will be expandable to 512 Kbytes (or 'half a meg', as it is termed) with future add-ons. This large memory is particularly useful for business applications, as it reduces the frequency with which the program must refer to off-line storage. This storage consists of two Microdrives built into the casing, offering around 100 Kbytes each. Though this does make the QL a self-

IAN McKINNELL

Serial Ports
Two RS232 ports are incorporated, suitable for driving a printer and a modem. The more common (Centronics) printer interface must be purchased as an add-on

Keyboard
Though the keyboard is based on a membrane construction (thereby guarding it against coffee spillages, etc.) it features 65 full-travel keys, and the 'feel' is every bit as good as some of the most expensive business machines. There are four cursor control keys, and five programmable function keys. The copyright symbol and pound sign are also included

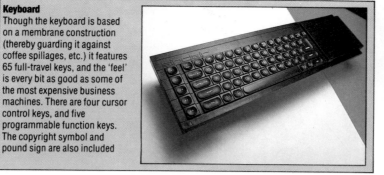

TV Socket
The QL will work with a TV set, but will normally only display 40 or 60 columns, where 85 are possible with a monitor

Monitor Port
Unlike the Spectrum, the QL can drive an RGB monitor directly, and indeed this is needed to take advantage of the maximum resolution of 512×256 pixels in four colours

Network Interface
Up to 64 QLs and Spectrums (the latter with Interface 1 added) can be linked together into a Local Area Network

Microdrive Extension Slot
Like the Spectrum, the QL can handle up to eight microdrives

Microdrives
Each of these uses a tiny wafer cartridge, containing a continuous loop of tape to store up to 100K each

Second Microprocessor
This Intel 8049 controls the keyboard, sound, and serial ports, leaving the 68008 free for running user programs

PROTOTYPE BOARD

The photograph shows the PCB of a pre-production QL, so elements of the design may change for the production models

Sinclair QL

PRICE	
£399 inc VAT (approx)	
SIZE	
472×138×46mm	
CPU	
Motorola 68008	
CLOCK SPEED	
7.5 MHz	
MEMORY	
128K RAM, expandable to 512K 32K ROM, expandable to 64K	
VIDEO DISPLAY	
25 lines of 85 characters (with monitor), high resolution graphics: 512×256 pixels (4 colours), 256×256 (8 colours)	
INTERFACES	
Serial RS232 (2), Joysticks (2), Microdrives, LAN, TV, RGB monitor	
LANGUAGE SUPPLIED	
BASIC	
OTHER LANGUAGES AVAILABLE	
Several are planned, most notably the 'C' language	
COMES WITH	
Instruction manual, four applications programs	
DOCUMENTATION	
The provisional manual is of a high standard, comes in a ringbound folder, and includes manuals for the standard software	

contained business system, the Microdrives must be viewed as something of a weak point when compared with the remarkably efficient processor. It takes an average of 3.5 seconds to locate a data item on the Microdrive, compared with perhaps half a second for the new generation of mini floppy drives.

Sinclair say that they intend to produce an interface to a hard (Winchester) disk unit, but there are no plans for floppy disks — though some independent manufacturer will undoubtedly offer them. Without disks, unfortunately, the QL will be unable to run the Unix operating system, which is usually considered to be one of the main reasons for choosing a Motorola 68000 CPU, and is tipped to replace CP/M as the standard operating system for business software.

The QL comes with four business packages as standard, all developed by the software house

Psion. Quill is a word processor; Abacus, a spreadsheet package; Archive, a database; and Easel a graphics package. All run under the resident operating system, which Sinclair have dubbed QDOS. The popularity that this machine is likely to achieve means that a lot of software will be developed for it, though it will not be easy for software houses to transfer their existing packages onto the QL. Still, it might be argued that if Sinclair adopted industry standards, its products would not have the market lead that they do have.

The resident BASIC has been upgraded from the Spectrum version, and as if the name Quantum Leap weren't immodest enough, Sinclair have called this SuperBASIC. It includes facilities for handling procedures (thereby encouraging structured programming) and for accessing the operating system from within a BASIC program. Both the BASIC and QDOS are contained in the 32 Kbytes of ROM as standard.

The Sinclair QL is without doubt a very impressive machine and, perhaps more important, has sufficient expansion possibilities to guard against obsolescence. It is a fitting addition to a long line of Sinclair milestones: the ZX80, the ZX81, and the Spectrum.

Questions And Answers

What is the 'fifth generation' of computers, and what were the first four?

The fifth generation is the stage of computer development towards which computer engineers and programmers are currently working. Such computers are expected to represent a significant leap beyond present technology.

The term 'fifth generation' was adopted by the Japanese to describe their long term research projects. Computers of the fifth generation will not have keyboards, and they will not have to be programmed in computer languages such as BASIC and PASCAL. Instead we can expect to be able to talk to our computers and they will answer back in whatever language we require. These fifth generation computers are also likely to be able to write their own programs as solutions to problems we present them with.

The first generation of computers were the first all-electronic computing devices, invented just after the Second World War. The second generation used essentially the same concepts with transistors instead of valves and relays, making computers smaller and cheaper. The third generation used integrated circuits (electronic circuits mounted on silicon). These integrated circuits were the earliest form of the microchip and marked the beginning of the reduction in price of computers. However these computers were still too expensive for the average home or office.

The fourth generation represents current technology. These computers use LSI (Large Scale Integration) circuits. The development of these microchips has brought the computer within the range of most people's budgets.

Where is Silicon Valley?

Silicon Valley is the name given to an area of land around San Jose to the south of San Francisco, where the headquarters or research departments of most of the large American computer and microelectronics companies are situated. The reason why so much expertise is collected together in such a small area is purely historical — there are no natural resources beneficial to the manufacture of microchips! Until 20 years ago the area was known only for producing fruit.

Is all the loose 'untidy' wiring at the back of some computers necessary?

Most of today's microcomputers are designed with as much thought put into the outward appearance as that of the electronics. 'Untidy' wires are normally hidden away. But with some advanced research computers, the loose wiring is very important. Electricity moves at the speed of light, but it still takes a certain time to travel down a wire. These research computers work so quickly that the information has to arrive at the right place at exactly the right time. The lengths of the wires are calculated precisely to ensure the timing is perfect.

Computers are often advertised as having a Z80 or 6502 microprocessor. What is the significance of these numbers?

The numbers themselves have no significance — '6502' is merely the identifying reference or 'name' for a particular microprocessor chip; 'Z80' is another. All computers which are based on the same microprocessor understand the same set of fundamental instructions (called Machine Code) from which programs are built up. However, programs are usually written by the user in a high level language such as BASIC and then interpreted into machine code by the computer. So unless you specifically want to write programs directly in machine code, it doesn't make any difference what sort of microprocessor your computer has.

Though some types of microprocessor operate at a higher speed than others, the rate at which you see things happen in a typical application is far more dependent on the way in which the software has been written.

DAVID HIGHAM

How can computers help in the fight against crime?

The Police National Computer Unit was set up in 1968 and the first file of information (stolen and suspect vehicles) was installed in 1974. Since this time, data has been included to list the details of all people with criminal records. The police are currently exploring the possibility of using microcomputers in 'incident rooms' to cope with emergencies. At present a few police cars have computer terminals through which they can access information from the central computer. The current state of storage technology means that it would be feasible for the police to store the personal details of every citizen. Fortunately, the government has implemented various 'watchdog' committees to safeguard the interests of the innocent.

Atari 400 & 800

Game-playing is the special strength of the Atari range of computers

CHRIS STEVENS

The fortunes of Atari, now with headquarters in Sunnyvale, in California's Silicon Valley, rest on the phenomenal success of their arcade games. The first of these was 'Pong', played in black-and-white on the television screen.

From this humble beginning, Atari grew, and eventually became part of the vast Warner Communications Group, and now, some six years later, is among the largest manufacturers of home computers, as well as having a very large slice of the arcade market.

With its excellent standard of construction, and reassuringly heavy feel, the Atari range of home computers, comprising the 800 and 400 models, has set standards which others seek to emulate. Superb graphics, well-developed software and — until recently — a very high price tag all contribute to this quality image.

Selling for around £150, the 400 differs from the larger model in price – the 800 costs £300 – maximum memory size – fixed to 16 Kbytes in the 400, expandable to 48 Kbytes in the larger model – in having one instead of two cartridge ports, and, perhaps of less immediate importance, being restricted to use via a domestic television, where the 800 has the option of display via a monitor. Most obvious, and perhaps most critical, amongst the differences, however, is in the keyboard.

In order to overcome the problem of inconsistent signal levels, Atari home computers do not use domestic cassette recorders, but rather require Atari's own model. A large proportion of users however, have at least one disk drive, in order to take advantage of the wide range of software packages available on disk.

Atari Keyboards
The striking difference between these two Atari models lies in their keyboards. While the larger 800 model is equipped with a full typewriter-style keyboard the smaller model has a membrane type which, while better than some, still suffers from the in-built faults of other similar units – notably a lack of 'feel', and sometimes unpredictable response. It is as well to bear in mind, however, that very expensive 'ruggedised' machines, produced for industrial and military applications, use this method to secure against dust and the occasional spilled cup of coffee!

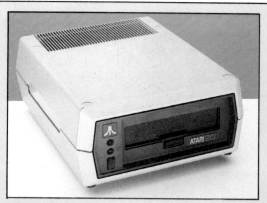

The Disk Drive
Generally considered to be the most useful peripheral, the Atari 810 is now beginning to show its age. At only 88 Kbytes per disk, it's rather small, and since it connects to the machine via a serial interface it's also fairly slow. However, it has a sophisticated operating system which has many features derived from other programs

The Cassette Unit
Being a special unit, designed to work with the Atari computers, the Atari 410 Cassette Unit is more reliable and easier to operate than the regular domestic variety. For the same reason, it doesn't have a speaker, which reduces size and weight, and neither can an 'ordinary' cassette be used instead. Shortcomings of the system are principally the lack of named cassette-files

The Atari Joystick
The Atari Joystick is one of the poorer add-ons for the machine. It's a switch-type, so there is no variability. It gives just a push in the required direction, and it's rather stiff, so other makers have produced alternatives

CPU BOARD

ANTIC
One of the specialised chips that give the Atari its impressive features, ANTIC controls the screen-scrolling, lightpen and one of the interrupts

Colour Clock
Turning this control will alter the colour. The various graphic resolutions are selected by varying the speed of this clock

CTIA or GTIA
This chip, unique to the At handles colour, some miscellaneous I/O and the Player-Missile graphics

6502 CPU

Colour Adjustment

RAM BOARDS

The Atari can hold up to three RAM boards. In this way the memory can be expanded to 48 Kbytes

Master Clock

POKEY
The third of the custom-n chips, POKEY takes care the keyboard, serial I/O, t system-timers and also controls the sound

6520 Peripheral Interface Adaptor
This chip looks after the Hand Controllers

Speaker

PERSONALITY BOARD

The Atari can be made into quite a different machine by replacing these ROMs with others. For example, alternative languages could be used.

MOTHERBOARD

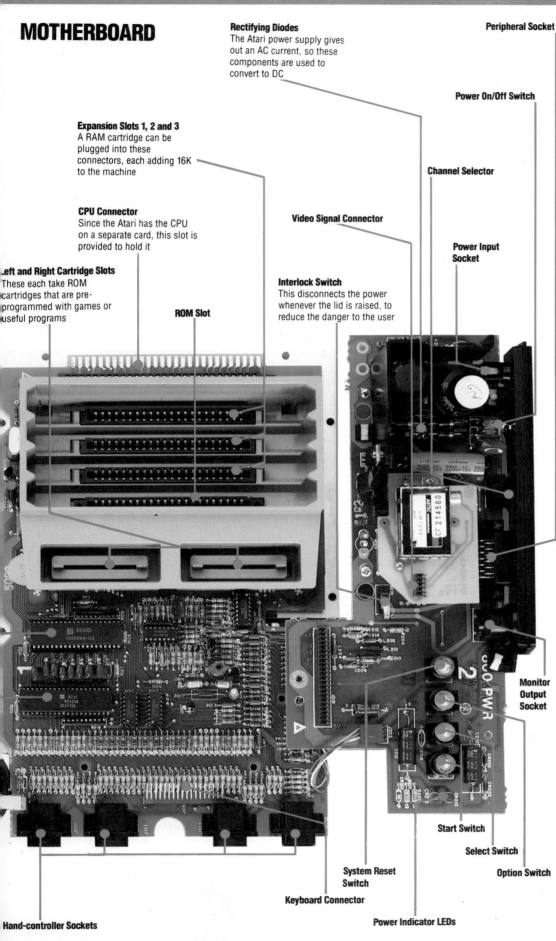

Rectifying Diodes
The Atari power supply gives out an AC current, so these components are used to convert to DC

Expansion Slots 1, 2 and 3
A RAM cartridge can be plugged into these connectors, each adding 16K to the machine

CPU Connector
Since the Atari has the CPU on a separate card, this slot is provided to hold it

Left and Right Cartridge Slots
These each take ROM cartridges that are pre-programmed with games or useful programs

ROM Slot

Interlock Switch
This disconnects the power whenever the lid is raised, to reduce the danger to the user

Video Signal Connector

Channel Selector

Power On/Off Switch

Peripheral Socket

Power Input Socket

Hand-controller Sockets

System Reset Switch

Keyboard Connector

Power Indicator LEDs

Start Switch

Select Switch

Option Switch

Monitor Output Socket

ATARI 800

PRICE	£280 (approx)
SIZE	405 × 330 × 110mm
WEIGHT	4,200g
CPU	6502
CLOCK SPEED	1.79MHz
MEMORY	16 K to 48 Kbytes
VIDEO DISPLAY	Text screen: 40 × 24 characters, graphics screen maximum of 329 × 192 dots including 16 colours and 8 shades
INTERFACES	TV connector, monitor, cassette recorder (dedicated unit), 4 joysticks, serial port
LANGUAGE SUPPLIED	BASIC
OTHER LANGUAGES AVAILABLE	BASIC A+, PILOT, C
COMES WITH	Power supply unit (without plug), manual
KEYBOARD	57 individual moving keys, plus 3 function keys
DOCUMENTATION	The introductory manuals are clearly written, accurate and well produced. Atari will supply full technical notes for the more experienced user. This advanced manual is exactly the same as used by Atari's engineers, and not only contains the full circuit diagram, but also listings of many of the programs that control the inside workings of the computer (the system software). The only shortcoming of the manual supplied is the format, which is in pages for a 3-ring binder that is not provided

Acorn Electron

In the two years that elapsed between Acorn's BBC Model B and Electron, microcomputer technology has developed dramatically

The Acorn Electron is an elegant computer that lives up to its initial impression of being a robust and well designed machine. As a scaled down version of the BBC Micro, it isn't quite as impressive in performance, but feels more comfortable to use. Most of the features of the BBC Micro have been incorporated into the Electron. For example, the SOUND command is used in conjunction with the ENVELOPE command to synthesise different types of musical instruments on both machines.

All of the BBC Micro's graphics modes are available on the Electron, with the exception of Teletext (MODE 7), which is generated in the BBC machine by a special chip. This chip is not available on the Electron's circuit board, and so Teletext-like displays can only be produced by redefining most of the characters and imitating Teletext using MODE 6 (which is, however, restricted to two colours). This is a pity, because the Telextext mode on the BBC Micro is a very economical way of producing quite complex displays without using a lot of memory.

Input and output facilities are also less impressive than on the BBC Micro. Visual output is via TV channel 36, as well as through composite video and RGB sockets to monochrome or colour monitors. But apart from the cassette port there is no immediately usable interface.

Expansion is clearly possible through a large edge connector at the back of the machine. Unfortunately, this protrudes from beneath a

Dynamic Duo
The brains behind the Electron were Chris Curry (left) and Herman Hauser (right), who were also largely responsible for the design of the BBC Micro. Curry was a development engineer working for Clive Sinclair, when he employed Hauser. The two men subsequently founded Acorn

Master Clock Crystal

TV Signal Control Crystal
A major reason for the stability of the image generated by the Electron is the fact that it has a special separate crystal, which is used to time the display

TV Modulator And Output Socket

Composite Video Socket

RGB Socket

Cassette Socket

Cassette Motor Relay
The voltage used in the motor of a cassette deck is higher than the computer can handle, so it is isolated from the computer's electronics by this miniature relay

Speaker

ledge in the casing, and on an unexpanded machine the only protection provided for it is a plastic cover. No details are given in the manual about what signals it produces, nor any suggestion as to what may be connected to it. But it is clearly intended that some kind of expansion box will plug into it because there are threaded brass sockets moulded into the casing nearby, which are used to provide a mechanical link between the computer and the add-on.

The built-in BASIC is the now well-known BBC dialect; but this has been considerably expanded and here has many features that make the machine

Keyboard Connector
The number of pins (22) reveals that the keyboard's output is not decoded into ASCII. If it were decoded, there would be only 10 pins at most (eight for the data, plus the 5v and the ground). This is probably a function of the ULA

Keyboard
The keyboard is among the best of any home computer, with real typewriter-style keys of very high quality. In practice the keyboard is very similar to that on the BBC Micro. There are no separate function keys, but the same facilities are provided by the Caps Lock key, which if pressed in tandem with a number key, converts it into a function key.

This is extended to the letter keys and three of the punctuation keys, which produce BASIC keywords if they are pressed while the Caps Lock is held down

Expansion Connector
No details of pin values or signal timings are given, but it is obvious that most of the system bus will be available through this connector, as well as TTL and power lines. Therefore, considerable expansion should be possible

CPU
Controlling the machine is a standard 6502A processor, clocked at 1.79 MHz. This actually makes the decisions, something which the ULA cannot do by itself

RAM
Bytes are loaded from RAM into the CPU in two halves. First, the lower four bits are accessed (one bit coming from each of the four chips), followed by the upper four. In most machines all eight bits of each byte would be stored in the same chip

Uncommitted Logic Array
This is the biggest ULA ever manufactured. Apart from the ULA, the 6502 CPU, the ROM and the RAM, there are only nine other chips on the board, all of which are standard TTL logic, each providing just a handful of logic gates

CHRIS STEVENS

Power Conditioning Circuitry
The Acorn Electron is unusual in requiring a 19v AC supply. This has the advantage of being more stable, but needs a more complex circuit to modify it for computer usage

Blank 28-Pin Area
This 28-pin area, marked out for a chip and with an unfilled link nearby, would suggest that either additional bank switched ROM may be added, or that a different type of chip may be used

a pleasure to use. Particularly useful is the OSCLI routine, which allows a BASIC program to send commands directly to the operating system, and this permits experienced users to remove some of the constraints of BASIC. The assembler package, which is a feature unique to BBC BASIC, has also been expanded. It has additional keywords for defining variable storage and string printing, both of which are a chore in Assembly language.

In performance the Acorn Electron is better than average. The picture is very steady and sharp, with good clear colour and definition. When some serious expansion facilities, such as disk drives, are available, the Electron will certainly become a justifiably popular machine.

Acorn Electron

PRICE
£199 (approx)

SIZE
340×160×65mm

CPU
6502

CLOCK SPEED
1.79MHz

MEMORY
64 Kbytes of ROM
32 Kbytes of RAM (with no on-board expansion)

VIDEO DISPLAY
Up to 32 lines of 80 characters. Eight colours with background and foreground independently settable. 127 pre-defined characters and 255 user-definable characters

INTERFACES
Channel 36 TV, composite video, TTL RGB, cassette, system bus (undocumented)

LANGUAGES SUPPLIED
BBC BASIC with in-line assembler

OTHER LANGUAGES AVAILABLE
Should run some other AcornSoft languages such as FORTH and LISP, provided that they are RAM-based. ROM-based languages such as BCPL and PASCAL are incompatible with the unexpanded machine

COMES WITH
Installation and BASIC manual, TV lead, power transformer, introductory cassette

KEYBOARD
56 typewriter-style keys. Single key BASIC keyword entry. 10 user-definable function keys

DOCUMENTATION
Simply excellent. There is plenty of real detail available for the experimenter or the serious programmer. Every BASIC keyword is separately explained; and there is a good section on the Assembly language, which is very important considering the in-line assembler. The functions of the operation system are also well described. Thanks to this wealth of information, most tasks should be relatively easy to accomplish with the machine

The Language Of Computing

Like any other area of specialist knowledge, computing has its own language to explain how the computer works. To the uninitiated, these key concepts may seem baffling.

Bits And Bytes

The computer understands nothing but numbers — but they're numbers with an unfamiliar look about them

The words 'bits' and 'bytes' are used whenever computers are written about. They are terms that describe the way computers store and use numbers.

They do this quite differently from the way that people do. We represent numbers with 10 different symbols (0 through to 9) and manipulate them in multiples of 10. (This is known as a 'base' of 10). Computers, on the other hand, and for all their mathematical wizardry, use only two numbers — zero and one. Bits and bytes are ways of representing combinations of these two numbers.

A bit is the smallest piece of information a computer can handle. It is the computer's way of representing the two numbers zero and one. A group of eight bits is called a byte; a byte allows the computer to represent quite large numbers.

First, let's look at bits, what they are, and why they are called 'bits'. Computers are electronic devices and, consequently, everything they do is done ultimately with electrical signals. A single electrical signal can either be 'on' or it can be 'off'; it is this principle that allows ordinary electrical signals to represent numbers.

The illustration shows a piece of wood with a hole in it, which can be filled with a peg. Even though it is a single hole, it can represent two numbers and is an excellent analogy for the way a computer works. Either the hole has no peg in it — in which case it represents a zero — or it does have a peg in it, and this represents a one. A single board can thus symbolise a zero or a one.

In a computer, the same effect is achieved with an electrical signal: when it is off, it represents a zero; when it is on, it represents a one. A single wire, or a one-hole board, can therefore be used to represent two states: no peg or with a peg; absent or present; off or on; 0 or 1.

This smallest piece of information is called a bit. The word itself suggests its small size and represents two possible states. The word is derived from **BI**nary digi**T**. Thought of in another way, a bit can

Bits And Bytes

A bit (binary digit) is the smallest unit of mathematical information a computer can handle. Here, a board with just a single hole can represent either zero or one depending on whether it has a peg in it or not. A computer does the same thing with an electrical signal that is either off (to represent 0) or on (to represent 1). If the board has two holes, there are four possible combinations of holes and pegs. If eight holes are used there are 256 different combinations and these are all shown in the table. Computers use groups of eight bits and such a group is called a byte. Each byte can represent a number ranging from 0 to 255

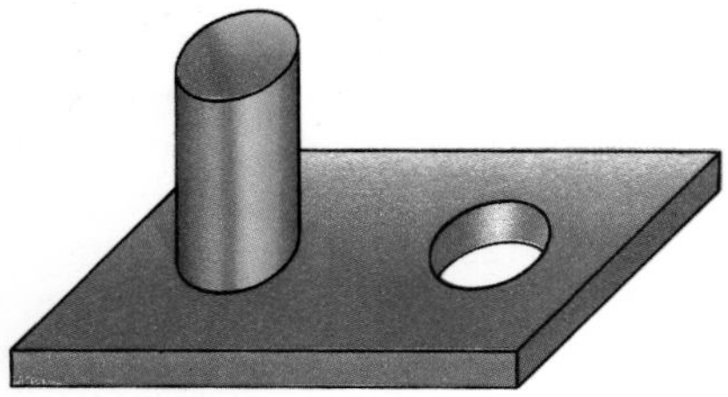

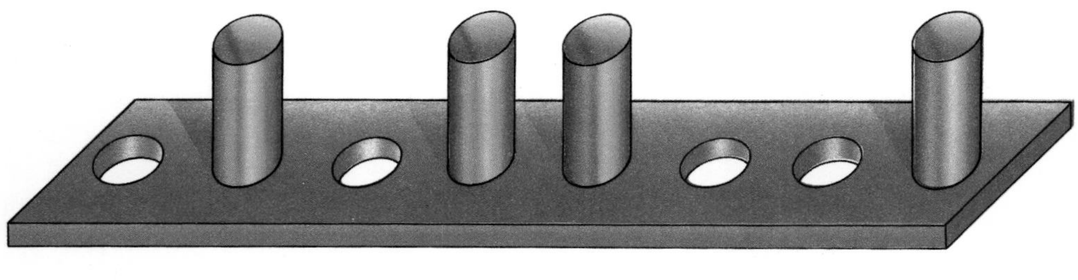

TONY LODGE

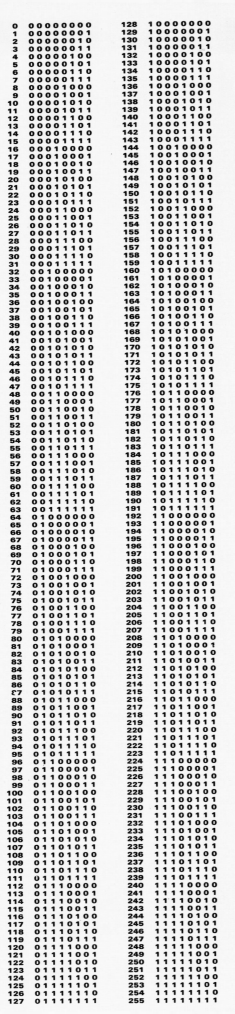

0	00000000	128	10000000
1	00000001	129	10000001
2	00000010	130	10000010
3	00000011	131	10000011
4	00000100	132	10000100
5	00000101	133	10000101
6	00000110	134	10000110
7	00000111	135	10000111
8	00001000	136	10001000
9	00001001	137	10001001
10	00001010	138	10001010
11	00001011	139	10001011
12	00001100	140	10001100
13	00001101	141	10001101
14	00001110	142	10001110
15	00001111	143	10001111
16	00010000	144	10010000
17	00010001	145	10010001
18	00010010	146	10010010
19	00010011	147	10010011
20	00010100	148	10010100
21	00010101	149	10010101
22	00010110	150	10010110
23	00010111	151	10010111
24	00011000	152	10011000
25	00011001	153	10011001
26	00011010	154	10011010
27	00011011	155	10011011
28	00011100	156	10011100
29	00011101	157	10011101
30	00011110	158	10011110
31	00011111	159	10011111
32	00100000	160	10100000
33	00100001	161	10100001
34	00100010	162	10100010
35	00100011	163	10100011
36	00100100	164	10100100
37	00100101	165	10100101
38	00100110	166	10100110
39	00100111	167	10100111
40	00101000	168	10101000
41	00101001	169	10101001
42	00101010	170	10101010
43	00101011	171	10101011
44	00101100	172	10101100
45	00101101	173	10101101
46	00101110	174	10101110
47	00101111	175	10101111
48	00110000	176	10110000
49	00110001	177	10110001
50	00110010	178	10110010
51	00110011	179	10110011
52	00110100	180	10110100
53	00110101	181	10110101
54	00110110	182	10110110
55	00110111	183	10110111
56	00111000	184	10111000
57	00111001	185	10111001
58	00111010	186	10111010
59	00111011	187	10111011
60	00111100	188	10111100
61	00111101	189	10111101
62	00111110	190	10111110
63	00111111	191	10111111
64	01000000	192	11000000
65	01000001	193	11000001
66	01000010	194	11000010
67	01000011	195	11000011
68	01000100	196	11000100
69	01000101	197	11000101
70	01000110	198	11000110
71	01000111	199	11000111
72	01001000	200	11001000
73	01001001	201	11001001
74	01001010	202	11001010
75	01001011	203	11001011
76	01001100	204	11001100
77	01001101	205	11001101
78	01001110	206	11001110
79	01001111	207	11001111
80	01010000	208	11010000
81	01010001	209	11010001
82	01010010	210	11010010
83	01010011	211	11010011
84	01010100	212	11010100
85	01010101	213	11010101
86	01010110	214	11010110
87	01010111	215	11010111
88	01011000	216	11011000
89	01011001	217	11011001
90	01011010	218	11011010
91	01011011	219	11011011
92	01011100	220	11011100
93	01011101	221	11011101
94	01011110	222	11011110
95	01011111	223	11011111
96	01100000	224	11100000
97	01100001	225	11100001
98	01100010	226	11100010
99	01100011	227	11100011
100	01100100	228	11100100
101	01100101	229	11100101
102	01100110	230	11100110
103	01100111	231	11100111
104	01101000	232	11101000
105	01101001	233	11101001
106	01101010	234	11101010
107	01101011	235	11101011
108	01101100	236	11101100
109	01101101	237	11101101
110	01101110	238	11101110
111	01101111	239	11101111
112	01110000	240	11110000
113	01110001	241	11110001
114	01110010	242	11110010
115	01110011	243	11110011
116	01110100	244	11110100
117	01110101	245	11110101
118	01110110	246	11110110
119	01110111	247	11110111
120	01111000	248	11111000
121	01111001	249	11111001
122	01111010	250	11111010
123	01111011	251	11111011
124	01111100	252	11111100
125	01111101	253	11111101
126	01111110	254	11111110
127	01111111	255	11111111

Bytes In Memory

Bytes are groups of eight binary digits (bits). Each byte is used by the computer to store numbers which can range from 0 to 255. Each byte is stored in separate memory 'cells' which are arranged systematically so that the computer can find the byte it needs. To do this it needs to know the location of the memory box containing the byte

1st memory location ▶

2nd memory location ▶

3rd memory location ▶

TONY LODGE

count, but only from zero to one.

A board with two holes can show four different states, or count from 0 to 3. Both holes can be empty; the right hole can have a peg; the left hole can have a peg or both holes can have pegs. The bottom of the picture shows a board with eight holes. There are 256 possible permutations of pegs and holes and these are shown in the table using ones to represent pegs and zeros to represent holes.

Such a group of eight binary digits (bits) is called a byte. A single byte can therefore represent 256 different states (it can count from 0 to 255).

When we say a computer 'stores' a byte, we mean that a number (ranging from 0 to 255) is kept in the computer's memory, to be used when required. Each byte has its own 'box' and these 'boxes' are arranged in sequence (the picture above shows them stacked one on top of the other). When the computer needs to retrieve a number from a memory box, it simply needs to know in which box the byte is stored.

All the numbers from 0 to 255 can be represented using unique combinations of ones and zeros (table on left). Bits are stored and used by computers in groups of eight. Eight bits together are called a byte.

When 1 And 1 Is 10

Computers achieve their prodigies of calculation with just two digits — 0 and 1

Converting To Binary

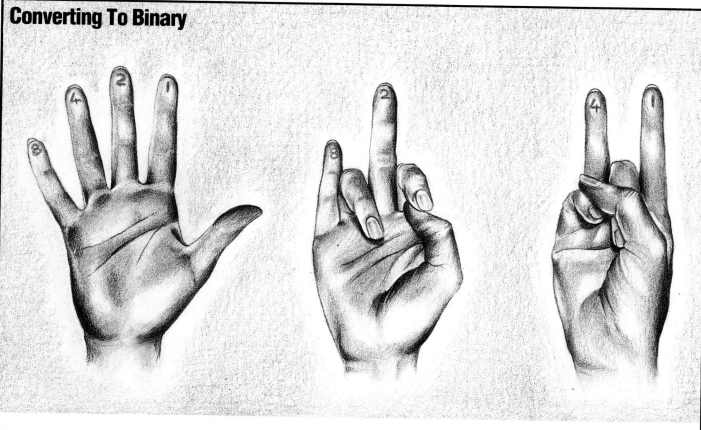

The easiest way to convert small binary numbers to their decimal equivalent is to imagine writing the 'place value' of each binary column on the fingers of the right hand. As long as the binary number is not more than four digits long, all you have to do is to hold up the appropriate finger if the corresponding binary digit is a 1 and to hold the finger down if it is 0.

Hold up the appropriate fingers for 1010 and you get an 8 and a 2, which add together to give the decimal number 10. The third illustration shows how to

decode 0101 — it gives a 4 and a 1. which comes to 5 in decimal form. Try using the method to compute the decimal equivalent of 1110 and 0110.

The method can be extended using both hands to figure out longer binary numbers. To do this, the fingers of the left hand (palm facing you) will need to be labelled 16, 32, 64 and 128, with the 16 on the little finger and the 128 on the index finger

ELAINE KEENAN

Most people take our system of using numbers so much for granted that it never occurs to them that any other system is possible.

The Romans thought up a system for representing numbers, using letters of the alphabet. X stood for 10, L stood for 50, C stood for 100, D stood for 500 and so on. The Roman system worked well enough as a way of recording simple numbers. It did not lend itself, however, to computations. Even additions in Roman numerals are difficult, for one reason: there is no concept of 'place value'. The position of a numeral in a Roman number tells us nothing about how much it is 'worth'.

Look at the two numbers 506 and 56. The only apparent difference is the zero in the middle. Its role is that in the number 506 it tells us that there are no 'tens', only five 'hundreds' and six 'ones'.

Every 'column' or position in a conventional

number has a 'value' associated with it. The column on the right of the number is the 'ones' column, the next one (moving to the left) is the 'tens' column, the next one is the 'hundreds' column and so on. The digit used in any 'column' merely signifies how many of that column's value are involved.

You may be wondering what all this has to do with computers and the binary system. Computers are electronic machines, which can easily deal with numbers by using voltage levels. Five volts represent a one and zero volts represent a zero. As we learnt in Bits and Bytes (page 43), ones and zeros are perfectly adequate to represent any number, however big.

Using the familiar decimal system based on 10 (also known as the denary system) the number 506 is a concise way of representing the equivalent of five hundred and six knots in a string or five hundred and six notches on a stick. In binary arithmetic, the same number is represented as a clumsy 111111010.

Because the system used here is 'binary', the place value of each digit in each column is different. Instead of increasing in value in powers of 10, the columns go up in powers of 2.

The column on the right is still the 'ones' column, but because there are only two symbols (0 and 1), we run out of digits as soon as we add 1. In the decimal system, we only run out of symbols when we get to 9; the next column uses a digit which says: we have run out of symbols — we don't have anything for numbers bigger than 9 — so we'll use the 'tens' column and use a 1 to indicate that we now have one 'lot' of ten.

The binary system works in exactly the same way. Instead of grouping in tens and writing 10 for ten, binary groups in twos, so the binary digits 10 represent the decimal number 2.

Showing the number five hundred and six written in decimal and in binary illustrates the essential similarity clearly:

Hundreds	Tens	Ones	
5	0	6	
= 5x100 +	0x10 +	6x1	(= 506)

256s	128s	64s	32s	16s	8s	4s	2s	1s
1	1	1	1	1	1	0	1	0

= 1x256 + 1x128 + 1x64 + 1x32 + 1x16
+ 1x8 + 0x4 + 1x2 + 0x1   (= 506)

The rules of arithmetic in the binary system are exactly the same as the familiar rules of the decimal system — the only difference is that we run out of counting symbols after 1 instead of after 9. Let's try some additions to prove it. Decimal equivalents are printed in brackets.

```
 (3)     11
+(5)   +101
─────────────
 (8)   1000
```

(1 +1 = 0 carry 1)
(1(carried) + 1 = 0 carry 1)
(1(carried) + 1 = 0 carry 1)
(1(carried) + 0 = 1)

In binary, as we have just seen, adding 1 to 1 means we have run out of symbols as only zeros and ones are allowed. So we say 'one and one equals nought carry one' (just as in decimal adding 1 to 9 means we have run out of symbols — there are no symbols larger than 9 — so again we say 'nine and one equals nought carry one'). Here's another addition, worked out for you, with two more to try for yourself.

```
 (4)    100      (7)    111    (3)     11
+(6)   +110     +(2)   + 10   +(12)  +1100
──────────────  ───────────────────────────
(10)   1010      (?)     ?     (?)       ?
```

By now you will have noticed that binary numbers are much longer than their decimal equivalent. See if you can add 11010110 to 1101101 — remember to keep the rightmost columns lined up just as you would when adding a longer decimal number to a shorter one!

The History Of Numbers

Babylonian

Roman

Hindu

Binary

The ancient Babylonians had an advanced number system, based on 60 rather than 10. Their representation of the number 59 in Babylonian 'cuneiform' script is shown above. The use of 60 as a number base had many advantages and there are still traces of their system in use today. There are 60 seconds in a minute, 60 minutes in an hour and six times 60 degrees in a circle — all vestiges of a mathematical system perfected 4000 years ago.

The Roman system was a considerable step backwards. Letters of the alphabet were used to represent numbers, but the position of each Roman numeral gave no indication of its value, making even simple arithmetic almost impossible.

The Hindus used nine signs for the numbers 1 to 9 and later added a sign to represent zero. Their vital contribution was 'place value' — the idea that a digit's position in a number determines how much that digit is 'worth'. Thus the 3 in 30 is 'worth' three tens. The Hindu system was adopted by the Arabs and gradually spread to Europe. One of the leading Arab mathematicians was called Al Khowarizmi. The Latinised pronunciation of his name gave us the mathematical term algorithm and his book 'Al-jabr wa'l Mugabalah' is remembered in the word algebra.

Computers use the binary system because numbers of any size can be represented using only ones and zeros

ANDY LESLIE

When Minus Equals Plus

Computers like their circuits simple and so must employ a clever trick to perform subtraction by means of addition

COURTESY OF THE SCIENCE PHOTO LIBRARY

Voyager 2
The spectacular Voyager was the first space explorer to go beyond our solar system. It travelled through space, taking pictures and gathering information, while the on-board computer converted the data into binary digits. The data were sent back to earth at the staggering rate of 116,000 bits per second. They were then processed by the NASA computer in Houston, Texas

In the previous few pages we discovered that binary digits could be used to represent any decimal number. Binary numbers have the disadvantage of being longer than their decimal equivalent, but are convenient for the computer as the zeros and ones may be represented by zero and positive voltages. We also saw that binary numbers can be added together very simply.

On paper, binary numbers can be subtracted as easily as decimal numbers, following the same rules used in decimal subtraction. Computer designers realised long ago, however, that adding circuits (electronic circuits that perform addition)

could both add and subtract without the need for special subtraction circuits. We shall find out how this is done.

Two's Complement

One method of representing negative numbers in computers is known as 'Two's Complement'. With this the process of subtraction appears as just another part of the addition. Consider the following arithmetical problem:

$$16 - 12 = 4$$
$$\text{or } 16 + (-12) = 4$$

47

Here 12 is taken away from 16 but the process of subtraction can equally be seen as an addition: the addition of 16 and negative 12. In both cases the answer is the same and the only difference is the use of arithmetic signs and brackets. This slight modification can be used by the computer to both represent negative numbers and simplify the problem of subtraction.

For simplicity assume our computer is only large enough to handle 5 digits. Of course real computers can handle numbers with thousands of digits. Our 5-digit computer adopts a method of working: the leading digit on the left hand side is to be considered separately from the other 4. If the leading digit is 1 it is to represent negative 16 and if it is 0 then it is of course a zero. The remaining 4 digits are positive and follow the binary conventions we saw in When 1 And 1 Is 10 on page 45.

[ ]	[ ]	[ ]	[ ]	[ ]
−16 or 0	8s	4s	2s	1 or 0

So for example the binary number 01000 is decimal 8 and 10000 is decimal −16. But what about 10100? This includes −16 and +4 giving −12.

How many numbers can be represented with only 5 digits using this convention? The largest positive number is 01111 or decimal 15 and the greatest negative number is 10000 or −16. With a little experimentation you will see that every number between −16 and +15 can be represented.

Binary	Decimal
10000	−16
10001	−15
10010	−14
10011	−13
10100	−12
etc.	
11111	−1
00000	0
00001	1
00010	2
etc.	
01110	14
01111	15

If we increased the number of digits our computer was able to handle, we could of course expand the range of numbers.

Early on in the development of binary computer arithmetic, a very simple trick was discovered for finding the Two's Complement, or negative form, of a number. There are two steps to this trick.

First, invert each digit. So whenever you see a 1 put a 0 and wherever there is a 0 change it to a 1. Secondly, add 1 to the reversed number.

Follow the method as it is laid out in the example below. We are using +12, the binary equivalent being 01100. (The leading 0 on the left hand side is not strictly necessary as 01100 is the same as 1100. But since our computer has 5 digits we must fill up every one.)

	01100 (= +12)
First Step:	10011
Second Step:	00001 (+1)
	10100 (= −12)

Now let's look at how our computer tackles a problem of subtraction; for example: 12 minus 4.

+ 12 is	01100
−4 is	11100 (using Two's Complement)
12+ (−4)	101000

Notice that we now have 6 digits. Since our computer is only large enough to register 5 digits, the leading left hand digit is called an overflow digit and is ignored, leaving 01000 or 8 in decimal, the correct answer! A slightly more complex example is: 4 minus 12.

+4 is	00100
−12 is	10100
4+(−12)	11000

As a final example let's try dealing with two negative numbers together: −3 −4 = −3+ (−4) = −7

3 is	00011
so −3 is	11101 (using Two's Complement)
and −4 is	11100
	111001

Again we are left with a 6-digit number. Once the overflow is discarded, we have the binary number: 11001 or −7 in decimal.

These subtractions used only addition and the trick of the Two's Complement (which itself uses only reversal of digits and addition). The advantage to the computer is that binary digits can easily be reversed using a NOT Gate (see page 50).

A NOT Gate has one input and one output. It is a very 'perverse' Gate because whatever value you feed in, the output is the opposite. So if the input is 0 the output is 1 and if the input is 1 the output is 0. This characteristic of 'inverting' is exactly what is needed for the first (the inversion) step in the trick of the Two's Complement. In Gates And Adders (page 52) we will see how addition can easily be carried out by a computer using a combination of logical Gates.

Dots And Dashes
Morse code is one of the earliest illustrations of binary coding in electronics. In 1837 the first electric telegraph was laid in London with two miles of cable joining Euston to Camden Town railway stations. Later the same year in America, Samuel Morse demonstrated his celebrated code for transmitting messages. Each letter was a combination of two signals: dots and dashes

Two's Company

Although computers give speedy answers to complex arithmetical problems, they deal with them in the simplest way

Up to this point we have seen how computers can add and subtract. Now we look at the process of multiplication.

If you had to multiply 14 by 12, a simple way would be to do a multiple addition, for example $14+14+14+14+ \ldots$ (12 times). Since multiplication is in one sense a form of repeated addition, this approach would certainly work, and is how the first computers dealt with multiplication. However, the method is awkward and time-consuming, so computer designers evolved a more efficient method.

When two numbers are multiplied, the operation is usually written down on paper like this:

$$\begin{array}{r} 14 \\ \times 12 \\ \hline 28 \\ +14 \\ \hline 168 \end{array}$$

(a final 0 is often written to keep the digits in the correct column)

Exactly the same process works in any base of numbers. Let's look at an example in base two or binary:

$$\begin{array}{r} 101 \\ \times 11 \\ \hline 101 \\ +101 \\ \hline 1111 \end{array}$$

With larger numbers the method is exactly the same, so let's go back to the example of 14×12 and do it in binary:

$$\begin{array}{rl} 1110 & (14) \\ \times 1100 & (12) \\ \hline 0000 & \\ 0000 & \\ 1110 & \\ 1110 & \\ \hline 10101000 & (168) \end{array}$$

Multiplication is even simpler in binary than in decimal because there can never be a carried digit. When you multiply a number by 1 the number is unchanged, $14 \times 1 = 14$ and when you multiply a number by 0 the answer is 0, $14 \times 0 = 0$. This is true in binary, decimal and all number systems.

When mathematicians looked at similar calculations to the one above they saw a simple

$$37 \times 15$$
$$\downarrow$$
$$100101 \times 1111$$
$$\downarrow$$

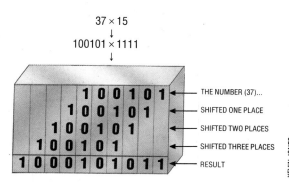

THE NUMBER (37)...
SHIFTED ONE PLACE
SHIFTED TWO PLACES
SHIFTED THREE PLACES
RESULT

KEVIN JONES

pattern emerging: binary multiplication consists of only two operations, 'shifting' and addition. And this is exactly how the computer does a multiplication. First it shifts 'copies' of the upper line into their correct position (determined by the 1s and 0s in the lower line) and then it adds all the 'copies' together.

The computer needs to have a large digit capacity to perform multiplications. When the 4-digit number 1110 was multiplied by the 4-digit number 1100 the answer contained 8 digits (10101000) and in general the result of a multiplication can be up to twice the length of the largest number.

It may come as a surprise to learn that a computer's multiplication can return an incorrect result. Nearly all these errors can be traced back to the amount of space the machine's designer has allowed to hold the answer. If insufficient space has been allocated, 'overflow' will occur, the least significant digits will be lost, and the result will thus be erroneous.

Shifting Into Multiplication

Multiplication is much easier in binary than it is in decimal. The same process of long multiplication used in the decimal system is applied, but because there are only two numbers involved in the multiplying (0 and 1), the operation is very simple. When a number is multiplied by 1 the result is obviously the same number. In the illustration, where 100101 (37) is multiplied by 1111 (15), four copies of 100101 appear. Each copy is shifted to the left according to the position of the 1 that multiplies it. Finally all the copies are added together to give the answer 1000101011 (555)

Gottfried Wilhelm Leibniz

Leibniz (1646–1716) was a contemporary of Isaac Newton and made contributions to mathematics, science and philosophy. He invented a machine that could multiply and divide. He also investigated the possibilities for using binary arithmetic in calculating devices, though the first known reference to binary numbers was by Francis Bacon in 1623. In his later years he fell into dispute with Newton over the invention of the calculus

True Or False?

Computers may not be able to 'think' yet, but they can certainly follow the laws of logic

The CPU (Central Processing Unit) is often descibed as the heart of a computer. It's the place where all the computations and logical decision-making take place. But how are these decisions and calculations made?

To understand, we need to know the basics of binary arithmetic and be familiar with logic gates. In computers, these gates are simple electrical circuits able to make logical decisions and comparisons. This may sound more complicated than it is, and the principles can easily be illustrated using examples from everyday life.

There are three fundamental types of gate — the AND gate, the OR gate and the NOT gate. Capital letters are used when writing about gates to differentiate the words from the usual English 'and', 'or' and 'not'.

Logical Connections

An AND gate is a circuit that gives a 'true' output if all the inputs are 'true'. Let's see what this means. Suppose you would like a trip to the country. If you have a car AND some petrol, you can have the trip. If you have some petrol but no car, you can't go. Similarly, a car but no petrol means no trip.

In this AND 'circuit', there are two input conditions and both need to be 'true'. To get the trip (the 'output') it must be true that you have a car AND it must be true that you have some petrol. Then the output becomes 'true'— it is true that you get the trip to the country. Later, we'll see how this logic diagram can be shown as a logic equation and also how it can be represented in a 'truth table'.

Imagine a slightly different situation. Somebody would like to take a trip to the country. The trip will be possible if they have either a car OR a bicycle (we'll assume the car has petrol this time). If they have a car, they can go. If they have a bike, they can go. It is only if neither of the input conditions is true that the trip becomes impossible — in computer jargon, the output becomes false (i.e. it is not true that he gets the trip to the country).

There is one more essential logic gate to consider, the NOT gate. This gate simply gives as an output the opposite of the input. If the input is true, the output will be false. If the input is false, the output will be true. Extending our metaphor of a trip to the country, whether by car or by bike, it must be false that there is a flat tyre to get a trip to the country. If the input (a flat tyre) is true, then the output (a trip) will be false.

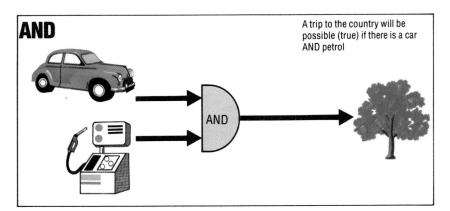

AND

A trip to the country will be possible (true) if there is a car AND petrol

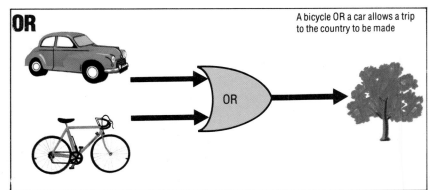

OR

A bicycle OR a car allows a trip to the country to be made

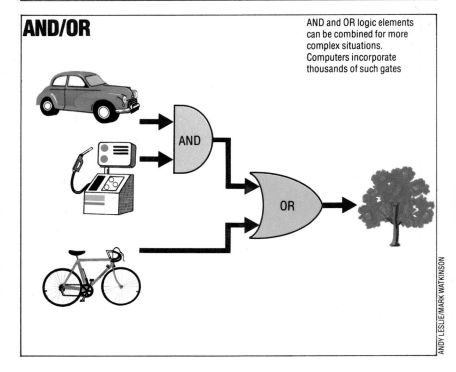

AND/OR

AND and OR logic elements can be combined for more complex situations. Computers incorporate thousands of such gates

ANDY LESLIE/MARK WATKINSON

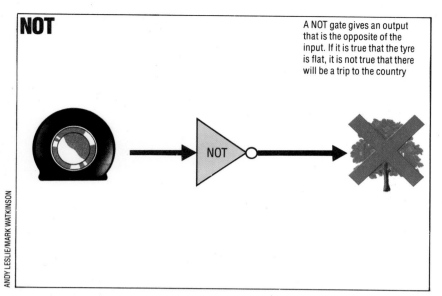

NOT

A NOT gate gives an output that is the opposite of the input. If it is true that the tyre is flat, it is not true that there will be a trip to the country

ANDY LESLIE/MARK WATKINSON

These logic elements can be combined and we have illustrated this using the trip to the country example. Combinations of AND, OR and NOT allow all decisions based on conventional logic to be made. It is interesting to work out the logic decisions (gates) needed for other problems. Try working out what would be required for a garden barbecue, for example. It can become quite complicated. To have the barbecue in the garden (the true output) we would need various input conditions: money OR a cheque book OR a credit card (to buy the food and drink) AND a free evening AND fine weather AND a grill AND charcoal.

Truth Tables

The symbols we have used in the illustrations are the same as those used in computer circuit diagrams. To see just how easily logical decisions can be implemented using electrical circuits, let's look at the 'truth table' for the AND illustration. If we use the letter c to represent the 'having a car' input condition and the letter p for the 'having petrol' input condition, we can represent the 'having a trip to the country' output condition using a t. We can then use T to stand for true and F to stand for false. The truth table shows all possible combinations of input conditions and the effect of using AND on the output. It looks like this:

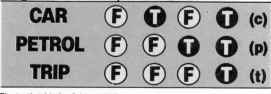

CAR	F	T	F	T	(c)
PETROL	F	F	T	T	(p)
TRIP	F	F	F	T	(t)

The truth table for 2-input AND

CAR	0	1	0	1	(c)
PETROL	0	0	1	1	(p)
TRIP	0	0	0	1	(t)

The same truth table using 0 and 1 for False and True

In computers we use the binary digits zero and one to stand for false and true respectively. The computer interprets a plus voltage as one and a zero voltage as a zero. An AND circuit can easily be made using transistors so that if both inputs are plus voltages, the output will also be a plus voltage. If either or both of the inputs is a voltage of zero, the output from the circuit will also be a zero.

An electronic OR circuit gives a positive voltage output if either or both of the inputs is positive. If both the inputs are zero, the output will also be zero. In a NOT circuit, the input is simply reversed: if the input is positive, the output will be zero; if the input is zero, the output will be positive.

The 7408 Chip
Large silicon chips often contain thousands of gates to perform AND, OR and NOT logic. The small 7408 chip illustrated contains all the transistors and circuitry for four AND gates. The gates are represented using the logic symbols, rather than showing the actual circuits

TONY LODGE

Gates And Adders

Binary numbers, 1s and 0s, can be added together using the simple logic of AND, OR, and NOT

We have seen in True Or False? (see page 50) how relatively simple transistor circuits can be used to make logical decisions such as AND, OR and NOT. The surprising thing is that these same 'logic gates' are also the building blocks used to perform arithmetic inside the computer. In logic, the inputs to the gates are either zero volts, to represent 'false', or a positive voltage, to represent 'true'. The absence of voltage is usually symbolised by a zero (0) and a positive voltage is usually symbolised by a one (1). When logic gates are used to perform arithmetic, the same zeros and ones are used, but this time they literally represent the ones and zeros being added.

If we want to add two binary digits, there will be only two inputs to the adding circuit, and there can be only four combinations of input — $0 + 0$, $0 + 1$, $1 + 0$ and $1 + 1$. From our studies of binary arithmetic, we have learnt that 0 plus 0 equals 0 (as in decimal arithmetic). We also know that 0 plus 1 (or 1 plus 0) equals 1 (again as in decimal arithmetic). The difference from the arithmetic we learnt in school is that in binary, 1 plus 1 equals 0 carry 1. Showing these four additions arithmetically, they would look like this:

X		Y		Z
0	+	0	=	0
0	+	1	=	1
1	+	0	=	1
1	+	1	=	10

If we were to use an OR gate to do the addition, we would get a false output (0) if both inputs were false (0), and a true output (1) if either of the inputs were true ($0 + 1$ or $1 + 0$).

So far, using a simple OR gate would seem perfectly adequate for adding two binary digits. But wait. If both the inputs are true, the output of a simple OR gate would also be true, but that would be the wrong answer in binary arithmetic. The answer should be a 0 and a carry 1. A simple OR gate would get it right for three out of the four possible input combinations, but three right out of four isn't good enough.

What is needed is a circuit that will give an answer of 0 if both inputs are 0, and an answer of 1 if either of the inputs is 1 and the other is 0, and an answer of 0 if both inputs are 1 (as in the truth table above). This is not as hard as it may seem. If we have two AND gates, with the two inputs going to both gates, but with one input being inverted

The Desk-Top Adder
Until the recent invention of the electronic calculator, the mechanical adding machine (or cash register) was a common feature in shops and offices. With the exception of a few refinements, it has remained essentially unchanged for 300 years; working through an arrangement of toothed wheels and cogs. The commercial potential for a calculator was quick to be seen. Pascal invented the first adding machine for use in his father's tax office. With division and multiplication developed by Leibniz, the calculator was ready for business.

through a NOT gate to one of the AND gates. And if the other input is being inverted through another NOT gate going to the other AND gate (see illustration), we have a situation where a 0 on both inputs will give a false output from both AND gates, and a 1 on both inputs will similarly give a false output from both gates. On the other hand, a 0 on one input and a 1 on the other will give two true inputs to one of the AND gates. One of these gates will therefore produce a true output. If the two AND gates have their outputs connected to an OR gate, the output of the OR gate will be true only if one, and one only, of the two inputs is true.

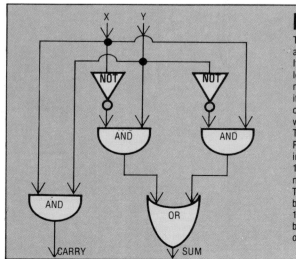

Half Adder

The half adder is a device for adding two binary numbers. It uses an arrangement of logical gates to do this. It is named the half adder because it cannot cope with the carried digit that often results when adding numbers. Try adding 1 and 1. Remember that a NOT gate inverts a 1 to a 0 and a 0 to a 1. Both inputs to an AND gate must be 1 for an output of 1. The output of an OR gate will be 1 if one or both inputs are 1. The output will only be 0 if both inputs are 0. The journey of the digits is illustrated here

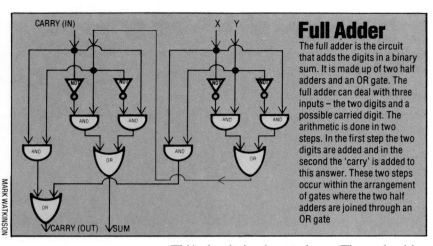

Full Adder

The full adder is the circuit that adds the digits in a binary sum. It is made up of two half adders and an OR gate. The full adder can deal with three inputs – the two digits and a possible carried digit. The arithmetic is done in two steps. In the first step the two digits are added and in the second the 'carry' is added to this answer. These two steps occur within the arrangement of gates where the two half adders are joined through an OR gate

CARRY (IN)   X Y
CARRY (OUT)   SUM

MARK WATKINSON

This circuit is almost there. The only thing lacking is that an input of two 1s, although giving a 'sum' of 0, correctly, fails to produce a carry signal. However, an additional AND gate, wired in parallel to the two inputs, produces a carry signal when, and only when, both inputs are true. The truth table for the circuit in the illustration, called a half adder, is as follows:

Z (input one)	Y (input two)	C ('carry' output)	S ('sum' output)
0	0	0	0
0	1	0	1
1	0	0	1
1	1	1	0

It is called a 'half adder' because, in a sense, it is only half adequate. If all we wanted to do was to add a single column of two binary digits, it would be fine. Usually, however, we will want to add two bytes of data together, and each byte contains eight bits. The adder looking after the rightmost column of binary digits would indeed need to be nothing more than a half adder. However, all the

adders to the left of that need to be able to accept three inputs — the two digits from 'their' column and any carry from the next column to the right. Consider this addition:

$$011$$
$$+111$$
$$\overline{1010}$$

When adding the 'ones' column, we say 1 and 1 is 0, carry 1' and write a 0 under the 'ones' column. When we add the 'twos' column, we say 1 and 1 is 0, carry 1, plus the carry from the 'ones', is 1, carry 1. We write a 1 under the 'twos' column and carry 1 to the 'fours' column. Here we say 0 and 1 is 1, plus the carry from the 'twos' column, is 0, carry 1. We write the 0 in the 'fours' column and carry 1, which we write under the 'eights' column. In other words, the truth table for a 'full adder' able to handle carries as well as two binary digits, would look like:

X	Y	C(in)	C(out)	S
0	0	0	0	0
1	0	0	0	1
0	1	0	0	1
0	0	1	0	1
0	1	1	1	0
1	0	1	1	0
1	1	0	1	0
1	1	1	1	1

A full adder can be made using two half adders and an additional OR gate. The 'carry out' of each full adder is connected directly to the 'carry in' of the adder on its left and as many full adders can be chained together in this way as required.

In modern microcomputers, most additions and other arithmetical operations are carried out in large numbers of adder circuits conceptually identical to the ones we have described above. For the most part, though, these adder circuits are included in, and form just a part of, the circuitry of the CPU (the Central Processing Unit). Before the days of large scale integration that culminated in the microprocessor, simpler integrated circuits containing just a few gates were in common use. These circuits are usually called TTL chips (TTL stands for transistor-transistor logic because of the way most of the logic switching is performed by transistors directly coupled together). The inside of a typical CPU consists of a single silicon chip incorporating small areas of RAM and ROM memory, very large numbers of switching circuits and a part known as the ALU or Arithmetic and Logic Unit. The ALU is the part of the CPU containing all the logic gates and adders needed for the computer to perform computations and make logical decisions.

8-Bit Adder

When you add large numbers carefully together the addition is done digit by digit. The computer does the same. In the illustration, two 8-digit binary numbers are being added. The top row contains the first number and the second row the other. Working from the right-hand side, there can be no 'carry' to add to the sum of the first two digits, so a half adder is sufficient. But for the second and subsequent pairs of digits, full adders must be used (any 'carry' is indicated by a 1 below the adder). Try working through the process as the computer does and check your answer in the bottom row

0	1	1	0	0	0	1	1
0	1	0	0	0	1	1	0
F/A	F/A	F/A	F/A	F/A	F/A	F/A	H/A
1	0	1	0	1	0	0	1

F/A = Full Adder
H/A = Half Adder

Total Recall

How the computer keeps careful track of all the information stored in its memory — and makes sure that it never forgets

RAM Memory

The RAM chip (below) is one of the major recent advances in computer technology. RAM (Random Access Memory) is one of the varieties of completely electronic memory, a category that also includes ROM (Read Only Memory). Cassette tapes and magnetic floppy disks are examples of the other main kind, electro-magnetic memory.

RAM memory is fabricated from silicon using a photographic process and chemical etching to create thousands of tiny transistors. Each 'bit' of memory requires at least one transistor in a storage cell circuit.

The time taken to 'write' a single bit into any one of the 16,384 storage cells is about 200 nanoseconds — a five-millionth of a second

In human terms, memory is the storehouse of the mind, the place where details of experience are stored for later use. And in computer terms 'memory' means pretty much the same thing, only a computer's memory is more limited in what it can do.

For a human being, poor memory is an inconvenience or an embarrassment. For a computer, it is disastrous. Without memory, the computer would have nothing to work on and nothing to tell it what to do, since it also uses its memory to store the programs that drive it.

In both cases, the word 'memory' implies two things; storage and recall. Storing information without being able to get it out again is not very useful, and trying to recall information that hasn't been stored is obviously futile.

The two kinds of memory are similar in another way too. Human memory appears to be of two general types, short-term and long-term. A man crossing the road, for example, will remember to wait until the approaching car has passed by. But when he is safely on the other side of the road, the vehicle is forgotten. His memory of the car was short-term.

However, had the same car contained two masked men in the back seat, and the man's wife in the driver's seat, he may well have remembered the whole incident, including the type and colour of the car, and possibly its registration number! This was a long-term memory.

Stretching a point a bit, computers have short-term and long-term memories as well. The long-term or 'non-volatile' type contains programs and information that the user wants to keep; these are stored as magnetic recordings on the surface of cassette tape, floppy disks, or ROM packs.

The short-term or 'volatile' type is the RAM chip inside the computer itself, and is only used temporarily while the computer is working. The moment the power supply is removed, even for a fraction of a second, all the contents in the memory disappear instantly.

The analogy with human memory is not exact, however. For the computer to work, the right programs and data need to be transferred from long-term storage into short-term storage so that the computer can have instant access to them. And the *way* data are stored and recalled to and from a computer memory is completely different too from the methods human beings use.

The way human memory works is still a mystery, since memories of a particular incident do not seem to be stored in any identifiable tiny segment of the brain. We do not have to figure out where a particular item of memory is to recall it to the foreground of the mind. And when we have finished with a memory, we do not have to worry about putting it back in its particular slot in the brain.

Organised Chaos

In computer memory, it is the *location* of each item that is vital. The computer has to be able to find a particular byte of information, whether it is part of a program or part of the program's data. The computer also needs to keep a 'note' of where it puts the information.

Human memory seems more like a box crammed full of information, but not organised. The pieces of information are just stuffed in, apparently at random, tangling up with each other and being shoved around inside the brain as more and more images and experience are crowded in. Somehow or other, the brain can make sense of this and pull out what it needs, when it needs it.

Computer memory is more like a giant rack of pigeonholes, each hole completely separate from the rest. Everything is very orderly; each pigeonhole has a number (called its 'address') and contains just one byte, no more and no less. The computer finds information by pigeonhole number, not by what is stored in that pigeonhole.

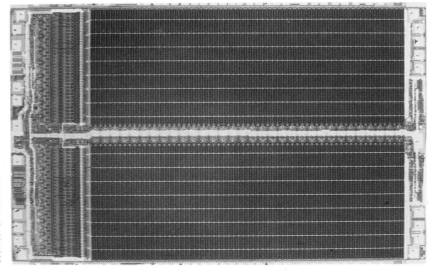

COURTESY OF MOSTEK LTD

Memory

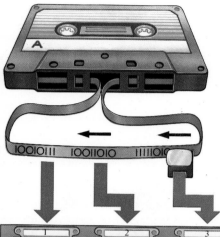

Programs recorded on tape are stored 'sequentially', with every bit from each byte recorded one after the other. When the tape is replayed, the computer 'reads' each bit but stores them in groups of eight (bytes) in each memory cell. The first byte on the tape is placed in the first available memory cell, the second byte in the next one and so on. When the computer needs to 'run' the program, all it needs to know is the 'starting address'. The computer transfers the contents of each memory cell into the CPU in sequence and these bytes cause it to 'execute' or perform the actions required by the program.

Part of the computer's memory is occupied by 'housekeeping' programs responsible for fundamental aspects of its operation — checking which keys have been pressed, displaying characters on the screen and so on. Such 'built-in' software may also include the BASIC programming language. These internal programs take up space in the memory and leave less for the storage of the user's own or commercial software. Some BASIC

versions, for example, are stored in 16 Kbytes of memory. If the computer is supplied with 64 Kbytes of memory, only 48 Kbytes will be left for other programs. When a program is loaded from cassette tape, the first available (empty) memory location will clearly not be the first location in RAM. It is one of the duties of the housekeeping software to know and remember where the first memory location available to the user is. After the program has been loaded into the computer's RAM, the housekeeping software says, in effect, 'start by looking at memory location x and then continue by examining each successive memory location, entering the contents of that location into the CPU and doing what it says'. The original order in which the program was entered on the keyboard by the programmer is the same as the order recorded on the tape. When the program is transferred from the tape to the computer's memory, it is put into the memory cells in the same order. To the computer, the effect is the same as if the program had just been typed in on the keyboard

Computers have no intelligence, and cannot organise their memories for themselves. The only reason a computer can store anything is because someone has put it into the right pigeonhole in the right order, and at the right time. How does that happen in a typical home computer system?

When you turn your home computer on, a message usually appears on the screen to tell you it is working. In most cases, it also informs you that you can start writing a program. This message, and the facilities that let you start programming, are stored in part of the computer's internal memory; they need to be stored in the long-term memory (usually in a Read Only Memory or ROM chip — see page 13).

This portion of the computer's memory contains programs that check if keys have been pressed, 'print' letters on the screen, and perform other essential 'housekeeping' jobs. It also contains a special program that translates commands usually written in BASIC into the much simpler binary language of ones and zeros understood by the computer.

When the home computer is switched on, the message on the screen often says 'x bytes free', where 'x' is something like 15,797 or another such strange number. What this tells you is the number of pigeonholes in the computer's memory that are

free for you to use. Hitting keys on the keyboard starts to fill these free pigeonholes up — and here we come to the other important thing about computer memory, the *order* in which information is stored.

Pressing a key on the keyboard sends one byte (representing the letter pressed — see page 7) to the memory for storage. Hitting the 'k' key, for example, puts the letter 'k' into a pigeonhole in memory in binary form.

But which pigeonhole does that 'k' go into? It goes into the first free slot in the computer's short-term memory. If you think of a block of empty pigeonholes hung on a wall, the 'k' would go in one in the top left-hand corner.

Hit another key, say 'e', and the appropriate pattern of bits goes into the second empty hole, to the right of the 'k'. Hit a third, a 'y', and it goes into the third hole next to the 'e'. Looking at our block of pigeonholes, the codes for the word 'key' appear on the top row.

The computer has an internal 'counter' to assess which pigeonhole it has reached; it knows where to start because the built-in 'housekeeping' program tells it where the free area of memory starts. As each letter is stored, the counter is increased by one to nominate the next pigeonhole for the next letter typed.

Safely Stored

The computer can store thousands of bytes of information in its memory and remember where each one is stored

One way of describing computer memory is in terms of long-term and short-term storage. The long-term type does not lose the information stored and can retain it for long periods even when the power is switched off. Magnetic tape and floppy disks come in this category (see page 54).

Computers also need fast short-term memory for the temporary storage of programs and results.

Another way of looking at computer memory is to think of it as being either internal or external memory. The internal memory is located inside the computer and is usually fully 'electronic' while external memory is peripheral to or outside the computer. External memory is usually partly mechanical, involving mechanisms such as cassette decks, floppy disk drives or even paper tape punches and readers.

The internal electronic memory is usually called the main memory, while the external memory is referred to as secondary memory or backup

EPROM
The problem with ordinary ROMs is that the memory contents are 'built in' at the manufacturing stage and cannot be changed. EPROMs (Erasable Programmable Read Only Memory) are considerably more flexible. Once programmed, they can be reprogrammed by first erasing the contents and then 'writing' in a new program. EPROMs incorporate a 'window' of silica that allows ultra violet rays to pass through to the interior, causing the capacitors that store the bits in the EPROM to discharge. In the absence of ultra violet light, the capacitors retain their charge indefinitely and the memory contents are retained.

memory. These days, internal memory comes in two main varieties – RAM and ROM.

Both RAM and ROM are completely electronic devices fabricated in the form of silicon chips and packaged in rectangular plastic cases with sets of parallel tin or silver plated leads. There are further similarities in the way they are selected and 'addressed' by the computer's CPU, but we shall come to that shortly.

The chief functional difference is that ROM memory chips are used to store programs in a permanent form. The pattern of ones and zeros in

each memory location is fixed and set at the time of manufacture and cannot be subsequently changed. ROMs are the 'reference libraries' of the computer world. The computer can refer to the contents of the ROM, but is not able to 'write' anything there.

ROM stands for Read Only Memory, read being the term used to describe what the computer does when it 'accesses' or retrieves information from memory. ROMs come in a number of slightly different types, some of which can have the internal program specially removed or erased and can then be re-programmed. A reasonably typical ROM, however, is the 2364 from Intel. This chip is described as being a 65,536 bit ROM, organised as 8 Kbytes of 8 bits. What this means is that the 64 Kbits are grouped together into 8-bit bytes and each 'addressable' location accesses or reads one whole byte. In mathematics $1K = 2^{10}$ (two to the power of ten) or 1,024 so $64K = 64 \times 1,024$ or 65,536.

The computer therefore has to be able to select any one of 8,192 (8K) address locations. A close look at the specifications for the 2364 chip reveals that it has 28 pins with one reserved for the +5 volt power supply and one for the ground (earth) connection. This leaves a total of 26 pins. Each byte contains eight bits, so when a byte is read from the chip, the eight bits in that byte have to be conveyed by wires from the chip to the CPU. Consequently, there are eight wires to convey the bits in the byte being read to the CPU. These wires are called the 'data bus'. Eight of the pins on the chip are dedicated to this, one for each bit in the byte.

This leaves 18 pins. One pin is not needed and is not connected. It is retained because it is easier to manufacture chips with an even number of pins. Four pins are used for 'selecting' the chip in various ways. These are the 'output enable' pin, the 'chip enable' pin and the two 'chip select' pins. These pins take signals from the computer to enable the chip to know when it is required.

The remaining 13 pins are the 'address' pins. Each pin is connected to an 'address bus' wire and these carry the address of the byte required, coded in binary form. Thirteen binary digits can give 2^{13} or 8,192 unique combinations of one and zero, so the 13 address lines are just enough to select uniquely each and every of the 8,192 bytes stored in the ROM.

RAMs are the blackboards of the computer world. Programs and data can be stored in them

ROM and RAM

Long-Term Memory
The ROM (Read Only Memory) is analogous to a book in that it is a place where information is stored permanently. You cannot change or remove the data any more than you can alter the words on a printed page

Short-Term Memory
The RAM (Random Access Memory) is more like a filing system than a book, since the information can be changed and the data is not permanent — the RAM is wiped clean when the computer is turned off

temporarily, while the computer is working, and results and other data can also be 'written' there temporarily. RAM memory is generally more complex internally than ROM because every bit in every byte of RAM must be capable of being changed if it is 'written to'. A fairly typical RAM chip is the Intel 2114. Each 2114 RAM chip holds 4,096 bits of memory, and these are organised as 1024 'nibbles' (half bytes) of four bits. This means that each location address will output four bits of data. Two of these chips will therefore be needed to produce a whole Kbyte of data. Each 2114 chip has just 18 pins, two of which are used for the ground and power supply. Four are used for the input/output data lines. One is used for the chip select signal (the signal that tells the chip when it is required or 'selected') and one is used to tell the chip, once it has been selected, if it is being written to or read from. The remaining ten pins are used for the address bus. Ten address lines can uniquely identify 2^{10} locations, or 1,024. If a computer were supplied with 64 Kbytes of RAM, and if Intel 2114 chips were used, a total of 128 RAM chips would be required as two chips are needed for every whole byte. These days it is more usual to use higher density RAM chips that pack more memory into the same space. Using more modern RAM chips, such as the 4164, it is possible to get 64 Kbytes of RAM with just eight chips.

RAM and ROM chips are becoming cheaper and more compact year by year and it is now possible to get 128 Kbits on a single chip. Progress in packing even higher densities into single chips is slowing down, however. The circuitry on the silicon is becoming so minute that the optical techniques used to 'etch' the circuits are barely up to the job. The 'high density' memory chips of the future are likely to be manufactured using electron beam or X-ray etching methods.

Broadly, there are two types of RAM memory in use, known as static and dynamic RAM. There are advantages and disadvantages to both types, but dynamic RAM is now used more commonly than static. Both types lose the memory contents as soon as the power supply is switched off, but dynamic memory needs to have the contents 'refreshed' every few milliseconds. Every bit in memory needs to be refreshed or rewritten without slowing down the CPU's ability to access data here. This means that special and very critical timing circuitry has to be designed, making the circuit designer's job more difficult.

Dynamic memory offers two distinct advantages over static memory. Dynamic memory requires only one transistor per bit, compared with the three transistors normally required for each bit in static memory. This allows more memory to be packed into smaller chips. Most dynamic RAM chips have only 16 pins. The other advantage of dynamic RAMs is that they use less power than their static counterparts. They therefore generate less heat and need smaller, cheaper power supplies.

The advantage of static RAM lies in the simplicity of circuit design. Once the contents of memory have been written, they stay in memory without needing to be refreshed. Each one-bit memory cell requires three transistors, so it is difficult to achieve the high densities that dynamic RAM allows. Static RAM also consumes more power and the extra heat generated complicates the computer's cooling system and may require the use of a cooling fan, making the design a lot more expensive.

Message Understood

Press a key, and hidden layers of software spring into action – decoding your instructions, searching the memory and all the while scanning the keyboard for your next command

A computer is an assembly of metal, plastic and silicon which, without a program in its memory, is incapable of performing any sort of useful task — just like a record player with no record on the turntable. The process of getting the computer to perform the specific task you require is therefore known as 'programming'. Even the relative beginner to programming will be able to identify two distinct phases to solve a problem. First the problem must be translated and written down in a form which the computer can understand. Secondly, this program must be fed into the computer and 'run'. These two phases can be further subdivided into two stages — the programmer himself goes through the first stage, while in stage two the computer must take the actions (usually without the user's knowledge or intervention).

Suppose that you want to write a program to prepare a payroll. The first thing you need is a perfectly clear understanding of the problem. What do you require as your output from the computer? What information will the computer need to produce the weekly payslips? This may entail salaries, hours worked this week, etc. The next essential is to specify the process by which this output is going to be produced, for example: 'How are tax and pension contributions calculated?'

In a large business application, this may well be done by a trained 'Systems Analyst' — whose speciality is analysing the way a business operates and writing it down in a form which can easily be translated into a program. For home or educational programs, all this would usually be done by the programmer himself.

If computers could understand plain English then this 'program specification' could be run straight away; but unfortunately they cannot, yet. Many beginners experience difficulties because they try to write the program from start to finish — in the same way that you might translate an English essay into French. Experienced programmers, however, break this stage down even further. They might divide the payroll specification into four 'modules': for inputting the week's data, calculation, storing the cumulative results like 'tax paid this year', and printing out the payslips.

Each module can then be broken down into smaller structures. This is called 'structured programming'; each of these smaller sections is simple and can be expressed as one or two lines in a program. Finally, the whole collection of lines — the program listing — is typed into the computer.

A good programmer always keeps notes from every stage and these reflect the many distinct levels from a problem written in English to a program written in a high-level language such as BASIC.

What happens from the moment you type RUN is entirely under the control of the computer and again involves many different layers or stages. However, the internal operations of the computer are 'hidden' — all the user is aware of is his program asking him for relevant information and producing the required output.

Because the microprocessor cannot understand a high-level language, the prime task ahead of the

From Problem To Program

The origin of a computer program begins with realising there is a problem that needs to be solved; in this case how to keep the temperature of the greenhouse at a constant level. In order to obtain the answer, this problem needs to progress through several layers of processing which results in the completed program

The problem arises . . .

The idea is scribbled down roughly on a piece of paper

A flowchart is formulated to analyse the problem and to develop the structure of the program . . .

It is then translated into one of the computer languages, for example, BASIC

computer is to translate the instructions into machine code. On home computers this is done by the interpreter which is stored permanently in the computer's ROM.

The interpreter is a sophisticated machine code program, executed directly by the microprocessor. When RUN is typed the interpreter starts examining the user's program, character by character. It looks up all the phrases it finds against its own dictionary. If it comes across a character which it doesn't understand (which may simply be because you made a typing mistake) it will stop trying to interpret the program and print a message on the screen such as SYNTAX ERROR.

If the word is in the interpreter's dictionary (e.g. PRINT) this immediately passes to the part of the interpreter which knows how to deal with that function. In this case the routine will now examine what comes after the word PRINT in the user's program and prepare this data as a stream of characters to display.

This is where the next level comes into operation. Somewhere else in the computer's memory is a routine which can accept a stream of characters, store them in another area of memory reserved for the screen, and arrange for them to be converted into the kind of signals needed by the television screen or monitor. This is something that has to be done continuously even while the program itself is purely engaged in calculation.

The same is true at the other end of the computer — the keyboard. A specially written program routine within the computer has to scan the keyboard to find out whether any keys have been pressed, and if so place the appropriate codes in another area of memory for use as the input to the user's program. And because you might want to halt the operation of the program at any time using the BREAK key, the keyboard must be scanned continuously — even while the program is running.

In fact the microprocessor found in most home computers can only do one job at a time so it effectively has to share its time between interpreting the user's program and its own

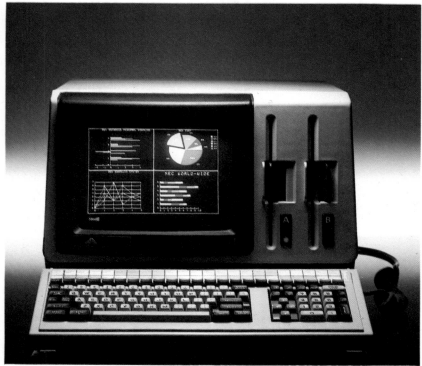

internal functions, such as checking the keyboard and controlling the screen. One method is 'interrupt-driven' where a special electronic circuit interrupts the microprocessor perhaps 50 times every second and 'reminds' it to perform its housekeeping tasks and other functions on the screen and keyboard, before resuming what it was doing.

So even when your program has been typed in, many levels of processing have to be carried out by the computer before the results are produced. Though the process may seem a complex one most of it is looked after by the computer.

Nowadays the trend is moving towards user-friendliness, with the computer doing as much of the routine work as possible. The next generation of computers will be able to write the whole program themselves from a plain English specification.

The Hidden Software
In any computer, there is a complex hidden software hierarchy continually working. Among its many tasks, it monitors and checks when and which key is being pressed, what is on the screen, what instructions are being given to the peripheral, and the status and content of the RAM memory. All these functions are continually in progress while the operator is simply concerned with the next function of his program. The principle of the hidden software hierarchy remains the same, in both sophisticated business computers (as pictured here) and in reasonably-priced home computers

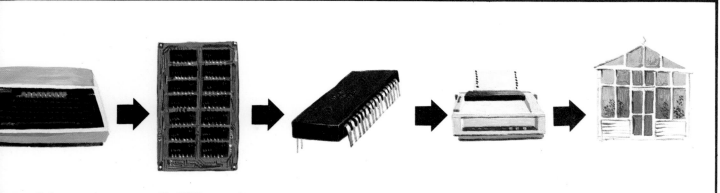

program is then entered the computer's memory via keyboard

The BASIC program then passes through an array of chips. These convert it into machine code that is relayed to the CPU

The computation is then made in the CPU. The resulting data are subsequently transmitted to a peripheral (e.g. a printer, monitor, disk drive etc...)

In this case the printer produces a printout or 'hard copy'

If the program is accurate, the problem is now solved

The Laws Of Thought

A century before the electronic computer was invented, George Boole published his ideas on mathematical logic

COURTESY OF THE ROYAL SOCIETY

In 1815, the year of Napoleon's defeat at the Battle of Waterloo, another significant event in the history of mankind occurred.

George Boole was born in Lincoln, England. The son of a cobbler, he was to become one of the geniuses behind the invention of the computer. Although he died in 1864, a century before the microcomputer revolution began, the modern computer could not have evolved without his ideas.

Boole knew that the processes of reasoning that people carry out in their everyday lives can be described in terms of the formal logic pioneered by the Greeks. He believed that if you tried hard enough you could go further and express human reasoning in a mathematical way. Boole set out to do just this; he taught himself mathematics and began his research into the logic of human decisions.

Sets Of Information

Imagine one night you go to a party. You want to dance so you find the room where people are dancing and look for a partner.

The people in the room are either dancing or they are not dancing — they cannot be doing both. The partner you approach must be either a boy or a girl. Obviously, a person can be male or female but not both.

Now Boole would have made a different approach. He would have seen a dance floor containing 'sets' of people, the male set and the female set, or M and F. Boole would also have seen D and W, or the set of people dancing and the set of people waiting to dance.

His partner would have to satisfy two conditions: be a female and also be waiting to dance. Boole noticed the importance of the 'and' connecting the two conditions and gave it a symbol — an upside down U. He was then able to list the set of possible dance partners as F ∩ W.

However, if he did not want to dance but just chatter to a friend, he could choose anyone from M or F because these two sets include everyone in the room. Again, he saw the importance of the innocent looking 'or' in the condition and gave it the symbol U. So in his logical algebra M∪F contains all the males and all the females in the room.

The logical gates found in computers are named after Boole's symbols, such as AND and OR. In BASIC programming we will soon discover two useful commands called AND and OR. But before we pursue these there is a very picturesque interpretation of Boolean logic — invented by the English mathematicians John Venn (1834–1923) and Charles Dodgson (1832–1892), better known as the author Lewis Carroll.

Let us take a practical problem. Imagine you have stored a list of your acquaintances in the memory of your computer. With each name is listed other information — such as the telephone

George Boole 1815-1864

George Boole was born before electronic computers were ever imagined yet he is one of the founders of the mathematical logic used by today's computers. He was the son of a cobbler and taught himself mathematics in his spare time. He was convinced that the everyday decisions that people make were based on reason, and that this reason could be refined into mathematical logic. He published his ideas in 1847 and almost overnight became famous and was invited to become the first professor of mathematics at the newly founded University of Cork

The Friends' Program

```
10 DIM N$(10),D$(10),F$(10),T$(10),C$(10)
15 REM NAME, TEL. NO., FRIEND?,TENNIS?,CAR?
17 PRINT "ENTER DETAILS IN THE FORM:"
18 PRINT "NAME, PHONE, YES/NO, YES/NO, YES/NO"
20 FOR K = 1 TO 10
30 INPUT N$(K),D$(K),F$(K),T$(K),C$(K)
40 NEXT K
45 REM SEARCH ROUTINE
50 FOR J = 1 TO 10
60 IF F$(J)="YES" AND T$(J)="YES" AND C$(J)="YES" THEN GOSUB 100
70 NEXT J
80 END
100 PRINT N$(J),D$(J)
110 RETURN
```

Venn Diagrams

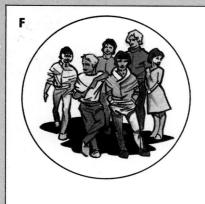

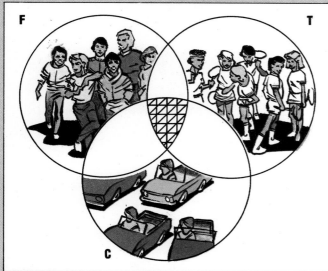

The square box represents the collection, or set, of all the people that are listed in the computer. Generally in Venn diagrams this is called the universal set. The circles within the square represent the individual sets. The friends are identified on the diagram as those people who lie within set F.

Not all the people will play tennis, but those who do are identified in set T. Since there will be some people who both play tennis and are friends, the two circles overlap (F∩T).

Set C identifies those people who own a car. This set overlaps the other two and the people who satisfy all three conditions are contained in the area where all three circles intersect (F∩T∩C). The last diagram represents the same sets, (F,T,C) but the conditions that need to be satisfied have changed. You have decided that you would like either to play tennis or go for a drive. The set of acquaintances who are friends and play tennis is shaded with diagonal lines. The set of acquaintances who are friends and own a car is shaded with horizontal lines. The combination of these two shaded areas represents the friends with whom you could play tennis or go for a drive

number, hobbies, etc. One afternoon you decide you want to play tennis at a court on the other side of town. You need a friend (as opposed to an acquaintance) who plays tennis and owns a car. Your computer is instructed to print out the name and telephone number of every person who satisfies all three conditions: plays tennis AND owns a car AND is a friend. The program on the left first asks for information about each acquaintance: are they friends, do they have a car, do they play tennis? It is assumed that you have 10 acquaintances but you can change the number of acquaintances to any you want (remembering to change the 10 in the bracket of the DIM statement in line 10). The list is then scanned using an IF...THEN command into which has been inserted a multiple condition. Most BASICS allow the IF...THEN command to work on a condition made up of separate subconditions joined by the commands AND and OR. Finally, the name and telephone number of any acquaintance who satisfies the condition — that they are a friend and play tennis and have a car — is printed.

Very complex combinations of logical functions are found in some programs. Boole's algebra, which was little more than a curiosity in his own lifetime, has come into its own in the age of the computer.

KEVIN JONES

The Nerve Centre

All paths of activity lead in and out of the computer's 'Central Processing Unit'

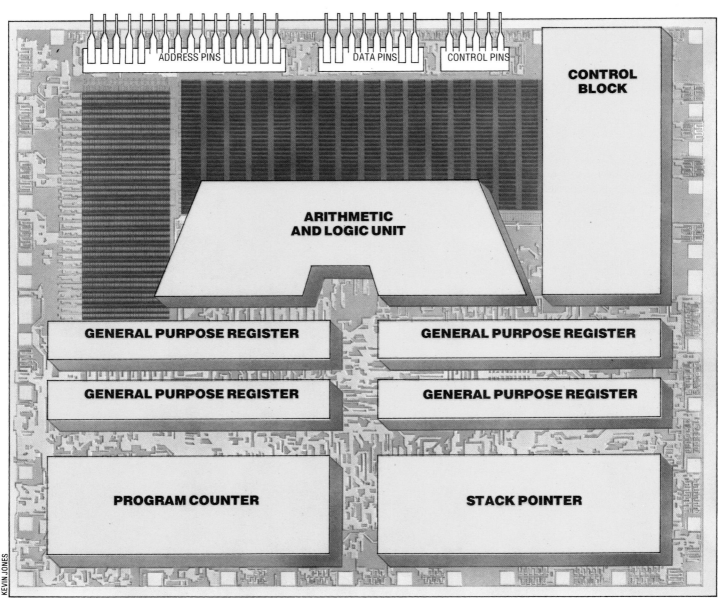

ADDRESS PINS   DATA PINS   CONTROL PINS

CONTROL BLOCK

ARITHMETIC AND LOGIC UNIT

GENERAL PURPOSE REGISTER   GENERAL PURPOSE REGISTER

GENERAL PURPOSE REGISTER   GENERAL PURPOSE REGISTER

PROGRAM COUNTER   STACK POINTER

KEVIN JONES

The computer's function is controlled by the CPU — the Central Processing Unit. The words can be interpreted fairly literally: Central — at the heart of the computer; Processing – it does the work; Unit – it stands alone. A very simple computer (see illustration) could consist of nothing more than a CPU, some memory and some I/O (input/output) circuitry.

The I/O is needed for the computer to communicate with the outside world. In a very simple application, a computer in a washing machine would need I/O in order to turn on motors and heaters. The memory is needed to store instructions for the CPU and data for the CPU to process. The data processed by the CPU may include numbers and binary codes that represent characters (letters, digits and signs such as @ and !).

If some of the memory locations contain instructions to the CPU, and some are data for the CPU to process, how does it know which ones are instructions and which ones are data? To answer this question, we need to take a look inside the microcomputer.

CPUs in 8-bit microcomputers (this includes almost all small home computers) are usually packaged in a single chip with 40 pins, 20 on each of the long sides. Every one of these pins (apart from the 0 and the +5v power supply pins) carries signals into and out of the CPU from other devices such as memory or I/O circuits.

Typical 8-bit CPUs have 16 'address' pins. These pins are connected to the 'address bus'. Each of these pins carries an output signal representing either a one or a zero. Between them, they can have 65,536 different combinations of ones and zeros. They are used to select specific memory locations.

There are also eight 'data' pins, which are connected to the 'data bus'. The data pins carry data into the CPU from memory or I/O, or data from the CPU to memory or I/O.

A number of other pins carry 'control' signals. Some of these signals are are outputs from the CPU and others are inputs. We will see how the control signals are used shortly.

Inside the CPU there are a few small one-byte or two-byte memory cells called registers, some of which are reserved for special purposes. The others are used for the temporary storage of information and are called general purpose registers. There are two other important functional 'blocks' in the CPU, the ALU and the 'control block'.

The abbreviation ALU stands for Arithmetic and Logic Unit. This part of the CPU performs arithmetical and logical operations, including (but not limited to) adding, ANDing, ORing and moving bits to the left or right within a byte.

The control block is a special circuit designed to make the CPU behave in accordance with the instruction received from memory. We can take a specific example, using the instruction codes for the popular Z80 CPU. If the coded instruction 11000110 is received from memory, the CPU will add the contents of the next byte in memory to the contents of one of the registers inside the CPU. If we then want to store the result of that addition in a specified memory location, the next instruction received by the CPU will have to be 00110010, followed by two bytes specifying the actual location in memory where we want the result to be stored.

Suppose that the result of the addition was 37 (using decimal notation), and that the two bytes following the instruction specified address location 33126 (again using decimal notation). The instruction code would cause the control block to set the address pins to the binary equivalent of 33126 (in binary this is 1000000101100110). It would then cause the control pins to send out signals telling the memory to expect some data and that the data must be stored (memorised). It would then cause the data pins to be set to the binary equivalent of 37 (in binary this is 00100101). This data would then pass down the data bus to the memory and would be stored in the memory location specified by the address bus. If, at some later stage, the CPU needed this data to process in some other way (to print on the screen, for example), a different instruction could be sent to the CPU. The control block would interpret this as meaning 'address memory location 33126, get the byte from it and store it temporarily in one of the internal registers'.

The number of registers or temporary memory cells inside the CPU depends on the CPU. They will either be eight-bit (one byte) registers or 16-bit (two byte) registers. The specialised registers are usually given special names such as the 'stack pointer', 'program counter' or 'accumulator'. The general registers are usually referred to as 'the X register', 'the Y register', 'the C register' and so on.

One of the 16-bit registers, and one of the most important, will be the 'program counter' register. This internal memory cell always contains the address (in binary) of the next instruction in memory due to be executed. When the time comes to get the next instruction for the CPU, the contents of the program counter will be put on the address bus, and the byte at the location will be transmitted (via the data bus) to the CPU.

The most important of the eight-bit registers is the 'accumulator'. This is the register that usually stores (temporarily) the result of operations performed by the ALU, bytes brought in from memory or I/O, or the place where bytes are temporarily stored immediately prior to being sent out to memory or I/O.

This introduction to CPUs has been very general; specific points will be covered in detail later. The aim has been to show that special instructions read in from memory cause the CPU to perform specified operations and to set the address pins to access particular memory locations. Data is fetched from these locations, or sent to them, over the data bus. The instructions also cause the control bus signals to indicate to memory or I/O whether data is to be 'read' or 'written'.

Under Control

The illustration shows a CPU with memory 'registers', an Arithmetic and Logic Unit comprising hundreds of logic gates (that perform such operations as adding, ANDing and complementing binary numbers), and a control block. The control block accepts the coded instruction (in binary), interprets it, and causes all the other parts of the CPU to behave appropriately. For example, if an instruction means that the contents of the accumulator should be stored in a particular memory location, the control block will put the address on the address pins, send control signals telling memory to store data, and put the contents of the accumulator on the data bus for transmission to the memory

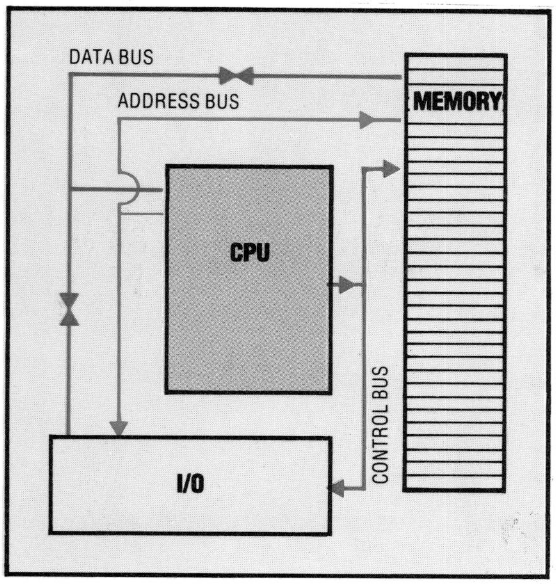

Following Orders

A very simple computer may consist of nothing more than a CPU, some memory and an I/O circuit. The memory will store special instructions that make the CPU perform specified actions. It will also store data for the CPU to process in accordance with the instructions. The I/O circuit will be needed for the CPU to communicate with the outside world. If the computer is controlling a washing machine, the I/O circuit will input signals from the buttons on the front panel and output signals to switch motors and heaters on and off.

The instruction codes for the CPU will be in binary. Each different model of CPU has its own set of instruction codes

DATA BUS
ADDRESS BUS
MEMORY
CPU
CONTROL BUS
I/O

Properly Addressed

The CPU has to locate instructions and data stored in thousands of bytes of computer memory. We reveal what goes on inside the CPU when program instructions are executed

The CPU receives its instructions and data from locations in the computer's memory by setting its address pins to the required binary code for the memory location and then reading the contents of the location into the CPU via the data bus. In actual operation, however, the operation is rather more complicated.

The problem is that the bytes (eight-bit binary codes) in any of the thousands of memory cells in the computer's memory might be instructions, telling the CPU to do something, or data, which the CPU must manipulate in some way. How does the CPU know which bytes are instructions and which are data?

Recognising Codes

First, let's consider what an 'instruction' is. It is a code, in binary, which causes a specific sequence of operations to be performed within the CPU. Thus the code 00111010, if recognised by the CPU as an instruction rather than as just a piece of data, might make the CPU address the next two bytes in

memory, read in the data from them, put that data in a special 'address register', set the address pins to the same number, go to the newly addressed memory location, get the contents of that location on the data bus and load those contents into the CPU's accumulator.

This can sound confusing when expressed in words, but what we have just described is one of the methods of memory addressing used in the popular Z80 CPU. The entire process of getting a byte of data from memory into the CPU is shown in the illustration. Suppose the CPU already knows that the next byte accessed from memory will be an instruction (not data) and that this byte resides in memory location 1053. (All the numbers used in this illustration are in decimal notation.) This address, 1053, will be put on the address bus. In binary, this is 0000010000011101. The 16 address pins are switched 'on' or 'off' to correspond to this number. When the 'address decoder' receives this address over the address bus, it 'decodes' it and switches on one, and only one, of its output lines. This is the line that selects

Chains Of Events

Many stages are involved in even the simplest CPU operation. Instructions, also called 'op-codes', are read into the CPU from memory. These instructions are decoded by the control block and cause specific operations to occur. In this example, instruction 58 is read in from memory location 1053. This particular instruction causes the following chain of events to occur: the byte in the next memory location (1054) will be read in and stored in one half of the CPU's 16-bit address register. The byte in the next location (1055) will be read in and stored in the other half. These two bytes now represent the address (elsewhere in memory) where some data is stored. The contents of the address register are now put on the address bus so that the next memory location accessed will be address 3071. The contents of this address are put onto the data bus and read into the CPU. This byte (96 in our example) is then placed in the CPU's accumulator, where it will stay until operated on by a further instruction. The address bus will then revert back to its previous address + 1, so that it will now be addressing location 1056. The CPU knows that whatever is contained in that location must be an instruction and a similar sequence of operations will be repeated. In this example, the next instruction is 84, which is interpreted by the control block to 'complement' or invert the bits in the accumulator. Since 84 is a 'one byte' instruction, the CPU knows that the byte in the next memory location, 1057, will also be an instruction

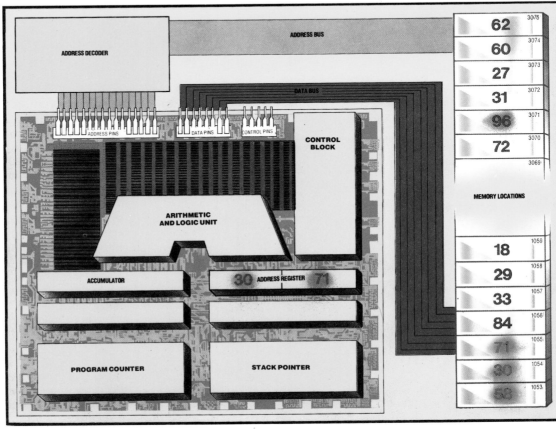

the memory location 1053.

The next stage is that the contents of this address, which is 58, or 00111010 in binary, is placed onto the data bus and 'loaded' into the CPU. Here, because the CPU is expecting an instruction, the byte is interpreted by the control block and causes a very precise sequence of operations to be performed. This particular instruction specifies that the next two bytes in memory will contain 16 bits to be used as a memory location, and that the contents of this location are to be loaded into the CPU's accumulator. As soon as the CPU recognises this instruction, it knows that the next two bytes in memory will specify an address and that the contents of that address will be loaded into the accumulator. It consequently knows that it will not receive another instruction from memory until after these operations have been performed, and that the next instruction will reside in location 1056.

The instruction we are using as an example causes the address bus to be incremented by one, so that the next memory location addressed is 1054. The contents of this location are then put on the data bus and loaded into the CPU. This time, however, they are put into one half of an address register. Having done that, the CPU increments the address bus again so that it now addresses location 1055. The contents of this location go on to the data bus and are similarly loaded into the CPU, this time to be stored in the other half of the address register.

Transferring Numbers

The next stage — and remember that all of these actions happen automatically as a result of the original instruction — is that the numbers in the address register are transferred to the address bus. These numbers, as we can see, are 3071. The memory location now being addressed is therefore 3071. This address (0000101111111111 in binary) is decoded by the address decoder and selects memory cell 3071. The contents of this location, 96, (01100000 in binary) are put onto the data bus and loaded into the CPU. This time, however, the data will be put in the CPU's accumulator. After this the address bus will be set to 1056 and the CPU will expect to find another instruction there.

Now that the CPU has one piece of data in its accumulator, what sort of instruction might be expected to be encountered next? It could be almost anything — CPUs have from a few dozen to a few hundred instructions they recognise, depending on the CPU — but suppose we wanted to invert the data in the accumulator. Inverting means changing each one into a zero and each zero into a one. The instruction to do this would be located at address 1056. On our imaginary CPU, the code for this instruction would be 84. When this number was received by the CPU, the data in the accumulator would be inverted. The number that

was in the accumulator was 96 (01100000 in binary). The instruction to invert would cause it to be changed to 10011111 in binary. The instruction to invert a number in the accumulator is a 'one-byte' instruction, so again the CPU would know that the contents of the next memory location, 1057, would again be an instruction rather than data.

This method of addressing a memory location to retrieve a piece of data is only one of several methods available to the programmer. The specific instruction bytes we used in the example (58 to load the accumulator and 84 to invert the contents of the accumulator) are the instructions for our hypothetical CPU, but the same principle applies to all other microprocessor chips. The only difference is that different codes are used for the various instructions and each make of CPU has slightly different 'instruction sets'.

I/O (Input/Output) locations must also have unique addresses, but the principles for addressing them by the CPU are the same. Usually, in eight-bit microprocessors, only eight of the address lines are available for addressing I/O locations, so the maximum number of I/O addresses is 256. This, however, is more than enough for most small computer applications.

Address Decoding
The 16 lines constituting the address bus are capable of uniquely identifying any one of 65,636 separate memory locations. The combination of ones and zeros on the address bus is decoded in address decoders. Part of the decoding is performed by address decoders built up from simple logic gates in chips mounted on the circuit; much of the decoding is performed by equivalent circuits inside the memory chips themselves. The illustration shows how two address lines can be decoded to select one, and only one, of four chips

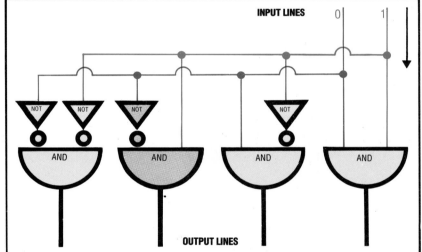

Address decoding is always needed so that the device selected by the CPU (whether it be a memory location or an I/O location) is made uniquely active while all the other memory or I/O locations remain inactive. This process is called 'enabling'. When there are only a small number of address lines to decode, it is possible to use simple logic gate chips to perform the decoding. The principle of a two-to-four line decoder is shown in the illustration. It is usual to use this type of simple decoding for selecting I/O devices. As the number of address lines increases, however, the complexity of the decoding circuit grows massively. When there are 65,536 separate memory locations that must be individually and uniquely selected, it is usual for most of the address decoding to be performed inside the memory chips.

Digital Dialogue

Input and Output are essential to the operation of any computer system

Analogue To Digital

In the real world, few pieces of information come in discrete, digital steps. Rather, they are infinitely variable like noise levels or the tides.

In order to make these data comprehensible to the computer, the signal must first be digitised. The Analogue-to-Digital (A/D) converter takes samples from the signal source at a known, constant rate — perhaps one hundred every second. Each of these samples is stored in a separate memory location as a digital value, thus allowing calculations of variance to be made, and out-of-limits conditions to be recognised.

Digital-to-Analogue (D/A) converters perform a similar function in reverse, statistical techniques being used to smooth out the peaks into a regular curve

Input/Output, or I/O as it is commonly abbreviated, is the term used to describe the transfer of information between the CPU (the Central Processing Unit forming the heart of the computer) and the 'outside world'. The 'outside world' in this context means any devices that may be connected to the computer. It does not include RAM and ROM memory, which are considered to be integral to the computer. The distinction between what is held to be 'inside' the computer and 'outside' it is somewhat arbitrary. But all of the logic circuits (see page 52), designed to work in close conjunction with the CPU and main memory, are considered to be part of the 'inside' of the computer.

External devices, which use I/O for communication with the computer, include a wide variety of peripherals ranging from the keyboard to floppy disk drives, joysticks, printers and video display units.

When the CPU wants to retrieve data from memory, it has first to 'address' the location where the byte of data is stored. Similarly, if the CPU wants to store a byte of data for later use, it must

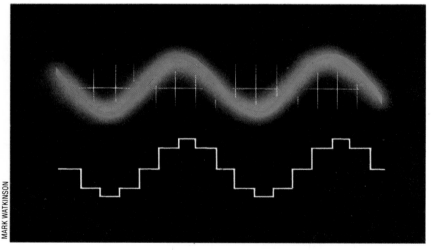

first address the location where the item of data is to be stored. This process is called 'memory addressing'. It involves the CPU putting the binary digits corresponding to the desired memory location on a set of 16 wires connected to the CPU's 'address pins'. These wires are called the 'address bus'. Special circuitry in the memory section is able to decode these 16 binary digits to select the correct memory location. (Sixteen binary digits can give 65,536 unique combinations of ones and zeros and can therefore

address that many different memory locations.)

If the computer wants to communicate with an external device, it also has to 'locate' that device in a similar way. Only eight address lines are available. This limits the total number of separate I/O locations that can be selected to 256. This is a small number compared with the addressing power of 16 address lines, but in practice 256 is more than adequate. There's usually no need for huge numbers of external devices to be connected to a computer.

Selecting Devices

To find out how the computer actually selects an external device and sends data to it, let's consider one of the simplest output devices possible — an LED (Light Emitting Diode) mounted on the keyboard of the computer to show when the 'caps lock' key has been pressed (there's a key and an LED like this on the BBC Microcomputer). To the computer, the LED is simply another external device to which it can send data. In the case of a single LED, the data will be either a single 1 (to turn the LED on) or a single 0 (to turn the LED off). Even though it is just a humble LED requiring a single bit of data, it still needs to have an address or location. The CPU can't spend its whole time addressing one LED. It needs to be able to select the LED once only to tell it when it needs to switch on, and again to tell it when to switch off. Suppose, for the sake of argument, the LED has an I/O address of 32. To select it, the address lines will have to be set by the CPU to the binary equivalent of 32. This is 00100000 in binary. The LED will have a special 'decoder' circuit that will ignore all other combinations of bits on the address lines. When the address line becomes 00100000, this decoder circuit recognises it and produces a high voltage and therefore a 'true' output. The next part of the circuit needed to switch on the LED is a small chip called a 'data latch'. This latches or holds the data sent to it so that the LED stays on or off until the next time it is addressed and new data is sent to it. This process is known as 'toggling'.

Most of the external devices with which the computer communicates are considerably more complex than a single LED. A printer is a typical peripheral and each time the computer communicates with it, the data transmitted will represent the code for a whole character to be printed. Usually, when large amounts of

MARK WATKINSON

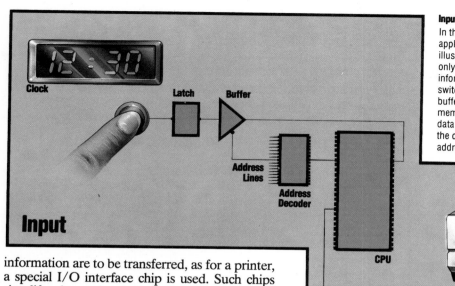

Input

CPU

Output

Video Recorder

Clock

Latch

Buffer

Address Lines

Address Decoder

Address Lines

Address Decoder

Latch

Input/Output
In the simplest control applications, such as that illustrated, the CPU handles only a single piece of information, whether or not a switch has been pressed. The buffer — itself a short-term memory — simply holds the data until the CPU next 'polls' the device in question. The address decoder indicates the source of each signal, and when a change of state is recognised, i.e., that the switch has been pressed, the CPU delivers an appropriate response, in this case changing the clock display from actual time to the time at which the VCR's auto timer will turn on the recorder. Within the output stage, the same procedure works in reverse

information are to be transferred, as for a printer, a special I/O interface chip is used. Such chips simplify the task of the computer engineer, because the interface circuit is designed to incorporate most of the circuitry needed into one chip. One of the most popular of these is the 8255 PPI (Programmable Peripheral Interface). This 40-pin chip contains three eight-bit I/O ports. That means there are 24 i/o pins on the chip, eight pins each for I/O ports A, B and C. Each of these ports can send eight bits (one byte's worth) of data at a time to a peripheral device such as a printer, or receive eight bits of data at a time from an input device such as a keyboard.

To send eight bits of data to a printer, the CPU will first address the PPI and then send it the eight bits of data on the data bus. This data will be stored in a temporary one-byte memory cell

The CPU stops running the program it is executing periodically and takes a quick look at all the input ports. If it finds data there waiting to be input, it instructs the port to put the data on the data bus. The process of enquiry of the input devices is known as 'polling'.

The other method uses 'interrupts'. The device

SERIAL RS232

IEEE 488

Serial And Parallel Ports
Most modern microcomputers provide both serial and parallel ports, the former passing data a bit at a time, the latter in whole bytes. The most common type of serial convention, known as RS232C, uses either a 'D-type' sub-miniature connector, a 25-pin example of which is illustrated here (left), or more rarely a DIN plug like those used in hi-fi systems.

The parallel port (right) follows the IEEE488 convention, developed by Hewlett Packard and adopted as an industry standard by the Institute of Electrical and Electronics Engineers in the USA

within the chip, called a register. The PPI will then make this data available on the appropriate set of I/O pins. A similar principle, but working in reverse, allows data from external input devices to be stored in a register in the chip, and then put onto the data bus when the CPU sends it the appropriate signal. As noted above, external devices cannot be allowed to put their data onto the computer's data bus continuously — it is needed to transfer data to and from memory and by other I/O devices. The I/O chip stores the data temporarily and only puts this data on the data bus (to be picked up by the CPU) when the CPU tells it to do so.

How does the CPU know if an external device is trying to send data to the computer? Briefly, there are two main techniques that can be used.

wanting attention sends an interrupt signal directly to the CPU and this forces the program being executed to stop while the input port is attended to. After the input port has off-loaded its data onto the data bus, the CPU resumes its former activity.

The I/O we have described so far is called 'parallel I/O' because data is input or output one byte at a time using eight I/O wires or lines (eight bits in parallel). Another technique is called 'serial I/O'. Here the information in each byte is fed in or out a bit at a time, one bit after the other. Some printers use serial interfaces, and the output from modems (see page 100) is also in serial form. The main advantage is that, essentially, serial communication allows a single pair of wires to be used instead of eight or more.

Waiting Room

Computers transfer information at a rate much faster than mechanical devices like printers can handle. This problem is solved by using a short-term memory called a buffer

The buffers used by trains are designed to cushion impact by absorbing energy in springs or damped pistons. Computers have buffers, too, and in some ways they function like the train's buffers by helping different parts of the computer system to 'get on together'.

The term is used somewhat loosely in the computer world and covers two quite distinct things. To the programmer 'buffer' means a specialised use of computer memory, while to the circuit designer it means a type of electrical signal amplifier. The second type, which we shall call signal buffers, is dealt with in the panel.

Memory Buffers

Imagine a word processor program that, among other things, can move a block of text from one part of a 'document' in the computer's memory to another part. The text consists of printable characters and spaces and certain 'unprintable' characters such as the Carriage Return. All these are represented in the computer's memory as ASCII codes in binary. One byte of memory is needed for each character. To move the characters in the block from their old positions in memory to their new ones means that another part of the computer's memory has to be set aside as a temporary text storage area. Such an area of memory specially set aside for a specific task is known as a buffer.

As a second example, consider the problem of printing a document created on a word processor. The document might consist of 15,000 separate characters, but they clearly could not all be sent to the printer for printing at once — most printers cannot print faster than about 80 characters a second. To overcome this, part of the computer's memory will be set aside, under the control of the word processor software, as a 'print buffer'. The software will first fill up this buffer with characters to be printed, and then send them out to be printed at a speed appropriate for the printer.

The print buffer may not be very big, perhaps only 128 or 256 bytes in capacity, but the principle remains the same however big it is. First a 'block' of ASCII characters is written into it, and then these are despatched out again, one byte at a time. The first byte to be written into the buffer will also be the first byte to be read out from it (obviously we will want the characters to be printed in the same order they were typed in). This type of buffer is called a 'First In First Out', or FIFO buffer. When all the characters have been read out from the buffer, the software will fill it with the next block of characters destined for the printer.

FIFO buffers of this type are an extremely common feature of most types of computer software. They are used wherever incompatibilities of speed exist, not only between computers and printers, but also between computers and floppy disk drives and between computers and computer keyboards. Although the phenomenal processing speed of computers means that they can usually identify which keys have been pressed faster than typists can type them, there may be times when the computer cannot identify the keys and display the corresponding characters fast enough. This can happen if the computer is momentarily busy doing something else (accessing a disk, for example). When this happens, it is common to incorporate into the computer's operating system a 'type ahead buffer'. This buffer 'remembers' which keys have been pressed and the computer displays them as soon as it can. Normally, the user will not notice

Temporary Stopover
One of the most common uses for a buffer is between the computer and a printer because the printer cannot output characters at the same speed that the computer sends them. Characters are consequently stored in the temporary memory until this buffer is full, whereupon a 'busy' signal is sent to the computer to stop it transmitting. The contents of the buffer memory are then sent to the printer in the same order that they were received, but at a much slower rate. When this has finished, the process begins again until the whole text has been printed

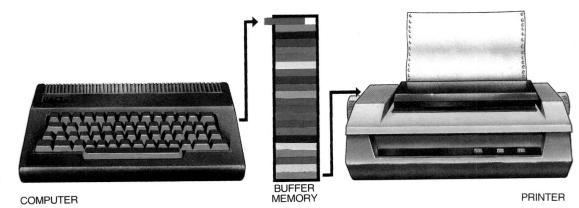

COMPUTER

BUFFER
MEMORY

PRINTER

Controlling The Flow

If we pour water into a tank from a bucket, a constant trickle will come from the outlet pipe. In just the same way, the computer 'pours' data into the buffer, which releases it at the much slower speed at which the printer, for example, works

buffer built in, this is often not more than two Kbytes and it will not allow the computer to send more data until this buffer is empty. The add-on hardware memory buffers contain more memory, so they can accept much more data before sending a 'busy' signal to the computer. If the buffer is big enough, it may be able to hold all the data to be printed in one go, so the computer will be able to get on with other tasks while the buffer sends the data at a slower rate to the printer.

Memory is often used rather like a large trunk or pigeon-hole rack to store programs and data, but it may instead be organised into stacks or buffers. Stacks are 'Last In First Out' or LIFO structures, whereas buffers are 'First In First Out' or FIFO structures. The analogy often made for stacks is that of the pile of plates supported by a spring occasionally seen at self-service counters. Plates are piled on the stack and the last one placed there will be the first one removed. Like buffers, stacks are also temporary memory areas and differ from buffers only in the order in which the data is input and retrieved. Stacks are used 'internally' in high level languages (in BASIC interpreters, for example) when information needs to be stored temporarily and recalled later. Consider this BASIC program fragment:

```
FOR X = 1 TO 10
PRINT "X = ";X
FOR Y = 1 TO 10
GOSUB SCAN
NEXT Y
PRINT "C$ = ";C$
NEXT X
```

This is an example of nested FOR. . .NEXT loops. When the BASIC interpreter gets to the second FOR statement, it needs to remember which variable is used by the previous FOR (X in this case), and so it 'pushes' the information about the first FOR onto a stack. When the inner loop has been completed, it 'pops' the information from the top of the stack and knows that the current FOR uses variable X. Since FOR. . .NEXT loops can be nested as deeply as required, it may need to push information for several FORs onto the stack. When it pops the information from the stack, it clearly needs to have the information in the inverse order from that in which it was pushed.

Buffers, on the other hand, organise memory so that the first information entered is the first information output. Buffers are often used in input/output routines and are used as 'interfaces' between routines or devices working in different units or at different speeds. For example, an input routine in BASIC might work in units of lines, terminated by a Carriage Return <CR>, but the interpreter may work on the lines in units of one character. Buffers usually need a 'pointer' to indicate where in the buffer the next character should be written. The pointer would be a byte or several bytes containing the address of that character. The address would be incremented after each character had been stored.

Strong Signals
The logic inside your computer works at TTL levels. Transistor-Transistor-Logic signifies a binary 1 with five volts, and 0 with zero volts. However, though devices such as the CPU are capable of producing these voltages, they can't generate enough current to drive all the other chips that might be connected to each pin. Signal buffers are therefore connected to the CPU's output lines to magnify the amount of current available. Signal buffers are themselves small chips, each typically capable of acting as a buffer for six signals

this happening, but with certain disk operating systems, or with certain types of applications software (involving a lot of processing of information) there may be a slight delay between a key being pressed and its appearance on the screen. A few operating systems allow the type ahead buffer to be turned on or off, or even allow the size of the buffer to be altered by the user.

The precise way in which the software is organised to handle buffers varies depending on what the buffer is supposed to do, but generally it will be necessary to set aside a few bytes to be used as counters and flags. It will be necessary to know how many bytes have been read out from a full buffer before more are written in, otherwise important data may be destroyed before it has been used.

Hardware Memory Buffers

Readers with printers may have noticed how slow they seem to be, especially when printing out a long program listing or document. Most computer operating systems are not able to do anything else while the printer is in use, so if it takes a long time to finish printing, the user will just have to sit at the screen waiting for the printout to end. Many manufacturers now offer add-on print buffers, usually in the form of a box that connects between the computer and the printer. These boxes effectively speed up the printer from the computer's point of view. Although the printer does not actually print any faster, the box contains extra, dedicated memory (sometimes as much as 16 Kbytes) with its own built-in software. To the computer it appears exactly like a faster printer. When the computer has to print a file, it sends bytes out to the printer until it receives a 'busy' signal, meaning that the printer cannot accept any more bytes. The computer then has to wait until the 'busy' line goes 'false', indicating that the printer is once again able to accept data. Even though printers usually have a small memory

Alternative Translation

Computers 'think' in machine code; programmers prefer to write in a high level language such as Basic. Compilers and interpreters offer different methods of translation between them

When computers were first developed they didn't have keyboards. Program instructions had to be entered one step at a time by setting each of eight switches to 'up' or 'down', to represent a single operation. These patterns of 'up' and 'down' were examples of machine code.

It was logical to replace the switches by a typewriter keyboard, and replace the patterns of switch settings by real English words. The result was the 'high-level' language such as BASIC, replacing the low-level machine codes.

As processors, however, computers did not change, but continued to work on the original patterns of switches (and still do), so programmers had to develop programs written in the original low-level notation to translate these high-level programs into patterns that the processors could work on. These low-level programs came to be called interpreters or compilers, according to their method of translation.

In computing (as elsewhere), any gain in power or speed has to be paid for — in money, time or freedom of action. So it is with interpreters and compilers. Together they provide all the program translation facilities that a programmer needs. Interpreters are strong in some areas and compilers in others, but each pays for its advantages with compensating disadvantages.

Interpreters, usually built into the home computer, are the cheap way of translating high-level language programs into something a computer can understand. They don't use up much memory — leaving more space for your programs.

Micros costing less than about £400 almost invariably feature a BASIC interpreter: you type in a BASIC program, type RUN, and either the program works, or it stops with an error message from the system — something like:

SYNTAX ERROR ON LINE 123

So you type LIST, find the error, correct it, type RUN, and it either works or stops again, and so on. Note that some of the more sophisticated BASIC interpreters actually check for syntax errors as each line is entered.

You may have done this sort of thing hundreds of times without having given a thought to the interpreter. Its chief virtue is precisely that it is an invisible device that allows you to work on your program without ever bothering about where it is in memory or how to execute it — the program is at your fingertips, and you can RUN it, LIST it, or EDIT it immediately.

The interpreter is easy to use, but not very sophisticated: every time you type RUN, the interpreter has to find your BASIC program in memory and translate and execute it line by line. If your program contains this loop:

```
400 LET N=0
500 PRINT N
600 LET N=N+1
700 IF N<100 THEN GOTO 500
```

the interpreter has to translate and execute lines 500 to 700 a hundred times, as if it had never encountered them before.

Compilers are different. They're expensive, difficult to write, and occupy and use a lot of memory. They are almost always disk-based software, so the user needs an expensive system.

What they offer is flexibility, power and speed; faced with the four lines of BASIC above, a compiler would translate them all once, then execute that code a hundred times.

This allows quite a saving in time — but at a price. Suppose you have a BASIC compiler and you want to enter and run a BASIC program.

First you load and run the File Creation Program (called the Editor), which allows you to type in the program and save it to disk as a 'source file'.

Files must be named so that you can find them once you've created them (just like files in a real filing cabinet), so the Editor asks you to name the source file. File names often consist of two parts: the first is a label, any name you choose – say MYPROG – and the second part is usually a three-letter code indicating the nature of the file contents; this code is the 'extension'. A BASIC file might have the code BAS as its extension. Your source file is now on disk under the name MYPROG.BAS. Now, typing:

COMPILE MYPROG.BAS

will cause the computer to LOAD and RUN the BASIC compiler on a BASIC source file called MYPROG. BAS.

You wait a few seconds, depending on the length of your program while the compiler translates your program into an 'object file', which it saves on disk under the name **MYPROG.OBJ** — the **OBJ** extension indicating that this is the object file, a machine code translation of a source file.

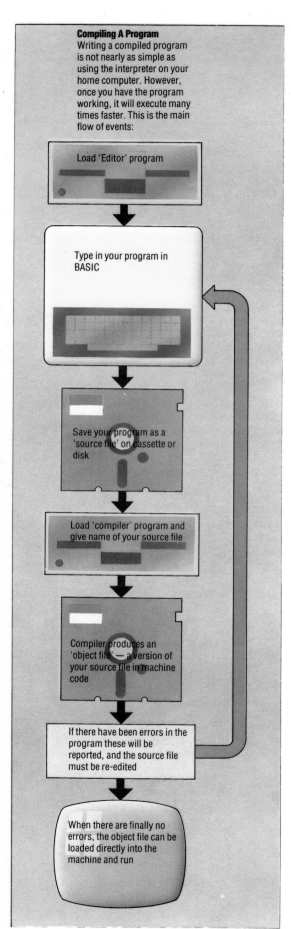

Compiling A Program

Writing a compiled program is not nearly as simple as using the interpreter on your home computer. However, once you have the program working, it will execute many times faster. This is the main flow of events:

Load 'Editor' program

Type in your program in BASIC

Save your program as a 'source file' on cassette or disk

Load 'compiler' program and give name of your source file

Compiler produces an 'object file' — a version of your source file in machine code

If there have been errors in the program these will be reported, and the source file must be re-edited

When there are finally no errors, the object file can be loaded directly into the machine and run

While the compiler translates your file, it checks it for syntax errors. If it finds any, then you'll get a message like this:

```
100 REED X:IF X=3(N+2) LET P=Q
    1            2        3
```

FATAL ERROR:-
1) //REED// UNRECOGNISED COMMAND
2) ///(// ILLEGAL OPERATOR HERE
3) ??'THEN' OR 'GOTO' EXPECTED HERE

You get this kind of message for every line that contains an error. In other words, the error reporting is far more comprehensive than on a BASIC interpreter. Now you must load and run the Editor again, recall the source file from disk, make the changes and try to compile again. If there are no more errors you can type:

RUN MYPROG

and it either works as you expect or it doesn't. There are no syntax errors at this stage, because you've corrected them, but you might still want to change the program anyway, in which case you load and run the Editor, change the source file, recompile it...and so on.

The virtues of a compiler are not obvious in the program development stage, though informative error reporting is valuable. Compilers start to earn their keep after you've got a working program and typed RUN, which is precisely where interpreters start to let you down.

Compiled programs are fast — anything from five to 50 times faster than interpreted programs, depending on the efficiency of the compiler, but the compiled program's speed of execution is bought at the expense of its speed of program development.

Comparing compilers and interpreters by contrasting typical sequences of user commands like those above is unfair to compilers, since they are written mostly for more powerful, less specialised machines, the users of which might want to write and run programs in many different programming languages.

COBOL (for writing commercial data processing programs to handle accounts, payroll and inventory), for example, was invented with compilation in mind, whereas BASIC really demands an interpreter. If you're going to compare a Jensen with a Jeep, you ought to do so on both ploughed fields and metalled roads.

Once you've developed and compiled a program, you don't need the source file except for reference. So the source program can be fully commented on and written with readability in mind, while the object file may be a much smaller file, occupying less space on disk and memory.

The fact that the object files created by a compiler consist of unreadable machine code, can, surprisingly, be an advantage. If you're marketing software you don't sell the source file but only the object file, which makes it much harder to pirate, copy or alter.

Slow
In an Adventure-style game speed is not critical, and most of the program consists of manipulating strings of text. Therefore it is written in BASIC and interpreted as it runs on the computer.

Faster
Many business programs (particularly spreadsheets) are difficult to write in machine code because they involve a lot of mathematics. However, an interpreted language would be too slow, so they are often written in BASIC and then compiled.

Fastest
For fast action arcade-style games, which involve the manipulation of graphics, even a compiled program would not be nearly fast enough. Such packages have to be written directly in machine code – a slow and painful task.

Peek And Poke

These two commands are used whenever you want to program something that Basic can't cope with, but every machine uses them differently

POKEing

The POKE statement needs to be used with care as it changes the contents of memory locations and this could affect the running of the computer. No damage can be caused by this, but it could mean the loss of a program. Here are a few 'safe' POKE statements for you to try.

On the Atari 400 or 800, POKEing a 1 into location 751 will turn the screen cursor off; try POKE 751,1.

On the Commodore 64, try POKE 1024,1. 1024 is the address of the first screen location.

On the Sinclair Spectrum, try:

```
100 FOR N = 0 TO 6 STEP 2
110 POKE USR"A" +
    N,BIN01010101
120 POKE USR"A" + N +
    1,BIN10101010
130 NEXT N
140 PRINT "AAAAAAAA"
```

The As in line 140 must be typed in the graphics mode. Running the program will produce a line of miniature checkerboard symbols. However, it should also result in some interesting interference patterns on your TV set

PEEK and POKE are two 'statements' from the BASIC language used in more advanced programming when individual bits and bytes need to be manipulated in memory. The PEEK statement is used to examine (peek at) the contents of a specific address (location) in memory, and POKE is used to store a number (ranging from 0 to 255) in a specific memory location.

PEEK and POKE statements allow the BASIC programmer to gain access to the inner workings of the computer in a way that is not otherwise possible. Normally, the built-in BASIC in your computer takes care of the actual locations where such things as variables and the data defining the characters to be displayed on the screen are stored. Although we do not usually worry about where such things are in the memory, occasionally we need to find out. The PEEK statement allows us to do this.

A short program to examine any memory location can easily be written:

```
10 REM LOOKING AT MEMORY LOCATIONS
20 PRINT "ENTER MEMORY LOCATION IN
   DECIMAL"
30 INPUT M
40 P = PEEK(M)
50 PRINT "CONTENTS OF LOCATION ";M;" ARE ";P
60 GOTO 20
70 END
```

This will print the contents of the specified address expressed as a decimal number. (In fact, of course, the computer stores it in binary.) If you would like to see what the contents are equivalent to in terms of 'printable' characters, BASIC includes a function to convert decimal numbers into their character equivalents. This is the CHR$ function and changing line 50 will print character equivalents of the memory locations instead:

```
50 PRINT "CONTENTS OF LOCATION ";M;" ARE ";
   CHR$(P)
```

To examine the whole of memory, a FOR...NEXT loop can be added by deleting line 30, changing line 20 to FOR X = 0 TO 65535 and replacing line 60 with NEXT X.

To give enough time to see each character as it is printed, you may need to add a delay loop after the PRINT statement and before the NEXT X statement. Note also that the upper limit of the FOR...NEXT loop assumes you have a 64 Kbyte memory. This number can be changed for smaller memories: 16 Kbytes requires 16383 in decimal,

32 Kbytes requires 32767, and 48 Kbytes requires 49151. A full listing of this program is:

```
10 REM PEEKING AND PRINTING ALL MEMORY
   LOCATIONS
20 FOR X=0 TO 65535
30 LET Y=PEEK(X)
40 PRINT "LOCATION ";X;" = ";Y;" = ";
50 PRINT CHR$(Y)
60 FOR D=1 TO 200
70 NEXT D
80 NEXT X
90 END
```

Although the CHR$ function converts decimal numbers into their character equivalents, printable characters are represented by the numbers 32 to 127. Most computers use the numbers between 128 and 255 (the largest number representable in a single byte) for special graphics characters. Many of the numbers between 0 and 31 have special screen control functions. When these are encountered in memory as the program is run, they will be converted by CHR$ into curious screen effects. These may make the screen go blank, for example, or cause the cursor to move to the top left-hand corner of the screen.

The POKE statement is essentially the opposite of PEEK. It allows you to 'write' a byte of data (any number between 0 and 255) into any memory location. POKE must be used with care: if you POKE a number into the wrong part of memory you could 'crash' the computer by corrupting part of an essential program. The only way to recover from this is to reset the computer (switching it off and then on, unless it has a reset button), and this risks destroying one of your programs. Before using POKE, therefore, check the manual to find an area in the memory map designated a 'user area'.

Most home computers make the video memory (the memory used for storing the characters to be displayed on the screen) available to the user. Normally, the computer gets the shape of the characters to be displayed from a special ROM called a character generator, which stores the patterns of dots for each character. But it is usually also possible to use RAM as well. When the pattern codes for characters are stored in RAM, new patterns, specified as decimal numbers, can be POKEd to the appropriate RAM location and used to define completely new displayable characters.

Against All Odds

'Even parity' ensures that the number of 1 bits in a byte is always even. This makes transmission errors easier to detect

One of the main advantages of digital computers over analogue devices is that the errors and inaccuracies that occur in all electrical circuits do not accumulate as a signal is passed through a number of circuits. However, when data is transmitted over any distance — whether by means of a serial interface and a pair of wires, or over a telephone line — the background electrical 'noise' in the line can sometimes be enough to flip a single bit from 0 to 1, or vice versa. Normally, the receiving computer would have no way of knowing that this had happened, and would accept the erroneous data as being correct.

Look at what happens if one bit in the ASCII code for the letter Q becomes corrupted:

[ ] 1 0 1 0 0 0 1 (Transmitted ASCII code for Q)
[ ] 1 0 0 0 0 0 1 (Received ASCII code for A)

An error such as this in the transmission of data would, at the least, be a nuisance and could be potentially catastrophic. However, you will remember that ASCII codes are assigned only to values up to 127, which requires only seven bits (numbered 0 to 6). The Most Significant Bit (bit seven) is therefore often used as a 'parity' bit, to detect when an error has occurred.

There are two conventions for using parity bits: 'even parity' and 'odd parity'. We shall consider the former. 'Even parity' means that the parity bit (bit seven in an ASCII code) is set so that the total number of 1 bits in the byte is always an even number. Here's how the letters A and Q would look with even parity:

[0] 1 0 0 0 0 0 1
(the ASCII code for A with even parity)
[1] 1 0 1 0 0 0 1
(the ASCII code for Q with even parity)

There are two 1 bits in the ASCII code for A, so the parity bit is made 0 so that the total of all eight bits is even. In the ASCII code for Q, there are three 1 bits, so the parity bit is made a 1. This brings the total number of 1 bits to four, which is an even number.

Now let's see what would happen if bit four in our ASCII letter Q became corrupted as in the example above.

[1] 1 0 0 0 0 0 1 (corrupted ASCII Q)

When the parity of the byte is checked (either by software or by special hardware) it is seen that the correct Q has an even number of 1s in it (including the parity bit). The corrupted Q, by contrast, accidentally had bit four changed from a 1 to a 0, but the original parity bit — bit seven — is still a 1. When the parity of this corrupted byte is checked, it will be found to have an odd number of 1 bits, and so this byte is known to be corrupted and can be rejected. If you think about it, you will see that even if the parity bit itself were to become corrupted in transmission, the fact that an error had occurred would still be picked up by the parity checking process, and the byte would be rejected.

If you look at the ASCII codes used in your own computer, you will probably find that bit seven (the Most Significant Bit, or MSB) is in fact used, but not as a parity bit. This is done to enable the computer to have an additional character set (usually a set of graphics characters), and because errors in data transmission *inside* a computer are very rare. Parity is normally used only when transmitting data over long distances, or when recording data onto a magnetic recording surface (such as tape or disk) which is equally susceptible to 'bit errors'.

Parity checking is fine for indicating that a given byte has been transmitted incorrectly, but it does not indicate which bit in the byte was wrongly transmitted, so the error cannot be corrected by the receiving computer. Worse still, if two bits in a byte become corrupted, an incorrectly transmitted byte could be taken as a correct one.

But in cases where the receiving device detects an error, it can send back an error message and the software can arrange for the incorrect byte to be transmitted again. More sophisticated error detecting and correcting schemes have been devised that can pin-point which bit or bits were in error, enabling them to be corrected automatically. Error correcting codes are looked at in more detail on page 74.

Just Checking
The last digit in an International Standard Book Number (ISBN) is a check digit — equivalent to parity in a computer. Multiply the first digit (0 here) by 10, the second (5) by 9, and so on, then add the results together. You will find that the check digit has been set such that the result is exactly divisible by 11

LANGUAGE

PUBLISHER'S NUMBER

BOOK NUMBER

CHECK DIGIT

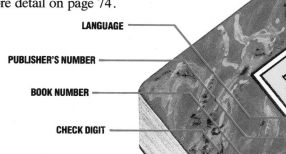

Illustration
Caroline Hol...

ISBN 0 571 09978 5

Detective Work

When data is passed from one computer to another it runs the risk of becoming corrupted. Hamming codes can detect and correct these errors

We must all have heard stories about computers making dreadful mistakes — like mailing 500 copies of the same company leaflet to one person. The truth is, of course, that the machine is not to blame: the mistake will have originated from a human failing, perhaps as simple as a typing error. The computer merely serves to amplify the problem. Occasionally, errors arise because the applications program hasn't been written to cope with all eventualities — as in the case of computer-generated final demands for gas bills of £0.00.

Sometimes, though, computers make mistakes that can't be attributed to human intervention, and these are usually manifested in the form of 'bit errors'. A bit error occurs when a single bit in a section of data is transposed from a 1 to a 0 or vice-versa. Bit errors can be caused when a hardware component, such as a RAM chip, fails. That's why many home computers go through a 'diagnostic' error checking software routine whenever the power is turned on.

Most bit errors, however, are 'soft errors' — bits get 'flipped' even though all the RAM has passed the diagnostic test. Home computers are designed to operate in domestic environments, but during a summer heatwave it is quite possible for the temperature to exceed the operating temperature range of the components. Damage is unlikely to be permanent, but bit errors may result in a character on the screen suddenly changing from an 'A' to a 'B', for example, or if the bit happens to form part of an important pointer, it may 'crash' the program, requiring the computer to be reset.

Bit errors can also arise during periods of high sunspot activity, when sub-atomic particles can penetrate the atmosphere and interfere with the flow of electrons in a miniature circuit. In applications such as military systems, industrial control, scientific experimentation or international banking, errors could bring disastrous consequences, so a variety of methods

have been adopted to detect them.

The simplest is parity checking (see page 73). An alternative method is the 'checksum', which is widely used when writing data onto magnetic tape or disk. Data is typically handled in blocks of 128 bytes, the last of which to be read or written will be a checksum byte. This byte represents the sum of all the other bytes (each having a value in the range 0 to 255) modulo 256 — meaning the remainder of the sum when divided by 256. Here's an example:

Data: 114,67,83...(121 other values)...
36,154,198
Total of these 127 bytes = 16,673
Total divided by 256 = 65, remainder 33
Therefore checksum = 33

The total of the bytes (16,673) is equal to 65 lots of 256 plus a remainder of 33 — the value that is written into the 128th byte as a checksum. When the computer reads the block back again, it performs its own checksum calculation on the data and if this value differs from 33 then it knows that a bit error has occurred in the recording process.

With both parity and checksum, the computer has no way of knowing which bit of the data has been corrupted. If the error occurred in transmission, then the receiving computer can request a particular byte or block of bytes to be transmitted again; in the case of a recording error, there may well be no way of retrieving the uncorrupted data.

Where errors would be unacceptable, a system must be used that will both detect and correct them. Hamming codes, named after their inventor R W Hamming of Bell Telephone Laboratories, perform this function.

All error correction systems work on the principle of redundancy. Human languages contain a high degree of redundancy — if a typing

Exclusive-Or
A simple Exclusive-Or gate has two inputs and one output. If both inputs are at logical 0 then the output is 0. If either input is 1 then the output is 1. However, if both inputs are 1 then the output is 0. This last condition differentiates the Or gate from the Ex-Or (for short). The operation can be represented by a truth table. Where an Ex-Or has more than two inputs, the output will be 1 if there is an odd number of 1s at the input. Such devices are the means by which parity and error-checking bits are created

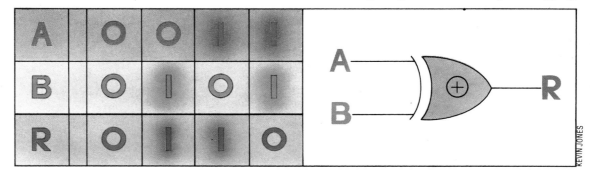

error occurs in a manuscript, or a crackle obliterates words in a telephone conversation, it is often possible to recreate the words by considering the context of the sentence. Sometimes we build in extra redundancy for use in 'noisy' environments: the use of 'alpha', 'bravo', and 'charlie' in place of 'a', 'b', and 'c' in radiotelephony, for example.

Suppose that on our computer we send a word of x bits in length, consisting of y bits of real data and z redundant bits (i.e. x = y + z). In our explanation of parity we had a value of seven for y and one for z. For Hamming codes, z will need to be proportionately larger. Now let's assume that a single-bit error can occur in any of the x bits (our z redundant bits are of course just as prone to error as the y data bits). If the chance of a bit error in a word is, say, one in a million, then the chance of two errors in a word is one in a million million, so we'll ignore this possibility.

When the data is received at the other end, there will be x+1 eventualities. Either there will be no errors, or the first data bit will be in error, and so on up to the xth bit. Now, with z redundant bits we can represent 2^z situations, so that for the word to be proof against one bit error:

$$2^z \geqslant y+z+1$$

If y is seven (for ASCII codes), then z will need to be four. If y is four (as in our example in the panel) then z will need to be three. However, if y is 16 then z need be increased only to 5. It follows that Hamming codes are far more efficient for longer word-lengths than for short ones.

In a Hamming code, each of the redundant bits acts as an even-parity check on a different combination of bits in the word. If any bit is flipped in transmission then one or more of the check bits will be wrong and the combination of these bits will point to the erroneous bit in the word (see example). The receiving computer's software can then simply flip that bit back again.

The key to the way that Hamming codes work is the different combinations of bits upon which each Hamming bit acts as a parity check. The total number of bits is effectively divided into several different but overlapping sets — devised so that no two bits appear in the same combination of sets. The receiving computer performs parity checks on the same sets as the sending device did to create the Hamming code. If any one of the bits, including the Hamming bits, has been flipped in transmission, then one or more of these sets will not pass the parity test. The combination of tests failed points to a unique bit.

Some computers employ Hamming codes even for their internal memory operations. When this is the case, it is possible to remove one whole RAM chip and watch the computer continue to function! Some military computers take the principle of redundancy to the extreme of duplicating every single component in the computer, and comparing the results from the two halves after each operation.

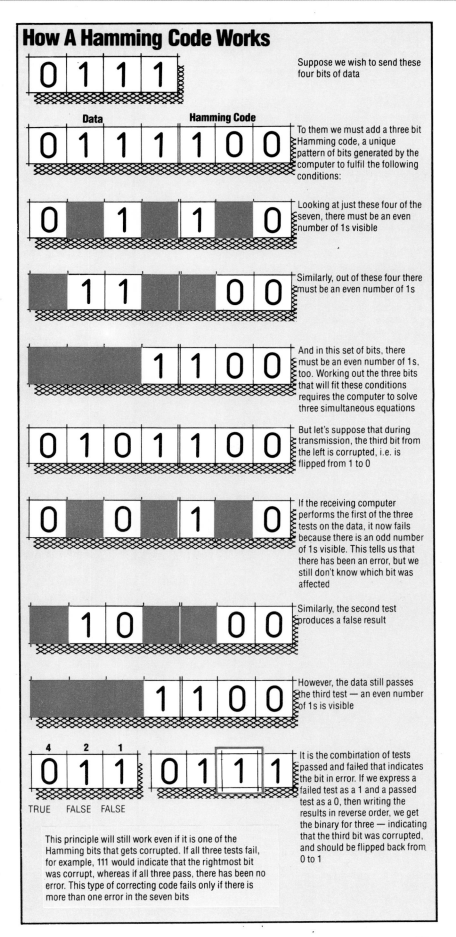

How A Hamming Code Works

Suppose we wish to send these four bits of data

Data   **Hamming Code**

To them we must add a three bit Hamming code, a unique pattern of bits generated by the computer to fulfil the following conditions:

Looking at just these four of the seven, there must be an even number of 1s visible

Similarly, out of these four there must be an even number of 1s

And in this set of bits, there must be an even number of 1s, too. Working out the three bits that will fit these conditions requires the computer to solve three simultaneous equations

But let's suppose that during transmission, the third bit from the left is corrupted, i.e. is flipped from 1 to 0

If the receiving computer performs the first of the three tests on the data, it now fails because there is an odd number of 1s visible. This tells us that there has been an error, but we still don't know which bit was affected

Similarly, the second test produces a false result

However, the data still passes the third test — an even number of 1s is visible

It is the combination of tests passed and failed that indicates the bit in error. If we express a failed test as a 1 and a passed test as a 0, then writing the results in reverse order, we get the binary for three — indicating that the third bit was corrupted, and should be flipped back from 0 to 1

TRUE   FALSE   FALSE

This principle will still work even if it is one of the Hamming bits that gets corrupted. If all three tests fail, for example, 111 would indicate that the rightmost bit was corrupt, whereas if all three pass, there has been no error. This type of correcting code fails only if there is more than one error in the seven bits

Influential Connections

You can't plug a square peg into a round hole, and you can't connect two computer devices together unless they have compatible interfaces

Parallel Port
This is a general-purpose parallel interface for connecting a micro to peripheral devices. All eight bits of each byte transmitted are sent together (in parallel) over eight wires. Other signals are provided for synchronising the transmission of data, ensuring that data is transmitted only when the receiving device is ready to receive it

Disk Drive Interface
Disk drives are usually connected to computers using a parallel interface. There is no standardisation and, as a general rule, it is only possible to connect disk drives specially manufactured for a particular model of computer

Cassette Interface
The cassette port or interface provided on most home computers is really a kind of serial interface. Because the data has to be recorded on ordinary audio cassette tape, using audio frequencies, high data-transfer rates are not possible. The interface circuitry takes bytes of data to be recorded from memory and converts each one into a stream of bits. 0 bits and 1 bits are rendered into two different audio tones. When tapes are loaded into memory, the tones are decoded by the interface circuitry and the resulting 1s and 0s assembled into eight-bit bytes for storage in memory. The cassette interfaces on most home micros are universal in the sense that any domestic tape recorder may be used successfully. The connector used is not standardised, but DIN sockets or mini-jacks are the most common

Analogue Input
Usually only found on the more expensive computers that are intended for educational use, an analogue input is useful for connecting the computer to devices in a laboratory, such as electrical temperature gauges or light-sensors. The interface will merely feature one or more lines that can accept and read a voltage in a specified range. It is up to the user to ensure that he doesn't connect the computer to a voltage outside this range, which could result in serious damage

Memory Expansion Port
This usually supports most if not all of the lines that come directly from the microprocessor — i.e. the address, data and control busses. This is where any additional memory will be plugged in and, on some computers, the manufacturer's peripherals as well. The connector is usually just a PCB edge-connector, though in some cases it may be a socket that can take an edge-connector, such as that on a games cartridge (which is really a form of ROM expansion)

Joystick Ports
There is no standard interface for joysticks, though many manufacturers have adopted Atari's standard so that they don't have to manufacture their own joysticks. Most such interfaces simply have five active lines — one from each switch at the four extremities of the joystick's movement, and one for the fire button. Analogue joysticks, however, require a different interface that can accept a whole range of voltages to indicate the stick's exact position. Most computers feature more than one joystick port, though sometimes the same socket is shared by more than one device

Printer Interface
Printer interfaces are reasonably well standardised, following the system developed by the Centronics Corporation, so there is usually little difficulty in getting a printer with a Centronics interface to work with the printer interface on most computers. The signal levels, as well as signal functions, are also standardised at 0 and 5 volts for binary 0 and 1 respectively. The connectors used and the assignment of the signals to the various pins are not standardised, so you may have to wire up a special connector lead to connect a printer to the computer

Video Interface (RF)

All home computers are designed to be connected to a video display unit and for most this means a domestic black and white or colour television set. If the ordinary aerial input socket of the television is to be used, the video signal must first be RF (radio frequency) modulated so that it resembles a broadcast television signal. This is then demodulated by the tuner in the television

RGB Interface

Even better results are possible if the elements needed by the video monitor are kept separate. The RGB interface provides separate red, green and blue video signals, plus a horizontal synchronisation and vertical synchronisation signal

Video Interface (Composite)

Some televisions and many video monitors incorporate a composite or 'video' input that by-passes the RF demodulating stage, enabling better-quality pictures to be produced. All the elements of a standard video signal (chrominance, luminance, synchronisation signals, etc.) are present in the computer's output but this 'composite' signal does not need to be further modulated for processing by the television tuner

RF   RGB   COMPOSITE

RS 232

IEEE

ORT

TONY LODGE

Serial Interface

Unlike many interfaces, the RS232 serial interface is theoretically precisely defined in a standard of the Electrical Industries Association. This standard specifies the type of connector to be used (a 25-pin 'miniature D' connector), the signals allocated to each pin, and the signal levels. Unfortunately, few manufacturers stick to the standard, and making serial devices work with a given computer can be difficult. Of the many pins present on the standard interface, usually only three are used: pin 2 to transmit serial data from the computer to the peripheral device; pin 3 to receive data transmitted from the peripheral device; and pin 7, the ground (earth) signal. Both transmitting and receiving devices need to be set so that the rate of data transmission and the format of the transmitted data are the same

IEEE Interface

The IEEE interface is a universal parallel interface based on the Hewlett-Packard Interface Bus, and now adopted as a standard by the Institute of Electrical and Electronics Engineers. The standard is well defined, both physically and electrically. Unlike other data interfaces (e.g., Centronics parallel and RS232 serial), which can connect only to one peripheral device at a time, the IEEE bus can connect up to 15 instruments (including the computer itself) simultaneously. Devices incorporating IEEE interfaces include printers, floppy disk drives, plotters, signal generators, voltmeters and other test equipment. Because it lends itself so well to use with test and measuring equipment, the IEEE bus is much favoured for use in laboratories and industrial establishments. At present only a few home computers offer an IEEE interface and some of these use a printed circuit board edge-connector instead of the standard IEEE connector

The term 'interface' is used loosely to mean the port or socket where external devices are plugged into the computer. Strictly speaking, however, the term refers to the circuitry and associated software that makes possible the connection between any two computer-related devices.

Internally, the computer communicates by sending data over 'busses' — sets of parallel conductors, each of which conducts a single binary signal. In most microcomputers there are three internal busses: an eight-bit data bus, a 16-bit address bus, and a control bus with, usually, signals consisting of between five and 12 bits that indicate the current condition of the CPU. Some of the control signals advise memory and peripheral devices whether the CPU wishes to retrieve data (read) or to deposit data (write). Others convey information from the outside into the CPU, informing it, for example, that a peripheral device has some data to input and requires attention.

Internally, the computer generally handles information consisting of either eight bits or 16 bits at a time. Thus, if the CPU wants to retrieve the data in memory location 65535 (or FFFF, expressed in hexadecimal) it will set all 16 wires of the address bus to one to identify that location. If the contents of this memory location happen to be 182 (B6 in hexadecimal), this data will be placed on the data bus as the eight binary digits 10110110.

When data is transferred like this, eight or 16 bits at a time, the transfer is said to be 'parallel'.

Many peripheral devices are also designed to transmit or receive data in parallel. The interfaces provided for peripherals of this type are called 'parallel interfaces' and most computers provide at least one socket or connector specifically for 'parallel' devices.

Not all peripheral devices are able to receive or transmit data in parallel. Some use a single wire to communicate with the computer a bit at a time. Internally they still use the data as eight or 16-bit bytes, but the bits in each byte will be transmitted or received one at a time, starting from the 'least significant' bit in the byte and ending with the 'most significant' bit. Each byte is split up into a stream of bits, sent off one after the other, and re-assembled into a byte at the other end, using special parallel-to-serial and serial-to-parallel converter circuits.

Both serial and parallel interfaces can be made to convey information either out of the computer or into it. Computers usually include other interfaces, which either always send information out (for example, the television output circuit) or always accept incoming information (for example, joystick ports).

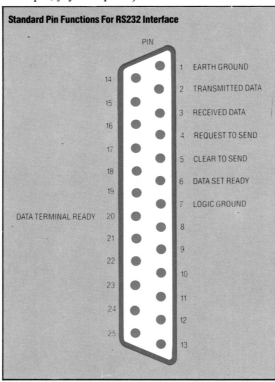

Standard Pin Functions For RS232 Interface

PIN

1	EARTH GROUND
2	TRANSMITTED DATA
3	RECEIVED DATA
4	REQUEST TO SEND
5	CLEAR TO SEND
6	DATA SET READY
7	LOGIC GROUND

DATA TERMINAL READY 20

Serial Interface

There is a standard serial interface, known as the RS232 interface, for which every detail of the signal levels and pin assignments is defined. Even the type of connector is specified. Unfortunately, the standard is seldom fully adhered to and making serial connections work can be difficult. RS232 is a 'bi-directional' serial interface, with one pin (terminal) for transmitting data from the computer and one for receiving data.

The data is sent one bit at a time via the 'transmitted data' terminal and received via the 'received data' terminal. The stream of bits may take a number of standard formats but it doesn't matter which is used as long as both transmitting and receiving devices use the same one.

Since each byte of information is sent out as a serial stream of bits, the software controlling the interface must have a way of indicating when the first bit of the data starts and when the last bit has ended. The convention most commonly used has a single 'start bit' (0 in Boolean logic), followed by eight bits of data, followed by a single 'stop bit' (a logical 1).

The rate at which the data is transmitted needs to be specified in advance, otherwise the pattern of pulses representing the eight bits of data in 0s and 1s could be misinterpreted. This data transmission rate is known as the 'baud rate', named after the 19th-century French inventor Baudot, and pronounced 'bored'. Baud rates range between 75 baud and 9,600 baud. These figures correspond to 75 and 9,600 bits transmitted per second, and as there are usually 10 bits (including the start and stop bits) for each character, the character transmission rate is one tenth of the baud rate.

Parallel Interfaces

The parallel interface transmits or receives information one byte at a time, but in addition to eight 'data lines' it will also need to provide other signals so that the computer and the peripheral know when it is possible for data to be transmitted and when it is not. The commonest type of parallel interface is the 'Centronics' interface (named after an American printer manufacturer, Centronics Corporation), but this so-called standard is not rigidly adhered to. The type of connector used and the assignment of signals to particular pins differ widely from one manufacturer to another. Most Centronics interfaces provide at least the following signals:

DATA 0 to DATA 7	Eight wires to carry the eight bits of the byte being transmitted.
ADK	An input signal to the computer to indicate that the receiving device is ready to accept data.
GND	The 'ground' or earth lead that gives a common reference of 0 volts for both the computer and the peripheral device.
BUSY	A signal from the peripheral device to the computer indicating that the peripheral cannot accept data.
STROBE	An output signal from the computer that indicates to the peripheral that data is ready and should be read in.

Many other devices apart from printers adopt the quasi-standard Centronics parallel interface, and connection with the computer may involve no more than buying a special connecting lead or wiring up one of your own. As a general rule, no changes in the software needed to 'drive' the peripheral will be necessary.

Track Record

The function of the Disk Operating System (DOS) is to keep tabs on where everything is kept on the disk. Without a DOS, programming would be very hard work

Before a computer is able to run any kind of applications program, it first needs its own internal set of programs to manage the various parts of its system, and to make sense of the instructions that comprise the user's program. This internal set of programs is called the Operating System (OS), and on most home computers this resides permanently inside the computer in the form of ROM memory. Generally, we are totally unaware that the Operating System is functioning, which is why we refer to it as being 'transparent in operation'.

If your system includes a disk drive then a large part of that OS will be concerned with the various disk operations. We call that set of routines the Disk Operating System, or DOS. You might see those three letters used in the names of proprietary products — Microsoft's operating system, for example, is called MSDOS. A DOS will typically come in one of three forms. It may comprise part of the ROM inside the computer. An example of this is the Sinclair Spectrum, which has the commands for operating the Microdrive (not really a disk, of course, but similar in operation) built in.

but offer considerable advantages over 'non-intelligent' disk units. For instance, they don't eat up valuable user memory, and can be left to execute a complex disk operation while the computer itself continues with the applications program.

Thirdly, the DOS may reside inside the computer RAM. This technique is increasingly popular in business systems, in which the disk drives are built into the computer, and there is plenty of RAM available (say, more than 128 Kbytes as standard). For the manufacturer, this has the advantage of eliminating the need to create a completely new set of ROMs every time there is a minor modification to the DOS, and the user benefits from a choice of one of a number of proprietary operating systems that will run on the same hardware.

But how does the DOS get into RAM in the first place? This question immediately arises when the system is switched on. The DOS needs to be transferred from the disk into RAM, but if there is no DOS in the computer to tell it how to control the disk, how can it load something into RAM? A program cannot 'pull itself into RAM by its own

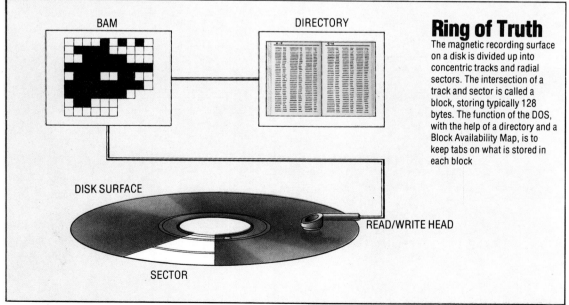

BAM

DIRECTORY

Ring of Truth
The magnetic recording surface on a disk is divided up into concentric tracks and radial sectors. The intersection of a track and sector is called a block, storing typically 128 bytes. The function of the DOS, with the help of a directory and a Block Availability Map, is to keep tabs on what is stored in each block

DISK SURFACE

READ/WRITE HEAD

SECTOR

KEVIN JONES

Another type stores the DOS in ROM within the disk unit itself. This is only applicable when the disk is an 'intelligent' device (such as the Commodore Disk Unit), meaning that it incorporates its own microprocessor ROM and RAM. These are more expensive to manufacture,

bootstraps', so the computer has to have a tiny program built into ROM, which it executes whenever the machine is switched on. This program is called the 'bootstrap' (from the analogy above) and is itself a very simple form of DOS. The bootstrap's job is simply to find the main DOS on the disk, and transfer it byte by byte into RAM, whereupon that DOS can take over and perform some far more sophisticated functions. This process of switching the computer on, then waiting for the DOS to take over, is called 'booting-up'. When it is finished, a greeting is printed on the screen with a prompt to indicate that the computer is ready for a command from the user.

Whichever form the DOS in a system takes, its main function is looking after the locations of the contents of the disk. You may already know that a disk (page 88) is divided into concentric rings, called tracks, which are in turn divided into sectors; and the intersection of a track and sector is called a block. A block can typically hold 128 bytes of information, and is the smallest unit that the disk can read or write at a time. One of the main reasons for having a DOS is to enable the computer to remember the exact location of everything on the disk. This task is more awesome than it sounds. Let's suppose our disk drive has a capacity of 320 Kbytes — enough to store 20 programs of 16 Kbytes each. With each block holding 128 bytes, loading one of those programs without the benefit of a DOS would require you to specify 128 different blocks, each with its own track and sector number!

Local Directory

Filename	Type	Location (Track-Sector)
Invaders	Prog	20-1,20-7,20-2...
Temperat	Prog	25-11,26-5,26-12...
Budget	Prog	23-12,24-3,24-9...
Budgetdat	Data	27-1,27-7,27-2...

The directory on a disk typically occupies the centre track. It contains a list of the filenames, file types (program, data, and perhaps other categories) and track and sector numbers where the file is stored

In order to perform this function, the DOS keeps a disk directory. This is usually located in the middle track of the disk because it has to be referenced frequently, and this minimises the distance the read/write head has to move. The speed of operation of a disk is far more dependent on the time taken to move the head from track to track than on the speed at which the disk spins.

The directory is a list of all the files (which may be programs or files of data) currently on the disk, with details of the file name, file type, and a list of the blocks (each specified by track and sector) where that file is stored. There may be some other entries, such as the date when a back-up copy of the file was last made, or a list of the users who can access a particular file.

When a new file is to be stored, the DOS must first look up something called the Free Sector List or the Block Availability Map (BAM). This has a single bit corresponding to every block on the disk, and as a block is used the value of its bit is changed from zero to one. Some home computers with disk drives feature a utility program that

displays the BAM on the screen, and you can watch the entries being made as you save a program. When a file is erased, the DOS doesn't bother to wipe clean all the blocks used in that file; it simply changes the entries in the BAM to indicate that the contents of those blocks are now unwanted.

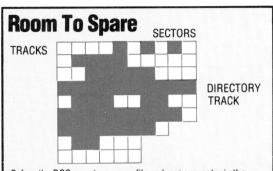

Room To Spare

TRACKS — SECTORS — DIRECTORY TRACK

Before the DOS can store a new file and make an entry in the directory, it must first consult the Block Availability Map (BAM) or Free Sector List. This is a section of memory in which each bit corresponds to a block on the disk. A binary 1 indicates that the block is in use, 0 that it is free (we've shown it as solid or empty squares). Notice that the innermost tracks (at the bottom of the map) have fewer sectors than the others, because they are so much shorter

Another feature of this system is that files are not stored, as would be expected, in consecutive neighbouring blocks. Suppose, for example, that a track consists of 12 sectors, numbered 1 to 12 clockwise. The first 128 bytes of a program might be found in sector 1, the second in sector 7, the third in sector 2 and so on. This is because there is a small time lapse while a block's contents are transferred to the memory buffer used to write each block. If the DOS had to write consecutive sectors, it would have to wait for one complete revolution of the disk between each write — thus slowing the system down. Furthermore, a disk

CHRIS STEVENS

I.Q. Test
Some disk drives contain their own microprocessor and RAM. These are called 'intelligent' drives, and the DOS is incorporated in the form of ROM. Where 'non-intelligent' drives are used, the DOS is stored inside the computer

that has been in use for some time, with files that change in length each day, will end up with a BAM looking like a piece of Gruyère cheese, and new files will have to be fitted into the holes.

A Disk Operating System has many other functions, including formatting new disks (marking out the tracks and sectors on a blank disk and creating an empty directory), making back-up copies, and 'tidying-up' full disks. More sophisticated versions include a variety of data handling structures (see page 144).

Section 4

The Computer System

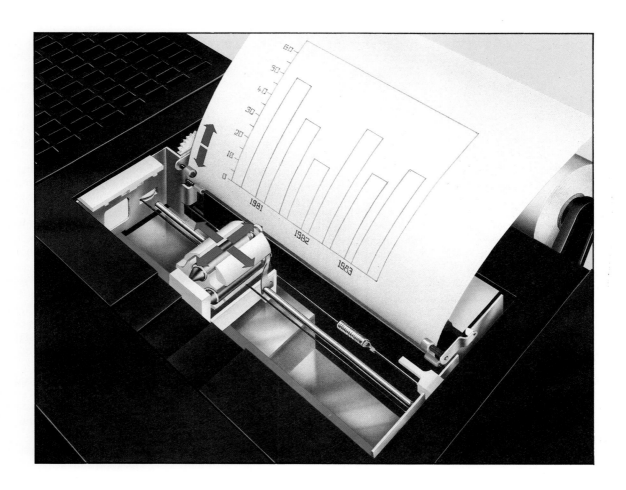

By itself the computer can do nothing. What is
needed is a comprehensive guide to the add-ons
available that can transform your computer
into a working tool.

Getting In Touch

Keyboards at first seem much alike. But some are distinctly better than others, and work in quite different ways

A computer's keyboard is an important part of the system. It is, after all, the way you communicate with the computer. The keyboard must be given as much consideration as the memory capacity, or the quality of the graphics.

Microcomputers have inherited the typewriter's Qwerty-style keyboard — so-called because the first six letters on the top row of keys spell QWERTY. In the early part of this century, the individual characters were positioned on the keys in such a way as to slow typists down so that they wouldn't wreck the flimsy mechanisms!

By the early 1950's when computers first came into commercial use, the QWERTY layout was the standard system for typists and became the standard entry device for computers as well. Today's microcomputer owner is stuck with the QWERTY system which is fine for trained typists, but sometimes difficult for the newcomer to master.

When computers were costing tens of thousands of pounds, the cost of a mechanical keyboard was negligible. But developments in microprocessor technology dramatically reduced the cost of the microcomputer's electronic components.

By the time the Sinclair ZX81 came along, a typewriter-style keyboard could make up a significant proportion of a microcomputer's manufacturing cost. The mechanical moving keyboard, found on models such as the Dragon or the BBC Microcomputer, uses actual switches under the keytops (see illustration on opposite page). When the key is pressed, the internal contacts close to complete a circuit. Switches like this contain numerous components and raise the cost of the keyboard considerably. The BBC computer has 74 keys and some models have more.

One solution to the problem is a new, cheaper type of keyboard. The thinking behind the 'touch-sensitive' keyboard of the ZX81 was that most of the people who bought microcomputers would be mainly interested in playing games and writing small programs.

These activities involve a fairly minimal amount of keyboard work, so it seemed logical that potential micro users would be prepared to settle for a lower quality keyboard. If the advantages of a conventional typewriter-style keyboard could be sacrificed considerable savings could be made.

The ZX81 was designed with a touch-sensitive keyboard, eliminating most of the bits and pieces. This brought the price of the model down, but it didn't provide the ultimate solution. The trouble with a touch-sensitive keyboard is that it doesn't provide much 'tactile feedback' (i.e. you are never quite certain that the key you have just pressed has registered in the computer unless you watch the screen).

Sinclair introduced, for its next product — the Spectrum — the membrane keyboard (see diagram). This kind of keyboard is an improvement, but it still lacks the tactile feedback of the typewriter style.

Several relatively low cost computers (including the BBC, the Dragon and the Lynx) have 'professional' typewriter keyboards. The advantages of typewriter keyboards become apparent when the computer is subjected to heavy use for word processing. The familiar typewriter feel enables lots of work to be done quickly.

There is another category of keyboard that lies somewhere between the full moving keyboard and the membrane type of the Spectrum. These are often called 'calculator type keyboards' and are found, for instance, on the NewBrain and the Oric-1. The keys provide a better 'feel' but are small, stiff and are less suitable for touch typing than fully moving typewriter-style keys.

One way of partially overcoming the lack of

The Keyboard Matrix

The keys on a computer keyboard are actually switches connected to a grid of wires. The illustration shows how pressing a key connects two wires on the grid. For each key there is one, and only one, pair of wires involved. Each key therefore makes a unique connection on the grid, enabling the computer to figure out which key has been pressed

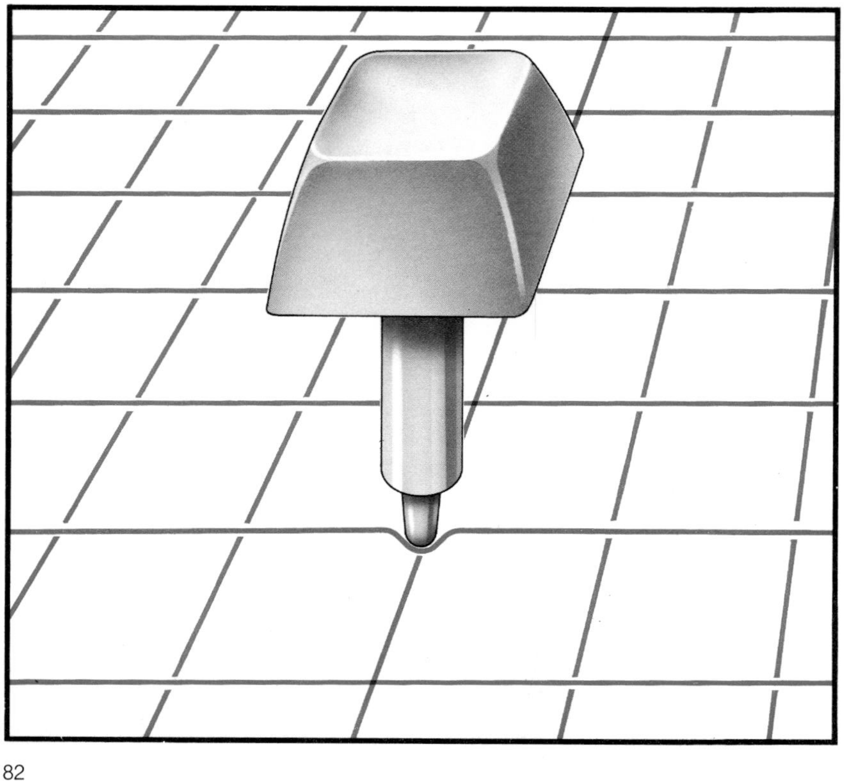

DAVID MALLOT

The Sinclair Keyboard

Sinclair advanced the art of keyboard design with the 'membrane' type used in the Spectrum. A moulded rubber sheet, with key-shaped protrusions, is mounted over a pad of contacts forming the keyboard grid or matrix. When a key like this is pressed, a protrusion under the keytop presses the contacts together. The computer checks which pair of contacts have been closed and is able to work out which key this corresponds to. The contacts closed by the key are normally held apart by an air bubble trapped between two plastic sheets. The restoring force to pop the keys back is provided by the elasticity of the the rubber which is stretched when a key is pressed. This original approach to keyboard engineering has certainly cut a few corners but it allows the product to be manufactured more cheaply and the benefit is passed on directly to the customer

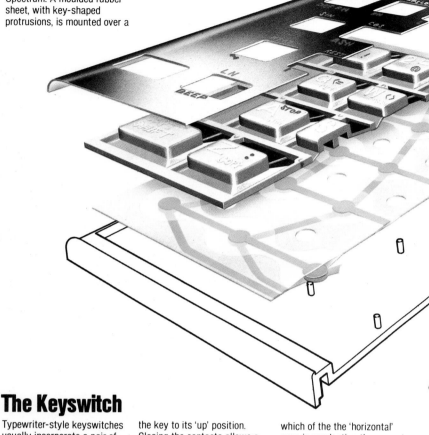

DAVID WEEKS

The Keyswitch

Typewriter-style keyswitches usually incorporate a pair of contacts. These are normally held apart and do not allow electricity to flow. When the key is pressed a plastic moulding (shown in mauve) moves down and allows the contacts to come together and close a circuit. An internal spring is provided to restore the key to its 'up' position. Closing the contacts allows a current to flow and the computer detects this. The wires connected to the contacts in each switch are arranged in a grid. The computer is able to know which key has been pressed by checking which of the 'vertical' wires on the grid and which of the the 'horizontal' ones is conducting the current. Keys of this type are mechanically complex and manufacturing costs are higher. They offer great reliability and have a more positive 'feel' than rubber membrane keys. This feel or 'touch' comes from the resistance provided by the spring. A well designed key gives a tactile feedback so that the user instinctively knows when the key has been pressed properly. The tops of the keys are also sculpted for more comfortable typing. Keyboards with this type of key are a better choice if the computer is going to be used extensively

tactile feedback from touch-sensitive and membrane keyboards is to make an audible 'beep' each time a key has been pressed. It reassures the user that the key has actually been pressed and recognised by the computer.

The designers of the Sinclair ZX81 and the Spectrum introduced a novel and very useful way of cutting down on the amount of typing required when entering in BASIC programs. Each key is made to represent more than just a single letter of the alphabet or a number. By using a special 'function' key in conjunction with the ordinary keys, whole BASIC words can be made to appear on the screen without the need to type out the word in full. For example, the BASIC word PRINT can be produced by simply pressing the special function key and the key for the letter P together. A similar idea is used by Sord in the M5 model.

The End of Typing

Not that long ago, the only way to get a computer to do anything was to key an instruction into it by way of the keyboard. This in itself was often a tedious business, made worse if one did not have much skill as a typist. Faced with the fact that these barriers were actually putting people off using (and therefore buying) computers, the manufacturers came up with the brilliantly simple solution of the 'mouse'. The mouse can be shuffled around on any flat surface and, as it moves, the cursor moves around the screen display. One can thus move very rapidly to any part of the screen one wants, press the button, and the operation one wants starts to roll. Mice can also be used in graphics to draw lines or 'paint' colours on the screen

On Record

A programmer's nightmare is losing the masterpiece he has created on screen. With the use of cassettes, the problem is solved

Loudspeaker
The speaker in most cassette recorders is disconnected if the unit is connected to a computer or a hi-fi system

Erase Head
Removes any signal previously recorded on the tape when in record mode

Tape Counter
An essential 'extra' if several programs are going to be stored on each tape

Record/Playback Head
This dual-purpose head records the audio signal onto the magnetic tape and replays it

The Hobbit
Ikon's Hobbit is a dedicated cassette player – one that is designed solely for storing computer programs. It is superior to a music cassette player as the Hobbit is completely under software control. No need to use wind, rewind, play or record, the Hobbit does all that for you. If you want to LOAD a program you type in the name, and the Hobbit searches its catalogue to find the program and its position. It then races through the tape to the right location

Capstan
A precision-made spindle that rotates at a carefully controlled speed in order to move $1\frac{7}{8}$" of tape a second past the Record/Playback head

Volume
This sets the replay volume and needs to be set carefully or cassettes may not LOAD correctly

When you type a program into your home computer, whether from a book, magazine or your own idea, the information is stored in the computer's RAM. As long as the power is turned on, the program should be quite safe but the instant you turn the computer off it all disappears. This can be something of an irritation, an entire programming session has now disappeared for ever! The next time you want to use that program you must type it all in again. To overcome this problem the makers of home computers generally incorporate a method by which the contents of the computer's memory can be stored in a more permanent form.

IAN McKINNELL

Motor
The motor drives the capstan at a constant speed and also turns the 'supply' and 'takeup' reels to wind and rewind tape

Remote Control
A useful facility that allows home computers to control the cassette recorder

Earphone Socket
Many micros use this output to feed the tones back into the computer

Microphone Socket
Often used as the input for computer data to the recorder. However, it should only be used if the Auxiliary and DIN sockets are not fitted. Careful adjustment of the tone and volume controls are usually needed when this input is used

The most common method of storing the program is a cassette tape. Originally chosen because it was both readily available and inexpensive, the system is now used on almost every home computer sold. The way in which each computer stores its information tends to vary slightly; a program created and stored on a Commodore computer won't load on a ZX Spectrum, for example. However, the method used to convert the program into a storable form is almost universal.

An audio cassette recorder of the type used by most home computers is obviously best suited to storing sounds, yet the program is stored inside the computer in the form of binary numbers. These must be turned into sounds in a way that will allow the computer to recognise the difference between a bit that is set 'on' and a bit that is set 'off' — the zeros and ones of binary. The simplest method of doing this is to create one sound that represents a 1 and another that represents a 0. Typically, these are chosen to be a tone of 2,400 cycles for 1 and a tone of 1,200 cycles for 0.

When the command SAVE is typed into the computer the first thing to be recorded on the tape will be a number of seconds of a constant tone. This is done so that when that tape is being played back into the computer at a later date it can tell the difference between the blank tape and the section that holds the program. The first real information to be recorded is the series of tones that represents the characters of the name that we have given to the program. Each character consists of one byte

— a total of eight bits — so each character needs eight tones to represent it. However, in order to indicate the beginning and end of each byte the computer usually puts one extra tone at each end. These are called the start and stop bits and their value is always the same: either 1 or 0 depending on the particular computer

The program itself is stored in much the same way, except that it is often broken down into segments. Typically these are 256 bytes long and they will often include extra information which enables the computer to be sure that it is reloading the correct information. The system used here is quite simple and is called a 'checksum'. The first byte of the segment contains the number of bytes that are held in the segment and the last byte contains a specially calculated number representing the total of all the bytes added together. When the computer reads the cassette back it checks the figures found on the tape with those it has calculated for itself and, if they don't match, informs the user of the mistake.

Certain cassette systems, like the one found on the BBC Micro, extend this checking to the extent of naming and numbering every segment. If an error occurs it is possible to simply wind the tape back a few inches and try again. Other systems, in strong contrast, don't even show the name of the program that is being loaded.

The Baud Rate

The speed at which the tones are produced and recorded on the tape is usually (and incorrectly) referred to as the Baud rate. The name originates from the Baudot code used in the earliest forms of the electric telegraph and actually relates to the number of times the signal changes per second. A more accurate measure would be the number of bits that are recorded per second. The faster the quoted speed – they range from 300 to 1,200 bits per second – the quicker your programs will be stored on the tape and the less time it will take to load them back into the computer. Unfortunately, the reliability of the system suffers the faster the tones are stored; a speed of 1,200 bits per second is both reliable and sufficiently fast to prevent frustration. Some systems offer two speeds, usually an ultra-reliable slow speed of 300 bits per second and a fast speed of either 1,200 or 2,400 bits per second. Copies of valuable programs can be held in both forms in case of accident.

The cassette tape itself should be of good quality: there is nothing wrong with using audio tape rather than the specially packaged cassettes, but care should be taken to choose a reputable brand and length in excess of C-60 should be avoided. The approximate capacity of a given length of tape can be established by dividing the speed of the cassette interface by 10. This gives the number of bytes that will be stored on the tape each second; a C-60 with 30 minutes on each side where the interface works at 1,200 bits per second, could hold some 432 Kbytes of program.

Fast Reactors

Some add-ons that will help the computer games enthusiast to speed up the action

IAN McKINNELL

Joystick

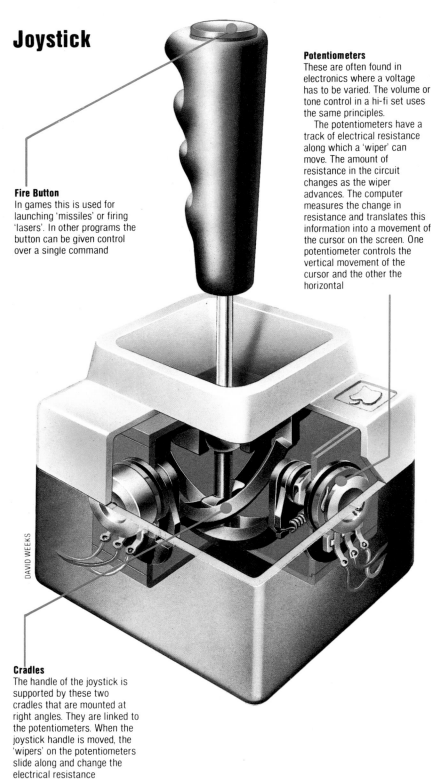

DAVID WEEKS

Fire Button
In games this is used for launching 'missiles' or firing 'lasers'. In other programs the button can be given control over a single command

Potentiometers
These are often found in electronics where a voltage has to be varied. The volume or tone control in a hi-fi set uses the same principles.

The potentiometers have a track of electrical resistance along which a 'wiper' can move. The amount of resistance in the circuit changes as the wiper advances. The computer measures the change in resistance and translates this information into a movement of the cursor on the screen. One potentiometer controls the vertical movement of the cursor and the other the horizontal

Cradles
The handle of the joystick is supported by these two cradles that are mounted at right angles. They are linked to the potentiometers. When the joystick handle is moved, the 'wipers' on the potentiometers slide along and change the electrical resistance

In a computer game you might have to pilot a spaceship through enemy lines and fire your missiles to destroy a target. The joystick transfers the control of the spaceship from a finicky typewriter keyboard into your own hands. It is modelled on the original pilot's joystick found in aeroplanes.

The joystick plugs into the back of the microcomputer and is most often used in arcade-style games. The spaceship, or whatever object the joystick controls, moves in the same direction as the joystick. Usually the joystick can move in any of four directions. When you ease the joystick forward, the spaceship moves up the screen. Electrically there are four switches inside the device arranged in such a way that when the joystick is moved one, and only one, of the contacts is closed. Each switch sends its own message to the computer: either up, down, right or left.

Some joysticks also have a button for firing missiles. The button is beside the joystick where it is operated with the other hand. Or, in the pistol grip design of joystick, missiles are released by squeezing the thumb-trigger.

The cheaper microcomputers, notably the Sinclair ZX81 and the Spectrum, don't always have joystick facilities. You either have to type in the desired directions of motion, using the allocated keys or else purchase a joystick interface.

The interface is an adaptor that allows a joystick to be connected to the computer. Some independent companies have produced interfaces for these machines, but even with such a device the game's programs have to be written to include joystick control as well as keyboard control.

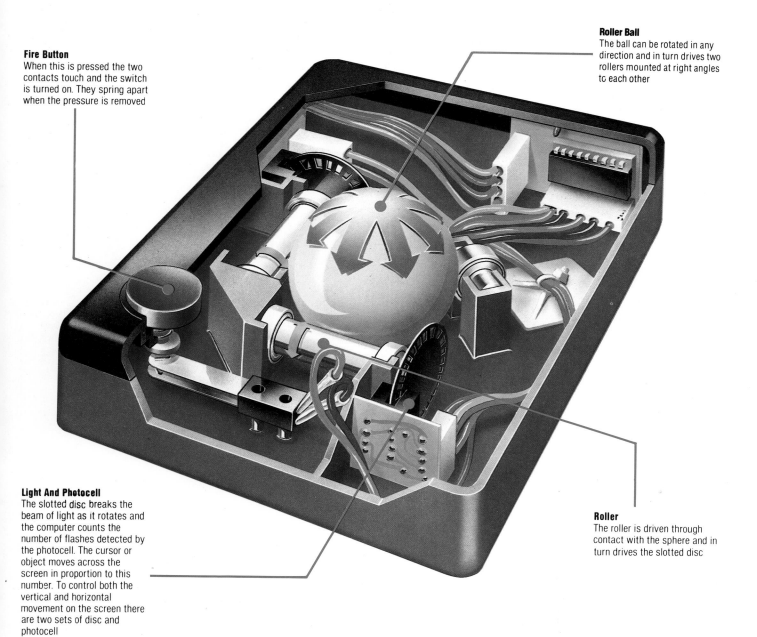

Fire Button
When this is pressed the two contacts touch and the switch is turned on. They spring apart when the pressure is removed

Roller Ball
The ball can be rotated in any direction and in turn drives two rollers mounted at right angles to each other

Light And Photocell
The slotted disc breaks the beam of light as it rotates and the computer counts the number of flashes detected by the photocell. The cursor or object moves across the screen in proportion to this number. To control both the vertical and horizontal movement on the screen there are two sets of disc and photocell

Roller
The roller is driven through contact with the sphere and in turn drives the slotted disc

Track Ball

Imagine you are guiding the screen cursor through a maze. You have to be able to advance the cursor and direct it through the passages as they twist and turn. The trackball is designed for this type of problem. The trackball uses a sphere the size of a billiard ball that you roll in the palm of the hand. As the ball rolls, the object moves in the same direction giving you complete and immediate control. Inside the device are two wheels set at right angles, which rub against the ball. As you roll the ball in the palm of the hand one wheel picks up the vertical part of the motion and the other the horizontal. The computer unites the two signals to recreate the movement.

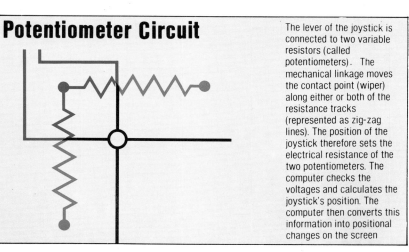

Potentiometer Circuit

The lever of the joystick is connected to two variable resistors (called potentiometers). The mechanical linkage moves the contact point (wiper) along either or both of the resistance tracks (represented as zig-zag lines). The position of the joystick therefore sets the electrical resistance of the two potentiometers. The computer checks the voltages and calculates the joystick's position. The computer then converts this information into positional changes on the screen

Flat Spin

Magnetic disks spin at high speed, within disk drives, carrying information that can be 'read' by your computer

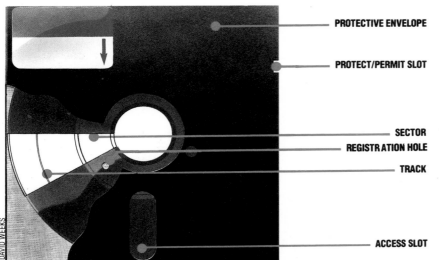

PROTECTIVE ENVELOPE

PROTECT/PERMIT SLOT

SECTOR

REGISTRATION HOLE

TRACK

ACCESS SLOT

DAVID WEEKS

The Floppy Disk
The surface of a disk is divided up into a number of separate bands called tracks. These tracks are further subdivided into sectors. On the Apple II, for example, each track is divided into 16 sectors. Each sector has an address field and a data field.

The Disk Operating System accesses the individual sectors on a track by using the address field, which contains the track and the sector numbers, and an identifier (to check that the user is reading the right disk). Thus it can retrieve information in much the same way as it is retrieved from a memory location (by using its address)

Analogue Board
This circuitry converts the signals coming from or going to the head. It translates the digital form used in the machine to the analogue form that goes on the disk

IN USE ▶

Indicator
This Light Emitting Diode shows whether access is being made to the disk drive.

Driving Hub
This engages with the plastic disk and spins it round inside the envelope

Home computers will 'forget' everything you have programmed them with once the power is switched off. At best this can be a minor irritation, at worst a major disaster as an entire evening's programming disappears for good. For this very reason, the makers of home computers incorporate a method by which the contents of the computer's memory can be permanently stored. This usually takes the form of a cassette tape on which the program is stored digitally as a series of tones (see page 84).

However, when dealing with long programs, or a collection of small programs that need to be frequently used, the time taken to find and load the program from a cassette can be a major setback. There are two reasons for this. This first is that a tape must be started at the beginning in order to locate a program recorded on it – although cassette recorders with tape counters greatly assist here.

The second cause of the problem is the way in which the program is stored. The patterns of bits held in the memory have to be converted into a corresponding sequence of tones: a high tone represents a bit that is on (or set to one), and the lower tone represents a bit that is off (or set to zero). These tones must then be recorded onto the cassette tape. The fastest practical rate at which this transfer can occur is 150 bytes a second. Any

faster, and the possibility of errors increases to the point where the system fails to be reliable.

A conventional cassette system using C-10 tape can take as long as five minutes on each side to find and locate a program. This is assuming that a fast loading system is being used. Some systems work as slowly as 30 bytes a second. For those long programs you really need a recording system that will find the beginning of the program and load it in a matter of seconds.

Such a storage system is the floppy disk and it can be used on most of today's home computers. If you imagine the yards of tape stored inside a cassette tape laid out in the form of a spinning disk some five inches across, you will appreciate how quickly any information stored on the disk can be located. This disk is placed inside a protective envelope and slotted inside a disk drive.

The drive's function is to spin the disk (inside its envelope) at a constant speed, and to provide a means of transferring programs on and off the disk from the computer. It does this through a recording and playback head, similar to that on a cassette recorder, but very much smaller. This head can move backwards and forwards across the surface of the spinning disk, unlike the cassette, which can only move the tape past the head.

Care Of Your Disk
Floppy disks are delicate and should be handled with respect. Follow the manufacturer's recommendations carefully

DON'T BEND!

DON'T STACK!

KEEP AWAY FROM MAGNETS

STORE CAREFULLY

KEEP AT ROOM TEMPERATURE

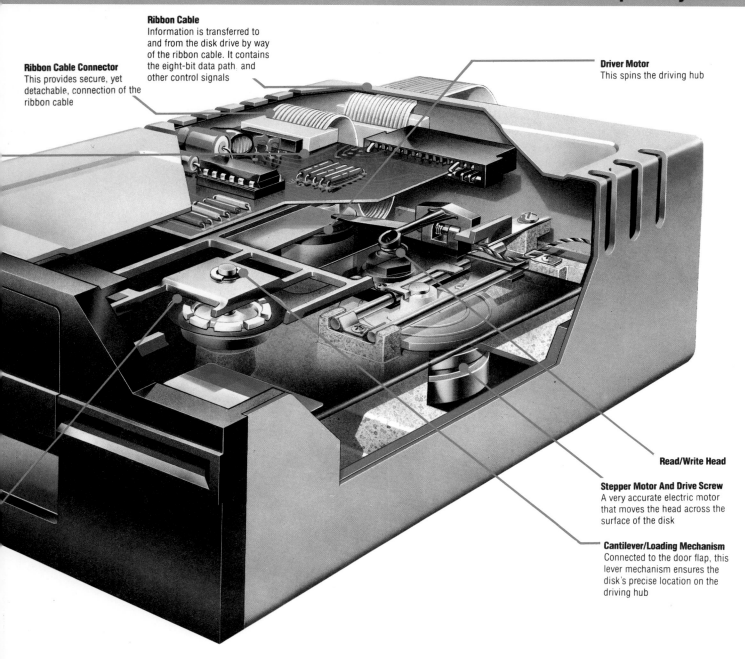

Ribbon Cable Connector
This provides secure, yet detachable, connection of the ribbon cable

Ribbon Cable
Information is transferred to and from the disk drive by way of the ribbon cable. It contains the eight-bit data path, and other control signals

Driver Motor
This spins the driving hub

Read/Write Head

Stepper Motor And Drive Screw
A very accurate electric motor that moves the head across the surface of the disk

Cantilever/Loading Mechanism
Connected to the door flap, this lever mechanism ensures the disk's precise location on the driving hub

COURTESY OF NEWBURY DATA

Read/Write Head
This is a highly magnified picture of the head that reads and writes data to the surface of the disk. It is similar to the head on a cassette recorder, but almost invisible to the naked eye.

Unlike a tape that is just one long string of bytes, a disk is 'formatted' in a series of concentric circles, each of which is treated by the system as small chunks, usually 256 bytes each. Each of these 'sectors' has an address.

When a program is to be written to the disk, the first thing that happens is that the head is moved to the directory, a special file which acts as an index to the whole disk. This is examined to find out where to put the file. If it's being re-written, the first sector of the old copy is found, and the new data is stored starting there. A new file won't have an entry in the directory, so one must be made, then the first empty sector is filled with the data, with more sectors being filled as required.

The advantages of high-speed efficiency and large storage capacity offered by the disk explain the substantial difference in price between the two systems. Disk drives sell from about £120, whereas a cassette player is usually less than £20.

The most important factor in this price difference is the precise engineering that is required. The recording and playback head of a disk drive is almost invisible and must be placed to within hundredths of an inch.

The mechanism that moves this minute head is based on an electric motor, which can turn by fractions of a degree. This is coupled to a shaft that carries the head and moves it across the surface of the disk in minutely calculated steps. To ensure that the disk spins at a constant speed, complex electronics are used and all the components are mounted on a rugged die-cast frame to reduce the effects of heat and vibration.

Staying In Focus

You can now buy a dedicated screen for your computer, which will give you high quality display for graphics and games

As more and more people begin to use computers, videos, and other equipment which needs screens, the prices of specialised monitors are starting to fall.

Originally a good colour monitor would cost six or seven hundred pounds, but nowadays it is possible to buy one for about £350, or even less. Monochrome monitors are much cheaper, typically in the £100 to £150 range.

With the ever-expanding graphic capabilities of microcomputers, most of which have colour, it is a very good idea to get a colour monitor.

There are two main types of colour monitor, one type being known as RGB (standing for Red — Green — Blue), and the other as composite video. An RGB monitor is controlled directly, with the three guns which actually produce the colours being turned on and off by the computer. The pulses which are used to synchronise the computer with the monitor are also produced directly by the computer.

There are two types of sync-pulse, one for each line of the picture, and one for each complete picture. At the end of each frame, the monitor is sent a short pulse, which tells it that the frame is now complete, and that the electron-beam (and thus the dot which it produces) must be returned to the top left-hand corner of the frame.

A similar process occurs at the end of each line, indicating that this particular line is complete, and that the electron-beam must be returned to the left-hand side of the screen, ready for the next line. In an RGB monitor, each of these signals (Red gun, Green gun, Blue gun, line-sync and frame-sync) are sent to the monitor down individual wires.

A composite monitor, on the other hand, is a closer relation to a television, since all the signals are combined into one, then sent to the monitor via a co-axial cable. Once inside the monitor, the line-sync, frame-sync and the three colour signals are separated again and used to control the image.

A monitor is a television without a tuner. In fact, it's possible to turn a monitor into a television by adding a tuner, or to modify an ordinary television by taking the channel selection mechanism out.

However, this is definitely not recommended, because there are dangerously high voltages inside any piece of equipment that contains a cathode ray tube. Even professional technicians would approach this problem with trepidation.

Screen Grid
To ensure that the electron guns are pointed at exactly the right place on the screen, a grid or mask is incorporated into the surface of the tube

Screen Phosphor
The coloured image is made up (as shown in the diagram) of three colours. Different substances are laid on the glass. When irradiated by the electron beam, they glow in either red, green or blue, thus giving the coloured image, depending on the intensity of the beam at that point

Electron Beams
There are three electron beams in the tube, each of which 'excites' a different phosphor to produce a coloured dot

The other main reason is that the design of the circuits is slightly different, so even if the tuner is removed, the result will not produce a very good monitor.

The reason for using a colour monitor rather than a television as the output device is that a television will only work with a signal which is overlaid with an Ultra-High Frequency carrier-wave, from which we get the acronym UHF. This means that the nice clean signal generated by the computer has to be encoded, sent down the wire, and then decoded again. Doing this results in a 'messy' signal, which gives a fuzzy picture.

A monitor, on the other hand, does not need the same modulation and de-modulation of the signal, and thus produces a cleaner, sharper picture. This is much easier on the eye, and makes your programs look much more professional.

Controls
As on a television, there are various controls. Vertical and horizontal hold are commonly accessible to the user. Colour intensity and other variables are usually not meant to be adjusted and are kept under the cover

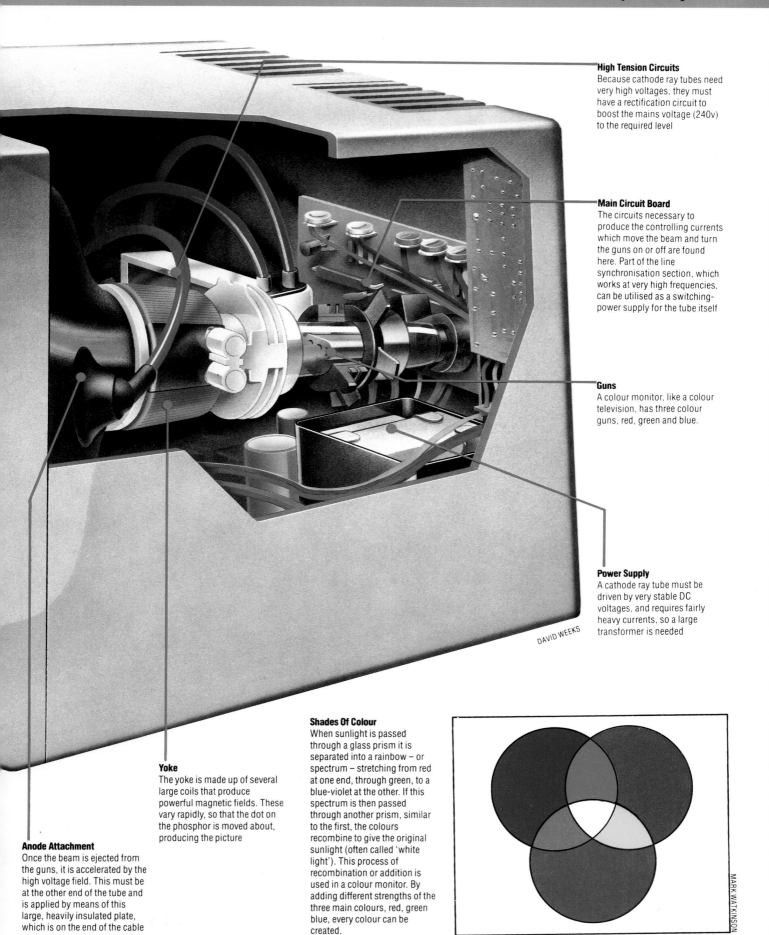

High Tension Circuits
Because cathode ray tubes need very high voltages, they must have a rectification circuit to boost the mains voltage (240v) to the required level

Main Circuit Board
The circuits necessary to produce the controlling currents which move the beam and turn the guns on or off are found here. Part of the line synchronisation section, which works at very high frequencies, can be utilised as a switching-power supply for the tube itself

Guns
A colour monitor, like a colour television, has three colour guns, red, green and blue.

DAVID WEEKS

Power Supply
A cathode ray tube must be driven by very stable DC voltages, and requires fairly heavy currents, so a large transformer is needed

Anode Attachment
Once the beam is ejected from the guns, it is accelerated by the high voltage field. This must be at the other end of the tube and is applied by means of this large, heavily insulated plate, which is on the end of the cable

Yoke
The yoke is made up of several large coils that produce powerful magnetic fields. These vary rapidly, so that the dot on the phosphor is moved about, producing the picture

Shades Of Colour
When sunlight is passed through a glass prism it is separated into a rainbow – or spectrum – stretching from red at one end, through green, to a blue-violet at the other. If this spectrum is then passed through another prism, similar to the first, the colours recombine to give the original sunlight (often called 'white light'). This process of recombination or addition is used in a colour monitor. By adding different strengths of the three main colours, red, green blue, every colour can be created.

MARK WATKINSON

Fit To Print

Daisy wheels, ink jet and dot matrix printers are among the newest developments in print technology that are finding their way into the home and office

Paper Guides
The paper is fed through the printer by a rotating spiked wheel that catches the perforations on the edge of the paper.

The Daisy Wheel
The daisy wheel has the characters attached to the end of the 'petals'. Hitting a key moves the wheel to the appropriate petal so the character can be printed

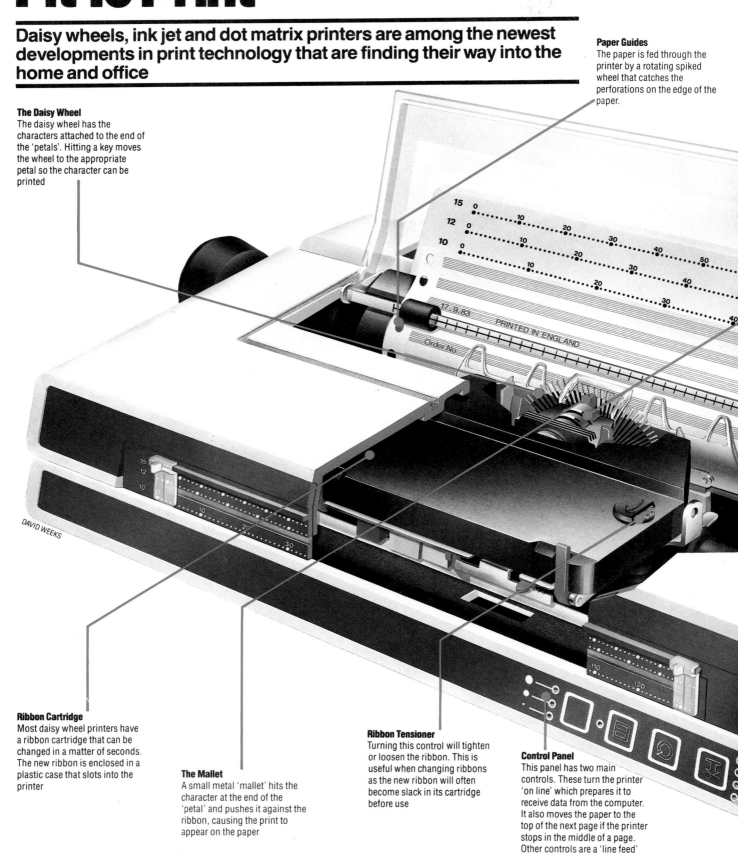

DAVID WEEKS

Ribbon Cartridge
Most daisy wheel printers have a ribbon cartridge that can be changed in a matter of seconds. The new ribbon is enclosed in a plastic case that slots into the printer

The Mallet
A small metal 'mallet' hits the character at the end of the 'petal' and pushes it against the ribbon, causing the print to appear on the paper

Ribbon Tensioner
Turning this control will tighten or loosen the ribbon. This is useful when changing ribbons as the new ribbon will often become slack in its cartridge before use

Control Panel
This panel has two main controls. These turn the printer 'on line' which prepares it to receive data from the computer. It also moves the paper to the top of the next page if the printer stops in the middle of a page. Other controls are a 'line feed' which moves the paper up a line at a time

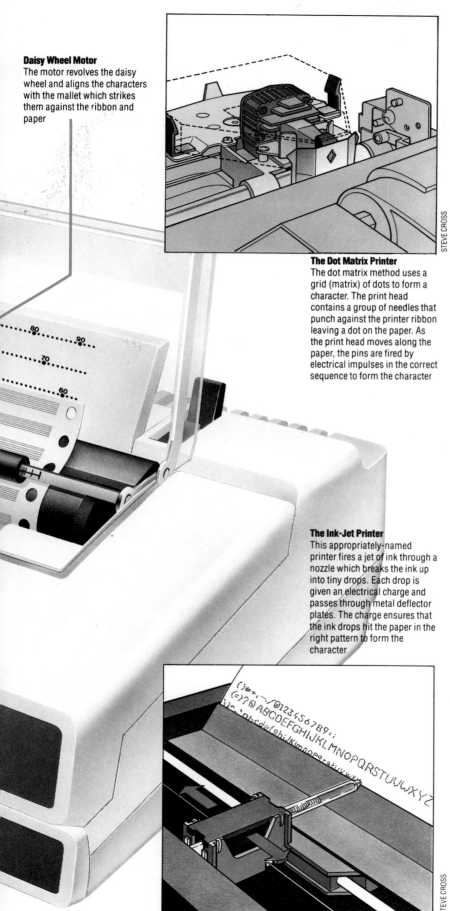

Daisy Wheel Motor
The motor revolves the daisy wheel and aligns the characters with the mallet which strikes them against the ribbon and paper

The Dot Matrix Printer
The dot matrix method uses a grid (matrix) of dots to form a character. The print head contains a group of needles that punch against the printer ribbon leaving a dot on the paper. As the print head moves along the paper, the pins are fired by electrical impulses in the correct sequence to form the character

The Ink-Jet Printer
This appropriately-named printer fires a jet of ink through a nozzle which breaks the ink up into tiny drops. Each drop is given an electrical charge and passes through metal deflector plates. The charge ensures that the ink drops hit the paper in the right pattern to form the character

Up to now you probably haven't given much thought to using a printer. After all, if you are quite happy using your home computer to play games or calculate your home finances there isn't much need for a printed copy of what your television screen or monitor displays.

But as you become more skilled at using a home computer the limitations of doing serious work without a printer become obvious. If you are interested in writing your own programs, you will want to keep copies of your program lists. If you use your computer for your accounts, a printed record of the calculations will be needed.

Choosing a printer for your needs is a fairly tricky job. How much you have to pay depends on the speed at which the printer can produce words and the quality of the results.

Choosing Your Printer

There are three main types of printers for home computers: the dot matrix, daisy wheel and thermal printer.

The most common method of printing is the dot matrix. This works through a print head that contains a group of needles. Characters are printed by combinations of these needles striking the ribbon. The advantage of the dot matrix method is that it is very fast and the printers are relatively inexpensive at around £300. However, because the letter or number is made up of a series of dots, the print quality tends to be poor. The printer is also rather noisy.

Some dot matrix printers overcome the problem of poor print quality by overprinting the dots two or three times. In this case, the print head moves slightly so that the new dots fill in the spaces between the dots that were first printed.

Dot matrix printers are acceptable if you want to keep rough copies of what your computer has produced. They will also produce charts and graphs, as the print head can be made to print patterns as well as characters. But you will need a different printer if you need high quality printing for, say, a letter to your bank manager.

For typewriter-style quality you must turn to a daisy wheel printer; so-called because the printer uses a wheel with long 'petals' that look like a daisy. At the end of each petal is a letter, symbol or number. To print out, the wheel turns to put each petal in line with a little metal 'mallet' that pushes the character at the end of the petal against the printer ribbon and printer. The daisy wheel is made of either plastic or metal. You may also change daisy wheels for different varieties of print face as you would with a golfball typewriter.

The problem with daisy wheel printers is that they are much slower in operation than dot matrix printers and tend to be more expensive. They are also not as suitable for charts and graphs, as several wheels would be required to produce the various graphics shapes. You can expect to pay at least £400 for a daisy wheel.

Higher up the price scale are ink jet printers.

STEVE CROSS

The 'Ball-Pen' Printer
This represents a new development in printing techniques. The print head holds four specially designed ball point pens. When the PRINT command is given, the paper moves up and down to create the vertical strokes in the character while the pens move sideways to create the horizontal strokes. The advantage of such a system is that it can be used for printing coloured charts and graphs. It also offers higher print quality than the dot matrix method as its characters are formed by single pen strokes. However this system is comparatively slow and the pens need to be replaced regularly if long pieces of text are continually printed

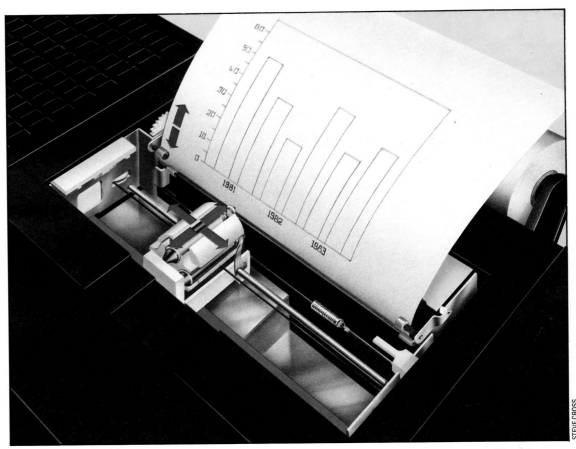

These eject drops of ink that form the shape of the character to be printed. The ink is forced through a nozzle which breaks it up into tiny drops. These drops then pass through an electrode and are given electrical charges. A pair of metal plates then deflects the drops in different directions, so as to form the shape of the character. Ink jet printers are so fast that they can print around 20 metres of characters every second!

An alternative method, the thermal printer, uses heat-sensitive paper. The print head transfers its heat to the paper in such a way that the paper turns black in the area touched to form the appropriate character. Thermal printers are very quiet and fairly fast. One of the most popular is Apple's appropriately-named Silent Type model. Thermal printers are reasonably priced at approximately £300, but you will have to use special heat-sensitive paper that is more expensive than ordinary paper, and the print quality is not as good as that from the daisy wheel.

The Right Interface

When you decide to buy a printer, as well as determining exactly what you want to use it for, in terms of quality and speed, you must also be certain that it can be used with your particular computer. The connecting plug from the printer must be compatible with the computer. The socket for plugging in a printer is usually found on the back of the computer and is called an 'interface' (see page 76).

The three most common types of interface are Centronics, IEEE488 and RS232. Centronics is also referred to as a 'parallel' interface. Your computer will have an opening carrying at least one of these three interface names.

However, the computer industry is notorious for its incompatibility, and you may find that a printer and a computer using the same connection might still not be compatible. This is because the interface must be set to work at the same speed on both the micro and the printer. This speed is known as the 'baud' rate and is the speed at which bits from the computer's memory can be transferred to the printer. The bits are sent to the printer in one of two ways: either they follow each other down a single wire, as in the RS232 interface ('serial' method) or they are transmitted together down several wires, as in Centronics and IEEE488 interfaces ('parallel' method).

Printers use two main methods of handling paper. Paper can be fed one sheet at a time as with a typewriter. Alternatively it can be 'tractor'-fed with the two sprockets catching the paper in perforated holes on each side of the sheet; in much the same way as a camera moves the film from frame to frame. Tractor or sprocket-fed paper is more convenient as you can leave the printer to feed itself with paper. However, this method will not accept headed paper which must be fed into the printer one sheet at a time.

When buying a printer, you should decide what you wish to use it for and then choose the best model that you can afford for your computer.

On Two Wheels

Robot technology is developing fast. Floor robots such as the BBC Buggy can even be programmed to detect obstacles

Floor robots and turtles are more than just educational, they are fun! The principles involved in controlling a device like the BBC Buggy are the same as those needed for full-sized industrial robots. Although they won't actually do the housework yet, they could become the next generation of domestic aids.

Robots need to be capable of being precisely positioned in relation to their surroundings and for this reason are usually driven by stepper motors. Unlike conventional motors, stepper motors do not rotate when power is applied. The spindle turns by a predetermined fraction of a complete rotation for each pulse of power that is applied. The number of pulses needed to make a complete revolution depends on the particular motor. The direction of rotation can also be controlled. It is possible to make a floor robot or turtle move in very precise distances, in any direction, by letting the computer drive the motors separately. A floor robot can turn on the spot simply by driving the two wheels in opposite directions.

However, it is equally important for the robot to be able to report back to the computer when it encounters something. Collisions are usually detected by mounting bumpers around the body of the vehicle, which are connected to microswitches. These, in turn, are connected back to the computer's input port and the closing or opening of each switch will cause one of the bits to change between '0' and '1'.

Other sorts of input from the robot are often required. An ability to follow white lines on a black floor may be useful. This is achieved by arranging a light source on the robot to shine down, with a detector next to it to measure the amount of light reflected back. This amount will vary according to the surface that the robot is passing over at the time; it is an analogue quantity rather than a digital one. The BBC Micro is fitted with an analogue input which enables a detector of this sort to be used directly. Most other systems will have to convert the signal to a digital one before sending it back to the computer.

Another use for this sort of detector is as a bar code reader. Codes relating to the nature of items stored in a warehouse could be scanned as the robot searches for the correct item. The BBC Buggy is supplied with some demonstration software that uses its bar code reader to play music; the principles are the same.

Other kinds of analogue signal that the floor robot might like to follow are light, sound and

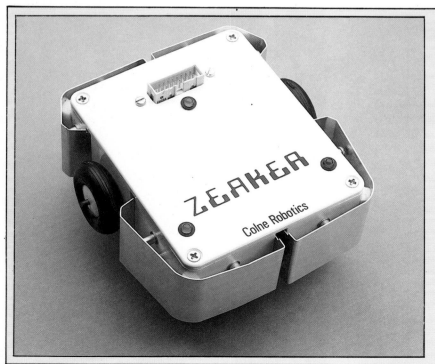

On Course

This 'micro-turtle' is really halfway between a floor robot and a purpose-designed turtle in that it possesses collision detectors and so can be given a degree of 'intelligence'. The Zeaker is capable of moving forwards, backwards, left and right and moving a pen up and down. Control is made very simple by the provision of a version of the LOGO language called 'SNAIL LOGO', so commands such as FORWARD and BACKWARD can be used directly. Computers other than the BBC Micro will require an interface unit. This is an extra expense, but the interface unit does have its own power unit and therefore doesn't place any strain on the computer's power supply

CHRIS STEVENS

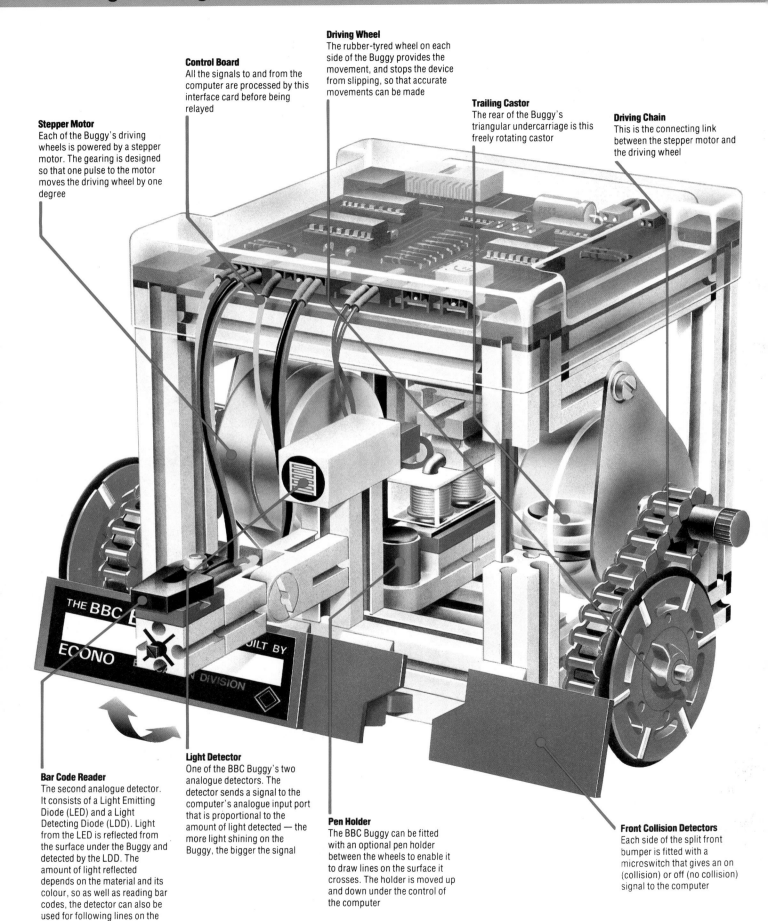

Driving Wheel
The rubber-tyred wheel on each side of the Buggy provides the movement, and stops the device from slipping, so that accurate movements can be made

Control Board
All the signals to and from the computer are processed by this interface card before being relayed

Trailing Castor
The rear of the Buggy's triangular undercarriage is this freely rotating castor

Driving Chain
This is the connecting link between the stepper motor and the driving wheel

Stepper Motor
Each of the Buggy's driving wheels is powered by a stepper motor. The gearing is designed so that one pulse to the motor moves the driving wheel by one degree

THE BBC
ECONO

JILT BY

DIVISION

Bar Code Reader
The second analogue detector. It consists of a Light Emitting Diode (LED) and a Light Detecting Diode (LDD). Light from the LED is reflected from the surface under the Buggy and detected by the LDD. The amount of light reflected depends on the material and its colour, so as well as reading bar codes, the detector can also be used for following lines on the floor

Light Detector
One of the BBC Buggy's two analogue detectors. The detector sends a signal to the computer's analogue input port that is proportional to the amount of light detected — the more light shining on the Buggy, the bigger the signal

Pen Holder
The BBC Buggy can be fitted with an optional pen holder between the wheels to enable it to draw lines on the surface it crosses. The holder is moved up and down under the control of the computer

Front Collision Detectors
Each side of the split front bumper is fitted with a microswitch that gives an on (collision) or off (no collision) signal to the computer

magnetic fields. These fields are often used in industrial applications where a robot must follow a fixed path through a warehouse or factory floor. Special cables are buried in the floor which leave a magnetic 'path' for the robot to follow.

Control of the floor robot is generally handled through a set of specially-written program routines. These handle the sending and receiving of information over the cable link from the computer's user port to the device. In the case of the BBC Buggy four bits are used to control the motors. Data is sent from the Buggy along the same cable. The analogue outputs from both the light sensor and the bar code reader go to the analogue port, and the two collision detectors are connected to two other input lines on the user port.

An I/O port such as the user port can be examined by looking at a certain location in the computer's memory map. The BASIC command PEEK is generally used to read the current contents of the location. To alter the contents, in order to change the direction of one of the motors, and turn the robot, for example, the programmer must alter the value of the appropriate bit in the location. The command POKE will achieve this in a BASIC program (see page 72).

The analogue information can be examined in much the same way, provided the computer being used has an analogue-to-digital converter built in. If no such device is available then an interface unit must be added to the robot which converts the analogue signals to digital information before sending them back to the computer.

A turtle is really a form of floor robot intended for use in conjunction with the LOGO language, though the distinction between a robot and a turtle is becoming somewhat blurred (see page 111). Many of the latest turtles are equipped with collision detectors, just as many of the floor robots are being fitted with pen holders to enable them to act as turtles. The idea of being able to create large-scale drawings by moving a wheeled pen over the surface originates from the teaching of the relationship between distance, angle and shape. If a person moves 10 units forward, turns left, moves 10 units, turns left, moves 10 units, turns left and moves another 10 units, he will have walked around a square. To illustrate these shapes and the relationship they have with movement we can attach a pen to the robot or turtle and create the shape on paper.

The BBC Buggy comes in the form of a construction kit, so you have to assemble it before you can explore the world of robotics. The Buggy is based on the commercially available Fischer Technik system and so can be expanded and enhanced very simply.

Putting together a device like the Buggy is an education in itself. A lot can be learnt from examining the way the various pieces to together. However, the real learning begins when the user tries to take control of his new 'toy'. Although many of the commercial floor robots come with

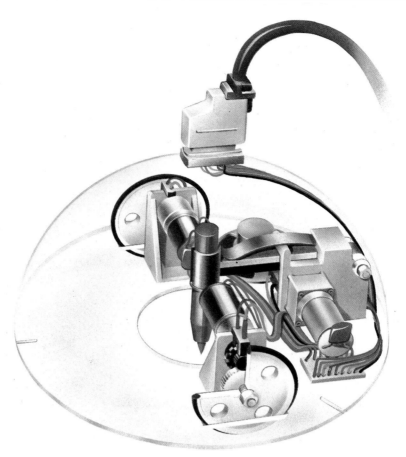

DAVID WEEKS

controlling software it is much more fun to write your own. A completely new approach to programming is required — that of control.

While the robot is active the program must constantly monitor its sensors to see whether it has found a line on the floor, detected a strong light source, bumped into a chair and so on. The instant the detector signals something the computer must react to protect the robot from potential damage. Programs of this type are typically called 'real-time' because their responses must be immediate.

In theory there is little difference between a program that can allow a floor robot to roam around a room without hitting objects and one that can control a power plant. The techniques learnt by playing with devices such as the BBC Buggy can also develop an understanding of artificial intelligence. Programs can be written that allow a floor robot to carry out a pre-determined task until a detector senses that its batteries are running low. The robot then searches for a suitable power supply to recharge itself, so that it can carry on functioning.

The next generation of floor robots will offer even more remarkable facilities. They will probably be equipped with grab arms to allow them to fetch and carry small loads. Light sensors may also be replaced by miniature solid-state cameras that will allow the robot to 'see' where it is going. Speech synthesis units will allow the robot to communicate with its operator and speech recognition will open a new channel of control over the robot's actions.

Dedicated Robot
A turtle is a dedicated form of robot which draws on the floor with a retractable felt-tip pen under the instruction of the computer. Turtles are usually associated with the LOGO educational language (see page 111), though they can be driven by BASIC

Intricate Plot

A plotter is the best means of producing high quality graphic output from your computer. Working with fibre-tip pens, some can change colour automatically

The ability to create printed copies of diagrams that appear on a computer screen is an essential requirement for many serious computer users. Engineers, scientists, technical artists and businessmen all need accurate diagrams and charts that conventional printers are not capable of producing. The only device that can create these images is a plotter and, until recently, these have been too expensive for the home computer user.

However, with the introduction of devices like the four-pen printer/plotter mechanism used in the Tandy/CGP-115 and Oric MCP-40 printer, graphical output is at last within reach of the emptiest wallets. A whole range of plotters has recently appeared on the market that offer features previously only found in machines costing thousands of pounds.

The need for a plotter is generally governed by the type of output being generated by the computer. An engineer or draughtsman will need accurate drawings of equipment and installations, a businessman might want charts and graphs showing sales figures. Producing these on conventional printers is a very laborious process and the results will appear only in black and white. The only other low cost option is to take a colour photograph of the screen and while this might suffice for business charts, it certainly won't be accurate enough for a designer or architect.

Plotters work in an entirely different way from printers: they draw lines between two points rather than creating their output from preformed characters or patterns of dots. The basic principle behind all the various systems is that of the X, Y coordinate. Just as a graph can be plotted by defining the coordinates through which the line must pass, so any shape can be broken down into a series of coordinates. To be able to join these coordinates together in order to recreate the shape, there must be some form of movement. So the pen is fixed to a travelling gantry that can move in the X direction (left and right) while the pen moves along the gantry in the Y direction (up and down).

The traditional type of plotter is known as a 'flat bed' plotter because the paper is fixed to a flat plate with the gantry travelling over the top — this is shown in the illustration. Its disadvantage is that the plotter must be at least as big as the piece of paper.

One method of reducing the size is to adopt a large-scale version of the four-pen plotter idea

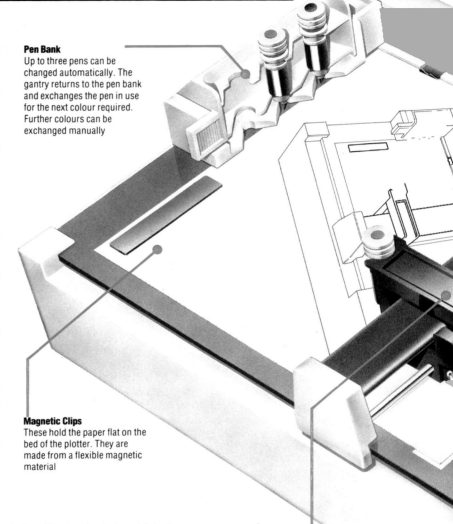

Pen Bank
Up to three pens can be changed automatically. The gantry returns to the pen bank and exchanges the pen in use for the next colour required. Further colours can be exchanged manually

Magnetic Clips
These hold the paper flat on the bed of the plotter. They are made from a flexible magnetic material

Pen Holder
The currently selected pen is clamped — in this case magnetically — into this holder, which moves down and places the pen in contact with the paper

(see illustration), in which the paper moves in one direction and the pen moves in the other. Examples of this are the Strobe 100 and the Hewlett Packard Sweetlips plotters. The movement of the paper must be as precisely controlled as the motion of the gantry in the flat bed type, and is achieved by using a stepper motor. A stepper motor is a very special type of motor that only rotates by a fraction of a turn for each pulse of power that is applied. It is mainly found in disk drives, where it controls the positioning of the head on the surface of the disk, and in robot devices (see page 95).

Connecting a plotter to a computer is generally the same as connecting a printer, at least in terms of the interface. Plotters are usually available with either serial (RS232) or parallel (Centronics or IEEE488) interfaces, which can be connected to the port normally used by a printer. The

Pen Gantry
The gantry can be positioned at any point across the page (the X axis) and the pen holder is then moved into position along its length (the Y axis).
Combinations of left to right and up and down motions allow any point on the page to be reached

programming is often a little more complicated in that, instead of just sending the results of a program to be printed, information about the way the results are to be presented must also be sent. This is generally done in much the same way as a diagram would be built up on the screen.

Because of the complicated way in which plotters build up their output they are usually 'intelligent'. This means they have built-in microprocessors that convert the characters and instructions from the computer into a series of coordinates, which the plotter then draws. Many of the more sophisticated plotters also allow complicated shapes such as circles and curves to be drawn by simply supplying the starting points — the plotter does the rest. The labelling of graphs

and diagrams and the colouring-in of pie charts and bar graphs are often automatic processes, making the programming much simpler.

Many plotters come complete with software that allows them to be used directly from within a program rather like a paper copy of the screen. If this type of program is not provided, the user will have to work out the necessary routines to translate screen information into the appropriate codes in order to drive the plotter. Some plotters don't feature built-in character sets, so even the codes for the letters and numbers will have to be created. This does at least allow the user to design his own characters and typefaces. Once a shape has been generated, it can be plotted at any position and in any orientation or size, so a library of shapes can be built up for repeated use. Routines to plot circles and curves and shapes in sections of graphs are often very useful, especially in the field of business graphics and these may also have to be created. However, the principles of creating a drawing from coordinates on the screen are just the same as those required to create the shape on paper, so the programming is usually quite simple.

Stepper Motors
These motors turn through a few degrees for every electrical pulse applied. With suitable gearing they provide the fine movement of the pen and gantry

Circuit Board
Plotters are usually 'intelligent' devices – they can be given a high-level command such as 'draw a circle with specified radius and centre', and the plotter works out how to move the pen. The circuit board contains its own microprocessor, ROM and RAM

DAVID WEEKS

Interface Connection
Plotters connect to the computer by means of a standard interface such as RS232 (serial) or Centronics (parallel). To the computer it appears just like a printer, though different commands will be needed to drive it

Pen Lift Control
This allows the pen to be manually placed in contact or lifted off the paper

Pen Motion Controls
The pen can be manually positioned on the page by these controls

ERROR

CHRIS STEVENS

The Four-Pen Plotter/ Printer

This mechanism captured the attention of the micro industry when it first appeared in the Sharp CE-150 printer. Its bigger brothers in the form of Tandy's CGP-115 and the Oric MCP-40 have helped bring low-cost colour printing to the home computer user.

Like all good ideas the system is amazingly simple in concept. A roll of paper is pulled through the mechanism by a spiked roller. The paper is moved both backwards and forwards in very precise steps while a pen carrier holding four miniature ballpoint pens moves across the surface from left to right and vice versa.

To create the output, which can be text or graphical, the pen carrier is rotated until the correct colour is in position and then the pen is pressed against the paper. Horizontal lines are created by the pen moving while the paper is stationary, vertical lines use the movement of the paper with the pen fixed in place. Combinations of the two movements produce diagonals and curves. The quality of the printing is very high, although the restricted paper width makes it unsuitable for word processing and other serious uses

Dialling Tones

An acoustic coupler will convert digital data into audible tones and back again. Plugged into a telephone handset, it can be used to communicate with other computers

Microphone
This picks up the signal from the telephone's speaker and feeds it to the circuit board

Connecting your home computer to a printer or a set of disk drives is relatively easy as they will usually be in the same room, if not on the same table. To connect your computer to its bigger brothers in your office or halfway round the world is a slightly different proposition. Fortunately, we already have a means of global communication — the telephone system. All that is needed is a means of connecting our computers to it.

Because the telephone system is so widely used by large computer systems (airline booking systems, for example), the technology is already well established. All the home computer user needs is a simpler and cheaper version of it. The conventional method of connecting computers to the telephone system is a device called a modem. This odd name is simply an acronym formed from the words modulator/demodulator.

The device works in much the same way as the cassette interface on a micro. The patterns of binary 1s and 0s are converted into electrical signals at two different audible frequencies and then sent down the telephone lines (this is the modulation process). At the other end they are 'demodulated' from audible frequencies back to 1s and 0s. The modem sends a constant frequency (called the 'carrier tone') whether or not data is actually being sent, which is how the receiving computer knows that the line is still connected.

The main disadvantage of a modem is that it has to be permanently wired into the telephone system, monopolising its use, which is something of an inconvenience for the home user.

An alternative method of communication is an acoustic coupler. Because the system uses tones that can be heard, there is nothing to stop these being generated acoustically, using a loudspeaker. This could then be coupled to the telephone handset and transmitted in that way. At the other end, a microphone placed in contact with the handset's earpiece could pick up the transmitted signal. This is what an acoustic coupler was designed to do. Unlike the modem, it does not need to be permanently attached to the telephone.

There are several types of acoustic coupler available, ranging from the device shown in the illustration, which is compact enough to be used with a portable computer, to large table-top units. Sophisticated units may be used to answer incoming calls automatically, without the need for a computer operator to be present, by constantly listening for the carrier tone. Just as cassette interfaces vary in the speed at which they can store

and retrieve the information, so do acoustic couplers. The range of speeds is, however, strictly limited. The transmission characteristics of a telephone cable prevent any signal faster than 1,200 characters per second (cps) being transmitted with reasonable reliability.

Low-cost units may work at speeds as low as 30 cps, with more expensive models featuring a switch to select a variety of speeds. The important thing to remember, however, is that the devices at both ends of the telephone line must be operating at the same speed — otherwise no transmission can take place.

The tremendous increase in the use of personal computers in business and the removal of British Telecom's monopoly on the production of modems has resulted in the development of a large number of new products. Devices like the Sendata and its near relatives allow portable computers like Tandy's Model 100 and Epson's HX-20 to be used as remote computer terminals by anyone from sales representatives to journalists. Orders, articles and correspondence can be entered into the computer's memory and then sent down the telephone lines to head office.

Power Socket
Supplies power to the coupler from a suitable transformer. It is also used to re-charge internal Ni-Cad batteries

Interface Cable
Connects to the computer's RS232 (serial) interface socket

MARCUS WILSON-SMITH

Phone Boxes
Light-weight acoustic couplers allow the travelling computer user to be in communication with any other computer, anywhere in the world by means of the public telephone network

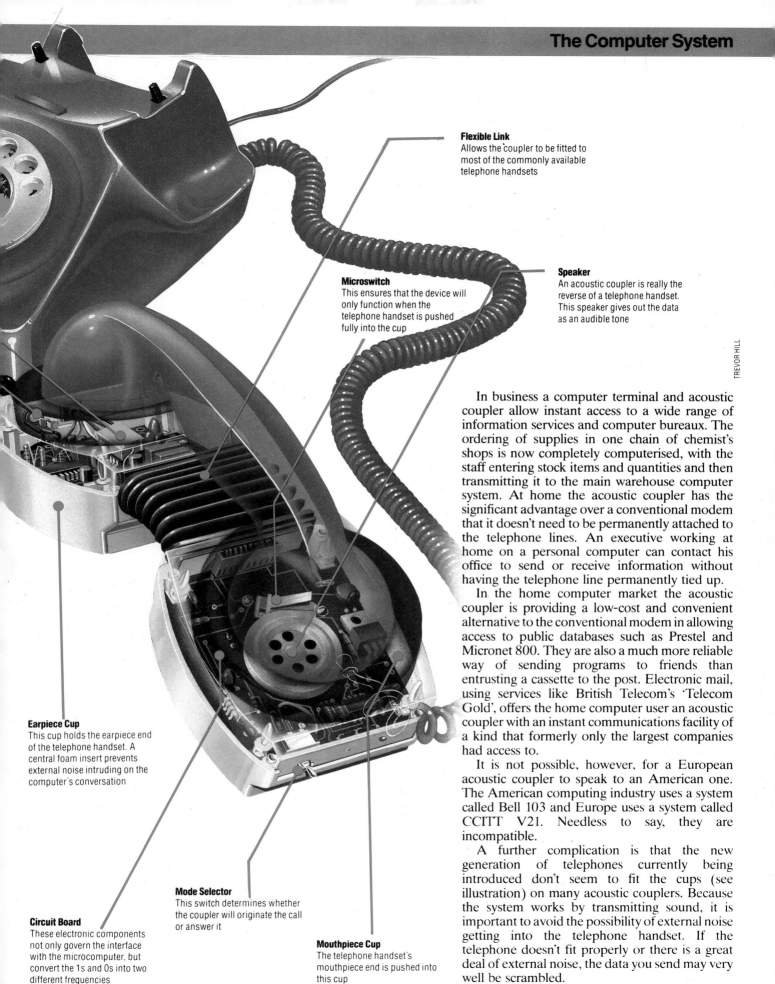

Flexible Link
Allows the coupler to be fitted to most of the commonly available telephone handsets

Microswitch
This ensures that the device will only function when the telephone handset is pushed fully into the cup

Speaker
An acoustic coupler is really the reverse of a telephone handset. This speaker gives out the data as an audible tone

TREVOR HILL

Earpiece Cup
This cup holds the earpiece end of the telephone handset. A central foam insert prevents external noise intruding on the computer's conversation

Mode Selector
This switch determines whether the coupler will originate the call or answer it

Circuit Board
These electronic components not only govern the interface with the microcomputer, but convert the 1s and 0s into two different frequencies

Mouthpiece Cup
The telephone handset's mouthpiece end is pushed into this cup

In business a computer terminal and acoustic coupler allow instant access to a wide range of information services and computer bureaux. The ordering of supplies in one chain of chemist's shops is now completely computerised, with the staff entering stock items and quantities and then transmitting it to the main warehouse computer system. At home the acoustic coupler has the significant advantage over a conventional modem that it doesn't need to be permanently attached to the telephone lines. An executive working at home on a personal computer can contact his office to send or receive information without having the telephone line permanently tied up.

In the home computer market the acoustic coupler is providing a low-cost and convenient alternative to the conventional modem in allowing access to public databases such as Prestel and Micronet 800. They are also a much more reliable way of sending programs to friends than entrusting a cassette to the post. Electronic mail, using services like British Telecom's 'Telecom Gold', offers the home computer user an acoustic coupler with an instant communications facility of a kind that formerly only the largest companies had access to.

It is not possible, however, for a European acoustic coupler to speak to an American one. The American computing industry uses a system called Bell 103 and Europe uses a system called CCITT V21. Needless to say, they are incompatible.

A further complication is that the new generation of telephones currently being introduced don't seem to fit the cups (see illustration) on many acoustic couplers. Because the system works by transmitting sound, it is important to avoid the possibility of external noise getting into the telephone handset. If the telephone doesn't fit properly or there is a great deal of external noise, the data you send may very well be scrambled.

Tracing Paper

Images drawn on paper can be transferred into your computer by means of a digitiser or graphics tablet

Among the most powerful features found in the current generation of home computers are the graphics capabilities. With a few simple commands, designs and patterns can be created and colours changed. All this requires programming knowledge, as it is not yet possible to create an image on paper first and load it into the computer as a completed work. Hand-held light pens facilitate the editing and manipulation of an image once it is on the screen, but they cannot be used to copy a picture from a sheet of paper.

Designers of cars, aeroplanes and microprocessors as well as interior decorators, landscape gardeners and fashion designers can all benefit from a computer graphics system. Once the design is safely stored in the computer's memory, additions and alterations can be tried without wasting valuable raw materials. So what is needed is an input device that can translate the lines and curves of the drawing or design into a language that a computer can understand.

In the professional market the 'graphics tablet' has been around for almost as long as the computer. However, low-cost alternatives for the home user have only recently become available. High-precision graphics tablets, also known as 'digitisers' because they convert analogue shapes and images to digital information, use a wide variety of techniques to produce the required information. The most accurate systems can resolve an image to around 1/4mm (1/100th of an inch) — sufficiently accurate for engineers and draughtsmen. All digitisers feature a flat baseboard, onto which the image drawn or painted on paper is laid. A stylus, which may be an ordinary pen or a sophisticated electronic device, is then traced over the image. The position of the stylus is detected by the digitiser and transmitted as a changing pair of co-ordinates to the computer.

The two most accurate systems — magnetic and capacitive — work by having a series of wire grids embedded in the baseboard of the tablet. In the magnetic system the stylus consists of a small magnifying glass with cross-hairs that is traced over the image. Surrounding the glass is a coil of wire that transmits a low-power, high-frequency signal. The signal is detected by the grids in the baseboard and provides a direct measure of the position of the stylus. The capacitive system works the other way around: a series of coded pulses is fed into a grid of wires and the signal is picked up by the stylus.

An alternative to these is the acoustic system. The stylus is electrostatically charged, and when touched to the baseboard, gives off a tiny spark. The time taken, for the acoustic wave created by the spark to reach two microphones, gives a measure of the stylus position. Amongst other things, this offers the possibility of digitising the third dimensions, by means of a signal passing

Data Entry Buttons
Most cursors feature more than one push button — the means by which the operator can indicate that a particular point needs to be recorded. In an alternative mode, the digitiser will take continuous readings as the cursor is moved

Cross-hairs
Cross-hairs and a magnifying glass help to position the cursor more accurately. Resolution to within 0.25mm is by no means uncommon

DAVID WE

Cursor
This device is moved by hand to trace over the image that is being digitised

Emitting Coil
A high-frequency signal is given out by this coil and is picked up by the grid

Interface
Digitisers are usually interfaced to a computer by a standard serial or parallel port

Baseboard
The image to be digitised is placed flat on this board. On some systems, an electrostatic charge is applied to the board to 'glue' the paper temporarily flat. It is very important that the image doesn't move relative to the board

through the object.

At the lower end of the scale is the pressure-sensitive tablet: the image is placed on it and then traced with a stylus. This requires more pressure than the other systems. Two electrically conductive sheets are separated by a cellular insulator and two different high-frequency signals are fed into the layers. The signal detected by the stylus when it makes an electrical connection between the two sheets provides a measure of its position. Typical problems encountered with this type of system include changes in the surface

SIMON LEWIS

Mapping It Out
One of the most widespread professional uses for digitisers is collecting data from maps and surveys. Here, the computer is being used to predict the location of new oilfields from digitised geological data

Processing Board
This PCB contains a microprocessor, some ROM and some RAM. This is so that it can present the computer with information in the form of pairs of X-Y co-ordinates

Receiving Grid
Embedded in the baseboard is a grid of wires that can pick up the signal given out by the coil. The spacing of the grid is considerably coarser than the finest resolution of the digitiser, because the processing circuitry can interpolate from the relative strength of the signal picked up by adjacent wires

resistance due to damage or the differing pressure of a hand. Given the limited resolution of home computer graphics, the accuracy of this method is more than adequate for today's home computers.

The cheapest and simplest digitisers are the pantographs — based on the principle of the old-fashioned drawing aid, constructed from linked arms. They use co-ordinate geometry to provide a direct measure of the position of the stylus. Variable resistances mounted at the two joints provide voltages proportional to the angles in the 'shoulder' and 'elbow' of the jointed arm. The resolution of the pantograph is limited by the accuracy of both the variable resistances and the mechanical linkages; typically it is only around

five per cent. However, sophisticated pantographs based on optical measurement of the rotation of the joints can offer much better results although they still fall short of the capabilities of the magnetic and capacitive systems.

Optical tablets use an intersecting grid of infra-red beams to detect the position of a stylus. They are not nearly as sensitive as the other systems but are quite adequate for allowing a finger to be used to select an item from a program menu. In some applications the infra-red sources and detectors are placed around the edge of the visual display unit — providing a truly interactive screen on which images can be drawn simply by moving your finger.

The actual data produced by a graphics tablet or digitiser must be converted into information suitable for display on the screen and to this end most of the commercial products come with all the necessary software. However, just entering the data isn't the end of the usefulness of graphics tablets. Once the information is stored in the computer the tablet can be used as an editing tool, allowing colour to be added or changed and shapes to be modified. The surface of the tablet can be programmed to act as a menu that selects standard options from the program so that the keyboard need only be used for selecting the main functions. Very efficient computer animation systems all have a high-quality graphics tablet as their main form of input.

Purpose Designed

Uncommitted Logic Arrays (ULAs) can handle all the functions of a home computer, apart from the CPU, ROM and RAM

Of the many advances in electronic design that have resulted from the microcomputer boom, one of the most significant has been the development of a type of chip called an Uncommitted Logic Array (ULA). Though largely unrecognised by the general public, this quiet revolution has been going on for some years now, to the point where it recently became possible to build very sophisticated computers and other devices with no more than four major components: a CPU, some RAM, some ROM and — to tie these all together — a ULA.

So what is a ULA? As the name suggests, it is a large number (an array) of logic gates, which are initially uncommitted but can be modified to carry out almost any operation that the designer needs. The ULA can be considered as a development of the ROM, since the contents of both of these components can only be specified by the chip manufacturer, not by the user.

Before a ROM or ULA is 'programmed' it consists of no more than a large number of simple electronic circuits or cells, which are not connected and therefore cannot perform any action. All chips are constructed by building up layers of semi-conductor materials by etching. The final

layer is usually made of conducting material, and forms the connections between the various cells. It is the wide variety of possible interconnections that gives the ULA its flexibility; and though each cell is quite simple, consisting perhaps of a couple of transistors or a single resistor, they can be connected to each other by the final layer to build fairly complex circuits such as flip/flops.

Such circuits, called 'modules', can usually be built from less than half a dozen cells, and since a large ULA may have several thousand cells, the modules themselves can be interconnected to build complex circuits, such as registers, counters, and timing circuits. The functions performed by these circuits are normally carried out in a home computer by a collection of general purpose logic chips.

A ULA can be programmed to perform an extremely diverse range of activities. Any given ULA could be made to synthesise sound, or control the exposure, focus and motor in a camera, or do most of the work in a digital thermometer. And besides the ULA, almost no external circuitry is needed — except for a battery, a switch and some sensors or control buttons.

As might be expected, computers are extensively used in the process of designing the layer that interconnects the cells of a ULA. A mini-computer, such as a DEC PCP11/23, running a Computer Aided Design system, first builds up an encoded diagram of the desired logic. The system then draws, and similarly encodes, a map of the planned layout. This is done on a graphics terminal, and a hard copy of the design can be produced on a plotter.

Once the design is complete it is transmitted to a larger computer, which checks that the plan is acceptable, compares it with the original logic design, and ensures that it doesn't contain any serious errors. It is then submitted to another program that simulates the circuit which would result, using a test program provided by the customer. When the design is finalised, the computer can produce the artwork for the optical mask used in making the final layer.

How far can ULAs go? The idea of putting a lot of simple circuits in silicon and allowing the user to decide how they should interact is so appealing that it might become the recognised method of implementing most circuitry. However, at the present level of technology, ULAs are economic only when at least a couple of thousand identical circuits are needed. The PROM (Programmable Read Only Memory), EPROM (Erasable PROM), EEPROM (Electrically Erasable PROM), and EAROM (Electrically Alterable ROM) are all alternatives to the ROM that can be programmed by a user with suitable equipment. It may not be too long before user-programmable equivalents to the ULA appear, too.

Higher Plane
All semiconductor chips are built up from layers of semiconductor deposits, which are individually etched to create the circuit elements. The final layer determines the connection between elements. A ULA consists of an array of logic elements that can be combined to form a complex logic circuit

STEVE CROSS

Computers At Work-And Play

In business, in schools, in games arcades and in
the home – even on the battlefield – the
computer is being integrated into the very
structure of our daily lives.

Games People Play

Dungeons and dragons, stock markets and space flights, excitement and education — all are in computer games

Most people play games on their computers, and the world of computer games is a fascinating kaleidoscope of excitement, puzzling problems, and new challenges.

The video games machines in the arcades and in the home are being overtaken by cheap and powerful home computers that give more variety and thrills without taking all your savings while you learn how to play. These home computer games have introduced more people to the fun of computing than any business accounting software ever did or will. There's no need to feel you're misusing the machine. Games are there to be enjoyed.

Adventure

Not all games need to have colour pictures and sound to be addictive. A whole new range of games

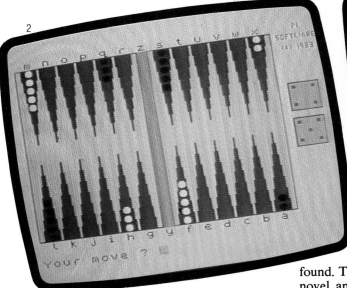

has appeared with the spread of cheap computer power; games that stimulate the imagination with words in the way that books have always done.

These are called 'adventure' games, after the first program that was written for programmers to play on their giant mainframe computers in their spare time. The idea is that the program creates a world that the player explores by guiding an alter ego; but the guiding is done with words typed on the keyboard rather than with joysticks.

The little character inside the computer's world is moved by typing directions like 'north' and 'up', and the computer gives word pictures of the surroundings and any objects lying around. The

player's character can 'take', 'drop', 'turn' or 'break' the objects, or can try any action that might seem helpful. The player can try anything. The only limit is the imagination.

The world inside the computer program can be a maze of caves and dungeons packed with treasures and monsters, as in the popular 'Dungeons and Dragons' role-playing games. Or it can be a deserted alien spacecraft, or even a country house where a murder needs to be solved.

Whatever the scenario, the player has to explore, find useful objects and treasure, and solve intellectual puzzles. The computer world needs to be mapped, and a full score comes only when all problems have been overcome and all treasures found. The best adventure games are like a good novel, and it can take much longer to complete one than to read the book.

Board And Table

It was natural for the old favourite board and table games to be transferred to home computers as soon as the technology could handle it. There is no need to find an opponent when the computer can handle that job, and if you make a wrong move you can correct it without the computer accusing you of cheating. The machine can also improve your game by pointing out and correcting any mistakes you make during play.

Computer chess has reached a very good stan-

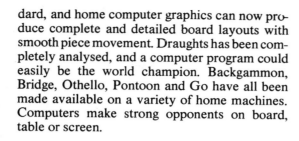

dard, and home computer graphics can now produce complete and detailed board layouts with smooth piece movement. Draughts has been completely analysed, and a computer program could easily be the world champion. Backgammon, Bridge, Othello, Pontoon and Go have all been made available on a variety of home machines. Computers make strong opponents on board, table or screen.

Learning Through Play

Several software companies specialise in educational games, with the computer setting tests and puzzles and providing the reward of a game if the answer is right. Or a game may just look like a game, but also have educational information embedded in it about adding up, spelling, or even

the law of supply and demand.

A favourite game is one in which children guide a pen-holding robot, known as a 'turtle' because of its shape, over a sheet of paper. In this way they have fun drawing pictures and are learning geometry at the same time.

Arcade-style

Arcade-style games are games for fast action and movement and have drawn billions of coins through the slots of video machines. On home computers you can play all the arcade favourites, with swooping invaders, hopping frogs, digging miners and giant gorillas.

But the software companies have games ideas of their own and have come up with games that match the arcades for excitement and spectacular graphics. With a home computer there is a wider choice of fast and thrilling arcade-style games, all ready to be played when you want, and with no hungry cash slot gaping. These games test home computers — and programmers — to their limits.

Grand Strategy

Games that require thought and planning, the deviousness and single-mindedness of a great general, have also moved onto the micro.

The player can be any general in any war, deploying armies and trying to out-think and out-plan the computer opponent. The computer is at its best acting as the umpire and the board controller, as it cuts out the densely written rules and easily lost cardboard pieces that have kept board wargames a minority cult.

Alternatively, the player can be the king of a small country, working out how to husband the crops and treasure while keeping the workers happy and fed and keeping robbers out of the fields.

1 Wizardry: Step into a mysterious world. Your companions can help. But who to choose? A warrior, a maiden or a scientist?

2 Backgammon: Your opponent in this game is backed by a formidable power — the relentless logic of the computer

3 ABC Dragon: An educational game for children

4 Zaxxon: One of the original arcade games. The screen becomes the pilot's windscreen as he weaves his way through missiles and dogfights to his goal!

5 Legionnaire: As a Roman general, your fate turns on the outcome of the battle

6 Aircraft flight simulation: Fly the plane or crash!

Equally, the player can be in charge of a country's energy supplies, weighing the costs of coal, oil and nuclear power against their dangers and long-term effects. The computer can help you take the long view, and perfect your world takeover schemes.

High Flying

Games programs can put you in the cockpit of a light aircraft, reading the instruments and handling the controls to make perfect take-offs and landings at a variety of simulations of real airports; they can make you pilot of a space shuttle mission, complete with views of the Earth through the portholes; or they can make you a Rockefeller-style tycoon on the stock markets of the world, making and breaking the giant corporations.

Accuracy is all in simulation games. Follow the rules of the real world, and the game will show you what would really happen. But make a mistake, and you don't find yourself trapped in tangled wreckage or having to take a plunge from a Wall Street balcony. Computers are more forgiving than the real world!

The Electronic Educator

Even the youngest members of your family will be keen to use your computer. Here's the best way to start them off

One of the most powerful computer aids for primary school children is the floor turtle. This robot is attached to a microcomputer and is operated by a program called LOGO. Children can draw with the floor turtle and it is very useful for teaching mathematical concepts such as shape, distance and the relationship between objects. It is also great fun!

IAN MCKINNELL

Many parents wonder if a home computer would be of benefit to their children. Most know that it is a good idea for teenage children to learn to use computers at home and at school, but can younger children gain anything from computing?

Yes! The answer is decidedly positive, but there are different ways of introducing a child to the concept of computing, and some are better than others.

The British Government, like many governments in developed countries, has decided that children should now use computers in primary schools. The 'Micros in Primary Education' project is costing £9 million and soon every one of Britain's 29,000 primary schools should have at least one micro. Now the teachers have to find out how to use their small amount of computer power properly.

Computers aren't just good at maths. With a good program — and there is a shortage of good programs for children at present — computers can help young children learn music, ballet, geography, foreign languages and, of course, maths-based subjects such as arithmetic and geometry.

There are two main ways in which a computer can be of help to young children. The child can use the computer to explore his or her world, or the computer can act as a teacher, instructing and drilling the child in a variety of educational subjects.

It isn't a good idea to try teaching your six-year-old how to program a computer in BASIC. Before the age of 12, a child can't really grasp the abstract concepts of such a language. Some children can write programs in BASIC at nine or even earlier, but the work of the French child psychologist Jean

Piaget has shown us that before the age of 12 or 13 most children have trouble grasping abstract ideas.

Reckoning with this problem, researchers have now found a way to let a child control and program a computer without needing to handle such abstract ideas (see the box on LOGO). The usual way teachers introduce children to computers is by a mixture of the two methods.

Turning Turtle

Even very young children can use computers to help them to learn. The picture on the facing page shows a young child playing with a 'turtle', a mechanical robot that is attached to a micro-computer. The turtles are expensive and are intended for school use, but the principle is simple: the turtle has two wheels and a pen. The child tells the turtle to move forward on a piece of paper and tells it whether or not to draw a line — a 'turtle trail' — as it goes. In this way the child draws, instructing the robot how to turn corners and join lines up. Because children are encouraged to work out exactly what moves the turtle has to make to draw a specific shape, they discover for themselves the elements that make up basic geometry. This 'self-help' approach is at the heart of the LOGO method. The belief is that lessons learned 'heuristically' (by trial and error) are better learned than when examples are shown.

These two schools of thought lie at the division in how we use computers with young children. In LOGO, older children, nine or ten perhaps, start using a version of the turtle on the computer screen, drawing intricate shapes and teaching the turtle how to remember various procedures. When a child is 'teaching' the turtle to do things, either on the floor or on the screen, he or she is, in fact, programming the computer. LOGO is a language that allows children to program before they have developed the abstract understanding necessary for most computer languages. Thus 'playing with turtle' allows young children to become used to the idea of controlling the computer and helps them explore their environment.

The other approach uses the apparent 'patience' of the computer to teach children by example.

Children who are having difficulty in understanding a subject or an idea are often helped by 'drill and practice' programs that ask the child questions and then provide a score to show how well he or she has done. Many of these programs are extremely attractive to look at, with good colour graphics and interesting tunes or sound effects. Children are encouraged to learn with these programs and the computer never gets tired or gives up if the child persistently provides the wrong answer. This patience has proved valuable in teaching slow learners, and drill and practice programs that, for example, ask a child to pick a noun out of a group of words, or make up a word out of a set of letters, are very useful educational tools. But to use a computer in this way is to sub-stitute it for the human teacher, and this leads us to an important statement: no computer can replace the human teacher. Human contact is the most important element in teaching and, although a computer is the most powerful educational aid there is, it is no substitute for caring instruction.

If you are thinking of buying a computer for your children to use, it is worth finding out which type of computer is in use at your child's school. Buying a similar model will allow your children to use the same programs at home and will forge a link between computer activity at school and in the home.

Computers are fun, and it is quite all right to allow children to play games with them. A lot of parents are worried about the possible addictive effects of games such as Space Invaders or Pac-Man, but although these games are particularly enjoyable, there is no evidence whatsoever to suggest that their appeal goes beyond fascination.

Under seven, children need help and supervision in turning on a computer and television set and loading a program. If the program is good

LOGO Logic

Here we show how shapes are built up on the screen using the LOGO language.

LOGO is a computer language developed specifically to allow young children — as young as four or five — to program a computer. It was developed at the Massachusetts Institute of Technology in the late 1960s by a team led by Seymour Papert, a mathematician who had worked with the world-famous educationalist Jean Piaget at his Geneva Centre.

For the youngest children, LOGO takes the form of a 'turtle', that is either a mechanical robot on the floor or a triangle of light on a computer screen. The command FORWARD 10 causes the turtle to move forward 10 units, drawing a line behind it. The command RIGHT 90 causes the turtle to make a right angle. Chains of commands can be built up that cause the turtle to draw squares, triangles, circles and unorthodox shapes as well. The turtle can be also taught to 'remember' the commands. Without realising it, children teaching a turtle are, in fact, programming a computer

One way to draw a square box:

FORWARD 50
RIGHT 90
FORWARD 50
RIGHT 90
FORWARD 50
RIGHT 90
FORWARD 50
RIGHT 90

Constructing a 'BOX' command:

TO BOX
REPEAT 4 [FORWARD 50 RIGHT 90]
END

The STAR command:

TO STAR
REPEAT 12 [BOX RIGHT 30]
END

Other shapes can easily be built up by combining the BOX with similar commands

Eye Strain

Some adult workers staring at computer screens do suffer from eye-strain and fatigue, but children don't have long enough concentration spans for this to become a problem. The problem for adults seems to be 'accommodative lock', a phenomenon in which the eye gets fixed at one focal length and takes a time to re-adjust. If you think that your child might be so keen on computing that he or she will stare solidly at the screen for long periods, problems can be avoided by ensuring that a short break is taken every 15 minutes.

One technical problem about old domestic televisions needs to be mentioned. It has been found that a few colour televisions made before 1970 are capable of emitting a low radiation dose when used regularly for close-up work that could be dangerous. If you are considering using an old colour television set for computing purposes it is worth ensuring that it was made after 1970

enough, they may then be left to use it, although this depends on their reading skill and ability to provide answers to the program's questions. Hardware requirements are pretty simple. A microcomputer has to be robust: children *do* hit the keyboard with clenched fists, they pull at the electrical connections and they constantly touch and prod the screen. If a system is flimsy, poorly connected or hard to use, it will fail to interest a young child. Some experts consider that a computer keyboard for a very young child must have large, clearly defined keys. But as children's motor movements become fully developed (usually by the age of seven), they are capable of dealing with 'fiddly' keyboards that would seem difficult even to adults. The touch-sensitive keyboards found on the cheapest Sinclair microcomputers are not really suitable for children under nine or ten, although the larger versions of the printed keyboard, such as the one on the Philips Videopac 7000, are suitable for four-year-olds. It is a question of size and ease of use.

Young Programmers

Software choice is more difficult for young children. If you intend using a cassette-based system you will have to supervise all loading and storage. If your system is disk-based you will find that young children are able to handle floppy disks very well. One of the best forms of program storage for the very young, those under seven, is the ROM cartridge, a plastic case that contains a chip with an electrically-embedded program. The disadvantage of such a system is that it doesn't allow the user to store any work, but cartridges are virtually indestructible and allow young children to use computers without any supervision.

If you make the decision to buy a computer specifically for your children, do try to provide it with a permanent home. Moving a computer from room to room, with the connection and disconnection of leads that involves, won't do a computer

any harm (unless you drop it), but it is likely to be skipped by the child in favour of something less tedious — like watching television.

The Ideal Work Station

In an ideal world, the child's computer should be set up in his or her bedroom complete with its own television screen. If you are serious about your children developing a positive attitude to computers, consider setting up a work-station in one of their bedrooms and supplying a second-hand television exclusively for their use. (Put the computer centre in the oldest child's bedroom. He or she may want to use it after the others have gone to bed.) Old black-and-white televisions can be purchased very cheaply and, provided there is a facility for channel tuning, they are perfectly capable of displaying computer information. There is a great deal of argument about the value of colour in computing for young children; some experts say it is vital, others consider it a bonus, but unnecessary. It seems obvious that if the choice is between a permanent connection to a black-and-white television set in a bedroom, or a temporary connection to the family's colour television, the permanent set-up is infinitely more desirable.

If you are able to set up a permanent, or semi-permanent, computer work/play centre in one of the children's bedrooms, it is a good idea to arrange things so that the computer can be removed without disturbing the set-up. When organising the computer table or bench, tape down all the leads and connections so that the children won't accidentally pull out a lead. (Ensure that all mains connectors are safely protected and taped down in such a way that they cannot become unsafe. And don't supply an aerial connection to the television, otherwise the late film may 'accidentally' appear on the screen after bed time.) It is important that the microcomputer is stable and doesn't bounce around. Sinclair can supply a tray that holds its very light Spectrum computer steady and, if your children are boisterous, you might consider building a clamp or other means of holding the microcomputer down. Of course, the computer you buy for your children will also be of use to the whole family so, if the family is sharing one computer, it is worthwhile buying duplicate leads and (if necessary) a second mains supply pack for the computer. These are relatively inexpensive and they will allow you to say a firm good night to your kids, unplug the computer and cassette recorder (or disk drive) from their bedroom centre (leaving all leads taped in place) and scuttle downstairs to plug them into your own television using your duplicate leads. If a computer has to be set up and taken down in the living room whenever your children wish to use it, the fuss of lead connections and the possible disputes with members of the family who would prefer to watch an early-evening soap opera may, unless carefully controlled, kill the idea of computing as a leisure activity for children even before it begins.

The Big Trak

It looks like a toy tank, but in fact it's a powerful learning tool. The Big Trak is a computer-based programmable toy that allows a child to plan out precisely what moves he or she wants the tank to do. The tank can remember up to 16 steps and may be programmed to wander from room to room around the house before returning to base. The child has fun, but the computer is helping him or her to explore the physical world and work out the individual steps necessary in a simple computer program. Despite its aggressive looks, girls love Big Trak as much as boys do!

Microworlds

Computers are widely used in schools, but most educational programs are merely electronic textbooks. Logo is different — it uses a computer to provide a new kind of 'learning environment'

Walking Turtle
The turtle was designed as a device to think with — particularly in the course of learning about geometry and spatial relationships. When children are unsure how to instruct the turtle to perform a particular manoeuvre, they tend to act out the role of the turtle by walking around the floor and obeying the LOGO instructions. This makes learning a far more 'real' experience

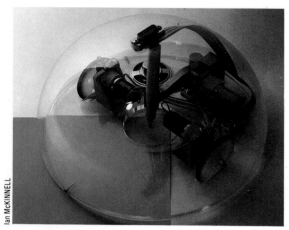

Ian McKINNELL

Since the micro first appeared in 1977, far-sighted educators have been quick to identify its potential as a teaching aid in schools. Most schools now have at least one machine, and many offer computer studies as part of the curriculum. Nevertheless, the micro has made few inroads into traditional teaching methods.

The strongest evidence for this lies in the range of educational programs currently available for home computers, which in the main exhibit a remarkable lack of imagination. The majority can be described as 'electronic textbooks', in which the computer presents the pupil with a series of 'frames' on the screen (equivalent to pages in a textbook) and then tests how well the information has been absorbed by means of a series of multiple-choice questions, which the computer marks automatically without the need of a teacher.

Such packages are easy to write on a home computer and offer the benefits of colourful — perhaps even animated — graphics as an accompaniment to the text. This is, however, merely automating the existing process rather than applying the power of the microcomputer in new ways.

LOGO is different. Primarily the work of Professor Seymour Papert, of the Massachusetts Institute of Technology, LOGO is defined as being 'a philosophy of education, and a family of computer programming languages designed to help implement that philosophy'.

Many people have mistakenly viewed LOGO purely as a programming language and compared its commands and facilities with those of BASIC, concluding that LOGO is a far better language for beginners. This misses the point. Papert never intended his system to be a method of teaching children to learn programming. He conceived it as

an environment in which children could learn diverse subjects — one in which they could, in fact, learn how to learn.

Much of this philosophy derives from the eminent Swiss educational philosopher Jean Piaget, who argued that, given the right environment, children can learn any subject for themselves in the way that they learn to walk and talk. Piaget's work, however, was entirely theoretical, and Papert set out to produce a practical environment for Piagetian learning.

That traditional education methods don't achieve this is evident from the fact that the majority of adults are afraid of learning and do not enjoy the idea of having to acquire new skills or areas of knowledge. The most common symptom of this, argues Papert in his book *Mindstorms — Children, Computers, and Powerful Ideas,* is the widespread fear of mathematics — or 'mathophobia', as he calls it.

One of the reasons for this is that most subjects are taught in the same way, whereas their applications are completely different. Children are taught, for example, to multiply in the same way they are taught the capital cities of the world — by rote learning. The learning process has been divorced from what is being learned, when it should be inseparable.

Papert himself views learning a new skill, whether it's flying, cooking or a foreign language, as a hobby. He attributes this attitude to his childhood, when he discovered how gearwheels work at an early age and applied this concept whenever he came across a new problem. Albert Einstein, too, used to say that when he encountered something he didn't understand, he would break it down into concepts that he had grasped before the age of five.

These powerful notions were incorporated into LOGO, as can be seen in our example of LOGO in action. The first important feature of LOGO is the turtle, which was designed as 'a device to think with' in the same way that Papert used gears as a child. For young children, the turtle takes the form of a specially designed floor robot (see page 95), which is linked to a micro and can be moved around the floor by typing in commands in LOGO. The turtle usually carries a pen for marking shapes on the floor, and it can also feature a small loudspeaker and collision detectors that guide it through an obstacle course.

Children usually graduate from using floor turtles to screen turtles — shapes that can be moved around the computer's screen. The turtle is

Learning Curve

This fictitious but typical example shows how LOGO encourages a group of children to solve problems they haven't encountered before.

```
TO CURVE
REPEAT 80
    FORWARD 1
    RIGHT 1
END
CURVE
```

'If we want petals then we need to draw a curve.'
'But the turtle always moves in straight lines.'
'What if we made it move a short distance, turn just a little bit, then move forward again, and so on — that would be like a curve.'
'OK, the smallest distance is one, and the smallest angle is one. Let's try doing that eighty times.'

```
CURVE
CURVE
```

'There, that's just what we want.'
'Two of them will make a petal — let's try it.'

```
TO PETAL
CURVE
RIGHT 90
CURVE
END
PETAL
```

'That's nothing like a petal — what happened?'
'It just carried on from the last curve — we should have told it to go in another direction.'
'But how much do we make it turn?'
'Let's try ninety — that often works.'
'And let's make a new word — PETAL — that will save time.'

```
TO PETAL
CURVE
RIGHT 100
CURVE
END
PETAL
```

'That's better, but ninety wasn't enough — what shall we try next?'
'Let's try and work it out, instead of guessing.'
'Yes — remember we learnt that if the turtle goes right round anything it turns through a total of three hundred and sixty.'
'Well, we know it turns through eighty on the first curve, so it must turn through eighty on the way back — that makes one hundred and sixty.'
'Leaving two hundred to be turned at the point of the petal.'
'No, because to get back to the position it started from, it would need to turn round at the other end too.'
'So we should try half of two hundred.'

```
PETAL
PETAL
PETAL
PETAL
```

'Great — four of those will make a flower.'

```
TO FLOWER
REPEAT 4
    PETAL
    RIGHT 10
END
FLOWER
```

'That's not much good, it's lop-sided.'
'We forgot to put in any turns between the petals.'
'But why didn't it draw them on top of each other, then?'
'Because when it's drawn one petal, the turtle is facing one hundred to the left of where it originally started.'
'So the petals are turned round by one hundred to the left each time.'
'That looks about right — what we want is ninety, so let's add in a right turn of ten between each petal.'

```
FLOWER
RIGHT 180
FORWARD 100
RIGHT 180
PETAL
```

'At last! Turn the turtle round and we can draw the stalk.'
'One hundred ought to be long enough.'
'Let's have a leaf on the end — it can be the same as a petal.'
'But remember the angle this time — the turtle needs to be turned right round.'

LIZ DIXON

a powerful device with which children can learn the basic concepts of spatial relationships, taking them up to advanced geometry.

Control of the turtle, however, is only one small application of LOGO, but because it is the most visually interesting it is the most publicised aspect. Of greater importance is the concept of building up simple ideas into more sophisticated ones, and conversely the breaking down of large problems into smaller problems of a kind that have previously been tackled.

These processes can be clearly seen in the imaginary conversation of a group of children learning to instruct the turtle to draw a flower (see box). They start off with only three available commands: FORWARD — which moves the turtle forward by a specified amount; RIGHT — which turns the turtle through a specified angle; and REPEAT, which repeats the lines indented in the program a specified number of times.

From these fundamental ideas the children first construct a 'tool' — a program — for drawing a curve (TO CURVE . . . END). This whole sequence can now be called up simply by typing CURVE. Similarly, after experimentation and further learning, a PETAL command is defined, which makes use of the CURVE command. Eventually a command FLOWER, which will draw the complete picture, is developed.

LOGO is not the only language to incorporate such structures (another common example is FORTH), but it is the only one designed to be used by young children. It does away with many of the formal procedures associated with programming in other languages. Indeed, the aim was that the child shouldn't be aware that he is programming a computer — only that he is solving a problem.

In some learning situations, the pupil does not even get involved at this level. The teacher sets up a series of powerful tools using LOGO, which all relate to a particular subject or area of knowledge. The child is then allowed to explore the subject using the tools and discover it for himself. These areas are called 'microworlds' — limited environments in which the computer is used to simulate something in the real world or some area of knowledge.

The best example of a microworld is probably the LOGO model of Newtonian physics. Though Newton's First Law states that without the influence of external forces a body will continue to move in a straight line at a constant speed, young minds observe that in the real world everything slows down. This causes a blockage to learning. Using LOGO, however, a microworld can be set up in which everything behaves in true Newtonian fashion, and with the aid of tools to push objects around the screen, children soon learn all three of Newton's laws for themselves.

LOGO is a powerful concept well worth learning about with a home computer. Floor turtles are available but are not cheap. Versions of LOGO that use screen turtles are becoming available for several popular home computers.

IAN McKINNELL

Portable Processor
Word processing is rapidly becoming one of the most popular applications for microcomputers. New machines are being designed with features specifically geared to this function. These include 80 column screens (to display the full width of a typed letter), built-in disk drives (sometimes a word processing disk is even included in the price) and programmable function keys which are used to manipulate the text. Some machines, like the Ajile pictured here, are designed to be portable — ideal for journalists or jet-setting executives!

Word Perfect

With the right software, your micro is transformed into a word processor, editing, organising and storing your words and even correcting your spelling mistakes

Word processing is one of the most useful tasks that can be performed on a microcomputer. But the phrase 'word processing' has hindered public understanding of this powerful tool. 'How can you process words?' is the usual reaction.

Until very recently tube and bus advertisements offered 'word processors for your office'. What these ads neglected to say was that their expensive hardware was no more than a microcomputer specially adapted to run word processing programs. Word processors are less flexible than the ordinary microcomputer, because they can only perform one task.

Perhaps the kind of program that the phrase 'word processing' describes should have been called 'computer-assisted typing'. With the

addition of a printer, most home computers can now run some form of word processing or text editing program. But it is not until computer owners try word processing for themselves that they realise how useful such a program is.

When used as a word processor, a computer displays words on the screen as they are typed in, just as a typewriter prints them on paper. The larger microcomputers can display 80 characters across the screen, representing your 'page'. On smaller computers the user requires more patience. He has to put up with a much narrower screen and on some models has to allow for the lack of lower case (small) letters. The user also has to remember that the smaller machine can only store a limited amount of text.

The program offers several sophisticated aids. All word processing programs sense the end of each line as it approaches and automatically 'wrap round', carrying the whole of the last word down to the beginning of the next line. This means that the typist no longer has to be concerned about 'carriage return' at the end of each line. Instead, he or she can type in an endless stream, while the program creates each new line as necessary. Where a new paragraph is to be started, however, the typist has to press the RETURN key.

On a conventional typewriter, you are faced with the prospect of correcting a mistake mechanically, usually by whiting out the error and typing over the top. It is pretty messy. If there are one or two corrections, the only alternatives are to send out a messy letter or to start again. With word processing, the problem is solved. The flashing cursor on the screen is, as always, the indicator of your current position. You move it back along the already written words until it is at the point where, say, you have typed the wrong word. You are then able to make the mistake disappear and type in the correction.

Once the editing power of a word processing program is realised, users are motivated to be more thoughtful in the preparation of the text. For example, it is possible to use the INSERT command to add a word, a whole sentence, or a paragraph just as easily as a single letter. This encourages the user to reconsider what is being said in the letter or

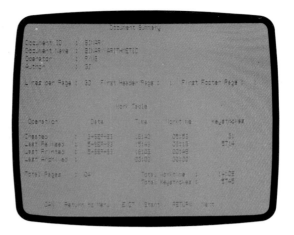

Seeing The Menu
The photograph shows the 'menu' from a sophisticated word processing package. The menu will appear on the screen as soon as you insert the software and guides you to the various editing functions available on the word processor. Examples of editing functions are: tab setting and margin positions, line spacing, counting the number of words in the document, rearranging paragraphs and creating an index

some degree of word processing power. The Sinclair ZX81 can operate with a simple text-editing program, which allows the user to write a letter or document on the screen and then edit out corrections. Text editing is the phrase usually applied to a limited word processing program, which may be able to handle a page or two of text but which is unable to manipulate and store longer documents. The small RAM in the ZX81 and similarly-sized computers severely limits the amount of text that can be displayed and worked on.

One problem with the ZX81 is the touch-sensitive keyboard, which prohibits any real

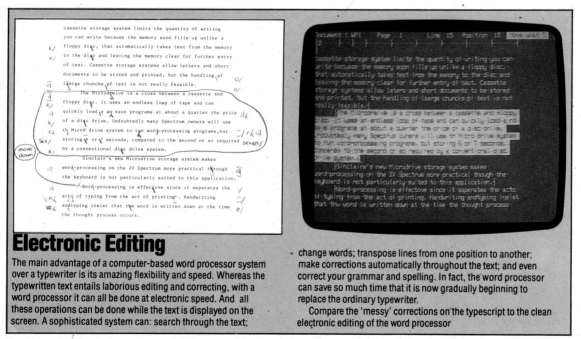

Electronic Editing

The main advantage of a computer-based word processor system over a typewriter is its amazing flexibility and speed. Whereas the typewritten text entails laborious editing and correcting, with a word processor it can all be done at electronic speed. And all these operations can be done while the text is displayed on the screen. A sophisticated system can: search through the text; change words; transpose lines from one position to another; make corrections automatically throughout the text; and even correct your grammar and spelling. In fact, the word processor can save so much time that it is now gradually beginning to replace the ordinary typewriter.

Compare the 'messy' corrections on the typescript to the clean electronic editing of the word processor

document. The instruction to delete text is also easy. A command causes unwanted words and letters simply to disappear off the screen and remaining text to close up, restoring the perfect appearance of the page. Many professional authors and journalists are now using word processors and they generally report that both the quality and quantity of their work has improved.

Even the smallest microcomputers can offer

attempt at fast typing. Although the keyboard on the ZX Spectrum is considerably better, it is still not the mechanical kind that typists are used to. If you are considering buying a micro for word processing use, it is a good idea to examine the keyboards of the machines under consideration as these have a significant effect on typing speed and comfort (see page 82).

A computer of 16 Kbytes or 32 Kbytes,

however, is capable of quite useful word processing. After the purchase of a printer, the main hardware problem becomes one of having enough memory in which to store your text. It is possible to run a word processing program using a cassette for storage. However, a cassette storage system limits the amount of text you can write because the memory quickly fills up. This is unlike a floppy disk that automatically takes text from the memory leaving it clear for further entry of text. Cassette storage allows letters and short documents to be stored and printed, but the handling of large chunks of text isn't really feasible.

Sinclair's new Microdrive system makes word processing on the ZX Spectrum or QL more practical. The Microdrive is a cross between a

of a letter or a poem. (See the article on printers on page 92).

Manufacturers are striving to produce inexpensive word processing systems and some chip programs are now becoming available for home computers. These store word processing programs' instructions on a chip that can be plugged into the computer's circuit board. They are very useful when there is no disk drive unit available. The advantage is that the program may be loaded quickly and is ready for instant use without waiting for it to load via a cassette tape or disk. If the computer's RAM is large enough (from 32 Kbytes upwards), you will be able to create a document of up to perhaps 5,000 words in length and edit it to your heart's content.

MICROCOMPUTER	PRICE (APPROX)	SOFTWARE	SUPPLIED ON CASSETTE	SUPPLIED ON DISK	TYPEWRITER STYLE KEYBOARD	PRICE (APPROX)
Sinclair Spectrum	£100	Wordprocessor	●			£9.95
Commodore Vic 20	£130	Vicwriter	●		●	£19.95
Dragon 32	£175	Gemini	●		●	£19.95
New Brain	£269	Propen	●			£40.25
Commodore 64	£200	Visawrite		●	●	£79
Atari 800	£280	Keyword		●	●	£115
BBC Micro	£399	View		●	●	£59.80
Epson HX20	£486	Deckmaster	●		●	£34.50

The Price Of Word Processing

The table above shows a selection of the word processing packages available for a range of microcomputers at both ends of the market. If you plan to use your word processor for long periods of time, make sure that you can type comfortably on your computer's keyboard. Calculator or membrane-style keyboards were developed to reduce the cost of manufacture and are best suited for games playing and writing short programs. It is also an advantage if your computer has the special programmable function keys. These are often employed on the more sophisticated word processing packages and reduce the number of commands you need to type into your keyboard. The prices quoted are typical of what you can expect to pay. Obviously the purchase of a printer is essential if you want a printed copy. Printers vary tremendously in the way of print quality and speed of execution (see page 92). Ensure that your word processor and printer are compatible for the various tasks you wish them to perform. If you wish to write letters, a reasonably-priced word processor and printer would be adequate. But for lengthy text, a more expensive combination would be necessary.

cassette and a floppy disk. It uses an endless loop of tape and can quickly load and save programs at about a quarter of the price of a disk drive. Undoubtedly many Spectrum owners will use the Microdrive system to run word processing programs, but storing and recalling pages is likely to take six or seven seconds, compared with the one second or so required by a conventional disk drive system.

Word processing is effective because it separates the act of composition from the act of printing. Both handwriting and typing demand that the word is written down at the same time as the thought process occurs. With word processing, no words appear on paper until the composition on the screen is right. But getting the words onto paper demands a printer, and the cheap printer that is adequate for listing computer programs is unlikely to be able to produce a satisfactory copy

If you wish to store the edited text after you have printed it, you will need to save it onto a cassette tape; a process that will take some minutes. The word processing chip is unable to store the text you create. If you want to write your novel with a word processing program, you need to know how well the program can handle very large chunks of text.

Some sophisticated word processing programs can perform useful extra functions. The automatic dictionary, or spelling checker, is among the most popular inclusions. For this facility you really need a disk system. The dictionary checks the words contained in a document against its own stored words. It indicates the words it doesn't recognise, and invites the user to correct them.

As the use of word processing spreads, it is likely to be regarded as an essential office skill and an ideal device for correspondence.

Planning Ahead

	A			B			N	
1	JANUARY			FEBRUARY	1		TOTALS	
2	42.41			18.75	2		388.4	
3	160.35			149.89	3		1732.7	
4					4			

Fields Of Play

A spreadsheet is divided into rows and columns, and the intersection of a row and column is called a 'field' or 'cell' that can be addressed by its coordinates (A1, B3 etc.). Each field may contain a title (e.g. JANUARY), a number (e.g. 149.89) or a formula. Field N2 contains the formula 'SUM(A2:M2)', which is the sum of the top row of figures from January to December. The result of this calculation is displayed: 388.4. Note that the spreadsheet has been divided into two windows so that March to December are not currently visible

A 'spreadsheet' program can help you put your computer to profitable use. Planning , budgeting and forecasting are its main applications

It has been estimated that managers spend anything up to 30 per cent of their time preparing budgets – an activity that always calls for many 'what if…' questions to be asked. Traditionally, a sheet of paper, usually the approximate size of a whole double-page spread in this size book, was used. This was ruled vertically into a dozen or more columns, each of these columns was headed with a month number, and all the types of expenditure entered down one side. In each column the month's expenditure in the various categories was entered. By this means, one could sum the columns to arrive at a total expenditure by month, and add up the rows to find the total spending under one heading for the whole year.

The problem came when one had planned to spend too much — or worse still, too little — and had to go back and alter a large number of figures, and re-calculate the row and column totals accordingly.

By using a spreadsheet program, one is able to re-calculate the entire page of figures every time a single basic element is altered. If, for example, the cost of Transport in January is changed, this alteration will cause the total expenditure for that month to change, and the whole of the expenditure under that heading to change with it — at the touch of a key. No wonder that spreadsheet packages are the world's largest selling type of software!

In common with most pieces of commercial software, spreadsheets are normally written with 'overlays' — that is not all of the program is actually resident in the machine all the time. If you think of the program as being divided into sub-routines (see page 176), a subroutine that is not required in the current operation will not be called up from backing storage (disk, or perhaps tape) until a 'call' is made into it. The operating system will then *lay* that subroutine *over* one that has become redundant (hence, overlay). As you can imagine, this method of stretching available memory is very useful indeed, but it does mean that one is often waiting while the back-up storage medium is transferring information into main memory.

Spreadsheet packages — you can usually spot them by their name, which more often than not ends in 'calc' — are available for a wide variety of home and business computers. Most popular, in terms of the number sold, is Visicalc, originally written for the Apple II and made available in mid-1979. The world of microcomputer software is never slow to react to the success of one of its members, and here was no exception. Before you could say 'spreadsheet' they were everywhere, for every type of machine, appropriate to the purpose or not.

To be of any real use a spreadsheet has to have two attributes — size (not necessarily what you see on the screen, because, as we will see later, what you see is just a 'window' on the whole), and a good range of formatting and control commands.

This means that there are severe limitations on the sorts of machine that could hope to run a spreadsheet program to its best advantage. As a rule of thumb, 32 Kbytes of RAM and an 80-character screen are minimum requirements for a business application, though a 40-character screen would probably suffice for domestic purposes.

Home computer users will find that many of the packages available for cassette-based machines like the Spectrum or Vic-20, while naturally being limited in size and power, will prove very useful.

Because spreadsheets have the ability to answer 'what if…?' questions, they can obviously be used to set up simple computerised models of the real world we find all around us. And if you are in the type of position where you use a spreadsheet package yourself, the need for very careful planning will soon become obvious. Database software consists of a mass of raw information that is ordered according to the user's particular requirements when the data is retrieved. Word processors, the other big-selling type of software, exist to allow the user to shift around single words or whole blocks of text at run time. But spreadsheets are a little different, in that they really do require the user to go through a planning process.

For instance, if you are using a spreadsheet to

The Bottom Line

The cursor is the rectangular block currently occupying field N2. If something is typed it will appear in the field where the cursor has been positioned. The full contents of that field will also be displayed on the command line of the spreadsheet, which in this case is at the bottom of the page

analyse your living costs, you might well wish to group together all expenses relating to the house — rent or mortgage repayments, rates, insurance, etc. and then use the result of that calculation in a larger table within the same sheet. You must be careful to sum all the household expenses before carrying forward any figure into the larger table.

Each individual location of the spreadsheet, known as a cell, is addressed and located by its X and Y coordinates. Horizontally they use the letters A – Z, AA – AZ, and perhaps BA – BM, to allow for the total possible width of the sheet — 65 cells in popular versions. Vertically, numbers 0 – 256 might be used. Each cell may contain a label (such as 'Sales' or 'Profit'), a value that is either entered or derived from a calculation (such as 1,000) or the formula for that calculation, such as B4+B6*B5. Formulae, because they often exceed the displayed size of the box, are usually displayed on a separate line at the top of the screen. On starting a fresh spreadsheet, the size of the cell will be preset, perhaps to eight or nine digits or characters. This is known as the default size. You are normally allowed to shorten or lengthen the cells to suit the type of calculation you are doing. Some packages will allow the leftmost column (usually your titles or descriptions) to be wider than the others. And you don't have to decide immediately how big you want your cells to be. Most versions allow you to expand or contract them even when you've got data in them. Should you reduce the size below that of the length of the contents, the non-displayed part is not erased, but only lost from view.

The last major component of the sheet is the command line, which appears at the top or bottom of the screen in response to the 'command' key: / for example. These commands are for use in formatting and manipulating the layout of the piece itself, not the data, although they may well affect how it appears. Most popular versions of spreadsheet software allow a wide variety of operations on the database. You can, for instance, clear, move or copy whole rows or columns. You can split the window to display together parts of

the sheet that are normally too far apart for the window to cover, and you can then scroll (move across) these windows separately.

Normally, movement between cells is by means of the cursor control key, but yet another command key allows a jump to a specified cell. Loading and saving, clearing, protecting are all performed by the use of command keys, and while on this subject it is worth stressing yet again the importance of regularly saving one's work. It takes a longish time to set up a spreadsheet — normally a lot longer than it does to enter the data. As a general rule, *always* save a sheet before you start to enter into it. Then, if you do make some ghastly mistake, you will have minimised your loss.

Results are transmitted to the printer on a command key, but care must be taken to define which part of the sheet one wants printed by use of the parameters. Just as the screen is a window, or portion of the whole sheet, so, of course, will be the printed page from an output printer. If you need to print a sheet that is wider than your printer, the recommended course is to do two print runs and then stick the pages together.

The use of windows, as we have noted, allows one to have two different parts of the sheet displayed at the same time. A sheet with a split window can also be printed. This is particularly useful when entering information, as one can refer back to any earlier entry. Most packages allow the user to 'hold' either or both the top and first lines, useful for the same reason, as these usually contain the titles or labels.

Up until now, we have considered the sheet as a table, which one could access only serially (one item after the next, along a row or column), but if one were to dispense with the luxury of summing rows or columns, there is little reason why the sheet should not be laid out in any pattern, if that pattern helped ease the user's thought paths. Bear in mind, though, that such sophistication within the database will require an even more thorough job of systems analysis than ordinarily.

The business-oriented spreadsheets, like Visicalc, Supercalc and Masterplan, all offer the

What If . . . ?
If the contents of any field are changed, the spreadsheet will automatically recalculate all other fields which in some way depend on that figure. The speed and ease of this process, encourages the user to test out the validity of his budgets, forecasts and projections to see what happens to, say, the overall profit if certain conditions change. Take this example of a fruit seller...

If the price of petrol were to rise by X%...

Then the monthly transport costs would go up by Y%...

This in turn would increase the wholesale cost of apples...

Which would be passed on to the customer in the form of higher prices...

user the ability to pass information from the spreadsheet to word processing or database management packages, and there are many complementary programs available to allow output to be in a variety of graphic forms: pie-charts, for example, or bar charts.

We have already mentioned one possible application of spreadsheets to the home computer user: analysing domestic expenses and budgeting. Another very appropriate use in the home might be in the installation of central heating, where there are a large number of variables to be taken into consideration: the type of fuel to be used, number and type of radiators, boiler output, etc. In fact, any decision-making process can be helped considerably by the use of a spreadsheet, not least because the user is almost forced to cover any and all possibilities.

Perhaps the most impressive feature of a business oriented spreadsheet run on an appropriate machine is the sheer speed of its operation. This is a function of machine code programming, and, not surprisingly, the speed of a package written in BASIC for a small home computer might, in contrast, give some cause for alarm.

It is perhaps worth considering some of the problems that one would encounter if one were to attempt to write such a program in BASIC, if only as an indication of the complexity of the task.

To start with, each cell must be defined in three ways. It must be capable of holding 'string variable' data, like 'January' or 'Rates'; it must be capable of holding numeric data for use in arithmetic operations, the amount of rates paid in January, for instance; and it may be required to hold a formula which is, in essence, a line of programming code, like 'annual rates/12' to give the monthly rate. Then, each cell must be expandable and contractable in size, but without losing the least significant part, so they must all be duplicated: one to appear on the screen, the other always to hold all the data, hidden away inside the program.

As you can see, the data handling alone is a very complex task — and remember that the more sophisticated packages may have up to 16,000 individual cells! The techniques used in writing such software are very much akin to the writing of interpreters for languages such as BASIC or FORTH, and similar techniques are also used in database management software.

All this goes some way towards explaining the high cost of such purpose-written business software. A package like Visicalc or Supercalc may cost hundreds of pounds, but one should perhaps bear in mind the savings that its use can bring about. The fairly simple application that we considered earlier, that of a manager compiling budgets, for instance, can lead to savings of perhaps 15 or 20 per cent in a year. The cost of the software is a very insignificant part of such an economy, even before one starts to think about the savings in time and energy. Indeed, the Visicalc package has probably been the Apple salesman's best friend.

Windows On The World
Just as we can move the cursor around the screen, left or right, up or down, under keyboard control, in a spreadsheet we can move the screen around the sheet. This sophistication allows an area much larger than that of the screen to be displayed.

Some portable computers with limited screen size, like the Epson HX-20 and the Osborne-1, use this same system in all their operations

The Age Of Portables

As computers become more sophisticated they can be squeezed into smaller packages, so that truly portable micros are now possible

IAN DOBBIE

No Executive Toy
Portable computers such as the Epson HX-20, with up to 32 Kbytes of memory, built-in peripherals and a wide range of software, have greatly increased the amount of information available to a business executive, no matter where he may be. Each microcassette can hold up to 230 Kbytes (perhaps 40,000 words, equivalent to a powerful database), while standard word processing and spreadsheet software allows work to be done almost anywhere — even in a taxi cab!

Development of the portable micro as we know it today has come from two directions. One has been the augmentation of the pocket calculator, as in the Sharp PC1251 and the Casio FX700P. The other has been an evolutionary process of miniaturisation, which has resulted in such machines as the Tandy TRS80 Model 100 Personal Computer and the Epson HX-20 (illustrated above).

These advances were a result of the development of more densely packed chips, allowing a great deal more information to be contained in the same physical space.

With the advent of the single-chip microprocessor in 1972 it became theoretically possible to build an entire computer into a box no bigger than a cigarette packet. However, the size of the display and the prime means of access — the keyboard — imposed practical limitations on this miniaturisation.

Pocket calculators did indeed become smaller, and today digital watches are available that double as calculators, requiring use of a matchstick or a purpose-built stylus to operate the 'keys'. But it is difficult enough to perform a simple arithmetical operation on these and even the most enthusiastic would shrink from entering a 50-line program in

BASIC. So personal computers are unlikely to become as small as a wristwatch. But they have become calculator-sized.

Once pocket calculators became programmable, albeit in their own programming notation, it was only a short step to the incorporation of a high level programming language, and the obvious choice was BASIC. At about the same time manufacturers started to use 'non-volatile' RAM — a type of memory that, by retaining a small electrical charge, doesn't lose its contents when the power is turned off — and a more comprehensive character generator, to allow for alphabetic characters to be displayed in addition to numerals.

Reasonably priced devices such as the Sharp and Casio pocket computers, which have a range of BASIC commands comparable to home computers and similar memory capacities, are fast taking over the programmable calculator market. Packaged to fit comfortably into a pocket — even a shirt pocket — some offer the possibility of being directly interfaced to both a printer and a cassette recorder. Doubtless, a built-in communications facility will follow if there is sufficient demand, allowing the transfer of information over telephone lines. The Casio range, especially, is attractive to scientists and engineers, as it retains the wide range of mathematical and scientific functions that made that company's calculators desirable.

Other models are available with a built-in printer and, complete with cassette interface, cost around £125. Sharp's PC1251 is similarly priced for a similar specification.

The next major step is represented by the 'lap-held' models such as Epson's HX-20, the Tandy 100 and the NEC 8220. These micros offer a full implementation of BASIC (in all cases Microsoft), 16 to 64K bytes of usable RAM, an inbuilt liquid crystal display (LCD) of a reasonable size (20×4 characters on the Epson, 40×8 on the other two) and the ability to connect to a wide range of industry-standard peripherals.

Indeed, couple them to a regular monitor (you may need to buy a special interface) and you have a micro comparable in capacity and performance to a conventional home computer at the same reasonable price. The essential difference lies in the fact that these machines rely on their own internal power supply, thus allowing absolute portability.

The Epson, for example, has built-in nickel

cadmium cells, one full charge of which lasts up to 50 hours, and the system is designed so that when the cells are running low it shuts itself down to preserve essential data.

In contrast, the NEC and Tandy use complementary metal oxide semiconductor (CMOS) circuitry, which requires much less power and enables them to run on ordinary pen-light cells.

The Epson, subject of the first mass-appeal advertising campaign in the marketing of micros, was originally seen as an 'executive aid', but it is more likely to be used outside the office than inside it. It is perfectly suited to data capture (the gathering of information) on the factory floor, on remote sites or even while walking down the street — to be processed back in the office.

In practice the Epson offers various ways of transmitting data. Proprietary add-ons allow it to be used as a Telex terminal; through a modem it can be connected to another machine via the telephone lines; or at the cheapest and simplest, data can be stored on cassette tape and sent through the post.

It is just this flexibility and versatility that makes these machines so attractive to people who had not previously considered that computers could be used in their everyday work. A salesman, for example, making 20 or more visits a day simply to record regular orders, might use a portable machine of this capacity and power rather than fill in order forms. The program to process orders would 'prompt' him with a product list and when the customer placed an order he would log the quantity. At the end of each call the order data would be dumped onto tape, and at the end of the day the salesman could post the tape to head office or transmit the information directly into the company's main computer system.

The micro's own printer would provide the salesman with a copy of his day's orders and his customer with an immediate confirmation.

Slightly more sophisticated versions might also refer to stock levels and give a warning when these fall dangerously low, though where more than one salesman was employed the micro would have to be connected to the mainframe at each call. This would present no problems, given a cheap, lightweight acoustic coupler. At this point our cheap portable turns into an interactive terminal, allowing the whole of the company's database to be interrogated with an immediate response.

Apart from the obvious benefits of immediate access to up-to-date information, the savings in time and cost brought about by this sort of on-line data entry can pay for a complete portable system in a matter of months.

Just as smaller pocket computers are ousting programmable calculators, lap-held machines are taking over from hand-held data-logging/data-collecting devices. These battery-powered 'dumb terminals' — which cannot be programmed — have been available for some time, but they have never been popular or successful due to high cost

and difficulty of operation.

Given suitable software, the ability to plug in to office-quality monitors and printers, and perhaps disk or cassette tape drives with faster access, lap-held portable computers are likely to become common. Portable machines of this sort provide the first real market for bubble memory — a self-contained, non-volatile memory based on a radically different type of chip, which offers huge storage capacity in a small package. Typical applications, such as Sharp's PC5000, provide 128 Kbytes of storage per plug-in cartridge, with an access time rather quicker than disk. The prospect of small machines with a million bytes of memory incorporated is very attractive.

This storage capacity is currently available on disk in the third type of portable machines such as the Osborne Executive, the Ajile Hyperion and the Portico Miracle. Costing up to five or six times

as much as the HX-20 or TRS100, these machines are better described as transportable, because they need mains power. Battery packs are available for some machines, but these rarely offer more than a couple of hours' use.

Their specification usually includes twin floppy disk drives, built-in television monitor, detachable

IAN McKINNELL

A Machine For All Seasons
(Clockwise, from top right.) Epson's HX-20, first of the new breed of 'lap-held' self-contained computers, offers up to 32 Kbytes of RAM and a wide range of peripherals.

Least powerful — and least expensive — among the available range of portable computers are the Sharp PC1251, shown here with printer and microcassette drive, and the Casio FX700P which uses a standard domestic cassette recorder.

After capturing a large share of the market for 'transportable' computers, the Osborne Computer Company's second model, the Executive, offered a larger screen and other refinements

Joined-up Writing
The concept of an 'electronic notebook' has come one step closer with the introduction of the Microwriter, a purpose-built word processor suitable for one-handed operation. The six keys are pressed in different combinations to achieve the full alphabet. Output can be either direct to a printer, with some formatting commands to allow you to arrange the text, or into a desktop word processor for storage

Tools Of The Trade
Inexpensive portable computers have found uses in areas previously inaccessible to information processing systems

Journalists can enter into their portable machine the questions they wish to ask at interviews, enter the answers alongside, and then edit the piece into shape on the train, perhaps, on the way home

Pharmacists have a cheap and easy way of labelling prescriptions legibly that also eases the task of controlling their stock

Salesmen can give estimates on the spot even for complicated calculations like central heating installation or life insurance

Stock control is very important even in a small business, but in industry, where stock values run into many millions of pounds, it is vital to keep an accurate record. Portable micros, with 32 or 64 Kbytes of RAM, back-up storage on cassette tape, and communications facilities, are ideal for this purpose

DAVID HIGHAM

keyboard and an operating system such as CP/M.

First on the market was Adam Osborne's model 1, which offered a complete range of software, including BASIC, Wordstar, and Supercalc and CP/M utilities, for less than £2,000.

Its weak point was a small screen — 100 × 85mm (4 × 3½ins) — which made the characters rather small and demanded the use of horizontal scrolling to achieve a readable display size when a word processing package such as Wordstar was used. Users, however, soon accustomed themselves to it and the Osborne 1 became a market leader.

Competitors came to offer more facilities, especially in terms of microprocessor power and speed, and capacity of disk storage, until this class of machine became indistinguishable in all but looks from sophisticated office/business systems. In many cases they offer full compatibility with specific machines, notably the IBM Personal Computer, which perhaps encourages their use as a 'second computer'.

The real difference between these portables and office systems lies in their packaging. An applications program that runs on a normal office system will run on a portable with a similar microprocessor. The only limitation is still likely to be the size of the monitor screen and hence of the individual characters.

All this has been made possible by the development of the single chip microprocessor. The limitations on input and output accessibility are a reflection on our dependence on the keyboard as the main input device and the cathode ray tube as the main output device. But what if we suggest voice recognition and speech synthesis as an alternative? There is then no reason why a

micro of similar power to the Ajile Hyperion, for instance, should take up any more space than a Sony Walkman — and the chances are that, had we the technology available, it would look just iike that, with the addition of a miniature microphone.

In the present climate of high-speed technological advance the developments in this field are likely to be considerable, even if we don't stray into the fantasy world of speech input and output. Imagine, for example, combining the Sinclair ZX Spectrum with Sinclair's flat-screen television and Microdrive, and powering the system from a nickel cadmium rechargeable pack: there is no reason why one should not put this together for oneself — though perhaps Sinclair will do it for us...

Because of its small size, the ZX Spectrum is an obvious machine for this application, but most computers operate on the sort of voltage obtainable from standard dry cells: there is little reason why almost any computer could not be made portable in this way.

An interesting trend is typified by the ACT Apricot, which is a normal office system, though small in size. Leave aside the monitor and the Apricot becomes a portable system. 'Portability' is, of course, a vague term. Many micros that are so described are merely fitted with a carrying handle and were never conceived as purpose-built, self-contained units.

With the introduction of a wide range of portable micros, the industry has taken a huge step towards fulfilling its real potential — making computing power available to all at low cost and in a form requiring no prior knowledge or training. Admittedly, it will be some time before these criteria are properly met, but the goal is in sight.

Talking Back

It used to be pure science fiction. Now with a speech synthesiser your computer really can talk to you. And it needn't sound like a Dalek, either

While the science of speech recognition has yet to be fully developed, the generation of electronic speech has been mastered. Until recently, however, the computing power and memory capacity needed to produce human-like utterances were substantial. Now, with the aid of a suitable add-on, almost every home computer and electronic toy is capable of talking back. The rapid advances in technology and the fall in the cost of computer components have made the talking computer commonplace.

When people talk, sounds of three distinctly different types are produced. The first is 'voiced' or vowel-type sound — *oo, ar, ee* and so on. These are produced by the vibration of the vocal chords in the throat, the frequency of this vibration determining the vowel sound. The second is the 'fricative' or unvoiced sound, such as *ss, sh, t* and *ff*. Here air from the lungs bypasses the vocal cords and the frequency of the sound is controlled by the positioning of the lips and tongue. The third 'sound' is silence or — to be more precise — the gaps occurring within words like six, eight and so on. You may not realise that there are gaps in these words, but if you try to pronounce them slowly you will realise that it is impossible to run smoothly from the sound of *i* into *x*.

Building Blocks Of Sound

There are two ways of generating speech-like sounds electronically. The first, until recently the most common, is that of synthesis by rule. By analysing the frequencies contained within speech it is possible to devise a system of rules that allows us to create any given sound from its components. For example, the word 'too' could be defined as so many milliseconds of the mixture of frequencies that make up the sound *t*, followed immediately by the *oo* frequencies.

These individual building blocks are called 'phonemes' and by using them in various combinations any word can be constructed. The individual characteristics of a human speaker tend to be lost when speech is generated in this way, but the words can be recognised and understood. Because the rules for generating the phonemes are built into the equipment itself, the user is able to enter a list of the phonemes into the system. These are reproduced through a small speaker. With a little practice it is possible to generate complete sentences instantly by calling up sequences of phonemes, which can usually be stored in BASIC strings.

The second method of speech synthesis relies

The Flow Of Sound
Speech can be digitised and stored in memory, either RAM or ROM. Electrical output from a microphone is passed through an analogue-to-digital convertor. The output from this chip is a digital pattern of 1s and 0s. The speech can be recreated using a digital-to-analogue convertor, an amplifier, and a loudspeaker

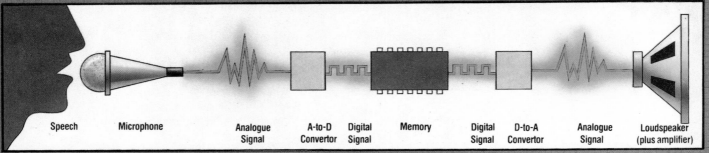

Speech | Microphone | Analogue Signal | A-to-D Convertor | Digital Signal | Memory | Digital Signal | D-to-A Convertor | Analogue Signal | Loudspeaker (plus amplifier)

on the human ear and brain to fill in gaps. For example, the range of frequencies that can be transmitted over a telephone line gives only one-fifth the quality we would expect from a reasonable hi-fi system, yet the speech we hear through the ear-piece is perfectly understandable. This is because our brain fills in the gaps.

The second method of synthesis, called 'digitised speech', uses the same phenomenon. With the reduction in cost of computer memory it is now possible to convert speech into digital information by means of an analogue-to-digital converter. The resulting data is then compressed many hundreds of times and stored in a ROM — thereby creating the gaps which your ear can compensate for.

To cause any of the stored words to be spoken we simply give the computer the address of that word in the ROM, and the digital information is recovered and converted back into sound. Because the original speaker's words are stored, the personal characteristics remain. Acorn's speech chips for the BBC Micro, for example, can be clearly identified as the voice of newscaster Kenneth Kendall.

Some computers, notably the Sirius 1, feature built in hardware and disk-based software to allow the user to digitise his own voice using a microphone. The resulting data is stored on disk — one second of speech occupies about one Kbyte — to be recalled from an applications program as verbal messages and warnings.

The uses for speech synthesisers are so many and varied that it is almost impossible to list them. To start with, speech synthesis can replace taped announcements at railway stations, airports and other terminals. In the USA it is widely used on the telephone system to inform callers of wrongly dialled numbers, engaged numbers or withdrawn services. Many automated ordering systems now feature speech response. An order number is keyed in to a computer, which speaks the description as a double-check. The computer can also inform the customer of the current stock level or the likely waiting period so that the order may be modified at the time it is placed.

Speech synthesis units are now incorporated into cars — the BL Maestro, for example — as part of the standard instrumentation. More than a mere sales ploy, the synthesiser provides warnings that the driver can hear and act on without having to take his eyes off the road.

In the home computer and electronic games market speech synthesis is used to enhance games: scores are called out and warnings of enemy attack can be given verbally, leaving the player free to concentrate on the tactics of the game rather than having to consult messages printed at the bottom of the screen.

Finally, there are educational devices such as Texas Instruments' Speak'n'Spell, which recites a word that must then be spelt correctly, and foreign language dictionaries that speak the words as they are displayed.

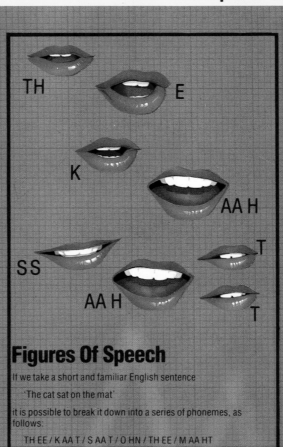

Figures Of Speech

If we take a short and familiar English sentence

'The cat sat on the mat'

it is possible to break it down into a series of phonemes, as follows:

TH EE / K AA T / S AA T / O HN / TH EE / M AA HT

Different chips require that phrases are broken down and specified in different ways. For the same sentence, another chip might require the following phonemes:

THV E / K A T / S A T / UH$_3$ N / THV E / MAT

The Votrax chip, for example, contains some 60 phonemes and rules for using them, which can be directly accessed by a simple number. To make the system more usable, a set of programs is provided that allows the user to type in the utterance required in the form of the phonemes it contains, as in the example above. However, with devices such as the Braid Speech Synthesiser or Votrax's own Personal Speech System, which incudes a dedicated microprocessor and some sophisticated software, the user can type in the plain English text and get the spoken equivalent back

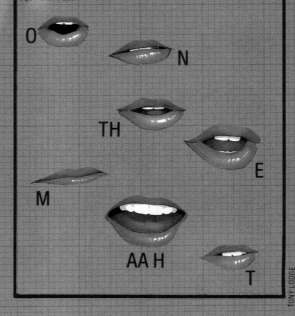

TONY LODGE

Mice And Men

Computer designers want to abandon the keyboard in favour of something easier to use. One approach is the mouse

Not long ago computers could only be accessed through large electromechanical typewriters called 'teletypes'. These were noisy, cumbersome and unreliable devices that have since been replaced by the swift and silent Visual Display Unit (VDU) with keyboard. The VDU eliminated many of the problems associated with the teletypes — not least of which was the production of large amounts of punched tape waste paper as the information was keyed in. However, both the mechanical terminal and the VDU-plus-keyboard are restricted by their character-by-character, line-by-line format. The user cannot move quickly around the screen — selecting items from a menu here, altering data there, or changing files and programs — without being faced with the limitations of the keyed cursor format. Freedom from the keyboard is attained when using graphics terminals or playing computer games with trackballs and joysticks, but how can a serious user benefit from these?

Most of the home computers currently available are equipped with four direction cursor controls that can be moved around a program listing or a text document to the position where an amendment needs to be made. But the cursor can be moved only in character- or line-sized steps; the user cannot move it directly to its destination. If the text cursor could be moved like a graphics cursor, which can be freely manipulated under the control of a joystick or trackball, movement of data would be considerably faster.

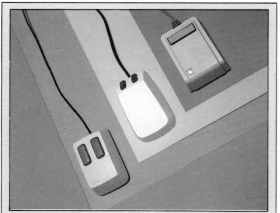

Three Blind Mice
Many of the most recent business microcomputers feature a mouse as standard, and some companies offer units as add-ons to existing machines. Most work by means of a rotating ball on the underside, and feature either one, two or three 'SELECT' buttons on the top

IAN McKINNELL. MICE COURTESY OF MICROSOFT, APPLE & XEROX

Main Ball
A large steel ball-bearing rests on the surface across which the mouse is moved. On some mice the ball is made from hard rubber to prevent it from slipping

Encoding Wheels
These two wheels make constant contact with the ball to pick up its movement in two directions. The wheels are mounted on shafts; at the end of these shafts are encoding devices that produce electrical pulses as the shafts are turned

Buttons
The function of the two buttons will depend on the software package in use. Usually, one is used to select an item, and the other to move objects around the screen

Microswitches
These are mounted on the PCB beneath the buttons, and require only a tiny movement to make or break the circuit

Rubber Grommet
The mouse must be free to be moved around the desk, and the rubber grommet is particularly important in preventing strain on the connection between the cable and PCB

A solution to this problem was first explored in the 1960's at the Stanford Research Institute in California; and the first 'mouse' — as the new kind of controller that was developed was called — was patented in 1970. The device was given the name 'mouse' because of its appearance: a mouse is small enough to fit into the palm of the hand; it has a 'tail' (the cable); and the first devices usually had two 'ears' (control buttons). Conventional trackballs and joysticks aren't used because the precision that they provide in positioning the cursor isn't needed.

The mouse operates by detecting its motion across any flat surface in the up/down and left/right directions, as well as combinations of the two. These movements are directly converted to movements of the cursor — or pointer, as it is often called — on the screen. There are two main methods of generating the electrical signals from the movement of the mouse. In both cases, the underside of the mouse features a large ball that rests on the surface across which the mouse is being moved.

The rotation of the mouse's ball-bearing is transferred to internal cylindrical rollers. In one system, the ends of these cylinders are fitted with code wheels that have alternating tracks of conducting and non-conducting material. The pulses received are counted by the mouse's operating software and enable it to give a direct reading for the cursor's position on the screen. In

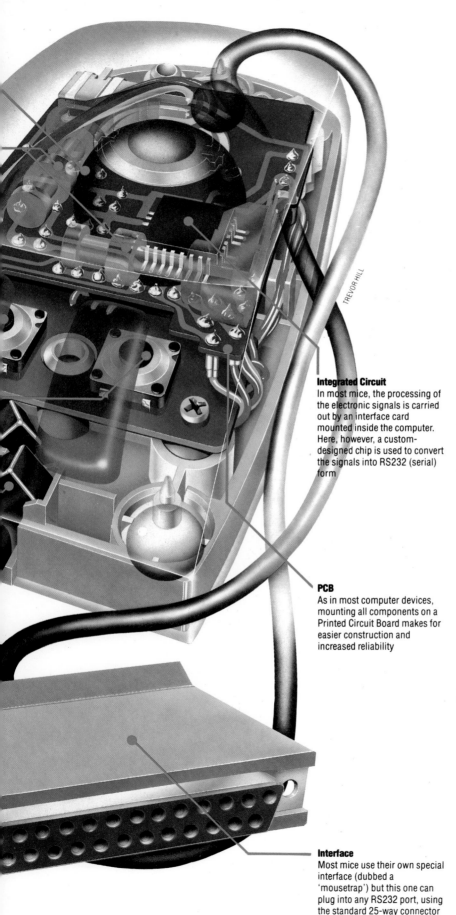

Integrated Circuit
In most mice, the processing of the electronic signals is carried out by an interface card mounted inside the computer. Here, however, a custom-designed chip is used to convert the signals into RS232 (serial) form

PCB
As in most computer devices, mounting all components on a Printed Circuit Board makes for easier construction and increased reliability

Interface
Most mice use their own special interface (dubbed a 'mousetrap') but this one can plug into any RS232 port, using the standard 25-way connector

the other system, two slotted discs are fitted to the rollers. A light is continuously directed at the discs and the beam is detected optically on the other side of them by a photocell. The pulses of light passing through the slots are then converted to electrical signals, which are treated in the same way as those of the mechanical system.

There are other systems, as well. In one case, for example, the mouse is used in conjunction with a special pad covered with a pattern of dots. A light inside the mouse's body illuminates the area of the pad covered by the mouse and this pattern is detected by a special optical processing chip. Any movement of the mouse will change the pattern that the chip detects and it can instantly calculate how far the device has moved in any direction. This system has the advantage of having no moving parts, but it is much more expensive than the others.

Once the cursor has been moved to the required place on the screen its position can be entered into the computer by pressing one of the 'ears' (buttons) on the mouse. The number of buttons fitted varies from one manufacturer to another. Some systems use as many as three; Microsoft have chosen to fit two, while the Apple Lisa mouse has only one. The buttons can also be used to select items from a menu — programs such as Microsoft's MultiTool Word use this facility — and give the mouse control of the normal cursor motion. These devices can be used with highly sophisticated software such as that provided on the Apple Lisa. Here the button is pressed once to select an 'icon' (or symbol) from a screen menu, and twice to open out that particular application.

The main advantage of all mice, and the software that has been produced to complement them, is that they can be used by those who have no keyboard skills. Rather than having to type in the name of a program or press certain letters or numbers to select a function, the user simply moves the mouse so that the screen cursor points to the application or course of action that is required, and presses a button to activate it.

Unfortunately, the mouse doesn't completely eliminate the need for a keyboard — new text and numbers still have to be fed into the computer — but it does make the manipulation of that information much simpler. Tests conducted by Apple during the development of the Lisa showed that a user entirely unfamiliar with a computer can learn to work with the Lisa's mouse-driven software in as little as 15 minutes. Similar software running on a conventional system takes nearly 20 hours to become familiar with, mainly because of the problems involved in learning to use the keyboard, and the need to learn lengthy and complicated commands. Electronic mice will soon be an integral part of home computers. They are efficient and simple to use and they don't frighten the faint-hearted as much as the sight of a traditional QWERTY keyboard.

One-Armed Bandits

Small robot arms can provide an insight into control programming, and they can be interfaced to any home computer with a parallel port

Have you ever wished there was some way that your computer could perform a simple task like make a cup of tea? There is no problem, given the correct interface, in programming a computer to switch the kettle on and off. But when it comes to physically manipulating objects, like tipping a kettle to pour hot water into a teapot, then a mechanical arm is needed. Recently, such devices — called robot arms — have become available for home computer users. These are smaller versions of the industrial arms used by companies like British Leyland and Fiat for welding and painting work on their car assembly lines. The Colne Robotics 'Armdroid', which was probably the first robot arm suitable for use with a home computer, first appeared in 1981. Although the arm is not mobile (unless you were to mount it on a floor robot), it does allow objects to be manipulated with a remarkable degree of precision.

The main components of the robot arm, apart from the metal sections themselves, are the stepper motors that facilitate movement of the sections by precise amounts. There are six motors: one to rotate the arm at the 'waist', one each to control the 'shoulder' and 'elbow' joints, and three to control movement in the 'hand'. All these motors can be controlled very simply by a computer.

All that is needed to interface the arm to a computer is a single eight-bit parallel port. One bit determines whether information is passed to or

from the robot. Three address bits are used to select the desired motor, and the other four bits control the direction and speed of movement. Clock signals are also sent to synchronise the movements of the robot arm with the computer's instructions. To speed things up and enable the arm to perform more complex manoeuvres, electronic latches are built into the circuitry that allow any combination of motors to operate simultaneously by 'holding' the instruction to one motor while the other motors are being instructed.

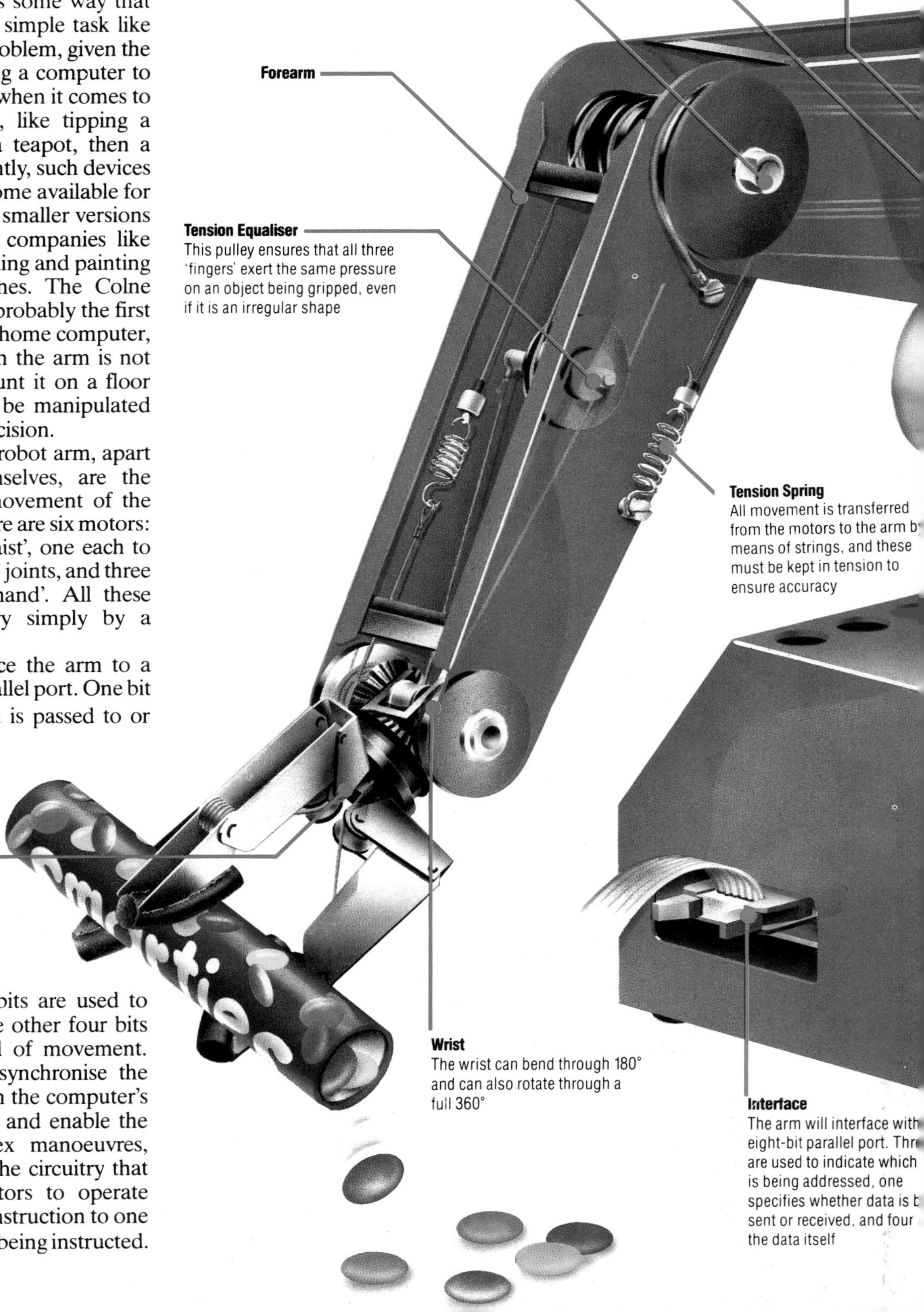

Spools
The spools of string are arranged in such a way that if the shoulder angle is changed, the elbow angle will automatically change, to keep the 'forearm' at the same angle to the horizontal

Upper Arm

Elbow
This has 270° freedom of movement

Forearm

Tension Equaliser
This pulley ensures that all three 'fingers' exert the same pressure on an object being gripped, even if it is an irregular shape

Tension Spring
All movement is transferred from the motors to the arm by means of strings, and these must be kept in tension to ensure accuracy

Hand
The three 'fingers' of the hand/gripper have spring-jointed knuckles, and rubber pads to help grip objects, when sensors are not fitted

Wrist
The wrist can bend through 180° and can also rotate through a full 360°

Interface
The arm will interface with eight-bit parallel port. Thr are used to indicate which is being addressed, one specifies whether data is b sent or received, and four the data itself

In order to make the arm move into position and grip an object, it is first necessary to divide the overall movement into a set of simple steps. Each motor will need to be instructed separately in a precise movement that will together compose the total motion of the robot arm. This information is then stored in the computer's memory and the arm can be made to repeat the operation as many times as required. Most robot arms currently available are supplied with programs to drive them that include routines to 'learn' sequences of movements.

If the arm is handling delicate objects — the normal testpiece is an egg — the computer must be made to monitor the pressure of the grip. If it is too light the egg will fall; if it is too tight the shell will be broken. Various methods are used to convey information from the arm to the computer, but the most common involve simple microswitches. These can be fitted to set the limits of travel of the arm (most low-cost arms don't include sensors), or they can be built into the grip to detect a pre-set pressure limit.

The main alternative system to microswitches, used on most of the bigger arms, is based on pressure sensing. Certain materials alter their electrical resistance when subjected to change of pressure and these fluctuations can be measured. Although this method is more expensive it does provide very accurate results.

If the program allows no feedback of information from the arm to the computer, it is known as 'open loop', or deterministic. In our example above, such a program would undoubtedly result in a broken egg. If there is, however, some form of feedback that adjusts the actions carried out under the program, then the system becomes 'closed loop', or stochastic. Here the microswitches or pressure sensors are used to limit the closing of the grip at a point where the egg is firmly gripped but not crushed.

Many of the more sophisticated robot systems include multiple sensors to measure light, heat and other variables. These sensors can be used to keep track of what is happening while the arm performs its task and report back if something is going wrong: a robot welder happily burning holes in itself, for example!

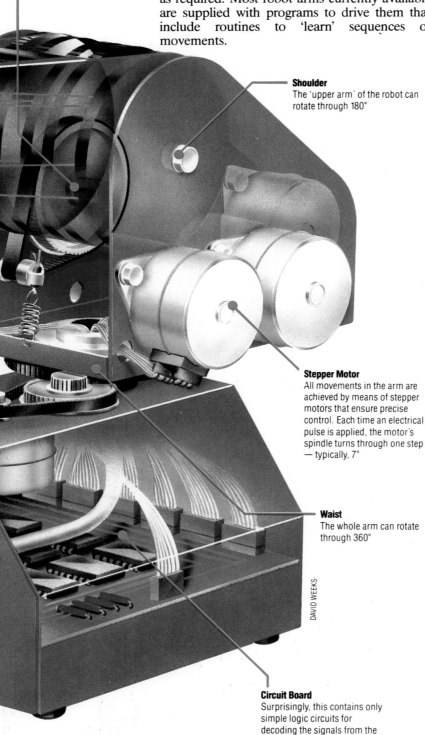

Gearing Mechanism
Toothed rubber drive-belts and large cog wheels provide a geared reduction so that the arm can be positioned repeatedly to within an accuracy of 2mm

Shoulder
The 'upper arm' of the robot can rotate through 180°

Stepper Motor
All movements in the arm are achieved by means of stepper motors that ensure precise control. Each time an electrical pulse is applied, the motor's spindle turns through one step — typically, 7°

Waist
The whole arm can rotate through 360°

DAVID WEEKS

Circuit Board
Surprisingly, this contains only simple logic circuits for decoding the signals from the computer. There is no microprocessor, ROM or RAM

IAN McKINNELL

Grasp Of The Language
It is relatively simple to write a program that will control a robot arm. In BASIC the main task would be to enable your computer accept control commands from the keyboard and pass these to the arm through the port using POKE. Similarly, input from the arm could be read from the associated port by the PEEK function. If speed is required above all else then machine code programming is essential. FORTH is a language that offers the programming ease of BASIC and most of the speed associated with machine code. This language is becoming available for an increasing number of home computers. Sections of a program, rather like subroutines or procedures, are given names that can be incorporated into the command set of the language. This makes it highly efficient for specialised applications such as robot arm control programs. A complete gripping operation, for example, could be controlled by the single command GRIP

Spirited Graphics

Large-capacity memories make it possible for home computers to produce colourful and fast-moving images

One of the most striking features of home computers is their ability to produce graphics and moving displays, commonly known as animation. On most microcomputers, the user can plot individual points, draw lines and circles, and change the background and foreground colours.

For fast-action games and simulations, we need to be able to simulate movement. The easiest way of doing this is to produce a series of still pictures, one after the other. This must be done rapidly enough to give the illusion of movement. Television pictures are produced using a similar method.

Speed Of Action

Another way of creating the illusion of movement is to print a character, erase it, and print it again in a position that is slightly displaced from the original. To achieve a smooth flow of movement, the distance moved at each step should be minimal. Similarly, the time taken to produce the shape and to blank it out should be as short as possible.

Using BASIC to produce animation results in

characters, as more and more are added to the screen scene.

Several computers, notably the Commodore 64, Sord M5, Texas Instruments TI99/4A, and the Atari range, overcome this problem by offering animation that utilises the same techniques that the coin-operated arcade machines employ. The technique is known as 'sprite graphics'.

Sprites are 'objects', or shapes, that can be moved independently of each other about the screen. This is done simply by changing the contents of a couple of memory locations, which specify the X and Y coordinates (the left-right and up-down positions). Typically, X can range from 0 to 255, and Y from 0 to 191. Some systems even permit you to specify the speed and direction of movement of each sprite, and the computer does the rest.

Sprites are normally implemented using special

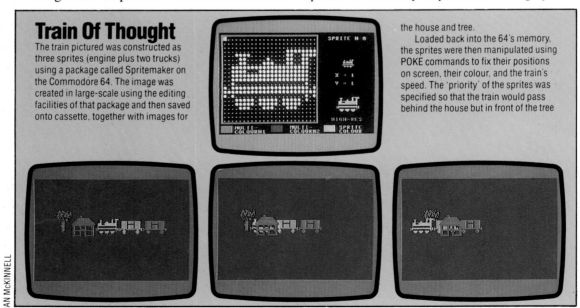

Train Of Thought
The train pictured was constructed as three sprites (engine plus two trucks) using a package called Spritemaker on the Commodore 64. The image was created in large-scale using the editing facilities of that package and then saved onto cassette, together with images for the house and tree.

Loaded back into the 64's memory, the sprites were then manipulated using POKE commands to fix their positions on screen, their colour, and the train's speed. The 'priority' of the sprites was specified so that the train would pass behind the house but in front of the tree

IAN McKINNELL

slow movement. One way to overcome this is to resort to Assembly language, an approach that requires a lot of practice, care and attention if you want flicker-free displays. Added to this, we have the extra problem of controlling the individual

chips or hardware circuitry within the computer. It is possible to buy software for other computers to achieve a similar result, but this is generally less satisfactory.

The speed at which sprites can move varies,

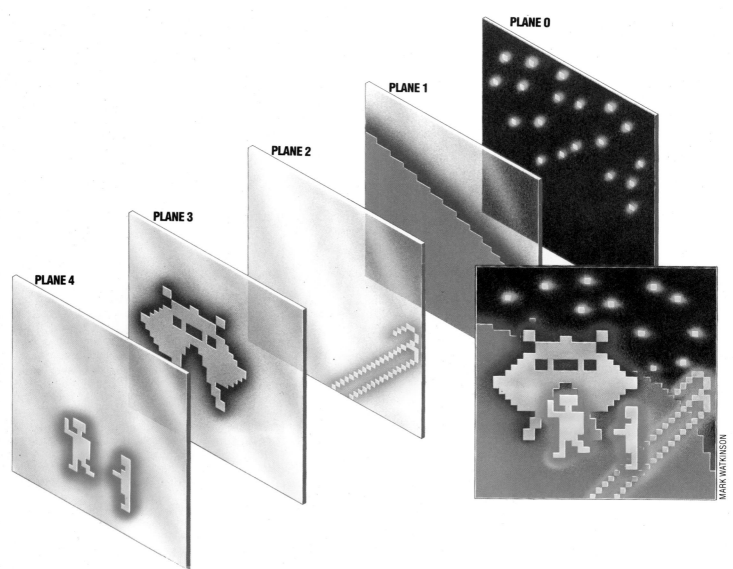

PLANE 0

PLANE 1

PLANE 2

PLANE 3

PLANE 4

MARK WATKINSON

because each one resides on what is known as a 'sprite plane'. A screenful of graphics is thus built up from a number of planes stacked behind each other, though the naked eye perceives them as one screen.

A three-dimensional effect can be achieved as sprites can pass behind or in front of one another. Sprites are numbered from zero to the maximum number available, which is, for example, 32 on the Sord M5. If two sprites overlap, the one with the lower number will be displayed. Therefore by careful ordering of your sprites, a three-dimensional effect can be easily obtained, such as a train passing a tree, obscuring it as it passes by. Alternatively, the train itself may be partially blocked out as it passes a house with a lower number.

Using the colour range that your computer offers, each sprite can be coloured individually. Sometimes a sprite can be expanded or shrunk, again by changing the contents of a memory location.

Obviously, sprites really show their worth in games programs, and a particularly useful feature

is known as 'collision detection'. When two or more sprites overlap (for example, when your missile connects with the enemy spaceship) the system can be programmed to jump to another part of the program to create the graphics for an explosion, and increase the player's score.

Before using sprites you have to create them in much the same way as you would design a new character. The letters of the alphabet, numbers, and special graphics symbols are stored inside the computer in a chip known as a 'character generator'.

Characters are, on most modern home microcomputers, generally built up on an eight by eight matrix of dots, or 'pixels'. The maximum size of a sprite varies from machine to machine, but will generally be several characters wide and deep. On the Commodore 64, for example, the maximum is 24 pixels wide by 21 pixels high.

The best way to construct a sprite is to draw up a

On Different Planes
Using sprite graphics, a complex image can be built up by placing component parts on different planes, which are stacked behind each other. Though they are viewed on the computer's screen as just one plane, the tremendous advantage of this system is that objects on different planes can move completely independently of each other. Planes are assigned an order of priority by the programmer, so that when two sprites overlap on the screen, the one with the higher priority is shown in front of the other — resulting in a three-dimensional effect.

Most computers with sprite graphics can also arrange for the program to be interrupted, whenever two sprites come into contact, to create the necessary explosion, or increase the player's score

Sprite Dimensions

Sprite graphics are available on only four of the popular home microcomputers, the Commodore 64, Sord M5, TI99/4A and the Atari range.

The 16 colours normally available are increased to 256 on the Atari because each colour comes in 16 degrees of 'luminosity'.

In games it is often useful to know when two sprites come into contact — for example when two spaceships crash — and for this a 'collision detection facility' is provided.

The 3-D effect is created by placing each sprite on a different plane; the more planes in a system the better. The maximum size of each sprite is expressed in pixels. Sprites can be made to expand or contract and can be moved about the screen.

To simplify the process of building up sprites special software 'utility packages' are available

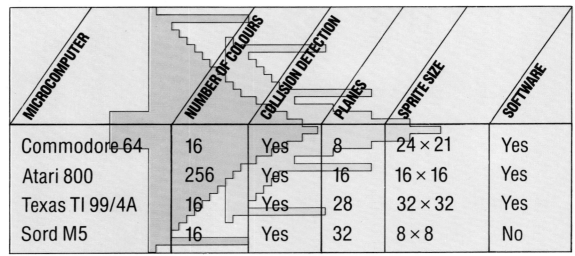

MICROCOMPUTER	NUMBER OF COLOURS	COLLISION DETECTION	PLANES	SPRITE SIZE	SOFTWARE
Commodore 64	16	Yes	8	24 × 21	Yes
Atari 800	256	Yes	16	16 × 16	Yes
Texas TI 99/4A	16	Yes	28	32 × 32	Yes
Sord M5	16	Yes	32	8 × 8	No

grid of squares to the maximum size, and make the required shape by filling in the appropriate blocks. You will already be aware that computers work using only 1s and 0s (see page 43). The black squares should be represented as 1s, and the white squares as 0s.

The computer handles most information in the form of bytes (a collection of eight bits). The computer's manual will show how the whole grid of dots making up a sprite needs to be broken up into groups of eight. Each byte in turn needs to be converted into a single decimal number, ranging from 0 to a maximum of 255, before it can be used in a BASIC program. This is done by multiplying the leftmost binary digit (bit) by 128, the next one by 64, and so on. The results are then added together.

The resulting collection of decimal numbers completely define the design of the sprite. These numbers are placed into memory locations using a

BASIC program; the exact procedure varies with each machine. The computer then needs to be instructed as to where in memory it can find the specifications for each of the sprites required.

Everything else can now be achieved using simple commands to specify the current position of each sprite on the screen, change its colour, expand or contract it, and detect when two or more sprites overlap.

Software packages, called 'utilities', are available for most machines with sprites. These make the process of creating the image less tedious. They show the grid on the screen in large scale, and allow the image to be drawn simply by moving the flashing cursor around the grid. All the arithmetic is handled automatically, and the results are then placed in the appropriate bytes. Finally the grid disappears and the sprite itself appears on the screen for manipulation.

Sprites have revolutionised home computer graphics by providing a simple and efficient method of producing fast-moving and colourful displays.

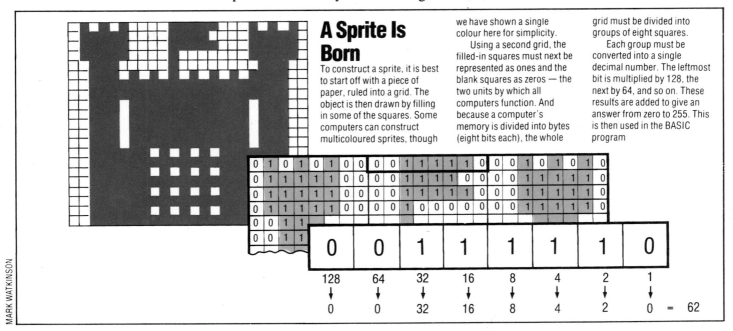

A Sprite Is Born

To construct a sprite, it is best to start off with a piece of paper, ruled into a grid. The object is then drawn by filling in some of the squares. Some computers can construct multicoloured sprites, though we have shown a single colour here for simplicity.

Using a second grid, the filled-in squares must next be represented as ones and the blank squares as zeros — the two units by which all computers function. And because a computer's memory is divided into bytes (eight bits each), the whole grid must be divided into groups of eight squares.

Each group must be converted into a single decimal number. The leftmost bit is multiplied by 128, the next by 64, and so on. These results are added to give an answer from zero to 255. This is then used in the BASIC program

MARK WATKINSON

War And Peace

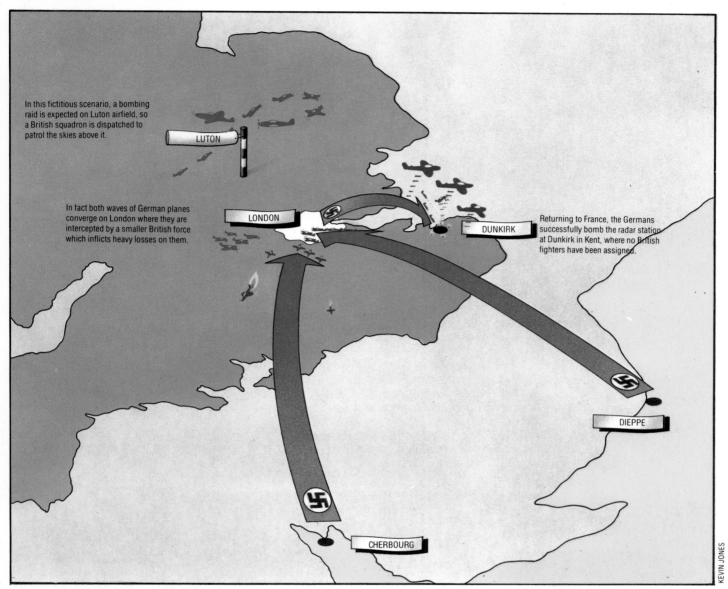

In this fictitious scenario, a bombing raid is expected on Luton airfield, so a British squadron is dispatched to patrol the skies above it.

LUTON

In fact both waves of German planes converge on London where they are intercepted by a smaller British force which inflicts heavy losses on them.

LONDON

DUNKIRK

Returning to France, the Germans successfully bomb the radar station at Dunkirk in Kent, where no British fighters have been assigned.

DIEPPE

CHERBOURG

KEVIN JONES

You can now purchase games that will test your skills as military strategist and tactician in both historical and fantasy battle simulations

Today modern generals place a great deal of importance on the war games that they play to test planned responses to anticipated attack or 'Threat Scenarios'. To play these sophisticated games complex hardware and software systems have been developed to simulate all the known aspects of a potential conflict, such as the initial deployment of friendly and enemy forces, supply states, availability of reserves, and so on. The system also allows for adverse weather conditions, changes in enemy tactics, the effects of fifth

IAN McKINNELL

Battle Of Britain
Fighter Command (from Strategic Simulations Inc. for the Apple) is typical of the sophisticated strategic war games available for microcomputers. Before the game commences, the player must select from a very wide range of options, including the type of aircraft used and the weather. Play is displayed in the form of moving symbols on the map, with additional information displayed as text. The packaging and documentation include a printed map with cardboard pieces for additional visual reference

column activities, or any number of variables that could possibly affect the successful execution of a military operation. One of the main functions of

Tactical Armour Command
TAC (from Avalon Hill) is available for the Atari, Apple, IBM PC and Commodore 64 computers and simulates armoured conflict during the Second World War. TAC can be played by one or two players who select from five different scenarios, and manipulate British, American, Russian and German forces

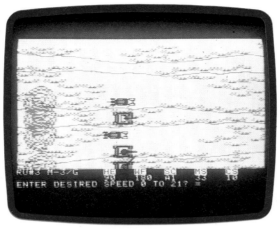

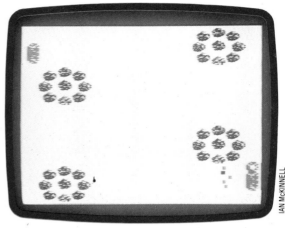

the NORAD radar defence system in the Cheyenne Mountains, Wyoming (featured in the film *(War Games)* is continually to assess, update, and evaluate the relative capabilities of the United States and the Soviet Union and to aid in the preparation of a response to any new developments.

Of course, war gaming for the amateur general has been somewhat less sophisticated. In order to create the appropriate degree of complexity, the war gamer has had to resort to sheets of tables, voluminous books of rules and innumerable dice. The sheer amount of hard work necessary to play war games has tended to restrict their appeal to a relatively small group of enthusiasts. However, with the arrival of the home computer and the availability of war game programs, all the tedious 'staff work' has disappeared and left in its place an absorbing game that offers both excitement and challenge, the equal of any other type of computer game currently on the market.

An immense variety of games is available. It is possible to recreate or simulate practically any type of warfare from the Ancient Greek to a theoretical clash between NATO and the Warsaw

or attempt to outwit Hitler by thwarting his invasion of Russia in 1941. The games set in outer space offer even more opportunity for invention. Not only do you manoeuvre fleets of starships round the galaxy, you also specify the type of ships you want. Compromises have to be made, of course. If you want more speed you may have to sacrifice weapon systems, and better protective screens could reduce the fuel supply. You have to

Legionnaire
This simulation of warfare between Caesar's forces (you) and the barbarians (the computer — Apple or Atari) is played in real time. Infantry, cavalry and other forces are represented by symbols, which can be selected and moved by means of the joystick-controlled cursor (white square). The game is produced by Avalon Hill

Pact sometime in the future. You can fight air battles, sea battles, wars in outer space, and even wars between mythological empires. The scope is limitless.

Historical games give you the chance to discover where Napoleon went wrong at Waterloo

choose the compromise that best suits your style of fighting a campaign.

Unlike their conventional counterparts, computer strategy games need no special skill or knowledge, and most come with short notes and hints for beginners. However, it's worth knowing that some games are classified as introductory, intermediate or advanced. If you are thinking of taking up strategy gaming you might be better advised to start at the introductory level, and pick up the basic concepts of war gaming and strategic simulation before advancing to games at the higher levels.

The game format varies to suit the differing needs of the various types of warfare represented. But, in general, the games are played across large maps. Where the map is too large to be displayed on a single screen, then the screen usually acts as a window that can be moved (by means of a joystick) across the map. For an historical simulation the game designers will have tried to reproduce, as faithfully as possible, the terrain over which the original battle was fought. In 'Computer Bismarck' by SSI, the action takes place mainly in the North Atlantic, and this did not pose too many problems in terms of graphics design. On the other hand, for another SSI game, 'Battle for Normandy', the designers' task was far more difficult. Not only did the general terrain have to be correct but so did specific features such as the beaches and the coast, the towns, villages and rivers. For non-historical games the designer has more scope to produce variety for the player to make full use of the forces he has available, but even here the designer must be careful to include sufficient checks and balances to prevent the game becoming too easy for one side or the other.

The map also has a grid superimposed on it. This grid subdivides the map in the same way that a chess board is divided into squares, though the grid on a war games map is often hexagonal rather than square. Each square or hexagon is given a value according to the type of terrain contained within it. This value represents the degree of difficulty a unit would have moving into or through that particular area. The effort of moving through the area would cause the movement allowance of the unit to be reduced by the corresponding value. When the movement allowance of the unit equals zero, or is less than the value of the area it is proposing to enter, it may not move any further that turn.

The game is usually divided into a number of 'game turns' that represent elapsed time, and each player is given a number of objectives that must be accomplished in the time available in order to win the game. In most cases it is not necessary, or even possible, to achieve all the objectives set. So the first decision the player has to make is to assess his chances and determine his strategic priorities accordingly. In such scenarios the role of the opponent is often to stop the attacker from gaining his set objectives. Once again it is probably not possible to protect everything, so the defender must decide when to abandon hopeless positions, how long to cling to strongholds, and whether or not to take the risk of launching counter-attacks to regain lost positions or disrupt his opponent's preparations for a fresh attack.

The player communicates with the program through the graphic and textual representation of the forces under his command that are on the map. The graphic display represents the location of a particular unit on the battlefield and the textual display supplies information relating to the unit's combat efficiency, and movement allowance. The player moves his units by nominating them with a cursor or by having the computer present them to him in rotation. Once a unit has been nominated, the command to move the unit is given. In the case of a map with a hexagonal grid, 1 would send the unit north, 2 would send it north-east, and so on around the points of the compass. An increasing number of these games work with joysticks or trackballs, in which case the unit can simply be 'picked up' and moved in the desired direction. To terminate the movement of an individual unit the command FINISH or F is often used. Even then some games will allow the player to renominate the unit and move it again, unless its movement allowance has been exhausted. When all movement has been completed, the player indicates the fact to the computer with the command EXECUTE or E. The computer will then initiate the combat phase.

COURTESY OF SOFT

IAN McKINNELL

Eastern Front
In this game the player takes on the role of the German army trying to reach Moscow in 1941, whilst the computer plays the defending Russian forces. Written by Chris Crawford and distributed by Atari, it incorporates radical new features, such as 'fine scrolling'

One of the most visually pleasing features of Eastern Front is the way the map changes as the year progresses. In autumn the forests defoliate, and then in winter the rivers freeze up and the ground is covered in snow. It is considered extremely difficult to reach Moscow in this game

During the combat phase the computer will indicate the friendly units that are in a position to engage the enemy and provide information about the relative strengths of the units involved. On the basis of this information, the player may accept or reject each combat suggestion as it is offered to him. Once all the combat has been resolved, and the effects calculated and displayed, the second player begins his turn.

For many people, the fascination of strategic games arises from there being no one 'correct' solution to the problems that are posed by the game. The player's enjoyment is derived from overcoming the physical and logistical problems of the terrain that he is operating in as well as meeting the intellectual challenge of using the resources available to defeat the enemy. Naturally, every strategist would like to win by using the most daring schemes and carefully laid traps, but above all the strategist wants to win!

Voice Of Authority

Speech recognition systems are being increasingly used in commercial and security applications. However, their powers are restricted by the computer's memory capacity

For a computer to be of any use it must have a workable means of allowing commands and information to be fed into it. The 'interface' that we normally use to communicate with a home computer is a keyboard (though mice and joysticks are possible alternatives). By using a keyboard, however, we find that we are forced to communicate with the system by means of an artificial language. Commands such as CLS, DIRECTORY, RUN, LOAD and SAVE may be meaningful to the operating system but they aren't 'natural'.

The natural communication system for humans is speech, not typing messages on keyboards and watching the replies on television sets. If a computer could be made to understand spoken commands — even if they were phrased in the same way as the ones given through a keyboard — it would be far easier to use, especially by those with a physical handicap. Before any computer system can 'understand' spoken words, it must first process the sound input: the analogue signals must be analysed and turned into a digital form that the computer can deal with. Although it seems to be an easy thing to generate electronically, speech is a remarkably complex combination of sounds.

Dreams of instant and complete speech recognition (as typified by the computer HAL in *2001 — A Space Odyssey*) are unlikely to be fulfilled for many years yet, if ever. The voice input typewriter is equally distant; yet the technology for both this and the 'understanding' computer already exists. But neither is available at low cost, because there is a major difficulty in creating speech recognition systems: words can sound the same but have different meanings, depending on the context that they appear in. The processing power needed to solve this problem is simply not available at a reasonable price.

Although researchers have created systems that approach this goal, they have discovered that increasing the number of speakers who can be recognised by the computer has the effect of reducing the number of words that can be recognised at any one time. Typically, a multi-speaker recognition system will allow between 20 and 30 words to be recognised at a time, with a success rate of around 85 to 90 per cent.

The potential uses of speech recognition systems are considerable. The German Post Office uses one to assist with sorting mail; and there are now many applications in aerospace, both military and civil, where pilots have literally not enough hands and feet to control their aeroplanes. In all these situations the number of words that can be recognised at any one time is limited to around 20. However, this doesn't mean that the overall system is restricted. The user is selecting one of the 20 words from a 'menu', and each recognised command produces a further menu of words to choose from. Only when the complete sequence has been successfully recognised will any action be taken by the computer. In the case of the sorting office the first level of sort could be by state, and once the correct state is selected the next sort could

Parts Of Speech

One technique of speech recognition simply involves digitising the signal and performing extensive 'pattern recognition' analysis. A more efficient method is to use hardware pre-processing, in which a number of independent circuits measure the signal for voiced sound (e.g. vowels), fricatives (s,f,t, etc), and short periods of silence (e.g. between syllables). The output from each of these filtering devices is a string of 1s and 0s, which the computer compares with a library of stored examples, selecting the nearest match as the word it recognises

VOICED

SILENT

FRICATIVE

DIGITAL

KEVIN JONES

be by town, then by village, etc. Only at the lowest level would the item finally be sent on its way, thus ensuring the maximum reliability of the operation.

Voice Analysis

Speech recognition is usually tackled in one of two ways. The 'quick' way is simply to feed all the speech through an analogue-to-digital convertor, and use the power of the computer to perform all the analysis. Unfortunately, this method has a number of drawbacks, most notably the time taken to perform the analysis. Systems using this method can take up to two or three seconds to recognise the input. For speech recognition to be of any real use the computer must 'understand' the speech as fast as another human, and the number crunching approach rarely achieves this.

The other method is to use pre-processing. Rather than analyse the speech signal mathematically, it is possible to do much of the work with standard electronics. What is then delivered to the computer is information about the spoken input: the frequency content, pitch, energy, etc. Frequencies can be measured by filtering the signal and detecting the level in each frequency band, rather like using tone controls on a hi-fi to 'bring out' the bass drum. Because all this electronic processing is done at the same time as the original speech signal is fed to the circuits, the analysis is almost instantaneous. Performing a similar operation on the digital data from an A/D convertor would require several computers working on the numbers at once. The pre-processing method is still at the research stage — no commercial system using it has yet been marketed — but it certainly appears to have more potential.

Once the information about frequency content, pitch, energy, etc. has been extracted from the original signal (regardless of the method), the actual recognition is performed by comparing the current set of figures with a number of models stored in the computer's memory. These models are created by 'training' the recognition system. The words that are to be recognised are spoken into the system one at a time and the resulting information is stored in a digital 'library' of examples. The complete set of words is then spoken again and the computer compares the input with its current model. If they agree, the second set of information is added to the first to form a more complete version of the model. This can be a continuous process, constantly adding new information to the library for more and more speakers.

To recognise a spoken word, the computer must match the pattern of information from the input with one or more of the models stored in the current library. In many cases, several possible matches will be found as parts of other words will match the input pattern. The first two syllables of 'international', for example, are the same as those of 'interpreter'. At the end of the search, one word

should stand out as being more perfectly matched than any of the other possibilities, and this is the one that the computer will interpret the input as being.

Speech recognition facilities are certain to find many applications in the future, but they are likely to be most readily used as a 'front-end' for complex software packages, such as databases, where the commands are selected from an on-screen menu. This type of application will remove the single biggest obstacle to computer usage by non-experts: the keyboard. Viewdata systems such as Prestel have reduced the input device to a simple numeric keypad, but this substantially limits the amount of interaction that a user can achieve. A speech-driven interface that can recognise a standard set of database interrogation commands, as well as numeric symbols and the letters of the alphabet, would provide a powerful facility that requires little, if any, conventional computer training to use.

There are now commercially available recognition units that can be plugged into home computers, but these are very unsophisticated devices. Systems like 'Big Ears' and Heuristic Inc's 'Speech Lab' use a lot of processing power to recognise just a few words spoken by one person. What is needed before speech recognition can become really useful is an ability to recognise words spoken by *any* person, regardless of dialect or accent. The limiting factor, at this stage, is the amount of memory available to hold the models. One interesting possibility is that of using a video disc to hold a standard set of models: this would use hardly any internal memory and the reduction in speed would be barely noticeable.

IAN McKINNELL

Environmental Control
Most recent applications of speech recognition are of an educational nature. One of these is called the 'limited environment', which involves a computer, a robot arm, and a number of simple objects that the arm can manipulate. Speaking into a microphone, the user can instruct the arm to 'PLACE THE EGG IN THE EGG CUP'. The computer will have to interpret the commands, and look up the positions of the objects in its memory

School On Screen

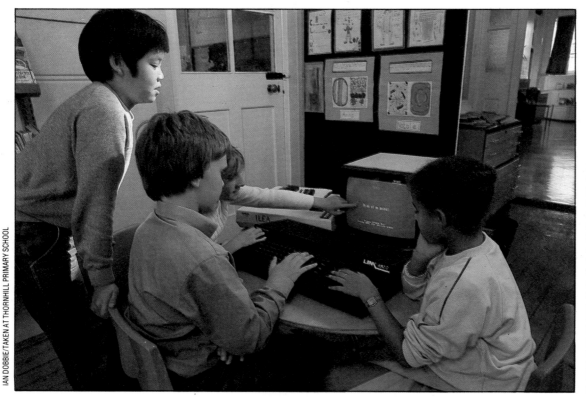

IAN DOBBIE/TAKEN AT THORNHILL PRIMARY SCHOOL

Computers In Primary Schools
Britain is preparing for the future with an educational policy to introduce computers to children in their first years at school. The idea is not only to familiarise school children with new technology, but to use the computer to teach a wide range of subjects — from biology to foreign languages. It is an ideal and patient teacher as it only moves on to new ground once a problem has been mastered, allowing both slow and fast learners to work at their own pace. The computer has a wider use as a learning aid — simply by using it the child discovers how a problem is analysed and solved

The classroom has now caught up with the computer age and an exciting choice of educational programs is on offer

Every one of Britain's 29,000 primary schools will soon have a computer and many secondary schools already possess one. Nowadays, computers are not simply on the curriculum under 'Computer Studies', but are being used by teachers for teaching numeracy and literacy, helping slow-learning children, and teaching foreign languages.

There are many educational programs for home computers on the market, but teachers frequently complain about their poor quality. The reason for this is that few programs have been written that observe both educational and computing disciplines.

Computer programmers rarely have teaching experience, and teachers, many of whom are new to programming, have sometimes been responsible for the most rudimentary of programming mistakes.

Although a teacher's program is likely to work in his or her own classroom, the moment it is sent out to another school problems arise. The actual program, whether stored on cassette or disk, is usually not sufficient by itself: good explanatory documentation should also be considered equally essential.

Without this, students may be unable to operate the program. 'Well of *course* you have to type LOAD!' might be the programmer's response to the problem, but to a computer novice all such details must be spelled out.

More seriously, good programming calls for an anticipation of all the mistakes that a beginner might make. This is as important as ensuring the program is a successful teaching aid. Good programming means more than 'de-bugging' the program to the point at which it does what it should when the right key is pressed. It also means ensuring that the program doesn't do anything it shouldn't when the wrong key is pressed. This is the hardest part of program writing. The program must be able to recover from the most careless of errors by a child, and still leave him thinking the computer is easy and fun to use.

Despite these problems, there is a wide range of educational programs suitable for home and school use. Computers are wonderful educational tools, and in choosing software for your children it is useful to understand the different ways in which a computer can be used.

A computer can be used to instruct a child in almost any subject. If the program is good, the child is likely to be fascinated by it and motivated to learn.

The usual type of educational program is best described as 'drill and practice'. Children are shown examples and then asked to solve similar problems. Usually the program keeps score of how well the pupil does. It even offers encouragement when the pupil gets the answer right, and makes a gentle suggestion to 'try again' when the answer is wrong.

Deciding which programs are right for your child depends on several things: the age of your child, the make of your computer and what your child is studying at school.

If you have yet to buy your home computer but you suspect that education will be one of its important roles in the home, it is worth finding out which type of computer is being used in your child's school. If you are able to purchase a similar model, the education programs your child is using at school will be available to you at home. Many schools are delighted to offer parents copies of the programs they are using in class and this 'homework' can have a considerable benefit. If

advertise in the computer magazines and home computer shops.

The Right Choice

For the under eights most programs concentrate on the basic skills of literacy and numeracy. One of the attractive ranges of educational software for very young children is produced by Texas Instruments. The TI-99/4A Home Computer has been slow to catch on in Britain, but many parents have been impressed by the range of TI educational software produced by both TI and Scott, Foresman & Co. in the USA. The 99/4A is actually a 16-bit computer and this means that programs written in machine code are likely to be very much better than programs written on the more usual 8-bit home computers.

This is proved by such TI programs as 'Begin-

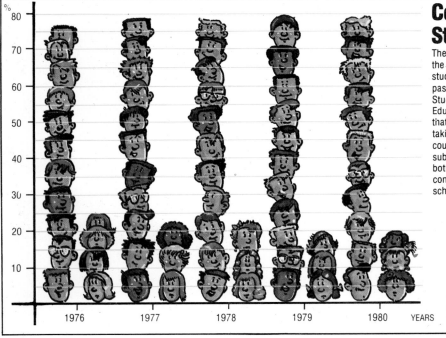

Computer Studies

The chart on the left shows the ratio of male and female students who achieved passes in 'A' level Computer Studies from 1976 to 1980. Educationalists are hopeful that the number of girls taking Computer Studies courses will rise substantially, as children of both sexes are introduced to computers early in their school careers

ANNI AXWORTHY

you have already bought your home computer and it is not compatible with the school's computers, don't despair; there is value in the very variety of computing experience your child is receiving.

It is natural that more educational programs are available for the better established computers, but some manufacturers have placed a particular emphasis on education. There are particularly wide ranges of educational programs available for the Apple, the Commodore PET, the Tandy, the BBC Micro, Sinclair and Texas Instruments but some of the newer manufacturers have yet to attract a really wide range of programs. Educational programs for any computer are likely to be available from several sources. The manufacturer of the computer is one, and the various independent software houses is another. The latter write programs for computers and

ning Grammar', 'Addition and Subtraction' (1 and 2) and 'Number Magic'. These programs are stored on a plastic cartridge, which slots into the TI 99/4A and is easy for very young children to use. And if you've splashed out on the marvellous little voice synthesiser add-on for the 99/4A, you will know that several of the programs talk in a Dalek-type voice children love. The problem is that the programs are American. The odd word is spelled differently and some British teachers would be likely to go into paroxysms over some of the TI programs. However TI has a stunning example of LOGO available (see page 111), although this really falls into the second category of discovery tools.

There is a good choice of programs available for home computers. A comprehensive selection can be found in *Educational Computing*. Here you will also find the program houses advertising their wares to teachers and you will find informed reviews of the various programs. The sort of programs for young children available for the BBC Microcomputer include the usual 'Number Fun' type and many basic literacy programs. Many useful programs are available from the British Micros In Primary Schools organisation. One is 'Cat and Mouse', which helps the child become familiar with the keyboard layout of the BBC Microcomputers.

As children get older so the number and range of programs increase. Programs for the 8 to 11 age group vary in complexity and quality, and most concentrate on reinforcing basic skills and stretching the child's ability. This age group acquires special interests such as music and foreign languages, which can be taught by computer. Most computers have this type of program available.

In the secondary school age group there is a plethora of programs. The only way to wade through them and to pick out the best is to speak to your child's teacher. It is important that your child's home study is not in contradiction to the work he is getting at school and most teachers will prove very helpful in guiding you towards the right type of program.

A further category of educational computer programs is primarily concerned with children under 13. At this age children are still discovering how to learn, and programs which induce them to use the computer to discover the world for themselves must prove very valuable. The best known program is LOGO, and a version of this language is available for computers made by Atari, Tandy, Apple, Texas Instruments, Research Machines, Commodore and the IBM. Versions are promised for the BBC and for Sinclairs, but they have yet to materialise. Using this program a child, between the age of 6 and 12, is encouraged to explore the computer's drawing power (and, in turn, geometry) with a 'turtle'. The child discovers how to teach the turtle to remember procedures (programs) and on some implementations the child progresses until he or she can draw a fantasy world of 'sprites' on the screen. Using this program children are actually teaching themselves the basic laws of mathematics, and much has been claimed for the power of this program to teach mathematical and spatial concepts.

It is not easy to choose good educational software, because there is so much to choose from. It is a good idea to attend one of the many computer exhibitions that are periodically held around the country. Here you will be likely to find both manufacturers and program writers showing off their wares, and you will have a limited opportunity to see, try and compare programs. The shortage of good programs that satisfy both educational and computing requirements is not likely to last for long. Each month more programs emerge that are likely to provide a valuable stimulus to your child's development.

The Secret Agent

There are many educational programs now on the market. This one is called Secret Agent and is published by Heinemann. Your mission is to catch a notorious enemy spy on the loose in Europe before he eliminates all your agents. The clues to his whereabouts have to be deciphered before you can catch up with him. The chase is on . . .

The master spy may only be apprehended in a city – but he won't stay in one place for more than a couple of hours. Once you think you know where he is, you have a choice of travelling there either by train or aeroplane. You have to decide for yourself whether speed is more important than cost

A light will flash on the map whenever a message is sent from one of your agents, showing the city from which it is being sent. If your agent is eliminated, the message will be intercepted before you can receive it. You may then wish to hire a new agent, but you will have to pay for it

Informers are happy to help you by selling their reports, but these will be sent in code so you may need to appeal to the boffins in London for help. At the end of the game you will have learnt the names and locations of all the European cities, and developed an understanding of timetables and the knack of careful budgeting

IAN McKINNELL

The Art Of Programming

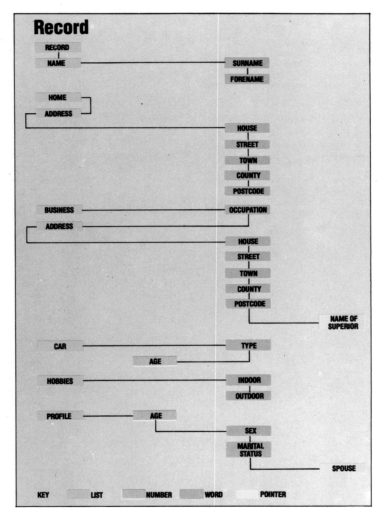

If you want to do more than simply run pre-packaged software, then you must understand how to control the flow of data and instructions in a computer program in the most efficient way.

Charting The Course

The conscientious use of flow diagrams leads to efficient and well-organised programs

The Flow Of Information

The real purpose of a flow diagram is to indicate in a simple, concise manner, the flow of information and control through a computer program.

Most important are the 'test' points, where control passes to a point other than the next in sequence. A simple graphical representation of this passage of control is much easier to grasp than a similar statement written out — a picture really can be worth a thousand words!

The 'TEST' symbol can be represented by either a flattened hexagon, as shown here, or by an elongated diamond shape

TERMINATOR
This symbol is used to indicate the beginning or end of a sub-program

INPUT/OUTPUT
This represents any process that performs an action internal to the program

PROCESS
Any data entry or display (I/O) is represented by the parallelogram symbol

TEST
This symbol is used when a choice is made between the alternative flow paths, TRUE or FALSE

LINK
Round symbols indicate links between paths

KEVIN JONES

A problem can be represented in a simple pictorial way by drawing diagrams to show the steps required in processing, and the flow paths or routes connecting them. These 'flowcharts' are useful as a means of understanding a problem, and in working out its solution.

Each box symbol in a flowchart represents a process or action, and the lines that connect these action boxes depict the possible paths through them. 'Traffic flow' is one-way, so arrows are used to indicate direction, which is normally top to bottom, and left to right across the diagram.

Whenever a choice is to be made, a hexagonal or diamond shaped 'decision box' is used. Control flows in by one path, as before, but may pass out in one of two directions, depending on the result of the test in question. If the test is to determine whether a single process is to be performed or not, then only one of the exit paths will contain a 'process box'. Here is an example of a test to decide whether or not to branch to a sub-routine:

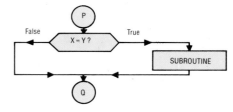

120 IF X = Y THEN GOSUB 300

The decision box is also used to indicate the test that terminates a loop. In the example given below, control is returned to the start of a program if there is a positive reply to the question 'AGAIN?':

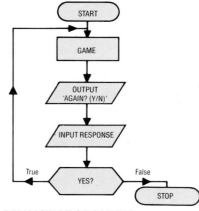

90 REM**START OF GAME**
100
800

```
810 PRINT "AGAIN? (Y/N)";
820 INPUT R$
830 IF R$ = "Y" THEN GOTO 100
840 END
```

We may wish to make a decision that will result in one of two distinctly different courses of action being followed. In the example shown below, we compare a player's game score to the highest previous score:

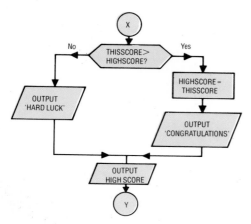

```
1200 IF THISSCORE > HIGHSCORE THEN GOTO
     1230
1210 PRINT "HARD LUCK. YOU HAVE TO BEAT";
1220 GOTO 1250
1230 LET HIGHSCORE = THISSCORE
1240 PRINT "CONGRATULATIONS! A NEW HIGH
     OF";
1250 PRINT HIGHSCORE
```

Note that the value of HIGHSCORE is printed in both events, and that the two possible flow paths rejoin in the process to become the single entry to this output operation.

All decisions are taken as a result of tests similar to this, which deliver a positive or negative, a True or a False result. As you can see, this purely binary decision-making process denies the possibility of a 'maybe' answer. You can use whatever terms you wish, but don't forget to label the two exit paths accordingly!

All programming languages have an inherent decision statement which, if the True condition is satisfied, cause a conditional branch, but which drops control through to the next statement if the result is False. In the case of a dialect of BASIC that allows only a simple IF-THEN, we must mimic the conditional branch by means of a GOTO statement, as in line 1200 of the last example. The statement in line 1210 will only be executed if the result of the test in line 1200 is False.

But what about the second use of GOTO in line 1220? As you can see, the use of GOTO at the end of the test, to solve the problem of the destination of the conditional branch, has forced us to use this method to 'join up' the two possible control paths again, in this case at line 1250.

The use of flowcharts usually encourages the introduction of GOTOs as a means of following the point to point graphical representation of the program. In general, this use of unconditional jumps is rather dangerous. If the version of BASIC that is being used forces this solution, then a flow diagram is an excellent method of assessing the way in which control passes out of the program's normal succession.

Let's use one last example to examine how the use of a flowchart allows us to represent accurately the necessary steps to perform a simple task: printing out all the numbers between one and one hundred.

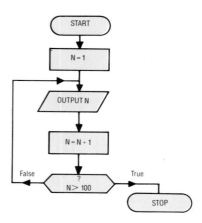

```
10 LET N = 1
20 PRINT N
30 LET N = N + 1
40 IF N > 100 THEN END
50 GOTO 20
```

The use of flow diagrams in this way tends to encourage a step by step approach to program writing which, especially in larger projects, often leads to a rather inelegant result. For those with even a passing knowledge of the BASIC language, the use of a FOR-NEXT loop is obviously indicated. For example:

```
10 FOR N = 1 TO 100
20 PRINT N
30 NEXT N
40 END
```

The flowchart is incapable of representing this piece of BASIC 'shorthand', and to follow it exactly would lead one to a less efficient way of solving the problem. It does, however, give us some information on the structure of the FOR-NEXT loop, and so is of value when we come to examine this and other BASIC functions, to determine how they are constructed.

Flow diagrams are particularly useful during the planning or conceptualising stage of programming, especially in the 'tricky' parts. Experienced programmers tend to use them less than beginners, and will often resort to a flow diagram to illustrate and document a piece of software written without their aid. But whether a flow diagram is drawn out on paper, or it simply exists inside the programmer's subconscious mind, the concept of charting the flow of information and control is central to the use of computers as a problem-solving tool.

Fact Finder

A computer can select facts and compile lists from the vast amount of information stored in a database

An accumulation of data that is held on and accessed by a computer is known as a 'database'. We all use various non-computerised databases as part of our everyday lives.

The telephone directory is an example of a non-computerised database. However, information does not have to be indexed or stored in a particular order to be a database. On a computer, such fixed ordering actually creates severe limitations.

A database program is a set of routines that allow selections to be made from the data. Such programs range from simple card-indexed systems to complete languages.

Typically, a computerised database will be large and contain data of many different types. But this does not mean that you have to be the owner of a huge machine. Any computer can handle a useful database. The only real limitation is the size and speed of the storage facilities.

We could, for example, make a list called 'people' containing facts about various persons. If we put these on an ordinary card index, we get a list that looks like the one called Personal Index. It is immediately apparent that there are several different kinds of information here. Within each category, many of the items are simple words, and some are numbers. There are limited possibilities within two of the categories: 'sex' can only be male or female and 'marital status' must be one of the set 'single, married, divorced, or widowed'.

It might be useful to make certain items into lists

AVAILABLE

TENNIS PLAYER

CRICKET PLAYER

READER

FOOTBALLER

ARTIST

DARTS PLAYER

WINE LOVER

CAR OWNER

PUBLIC TRANSPORT

CYCLIST

TONY LODGE

of words and numbers. For example: occupation, name of company, business address, business telephone, and name of superior could usefully be grouped under the heading 'business', and both types and age of car could be members of the car list.

By extending this idea, we can keep all addresses as lists. This is better than keeping an address as a single item, since we might want to know which town a person lives in, but not which street.

'Marital status' can also be extended by adding the name of the spouse where appropriate. This

Anyone For Tennis?
We have used the Rubik's cube as an analogy for a raw database — that is, one that contains all the information we may need, but as yet has not been manipulated into the right order. In this example we are looking for a tennis partner (the racquet symbol), who is a car owner (the car), and who is free on the day in question (the red squares)

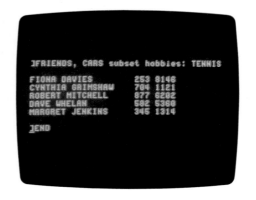

Asking The Right Questions

Most commercial database programs use codes that are almost programming languages in themselves. The code we've used here is typical. 'ACCESS' indicates to the program that we wish to 'interrogate' or ask questions of a file that we have previously created. 'Use' indicates that we are going to use a sub-set of the file called 'FRIENDS', and 'while' these conditions are true, we are going to pull out all the items that are tagged with 'CAR' or 'TENNIS'. The result is a list of friends, with their telephone numbers, who both drive cars and play tennis

IAN McKINNELL

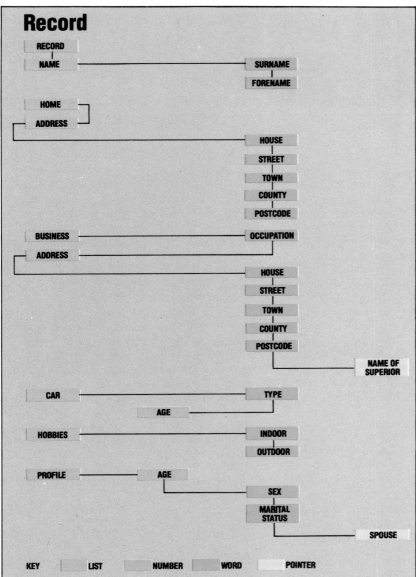

Record

RECORD		
NAME		SURNAME
		FORENAME
HOME		
ADDRESS		HOUSE
		STREET
		TOWN
		COUNTY
		POSTCODE
BUSINESS		OCCUPATION
ADDRESS		HOUSE
		STREET
		TOWN
		COUNTY
		POSTCODE
		NAME OF SUPERIOR
CAR		TYPE
	AGE	
HOBBIES		INDOOR
		OUTDOOR
PROFILE	AGE	
		SEX
		MARITAL STATUS
		SPOUSE

KEY LIST NUMBER WORD POINTER

Personal Index

SURNAME
FORENAME
ADDRESS
HOME TELEPHONE
OCCUPATION
BUSINESS ADDRESS
BUSINESS TELEPHONE
NAME OF SUPERIOR
AGE
SEX
HOBBIES
MARITAL STATUS
TYPE OF CAR
AGE OF CAR

Organised information
An hierarchical database leads the user from one piece of information to another, offering choices at every turn. No knowledge of the contents is assumed

could just be a single word, but since this refers to a person, and the file is about people, it would be useful if we could somehow refer to another record instead.

Since each record is in a particular place in the file, it has a number. So we can use the number of the record that describes this person, instead of the person's name, to establish a cross reference.

Such an item of data is called a 'pointer' record. If we use this technique to refer to the person's business superior, the result is a structure that looks like the one called Record.

The difference between a card index and a computerised database is that the former can have only one ordering, usually alphabetical.

The card index is adequate if we want to find out – for example – what company employs a specific person. But what do we do if we want the names of all the employees of a particular company?

Using a card index, we would have to look through all of it, extracting each card for the required data. To do so is not only time-consuming, but is likely to result in errors.

With a computerised system, however, we can ask the machine to look at each record in turn, and to print out the name of every person who works for the company in which we are interested.

Alternatively, we could have the machine re-order the file, with the company field being the most important item. This will result in the same database with the same data, but with a completely different 'shape'. The reordering will place all occurrences of a given company in one group, and that section will give us the names of all employees. In a card index, there is only one primary item, the surname. But in a computerised system, any item can be primary.

Using this principle, we can 'reshape' the database. For example, the cars owned by people could be primary, or the names of towns in which the people live. This is the great advantage of the computerised database system.

Today's Encyclopædia
Services like Prestel are an attempt to make huge databases available to the general public by means of services that they already have in their own homes. Viewdata systems use the domestic TV as the monitor screen, and a specially devised keypad, connected to the central computer over an ordinary telephone line, as the keyboard. Access to the database is by means of a 'menu' of available services. The choices are displayed on the screen, and the user arrives at the desired 'page' of information by working his way through the hierarchical tree. By entering a Credit Card code, purchases can even be made from home

COURTESY OF PRESTEL LTD

Classified Information

When designing any program that involves the storage or manipulation of information, it is important to pay close attention to structure, so that items of data needn't be duplicated

Shortest Route

A Midlands firm has interests in six towns, and has to send a lorry around them every month. The firm's computer can work out the most efficient route.

Town$(1)	"Barmouth"
Town$(2)	"Carlisle"
Town$(3)	"Margate"
Town$(4)	"Nottingham"
Town$(5)	"Perth"
Town$(6)	"Truro"

The names of the towns are in a sequential file on tape in alphabetic order. They are read from the file in this order into the array Town$( ). The computer works out that the best order is:

Nottingham	Town$(4)
Perth	Town$(5)
Carlisle	Town$(2)
Barmouth	Town$(1)
Truro	Town$(6)
Margate	Town$(3)

Rather than store the town names again in this order, using up more memory, the computer stores only the position numbers of the towns in the array Town$( ). Like this:

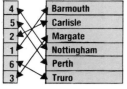

The list of numbers is an index to the array Town$( ). Other such indexes to the array could be created, each giving a different order to the names. The advantage of indexing like this is that the original file does not have to be sorted or duplicated: only the indexes need be sorted and stored

Anyone who has ever used a card index system (a library catalogue, for example) knows how useful it can be. If you have ever dropped the card box you know that the same cards out of order become maddeningly useless. A library contains a vast amount of information, but unless it's arranged in some sort of order its value as an information system is almost nil.

The essence of an information system is not the information itself but, rather, its organisation. Take, for example, this (fictional) item in a trade directory:

Smith, J., 15 High Street, Middletown.

On its own, its value as information is limited; if, however, you know that it comes from the Ironmongers' section of the directory, then it has a new significance that comes from the structure in which it is placed.

The simplest data structure is in the form of a file: a collection of data with common features. The name of the file reveals something about the information in it, and putting all that information together under that name makes it much easier to use. The file can be treated as one large unit of information, or as a particular grouping of smaller units. A book is a file; Mrs Beeton's autobiography is usually read as a whole, while her cookery book is usually read as a collection of individual recipes.

If the file is large, finding a particular piece of information may mean starting with the first item of the file, and scanning each item in turn until the right one is found. This is called sequential search or serial access, and a file arranged this way is a sequential file. A television programme is a sequential file of information, and so is a human conversation.

Sequential files are common because they are useful and cheap to implement, and because in many ways they mirror human methods of thought. However, they can become unwieldy and slow to use, so they are frequently divided internally into sub-files, which can be found directly without searching through the whole file. Books were once simple sequential files, but the invention of chapters, page numbers, and indexing transformed them. The chapters are sub-files of the book, and the pages are sub-files of both the chapters and the book.

A file that does not require sequential searching is called a direct access file. An album of songs on magnetic tape is a sequential file, while the same album on a long playing record is a direct access file: finding a song on the tape requires starting at the beginning and winding forward, while any track on the LP can be accessed directly by moving the pick-up arm across the LP to the start of the track.

Direct access depends on knowing where things are: in a book the index tells you what is where. Knowing exactly where things are means work (and, therefore, costs money). Indexing a book is an extra task for the author or publisher, and the information in the book may not warrant this expense; novels, for example, are not indexed, whereas textbooks usually are.

Computers process large quantities of information at speed, using a variety of data structures. Data has to be stored permanently on magnetic tape or disk in some structured way — typically in a sequential file — but in quite different ways in the computer's main memory.

Suppose that a bakery has the addresses of all its shops in a sequential file on tape, and wants the computer to print delivery schedules for the drivers who take bread to the shops. The file on tape might look like this:

```
Atkinsons   22 High Street
Brown & Co   108 Alma Road
Edwards   49 Barking Lane
Wilson Bros   7 High Street
Wrights   65 Lower Road
Youngers   31 Parsons Hill
```

When the file is read from tape into main memory, each name and address will be stored in a numbered location of its own, and all these locations together form a block of memory with its own name, so the file in memory looks like this:

```
BLOCKNAME: Shops
1) Atkinsons   22 High Street
2) Brown & Co   108 Alma Road
3) Edwards   49 Barking Lane
4) Wilson Bros   7 High Street
5) Wrights   65 Lower Road
6) Youngers   31 Parsons Hill
```

Now the data items can be accessed individually by naming the block and the location within it. Shops(4), for example, contains Wilson Bros, 7 High Street. This structure is called an array (see page 196), the data structure most commonly used by computers for internal data processing. It is like a book with one piece of information on each page. Notice that this simple structure immediately

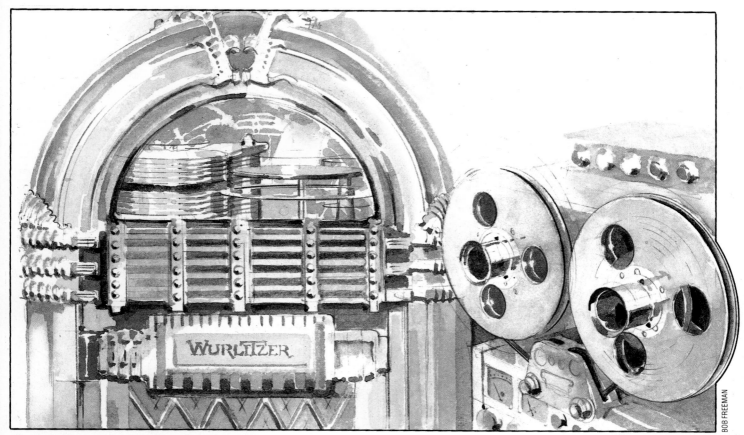

BOB FREEMAN

changes the way we look at data. A file of recognisable names and addresses has become a block of anonymous data. Computers do not need to know what a data item means, only where it is, and what to do with it.

The data in the array Shops( ) is in alphabetic order, but this is unlikely to be the most economical order in which to visit the shops. Suppose the computer works out that the best delivery schedule is:

1) Wilson Bros   7 High Street
2) Atkinsons   22 High Street
3) Edwards   49 Barking Lane
4) Brown & Co   108 Alma Road
5) Youngers   31 Parsons Hill
6) Wrights   65 Lower Road

This schedule might be stored in another array, but that would mean the same information is stored twice in the memory. Micro owners will know that RAM is limited, and it might be inconvenient or impossible to duplicate data in that way, so another method is needed.

If the actual data are replaced by their position numbers in the array Shops( ), then the delivery schedule looks like this:

BLOCKNAME: Deliveries
1)   4
2)   1
3)   3
4)   2
5)   6
6)   5

and what it really means is, 'First go to the shop whose details are stored in Shops(4), then go to Shops(1), then to Shops(3) . . .', and so on. The only significant information in the schedule is the order in which to visit the shops, so this is all that needs to be stored in the new array, Deliveries.

Deliveries( ) is now an index to the array Shops( ) for the purpose of deliveries. When printing this schedule the computer will use the numbers in the array Deliveries( ) to print the names and addresses from the array Shops( ) in the correct order.

In this simple exercise, information — the shops' names and addresses — has been manipulated but not changed by the different data structures imposed upon it. A data structure does not change the content of the data, but gives significance by associating it in an ordered way with other data.

Just as we can re-arrange the array Shops( ) by re-indexing it according to the array Deliveries( ), so can we construct other indexes to serve other purposes. When we discussed databases (see page 142), we noted that certain information could be selected by reference to pointers included in each individual record. In this way we can 'embed' in each record of the file Shops( ), a pointer that would indicate its place in the delivery schedule. We could further extend the record to include, for instance, a pointer into a file of standing orders — Atkinsons, for example, always have 48 white loaves, 12 wholemeal loaves, and so on. The production department could then run through the file extracting information relating only to the number of loaves that they need to bake.

On The Right Track
A juke box contains 200 songs on 100 record discs. It costs £2,000, and weighs 80kg (176lbs). To select any song, press three keys. Average time from SELECT to PLAY is 15 seconds. A reel of magnetic tape on a tape recorder may contain the same 200 songs. The tape recorder costs £500, and weighs 10kgs (22lbs). To select any song, rewind the tape, press PLAY, and wait. Average time from SELECT to PLAY is 1,500 seconds.

A juke box is a direct access device: it is fast, fairly specialised, and expensive. A tape recorder is a sequential access device: slow, much less specialised, but reasonably cheap. A cassette recorder connected to a microcomputer is a sequential access device, while a floppy disk drive is a direct access device, even though it may be used to store sequential files

Chain Mail

Indexing is one way of structuring large quantities of data, such as names and addresses. The Linked List or chain is an alternative with distinct advantages

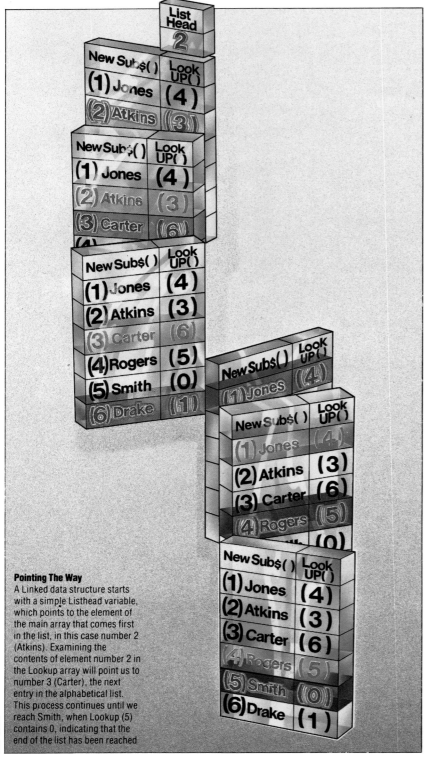

Pointing The Way
A Linked data structure starts with a simple Listhead variable, which points to the element of the main array that comes first in the list, in this case number 2 (Atkins). Examining the contents of element number 2 in the Lookup array will point us to number 3 (Carter), the next entry in the alphabetical list. This process continues until we reach Smith, when Lookup (5) contains 0, indicating that the end of the list has been reached

In a computer's memory there is only data, byte after byte of it, stored in thousands of voltage patterns. Meaning is given to those bytes by the data structure that the central processor imposes. Those various data structures decide whether any particular byte is interpreted as part of an instruction, or as digits belonging to a larger number, or as a character code.

From the user's point of view some kinds of data structure are virtually wired into computers. Programming languages usually demand that data be structured in a limited number of ways. BASIC imposes the idea of numeric and string data types, and supplies variables and array structures for manipulating those types. Other languages usually support those and additional structures. The strength and variety of its data types are major components of a language's power.

The BASIC data structures — variables and arrays — will be all that we need to simulate some other ways of looking at data.

The indexed array is a useful data structure, and easily implemented in BASIC. It has its limitations, however, particularly when the data to which it refers is likely to change often and/or unpredictably.

Suppose British Telecom keeps a file of its new subscribers for eventual inclusion in the next issue of the telephone directory. Until that time, the names and addresses have to be kept in alphabetic order for easy reference, but the file is constantly growing, and the additions arrive unpredictably. On Monday the file NewSub$ ( ) might look like this when it's read into the array:

NewSub$ ( )	Index ( )
(1) Jones	(2)
(2) Atkins	(3)
(3) Carter	(6)
(4) Rogers	(1)
(5) Smith	(4)
(6) Drake	(5)

The array Index ( ) shows the order in which to read NewSub$ ( ) so that the entries are in alphabetic order. Thus, the first item alphabetically is NewSub$ (2), Atkins. The second item is NewSub$ (3), Carter. In this example only the names are shown, but in fact a directory entry comprises name, initials, and address — typically about 60 characters. Moving blocks of 60 characters around in memory is slow (as sorting requires

TONY LODGE

many data moves) and wastes memory, so it is more efficient to leave NewSub$ ( ) unsorted, and create Index ( ) instead. Now a new name, Bull, has to be added to the file, so the arrays look like this:

NewSub$ ( )	Index ( )
(1) Jones	(2)
(2) Atkins	(7)
(3) Carter	(3)
(4) Rogers	(6)
(5) Smith	(1)
(6) Drake	(4)
(7) Bull	(5)

Notice that the contents of Index ( ) above the new insertion are unchanged, and its contents below the insertion are in the same order as previously, but have all been moved one place down in the array. Insertion to an index therefore requires: finding the position of the new element, moving every element between there and the end of the index down one, and writing in the new entry. This is preferable to doing the same thing with the actual data, NewSub$, but is still relatively slow, if the index is large.

Suppose, now, that we structure the data in a different way. Leave NewSub$ ( ) unsorted because manipulating it is slow and expensive, and establish a parallel array called LookUp ( ), whose contents are simply numbers referring to positions in NewSub$ ( ).

ListHead (2)

NewSub$ ( )	LookUp ( )	Index ( )
(1) Jones	(4)	(2)
(2) Atkins	(3)	(3)
(3) Carter	(6)	(6)
(4) Rogers	(5)	(1)
(5) Smith	(0)	(4)
(6) Drake	(1)	(5)

The first difference is that a simple variable called ListHead is needed: it points to NewSub$ (2) which is alphabetically the first element of NewSub$ ( ). The next difference is that the number (0) has been used in LookUp (5): this indicates that NewSub$ (5) is alphabetically the last element of the array.

The next difference is the contents of Index ( ) and LookUp ( ). Index ( ) has to be read: 'the first element is in NewSub$ (2), the second is in NewSub$ (3), the third is in NewSub$ (6)'...etc. while ListHead ( ) is read: 'the first element is in NewSub$ (2); Then LookUp (2) says that the next element is in NewSub$ (3); LookUp (3) says that the next element is in NewSub$ (6); and so on. LookUp (5) says that NewSub$ (5) is the last element.

Index ( ) gives an absolute position for elements of the file, while LookUp ( ) gives only relative positions — any item in LookUp ( ) tells you only where to find the next element, and says nothing about absolute position. The number in Index (4) points to the fourth item in the alphabetically ordered file, whereas the number in LookUp (4)

points only to the item that comes after NewSub$ (4) in the ordered file. LookUp ( ) implements the data structure called a 'Linked List'. Reading a Linked List is like following a treasure hunt: at the start you're told your first destination; when you get there you find a clue which points you to your next destination, and so on. Reading an Indexed Array is like being on a car rally: at the start you're told all your destinations and the order in which to visit them.

The great advantage of the List structure is its flexibility. Consider the List after insertion of the new element, Bull:

ListHead (2)

NewSub$ ( )	LookUp ( )
(1) Jones	(4)
(2) Atkins	(7)
(3) Carter	(6)
(4) Rogers	(5)
(5) Smith	(0)
(6) Drake	(1)
(7) Bull	(3)

The array LookUp ( ) has changed in only two places:

i) LookUp (2), which formerly pointed to NewSub$ (3) as containing the next alphabetic element after NewSub$ (2), now points to NewSub$ (7) since it is now the next alphabetic element after NewSub$ (2)

ii) LookUp (7), which was unused, now points to NewSub$(3) as the next item after NewSub$ (7) in the alphabetic ordering.

This illustrates the general process of insertion to a Linked List: find the element of the list which should come just before the new element, and make that element point to the new element; then make the new element point to the element that it has displaced. These simple operations will be all that is required for insertion to a Linked List, and only the first of these is affected by the size of the List. Inserting an element to a List is like inserting a new link into a chain — decide where to put the link, break the chain, join the preceding link to the new one, and the new link to the succeeding link. Linked Lists are sometimes called Chained Lists. The numbers in LookUp ( ) — the links — are sometimes called Pointers.

A striking feature of Lists is their strong seriality; it is impossible to find an element in a List except by starting at the beginning and inspecting every element until the target is found. The List is implemented here by using arrays, which are designed to be Direct Access structures, but the List has effectively turned them into Sequential Files. In other languages, such as LISP and PASCAL, the List facility is built-in.

Lists are useful structures for handling dynamic data (data that regularly changes), and can be powerful tools when dealing with either natural language (as in speech recognition) or artificial language (when compiling programs), where the data itself naturally forms a list of elements.

Order Of Play

The ability to sort information into order is essential to most programs, and there are many ways of doing it

Bubble Sort

This diagram illustrates the Bubble Sort for a reduced hand of nine cards (T is the Ten card). The ordered part of the hand grows from the right-hand end with each pass. The 1 and 2 underneath the hand of cards indicates the two cards currently being compared

```
Begin Sort
2 8 9 3 T 5 K 6 7  Begin Pass 1
1 2
8 2 9 3 T 5 K 6 7
  1 2
8 9 2 3 T 5 K 6 7
    1 2
8 9 3 2 T 5 K 6 7
      1 2
8 9 3 T 2 5 K 6 7
        1 2
8 9 3 T 5 2 K 6 7
          1 2
8 9 3 T 5 K 2 6 7
            1 2
8 9 3 T 5 K 6 2 7
              1 2
8 9 3 T 5 K 6 7 2  End Pass 1
9 8 T 5 K 6 7 3 2  End Pass 2
9 T 8 K 6 7 5 3 2  End Pass 3
T 9 K 8 7 6 5 3 2  End Pass 4
T K 9 8 7 6 5 3 2  End Pass 5
K T 9 8 7 6 5 3 2  End pass 6
End Sort
```

Insertion Sort

With the Insertion Sort, the ordered part of the list grows from the left-hand end. Cards are moved directly to their correct position in the list as they are inspected

```
Begin Sort
2 8 9 3 T 5 K 6 7
2 1
8 2 9 3 T 5 K 6 7
  2 1
9 8 2 3 T 5 K 6 7
    2 1
9 8 3 2 T 5 K 6 7
2       1
T 9 8 3 2 5 K 6 7
      2 1
T 9 8 5 3 2 K 6 7
2         1
K T 9 8 5 3 2 6 7
        2   1
K T 9 8 6 5 3 2 7
          2   1
K T 9 8 7 6 5 3 2
End Sort
```

Sorting is one of the most widely used computer operations, but it is a task at which computers are, by their own standards, highly inefficient. According to operational research, between 30 and 40 per cent of all computing time is spent in sorting, and if you add the associated tasks of merging data and searching for specific items, then the figure probably rises above 50 per cent.

Programmers have probably spent as much time inventing sort algorithms (general methods of solving problems) as computers have spent doing the actual sorting. Advanced sorting methods are extremely difficult to analyse, but it is quite easy to understand the simplest methods computers use to sort data with the aid of the example of sorting a pack of playing cards.

Lay 13 cards of the same suit on a table. Arrange them in a line, in no particular order, but the Ace and the Two should not be at the right-hand end of the line. The cards are to be sorted into descending order (King, Queen, Jack...Ace), starting at the left. This is an almost trivial task for us, and requires so little thought that it is difficult to describe exactly how we might do it. If, however, you were to specify that only one card can be moved at a time, that no card can be placed on top of another, and that the cards are to cover as little of the table as possible, the task becomes a lot less trivial, and an efficient method is hard to determine. In this analogy the cards are pieces of data, the maximum surface covered corresponds to the computer memory required, and you are the program. How do you solve the problem?

1) Put a coin below the leftmost card to act as a position marker and to remind you where you are in the sort. Compare the marked card with the card to its right. Are they in descending order? If they are not, swap their positions, leaving the coin where it is, and obeying the rule of only moving one card at a time and not placing cards on top of each other. Notice what you have to do to swap them.

2) When the two cards are in order, move the coin one place to the right and repeat Step 1. You are now in a loop that will end once you move the coin into the rightmost position. Reaching this position is called making a 'pass' through the cards.

3) At the end of the first pass look at the cards. The Ace, which is the lowest card in the suit, has found its way to the rightmost end of the line, and so is in its correct place. If you make a further pass through the cards, as detailed in Steps 1 and 2, the

Two card will be moved to its correct place. This is repeated, through pass after pass, until the whole suit is in descending order.

You may have noticed several drawbacks to this method. It is very tedious; it is not economical, as simply exchanging the positions of two cards requires three different operations; and, above all, many of the comparisons made between different cards are unnecessary. For example, after one pass the Ace is in its correct place, so there's no point moving the coin into position 13 (where no comparison is possible, anyway). On the second pass, because the card on the right is in its correct place, there was no need to move the pointer to position 12. In general, each pass will end one place to the left of the endpoint of the previous pass.

Knowing where to stop is another problem. A computer will continue comparing cards indefinitely unless it is told to stop. The only sure rule is: stop after a pass with no swaps. In other words, if you've gone through the data without altering its order, then it must be in order.

The method of sorting we have investigated is called the 'Bubble Sort'. Its advantages include simple programming techniques, little use of extra memory and reasonable efficiency with small amounts of partially ordered data. These are the criteria by which a sort algorithm must be judged, although when the data to be sorted is extensive, speed may have to be sacrificed for economy of memory simply because computer memory may not accommodate both the raw data and a sorted copy. For this reason, we'll ignore algorithms that require taking data from one array and moving it to the sorted position in a second array. The second method of simple sorting is based more directly on the way that we would sort cards.

1) Lay the shuffled cards out again and place a penny coin beneath the second card from the left. Whichever card the penny is beneath at the beginning of each pass, we will call the 'penny card'.

2) Push the penny card out of the line, leaving a gap, and place a twopenny coin beneath the card's immediate left. Call this card the twopenny card.

3) Compare the penny card with the twopenny card. If they're in order, then push the penny card back into place and skip to Step 4. If they're not in order, then push the twopenny card into the gap and move the twopenny coin one place to the left to mark a new twopenny card (if the twopenny card is at the extreme left, this will not apply, so

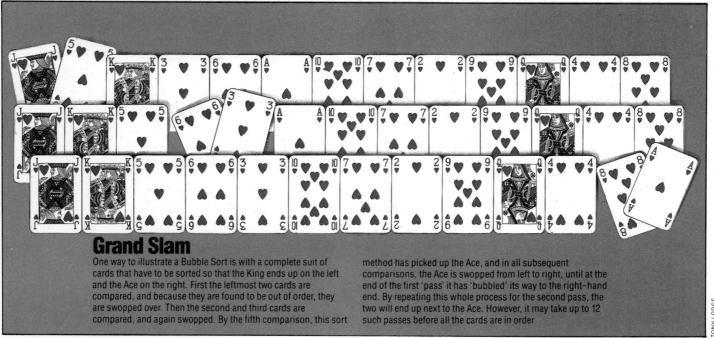

Grand Slam

One way to illustrate a Bubble Sort is with a complete suit of cards that have to be sorted so that the King ends up on the left and the Ace on the right. First the leftmost two cards are compared, and because they are found to be out of order, they are swopped over. Then the second and third cards are compared, and again swopped. By the fifth comparison, this sort method has picked up the Ace, and in all subsequent comparisons, the Ace is swopped from left to right, until at the end of the first 'pass' it has 'bubbled' its way to the right–hand end. By repeating this whole process for the second pass, the two will end up next to the Ace. However, it may take up to 12 such passes before all the cards are in order

TONY LODGE

place the penny card in the gap and proceed to Step 4).

Compare this twopenny card with the penny card (the displaced one). Now repeat Step 3 until the correct position for the penny card is found.

4) Move the penny one position to the right and repeat Steps 2 and 3. When you can't move the penny any further right, the cards will all be in order.

This is called an 'Insertion Sort', and is very similar to the way people sort a hand of cards. Although it is a little harder to program than a Bubble Sort it is a far more efficient method. Later in the book, we will look at some more complex algorithms for sorting data.

```
9    REM*********************
10   REM* SORT ALGORITHMS    *
11   REM*********************
100  INPUT"HOW MANY ITEMS TO BE SORTED";LT
150  IF LT<3 THEN LET LT=3
200  LET LT=INT(LT)
250  DIM R(LT),C(LT)
300  LET Z=0:LET Q=0:LET P=0
350  LET I=1:LET O=0:LET II=2:LET TH=2
400  INPUT"HOW MANY TESTS ";N
450  FOR CT=I TO N
500  GOSUB 4000
550  FOR SR=I TO TH
600  GOSUB 5000
650  PRINT:PRINT:PRINT:PRINT
700  PRINT "TEST #";CT+SR/10
750  INPUT"HIT RETURN TO BEGIN SORT";A$
800  PRINT "THE UNSORTED LIST IS"
850  GOSUB 3000
900  ON SR GOSUB 6000,7000
950  PRINT "THE SORTED LIST IS"
1000 GOSUB 3000
1050 NEXT SR
1100 NEXT CT
1150 END
2999 REM*********************
3000 REM*  PRINT THE LIST   *
3001 REM*********************
3100 FOR K=I TO LT
3200 PRINT R(K);
```

```
3300 NEXT K
3400 PRINT
3500 RETURN
3999 REM*********************
4000 REM*    RND GENERATOR   *
4001 REM*********************
4100 RANDOMIZE
4200 FOR K=I TO LT
4300 LET C(K)=INT(100*RND)
4400 NEXT K
4500 RETURN
4999 REM*********************
5000 REM*   RND REGENERATOR  *
5001 REM*********************
5100 FOR K=I TO LT
5200 LET R(K)=C(K)
5300 NEXT K
5400 PRINT:PRINT
5500 RETURN
5999 REM*********************
6000 REM*       BUBBLE       *
6001 REM*********************
6050 PRINT "BUBBLE SORT - GO !!!!!
6100 FOR P=LT-I TO I STEP-I
6150 LET F=-I
6200 FOR Q=I TO P
6250 LET Z=Q+I
6300 IF R(Q)<R(Z) THEN LET D=R(Q):
        LET R(Q)=R(Z):LET R(Z)=D:LET F=0
6350 NEXT Q
6400 IF F=-I THEN LET P=I
6450 NEXT P
6500 PRINT "BUBBLE SORT - STOP !!!!!
6550 RETURN
6999 REM*********************
7000 REM*     INSERTION      *
7001 REM*********************
7050 PRINT "INSERTION SORT - GO !!!!!
7100 FOR P=II TO LT
7200 LET D=R(P)
7300 FOR Q=P TO II STEP-I
7400 LET R(Q)=R(Q-I)
7500 IF D<=R(Q) THEN LET R(Q)=D:LET Q=II
7600 NEXT Q
7700 IF D>R(I) THEN LET R(I)=D
7800 NEXT P
7850 PRINT "INSERTION SORT - STOP !!!!!
7900 RETURN
```

High-Speed Sort
This BASIC program demonstrates the difference in efficiency between a Bubble Sort and Insertion Sort. The code has been written with speed in mind, so we have not documented the operation of the routines. The listing should run on most machines, but see page 201 for ON...GOSUB flavours, and page 195 for RND and RANDOMIZE

Sorting Code

The Shell Sort is more efficient than either the Bubble or Insertion Sorts for long arrays. It works by dividing the data into a series of 'chains'

On page 148 we looked at two methods of sorting an array into order — the Bubble and Insertion Sorts. Generally, the Bubble Sort is easier to carry out, but the Insertion Sort is faster. Experience of these two methods shows that what takes the time is swapping cards around over short distances: it's usually far better to swap once over a long distance than several times over short distances.

```
7999 REM*********************
8000 REM*        SHELL        *
8001 REM*********************
8025 PRINT "SHELL SORT - GO !!!!!"
8050 LET LK=LT
8100 FOR Z=0 TO I STEP O
8150 LET LK=INT(LK/II)
8200 FOR LB=I TO LK
8250 LET LL=LB+LK
8300 FOR P=LL TO LT STEP LK
8350 LET D=R(P)
8400 FOR Q=P TO LL STEP-LK
8450 LET R(Q)=R(Q-LK)
8500 IF D<=R(Q) THEN LET R(Q)=D:LET Q=LL
8550 NEXT Q
8600 IF D>R(LB) THEN LET R(LB)=D
8650 NEXT P
8700 NEXT LB
8750 IF LK=I THEN LET Z=I
8800 NEXT Z
8850 PRINT "SHELL SORT - STOP !!!!!"
8900 RETURN
```

To add this routine to the sorting demonstration program on page 149, change line 350 to:

350 LET I=1:LET O=0:LET II=+:LET TH=3

and change line 900 to:

900 ON SR GOSUB 6000,7000,8000

A better method than either of these two is called the 'Shell Sort' (named after its creator, D Shell). This method ensures that the disorder in the array is reduced early in the sort (so that items are not a long way from their true positions), and enables swaps to operate over relatively long distances. Here is a method for this sort:

1) Lay out all the cards of one suit in any order. They are to be sorted into descending order so that the King will be the leftmost card, and the Ace the rightmost. Count the cards, divide that number (in this case, 13) by two, ignoring any remainder, and write the result (i.e. six) on a piece of paper labelled 'The Link'.

2) Place a fivepence piece under the leftmost card (call this Position One), and a tenpence piece in the Link position (i.e. Position Six in the first instance). All of the cards from the First to the Link position are each to be the leftmost end cards in a series of 'chains' of cards. The number of chains will equal the current value of the Link. Each chain is formed by starting with its end card, adding the Link to the end card's position number

to get the position of the next card, adding the Link to get the position of the next card, and so on until the end of the array has been reached or exceeded. The first chain, therefore, comprises the cards in positions One, Seven, and Thirteen; the second chain is the cards in positions Two and Eight; the third is the cards in positions Three and Nine. The last chain is the cards in positions Six (the present value of the Link) and Twelve.

3) Now, having marked the boundaries with the five- and tenpence pieces, push the cards that comprise the first chain out of the array so that you can see them in isolation, and sort them into order using either the Bubble or Insertion Sort as described on page 148 (the listing on the left uses the Insertion method).

4) Push the ordered chain back into the gaps in the array, and repeat the above with the next chain, and the next, and so on, until all the chains whose leftmost cards lie between the five- and ten-pence pieces have been sorted.

5) When all the chains have been sorted, divide the Link by two, ignoring any remainder. If the Link is now less than one then the array will be sorted. Otherwise, repeat from Step Two above with the new value of the Link.

Shell Sort Panel

Position No.									Link Value	Comments
1 2 3 4 5 6 7 8 9										
2 8 9 3 T 5 K 6 7									(9/2)=>4	Begin Pass
* + @ $ * + @ $ *										Form chains
T 7 2										Sort Chain 1
8 5										Sort Chain 2
K 9										Sort Chain 3
6 3										Sort Chain 4
T 8 K 6 7 5 9 3 2										Begin Pass
T 8 K 6 7 5 9 3 2									(4/2)=>2	End of Pass
* + * + * + * +										Form Chains
K T 9 7 2										Sort Chain 1
8 6 5 3										Sort Chain 2
K 8 T 6 9 5 7 3 2										End of Pass
K 8 T 6 9 5 7 3 2									(2/2)=>1	Begin Pass
* * * * * * * * *										Form Chain 1
K T 9 8 7 6 5 3 2										End of Pass

KEY	
*	Member of Chain 1
+	Member of Chain 2
@	Member of Chain 3
$	Member of Chain 4

Shell Sort
The example of the Shell Sort for a reduced hand that we show in the panel demonstrates its unique method of dividing the array into a series of chains (with spacings based on the current Link number). These chains are separately sorted, in this case using the Insertion method, before a pass is completed.

The program listing for a Shell Sort given here must be used in conjunction with the testbed program on page 149. When we tested it, there was a significant improvement over the other sorting methods once the number of items to be sorted exceeded 40

Top Gear

By paying careful attention to variables and program structure, you can speed up the operation of almost any Basic program

BASIC is, despite what its critics say, a versatile language and a powerful educational aid. You can write any program in BASIC, provided your machine has enough memory and the execution time is not important. However, because BASIC is usually interpreted rather than compiled (see page 70), it can be painfully slow in executing programs — especially those that require the same instruction to be translated and executed repeatedly.

Sorting, for example, is a highly repetitive process: the procedure is carried out within a loop, and there are smaller loops nested inside the main loop (see page 148). If 100 items are to be sorted, the program may make between 2,500 and 5,000 iterations of the loop. A BASIC sort will always be slow, but the way the code is written can make a significant difference to the speed of execution. If an instruction is to be repeated 5,000 times, and if coding it properly can save one hundredth of a second of execution time for each repetition, then there will be a total saving of 50 seconds — a considerable improvement for the user.

To observe the difference that good and bad coding can make, you will need a timing mechanism and a 'testbed' program. If you own a Commodore computer, you can use the system clock, with the associated variables TI$ and TI, as part of the testbed program. If your computer doesn't have an accessible clock, you'll have to use a stopwatch to time the code in execution. It is also a good idea to make your program 'beep' at you when it starts and finishes, so that you'll know when it's operating.

The testbed program looks like this:

```
1000 L=500
2000 PRINT "***GO***":REM "BEEP"
        instructions here
2100 TI$="000000"
2200 FOR K=1 TO L
.................................................................
2900 NEXT K:T9=TI
2950 REM "BEEP" instructions here
3000 PRINT "******STOP******"
3100 PRINT "That took    "; (T9/60); "    seconds"
```

Lines 2100 and 3100 are for Commodore users. For other machines, delete or replace them with appropriate code. The space between lines 2200 and 2900 is where we will put the code to be timed. Notice that the timings will refer to L repetitions where L is the limit of the loop. Testing

only one execution of a piece of code would be very inaccurate because the system clock measures only in 60ths of a second, and there is a timing overhead imposed by the code of the testbed program as well.

Here are some general rules for writing efficient BASIC, roughly in order of importance:

1. Avoid all arithmetic in loops.

Exponentiation (x^3, meaning 'x raised to the power of 3', for example), and mathematical functions ($\cos(y)$, meaning 'the cosine of the angle y', for example) are particularly slow. Multiplication and division are slower processes than addition and subtraction, but even the quickest of these operations (addition) is relatively slow.

In the testbed program insert these lines:

```
900 Z=1.1
2300 X=Z↑3
```

and run it. On our test machine 500 repetitions took 27.95 seconds. Now replace line 2300 with:

```
2300 X=Z*Z*Z
```

and run it. This took 3.55 seconds — a dramatic difference!

Further investigation will reveal the level of exponentiation at which it becomes worthwhile replacing repeated multiplication by the exponentiation function. On our computer this was at the 18th power (when $X=Z↑18$). Remember, however, that to calculate $Z^{2.3}$, for example, repeated multiplication would be useless, whereas the exponentiation function (↑) works for all real numbers, including negative ones.

Use the testbed program to see how long the other arithmetic processes take, and compare alternatives. Is it quicker to divide a number by 2, or multiply it by 0.5, for example?

2. Use variables rather than numerical constants.

Every time a numerical constant (7,280 for example) occurs in a BASIC instruction, time is spent translating the number into usable form. Try this line:

```
2300 X=X+7280
```

On our machine that took 4.63 seconds to execute 500 repetitions, whereas:

```
900 C=7280
2300 X=X+C
```

took 2.75 seconds to do the same number of repetitions.

3. If you must use the GOTO statement, jump forward in your program rather than back. If you must jump back, however, jump to the start of the program rather than back a few lines.

The same is true for GOSUB. On meeting a GOTO or GOSUB instruction the BASIC interpreter compares the target line number with the current line number. If the target is greater than the current, the interpreter simply searches forward, line by line, until it is found. But if the target is less than the current, then the search always begins from the very first line of the program. This means that it may be more efficient to place subroutines and frequently used sections at either end of a program. Add 56 REM lines at the start of the program, to make it up to typical length, and try:

```
2300 GOTO 2400
2400 GOTO 2500
2500 GOTO 2900
```

This took 2.33 seconds for 500 repetitions, whereas:

```
2300 GOTO 2500
2400 GOTO 2900
2500 GOTO 2400
```

took 4.85 seconds.

4. Initialise all variables in order of access frequency.

Variable names are stored by the interpreter in a symbol table in the order in which they first appear in a program. The later a variable occurs in the table, the longer it takes to find it and access its contents. For the same reason you should avoid using a new variable in a program where you can resort to one previously used by the program but currently not in use.

If a variable is used inside nested loops — as is common in sorting — that variable is accessed frequently, so initialise it at the start of the program before any other variable, with a dummy value if need be:

```
1000 L=500:C=7280:X=0:Z=1.1
2300 A=0
```

took 2.2 seconds for 500 repetitions, whereas:

```
1000 A=0:L=500:C=7280:X=0:Z=1.1
2300 A=0
```

took 2.06 seconds.

5. Avoid using strings.

String operations use up memory in ways that arithmetic does not, and a system program called the Garbage Collector may have to be called every now and again by the interpreter to tidy up

Memory Map

This a simplified memory map of a typical home computer. Most microprocessors can address up to 64K (65536 bytes), which will be divided up into ROM, RAM, and unused space. When considering the speed of a BASIC program, one of the most important factors is the way in which strings are stored. Whenever the contents of a string are altered, a complete new copy of the string will be made in memory. Eventually, all the free memory will be used up and BASIC will have to invoke the Garbage Collector, which tidies up the string memory. This might take several seconds, and in a program that manipulates a lot of strings, this could slow down the program considerably

TOP OF MEMORY
BYTE NO. 65535

OPERATING SYSTEM
SCREEN MEMORY
STRING DATA
FREE MEMORY
NUMERIC VARIABLES
BASIC PROGRAM TEXT
SYSTEM DATA

BYTE NO. 0
BOTTOM OF MEMORY

This is the set of standard programs held in ROM, which the computer needs to operate internally

Each byte of this RAM corresponds to a character position on the screen

When a string is defined or altered, the characters will be stored in this section of RAM

As the variable list or the length of strings increases, the free memory is used up

Numeric variables typically occupy seven bytes each: two for the variable name, and five to hold the number in floating-point format

The text of a program is stored here, usually in the form of ASCII codes. However, to save memory, keywords like PRINT and INPUT are stored as one byte. This is called tokenising

All computers use up some of their RAM for internal variables and buffers for cassette and keyboard

the contents of string memory. This procedure can take a lot of time.

A general demonstration of this is difficult to write because computers vary so much in their memory management: you have to fill up most of the user memory with data — a large numeric array will do — then perform string manipulations that will cause the Garbage Collector to be called. On our machine we entered:

```
40 POKE 52,32:POKE 56,32:CLR
```

to reduce severely the amount of memory available to BASIC programs, and then entered:

```
1000 L=500:DIMT$(L)
1100 FOR K=1 TO L
1200 T$(K)="A"+"B"
1300 PRINT K
1400 NEXT K
```

which uses up a lot of string memory and provides a string array for later use. The PRINT statement is executed in every iteration, displaying the value of the loop counter. When we ran this version of the testbed program, the printing repeatedly paused as the Garbage Collector was called to rearrange memory. Sometimes the pause lasted more than three seconds. The program continues:

```
2300 A$=LEFT$(T$(L),1):B$=A$+RIGHT$(T$(L),1)
```

and this took 30.03 seconds for 500 repetitions. When we ran the same program with much more memory available, garbage collection was not visible, and the timed loop took 8.66 seconds.

Call My Bluff

Chess-playing programs are difficult to write, but it is possible even for beginners to construct a simple, 'intelligent' game program

COURTESY OF MILTON BRADLEY LTD

IAN McKINNELL

Invisible Hand
Dedicated chess-playing machines contain the same components as home computers: a CPU, RAM, and the program in ROM, and differ only in the method of input and output. The Phantom, shown here, uses a servo-mechanism and magnets that enable the computer to move the chess pieces automatically. When, for example, a knight jumps over another piece, a sophisticated algorithm is employed that removes any obstruction and then replaces it after the move

Many people, when they begin writing their own computer programs, dream of the day when they will know enough to be able to write a program that plays chess. This is not because chess programs are unavailable, of course. Such programs abound in number, both as packages available for home computers and in the form of dedicated chess-playing machines. But writing chess programs can become an obsession, even among programmers who are not particularly keen on chess as a game. A possible reason for this is that we regard the game as being a highly intellectual pursuit, and therefore a computer that can play chess is a step towards creating an intelligent machine. It would be very difficult to explain to you how to write a complete chess program from scratch, however. But we can explain some of the principles on which computerised 'intelligent' games are constructed, and to a level where you could write a fairly sophisticated program in BASIC.

It should be remembered, however, that the 'games' we are concerned with are not arcade games, adventures or simulations, all of which require different programming techniques and different imaginative skills. We'll begin our discussion of intelligent games with what you might consider to be a trivial example, but one that demonstrates many of the principles of intelligent game writing.

Most children (as well as grown-up children) are familiar with the game Scissors-Paper-Stone. The rules are simple: both players must think of one of these three objects, and then simultaneously hold up a hand in a shape representing the chosen object. The winner is determined according to three rules: scissors beats paper (by cutting), paper beats stone (by covering), and stone beats scissors (by blunting them).

Anyone, after following the Basic Programming chapter of this book, should find it a simple exercise to write a program to play the computer's part and keep the score. The RND function is used to select one element from a three-element string array containing 'SCISSORS', 'PAPER' and 'STONE'. The chosen element is then PRINTed when the space bar is pressed. The player types in his own choice (the program relies on his honesty), and the program calculates who won, displaying the result and an accumulating score for itself and its opponent. If the RND function is truly random, then the scores should even out over a large number of rounds, no matter what strategy the player adopts. Now we need to determine how we can improve the computer's strategy to ensure that it will win over a large number of rounds.

When you look closely at random functions, you will see that generating a truly random sequence of numbers is an impossible task for both humans and computers, though the latter make a much better approximation. Over many rounds of our game the human player will invariably favour one of the objects more than the others. You can write a subroutine in your program that keeps track of the player's choices, using an array with three elements called, let's say, CHOICE(1), CHOICE(2), and CHOICE(3). Each time the player makes a choice, one is added to the total in the corresponding array element. The computer can then establish which object is more often presented by its opponent, and play the object that beats this preferred choice.

the game. So rather than keep a record of his opponent's choices since the start of the game, it would be better that the program simply recorded, let's say, the last 20 choices. This will require a CHOICE array of 20-by-three elements, and a more sophisticated subroutine to add up the three columns and hence predict the best choice for the computer's next turn.

However, the most serious shortcoming of this algorithm becomes apparent if the player deduces the computer's strategy. Then it is relatively easy for him to play in a way that ensures that the computer will lose on more than half the turns. The player could, for example, consistently play the same object, and then switch to another unexpectedly, and so on. What we need is a different algorithm that avoids these problems. Nevertheless, it would be worthwhile developing programs that use both the fully random and the modified random methods, and observing the scores when these are used by unsuspecting players.

Because humans are incapable of making a totally irrational or random decision, it follows that

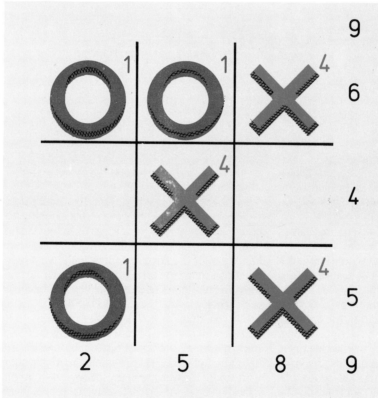

9

6

4

5

8 9

Winning Position

'Position evaluation' is fundamental to any board game program — even if the game is as simple as noughts and crosses. In this case, the board is represented as a three by three array, the player's noughts by the value one, and the computer's crosses by a four. Using these values, any position can be evaluated by adding up the totals for every row, column and diagonal. A total of 12 in any of these lines indicates that the computer has won; three means that the player has won; a total of eight shows that two crosses have been played and the computer can win; and so on. The values one and four are used because these ensure that every combination of noughts and crosses gives a unique total

LIZ DIXON

Three problems arise with this method. Firstly, if the computer consistently plays the same object then the player is very quickly going to take advantage of this. Therefore, the computer must generally be made to choose from the three objects using the RND function, while a routine should be added to ensure that it will more frequently choose the object that will beat the player's most preferred choice.

The second problem is that the player will tend to change his favourite object over the course of

every choice must be a function of the previous choices. That function may be extremely complicated, and the player almost certainly isn't aware of it, but if the computer can work out a good approximation to that function, then it should be able to win fairly consistently. Because each player will have an individual subconscious formula, and will probably change this formula over the course of a long game, the program must be made to interpret the formula while it is playing. Programs that can learn like this are called 'heuristic' programs.

An heuristic program enables the computer to detect alterations in its opponent's strategy, and modify its algorithm accordingly. Such a program would have to keep a record of, let's say, the last 50 choices of both opponents, in an array. It constantly scans through this track record applying a statistical technique known as 'correlation'.

This involves the computer in making hundreds of comparisons between the player's choice and his previous choice, or the one before that, or the choice made five turns ago. The computer performs the same operation on its own choices. Let's consider the correlation between the player's move and his previous move, for example. We'll call Scissors — element 1, Paper — element 2, and Stone — element 3. First we must set up a three by three array, called say CORR1, because it represents our first correlation test. Now we must work through our game history, looking at the player's choices for the last 50 moves. Every time he followed Scissors (1) by Stone (3), we add one to the element CORR1(1,3); when Stone (3) is followed by Paper (2), one is added to element CORR1(3,2) and so on.

If the player is making truly random choices, then there should be approximately equal values in each element of CORR1 — but this is very unlikely to be the case. So, if the player chose Paper last, then the element in row 2 (Paper) of CORR1 with the largest value will give us the best guess as to what he will choose next. The greater the difference between the elements in any row, the better the correlation is, and the more reliable the prediction will be. However, it is possible that there will be little correlation between the player's choice and his previous choice, in which case we must also perform correlation calculations on the second to last choice, or between the player's choice and the computer's previous choice.

A problem arises if the various correlation routines all predict different results for the player's next move. The program has to decide which is the most reliable advice. In this simple game, all it needs to do is see which test has the most pronounced correlation. For example, the CORR1 array might predict the following probabilities: Scissors 51%, Paper 29%, Stone 20%; whereas CORR2 (which, say, compares the player's choice with the computer's last choice) might give: Scissors 24%, Paper 60%, Stone 16%. Clearly CORR2 has the better correlation, so its prediction should be selected. An intelligent games program will in fact frequently consist of a number of subroutines, each working on different strategies, and each advising the main routine of the best move. The playing routine can regard these subroutines as a 'committee', and act on a majority decision. But as the game proceeds, it can award marks to each routine according to whether its advice was good or not.

If there does turn out to be some correlation between the player's moves or choices and the previous moves of the computer, then it is possible

```
5    CLS
10   DIM C1(3,3),C2(3,3),C3(3,3)
20   CR=0
30   FOR I=1 TO 3
40   IF C1(PL,I) > CR THEN BG=I:CR=C1(PL,I)
50   IF C2(PP,I) > CR THEN BG=I:CR=C2(PP,I)
60   IF C3(P3,I) > CR THEN BG=I:CR=C3(P3,I)
70   NEXT I
80   CT=BG-1
90   IF BG=1 THEN CT=3
100  GET PT: IF PT=0 THEN 100
110  REM LINE 100 WAITS FOR A DIGIT TO
120  REM BE PRESSED.
130  IF CT=PT-1 THEN CS=CS+1
140  IF CT=PT-2 THEN PS=PS+1
150  IF CT=PT+1 THEN PS=PS+1
160  IF CT=PT+2 THEN CS=CS+1
170  CLS
180  PRINT "YOUR CHOICE: ";PT
190  PRINT "MY CHOICE: ";CT
200  PRINT "YOUR SCORE IS ";PS
210  PRINT "MY SCORE IS ";CS
220  C1(PL,PT)=C1(PL,PT)+1
230  C2(PP,PT)=C2(PP,PT)+1
240  C3(P3,PT)=C3(P3,PT)+1
250  P3=PP
260  PP=PL
270  PL=PT
280  GOTO 20
```

to program in some kind of 'bluffing' factor that will deliberately mislead the player. This works best in gambling games, where the stakes increase as the game continues, and it is worthwhile losing the early rounds to win the later ones.

At the State University of New York at Buffalo (reported in *Scientific American*, July 1978) a collection of poker-playing programs (all of them with a learning capability) were set against each other for several thousand games. The overall winner was a program called the Adaptive Evaluator of Opponents (AEO), which made an initial judgement about the strength of its opponents' hands, and modified this estimate as each game proceeded. The SBI program, 'Sells and Buys Images', did surprisingly badly — its technique was to bluff in order to 'sell' a false image to its opponents, or effectively to 'buy' the playing style of others. The Bayesian Player (BP) tried to make inductive inferences, and improve its play by comparing the predicted consequences of its actions with the actual consequences. Finally, the Adaptive Aspiration Level (AAL) program attempted to mimic a feature believed to exist in human playing: adapting the level of aspiration (that is, the degree of risk it is prepared to take) according to its past record and current status.

No two chess programs or other artificially intelligent routines work in exactly the same way. But by experimenting with the techniques we've outlined here on progressively more complicated games, you may eventually be able to join the exclusive club of chess program writers.

Slow Learner
This program, based on the game Scissors — Paper — Stone, illustrates how a program can 'learn' as a game progresses. The computer selects from the numbers 1,2 and 3, compares its choice with the one you have typed in and adjusts the score. The GET statement has been used so that you can simply press the three number keys in rapid succession. If you attempt to make your sequence random, you should find that after a couple of hundred key-presses, the computer's score will pull ahead. It is possible to fool this program and hence continue to win, but more sophisticated routines can be added to it to prevent you from doing this

Subversive Elements

With careful planning and a step-by-step approach, the time taken to de-bug a program can be dramatically reduced

As you become more skilled at writing programs, you will also tend to become more accomplished at 'de-bugging' them. The syntactical mistakes and errors in logic, which even the most experienced computer programmers can make, become less frequent and less problematic as your experience increases. Here are some hints to help you avoid programming errors and become more efficient at de-bugging your code.

The first place to begin is at the precise point where a program begins — in your head! If the concept of a program is badly thought out at the beginning, then it is sure to be infested with bugs when it is written.

It is a far better idea to begin writing a program by first stating the problem as clearly as possible to yourself or someone else. Then divide the problem into logically complete parts — Input, Output, Algorithms, Data Structures, Processes, etc. — and consider each of those parts as a separate problem. If necessary, break down each of these problems into its component problems, and so on, until the original problem is a structured collection of sub-problems, each of which is easy for you to program. A formal approach, such as using a pseudo-language or a flowchart, is essential in the design stage as a way of keeping track of, and preserving, the program structure as a whole. You must try to stay away from the keyboard until you can honestly say that you know how to program every part of the problem This is called the top-down approach to programming, and the method can dramatically cut your de-bugging time.

Splitting problems into solvable tasks will lead you to write programs that are really collections of subroutines or procedures linked by a skeleton main program. This makes finding bugs easier, and it enables you to build a library of bug-free subroutines for use in later programs. The alternative is called 're-inventing the wheel': every time you write a program that sorts data, for example, you re-solve the problem of how to write a sort routine, and probably rewrite the same old bugs, as well! It is much easier to write and debug it once, save it, and recall it whenever you need it thereafter.

As far as BASIC allows, always try to use appropriate variable names, even if they have to be abbreviated. NET=GROSS−TAX, for example, explains itself; and NT=GR−TX isn't a bad substitute; but N=G−T is extremely ambiguous,

and gives no clue as to what variables are involved. It's good practice to keep a variable table, which shows you all the variables used in the program and what they're for. This can lead you to standardise your use of variables (such as, always using certain single letter variables as loop counters), and stops you using the same variable for different purposes. Similarly, it's good practice to store constant values in

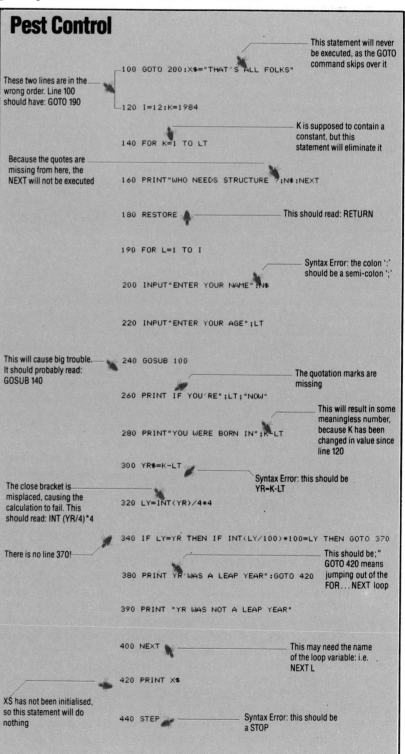

Pest Control

```
100 GOTO 200:X$="THAT'S ALL FOLKS"
120 I=12:K=1984
140 FOR K=1 TO LT
160 PRINT"WHO NEEDS STRUCTURE ";N$:NEXT
180 RESTORE
190 FOR L=1 TO I
200 INPUT"ENTER YOUR NAME":N$
220 INPUT"ENTER YOUR AGE";LT
240 GOSUB 100
260 PRINT IF YOU'RE";LT;"NOW"
280 PRINT"YOU WERE BORN IN";K-LT
300 YR$=K-LT
320 LY=INT(YR)/4*4
340 IF LY=YR THEN IF INT(LY/100)*100=LY THEN GOTO 370
380 PRINT YR'WAS A LEAP YEAR":GOTO 420
390 PRINT "YR WAS NOT A LEAP YEAR"
400 NEXT
420 PRINT X$
440 STEP
```

This statement will never be executed, as the GOTO command skips over it

These two lines are in the wrong order. Line 100 should have: GOTO 190

K is supposed to contain a constant, but this statement will eliminate it

Because the quotes are missing from here, the NEXT will not be executed

This should read: RETURN

Syntax Error: the colon ':' should be a semi-colon ';'

This will cause big trouble. It should probably read: GOSUB 140

The quotation marks are missing

This will result in some meaningless number, because K has been changed in value since line 120

Syntax Error: this should be YR=K-LT

The close bracket is misplaced, causing the calculation to fail. This should read: INT (YR/4)*4

There is no line 370!

This should be;" GOTO 420 means jumping out of the FOR...NEXT loop

This may need the name of the loop variable: i.e. NEXT L

X$ has not been initialised, so this statement will do nothing

Syntax Error: this should be a STOP

variables at the start of the program, and refer back to these variables thereafter. This makes the program faster and neater, and it means that you can change these values without having to hunt through the program for every occurrence.

Even with the sort of formal approach that we have outlined here, it's difficult to eliminate bugs entirely, so it's important to adopt a disciplined method for finding and eradicating them. The commonest bugs are syntax errors, and you can usually correct them as soon as you encounter them. But this is not always the case. Consider:

```
10 PRINT"BIG BUGS HAVE LITTLE BUGS UPON"
20 PRINT"THEIR BACKS TO BITE THEM"
```

Such lines often cause an error message when executed if they're not keyed in as two separate lines. Line 10 contains 40 characters, so when you type it on a 40-column screen, the cursor finishes up at the start of the next screen line, which can cause you to forget to hit RETURN on line 10 before you start typing line 20. If so, then what look like two perfect lines in your program will actually be one line with a syntax error (the number 20) in the middle of it. One way of trapping these errors is to list suspect lines individually rather than as part of a piece of program.

Error messages, when they're not incomprehensible, can be misleading. Take for example:

```
25 DATA 10.2,34,56.9,0.008,15.6
30 FOR K=1 TO 5: READ N(K):NEXT K
```

This may fail to execute because of an alleged syntax error in line 30; whereas the error is actually in the data on line 25 (One of the zeros has been mis-keyed as the letter 0).

Coding errors that don't result in syntax errors are the commonest bugs, and usually also the hardest to find. In this case, it is vital to be methodical. Begin by trying to find out roughly where the bug is in the program. This is reasonably easy with well-structured modular programs, and can be made easier by the TRACE utility, which causes the current program line number to be printed on the screen as it is executed. If your machine doesn't allow this, then you can create TRACE statements periodically throughout the program (PRINT "LINE 150" at the beginning of line 150, for example). Similarly, you can use the STOP command to halt program execution at significant places in the program so that you can examine the values of crucial variables. You can do this in direct mode using PRINT, or you can write a subroutine onto the end of your program:

```
11000 REM PRINT THE VARIABLES
11100 PRINT"SCORE,SIZE,FLAGS"
11200 PRINT SC;SZ;F1;F2
11300 PRINT"BOARD ARRAY"
11400 FOR K=1 TO 10:PRINT BD$(K):NEXT K
```

Consequently, when the program comes across a STOP command, you can type GOTO 11000, and

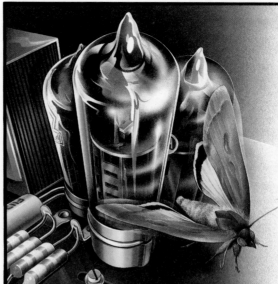

TONY LODGE

Early Bug

To new programmers, bugs often seem to take on animate characteristics, such as hiding from the programmer and deliberately undermining all his efforts to find them. However, the first bug (at least the one from which the term is derived) really was animate. In trying to eliminate an error from a program she was developing on the Harvard Mrk II in 1945, Captain Grace Hopper discovered that a large moth had got caught up in the electromechanical working of the computer and was causing the fault. As a result of that incident, the term 'de-bugging' was coined

have the current state of the variables displayed. You can even change them (by typing, say, SZ=17 and pressing RETURN), and then restart the program with the CONTinue command.

When you've found that the bug is lurking within certain lines, or in a particular variable, then you should be close to eliminating it, but tread carefully! Try one remedy at a time so that you can see what its exact effect on execution is. It's very easy to make several changes between runs, perhaps getting rid of one bug, but creating one or more new ones, and then forgetting exactly what it was you did!

Loops and branches, especially when they're nested, are particularly fertile ground for bugs, and require special care in both writing and debugging. Consider this piece of code:

```
460 IF SM< 0 AND SC< >-1 THEN IF SC>0 OR
    SM=SC-F9 THEN LT=500
470 FOR C1=1 TO LT:FOR C2=LT TO C1 STEP-1
480 SC=SM+SC*C2
490 NEXT C2:SM=0:NEXT C1
```

What does this all mean? Even if you know what it's meant to do, would you know if it were succeeding or failing? Putting statements inside a loop when they should be outside is a sure way to encourage bugs. And so is failing to cover all possible conditions when writing IF . . . THEN statements. A special case of this occurs when you write multiple statements after IF . . . THEN. For example:

```
655 IF A$="" THEN GOTO 980:A$=B$
660 PRINT A$
```

The statement A$=B$ will never be executed because either A$="", in which case control passes to line 980, or A$< >"", in which case the rest of line 655 is ignored.

Experience is the best teacher of de-bugging, but a step-by-step approach and a disciplined method are invaluable aids. Take your time, and — above all — DON'T PANIC!

Speaking In Tongues

Basic has a familiar mathematical construction, and so is relatively easy to learn, but it is clumsy in relation to some of the other languages

Unless your home computer is a Jupiter Ace (uses FORTH) then it will almost certainly feature BASIC as its resident programming language. But that doesn't mean to say that you are restricted to that choice, and though BASIC is acknowledged as being a particularly easy language to learn, there are other far more suitable languages for writing specific applications. To install these on your computer it will be necessary either to replace the ROMs containing the BASIC interpreter, or to load the new language into RAM — in which case you will need a machine with a reasonable memory capacity so that there is RAM left over to contain your programs. A few home computers, such as the Sharp MZ-711, have anticipated this problem by also having the BASIC interpreter cassette loaded.

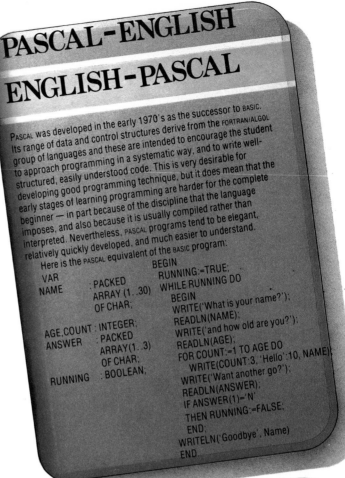

PASCAL-ENGLISH
ENGLISH-PASCAL

PASCAL was developed in the early 1970's as the successor to BASIC. Its range of data and control structures derive from the FORTRAN/ALGOL group of languages and these are intended to encourage the student to approach programming in a systematic way, and to write well-structured, easily understood code. This is very desirable for developing good programming technique, but it does mean that the early stages of learning programming are harder for the complete beginner — in part because of the discipline that the language imposes, and also because it is usually compiled rather than interpreted. Nevertheless, PASCAL programs tend to be elegant, relatively quickly developed, and much easier to understand.
Here is the PASCAL equivalent of the BASIC program:

```
VAR                       BEGIN
  NAME      : PACKED         RUNNING:=TRUE;
              ARRAY (1..30)   WHILE RUNNING DO
              OF CHAR;          BEGIN
                                 WRITE('What is your name?');
  AGE,COUNT : INTEGER;         READLN(NAME);
  ANSWER    : PACKED           WRITE('and how old are you?');
              ARRAY(1..3)      READLN(AGE);
              OF CHAR;         FOR COUNT:=1 TO AGE DO
                                 WRITE(COUNT:3, 'Hello':10, NAME);
  RUNNING   : BOOLEAN;        WRITE('Want another go?');
                             READLN(ANSWER);
                             IF ANSWER(1)='N'
                               THEN RUNNING:=FALSE;
                             END;
                           WRITELN('Goodbye', Name)
                           END
```

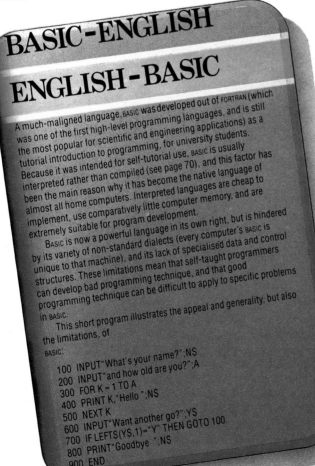

BASIC-ENGLISH
ENGLISH-BASIC

A much-maligned language, BASIC was developed out of FORTRAN (which was one of the first high-level programming languages, and is still the most popular for scientific and engineering applications) as a tutorial introduction to programming, for university students. Because it was intended for self-tutorial use, BASIC is usually interpreted rather than compiled (see page 70), and this factor has been the main reason why it has become the native language of almost all home computers. Interpreted languages are cheap to implement, use comparatively little computer memory, and are extremely suitable for program development.
    BASIC is now a powerful language in its own right, but is hindered by its variety of non-standard dialects (every computer's BASIC is unique to that machine), and its lack of specialised data and control structures. These limitations mean that self-taught programmers can develop bad programming technique, and that good programming technique can be difficult to apply to specific problems in BASIC.
    This short program illustrates the appeal and generality, but also the limitations, of BASIC:

```
100 INPUT"What's your name?";NS
200 INPUT"and how old are you?";A
300 FOR K = 1 TO A
400 PRINT K,"Hello ";NS
500 NEXT K
600 INPUT"Want another go?";YS
700 IF LEFTS(YS,1)="Y" THEN GOTO 100
800 PRINT"Goodbye ";NS
900 END
```

COMAL-ENGLISH
ENGLISH-COMAL

COMAL was developed to combine the accessibility of BASIC with the powerful structures and disciplined approach of PASCAL. It therefore resembles both, and may have been a model for the development of the BBC Micro's BASIC, which has almost developed into a new language. COMAL has been very successful in school computing and in Scandinavia (where it originated), but seems unlikely to displace either of its two forebears as the introductory programming language.
    This is the "Hello" Program in COMAL:

```
100    RUNNING:=TRUE
200    WHILE RUNNING DO
300       INPUT"What's your name? ";NS
400       INPUT"and how old are you? ";A
500       REPEAT
600          FOR K:=1 TO A DO
700             PRINT K,"Hello",NS
800          NEXT K
900       INPUT"Want another go";YS
1000      IF YS="N" THEN RUNNING:= FALSE
1100   ENDWHILE
1200   PRINT"Goodbye ";NS
```

LISP-ENGLISH
ENGLISH-LISP

LISP was developed in the early Sixties as a list processing language, and has since been widely used in the field of Artificial Intelligence, which involves continually searching and comparing lists of data, relationships and responses. Unlike BASIC, where the emphasis is on the flow of the program through a sequence of instructions and procedures, LISP is a 'functional' language, in which the elementary command set can be built up to form more sophisticated functions with names determined by the programmer. For example:

    (SETQ ARRAY1 '(4 7 2 5 1))

creates a list called ARRAY1 whose elements are the numbers (4 7 2 5 1).

    (CAR ARRAY1)

gives the first element of the list ARRAY1 (4, in this case).

    (CDR ARRAY1)

gives the list ARRAY1 with its first element removed — (7 2 5 1) in this case.

    (SETQ ARRAY1(CDR ARRAY1))

will turn the list ARRAY1 into a copy of itself excluding its first element.

LISP also lends itself to 'recursive' applications — problems that after a simple function is applied are reduced to a smaller but identical problem.

LOGO-ENGLISH
ENGLISH-LOGO

LOGO was developed by a psychologist working on Artificial Intelligence in the context of the classroom. It resembles FORTH in both its interactivity and its use of a number of 'primitives' that can be incorporated in user-defined functions. But the fundamental principle it embodies is that the way to learn something is to teach somebody else — namely the computer — how to do it. It is considered an innovative language that will create a completely new way of teaching children to think.

LOGO is usually called a 'turtle' language because it is often used to control a small wheeled robot called a turtle (see page 108).

Here is a LOGO fragment that draws a symbolic house as a square of specified size with a triangle on top:

```
TO TRIANGLE LENGTH
   REPEAT 3(FORWARD :LENGTH RIGHT 120)
END
TO SQUARE LENGTH
   REPEAT 4 (FORWARD :LENGTH RIGHT 90)
END
TO HOUSE LENGTH
   RIGHT 30
   TRIANGLE :LENGTH
   LEFT 90
   SQUARE :LENGTH
END
```

Now typing HOUSE 15 will cause a 'house' with a side length of 15 units to be drawn.

FORTH-ENGLISH
ENGLISH-FORTH

FORTH resembles LOGO in being a functional interactive language, but has the important distinction of being the first language other than BASIC to be implemented as native on a home computer — the Jupiter Ace. The language consists of a number of defined functions, called the 'primitives', and has the ability to define new functions in terms of these. Mathematical operations in FORTH are 'stack-oriented', which means that computer memory is treated as an expanding and contracting list of data and this results in the last operation always being at the head of the list. A further consequence of stack-orientation is that algebraic notation is not used. Instead of writing (12 + 4)/2 to find the mean of 12 and 4, in FORTH you must write 12 4 + 2 /, which is the same sum in Reverse Polish rather than algebraic notation.

All this makes FORTH a very different kind of language, forcing a very different view of problem-solving and computer processes. It's almost a step back down the high-level languages hierarchy.

This FORTH fragment defines two new words called SHOUT and CHORUS:

```
: SHOUT (prints "SHAZAM !")
     ."SHAZAM !";
: CHORUS (uses SHOUT in a loop)
     0 DO SHOUT LOOP;
```

Now typing n CHORUS will cause SHAZAM ! to be printed n times on the screen.

On these pages, we give you an overview of the most common programming languages available for home computers. As with human languages, the more programming languages you've mastered, the easier it is to adopt a new one.

TONY LODGE

Original Author

It is possible to write computer programs that will themselves generate other programs, or correct errors in human coding

'If computers are so smart, how come they need humans to program them?' Experienced computer users will tend to shrug off a question like this from a sceptical newcomer, but it is not as silly as it seems. Much research is being undertaken in writing programs that can generate other programs, and operating systems that can correct bugs in code written by humans.

Consider the SYNTAX ERROR? message, which is frequently encountered by home computer users. This can be infuriating because the message gives you so little information. A compiler on a large mainframe computer will generally give far more information as to the nature of the error encountered. For example, the error message could read:

```
1090 LET A=(C*2+F$)*((FG—C)*TH+1))
```

ERRORS: 1) MISMATCH — STRING VARIABLE F$
NOT ALLOWED
2) LAST CLOSE BRACKET NOT EXPECTED

There is no fundamental reason why such techniques cannot be used in an interpreter on a home computer — the cost of the extra ROM needed to store the routines would be minimal. But few home computers employ even cursory error monitoring procedures: most don't even check the syntax of the code as it is entered. However, it is often possible to buy additional ROM chips or plug-in software cartridges that will extend the range of BASIC commands available, particularly those related to the development and de-bugging of programs. These BASIC commands include:

HELP — prints out the program line and highlights the exact character position where program execution terminated. This will usually, but not always, indicate the source of the syntax error.

DUMP — prints a list of all variable names and their contents currently in use by the program. This is helpful in deducing how far the program had got in its task before the error occurred.

TRACE — displays (in a window in the corner of the screen) the line number (or numbers) currently being executed while the program is running. This helps the user to trace the flow of the program, and ensures, among other things that subroutines are being executed in the desired order.

Writing programs that allow a computer to correct human coding errors is, in general, not a simple task. But in the case of some errors it is fairly easy. For example, we know that all program lines have to start with a BASIC keyword (though some machines will allow you to drop the word LET). Therefore, if a line begins with PRUNT or PRONT, it would be easy to work out that it should say PRINT. In the Basic Programming chapter we will discuss the idea of fuzzy matching (algorithms for choosing the closest match to any phrase) and this could be applied to program keywords as well. Alternatively, the interpreter could simply include a list of common typing errors, and their correct equivalents. For safety, it would be desirable for the computer to check any alterations it makes with the operator.

But beyond these basic procedures, automatic correction becomes a great deal more difficult. In

Paper Money

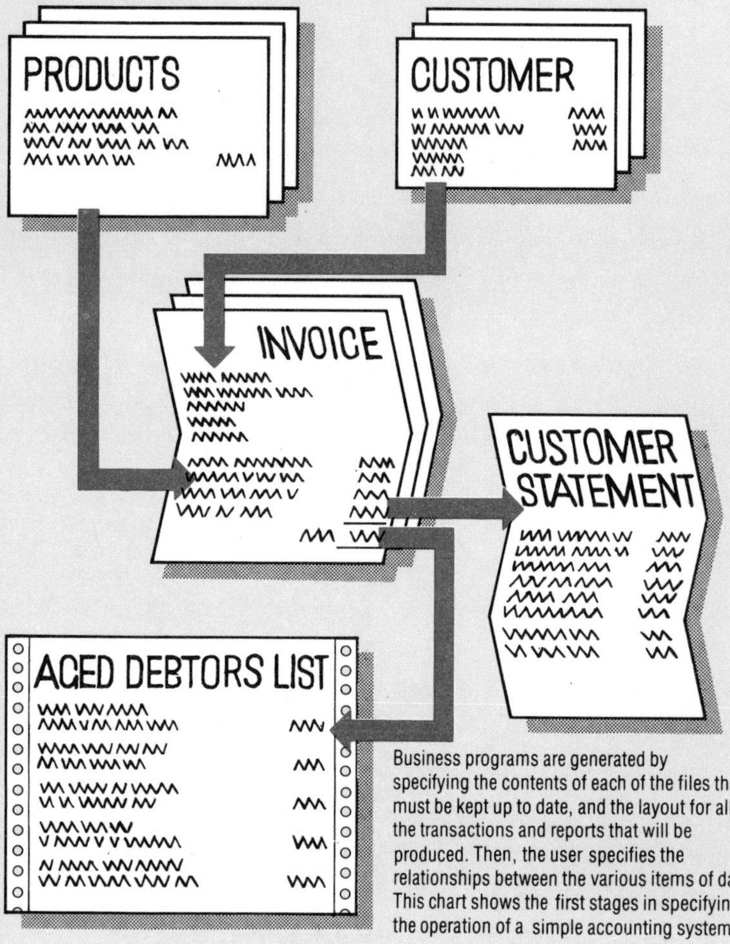

PRODUCTS

CUSTOMER

INVOICE

CUSTOMER STATEMENT

AGED DEBTORS LIST

Business programs are generated by specifying the contents of each of the files that must be kept up to date, and the layout for all the transactions and reports that will be produced. Then, the user specifies the relationships between the various items of data. This chart shows the first stages in specifying the operation of a simple accounting system

LIZ DIXON

the example we have given, is F$ a misprint for F or FS or F4? Or something entirely different? If you were to show the complete listing to another competent programmer, he should be able to identify the faults and make the corrections. He would use two criteria in making his decisions: the context in which the program line appeared, and his own experience.

Strangely enough, this technique has been more widely applied to correcting English text than to checking program code. A spelling checker package, for example, will work through a text and highlight any words that don't match the entries in its dictionary of perhaps 50,000 words, held on disk. Most of these packages have the facility to learn new words (such as the spelling of company or proper names) and add these to their dictionaries. The more sophisticated will even suggest the correct spelling if a close match is detected. Experimental word processors have also been developed that can apply the same processes to grammar and writing style — pointing out such things as incorrect punctuation, repetition of words within a paragraph, mixed metaphors, and inapplicable adjectives. Again, these work by examining the context of any phrase, and by reference to a library of previously used examples.

More effort, however, has been put into the development of systems that will *create* programs, rather than *correct* existing ones. In 1981, a software product was announced that set off one of the fiercest battles ever waged within the microcomputer industry. Cleverly named The Last One, it purported to be a program that could write any other program you might want, and hence was the last program you would ever need to buy. This proved to be an unjustified claim, but The Last One was a very useful aid in the development of certain types of program — mainly business applications. There are now several such products on the market for business microcomputers, and a few for home computers, and these are collectively called 'program generators'.

Let's now look at the basic concept behind a program that can write programs. Consider this trivial example:

```
10 PRINT "WHAT DO YOU WANT THE PROGRAM TO
   DISPLAY ON THE SCREEN?"
20 INPUT A$
30 PRINT "THE PROGRAM IS:"
40 PRINT "10 PRINT ";CHR$(34);A$;CHR$(34)
```

If you answer HELLO to the question, the program (which should run on most home computers) should print out the line:

```
THE PROGRAM IS
10 PRINT "HELLO"
```

If you apply the same technique to the input, calculation and output phases of the application you have in mind, then you could write yourself a very simple program generator. If all the questions that it asks are plainly worded, it should be possible for someone with no previous experience to develop a simple program using your generator.

Commercially produced program generators use the same techniques. Most business applications consist of a combination of five distinct processes: input of data, output to screen or printer, storage in a data file, retrieval, and calculation. The generator will have standard and very flexible subroutines for each of these. By asking you to specify the exact structure of the data you will be using, the calculations that go with that data, and the layouts you require on the screen and printer, the generator will change the values of certain variables in the subroutines, and string them together to create the program.

Although program generators are becoming more sophisticated, they are unlikely to replace human programmers in the immediate future because they suffer from the following limitations. First, the technique described is all very well for transaction-based business applications such as accounting or stock control, but generally these program generators can't be applied to writing word processor or games programs. Secondly, because the program generator has to make use of these standard flexible subroutines, the resulting listing won't be nearly as efficient (either in terms of speed or memory used) as it would have been if it had been purpose-written by a programmer. Thirdly, programs produced by generators generally aren't as user-friendly as the systems currently being produced by human programmers. For example, they seldom make good use of the graphics facilities offered by the latest machines.

Finally, the program generators that are now available can only really replace the final stage in programming — the writing of the code. The user still has to put the work into thinking out the exact form of the data, input and output that is needed. Generally, the earlier stages of programming are the most difficult, and require specific skills distinct from those of programming. Most large companies employ specialists called 'systems analysts' to specify the programs they need, and these specifications are then turned into code by programmers. Program generators have yet to acquire all the skills required to create a computer program.

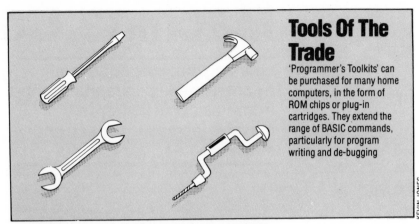

Tools Of The Trade
'Programmer's Toolkits' can be purchased for many home computers, in the form of ROM chips or plug-in cartridges. They extend the range of BASIC commands, particularly for program writing and de-bugging

KEVIN JONES

Machine Code

Learning machine code requires a considerable conceptual jump from Basic, but it offers a massive increase in speed and efficiency

A Step At A Time

The machine code program is stored in one area of memory, though the data that it operates on may well be elsewhere in memory. Note that the operands (e.g. $3F80) are stored in the form of two bytes, with the lower byte ($80) before the higher byte ($3F)

Memory Address

All machine code programs are made up from simple operations that transfer bytes of memory into the CPU's internal registers, process them, and return them to a location in memory. This diagram shows the program needed to add the contents of two locations, and store the result in a third

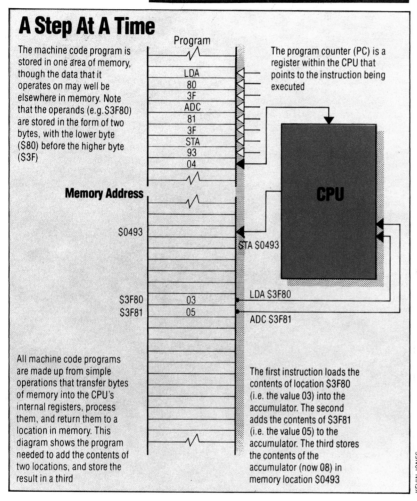

Program

LDA
80
3F
ADC
81
3F
STA
93
04

$0493

$3F80   03
$3F81   05

The program counter (PC) is a register within the CPU that points to the instruction being executed

CPU

STA $0493

LDA $3F80

ADC $3F81

The first instruction loads the contents of location $3F80 (i.e. the value 03) into the accumulator. The second adds the contents of $3F81 (i.e. the value 05) to the accumulator. The third stores the contents of the accumulator (now 08) in memory location $0493

KEVIN JONES

So far in this book, all our discussion of programming has been centred around the language BASIC, because it is both versatile and easy to use. However, as your experience grows, and the programming projects you tackle become more adventurous, it will not be long before you encounter the limitations of this language. You will soon find that graphics can't be moved around the screen as fast as you would like, and that you often have to resort to the confusing PEEK and POKE commands to make the best use of your machine's facilities.

By contrast, programming in machine code imposes very few constraints on what you can do, and compared with BASIC, gives the impression of almost infinite speed. However, comparatively few home computer owners make the jump from BASIC to machine code, partly because using machine code is a far more labour-intensive programming process, and also because it is conceptually quite different from BASIC or any other high level language. Nevertheless, it is extremely worthwhile to have an understanding of machine code; and in this article, the first of two, we look at the fundamental procedures involved in using it.

Machine code, as we have explained before, is the language understood by the microprocessor (the CPU) that forms the heart of your computer. This microprocessor can only perform very simple functions (it can add two digits of a number, for example, but can't multiply them). It does, however, perform these functions at very high speeds. Every operation of a microprocessor is specified in terms of the number of 'clock cycles' taken. If the CPU in your computer runs at 1 MHz, then a clock cycle is one microsecond, and an operation that takes four 'clock cycles' to perform does so in four millionths of a second.

As a consequence, any program written in machine code will consist of a large number of instructions, and any function must be built up 'by hand' from simple operations. All machine code programming consists of manipulating individual bits or bytes of memory, using simple logic functions like AND, OR and NOT, and elementary binary arithmetic.

This is one reason why writing machine code is a slow task; the other is that it is the programmer's responsibility to know where everything is kept in memory. In BASIC, whenever a statement like LET A=5 is encountered, it is the job of the BASIC interpreter to find a space in memory to store that variable. Furthermore, whenever A is referenced later in the program, it will remember where to look for the necessary data. When you first start programming in machine code you discover that you have to specify an address (a memory location) for every piece of data you need to store, and it is up to you to ensure that it is not accidentally overwritten with other pieces of data.

Let's look at what machine code consists of. (Incidentally, all our examples will refer to eight-bit CPUs, such as the Z80 and 6502; 16-bit devices work in a similar manner but process twice as many bits with each operation). The microprocessor is connected to the computer's memory by two busses (a bus is merely a group of wires or lines): the address bus and the data bus (see page 64). There is also something called the control bus, but this provides timing signals for the CPU and is not used by the programmer.

The address bus is 16 bits wide, and by placing a pattern of bits on this bus, the CPU can select any of the 65,536 bytes in its 'memory map' (see page 152). In a typical home computer, some of these locations will consist of RAM, some of ROM, some of special input/output chips, and some will be unused. If the CPU wants to read a memory location (one of the lines in the control bus indicates whether a read or write is to be performed), then the selected byte will place its contents on the data bus, in the form of a pattern of eight bits. Similarly, the CPU can write a pattern of eight bits into any chosen location. The CPU has no knowledge of which parts of memory are ROM and RAM, so getting the addresses right is another crucial responsibility of the programmer.

Inside the microprocessor, there are perhaps half a dozen 'registers', which are like individual memory locations and are used for storing temporary results and performing the logic and binary arithmetic functions. Most of these registers are equivalent to one byte of memory, though some are 16 bits wide. One of the latter type is called the Program Counter (PC) register, and this contains the address in memory of the machine code instruction that is currently being performed. You can think of this as being similar to the line number in a BASIC program.

Another of the most important registers (but this time just eight bits wide) is the 'accumulator'. As the name suggests, this register can accumulate totals (that is to say, bytes can be added to it or subtracted from it), and indeed this is usually the only register that can perform any kind of arithmetic. So, a very simple machine code program might be specified as follows:

1) Load the accumulator with the contents of memory location $3F80. Addresses in machine code are usually written in hexadecimal (base 16). Hexadecimal numbers are indicated in writing by prefixing a special sign, usually a $.

2) Add to the accumulator the contents of memory location $3F81, allowing for the fact that the result may be larger than can be stored in a single byte — in which case there will be a 'carry bit' as well.

3) Store the new contents of the accumulator (i.e. the result) in memory location $0493.

Each of these constitutes a machine code instruction, and the program would normally be written thus:

```
LDA $3F80    (LoaD Accumulator)
ADC $3F81    (ADd with Carry)
STA $0493    (STore Accumulator)
```

The comments in brackets, like BASIC REMark statements, have no effect. The first entry on each line is called the 'opcode', and this indicates the nature of the operation. The second column contains the 'operand' — the details of, or whereabouts of, the data that is to be operated on. A microprocessor will usually feature several dozen possible opcodes (that is to say, it can perform several dozen types of simple operation), and each opcode will occupy just one byte of memory when it has been entered into the machine.

An opcode can therefore by specified as a number in the range 0-255 (or, more properly, in the hex range $00 to $FF). However, while a program is being developed, it is more usual to make the listing more readable by using three

KEVIN JONES

Flashing Lights
The idea for the huge panels of lights often seen on computers in films came from the 'front panel' found on many mini-computers. This front panel was a line of lights and switches representing the CPU's address and data buses. Before keyboards were interfaced, all machine code programs had to be entered in binary in this form

letter mnemonics, such as LDA, ADC and STA.

Each of the three operands shown consists of a hex number in the range $0000 to $FFFF, and uses up two bytes of program memory space. However, some operands are just one byte long, and some opcodes don't have operands at all. The short program that we have given would therefore occupy a total of only nine bytes — not including the three memory locations ($3F80, $3F81, and $0493) that the program will operate on. For this trivial exercise, the following BASIC program would achieve exactly the same effect, but would occupy nearly 50 bytes and perform the operation at least a hundred times slower, because of all the time taken by the interpreter to translate it:

```
10 A = PEEK (16256)
20 A = A + PEEK (16257)
30 POKE 1171,A
```

N.B. The locations used by this particular program may not be suitable for your machine.

In the next two pages of The Art Of Programming, we'll look at how machine code is entered into a computer and run, and the different ways in which machine code is expressed.

LDA

STA

ADC

SBC

JMP

LDA — LoaD Accumulator
Transfers the contents of a single memory location (byte) into the internal accumulator register

STA — STore Accumulator
Performs the opposite process to LDA

ADC — ADd with Carry
Adds the contents of a memory location to the current contents of the accumulator, creating a carry bit if necessary

SBC — SuBtract with Carry
This is the inverse function of ADC

JMP — JuMP
Transfers program operation to a new location. This is similar in operation to a BASIC GOTO statement

Opcodes
These are just a few of the opcodes (types of operation or instruction) that a typical microprocessor can execute

Assembly Line

Continuing our introduction to machine code, we look at the many different forms in which programs can be expressed — from binary to Assembly language

One of the conceptual difficulties that most newcomers experience with machine code is that the programs can take various forms. Any data stored in computer memory ultimately takes the form of eight-bit binary numbers. However, when these are listed out on paper, they occupy a lot of space, are difficult to read and remember, and are prone to typing mistakes. So instead we usually make use of hexadecimal numbers. This has the advantage that the contents of any byte can be expressed as a two-digit number, and any address in the computer's memory range (0 to 65535 in decimal) can be represented by four digits.

When we write a hex number on paper we usually precede it with a $ sign to distinguish it from a decimal number, although the sign does not feature in the computer's memory when the program has been entered. Secondly, when an opcode has a two-byte operand (e.g. LDA $3F80) the two bytes are entered into the machine in the opposite order — i.e. the low byte followed by the high byte. In the example given, therefore, the three bytes would be AD (the hex representation of the LDA opcode in 6502 language) followed by 80, followed by 3F. This makes things easier for the processor, but it can be confusing for the user.

Usually a machine code program is printed as a 'hex dump' — a long list of two-digit hexadecimal values. In addition, a starting address will be given (either in hex or decimal) and the first hex value must be loaded into this location, the second into the next location, and so on. Loading can be achieved by means of the BASIC POKE command. If the starting address is $1000 (4096 in decimal) and the hex dump is:

AD	(173 in decimal)
80	(128 in decimal)
3F	(63 in decimal)

the program can be loaded with the three BASIC statements:

```
POKE 4096,173
POKE 4097,128
POKE 4098,63
```

Note how we have to convert all the values from hex to decimal before they can be used in the POKE statement — inside the machine they will be stored in binary.

For longer hex dumps it is normal to use a short BASIC program called a 'machine code loader'. This asks for the start address and then the hex values. As each is entered, the short BASIC routine converts the hex value to decimal, and POKEs it into the next location. Alternatively, the hex dump can be READ by the program from DATA statements.

Once the machine code has been loaded, the BASIC loader program can be dispensed with. It's therefore important to load the machine code somewhere in memory where it won't be 'trampled over' by the BASIC program, nor be

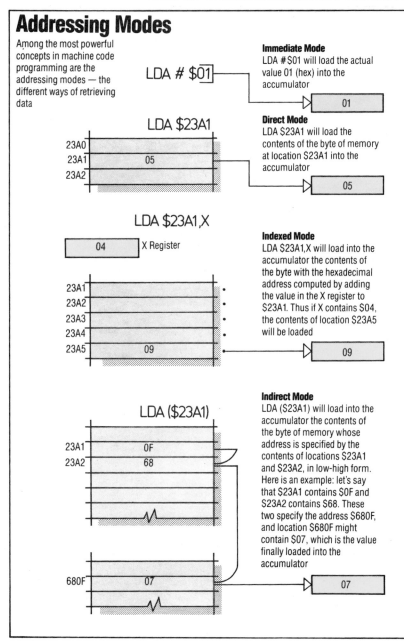

Addressing Modes

Among the most powerful concepts in machine code programming are the addressing modes — the different ways of retrieving data

LDA # $01

Immediate Mode
LDA #$01 will load the actual value 01 (hex) into the accumulator

LDA $23A1

Direct Mode
LDA $23A1 will load the contents of the byte of memory at location $23A1 into the accumulator

LDA $23A1,X

Indexed Mode
LDA $23A1,X will load into the accumulator the contents of the byte with the hexadecimal address computed by adding the value in the X register to $23A1. Thus if X contains $04, the contents of location $23A5 will be loaded

LDA ($23A1)

Indirect Mode
LDA ($23A1) will load into the accumulator the contents of the byte of memory whose address is specified by the contents of locations $23A1 and $23A2, in low-high form. Here is an example: let's say that $23A1 contains $0F and $23A2 contains $68. These two specify the address $680F, and location $680F might contain $07, which is the value finally loaded into the accumulator

Longhand/Shorthand

A machine code program can take on several different forms. It is usually written by the programmer in the form of Assembly language, which uses mnemonics for opcodes and labels for operands, thus:

```
LDA WEIGHT
ADC FUEL
STA WEIGHT
```

We must however specify the addresses of those labels. For example:

```
FUEL = $03EE
WEIGHT = $031F
```

An assembler package would transform this into a hex dump, using a disk drive. 'Pseudo assembly language', as shown below, is less easy to read, but can often be entered into a package called a 'spot assembler', which doesn't need disks.

```
LDA $031F
ADC $03EE
STA $031F
```

A hex dump consists of a starting address (at the left) and the sequence of two-digit hex values as they will appear in memory. Note that an operand like $031F is stored in reverse order (1F 03) and that opcodes have been replaced by the appropriate hex value:

```
19C4 AD 1F 03 6D EE 03 8D 1F 03
```

obliterated by BASIC statements such as NEW.

Most home computers have some BASIC command to tell the machine to stop executing BASIC and begin executing the machine code program that starts at a specific location. One form of this command is SYS 4096 (RETURN), meaning 'transfer control to the system starting at decimal location 4096'; another is CALL $E651, meaning 'call the machine code routine starting at hex location E651'.

The machine code subroutine or program will then execute this system or routine (it may or may not produce any visible results, depending on the nature of the program). If it is correctly written and incorporates the proper terminating procedure, control will be passed back to BASIC. This means, incidentally, that it is possible to call machine code subroutines from several places in the operation of a BASIC program, whenever a function needs to be performed at high speed.

One of the difficulties of programming in machine code is that if you have made a mistake in your code, the computer won't come back with a nice helpful SYNTAX ERROR. It will more than likely 'crash' instead: the machine won't respond to anything you type. This isn't harmful to the computer, but you will have to reset it (or switch the machine off and then on again), and that usually means having to enter the program again from scratch. That's why you can't experiment in machine code as you can in BASIC — the operation of the program must be thoroughly checked on paper before it is entered into the computer.

However, a software device that can assist greatly in the entering and checking of machine code is the 'machine code monitor' (which has nothing to do with a monitor screen). This is built

into the ROMs of a few computers but is generally purchased as a cassette or cartridge-based package. A machine code monitor is a simple operating system that will display on the screen the contents of any requested section of memory. These (hex) values can simply be altered or written over, so a monitor is by far the fastest way of entering a hex dump. Moreover, it usually allows you to load and save machine code programs directly onto cassette, without the need for the BASIC loader program. The most advanced machine code utility programs presently available show the precise contents of each of the central processing unit's internal registers.

Hex dumps are a convenient way of expressing machine code, but they aren't easy to read. Unless you happen to remember the hexadecimal equivalent of all the various opcodes, it's almost impossible to distinguish the opcodes from the operands. So programs are usually written using the three-letter mnemonics that we introduced in the previous article (page 162), and these are then translated into hex using a table of codes from the microprocessor's handbook.

However, a more sophisticated form of machine code monitor will allow you to type in the program in mnemonics, performing the conversions automatically. This is called a 'spot assembler' because it will assemble the mnemonics into numbers on the spot.

This leads us on to the final form in which machine code can be expressed — Assembly language — which not only makes use of mnemonics for the opcodes but can handle names (or labels) instead of hex numbers for the operands. Thus, if location $07B2 contains the current number of missiles fired in a game, we can load this into the accumulator with the instruction:

```
LDA MISSIL
```

At the start of the program we will have to specify the location of MISSIL=$07B2, and that this location should initially contain the value of $09 (nine missiles).

When we have finished developing this program in Assembly language (called the 'source code' of the program), we run a utility program called an assembler. This works through the code, replacing mnemonics and any labels with their hex equivalent, thereby creating a new version called the 'object code'. This code can then be entered into the computer's memory and run. The process is not dissimilar to compiling (see page 70), though in this case there is a one-to-one correspondence between the source and object code.

Assembly language, being a higher-level language than machine code, is considerably easier to write, but there is no loss in performance. However, assembler packages will usually only work with a disk drive, and so are not available to all home computer users.

JSR
Jump SubRoutine
This function is equivalent to BASIC's GOSUB. JSR $354D will change the contents of the program counter (PC) register so that it executes the code from $354D onwards

RTS
ReTurn from Subroutine
On encountering RTS, the processor will jump back to the location from which the subroutine was called (i.e. equivalent to RETURN in BASIC). RTS has no operand because the return address will have automatically been stored in a special area of memory called the Stack

BMI
Branch if Minus
This is one of several forms of conditional branching in machine code (in BASIC, IF . . . THEN GOTO is a conditional branch). If the result of the last operation resulted in a negative value in the accumulator, program execution will jump to a specified address. BPL specifies Branch if PLus

LDX
LoaD X register
X is another single byte register within the processor, and while it cannot perform arithmetic in the same way as the accumulator, it is used for 'indexed addressing' (see panel). LDX loads a value into X, and STX (STore X) will store it back in memory

INX
INcrement X
By adding 1 to the value of X (DEX — DEcrement X — will subtract 1), and using indexed addressing, it is possible to step through a number of locations in memory, performing the same process on each

Basic Programming Course

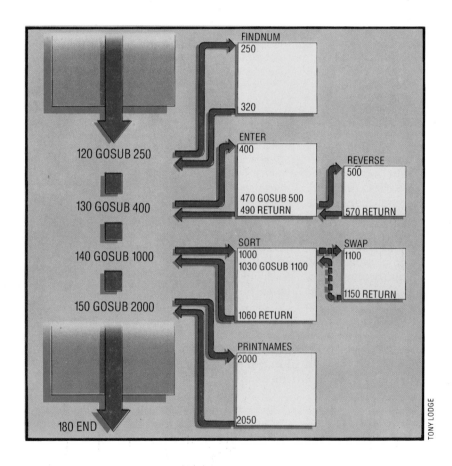

A thorough step-by-step course in BASIC, the most widely used programming language, followed by a major project – a computerised address book – with the emphasis on sound programming practice.

Simply Obeying Orders

Your computer will do exactly what you want when you 'talk' to it in the right way — and it won't make mistakes

Other Languages

BASIC is used by more people on more microcomputers than any other programming language. But BASIC is by no means the only one. Before the days of microcomputers, when most computing was done on room-sized mainframe computers, scientists and engineers used a language called FORTRAN. In the world of micros, other popular languages include PASCAL, FORTH, and LOGO.

Pascal

Like BASIC, PASCAL was developed primarily as a teaching language for student programmers. It is held in high regard by teachers of programming because it encourages the writing of well thought out and elegant programs. PASCAL is usually supplied on floppy disk and tends to be expensive. A low-cost cassette version is available for the Spectrum for under £30. The PASCAL language can be used for writing large and sophisticated programs

Forth

Programs written in the FORTH language look much less like English than BASIC or PASCAL. FORTH is also more difficult to learn. It has the advantage of great power in the sense that complex programs can be written in a few lines. FORTH allows you to define your own commands, whereas in BASIC they are pre-defined

Logo

LOGO is a relatively new language becoming popular in education. It has the great advantage of being simple enough for even quite young children to learn. It can help teach programming techniques and also encourages a logical approach to program design from an early stage. LOGO uses 'turtle' graphics which allow pictures to be easily produced on the screen. A mechanical turtle (see page 108) can also be connected to the computer. Simple commands typed in on the keyboard can move the turtle and make it draw lines and shapes

It is perfectly possible for anyone to use a computer — at home or at work — without knowing anything at all about how the computer works. Starting here, the Basic Programming Course begins a step-by-step series that explains, from the beginning, all you need to know to be able to create your own computer programs successfully.

Many people find that after a while, the pre-packaged programs and games they've bought for their computer start to become a little boring and they wonder if they can modify them or even write their own. But a computer can do nothing by itself. It must be given a list of instructions telling it in minute detail exactly what to do and how to go about achieving it. These instructions form what is called a *program* and the art of creating them is called *programming*.

There is nothing difficult about programming. You don't even have to be good at maths, unless, of course, you want to write programs to perform mathematical tasks. All you need to begin with is to understand BASIC.

Your First Language

Most home computers are provided with a built-in computer language called BASIC. As its name implies, it is designed to enable beginners to learn the rudiments of programming quickly and easily. Like any human language, BASIC has it own grammar, vocabulary and syntax, although the vocabulary is far smaller than that of English. BASIC uses a number of short English words that are easily recognisable and simple to learn. As a general-purpose language it is suitable for both the novice and the more experienced user.

But one drawback with the language is that over the years, different computer manufacturers have tended to include their own modifications. The result is that there are a large number of variations in BASIC, particularly regarding the commands for controlling the more recently developed aspects of the machine — such as colour, graphics and sounds. Any variations of BASIC which occur in the most popular computers are shown in the 'Basic Flavours' box in each lesson.

Because of the variations in BASIC from computer to computer, it is nearly impossible to write a BASIC program of any complexity that will run on every computer. Fortunately, however, the language has a common core, which is usually the same in all machines. We'll start by concentrating on that core, and as the course progresses we will work steadily towards more complex programs.

The Initial Steps

Let's begin by writing a small program and seeing what happens. This one will show the computer apparently making a mistake. Switch on the computer and type in the program exactly as shown, including all the spaces. The <CR> at the end of each line is to remind you to hit Carriage Return. On your computer, this key may be labelled RETURN, ENTER or even ↵.

```
10 REM COMPUTERS NEVER MAKE
     MISTAKES<CR>
20 PRINT "TYPE IN A NUMBER"<CR>
30 INPUT A<CR>
40 LET A = A + 1<CR>
50 PRINT "I THINK THE NUMBER YOU TYPED
     WAS   ";<CR>
60 PRINT A<CR>
70 END<CR>
```

After you have typed it all in, type LIST<CR>. The program you just typed should reappear on the screen. LIST is an instruction to the computer to 'print' a listing of the program in memory. If the program appeared on the screen properly after typing LIST, we could try to RUN it. If you make a mistake when typing in the program, don't worry. After you have LISTed the program, simply retype any line containing a mistake. Don't forget the line number. Try typing

25 REM HERE IS ANOTHER 'REM' LINE<CR>

and then LIST the program again. To get rid of the line, type the line number alone, followed by <CR>. When you are satisfied the program has been typed correctly, you can 'run' it by typing RUN<CR>. Try this and you should see on the screen:

TYPE IN A NUMBER

Go ahead and type a number. Try 7. (Use numerals — the computer won't recognise 'seven' as 7 unless we specially program it to do so.) If you typed in 7, the screen should look like this:

I THINK THE NUMBER YOU TYPED WAS 8

Did the computer really make a mistake, or was it simply obeying orders? If we look at the program line by line we can see what each instruction made the computer do. Here's the first line:

10 REM COMPUTERS NEVER MAKE MISTAKES

REM stands for REMark. Anything appearing on the same line after REM is ignored by the computer. Remarks are a handy way of reminding yourself what the computer is doing. This particular REM is just a title — it does not tell us what the program is doing. We'll see how helpful properly written REMs are later in the course. Now let's look at:

20 PRINT "TYPE IN A NUMBER"

When BASIC gets to the word PRINT, the part that follows it is 'printed' on the computer screen. Notice that the sentence is enclosed in double quote marks. One of BASIC's rules is that the characters (letters) appearing inside double quote marks after a PRINT statement will appear on the screen exactly as they were typed in. We'll see another way of using PRINT in line 60. Next comes:

30 INPUT A

We'll skip this line for now and come back to it after looking at line 40.

40 LET A = A + 1

The letter A is used here as a variable. A variable is like a labelled box that can contain either a number or some characters. Instead of having to remember what's in the box, all we have to know is what the box is called in order to reference it. It's like saying "Pass me the box labelled B" instead of "Pass me the box containing the 15mm cheese-head screws".

In this line we have a 'box' called A. This box is called a variable, because the value of what we put in it can vary. We can assign virtually any value to a variable. A value was assigned to variable A in line 30, so let's see how it was done:

30 INPUT A

Using the word INPUT is one of the ways in BASIC of assigning (giving) a specific value to a variable. When the BASIC program gets to a line starting with INPUT it waits for something to be typed in from the keyboard. INPUT A lets the computer know that we have a variable called A and that whatever is typed in at the keyboard will be assigned to that variable. Typing 7<CR> at this point puts 7 in box A, or to use computer jargon, assigns the value 7 to variable A. Now that we know what a variable is, and one of the ways of assigning a value to it, let's look at line 40 again.

40 LET A = A + 1

The name of the variable to which a value is assigned always appears on the left of the equals sign. Here we are giving a new value to A. The statement means 'LET the new value of A equal the old value plus 1.' The old value of A was 7. We have now made it 7 + 1, so the new value is 8.

50 PRINT "I THINK THE NUMBER YOU TYPED WAS ";

This is our print statement again. It 'prints' the character string (that is, the words or numbers you have typed) between the double quote marks. Notice the semi-colon at the end of the line. It helps to specify the positions at which things are printed on the screen. Later in the course we'll return to how the semi-colon is used in more detail. Now let's look at:

60 PRINT A

Here's another PRINT statement, but this time there are no quote marks around the A. We already know that the program will not print an actual A on the screen because we have seen that quote marks are needed to do that. Without the quotes, BASIC looks for a variable with the same label as the character after PRINT. If it finds one, it prints the value of the variable. (If it doesn't find one, it gives an error message!) This program already has a variable called A and so BASIC prints its value — what is it?

If you thought the answer was 7, remember that BASIC works through programs line by line,

The box below shows how 'variables' are used in BASIC. It also illustrates how the GOTO statement (see next page) is used to form a loop

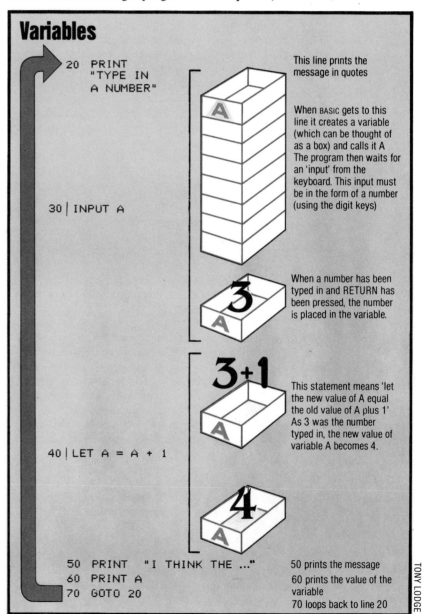

Variables

```
20   PRINT
     "TYPE IN
     A NUMBER"

30 | INPUT A

40 | LET A = A + 1

50   PRINT   "I THINK THE ..."
60   PRINT A
70   GOTO 20
```

This line prints the message in quotes

When BASIC gets to this line it creates a variable (which can be thought of as a box) and calls it A The program then waits for an 'input' from the keyboard. This input must be in the form of a number (using the digit keys)

When a number has been typed in and RETURN has been pressed, the number is placed in the variable.

This statement means 'let the new value of A equal the old value of A plus 1' As 3 was the number typed in, the new value of variable A becomes 4.

50 prints the message
60 prints the value of the variable
70 loops back to line 20

TONY LODGE

Basic Flavours

 Only the Sinclair Spectrum uses the LET part of the instruction. On other computers this is implied, meaning it can be left off. For example, line 20 can be written as A = A + 1 instead of LET A = A + 1

 This is not used on the Spectrum. The last line of the program typed in is assumed to be the end of the program. It can just be replaced by STOP

 Appears on the screen as two words (GO TO) on the Spectrum, although only one key is pressed. Most other computers, with the exception of the BBC, will accept the instruction typed as two words

following the order of the line numbers. By the time we got to line 60 the value of A had already been changed to 8, and that is what it will print. Finally we come to:

70 END

The END statement tells BASIC that the end of the program has been reached. Some versions of BASIC insist that all programs should finish with END while others do not (see the 'Basic Flavours' box).

Notice that when you run the program it only 'works' once. To get it to go through once more you have to type RUN<CR> again. Now we'll look at a way of getting the program to work as many times as we want by using the GOTO statement.

Using GOTO

The same program but with an extra line is given below. If you have switched off the computer to take a break, type it in. Otherwise all you need to do is to type in lines 70 and 80. These are shown in blue in the listing below.

```
10 REM COMPUTERS NEVER MAKE
   MISTAKES<CR>
20 PRINT "TYPE IN A NUMBER"<CR>
30 INPUT A<CR>
40 LET A = A + 1<CR>
50 PRINT "I THINK THE NUMBER YOU TYPED
   WAS " ; <CR>
60 PRINT A<CR>
70 GOTO 20<CR>
80 END<CR>
```

After you have typed it all in and LISTed it, see if you can figure out what will happen before you try to RUN it. Then type RUN<CR> and, as in the first version of the program, you should see:

TYPE IN A NUMBER

Type in any number (using the numeral keys) and hit RETURN. The computer will add 1 to the number and display it at the end of the message.

I THINK THE NUMBER YOU TYPED WAS 8

You will see that this is immediately followed by the TYPE IN A NUMBER message again. Entering another number and hitting return again makes the program cycle like this *ad infinitum*. The reason this happens can be found in line 70:

70 GOTO 20

When BASIC reaches a GOTO statement, instead of continuing to the next line, it GOes TO the line number specified. Here it is directed back to line 20 and the whole program is run all over again. It goes on looping back like this forever. If you want to stop the program from running you'll find there's no way of getting out of the loop. The program just goes on and on waiting for your input.

As you would expect, there are ways of writing the program so that we can get out of it if we want to, and we'll look at one of these in the next instalment of this course. Meanwhile, we still have to stop the program. If your computer has a BREAK key, it can be used to stop the program from running. Typing RUN<CR> will start the program again.

Notice that we still have the END statement at the end of the program. The way we have written this program, with the GOTO 20 statement creating an endless loop, we never do get to the end, but some versions of BASIC insist that we always use an END at the end!

If you can't find a way of stopping the program, try hitting the RESET key. That is almost certain to halt the program. Then try to LIST it again. If you get a list, you will be able to 'edit' the program in the exercises below. If you do not get a list, it means the RESET on your computer destroys the program in memory and you will then have to type the whole thing in again.

Exercises

These questions are carefully graded and are designed to be fun. Working through exercises is one of the best ways of checking that you have understood the material presented and are making genuine progress.

Before starting the exercises, try changing a few of the lines to see the effect on the way the program runs. You can't possibly do the computer any harm even if you make mistakes or hit the wrong keys. To change a line, type in the program and then check the result by LISTing it. The whole program will appear on the screen again. Type the number of the line you want to change followed by the new line. Try this:

10 REM COMPUTERS SOMETIMES MAKE
   MISTAKES<CR>

then type LIST again. Notice how the first line has been changed. If you want to get rid of everything in the line, just type the line number followed by <CR>. Try:

10<CR>
LIST

Line 10 should have disappeared. Put line 10 back in by typing out the whole line again — not forgetting the line number!

■ Rewrite the program so that the computer really does print out the number typed in. Hint: taking out one whole line should do the trick.

■ Retype line 70 so that the program goes to line 80. LIST the program. RUN the program. Why didn't it run the same way as before?

■ Change line 60 so that the computer prints an A on the screen instead of the value of variable A.

■ Rewrite line 60 so that the computer prints the value of variable A once again. Remove line 10 (the REM line) completely. RUN the program. Does it run any differently?

■ Put in a new REMark on line 25. New lines can be added by simply typing the new number followed by the new statement. Put in a remark on line 25 to remind you what will happen next — it could be something like 'expects an input from the keyboard'. After you have typed the new line and

hit <CR>, LIST the program again and check that your new remark appears in the right place.

■ Rewrite the program so that it multiplies the number you type in by 10. You'll need to change line 50 to print something like THE NUMBER YOU TYPED MULTIPLIED BY 10 IS. This time we will not want to add to the value of the old variable, we'll wants to multiply it by 10. BASIC uses the * sign to mean 'multiply'. (Don't use an X because BASIC only recognises it as a letter, not as a multiplication sign.)

We have now covered quite a lot of ground. We have seen how to write comments, which BASIC calls REMarks, how to PRINT character strings on the screen, how to PRINT the value of a variable on the screen, and how to make the program GOTO a specified line number.

Next we'll see how to get out of a loop by using an IF-THEN statement. We'll find out how to get the program to 'perform' for us a specified number of times instead of looping forever. And we'll also see how to slow the program down to make the computer look as if it's really having to think.

And Then There Was BASIC

Today, BASIC is the world's most popular programming language. Computer languages were invented to allow the human operator to communicate more easily with the machine, and BASIC is one of the easiest to learn and use. It consists of instructions in simple English combined, where necessary, with the mathematical symbols found on a typewriter keyboard.

BASIC is a quick language to master. Within a few minutes of unpacking a microcomputer you can be writing simple programs. It was devised in 1965 at Dartmouth College, New Hampshire, with the express purpose of simplifying existing languages. The inventors were two teachers, Thomas Kurtz and John Kemeny. The universal use of BASIC has meant slight variations in the language have crept in. But the core of BASIC remains common to all manufacturers.

A program is a sequence of instructions which the computer executes to perform a specified task. The task might be to produce a monthly financial forecast, or to move a Space Invader across the television screen. The program appears as a series of numbered lines. Each line contains one instruction and the number allows the computer to obey the commands in the right order. Commands are quickly learnt and even the most complicated

BASIC has taken the mystique out of programming and made computing accessible to everyone

program uses nothing more than combinations and repetitions of the elementary commands.

Most computers arrive from the manufacturers with BASIC built in. Computers can also be programmed in 'machine code' (described as a 'low' level language because it is close in structure to the logic found in the electronic circuits). BASIC is a 'high' level language as it is nearer to everyday English. There are many other high level languages devised for more technical and specialised applications, but BASIC is the best introduction to them all. It's a simple and powerful language.

Looping The Loop

Breaking out of loops, going round them a required number of times, and line numbering are covered in the second part of our programming course

We ended the last part of the 'Basic Programming' course with the program listed below. It worked fine but because of the GOTO in line 70 the program kept looping back to the beginning and never stopped. The only way to get out of the loop was to use the BREAK key or the RESET key.

Now we are going to look at one of the ways we can get out of a loop like this by incorporating a test in the program. The usual way it's done is to test for a number we would never actually want to use in the program. The program allowed us to type in a number that the computer then printed on the screen with a 1 added to it. We might decide that we would never want to enter a number bigger than 999. In that case we could test to see if the number that has been input is greater than 999. Type in the program and then add:

35 IF A > 999 THEN GOTO 80<CR>

Now run the program again and it will function as before — unless, that is, you enter a number greater than 999. Try typing 1000<CR> and see what happens.

Why did the program stop this time? The IF in line 35 is what made it happen. When BASIC finds an IF statement it knows that a logical test is coming. The > sign means 'greater than'. Line 35 therefore means IF (variable) A (is greater than) 999 THEN GOTO (line) 80. If you just typed in 1000, the value of A becomes 1000 which is greater than 999 so the program THEN GOes TO line 80 which is the end of the program. If A is not greater than 999, the THEN part of the line is ignored and the program continues to the next line.

When running this program, then, you can input numbers as often as you like, just as long as they are not greater than 999. As soon as a number bigger than 999 is input, the IF-THEN statement detects the fact and terminates the program by GOing TO the END. When a BASIC program has reached the end or been terminated, you will be given a 'ready' prompt on the screen. Depending on your computer, this prompt may take several forms. On the BBC Microcomputer the ready prompt is a sign like this: >. On the Dragon it's OK. On the Sord it's READY. Whatever form it takes, the ready prompt is BASIC's way of telling you that no program is running and that it is awaiting further orders.

There is a lot of variation in the way different versions of BASIC use THEN. Details are given in the 'Basic Flavours' box on page 173.

Other comparisons used in BASIC are < (less than), = (equals), >= (greater than or equal to), <= (less than or equal to) and <> (not equal to). We'll see these comparisons used often as the course progresses.

Before continuing any further, it's worth trying out a few exercises to get the feel of using these comparisons.

Exercises

■ Change one of the lines so that the program will be aborted if A = 1000.

■ Change one of the lines so that the program will be aborted if the number input is less than zero.

■ Change the GOTO line so that it makes the program loop back to the beginning if A is equal to or less than 500. Hint: you will not need a separate IF-THEN line and a GOTO line.

Discovering FOR-NEXT

When writing programs there will be many occasions when you would like some items in the program to be repeated a precise number of times. The GOTO in line 70 enabled the program to loop as many times as we wanted. We later added an IF-THEN statement in line 35 which enabled us to escape by entering an 'out of range' number.

```
10 REM COMPUTERS NEVER MAKE MISTAKES
20 PRINT "TYPE IN A NUMBER"
30 INPUT A
40 LET A = A + 1
50 PRINT "I THINK THE NUMBER YOU TYPED WAS ";
60 PRINT A
70 GOTO 20
80 END
```

The FOR-NEXT Loop In BASIC

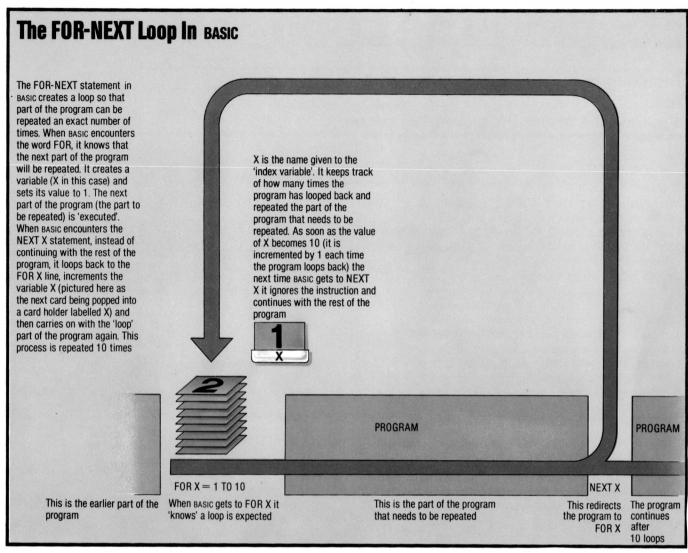

The FOR-NEXT statement in BASIC creates a loop so that part of the program can be repeated an exact number of times. When BASIC encounters the word FOR, it knows that the next part of the program will be repeated. It creates a variable (X in this case) and sets its value to 1. The next part of the program (the part to be repeated) is 'executed'. When BASIC encounters the NEXT X statement, instead of continuing with the rest of the program, it loops back to the FOR X line, increments the variable X (pictured here as the next card being popped into a card holder labelled X) and then carries on with the 'loop' part of the program again. This process is repeated 10 times

X is the name given to the 'index variable'. It keeps track of how many times the program has looped back and repeated the part of the program that needs to be repeated. As soon as the value of X becomes 10 (it is incremented by 1 each time the program loops back) the next time BASIC gets to NEXT X it ignores the instruction and continues with the rest of the program

PROGRAM

PROGRAM

FOR X = 1 TO 10

NEXT X

This is the earlier part of the program

When BASIC gets to FOR X it 'knows' a loop is expected

This is the part of the program that needs to be repeated

This redirects the program to FOR X

The program continues after 10 loops

However, there are occasions, as we learnt in the first part of the course, when using GOTO to make a loop is not the best way of doing things.

Let's return to our old program, modified now to tell the truth this time, to multiply the number input by 10, and do it exactly eight times.

```
10 REM MULTIPLY BY 10
20 FOR X = 1 TO 8
30 PRINT "TYPE IN A NUMBER"
40 INPUT A
50 LET A = A * 10
60 PRINT "YOUR NUMBER MULTIPLIED BY 10
   IS ";
70 PRINT A
80 NEXT X
90 END
```

Type this program in, LIST it to check for mistakes and then RUN it. You will be asked for a number only eight times. After that the program simply stops. The reason this happens is to be found in line 20.

```
20 FOR X = 1 TO 8
```

This is part of a FOR-NEXT loop. It is one of the most useful structures BASIC has to offer. It deserves careful study.

The way we have used it here, we have created a variable called X. (Variables are explained in the first part of the course on page 168.) We could have called it anything (except A — which we are using for something else). FOR must always be used with a corresponding NEXT, but the NEXT will appear later in the program — after the portion to be repeated. The FOR part of a FOR-NEXT loop always has the following form:

FOR variable = starting value TO final value

In our example FOR X = 1 TO 8 we have called the variable X and given it an initial value of 1. The next part of the program is then executed by the computer; the number we typed in is multiplied by 10 and then printed on the screen. After that we get to NEXT X and the program loops back to where variable X is — in line 20. As soon as it has done that it increments X by 1, so X acquires a value of 2. The part of the program within the FOR-NEXT loop is then executed again. On coming to NEXT again in line 80, the program loops back and increments X to 3.

The program continues to repeat like this until X has been incremented to 8. After that, the loop is terminated; NEXT X does not go back to FOR X and the program continues to the next line.

More Uses For FOR-NEXT Loops

FOR-NEXT loops are often used to create delays in the program. There are times when you don't want everything done at maximum speed and so you introduce a delay. You probably found that the answers in the MULTIPLY BY 10 program flashed up so quickly they seemed instantaneous. Let's make the computer look as if it's having to think before it answers by using FOR-NEXT to insert a delay. Add the lines shown in blue type to your program.

```
10 REM MULTIPLY BY 10
20 FOR X = 1 TO 8
30  PRINT "TYPE IN A NUMBER"
40 INPUT A
50 LET A = A * 10
52 FOR D = 1 TO 1000
54 NEXT D
60 PRINT "YOUR NUMBER MULTIPLIED BY 10
   IS ";
70 PRINT A
80 NEXT X
90 END
```

We have added another two lines, 52 and 54, inside our original FOR-NEXT loop. Let's look at them.

```
52 FOR D = 1 TO 1000
54 NEXT D
```

D is set to 1 and the program goes to the next line. This is the corresponding NEXT statement. Nothing actually happens inside the loop, the program simply loops back to line 52 and increments D to 2. This happens 1000 times before the program goes to the next part — which is printing the answer. Computers are fast, but everything takes a finite time, so looping back 1000 times takes a noticeable amount of time. Computers vary in the time they take to loop. On the Epson HX-20 this FOR-NEXT loop takes 2.9 seconds, while on the Spectrum it takes 4.5 seconds. Experiment by changing the number you use as the upper limit in line 52.

To make the computer behave more like a human being, add these three lines:

```
56 PRINT "NOW LET ME SEE. . ."
57 FOR E = 1 TO 1000
58 NEXT E
```

LIST the program and RUN it. We now have two delays that do absolutely nothing except waste time.

Add these two lines:

```
.51 REM THIS LOOP WASTES TIME
55 REM THIS WASTES MORE TIME
```

Now LIST the program and have a good look at it. Notice how all the extra lines we have added have fitted into exactly the right places. Which brings us to the last point in this part of the course — line numbers.

We started our original program with line 10 and went up in jumps of 10 for each new line, ending with line 90. We could have chosen any numbers, for example 1, 2, 3 . . . 9. But if we had done that, how would we have fitted in the extra lines? Programmers always have afterthoughts and improvements to make, so allow for these by leaving big gaps between line numbers in the 'Mark I' versions of their programs. You could even start with line number 100 and go up in jumps of 50 or 100 if you wanted.

Some versions of BASIC include a useful command called AUTO. BBC BASIC has it, so does the Epson HX-20. The Dragon, Sinclair computers and the VIC 20 do not. If your BASIC has AUTO you can save a lot of time by having the line numbers generated for you automatically. Find out if your BASIC has AUTO by typing:

AUTO 100, 10<CR>

If your BASIC does have AUTO you will see on the screen:

100

The screen shows the number 100 followed by a space and then the *cursor*. The cursor is a mark (sometimes a line, or a square) that shows on the screen where the next character will appear. You can start entering the first line of the program from the cursor position. When you hit <CR> the next line will appear automatically, starting with the line number 110. AUTO, if you have it, can either be used by itself, or with one or two 'arguments'. *Argument* is a mathematical term. In the expression $2 + 3 = 5$, the arguments are 2 and 3. With the AUTO command, it can be used just by itself (i.e. AUTO<CR>) or with one 'argument' (e.g. AUTO 100<CR>) or with two arguments (e.g. AUTO 300,50). AUTO by itself usually causes line numbers to start with 10 and to go up in increments (jumps) of 10. If only one argument is used (e.g. AUTO 100<CR>) the first number will be 100 (in this case) and then the numbers will go up in the 'default value' — which again is usually 10. If you specify two arguments, the first number specifies the starting line number and the second number specifies the increment. AUTO 250,50<CR> will give a starting number of 250, the next number will be 300 and so on in increments of 50. Even on the simplest micro, you're unlikely ever to run out of lines.

In the next two pages of this course we will look at various ways of improving the visual presentation of the program on the screen and different ways of printing out data.

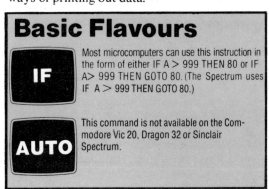

Basic Flavours

IF — Most microcomputers can use this instruction in the form of either IF A > 999 THEN 80 or IF A> 999 THEN GOTO 80. (The Spectrum uses IF A > 999 THEN GOTO 80.)

AUTO — This command is not available on the Commodore Vic 20, Dragon 32 or Sinclair Spectrum.

To The Point

Why you have to pay attention to every detail of punctuation when you write a computer program

You may well have noticed, in the program listing in the first part of Basic Programming (page 167) that there is a semi-colon at the end of line 50. The function of this punctuation mark in BASIC was not explained at the time, but is nevertheless very important. It is used in almost all versions of BASIC to concatenate printed sections ('concatenate' means 'join together'). Lines 50 and 60 on page 167 were:

```
50 PRINT "I THINK THE NUMBER YOU TYPED
   WAS ";
60 PRINT A
```

Line 50 printed the words inside the double quote marks. Line 60 printed the value of the variable A. Putting in the semi-colon caused the value of variable A to be printed directly after the words within quotes in line 50. If no semi-colon had been used, it would have been printed on the line following the words.

The program below has been designed to illustrate some of the useful properties of the semi-colon as it is used in BASIC. Try typing it in and running it. From now on, we will omit the <CR> reminder at the end of each line to indicate that you should press the RETURN key. This next program allows you to enter a range of temperatures in Centigrade (also known as Celsius) and have them converted automatically to their equivalents in Fahrenheit.

Enter this program, LIST it to check that it has been entered correctly, and then RUN it. First you will be asked to enter the lowest temperature. Try typing in −6. Then you will be asked to enter the highest temperature. Try typing in 10. The program will convert all temperatures at one degree intervals from −6 to 10 degrees Centigrade to their Fahrenheit equivalents. You should get a

'printout' on the screen looking something like:

Notice that the columns are not very even because of the decimal points, but that each value in Centigrade is printed with its equivalent in Fahrenheit on a single line. After you have run the program a few times, re-type line 80 just as it is, but substitute commas wherever we have printed semi-colons. RUN the program again. As you can see, the printout becomes a complete mess.

To see why this happened, let's try a very simple program to compare the effect of commas compared with the effect of semi-colons. Type NEW<CR>. Then enter:

```
10 REM COMPARE ; WITH ,
20 PRINT "THIS LINE USES SEMI-COLONS"
30 PRINT "H";"E";"L";"P"
40 PRINT "THIS LINE USES COMMAS"
50 PRINT "H", "E", "L", "P"
60 END
```

When BASIC prints line 30 it will appear on the screen as HELP, whereas line 50 will appear as H E L P. See the 'Basic Flavours' box for variations between different machines. The comma has many uses in BASIC, but in PRINT statements it has the effect of making the individual items appear on the screen (or on a paper printout) spaced out, usually by between 8 and 16 spaces depending on the version of BASIC. If the PRINT statement is used without either commas or semi-colons, the items will be printed out on separate lines.

Apart from illustrating BASIC's use of the semi-colon, our temperature conversion program also revises several statements covered in the first two parts of the Basic Programming course. Lines 30 and 50 set variables L and H to the values for the lowest and highest temperatures we want to convert. Line 60 is the first part of a FOR-NEXT loop. It seems to differ from the FOR-NEXT loop we have encountered so far by using letters instead of numbers. In fact, there is no difference. The letters we are using here, L and H, are variables with numeric values corresponding to the values typed in at the INPUT L and INPUT H stage of the program. If, as suggested earlier, you entered −6 and 10, the statement FOR X = L TO H is therefore equivalent to FOR X = −6 TO 10.

Line 80 in effect says: PRINT the value of X (which starts at the lowest temperature and increments by 1 each time up to the highest temperature) followed directly on the same line (that's why we used the semi-colon) by the words in quotes, followed directly again (another semi-colon) by the value of F. If you look carefully at F, you will see that it is the current value of the Centigrade temperature, converted into Fahrenheit by multiplying it by nine, dividing it by five and then adding 32. The NEXT X line ensures that we go through the conversions until the upper limit in the FOR-NEXT loop has been reached.

Before going on to look at a more sophisticated variation on the PRINT statement, it is worth taking a second look at line 70 in our temperature conversion program:

```
70 LET F = X * 9 / 5 + 32
```

This line assigns a value to the variable F (which stands for Fahrenheit). The program first takes the value of X (the temperature in Centigrade), multiplies it by 9, divides that by 5 and then adds 32. The way this formula would be presented in an ordinary arithmetic book is $F = C \times 9 \div 5 + 32$. BASIC uses * for multiplication, / for division, + for addition and − for subtraction.

In ordinary arithmetic, and in BASIC too, the order in which arithmetical operations are carried out is important. Multiplication always has top priority, followed by division, followed by addition, followed by subtraction. If parts of an arithmetic expression are enclosed in round brackets, they must be evaluated first. If you want an addition to be performed first, before a multiplication, the addition part must be enclosed in brackets. For example, if you wanted to know how much money you had in your current account plus your savings account in dollars, you might express it in part of a program like this:

```
D = (C + S) * 1.5
```

If your current account has £600 (C) and your savings account has £1,300 (S) and there are 1.5 dollars to the pound, you will want to add the pounds first (C + S) and then multiply by 1.5 to convert to dollars. Without the brackets, the value of your savings account would first be multiplied by 1.5 and then the value of your current account would be added to the result — not what you wanted at all! Always be sure to check that the arithmetic parts will be calculated in the right order.

Print Using

In order to look at a final refinement to our temperature conversion program, try typing it in again and RUNing it. Enter, say, −10 as the value for the lowest temperature and 10 as the value for the highest. As we have already seen, the printout on the screen is very ragged. This is because of the semi-colons used in line 80 in order to concatenate (run together) all the parts being printed, instead of printing them on separate lines. Which is fine, except that the space taken up by the figures —

both the Centigrade and the Fahrenheit ones — varies. This has the effect of pulling the columns out of alignment and making the printout look untidy.

Almost all versions of BASIC have a special PRINT feature called PRINT USING. It allows the appearance of the printed numbers or words to be 'formatted' or tidied up. If you want to print the value of X and that value is known in advance to range from, say, −99 to 99, the figures can be printed out correctly aligned by using PRINT USING "###";X. The three 'hash' signs allow up to three digits, or two digits preceded by a minus sign, to be printed. If more than three digits are entered, they will not be printed out correctly. If, however, only two digits are entered (or only one) they will be positioned correctly. If decimal points are required, they can be included in the appropriate position within the hash signs. For example, the statement can take the form PRINT USING "###.##";X. Use one 'hash' sign for each digit. All the decimal points will line up automatically.

Modify the original program by changing line 80 and adding lines 82, 84 and 86:

```
80 PRINT USING "###";X;
82 PRINT " IN CENTIGRADE IS ";
84 PRINT USING "###.##";F;
86 PRINT " IN FAHRENHEIT"
```

LIST the program again and then RUN it. All the columns should now be lined up perfectly.

We will find out how to 'save' programs, so that they do not need to be re-typed every time, in the next instalment of the course.

Exercises

■ Try entering a 'lowest temperature' of −1000. Why doesn't the program work this time? How would you modify the PRINT USING statement in line 80 to make it work?

■ Alter line 84 so that only whole numbers (no decimal fractions) are printed.

■ Write a program to convert a range of figures in pounds to dollars, using an exchange rate of $1.50 to the £.

Basic Flavours

PRINT USING This facility is not available on the Commodore 64, Oric, Spectrum, ZX81 or BBC Micro. However, the BBC can limit the number of decimal places to be printed, and this is achieved by using the following instruction:
@%=131594

COMMA The use of a comma between print fields will separate the items to be printed by causing the second one to begin at the next pre-set tab position. The spacing that this gives rise to will vary according to the lengths of the print fields and the number of characters in one line of the particular computer's display

Routine Matters

Programs within programs: we introduce a new feature of Basic that will keep your programs neat and manageable

In previous instalments of our Basic Programming course we have typed in programs, run them, made modifications to them and then cleared the memory (using the NEW command) when we wanted to enter new programs. When we have needed to run the old program again, it has been necessary to type the whole thing in again.

To save this repetitious work, all versions of BASIC are provided with a command that allows any program to be stored on cassette tape. The program below can be saved on tape by using the simple command SAVE followed by a file name. The program calculates the number of tiles needed to tile a room.

```
10 REM THIS PROGRAM CALCULATES THE
   NUMBER OF TILES
20 REM NEEDED TO TILE A ROOM
30 PRINT "ENTER THE SIZE OF SIDE OF TILE IN
   MM"
40 INPUT A1
45 LET T = 0
50 REM LINE 60 FINDS AREA OF TILE
60 LET A2 = A1 * A1
70 PRINT "ENTER THE NUMBER OF WALLS"
80 REM W SETS LIMIT FOR LOOP
90 INPUT W
100 FOR X = 1 TO W
110 PRINT "LENGTH OF WALL NO."; X; "IN METRES"
120 REM D IS DIMENSION OF WALL
130 INPUT D
140 REM IT IS CONVERTED TO MM
150 REM IN THE SUBROUTINE
160 GOSUB 380
170 REM LINE 190 SETS L TO
180 REM LENGTH OF WALL IN MM
190 LET L = D2
200 PRINT "HEIGHT OF WALL NO."; X; "IN METRES"
210 REM LINES 230 TO 250 SET H
220 REM TO HEIGHT OF WALL IN MM
230 INPUT D
240 GOSUB 380
250 LET H = D2
260 REM LINE 270 SETS A3 TO AREA OF WALL
270 LET A3 = L * H
280 REM S (SUB-TOTAL) IS AREA OF WALL DIVIDED
290 REM BY AREA OF TILE
300 LET S = A3/A2
310 REM T (TOTAL) HAS THE NEW SUB-TOTAL
320 REM ADDED EACH TIME THRU THE LOOP
330 LET T = T + S
340 NEXT X
350 REM PRINT THE TOTAL
360 PRINT T
370 END
380 LET D2 = D*1000
390 RETURN
```

Having typed in the program, all you need to do to save it on cassette tape is to use the SAVE command. First, of course, the cassette recorder must be set up in accordance with the instructions in your computer's handbook. The SAVE command is extremely easy to use. Just type SAVE followed by a file name in double quotation marks. A file name is the name given to a file, and a file, in computer terms, is like a file in a filing cabinet — a program or set of data that can be stored away or retrieved when required. It is best to use a file name that will remind you of the function of the program. Since our program calculates the number of tiles needed to tile a room, we could call it "TILES". Once the cassette recorder is set up, insert a blank tape to hold the program.

Cassette decks with a remote control socket can usually have the motor controlled directly by the computer. Otherwise, set the recorder in the record mode and then put it in the pause mode. Type in the SAVE command, including the file name. Set the recorder running by releasing the pause control and then hit RETURN.

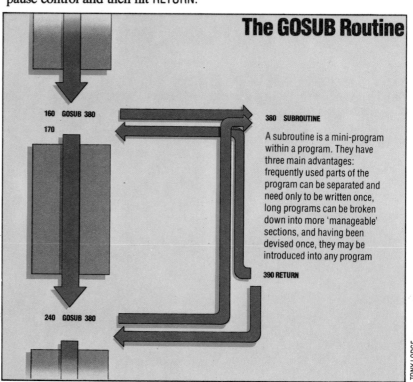

The GOSUB Routine

160 GOSUB 380
170

240 GOSUB 380

380 SUBROUTINE

A subroutine is a mini-program within a program. They have three main advantages: frequently used parts of the program can be separated and need only to be written once, long programs can be broken down into more 'manageable' sections, and having been devised once, they may be introduced into any program

390 RETURN

TONY LODGE

To test that the program has been recorded correctly, erase the computer's memory by typing NEW‹CR›. Rewind the cassette, put it into the play mode and then load the program back into the computer using the LOAD command. LOAD must be followed by the file name of the file wanted. Type LOAD "TILES" and then hit RETURN.

After the program has been loaded into the computer, a message on the screen such as READY or OK indicates that the load has been completed. LIST the program and check that it is the same as the one you typed in.

GOSUB

GOSUB is a statement that diverts the flow of a program to a subroutine. A subroutine is like a separate mini-program or program-within-a-program. In the program used to illustrate it here, the subroutine is very simple. It is included to show the principle, although other ways could easily have been devised to produce the same results without using a subroutine.

Our program calculates the number of tiles needed to tile a room by finding out the area of the tiles used. It then asks for the length and height of each wall to be entered. It works out the area of the wall after the length and height has been converted from metres to millimetres. The number of tiles needed is found by dividing each wall's area by the area of a tile and adding the results. The conversion of wall length and height into millimetres is done in the subroutine, which simply multiplies the length or height (in metres) by 1000 to find the equivalent in millimetres.

Subroutines have three advantages. Frequently used parts of programs can be separated off and only need to be written once — no matter how often the operation is required. They allow long and complex programs to be broken down into more manageable and easily understood units or sections. Finally, subroutines can be re-used in any program where its function is appropriate.

In our program, the subroutine starts at line 380 and consists of only one statement: LET D2 = D * 1000. This takes D, the wall dimension (length or height) and multiplies it by 1000 to convert from metres to millimetres. The result is assigned to variable D2.

The instruction that forces the program to go to the subroutine is GOSUB. It occurs first in line 160. Variable D was assigned the value of the length of the wall in line 130. Line 160 forces the program to go to the subroutine, where variable D2 is given the value of D multiplied by 1000. The RETURN instruction in line 390 is needed to make the program return from the subroutine to the main program. Subroutines always return to the line after the GOSUB statement, in this case, to line 170.

The next occurrence of GOSUB is in line 240, which 'calls' the same subroutine. This time, the subroutine RETURNs to line 250. Although this program uses only one subroutine, it is possible to use as many as are needed. In every case, the GOSUB statement will have to include the line number of the appropriate subroutine. Notice that the END statement occurs in line 370, before the subroutine. END indicates the end of the main program and also serves to stop the program from running on through the subroutines after it has been completed.

Although this program is a little longer than previous programs in this chapter, it is really no more complex. Try and follow it through, line by line, and see what is happening at each stage. Apart from GOSUB and subroutines this program introduces only one new concept — longer variable names.

It may be helpful to draw boxes with the variable names written on them and to write in the values at each stage.

Line 300: LET S = A3/A2 will sometimes give a number with a decimal fraction. Try running the program and entering the tile size as 110mm and the wall length and height as 2.3 and 1.8 metres respectively, using just one wall. You should get an answer of 342.149 tiles. Since tiles are never sold in units of less than one, this answer is not completely appropriate. Next time we will look at one of the ways of getting an appropriate answer in whole numbers.

Exercises

■ See what happens if you enter the size of the tile as 0mm. You should get an error message at the end of the run. Why is this? Why don't you get a similar error message when you enter the length of one of the walls as 0 metres? Hint: multiplying by zero and dividing by zero are not the same thing — try it on your calculator!

■ The program only works for square tiles. See if you can change lines 30 to 60 to find the area of rectangular tiles (just as we found the area of rectangular walls later in the program).

■ Add a statement at line 355 to increase the total number of tiles by five per cent to allow for wastage. Multiplying a number by 105/100 will increase it by five per cent.

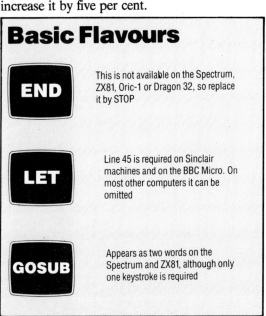

Basic Flavours

END — This is not available on the Spectrum, ZX81, Oric-1 or Dragon 32, so replace it by STOP

LET — Line 45 is required on Sinclair machines and on the BBC Micro. On most other computers it can be omitted

GOSUB — Appears as two words on the Spectrum and ZX81, although only one keystroke is required

Christmas In Basic

We introduce new commands for dealing with data and write a program to work out the number of days until Christmas

This program revises all the topics covered so far in our programming course, and also introduces several new and powerful BASIC statements. The purpose of the program is to calculate the number of days remaining until Christmas.

If you look at the program listing, you will see that it starts with a list of the variables used. This practice is certainly not essential, but is advisable as it can make your programs much easier to understand when you come to look at them later. Some versions of BASIC allow variables to have long names, DAY for example, rather than the single letters we have been using. If you are lucky enough to have a BASIC that allows long variable names, choose meaningful names. DAY, MONTH or DAYNUM are much better than A, X or D. If you have no choice in the matter because your BASIC does not allow long variable names, listing the variables at the top of the program makes it almost as 'readable'.

When the program is run, the first thing that will appear on the screen will be the PRINT statements starting at line 230. These state briefly what the program will do and then prompt the user to type in the date in the form shown, using commas to separate the day, month and year.

The first unfamiliar statement will be in line 300. This is a DIMension statement. It is used to set the number of items or elements allowed in the array labelled X. An array, sometimes called a subscripted variable, is like an ordinary variable except that the box contains several compartments. In line 300 we are creating a variable called X with 13 compartments inside the box. We shall return to the subject of arrays and the DIM statement in more detail later in the course.

310 INPUT D, M$, Y

This line is an ordinary INPUT statement except that it expects three inputs. D is a numeric variable that will contain today's date. Y is another numeric variable for the year. M$ is slightly different. It is called a 'string variable' and this is indicated by the $ (dollar) sign. A string variable accepts characters from the keyboard as well as numbers. If, for example, we type 23, JANUARY, 1983, variable D will be assigned the value 23, variable M$ will be assigned the character string JANUARY and variable Y will be assigned the value 1983.

330 GOSUB 560 REM 'NO OF MONTH' ROUTINE

This statement instructs the program to branch to the subroutine starting at line 560. Note, also that a REMark has been inserted on the same line. If there is room on the line, it is not always necessary to put REMs on a new line. This particular subroutine is only used by the main program once, and strictly speaking could just as easily have been incorporated into the main program. Making it into a subroutine just keeps this part separate from the rest of the program.

When the program was originally written, a number was used for the month and this part of the program was not needed. Later it was decided to allow the month to be entered as a typed word spelled out in full. In order to convert the spell-out month into its equivalent number, the extra program now forming this subroutine was written separately. The only change needed to the main (original) program was to add a single GOSUB statement. This subroutine illustrates the ease with which programs can be built up in blocks and linked together using the GOSUB and RETURN statements.

The subroutine itself is very simple, but illustrates how clever BASIC is at manipulating character strings. Suppose we had entered JANUARY as the month part of the INPUT statement. Variable M$ would then be assigned the character string JANUARY. The first line of the subroutine is:

560 IF M$ = "JANUARY" THEN LET M = 1

This statement compares the contents of M$ with the characters inside the double quotation marks. If they are the same (as they are in this case) the line goes on to set the value of numeric variable M to 1. Do not confuse variable M with variable M$. They are different. Only one can contain a string variable, the one with the $ sign! After checking to see if M$ is the same as the string JANUARY, the program moves to the next line and checks to see if the contents of M$ are the same as FEBRUARY. It is not, so M is not set to 2. Only where the match is correct will variable M be set to a value, and that value is the same as the number of the month — 1 for January, 3 for March and so on.

On getting to line 680 BASIC RETURNs to the main program, to the line after the GOSUB statement. This is line 340. It contains a REM but no comment. It is inserted simply to space out the program and to make it easier to read.

Lines 350 to 370 are a FOR—NEXT loop. This increments the value of I, starting with 1 and counting up to 13. The variable I is used as the subscript of the array X in line 360. It should be examined carefully.

360 READ X (I)

READ is a new statement we have not encountered before. READ is always used with a corresponding DATA statement. The DATA statement for this line is in line 510:

DATA 31, 28, 31, 30, 31, 30, 31, 31, 30, 31, 30, 25, 0

These numbers, except for the last two, are the numbers of days in each month of the year. The two lines are equivalent to 13 separate LET statements

LET X(1) = 31
LET X(2) = 28
LET X(3) = 31
LET X(4) = 30
LEX X(5) = 31
LET X(6) = 30
LET X(7) = 31
LET X(8) = 31
LET X(9) = 30
LET X(10) = 31
LET X(11) = 30
LET X(12) = 25
LET X(13) = 0

The loop set up in line 350 makes I count up from 1 to 13 so we were able to substitute X(I) for X(1), X(2), X(3) etc.

Before returning to this program, let's consider a far simpler small program:

10 READ A, B, C
20 LET D = A + B + C
30 PRINT D
40 DATA 5, 10, 20

Here, the READ statement in line 10 reads the first item of DATA in line 40 and 'writes' its value into the first variable. In other words, it assigns the value 5 to variable A. READ then reads the next item of data and puts it in the next variable. This program makes A = 5, B = 10 and C = 20. It then adds these and assigns the result to variable D. This result, 35, is then PRINTed in line 30.

Back to the 'Christmas' program. The first time round the loop starting in line 350, the value of I is set out to 1. Line 360 is therefore equivalent to READ X(1). The corresponding data item in line 510 is 31 (the first item). Consequently X(1) is set to 31.

The second time round the loop, I becomes 2 so line 360 is equivalent to READ X(2). The next data item in the DATA line is 28. This means that X(2) is set to 28. In this way all 13 'compartments' in the subscripted variable X are filled up with the number of days in each month; except for the 12th compartment, which has only 25 days in it, and the 13th, which has 0. (Can you see why?)

390 GOSUB 750 REM 'LEAP YEAR' ROUTINE

This line directs the program to a subroutine that checks if the year entered is a leap year or not.

```
100 REM   LIST OF VARIABLES
110 REM
120 REM   D = TODAY'S DATE
130 REM   M$ = NAME OF MONTH
140 REM   Y = YEAR
150 REM   I = INDEX 1
160 REM   X = ARRAY FOR DAYS IN EACH MONTH
170 REM   R = REMAINING DAYS
180 REM   M = NO. OF MONTH
190 REM   L = INDEX 2
200 REM   Z = INT. VALUE OF Y/4
210 REM
220 REM
230 PRINT "THIS PROGRAM CALCULATES"
240 PRINT "THE NUMBER OF DAYS REMAINING"
250 PRINT "UNTIL CHRISTMAS"
260 PRINT
270 PRINT "ENTER TODAY'S DAY,MONTH,YEAR"
280 PRINT "E.G. 12,JULY,1984"
290 PRINT
300 DIM X(13)
310 INPUT D,M$,Y
320 REM
330 GOSUB 560    REM 'NO OF MONTH' ROUTINE
340 REM
350 FOR I = 1 TO 13
360 READ X(I)
370 NEXT I
380 REM
390 GOSUB 750    REM 'LEAP YEAR' ROUTINE
400 REM
410 LET R = X(M) - D
420 FOR L = M TO 11
430 LET M = M + 1
440 LET R = R + X(M)
450 NEXT L
460 REM
470 IF R = 1 THEN GOTO 500
480 PRINT "THERE ARE";R;"DAYS LEFT UNTIL CHRISTMAS"
490 GOTO 520
500 PRINT "THERE IS 1 DAY LEFT UNTIL CHRISTMAS"
510 DATA 31,28,31,30,31,30,31,31,30,31,30,25,0
520 END
530 REM
540 REM
550 REM
560 IF M$ = "JANUARY" THEN LET M = 1
570 IF M$ = "FEBRUARY" THEN LET M = 2
580 IF M$ = "MARCH" THEN LET M = 3
590 IF M$ = "APRIL" THEN LET M = 4
600 IF M$ = "MAY" THEN LET M = 5
610 IF M$ = "JUNE" THEN LET M = 6
620 IF M$ = "JULY" THEN LET M = 7
630 IF M$ = "AUGUST" THEN LET M = 8
640 IF M$ = "SEPTEMBER" THEN LET M = 9
650 IF M$ = "OCTOBER" THEN LET M = 10
660 IF M$ = "NOVEMBER" THEN LET M = 11
670 IF M$ = "DECEMBER" THEN LET M = 12
680 RETURN
690 REM
700 REM
710 REM
720 REM NOTE: THIS ROUTINE DOES NOT CHECK
730 REM          FOR LEAP YEARS AT THE END OF
740 REM          EACH CENTURY
750 LET Y = Y / 4
760 LET Z = INT(Y)
770 IF Y - Z = 0 THEN GOTO 790
780 RETURN
790 LET X(2) = X(2) + 1
800 RETURN
```

```
750 LET Y = Y/4
760 LET Z = INT(Y)
770 IF Y−Z = 0 THEN GOTO 790
780 RETURN
790 LET X(2) = X(2) + 1
800 RETURN
```

A leap year is defined as one which is wholly divisible by the number 4. If it is a century, it must also be divisible by 400 to qualify as a leap year. To keep it simple, we have not attempted to check the century, only the divisibility by 4.

Line 750 sets Y to the old value of Y (the year) divided by 4. The new Y will be a whole number if the year is exactly divisible by 4. Otherwise it will have a decimal fraction.

Line 760 uses the function INT to find the 'integer' value of Y. Integer means whole number. While having no effect on integers, the INTeger function will round down fractional numbers to the nearest whole number. The number to be rounded down is placed in brackets after INT. Alternatively, a variable name can be put in the brackets. So LET Z = INT(496.25) would set Z to 496.

Line 770 subtracts Z from Y and checks to see if the result is 0. If it is, it means the year is a leap year (as there was no decimal fraction in the new Y). If that is the case, the program branches to line 790 using GOTO. Line 790 adds 1 to the second item in the array (the second item was 28, the number of days in an ordinary February).

If the result of the subtraction in line 770 was not zero, X(2) is left as it is and the subroutine RETURNs to the main program, to line 400.

Line 400 is another REM used just to space out the program to aid readability. The next line that actually does something is 410, where R is the variable holding the number of remaining days. It is set here to the number of days in the month entered minus the day entered. If we had entered, for example, 12, FEBRUARY, 1983, D would be equal to 12 and M would be 2. Therefore X(M) would be the same as X(2) and the second item in the X array is 28 (it would not have had 1 added to it as 1983 is not a leap year). Consequently R will be set to 28 − 12, i.e. 16, the number of days remaining in the current month, February.

Line 420 starts another loop. This one is designed to increment the value of M. Can you see why we say FOR L = 1 TO 11 rather than FOR L = 1 TO 12? If M was 2 because we had entered the month as FEBRUARY, line 430 will increment it to 3. Line 440 then sets R, the number of days remaining, to the old R plus X(M). The latter is now equivalent to X(3) since M has been incremented by 1. The value of X(3) is 31, the number of days in March. Line 440 therefore sets the new value of R to 16 + 31 (16 was the result of subtracting 12 from 28). The next time round the loop, M is incremented to 4 and the number of days in April, X(4), is added to the old value of R. The variable R therefore becomes 16 + 31 + 30.

The last circuit through the loop occurs when L = 11, and X(12)'s value, 25, is added to R.

What happens to the loop if a December date is input, so that M = 12? Because of the discrepancy in the limits, some machines skip the loop entirely, while others execute it once, so that X(13) is added to R. X(13) has been set to 0 to give the correct result.

```
470 IF R = 1 THEN GOTO 500
```

This line simply checks if there is only one day remaining to Christmas so that we get a grammatically correct sentence on the screen. If R is not 1, there must be more than one day remaining, so the PRINT statement in line 480 will be grammatically correct.

So that's all there is to it. The version of BASIC we have used should run on most computers (see the 'Basic Flavours' box) except possibly for the 'leap year' subroutine. BASIC is very inconsistent in the way it uses LET. If lines like IF M$ = "SEPTEMBER" THEN LET M = 9 do not work on your computer, the subroutine can be rewritten like this:

```
560 IF M$ = "JANUARY" THEN GOTO 900
570 IF M$ = "FEBRUARY" THEN GOTO 910
580 IF M$ = "MARCH" THEN GOTO 920
            :
900 LET M = 1
905 RETURN
910 LET M = 2
915 RETURN
920 LET M = 3
925 RETURN
(...and so on)
```

This solution is more space-consuming and less easy to follow with all its GOTOs and RETURNs. However, it does demonstrate that there are usually several ways of solving every problem.

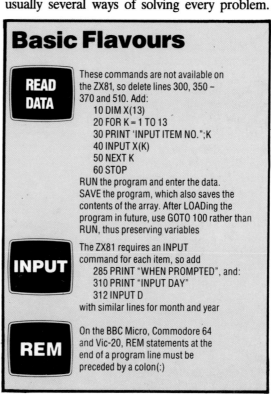

Basic Flavours

READ DATA

These commands are not available on the ZX81, so delete lines 300, 350 – 370 and 510. Add:
```
10 DIM X(13)
20 FOR K = 1 TO 13
30 PRINT 'INPUT ITEM NO.';K
40 INPUT X(K)
50 NEXT K
60 STOP
```
RUN the program and enter the data. SAVE the program, which also saves the contents of the array. After LOADing the program in future, use GOTO 100 rather than RUN, thus preserving variables

INPUT

The ZX81 requires an INPUT command for each item, so add
```
285 PRINT "WHEN PROMPTED", and:
310 PRINT "INPUT DAY"
312 INPUT D
```
with similar lines for month and year

REM

On the BBC Micro, Commodore 64 and Vic-20, REM statements at the end of a program line must be preceded by a colon (:)

Braving The Elements

Subscripted variables, unlike their simple counterparts, can contain any number of elements

In our earlier program for calculating the number of days to Christmas we encountered a new type of variable called a 'subscripted' variable. These differ from ordinary or 'simple' variables in that they can have any number of compartments or elements within the box. Simple variables recognise two letters or letters followed by a digit from 0 to 9 (some versions of BASIC allow whole words to be used as variable names). A, B, B1, C3 and R2 are all simple variables. Subscripted variables look like this: A(6), B(12) or X(20). The subscript is the number in brackets. The examples we have given would be read as: 'A sub six', 'B sub twelve' and 'X sub twenty'.

If we think of a simple variable as being a box with a name or label on it, we can think of a subscripted variable as a box containing a specified number of internal elements. If we want a variable with 12 elements, we create it initially using the BASIC DIM statement, like this: DIM A(12). Any letter of the alphabet may be used.

Assigning values to simple variables is straightforward, using either LET or INPUT statements, like LET A = 35, LET B1 = 365 or INPUT C3. Values can be entered in the elements of a subscripted variable in the same way. Let's see how we would assign values to a subscripted array. ('Array' is an alternative name for a set of subscripted variables.) For example:

```
10 DIM A(5)
```

creates a subscripted variable with five elements. We can now assign a value to each element:

```
20 LET A(1) = 5
30 LET A(2) = 10
40 LET A(3) = 15
50 LET A(4) = 20
60 LET A(5) = 100
```

To find out how these variables differ from simple variables, let's assign values to a few simple variables:

```
70 LET X = 5
80 LET Y = 6
90 LET Z = 7
```

Try entering all these on your computer and then check the contents of each variable using the PRINT command. Many of the statements in BASIC also function as commands. After you have entered the statements above, check them by LISTing them and then type RUN. Now you can type PRINT X<CR>. You should see 5 instantly

displayed on the screen. Next type PRINT Y. The computer will respond to this PRINT command by displaying 6 on the screen. If you want to check the elements in the subscripted variable, type PRINT A(1) to find out the value of the first element in the array. The computer should respond by printing 5 on the screen. Try PRINTing the values of A(3) and A(5).

The important difference between subscripted variables and ordinary variables is that the subscript can itself be a variable. To see what this means, type PRINT A(X). The screen will respond with the figure 100. Why?

Look at the list you have typed in and check the value of variable X. It is 5. A(X) is equivalent to A (the value of variable X) and this is equivalent to A(5). Typing PRINT A(X) is therefore exactly equivalent to typing PRINT A(5). What value would you expect if you typed PRINT A(Y — X)? Before actually trying it, see if you can work out the answer.

Assigning Values

If there are only a few simple variables, the LET statement is the simplest way of assigning values to them. Subscripted variables may well have a large number of elements in the array, so let's see what the alternative methods of entering the values are:

```
10 DIM A(5)
20 PRINT "INPUT THE VARIABLES"
30 INPUT A(1)
40 INPUT A(2)
50 INPUT A(3)
60 INPUT A(4)
70 INPUT A(5)
```

This method is just as tiresome to type in as using LET statements, though it would certainly work. If we know exactly how many variables there are (in this case there are five) it is easier to use a FOR-NEXT loop, like this:

```
10 DIM A(5)
20 FOR X = 1 TO 5
30 INPUT A(X)
40 NEXT X
```

This program would expect five values to be typed on the computer keyboard when the program was run. The RETURN key would have to be pressed after each figure had been entered. If we know beforehand what the values in the variable are, it is easier to enter them using a READ statement together with a DATA statement, like this:

```
10 DIM A(5)
20 FOR X = 1 TO 5
30 READ A(X)
40 NEXT X
50 DATA 5, 10, 15, 20, 100
```

Try this short program, and then test the contents of the array using the PRINT command (that is, use PRINT after the program has been RUN. For example, PRINT A(1)‹CR› and PRINT A(5). Now we can add a few lines to the program to print the elements in the array for us automatically:

```
60 FOR L = 1 TO 5
70 PRINT A(L)
80 NEXT L
90 END
```

RUN this program and check that the correct values are printed on the screen. Then retype line 50 using five different DATA items. Remember that the numbers in a DATA statement must be separated from each other using commas, but there must be no comma before the first number or after the last one.

The simplest way to assign values is to use READ and DATA statements. If the values will be different every time the program is run, using the INPUT statement inside a FOR-NEXT loop is probably the best way. If the total number of elements in the array is fixed, the number can be used as the upper limit in the FOR statement.

Let's use all we have learnt so far to build a short but powerful program. Suppose we wanted to sort some numbers into ascending order. Before setting out to write the program, the first thing to do is to figure out how to solve the problem in a logical way. When the way to solve the problem seems clear, write down the steps one after the other using clear, short English sentences.

Suppose we start with five numbers: 4, 9, 2, 8, 3. Sorting these into ascending order is a trivial problem. We just scan along the line and notice which is the smallest, and put it on the left, and then repeat the process for the remaining digits.

The computer, however, needs a very precise set of instructions, so we shall have to think very clearly about what steps are required. Here's one approach: Compare the first digit with the second digit. If the first digit is bigger than the second one, swap them. If the first digit is smaller than the second one, leave their positions unchanged.

Compare the second digit with the third digit. If the second digit is smaller than the third one, leave their position unchanged.

Repeat the process of comparing pairs of digits until the last pair of digits has been compared.

If there were no swaps, all the numbers must be in order. If there were any swaps, go back to the beginning and repeat the process.

If you think about this process, you will see that it will indeed sort any group of numbers into ascending numeric order. Look at what would happen to our original set of numbers as each pair of digits is compared:

```
4   9   2   8   3
4   2   9   8   3
4   2   8   9   3
4   2   8   3   9
```

All the pairs have now been compared and swapped where necessary. Since at least one swap took place, go back to the beginning and repeat the process:

```
4   2   8   3   9
2   4   8   3   9
2   4   3   8   9
2   4   3   8   9
```

There were still swaps, so go back to the beginning and repeat:

```
2   4   3   8   9
2   3   4   8   9
2   3   4   8   9
```

There were no swaps, last time through, so every number must be smaller than the number to its right. The numbers must be in ascending order and the operation can be terminated.

Using subscripted variables allows a sort routine like this to be implemented easily in BASIC, because the subscript itself can be a variable. If our original five numbers were the values in an array; so that A(1) = 4, A(2) = 9, A(3) = 2, A(4) = 8 and

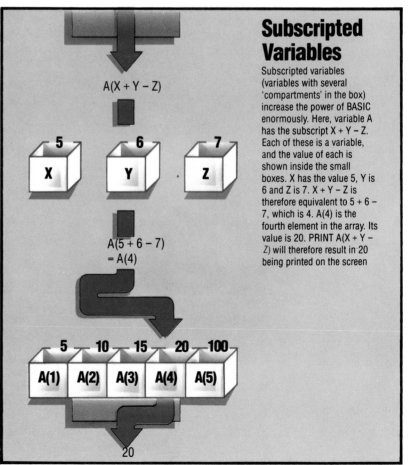

Subscripted Variables

Subscripted variables (variables with several 'compartments' in the box) increase the power of BASIC enormously. Here, variable A has the subscript X + Y − Z. Each of these is a variable, and the value of each is shown inside the small boxes. X has the value 5, Y is 6 and Z is 7. X + Y − Z is therefore equivalent to 5 + 6 − 7, which is 4. A(4) is the fourth element in the array. Its value is 20. PRINT A(X + Y − Z) will therefore result in 20 being printed on the screen

TONY LODGE

A(5) = 3, then if X has the value 1, A(X) will be the contents of A(1), which is 4. A(X + 1) will be the contents of A(2), which is 9, and so on.

Look at the program and see if you can see exactly what is going on. Line 20 sets variable N to the number of numbers we want to sort. Let's assume we want to sort five numbers: when the program is run we will type in 5 and then hit RETURN.

Line 30 is the DIMension statement. If N is 5, it sets the size of the array to 5. This line is equivalent to DIM A(5).

Lines 40 to 60 are a FOR-NEXT loop that allows us to type in the five numbers. Most versions of BASIC prompt the user with a question mark on the screen. RETURN will have to be pressed after each number has been entered. The numbers may be more than one digit, and may include decimal fractions.

Line 90 sets the variable S to 0. This variable is being used as a 'flag'. Later in the program, A is tested to see if it is 1 or not. It is only ever set to 1 if two numbers have been swapped, as we shall see in line 240. We shall investigate the use of 'flags' in more detail later in this chapter.

Line 100 sets up the limits for a loop; in this case from 1 to 4 (because N is 5 so N − 1 is 4). The first time through the loop, L is 1 so A(L) in line 110 will be A(1) or the first element in the array and A(L + 1) will be A(2), the second element in the array. The next time round the loop, L will be incremented to 2, so A(L) will be equivalent to A(2) and A(L + 1) will be equivalent to A(3). Line 110 tests to see if A(L) is greater than the number immediately to its right in the array. The sign for 'greater than' is ›.

If the first number is bigger than the next one, the program branches to a subroutine that swaps the numbers. If the first number is not bigger than the next one, there is no branch to the subroutine and BASIC simply continues to the next line, which is the NEXT L statement. After the loop has been repeated four times, it stops the program and goes to line 130 which tests the 'swap' flag, S, to see if it has been set or not. If it has been set (in the 'swap' subroutine), the program branches back to line 90 to repeat the comparison process. If S is not 1 it means no swap took place, so all the numbers are

in order. The rest of the program simply prints them out.

The swap subroutine needs a temporary variable to store one of the numbers to be swapped. After the two numbers have been swapped in lines 210, 220 and 230, the 'swap' flag S is set to 1 and then the program RETURNs to the main program.

```
10 PRINT "HOW MANY NUMBERS DO YOU WANT
   TO SORT?"
20 INPUT N
30 DIM A(N)
40 FOR X = 1 TO N
45 PRINT "NEXT NUMBER"
50 INPUT A(X)
60 NEXT X
70 REM
80 REM SORT ROUTINE
90 LET S = 0
100 FOR L = 1 TO N − 1
110 IF A(L) › A(L + 1) THEN GOSUB 200
120 NEXT L
130 IF S = 1 THEN 90
140 FOR X = 1 TO N
150 PRINT "A(";X;") = ";A(X)
160 NEXT X
170 END
180 REM
190 REM
200 REM SWAP SUBROUTINE
210 LET T = A(L)
220 LET A(L) = A(L + 1)
230 LET A(L + 1) = T
240 LET S =1
250 RETURN
```

Exercises

■ Extend the program to find the average value of the numbers input. The average is equal to the sum of items divided by the total number of items. The simplest way to do this is to insert a GOSUB just before the END statement in line 170. The subroutine should read each of the elements in the array and add the values to a 'sum' variable. After all the elements have been added, the sum should be divided by the number of elements. The sum is most easily derived by using the number of elements as the upper limit of a FOR-NEXT loop.

■ Change one line in the program so that the numbers will be sorted in descending order.

■ This exercise is directed mainly at owners of the TI99/4A which does not like having variables used as subscripts in subscripted variables. TI BASIC does, however, accept statements such as DIM A(12). Rewrite the program so that the INPUT statement expects an exact number of numbers to be input, 12, say. This will avoid the problem of using a variable name as a subscript. Lines 100 and 110 will also have to be changed. The swap subroutine will not work in TI BASIC for the same reason. This will have to be changed too.

■ A tough one. Our way of sorting numbers is by no means the only way to do it. See if you can think up an alternative method.

Basic Flavours

IF... THEN
If this program is to be run on the Spectrum, line 130 must be amended to read: 130 IF S=1 THEN GOTO 90

END
This is not available on the Spectrum, ZX81, Oric-1 or Dragon 32, so replace it by STOP

DIM A(N)
This program will not work on the TI 99/4A as subscripts, like X in line 50 and the L in line 110, must be specific numbers, and not variables

Organise Your Program

We sort a program using built-in functions to rearrange information

The program in this example illustrates how relatively complex programs can be broken down into simple sub-programs or subroutines that can be written and tested separately.

Apart from the advantage of being separately testable, the use of subroutines allows the development of the program to follow a logical progression. There are many approaches to writing a program in BASIC. One of the commonest is 'trial and error': you sit down at the computer and start entering lines of BASIC without having thought out carefully what is required to make the program work. This method leads to badly structured programs that will often not work the first time. If the structure of the program is not clear, it is not easy to find the mistakes or 'bugs'.

A much better approach is to sit down with a notebook and work out the structure of the program first, in steps of ever-increasing refinement, until a correct and working program can be written. A flow diagram will also help (see page 140). Let's see how this is done.

Problem: Write a program that will input a number of names, the forename followed by surname. Now reverse the order of each name so that the surname comes first, followed by a comma and a space, and by the forename. It will then sort the names into alphabetical order and print them out.

For example, if the names BILL JONES and FRED ASHTON were entered (in that order), the program would print out:

ASHTON, FRED
JONES, BILL

Before even attempting to write a program to do this, first write down the desired input and output in the most general terms:

Step 1
Input names in random order, first name first
Output names in alphabetical order, surnames first

This simply clarifies what we want to be done. This is an essential first step to a properly organised program. The next step is to refine the stages in the first step and make sure that the program still works. Do not, at this stage, get into too much detail. Simply write down in a little more detail, the stages involved:

Step 2
Find out number of names to be input
Enter names

Reverse names
Sort names
Print names

Look at the above list and check that it will work. Can you see anything wrong with it? Are there any flaws in the logic? If not, you are ready to go on to the next stage of refinement.

The stages we arrived at in Step 2 are small enough and simple enough to be written separately as small sub-programs. Sub-programs are called subroutines in BASIC. Let's give the subroutines names to make them easier to identify. Subroutine 1, to find out the number of names to be input, can be called FINDNUM. Subroutine 2, to enter the names, can be called ENTER. Subroutine 3, to reverse the names, can be called REVERSE. Subroutine 4, to sort the names, can be called SORT. Finally, Subroutine 5, to print the names can be called PRINTNAMES.

Step 3.1 FINDNUM
Prompt the user to input required number
Get the required number N
Use N to set up string array
Step 3. 2 ENTER
If number of names is less than N,
prompt user to input another name
Add name to string array
Step 3.3 REVERSE
Find length of string (name)
Find 'space' in string
Put characters in string up to 'space'
into temporary string variable
Put characters in string from 'space' to
end into another temporary variable
Add comma space to end of variable
Assign second followed by first
temporary variables to original string
Step 3. 4 SORT
Compare first item in array with next item
If first item is bigger than next one
(i.e. higher in the alphabet), swap
Compare second item with third
Swap, if necessary
Repeat until all pairs are compared
Go back to beginning of array and
repeat comparison of pairs until no swaps
have taken place

Note: This sort routine is exactly the same as the one used in the previous part of the Basic Programming course. The 'swap' part will be dealt with as a subroutine called from within the SORT subroutine.

Step 3.5 PRINTNAMES

Print each item in the array until all items have been printed

Each of the steps needed to build this program has now been worked out in a reasonable amount of detail. The SORT routine has only been sketched roughly since it was dealt with fully in the last part of the chapter. And SWAP, which is 'called' from within this subroutine, has been left out completely. Let's now see how easy it is to convert programs worked out in English into a program in BASIC.

Step 4
1. FINDNUM

The three lines in Step 3.1 translate directly into BASIC statements. The user is prompted by a PRINT statement, the number is found by using an INPUT statement and the array is dimensioned by using the DIM statement:

```
PRINT "HOW MANY NAMES DO YOU WISH TO
    ENTER?"
INPUT N
DIM A$ (N)
RETURN
```

The variable N now contains the maximum number of names to be entered. The DIM statement dimensions a string array. String variables contain strings of alphanumeric characters instead of numbers. A string variable name always ends with a 'dollar' sign. A$ alone could only contain one string. DIM A$ (N) creates an array that can contain 'N' strings. Subscripted variables have been dealt with earlier in the chapter.

The RETURN statement transfers control back to the main program at the line following the subroutine call. Values assigned to variables in the subroutine will be 'carried back' to the main program and can be used elsewhere in the program, even in other subroutines.

2. ENTER

As long as the number of names entered is less than N, the user needs to be prompted to enter a name and this name must be added to the string array. This calls for creating a FOR-NEXT loop; we know that the first name in the array will be its first element, and that the last one will be the Nth, so:

```
FOR X = 1 TO N
PRINT "ENTER NAME"
INPUT A$(X)
NEXT X
RETURN
```

That should suffice to enter all the names into the array. But sharp readers will have spotted what happens when we come to reverse the order of the first and last names in the REVERSE subroutine. Each element (name) in the array will have to be pulled out again, then reversed, and then put back in the array. Rather than complicate and lengthen

the program by doing that, it would be simpler to call the REVERSE subroutine from within the ENTER subroutine after each name has been typed in. The name can then be reversed before it is assigned to the array. To do that, we just have to add one line, thus:

```
FOR X = 1 TO N
PRINT "ENTER NAME"
INPUT A$(X)
GOSUB [REVERSE]
NEXT X
RETURN
```

All the names in the array will now be in reversed order (surname first, followed by forename) and will therefore be ready for sorting.

3. REVERSE

To reverse the order of names, we need to know where the 'space' is separating the first name from the surname. When we know where the space is, we can use various functions to pull out parts of the string and assign those parts to other strings. Functions in BASIC are commands that perform a predefined operation on the value following the function name. This part is always in brackets. Many functions are 'built in' but it is also possible to define your own. A typical 'built in' function is SQR ( ). This function 'returns' the square root of the value inside the brackets. So: LET A = SQR (9): PRINT A will print a 3.

REVERSE uses the functions LEN (to find the length of the string), INSTR (to locate the position of the space), LEFT$ (to remove a specified number of characters from the left of the string) and

Programs Within A Program
The main program this time is very short. All the real work is done in the sub-programs (called subroutines in BASIC). Each of the steps needed to make the program work are separated and written as short 'mini-programs'. These are then simply linked together by the main program.

When the program is run, each time a GOSUB statement is encountered, the program branches to the specified subroutine line number and that section of the program is then executed. The end of the subroutine is indicated by the RETURN statement. On reaching this, the program returns to the point immediately after the GOSUB that called the subroutine.

Subroutines can be 'nested' within subroutines. The ENTER subroutine calls another subroutine called REVERSE, and SORT sometimes calls another subroutine called SWAP.

Breaking down a problem into separate subroutines linked by a simple main program makes the development and testing of programs far easier

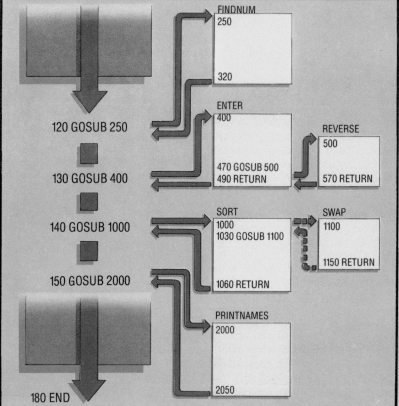

RIGHT$ (to remove a specified number of characters from the right of the string). We will not discuss in detail exactly how these functions work at the moment. We will take a more comprehensive look at functions in BASIC in the next part of the chapter (see page 188).

4. SORT

SORT, and the SWAP subroutine called from within it, follow closely the routines used last time.

5. PRINT NAMES

This is very straightforward:

```
FOR Q = 1 TO N
PRINT A$(Q)
NEXT Q
RETURN
```

Now all that remains is to write the main program. It's as simple as this:

```
REM MAIN PROGRAM
GOSUB [FINDNUM]
GOSUB [ENTER]
GOSUB [SORT]
GOSUB [PRINT]
END
```

We have put the 'names' of the subroutines in square brackets. A few BASICS are able to call subroutines by name, but most have to use line numbers. When the program is actually written out, the appropriate line numbers are inserted in place of the subroutine names. Appropriate REMs and PRINT messages are also added.

Exercises

Now that we have covered almost all of the most important features of BASIC, it is time to check your progress by working through these exercises. They range in difficulty from the very easy to the moderately difficult. Answers on page 191.

■ **Variables** Put a circle around the expressions below that are valid numeric variables, and draw a cross through the expressions that are not valid variable names at all. Leave the valid string variable names unmarked.

A B6 2Z D$ 15 X$ A12 D9 Q81 Q5 6F H$

■ **Arithmetic 1** Write a short program to assign the value 6 to variable B and then PRINT the value of B.

■ **Arithmetic 2** Write a short program to assign the value 5 to variable A, 7 to variable B and 9 to variable C. Add the values of these three variables and assign the sum to variable D. PRINT the value of variable D.

■ **Arithmetic 3** Look at these lines of BASIC and then work out what the value of C will be.

```
LET C = 5 + 4 * 3
PRINT C
```

```
10 REM   THIS PROGRAM SORTS NAMES
20 REM   INTO ALPHABETICAL ORDER
30 PRINT "FIRST DECIDE HOW MANY"
40 PRINT "NAMES YOU WANT TO ENTER"
50 PRINT "THEN ENTER THE NAMES IN"
60 PRINT "FIRSTNAME(SPACE)LASTNAME"
70 PRINT "ORDER."
80 REM
90 REM   THIS IS THE MAIN PROGRAM
100 PRINT
110 PRINT
120 GOSUB 250
130 GOSUB 400
140 GOSUB 1000
150 GOSUB 2000
160 REM
170 REM   END OF MAIN PROGRAM
180 END
250 REM   SUBROUTINE TO FIND NO. OF
260 REM   NAMES TO BE ENTERED
270 PRINT "HOW MANY NAMES DO YOU"
280 PRINT "WISH TO ENTER?"
290 PRINT
300 INPUT N
310 DIM A$(N)
320 RETURN
400 REM   SUBROUTINE TO ENTER NAMES
410 PRINT "ENTER NAME IN THIS FORM:"
420 PRINT "FIRSTNAME(SPACE)LASTNAME(CR)"
430 PRINT "E.G. JILL THOMPSON"
440 FOR X = 1 TO N
450 PRINT "ENTER NAME"
460 INPUT A$(X)
470 GOSUB 500
480 NEXT X
490 RETURN
500 REM   SUBROUTINE TO REVERSE ORDER OF NAMES
510 LET L = LEN(A$(X))
520 LET S = INSTR(A$(X)," ")
530 LET C$ = LEFT$(A$(X),S - 1)
540 LET F$ = RIGHT$(A$(X),L - S)
550 LET F$ = F$ + ", "
560 LET A$(X) = F$ + C$
570 RETURN
1000 REM   SORT ROUTINE
1010 LET S = 0
1020 FOR P = 1 TO N - 1
1030 IF A$(P) > A$(P + 1) THEN GOSUB 1100
1040 NEXT P
1050 IF S = 1 THEN GOTO 1000
1060 RETURN
1100 REM   SWAP SUBROUTINE
1110 LET T$ = A$(P)
1120 LET A$(P) = A$(P + 1)
1130 LET A$(P + 1) = T$
1140 LET S = 1
1150 RETURN
2000 REM   PRINT SUBROUTINE
2010 PRINT
2020 FOR Q = 1 TO N
2030 PRINT A$(Q)
2040 NEXT Q
2050 RETURN
```

■ **Arithmetic 4** What result will be printed in this program?

```
LET A = 3
LET B = 2
LET C = 9
LET D = 4
LET E = (A + B) * (C − D)
PRINT E

LET E = 5
LET E = E * E
PRINT E
```

■ **Comparisons 1** What value of X will be required for the PRINT message to be printed?

```
70 LET A = 5
80 LET B = X
90 LET R = B − A
100 IF R = 0 THEN GOTO 120
110 GOTO 10
120 PRINT "CONGRATULATIONS! YOU HAVE WON"
999 END
```

■ **Comparisons 2** What is the smallest value of X that will make the program jump to line 300?

```
250 IF X > 6 * 100 THEN GOTO 300
```

■ **Comparisons 3** What is the smallest value of Z that will make the program jump to the 'congratulations' message?

```
340 IF Z < 10000 THEN GOTO 500
350 IF Z >= 10000 THEN GOTO 520
    :
    :
500 PRINT "YOUR SCORE IS TOO LOW. TRY AGAIN"
510 GOTO 600
520 PRINT "CONGRATULATIONS, YOU ARE NOW A
MASTER"
530 GOTO 700
```

■ **Print 1** Assume that the value of T is 50. Write a PRINT statement that will print THE VALUE OF T IS 50. Hint: Put the 'message' in double quotes, use a semi-colon and the variable name.

■ **Print 2** Look at the following short program and complete the PRINT statement so that the program will print a score message like this:

SORRY, BUT YOUR SCORE OF 175 IS TOO LOW

Complete the line so that the actual value of the score can vary each time.

```
620 REM VARIABLE S IS THE SCORE SO FAR
620 IF S <= 500 THEN GOTO 640
630 GOTO 700
640 PRINT "SORRY"
```

■ **Print 3** What message will be printed when the program is run?

```
200 LET A$= "THE HOME COMPUTER COURSE ?"
210 LET B$ = "HOW DO YOU LIKE ";
220 PRINT B$
230 PRINT A$
```

■ **Input 1** INPUT is one way of assigning a value to a variable. If the following program is run, which key will need to be pressed for the program to print out an answer of 12?

```
60 INPUT N
70 LET N = N * 2
80 PRINT N
```

■ **Input 2** What will be printed here?

```
100 PRINT "PLEASE TYPE YOUR NAME"
110 INPUT N$
120 PRINT "HI ";N$;"I'M YOUR COMPUTER"
```

Basic Flavours

This program will not run on the Atari 400 and 800 because their string handling is so different from that of other machines

DIM

On the ZX81 and Spectrum replace line 310 by:
310 DIM A$ (N,30)
This creates a string array called A$ that has N elements, each of them 30 characters long.
On the Lynx replace line 310 by:
310 DIM A$ (30) (N)

GOTO

In line 1050 the command GOTO 1000 comes immediately after the word THEN. In this case, most computers allow you to omit the word GOTO; so line 1050 might be written
1050 IF S=1 THEN 1000

INSTR

This command is not available on the ZX81, Spectrum, Commodore 64, Vic-20 and Oric-1.
On the Commodore machines and the Oric-1 delete line 520 and replace it by:
515 LET S= 0
520 FOR P=1 TO L
523 IF MID$(A$(X),P,1)=" " THEN LET S=P
524 IF S=P THEN LET P=L
525 NEXT P
On the Spectrum and ZX81 delete lines 510 to 560, and replace them by:

INSTR

510 LET D$=A$(X)
520 LET L=LEN D$
530 LET S =0
540 FOR P=1 TO L
550 IF D$(P)=" " THEN LET S=P
560 IF S=P THEN LET P=L
570 NEXT P
580 LET C$=D$(TO S-1)
590 LET F$=D$ (S+1 TO)
600 LET A$(X)=F$+", "+C$
610 RETURN

LEFT$

RIGHT$

None of these commands is available on the Spectrum or ZX81. Their equivalents in Sinclair BASIC are:
LEFT$(Z$,N)	replace by Z$(TO N)
RIGHT$(Z$,N)	replace by Z$(LEN(Z$)−N+1 TO)
MID$(Z$,P,N)	replace by Z$(P TO P+N−1)

Fully Functional

There are built-in functions in Basic, which means that a lot of the programming has already been done for you. Knowing how to use them adds power to your computing

Suppose you wanted to calculate the square root of a number in one of your programs. There are a number of ways this could be done. The crudest and least satisfactory way would be to create a table of square root values and to use this to give you the value wanted for a particular number. You probably learnt how to do this in school. An alternative method is to use the square root 'function', built in to most versions of BASIC. Here, the arithmetic of the operation is taken care of by BASIC without the programmer having to worry about it. Let's see how it works:

```
10 REM THIS PROGRAM FINDS THE SQUARE ROOT
20 REM OF A NUMBER
30 PRINT "INPUT THE NUMBER YOU WANT TO"
40 PRINT "FIND THE SQUARE ROOT OF"
50 INPUT N
60 LET A = SQR(N)
70 PRINT "THE SQUARE ROOT OF ";N;" IS ";A
80 END
```

Type in this short program and see that it does indeed give you the square root of any number you type in. Let's look at the rules of how to use this 'square root' function.

A 'function' in BASIC is generally a command word (SQR in this case) followed by brackets that enclose the expression to be operated on. In this program, N is the number input from the keyboard. It is the number we want the square root of. Line 60 says 'let the square root of N be assigned to the variable A'. Line 70 prints out the value of A.

The expression inside the brackets is called the 'argument' of the function and does not always have to be a variable: it is equally possible to use actual numbers. Type this in and see what happens when you run it:

```
10 PRINT SQR(25)
20 END
```

You will see that this works just as well. Similarly, we can use more complex arguments inside the brackets. Try this one:

```
10 LET A = 10
20 LET B = 90
30 LET C = SQR(A+B)
40 PRINT C
50 END
```

This little program can be shortened by combining lines 30 and 40 like this:

```
10 LET A = 10
20 LET B = 90
```

```
30 PRINT SQR(A+B)
40 END
```

The way to think of functions is as short programs built in to BASIC that are available for the programmer to use at any time. Most versions of BASIC have quite a large number of functions as well as the facility of allowing the programmer to define new ones for use within a program. Later, we will see how this is done. Here we will look at a few more of the commonly available functions. They come in two varieties: numeric functions, in which the argument (the part inside the brackets) is a number, numeric variable or numeric expression, and string functions, in which the argument is a character string or expression made up from character strings. First we'll look at a few of the numeric functions.

Previously, on page 176, we used a program that calculated the number of tiles needed to tile a room. A small 'bug' in this program was that the answer could well involve fractions of a tile. 988.24 could represent a possible result of running this program. At times like this we want a way of rounding the answer to the nearest whole number. Whole numbers are referred to mathematically as 'integers' and one of the functions in BASIC will 'return' the integer part of any number. Here's how it works:

```
10 PRINT "INPUT A NUMBER CONTAINING A
    DECIMAL FRACTION"
20 INPUT N
30 PRINT "THE INTEGER PART OF THE NUMBER
    IS ";
40 PRINT INT(N)
50 END
```

If this program is run and the number you input is 3.14, the program will print on the screen:

THE INTEGER PART OF THE NUMBER IS 3

Of course, if we are dealing with tiles, we would then need to add 1 to the answer, to make sure that we bought more than the required amount, not less.

On other occasions, we may want to find the 'sign' of a number to see if it is negative, zero or positive. To do this, most BASICs incorporate a SGN function. Try this:

```
10 PRINT "INPUT A NUMBER"
20 INPUT N
30 LET S = SGN(N)
40 IF S = −1 THEN GOTO 100
```

```
50 IF S = 0 THEN GOTO 120
60 IF S = 1 THEN GOTO 140
100 PRINT "THE NUMBER WAS NEGATIVE"
110 GOTO 999
120 PRINT "THE NUMBER WAS ZERO"
130 GOTO 999
140 PRINT "THE NUMBER WAS POSITIVE"
150 GOTO 999
999 END
```

If you look at the values 'returned' by the SGN function to S in line 30 (these are tested in lines 40, 50 and 60) you will see that there are three possible values. -1 is returned if the argument in the brackets was a negative number, 0 if the argument was zero and 1 if the argument was a positive number. Using the SGN function in line 30 saves several lines of programming. We could have written:

```
IF N < 0 THEN LET S = -1
IF N = 0 THEN LET S = 0
IF N > 0 THEN LET S = 1
```

The action performed by a BASIC function can always be achieved through normal programming; using a function just saves time, space and programming effort.

Here are a few more numeric functions. ABS returns the 'absolute' value of a number. The absolute value of a number is the same as its real value with the sign removed. Thus, the absolute value of -6 is 6. Try this:

```
10 LET X = -9
20 LET Y = ABS(X)
30 PRINT Y
40 END
```

MAX finds the maximum value of two numbers. Thus:

```
10 LET X = 9
20 LET Y = 7
30 LET Z = X MAX Y
40 PRINT Z
50 END
```

MIN is similar to MAX but finds the smaller of two numbers. Try this:

```
10 PRINT "INPUT A NUMBER"
20 INPUT X
30 PRINT "INPUT ANOTHER NUMBER"
40 INPUT Y
50 LET Z = X MIN Y
60 PRINT Z
70 END
```

Notice that these latter two functions have two arguments instead of one, and they don't need to be enclosed in brackets. Most BASICS also have a number of other numeric functions, including LOG to find the logarithm of a number, TAN to find the tangent, COS to find the cosine and SIN to find the sine. We will look at some of the ways these 'trigonometrical' functions can be used later.

BASIC also has several built-in functions that operate on character strings. We used some of these in our name-sorting program (page 185) but at the time did not look closely at how they worked. Now we will look at these and a few other string functions in more detail.

One of the most useful string functions is LEN. This counts the number of characters in a string enclosed in double quotation marks or the number of characters assigned to a string variable. Try this:

```
10 LET A$ = "COMPUTER"
20 LET N = LEN(A$)
30 PRINT "THE NUMBER OF CHARACTERS IN THE
    STRING IS ";N
40 END
```

Why would we ever need to know how many characters there are in a string variable? To see why, enter and run this short program designed to build a 'name triangle'. It prints first the first letter of a word, then the first and second letter and so on until the whole word is printed.

```
5 REM PRINTS A 'NAME TRIANGLE'
10 LET A$ = "JONES"
20 FOR L = 1 TO 5
30 LET B$ = LEFTS(A$,L)
40 PRINT B$
50 NEXT L
60 END
```

Now run this program. Can you figure out what the printout will be? It should look like this:

```
J
JO
JON
JONE
JONES
```

This short program uses the LEFT$ function to extract characters from a string. LEFT$ takes two arguments. The first specifies the string and the second (which comes after a comma) specifies the number of characters to be extracted from the string, starting from the left of the string. A$ has been assigned the string "JONES" so LEFT$(A$,1) would 'return' the letter J. LEFT$(A$,2) would return the letters JO. The short program above uses an index, L, that ranges from 1 to 5, so that the second argument in the LEFT$ function goes up from 1 to 5 each time through the loop. We knew exactly how many characters there were in the word we wanted to print (JONES), so it was easy to decide that 5 should be the upper limit in the FOR-NEXT loop. But what would we do if we did not know beforehand how many characters there would be in the loop?

This is where the LEN function comes in. LEN takes a string (in double quotes) or a string variable as its argument. Here are a few examples to show how it works:

```
10 REM PROGRAM TO TEST THE 'LEN' FUNCTION
20 PRINT LEN("COMPUTER")
30 END
```

The program should print 8 when it is run. It has counted the number of characters in the word COMPUTER and returned this value. Let's do the same thing in a slightly different way:

```
10 REM FINDING THE LENGTH OF A STRING
20 LET A$ = "COMPUTER COURSE"
30 LET L = LEN(A$)
40 PRINT L
50 END
```

If this program is run, the computer should print 15 on the screen. There are 15 characters in this string, not 14. Don't forget that the space between the two words is a character as far as the computer is concerned. Now let's apply the LEN function in a modification of our earlier program to print out a 'triangular name':

```
10 REM THIS PROGRAM PRINTS A 'NAME
   TRIANGLE'
20 PRINT "TYPE IN A NAME"
30 INPUT A$
40 LET N = LEN(A$)
50 FOR L = 1 TO N
60 LET B$ = LEFT$(A$,L)
70 PRINT B$
80 NEXT L
90 END
```

Each time this loop is executed, the value of L increments from 1 up to N (which is the length of the name in the string). If you input the name SIMPSON, line 40 will be equivalent to LET N = LEN ("SIMPSON"), so N will be set to 7. The first time through the loop, line 50 will set L to 1 and line 60 will be equivalent to LET B$=LEFT$ ("SIMPSON",1) so B$ will be assigned one character from the string, starting from the left. This character is S.

The second time through the loop, L will be set to 2 so line 60 will be equivalent to LET B$ = LEFT$ ("SIMPSON",2). This will take the first two characters from the string and assign them to string variable B$. B$ will therefore contain SI.

The LEN function found that there were 7 characters in the string SIMPSON and assigned this value to variable N, so the last time through the loop B$ will be assigned all seven characters from the string and the whole string will be printed.

Note that LEFT$ has a companion function, RIGHT$, which takes characters from the right of the string variable in exactly the same way.

Finally, we will look at one more string function, also used in the name-sorting program. This is INSTR; it is used to find the location of the first occurrence of a specified string (called a 'substring') within a string. In the name-sorting program, INSTR was used to locate the position of the space between the first name and surname. Here's how it works:

```
10 LET A$ = "WATERFALL"
20 LET P = INSTR(A$,"FALL")
30 PRINT P
40 END
```

Before entering and running the program, see if you can anticipate what value will be printed for P. Remember, INSTR locates the starting position of the first occurrence of the 'sub-string' within the string. If the string is WATERFALL, the starting position of the sub-string FALL will be 6 — the F in FALL is the sixth letter in WATERFALL. Some BASICS do not use INSTR, but have a similar function called INDEX instead. Here's how to use INSTR (or INDEX) to locate a space within a string:

```
10 REM FINDING THE POSITION OF A SPACE IN A
   STRING
20 LET A$ = "HOME  COMPUTER"
30 LET P = INSTR(A$," ")
40 PRINT P
50 END
```

Notice that the second argument in the INSTR function (line 30) is " ". The quotes enclose a space — the character to be searched for. The program will print 5 as the value of P since the space is in the fifth position in the string. Work out what would be printed if line 30 were changed to:

```
LET P = INSTR(A$,"C")
```

Lastly, a handy function used with the PRINT statement. See what happens when you run this program:

```
10 PRINT "THIS LINE IS NOT INDENTED"
20 PRINT TAB(5); "THIS LINE IS INDENTED"
30 END
```

Can you see what happened? The second line was printed starting five places in from the left margin. TAB is analogous to the tabulator on a typewriter. Here is another short program using the TAB function:

```
10 REM  USING THE TAB FUNCTION
20 PRINT "ENTER THE TAB VALUE"
30 INPUT  T
40 LET W$ = "TABULATION"
50 PRINT TAB(T);W$
60 END
```

Now you can go back to the name-sorting program on page 186 and see how some of those functions were used there.

Exercises

■ **Loops 1** What will be printed when this program is run?

```
10 LET A = 500
20 FOR L = 1 TO 50
30 LET A = A −1
40 NEXT L
50 PRINT "THE VALUE OF A IS ";A
```

■ **Loops 2** What will you see on the screen if this program is run?

```
10 REM
20 REM THIS IS A TIMING LOOP
30 REM SEE HOW LONG IT TAKES
40 REM
```

Basic Flavours

On the Spectrum and ZX81 functions such as TAB, LEN, CHR$ can be used without brackets, so that TAB(30), for example, can be written TAB 30

None of these commands is available on the Spectrum or ZX81; their equivalents in Sinclair BASIC are:

LEFT$(Z$,N)   replace by Z$(TO N)
RIGHT$(Z$,N)   replace by Z$(LEN(Z$)– N+1 TO)
MID$(Z$,P,N)   replace by Z$(P TO P+N–1)

When N=1 in a MID$() command then the Sinclair equivalent is very much simpler than the above:

MID$(Z$,P,1)   replace by Z$(P)

MID$

INSTR

This is not available on the Spectrum, ZX81, Commodore 64, Vic-20, and Oric-1, but you can write a sub-routine to replace it. Suppose that a program line is:
20 LET P=INSTR(A$,"FALL")
Replace it by:
20 LET X$=A$: LET Z$="FALL":GOSUB 9930:LET P=U
9929 STOP
9930 LET U=0:LET X=LEN(X$): LET Z=LEN(Z$)
9940 FOR W=1 TO X–Z+1
9950 IF MID$(X$,W,Z)=Z$ THEN LET U=W
9960 IF U=W THEN LET W=X–Z+1
9970 NEXT W
9980 RETURN
On the Spectrum and ZX81 replace line 9950 by:
9950 IF X$(W TO W+Z–1)=Z$ THEN LET U=W

```
50 PRINT "START"
60 FOR X = 1 TO 5000
70 NEXT X
80 PRINT "STOP"
90 END
```

■ **Loops 3** What result will be printed if the following program is run and you type in the number 60 when asked?

```
10 PRINT "THINK OF A NUMBER AND TYPE IT IN"
20 INPUT N
30 LET A = 100
40 FOR L = 1 TO N
50 LET A = A + 1
60 NEXT L
70 PRINT "THE VALUE OF A IS NOW ";A
80 END
```

■ **Loops 4** What will happen if this program is run?

```
10 PRINT "I LIKE BASIC"
20 GOTO 10
30 END
```

■ **Loops 5** What will you see on the screen if this program is run?

```
10 FOR Q = 1 TO 15
20 PRINT "I'M FEELING LOOPY"
30 NEXT Q
40 END
```

■ **Read-Data 1** What result will be printed?

```
10 READ X
20 READ Y
30 READ Z
40 PRINT "WE'RE TESTING THE 'READ' STATEMENT"
50 DATA 50,100,20
60 PRINT X + Y +Z
```

■ **Read-Data 2** What will be printed on the screen if this program is run?

```
100 FOR L = 1 TO 10
110 READ X
120 PRINT "X = ";X
130 NEXT L
140 DATA 1,2,3,5,7,11,13,17,19,23
```

Answers on page 195.

Answers To 'Exercises On Pages 186-187
Variables

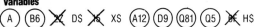

Arithmetic 1
10 LET B = 6
20 PRINT B

Arithmetic 2
10 LET A = 5
20 LET B = 7
30 LET C = 9
40 LET D = A + B + C
50 PRINT D

Arithmetic 3
17

Arithmetic 4
25
25

Comparisons 1
5

Comparisons 2
601 (integers are assumed)

Comparisons 3
10000

Print 1
PRINT "THE VALUE OF T IS ";T

Print 2
640 PRINT "SORRY, BUT YOUR SCORE OF ";S;" IS TOO LOW"

Print 3
This was a deliberate mistake.
The semi-colon at the end of the line will cause a syntax error at run time. The program should read:
200 LET A$="THE HOME COMPUTER COURSE?"
210 LET B$="HOW DO YOU LIKE "
220 PRINT B$;A$

And the result would then have been:
HOW DO YOU LIKE THE HOME COMPUTER COURSE?

Input 1
6

Input 2
PLEASE TYPE YOUR NAME
HI (YOUR NAME) I'M YOUR COMPUTER

Note that the answers to 'Variables' will differ for some machines, which do not allow more than one alphabetic character (i.e., no numeric suffix)

Leaving It To Chance

Continuing our look at Basic functions, we come to RND, which produces random (or nearly random) numbers for use in games or statistical programs

Now that we have seen how several of BASIC's functions work we shall look at one of the most commonly used — the RND function. RND is used to generate random numbers. It is also used in games whenever there is an element of chance.

Unfortunately, RND is one of the most variable 'words' in BASIC. Our description of it may differ from the way it is implemented in your home micro. Let's, therefore, clarify the differences between BASIC used in the Basic Programming course and your BASIC.

Most of our programs are based on Microsoft BASIC (or MBASIC). Microsoft is an American company and their BASIC was one of the first made widely available. BASIC is a language with no official standard, but Microsoft's version is as near to a standard as there is. Many other versions are modelled on Microsoft's, and the company has been commissioned to produce versions for several popular computers.

The chief difference between MBASIC and most of the more recent versions is that home computers now have powerful graphics capabilities that were not available when MBASIC was developed. Other versions of BASIC generally include a number of graphics commands and statements. To get the most from your computer, you will want to use its graphics capabilities to the full, and this will require a careful study of the owner's manual.

Of the various BASICS supplied with popular home computers, Sinclair BASIC (used in the ZX81 and Spectrum) and BBC BASIC probably differ most from MBASIC. Texas Instruments' version (used in the TI99/4A) also has a number of significant differences. As far as possible, we point out how to modify our programs in the 'Basic Flavours' boxes and you should refer to these if you have any problems running the programs.

As mentioned previously, the RND function differs from version to version. Check in your BASIC manual to see how it has been implemented in your version. We are illustrating its use in a very simple dice game. As with previous programs we have done most of the work in subroutines. This technique has the advantage of making the programs more readable, easier to write and easier to debug.

The main program starts with the statement

RANDOMIZE in line 20. Most, but not all, versions of BASIC need this statement to 'reseed' the RND function. It is actually quite hard to get computers to produce genuinely random numbers. Without this reseeding operation, the same sequence of supposedly random numbers would be produced each time by the RND function. Line 50 then calls a subroutine that uses RND to assign a random number to the variable D. The form we have used is:

320 LET D = INT(10 * RND)

This is the line most likely to need changing when you enter the program. Details of how different versions of RND work are given in 'Basic Flavours', so let's see what's happening in this Microsoft BASIC. The RND uses an expression (in brackets, as is usual with functions) as an option to alter slightly the sequence of numbers generated. With no expression — for example LET A = RND — the value of A will be a number between 0 and 1. We do not want a number smaller than 1 so we multiply the number by 10. This can be done like this: LET A = 10 * RND. If, for the sake of argument, RND had returned the value 0.125455, the value of A would now be 1.25455.

To eliminate the fractional part of the number and retain only the integer portion, we use the INT (integer) function like this: LET A = INT(10 * RND). Some versions of BASIC allow the upper limit of the random numbers generated to be specified in the expression used in the brackets after RND. For example, Dragon BASIC will print a whole number in the range 1 to 6 in response to: PRINT RND(6).

Since our Microsoft BASIC cannot do this, we check to see if the numbers returned are greater than 6 or less than 1 as such numbers are of no use in a dice game. This is done in lines 330 and 340:

330 IF D > 6 THEN GOTO 320
340 IF D < 1 THEN GOTO 320

If D is outside the limits 1 to 6, the GOTOs make the program jump back and try again.

Having chosen a random value for D between 1 and 6, the dice throw subroutine RETURNS to the main program. This prints the message YOUR SCORE IS A, followed by a picture of a dice. Notice how the appropriate picture of a side is selected. It is done in the SELECT subroutine. For example, if the dice (and therefore D) is a 1, line 410 calls the subroutine starting at line 530 thus:

410 IF D = 1 THEN GOSUB 530

CAROLINE HOLDEN

This subroutine is nothing more than a series of PRINT statements designed to produce crude graphics on the screen. Your BASIC may well have much better screen graphics, and if this is the case it would be better to substitute the appropriate graphics statements in place of our subroutines.

Once the program has chosen a dice for you at random, it will then repeat the process to select and display a dice for the computer. The part of the program that decides who has won has been incorporated in the main program; it could just as well have been written as a subroutine, but this would hardly be worth it since it is only four lines long. Line 200 compares M (my dice) with C (computer's dice) to see if they are equal. If they are, the words IT'S A DRAW are assigned to the string variable S$. Line 210 tests to see if M is greater than C. If it is, it assigns the words YOU HAVE WON to S$. Line 220 tests to see if M is less than C. If it is, it assigns the words THE COMPUTER HAS WON to S$. Line 240 simply prints the result and the game is over. Although this program is rather long, it is essentially very simple. It uses only one function, RND, has no loops, no subscripted variables and nothing more complicated than a few IF . . . THEN statements.

Given that the RND function is so variable, and that some versions of BASIC (Microsoft's, for example) require the RANDOMIZE statement to generate a new sequence of random numbers, is there any way we could generate truly random (i.e. unpredictable) numbers without using these functions? Several techniques are available.

One of the functions we have not looked at so far is INKEY$ (pronounced 'inkey-string'). Each time the word INKEY$ is encountered, the program inspects the keyboard to see if a key has been pressed. The program does not wait for a character to be input as it does when the command INPUT is used. So the command INKEY$ is usually placed in a loop. The program then continually scans the keyboard, waiting for something to be input. There is usually a test within the loop to terminate it, if an appropriate character has been input. This makes it possible to write a program to form a counting loop that will terminate when a specific character has been typed in. What would happen if we used this program?

```
10 PRINT "HIT THE SPACE-BAR"
20 FOR X = 0 TO 1
30 LET R = R + 1
40 LET A$ = INKEY$
50 IF A$ = "    " THEN GOTO 80
60 LET X = 0
70 NEXT X
80 FOR Q = 0 TO 1
90 IF R < 10 THEN GOTO 130
100 LET Q = 0
110 LET R = R / 10
120 NEXT Q
130 PRINT INT (R)
140 END
```

Would R be a random number? It should be, so let's look at the program and see why.

Line 10 prints the prompt HIT THE SPACE-BAR. Before we have time to respond to this prompt, the program has entered the FOR X = 0 TO 1 loop in line 20. 0 and 1 may seem like strange limits for the loop, but we will see how this structure is used shortly. Line 30 assigns the value 1 to variable R the first time through the loop. Line 40 assigns whatever character is typed in on the keyboard to the string variable A$ in line 40. This is done using the INKEY$ function. If you were to hit the letter R, R would be assigned to A$. Line 50 tests A$ to see whether it is a space (this is represented in BASIC as a space between double quote marks thus "   "). If A$ is a space, the program branches using the GOTO statement, but if A$ is not a space, the program continues to the next line.

This is line 60, which says LET X = 0. Now X is the index of the loop. The NEXT X statement in line 70 causes the program to return to the beginning of the loop in line 20. Since X has been reset to 0, the loop repeats it. In this way the FOR X = 0 TO 1 loop will be repeated indefinitely, as long as the IF A$ =

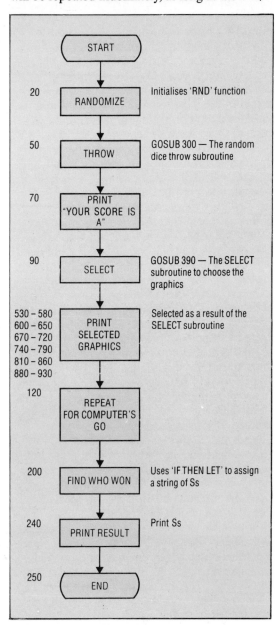

Program Flow
The flowchart shows the main actions performed by the program in simplified form. Corresponding line numbers are given on the left and short explanatory notes on the right. This is not a full flowchart as many of the 'decisions' and branches in the program are not shown

Line	Box	Note
	START	
20	RANDOMIZE	Initialises 'RND' function
50	THROW	GOSUB 300 — The random dice throw subroutine
70	PRINT "YOUR SCORE IS A"	
90	SELECT	GOSUB 390 — The SELECT subroutine to choose the graphics
530 – 580 600 – 650 670 – 720 740 – 790 810 – 860 880 – 930	PRINT SELECTED GRAPHICS	Selected as a result of the SELECT subroutine
120	REPEAT FOR COMPUTER'S GO	
200	FIND WHO WON	Uses 'IF THEN LET' to assign a string of Ss
240	PRINT RESULT	Print Ss
250	END	

" " test fails.

If at some stage the space bar is pressed, A$ will be assigned the character representing a space, and so the program will branch to line 80 and the loop will not be repeated.

But what will happen while the loop is repeating? Line 30 increments the value of R at each repetition of the loop. The first time through, R would be set to 1, the second time through it would be set to 1 + 1 and so on. When the loop has been broken out of by the test on A$, we could read R to see what we had counted up to.

Computers, however, operate very quickly and so R could be in the hundreds by the time we press the space bar. What would we do if we wanted values of R only between 1 and 10? Line 80 sets up another loop to enable us to test R and divide it by 10 if it is larger than 10. As long as R is larger than 10, the test in line 90 will fail, the value of Q will be reset to 0 and the loop will be repeated. Line 110 divides the value of R by 10 and a result is not printed out until the value of R has been reduced to a figure of less than 10. Line 30 ensures that the value of R can never be 0.

In theory, then, this program should produce a random number varying between 1 and 9 inclusive. But does it? The INT statement ensures that the decimal fractions have been removed, therefore the possible values of R would be 1,2,3,4,5,6,7,8,9. The average of these numbers is 5 (because their sum is 45, and 45 ÷ 9 = 5). Try it and see. You could do this by running the program a number of times, noting the value of R each time and then calculating the average. Alternatively, you could add some lines to the program to make it run, say, 100 times, adding the value of R to another variable S and then dividing S by 100.

When we tried this, we found that the average value of R was well below 5 and so the numbers could not have been random. It is instructive to consider why this could be.

The problem is that although BASIC is fast, it is not fast enough. The first loop lets the value of R increment until it reaches hundreds, or even thousands, before we press the space bar. Unless you make a deliberate effort to vary the amount of time elapsing between seeing the HIT THE SPACE-BAR prompt and actually pressing it, chances are you will press it after a fairly regular lapse of time. In this time, the value of R will probably have increased to several hundred.

The divisions that take place to reduce the value of R to a figure below 10 do not take place until after the space bar has been pressed. This means that R will almost always be in the low hundreds before the divisions take place and so the final value of R will tend to be low.

Is it possible to write a routine that overcomes this problem? The answer is yes, if we can make the counting process fast enough for our reaction time to the HIT THE SPACE-BAR prompt to be truly unpredictable. The solution is to make the test for the 'greater than upper limit' part of the first loop. Consider this program:

```
10 REM   GAME OF DICE -- MAIN PROGRAM
20 RANDOMIZE
30 REM   YOUR THROW
40 REM   GOSUB 'THROW' ROUTINE
50 GOSUB 300
60 LET M = D
70 PRINT "YOUR SCORE IS A"
80 REM   GOSUB 'SELECT' ROUTINE
90 GOSUB 390
100 PRINT
110 REM   COMPUTER'S THROW
120 REM   GOSUB 'THROW' ROUTINE
130 GOSUB 300
140 LET C = D
150 PRINT "THE COMPUTER'S SCORE IS A"
160 REM   GOSUB 'SELECT' ROUTINE
170 GOSUB 390
180 PRINT
190 REM   WHO WON?
200 IF M = C THEN LET S$ = "DRAW"
210 IF M > C THEN LET S$ = "YOU WON"
220 IF M < C THEN LET S$ = "COMPUTER WON"
230 REM   PRINT RESULT
240 PRINT S$
250 END
260 REM
270 REM
280 REM
290 REM
300 REM   RANDOM DICE THROW SUBROUTINE
310 REM
320 LET D = INT(10*RND)
330 IF D > 6 THEN GOTO 320
340 IF D < 1 THEN GOTO 320
350 RETURN
360 REM
370 REM
380 REM
390 REM   SELECT SUBROUTINE
400 REM
410 IF D = 1 THEN GOSUB 530
420 IF D = 2 THEN GOSUB 600
430 IF D = 3 THEN GOSUB 670
440 IF D = 4 THEN GOSUB 740
450 IF D = 5 THEN GOSUB 810
460 IF D = 6 THEN GOSUB 880
470 RETURN
480 REM
490 REM
500 REM
510 'GRAPHICS' SUBROUTINES
520 REM
530 PRINT "|        |"
540 PRINT "|        |"
550 PRINT "|        |"
560 PRINT "|    *   |"
570 PRINT "|        |"
580 PRINT "|        |"
590 RETURN

600 PRINT "|        |"
610 PRINT "|        |"
620 PRINT "|      * |"
630 PRINT "|        |"
640 PRINT "| *      |"
650 PRINT "|        |"
660 RETURN
670 PRINT "|        |"
680 PRINT "|        |"
690 PRINT "|      * |"
700 PRINT "|    *   |"
710 PRINT "| *      |"
720 PRINT "|        |"
730 RETURN
740 PRINT "|        |"
750 PRINT "|        |"
760 PRINT "| *    * |"
770 PRINT "|        |"
780 PRINT "| *    * |"
790 PRINT "|        |"
800 RETURN
810 PRINT "|        |"
820 PRINT "|        |"
830 PRINT "| *    * |"
840 PRINT "|    *   |"
850 PRINT "| *    * |"
860 PRINT "|        |"
870 RETURN
880 PRINT "|        |"
890 PRINT "|        |"
900 PRINT "| *    * |"
910 PRINT "| *    * |"
920 PRINT "| *    * |"
930 PRINT "|        |"
940 RETURN
```

```
10 PRINT "HIT THE SPACE-BAR"
20 FOR X = 0 TO 1
30 LET R = R + 1
40 IF R > 9 THEN LET R = 1
50 IF INKEY$ = "   " THEN GOTO 80
60 LET X = 0
70 NEXT X
80 PRINT R
90 END
```

In this program, R can never be less than 1 or greater than 9. By the time the space bar is pressed (and recognised by the INKEY$ function in line 50), R will have a value somewhere between 1 and 9 inclusive.

This program was tested 1,000 times and found an average value for R of 5.014. Since a perfect average would be 5 and the error is only 0.28% high, this suggests that the program does indeed generate a random number very close to the theoretical average. The point is, of course, that even when a program appears reasonable on paper, there may be unforeseen flaws in it. Actual testing is well worth while.

Some readers will have noticed that these random number programs could be shortened by using various GOTO statements in place of the FOR . . . NEXT loop. Our reason for avoiding GOTO statements will become clearer in future parts of the Basic Programming course.

Basic Flavours

RANDOMIZE

On the BBC Micro and the Oric-1, delete line 20, and replace line 320 by:

```
320 LET D = INT(10*RND(1))
```

On the Dragon 32, delete line 20, and replace line 320 by:

```
320 LET D = RND(6)
```

and delete lines 330 and 340.

RND

On the Lynx, replace line 20 by:

```
20 RANDOM
```

On the Vic-20 and the Commodore 64, replace line 20 by:

```
20 LET X = RND(-TI)
```

and replace line 320 by:

```
320 LET D = INT(10*RND(1))
```

On the Spectrum, the word RANDOMIZE is abbreviated on the keyboard to RAND, but it will appear on the screen as RANDOMIZE.

INKEY$

On the Oric-1 and the Lynx, replace INKEY$ by KEY$.
On the Vic-20 and the Commodore 64, replace line 40 by:

```
40 GET A$
```

Then replace line 50 by:

```
50 GET A$: IF A$="   " THEN GOTO 80
```

On the BBC Micro, replace INKEY$ by INKEY$(10). The number in brackets is the time in hundredths of a second during which the system will wait for a keypress; so for fast response use a low number, and vice versa

Exercises

■ **RND Function** Modify the last program in the text to give a random number in the range 1 to 6 (inclusive).

■ **Loop And Average** Add lines to the last program in the text to make it repeat 100 times and produce an average of the 100 results.

■ **Replace With Subroutine** Replace lines 50 and 130 in the main program (the random dice throw subroutine) with a GOSUB calling your 'random number generator' in the first exercise.

■ **INKEY$** Using the INKEY$ function, how would you write a program to read any key typed at the keyboard and print: THE KEY YOU HIT WAS: * as a result (* represents the key you pressed).

■ **Timing Loop** Write a timing loop (a 'counting' loop) and use the INKEY$ function to find how big the value of a variable becomes after 10 seconds (you'll need to use a watch). Write the program so that the final printout reads: THE VALUE OF R AFTER 10 SECONDS IS: * (* represents the value of R).

■ **IF-THEN Tests** Write a simple game program in which the computer generates a random number between 1 and 100 (inclusive) and the player has to guess what the number is. The player has five tries. Each time, the program responds with the messages YOUR GUESS IS TOO LARGE, YOUR GUESS IS TOO SMALL, or YOU ARE RIGHT, CONGRATULATIONS, or NO MORE GOES. YOU LOSE!

Answers on page 199.

Answers To 'Exercises' On pages 190-191

Loops 1
THE VALUE OF A IS 450
Loops 2
START
STOP
Loops 3
THE VALUE OF A IS NOW 160
Loops 4
I LIKE BASIC
I LIKE BASIC
I LIKE BASIC
:

Until you RESET or BREAK the program
Loops 5
I'M FEELING LOOPY
(15 times)
Read-Data 1
WE'RE TESTING THE READ STATEMENT
170
Read-Data 2
X=1
X=2
:
:
X=23

Another Dimension

One-dimensional arrays, as we have seen, store a collection of data that have something in common. Two-dimensional arrays are used for tables and charts

So far we have considered two types of variables, simple variables and subscripted variables. Simple variables are like memory locations where numbers (or character strings) can be stored and manipulated by referring to the variable 'label'. Simple variables can store just one value or string and have 'simple' variable names — N, B2, X, Y3 are examples. Subscripted variables, sometimes called one-dimensional arrays, can store a whole list of values or strings. The number of values or strings that can be held is specified at the beginning of the program using the DIM statement. For example, DIM A(16) establishes that the array labelled A can contain 16 separate values. It should be noted, however, that many BASICS accept A(0) as the first element, so that DIM A(16) actually defines 17 elements. These 'locations' are referred to by using the appropriate subscript. PRINT A(1) will print the first element in the array; LET B = A(12) assigns the value in the 12th element in the array to variable B; LET A(3) = A(5) assigns the value of the fifth element to the third element.

Sometimes, however, we need to be able to manipulate data that is best presented as tables. Note how closely this resembles a spreadsheet (see page 116). Such data could range from tables of football results to a breakdown of sales by item and department in a store. As an example of a typical table of data, consider this breakdown of household expenditure over a one year period:

	RENT	PHONE	ELECTR.	FOOD	CAR
JAN	260.00	25.10	41.50	161.30	50.55
FEB	260.00	35.40	43.75	145.90	46.20
MAR	260.00	29.05	50.70	151.20	43.40
APR	260.00	26.20	44.60	155.30	49.20
MAY	260.00	19.30	39.80	150.95	48.30
JUN	260.00	20.45	32.60	147.65	52.30
JUL	260.00	30.50	26.10	150.35	58.40
AUG	260.00	29.50	22.40	148.05	61.20
SEP	260.00	28.25	24.45	148.60	59.45
OCT	260.00	31.15	34.50	154.90	23.50
NOV	260.00	31.05	39.50	160.05	45.95
DEC	260.00	28.95	42.20	210.60	51.25

Arranging the information in this way allows it to be manipulated in a number of ways relatively simply. It is easy, for example, to find the total expenditure in March by simply adding up all the figures in the row for March. It is just as easy to find the total expenditure for the year on the telephone or the car by adding up the vertical columns. Similarly, it is easy to find monthly or yearly averages. This table is called a two-dimensional array. It has 12 rows and five columns.

Two-dimensional arrays such as this can also be represented in BASIC in much the same way as single-dimension arrays. The difference is that the variable now needs two subscripts to reference any location.

If we were writing a BASIC program using this table of information, the simplest thing would be to treat the whole table as a single two-dimensional array. Just as with ordinary subscripted arrays, we give it a variable name. Let's call it A (for 'Array'). Again, as with ordinary subscripted arrays, it will need to be DIMensioned. As there are 12 rows and five columns, it is dimensioned thus: DIM A(12,5). The order in which the two subscripts are put is important; the convention is that rows are specified first and columns second. Our table above has 12 rows (one for each month) and five columns (one for each of the five categories of expenditure), it is therefore a 12-by-5 array.

The DIM statement serves two essential functions. It sets aside enough memory locations in the computer's memory for the array, and it allows each of the locations to be specified by the variable name followed, in brackets, by the row and column positions. The DIM statement DIM X(3,5), for example, would create a variable X able to represent an array with three rows and five columns.

Look at the table and assume that the information has been entered as the elements in a two-dimensional array labelled A. Find the values present in A(1,1), A(1,5), A(2,1), A(3,3) and A(12,3).

It is possible to enter a table of information as an array in part of a program by using LET statements, for example.

```
30 LET A(1,2) = 25.1
40 LET A(1,3) = 41.5
50 LET A(1,4) = 161.30
      :
      :
610 LET A(12,5) = 51.25
```

But this is clearly a laborious way of doing things. A far simpler method is to use either READ and DATA statements or the INPUT statement with nested FOR...NEXT loops. Let's see how it could be done using the READ statement:

```
10 DIM A(12,5)
20 FOR R = 1 TO 12
30 FOR C = 1 TO 5
40 READ A(R,C)
50 NEXT C
60 NEXT R
70 DATA 260, 25.1, 41.5, 161.3, 50.55, 260, 35.4,
```

43.75
80 DATA 145.9, 46.2, 260, 29.05, 50.7, 151.2, 43.4, 260
90 DATA 26.2, 44.6, 155.3, 49.2, 260, 19.3, 39.8, 150.95
100 DATA 48.3, 260, 20.45, 32.6, 147.65, 52.3, 260, 30.5
110 DATA 26.10, 150.35, 58.4, 260, 29.5, 22.4, 148.05, 61.2, 260
120 DATA 28.25, 24.45, 148.6, 59.45, 260, 31.15, 34.5
130 DATA 154.9, 23.5, 260, 31.05, 39.5, 160.05, 45.95
140 DATA 260, 28.95, 42.2, 210.6, 51.25
150 END

There are a number of important points to note about this program. The first is that the DIM statement is right at the beginning of the program. A DIM statement should be executed only once in a program and so it is usual to place it near the beginning or before any loops are executed. The second point to note is that there are two FOR...NEXT loops, one to set the 'row' part of the subscript and one to set the 'column'. These two loops do not follow one after the other; they are 'nested' one inside the other. Notice the limits chosen. FOR R = 1 TO 12 will increment the value for the row from one to 12; FOR C = 1 TO 5 will increment the value for the column from one to five.

Right in the middle of the nested loop is the READ statement. The crucial part of the program is:

```
20 FOR R = 1 TO 12
30 FOR C = 1 TO 5
40 READ A(R,C)
50 NEXT C
60 NEXT R
```

The first time through, after lines 20 and 30 have been executed, the values of R and C will both be one, so line 40 will be equivalent to READ A(1,1). The first item of data in the DATA statement is 260, so this value will be assigned to the first row and the first column of the array. The choice of eight elements to each DATA statement is purely arbitrary.

After that has happened, the NEXT C statement sends the program back to line 30 and the value of C is incremented to two. Line 40 is now equivalent to READ A(1,2) and the next item of data, 25.1, will be assigned to the first row and the second column of the array. This process is repeated until C has been incremented to 5. After that, the NEXT R statement in line 60 returns the program to line 20 and R is incremented to two. Line 30 will set C to one again and so now line 40 will be equivalent to READ A(2,1).

Nesting loops in this way is very useful, but care is needed. Each loop must be nested completely within another loop and the order of the NEXT statements must be carefully observed. Notice how the first loop, FOR R, has the second NEXT statement. When there are two loops, one nested inside the other, the first loop is called the outer loop and the second is called the inner loop. The whole of the inner loop will always be completed before the index of the outer loop is incremented. It is possible to nest loops to as many 'depths' as required by the program, but such programs can become complex and difficult to follow and debug. It is bad programming practice to put branching instructions inside loops and GOTOs are to be avoided.

Let's look at the DATA statements. Notice that commas are used to separate data items, but there must be no comma before the first data item or after the last. We have inserted spaces between each data item, but this is not normal. Mistakes when entering the data are easy to make and difficult to spot later. As many DATA statements as required may be used. Each new line needs to start with a DATA statement. The data is read in one item at a time, starting from the beginning of the first DATA statement and working through until all the items have been read. Be sure that the number of data items is correct or you will get an error message when the program is run.

The program presented so far does not actually do anything except convert appropriate data into a two-dimensional array. After the program has been entered and RUN, nothing will apparently happen and all you will see on the screen will be the BASIC prompt. To test that the data is correctly placed, try a few PRINT commands. (A command in BASIC is a keyword that can be immediately executed without having to be within a program and does not therefore need a line number. Examples are LIST, RUN, SAVE, AUTO, EDIT and PRINT). PRINT A(1,1) <CR> should cause the number 260 to appear on the screen. What will be printed by the following commands?

```
PRINT A(12,1)
PRINT A(1,5)
PRINT A(5,1)
PRINT A(5,5)
```

To make the program do something useful, it will need to be extended. As it stands it forms an adequate basis for a 'main program'. To use it as part of a larger, more useful program, modules can be written as subroutines to be called by GOSUBs inserted at suitable points before the END statement.

In the early stages of designing a household accounts program, it is best to start with a simple written description of the general requirements. We might decide that we want to be able to have totals and averages calculated for monthly expenditure or by category (electricity, for example). We can work out the details of how to derive these results at a later stage. If there is a choice to be made within the program about which subroutines we wish to be executed we will probably want to be prompted by a 'menu' which will direct control to the appropriate subroutines as a result of our response. An early sketch of the program at this stage might look like this:

```
MAIN PROGRAM
(DATA ENTRY)

MENU
(SELECT SUBROUTINES)

END
```

A little further refinement may show that we will need subroutines to calculate totals for months or for categories (MONTHTOTAL and CATTOTAL), average monthly expenditure (MONTHAV) and average yearly expenditure by category (CATAV). The reason for using one-word names for these subroutines is to help us to plan the program without having to worry about details such as line numbers at this stage. On reflection we may decide that even the main menu selection part of the program should be dealt with as a subroutine in order to keep the main part of the program as a separate module. The next stage of refinement of the program will look like this:

```
MAIN PROGRAM (DATA ENTRY)
   MENU (CALL SUBROUTINE)
END

**SUBROUTINES**

1 MENU
2 TOTALS
3 AVERAGES

(2) TOTALS
4 MONTHTOTAL
5 CATTOTAL

(3) AVERAGES
6 MONTHAV
7 CATAV
```

This sketch of the program shows that the MENU subroutine will give us a choice of either TOTALS or AVERAGES. Both of these will themselves be subroutines. The TOTALS subroutine will give a further choice of MONTHTOTAL or CATTOTAL. These will be the subroutines that perform the actual calculations.

The AVERAGES subroutine will give a choice of MONTHAV or CATAV, and again these will be subroutines to perform the appropriate calculations. At this stage it should be possible to see whether our 'program' will do what we want, without doing any actual coding (detailed program writing in BASIC). If we can be satisfied that 'so far so good', we are ready to tackle the writing of the modules (subroutines) themselves. The only change needed to the main program will be a subroutine call before the END statement, so we could add:

```
145 GOSUB **MENU**
```

Note that we are still using 'names' for subroutines rather than line numbers. Many languages, PASCAL, for example, allow sub-programs to be called by name, but most versions of BASIC do not and actual line numbers are needed instead. However, these 'details' can be incorporated later.

Let's see how the MENU subroutine could be written (line numbers have been omitted and you can add appropriate ones if you wish to implement this program).

```
REM THE **MENU** SUBROUTINE
PRINT "WOULD YOU LIKE T(OTALS) OR
    A(VERAGES)?"
PRINT "TYPE EITHER A OR T"
INPUT L$
IF L$ = "T" THEN GOSUB *TOTALS*
IF L$.= "A" THEN GOSUB *AVERAGES*
RETURN
```

Note: we are marking the subroutines called by enclosing them within *——* marks. You will have to use line numbers instead. These can be inserted when you are in a position to know what they are.

Suppose you type T for TOTALS. The program will then call the TOTALS subroutine. This will then present another menu and could look like this:

```
REM THE **TOTALS** SUBROUTINE
PRINT "WOULD YOU LIKE TOTALS FOR"
PRINT "M(ONTH) OR C(ATEGORY)?"
PRINT "TYPE EITHER M OR C"
INPUT L$
IF L$ = "M" THEN GOSUB *MONTHTOTAL*
IF L$ = "C" THEN GOSUB *CATTOTAL*
RETURN
```

Suppose you selected M for MONTHTOTAL. Let's see how we could write a module to calculate the total expenditure for any month in the year.

```
REM THE **MONTHTOTAL** SUBROUTINE
REM THIS CALCULATES TOTAL EXPENDITURE FOR
REM ANY MONTH
PRINT "SELECT MONTH"
PRINT "1-JAN 2-FEB 3-MAR 4-APR 5-MAY"
PRINT "6-JUN 7-JUL 8-AUG 9-SEP"
PRINT "10-OCT 11-NOV 12-DEC"
PRINT "TYPE A NUMBER FOR THE MONTH"
LET T = 0
INPUT M
FOR C = 1 TO 5
LET T = T + A(M,C)
NEXT C
PRINT "THE TOTAL EXPENDITURE FOR MONTH"
PRINT "NUMBER ";M;" IS ";T
RETURN
```

The number representing the month is typed in and the INPUT statement assigns the number to the variable M (MONTH). M is used to specify the 'row' subscript of the two-dimensional array A. The FOR-NEXT loop increments the value of C (column) from one to five so the first time through the loop, if we had selected three for March, the LET statement would be equivalent to LET $T = T + A(3,1)$. The next time round it would be equivalent to LET $T = T + A(3,2)$ and so on.

This time we'll leave you to write the other subroutines, or try out the other exercises. Two-dimensional arrays are ideal for any program that involves tables of data, be they statistical, financial or any other quantity.

Answers To Exercises On Page 195

RND Function
```
40 IF R >6 THEN LET R = 1
```
Loop And Average
```
5 FOR L = 1 TO 100
    :
80 LET T = T + R
90 NEXT L
100 LET A = T/100
110 PRINT A
120 END
```
Replace With Subroutine
Delete lines 5, 80, 90, 100, and 110 in the solution above. Change lines 10 to 70 to (say) 1000 to 1070. Check that line 40 is as in the RND Function solution above. Then add 1080 RETURN. Incorporate the result into the main program. Change lines 50 and 130 in the main program to read 50 GOSUB 1000 and 130 GOSUB 1000.

INKEYS
```
10 PRINT "TYPE ANY KEY"
20 LET A$ = INKEY$
30 IF A$ ="" THEN GOTO 20
40 PRINT "THE KEY YOU HIT WAS";A$
50 END
```
(On the Spectrum add: 15 IF INKEY$ <>"" THEN GOTO 15)

Timing Loop
```
5 PRINT "HIT THE SPACE-BAR AFTER 10 SECONDS"
10 FOR L = 0 TO 1
20 LET R = R + 1
30 IF INKEY$ = "    " THEN GOTO 60
40 LET L = 0
50 NEXT L
60 PRINT "THE VALUE OF R AFTER 10 SECONDS IS
    ";R
70 END
```

IF...THEN
```
10 GOSUB 1000
20 PRINT "GUESS THE NUMBER"
30 FOR G = 1 TO 5
40 INPUT N
50 IF N >R THEN GOTO 110
60 IF N <R THEN GOTO 130
70 IF N = R THEN GOTO
80 NEXT G
90 PRINT "NO MORE GOES. YOU LOSE!"
100 GOTO 500
110 PRINT "YOUR GUESS IS TOO LARGE"
120 GOTO 80
130 PRINT "YOUR GUESS IS TOO SMALL"
140 GOTO 80
150 PRINT "YOU ARE RIGHT,
    CONGRATULATIONS".
500 END
1000 REM **RANDOM SUBROUTINE**
(Insert your subroutine here.)
1020 RETURN
```

Exercises

■ **Assigning Values** Write a program that assigns values to the elements ('Petrol', 'Service' etc.) of the matrix (see illustration below). Next, write a subroutine that asks for a month, and an expense heading, and prints the contents of the box thus specified. Finally, write a subroutine that finds the sum of each column, and places the result in the bottom box, does the same across the rows, and then calculates the grand total, which it stores in the lower right box.

■ **Bugs** The following program would not run properly and would produce an error message. There are two mistakes. Find them and make appropriate corrections.

```
●10 DIM A(3,4)
  20 FOR R = 1 TO 3
  30 FOR C = 1 TO 4
  40 READ A(R,C)
  50 NEXT C
  60 NEXT R
  70 FOR X = 1 TO 3
  90 FOR Y = 1 TO 4
  100 PRINT A(Y,X)
  110 NEXT Y
  120 NEXT X
  130 DATA 2,4,6,8,10,12,14,16,18,20,22
  140 END
```
Answers on page 203.

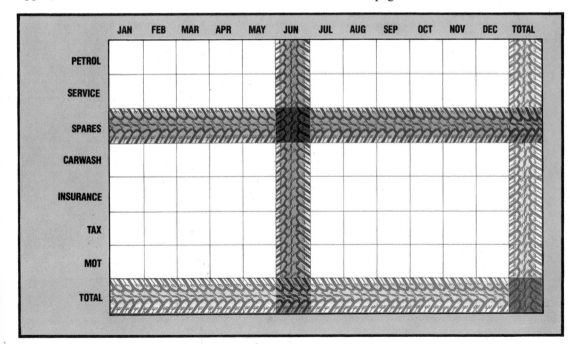

	JAN	FEB	MAR	APR	MAY	JUN	JUL	AUG	SEP	OCT	NOV	DEC	TOTAL
PETROL													
SERVICE													
SPARES													
CARWASH													
INSURANCE													
TAX													
MOT													
TOTAL													

Car Expenses
The picture shows a grid of 8 × 13 squares. The rows represent different elements of the cost of running a car, and the columns represent the different months of the year. Follow the exercise on 'Assigning Values' to calculate the yearly cost of running a car

Keeping Control

All versions of Basic feature 'control structures' that govern the flow of a program. Some machines, however, offer a wide range of alternatives, with subtle differences

The first 10 parts of the Basic Programming course have covered almost all of the more important aspects of the BASIC language. In this part we will present an overview of the topics we have covered so far, deal with a few interesting asides and give some pointers to where we shall go next.

First the overview: a high-level language such as BASIC provides the user with a set of instructions that are translated internally into a form the computer can understand. Any computer program can be written using just two simple patterns, called 'constructs'. These are 'sequence' constructs and 'control structures' of which only two are essential in BASIC: IF...THEN...ELSE and WHILE...DO. Most other computer languages provide considerably more.

The sequence construct allows the task to be broken down into a set of sub-tasks that perform the main task when executed in sequence. The size of the sub-tasks depends on the language; in BASIC the sub-tasks are represented by the statements written on each line, and the sequence is represented by the line numbers. Thus, if the task is to multiply the value assigned to a variable by 10, the sequence we could use might be:

```
110 INPUT N
120 LET N = N * 10
130 PRINT N
```

In addition to sequence constructs, we also need control structures. These are constructs that alter the order of execution of statements in a program.

The simplest control structure provided by BASIC is GOTO. This is an unconditional jump (or branch) that re-directs the execution of the program to a specified line number without a test or condition having to be satisfied. GOSUB is also an unconditional branch, but the program will always RETURN to the point immediately after the GOSUB and its use in structured programming is perfectly acceptable.

The IF...THEN...ELSE control structure is available in BASIC. It takes the form of the IF...THEN statement and has the following syntax ('syntax' is the computer jargon for 'form'):

IF (specified condition) is true THEN execute specified statement (ELSE) execute the next statement.

Note that in standard BASIC, the ELSE part of IF...THEN...ELSE is implied. In some BASIC dialects and in certain other languages, PASCAL for example, ELSE forms part of the statement.

IF...THEN...ELSE (IF...THEN in BASIC) performs one of two sub-tasks depending on whether a certain condition is true or not. Consider the following program, which is designed to find the square roots of numbers input from the keyboard unless a 'flag' value of −9999 is input (in order to terminate the program):

```
10 PRINT "INPUT A NUMBER"
20 INPUT N
30 IF N = −9999 THEN GOTO 70
40 LET S = SQR(N)
50 PRINT "THE SQUARE ROOT OF ";N;" IS ";S
60 GOTO 10
70 END
```

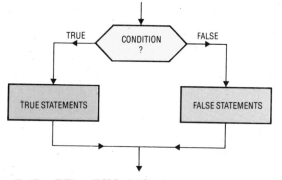

The IF...THEN...ELSE Control Structure
If the condition is True, the True statements will be executed. If the condition is False, the False statements will be executed

What line 30 is really saying here is 'IF it is true that N = −9999 THEN go to the end of the program ELSE (if it is not true that N = −9999) execute the next line of the program to find the square root'.

The other essential control structure (WHILE... DO) is not directly available in BASIC, but it can easily be simulated. WHILE...DO is a type of 'do-loop' and it means 'repeat a statement or set of statements WHILE a specified condition is true' or 'WHILE a condition is true DO something'.

WHILE...DO always tests the condition before the statements are executed, so if the test fails first time through, the statements (called the body of the loop) are not executed. As an example, consider a games program that prompts the player to 'PRESS SPACE-BAR WHEN READY'. This part of the program could be written (in 'pseudo-language' or simplified English) as:

WHILE space-bar is not pressed
DO scan keyboard
start game

In BASIC this could be written:

```
250 PRINT "PRESS SPACE-BAR WHEN READY"
260 IF INKEY$ < > "   " THEN GOTO 260
270 GOSUB *START*
```

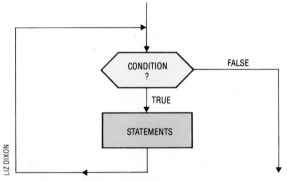

The DO . . . WHILE Control Structure
The loop is repeated as long as the condition is True. The statements may never be executed (if the initial condition is False)

Line 260 says IF INKEY$ is not equal to (< >) a space ("   ") THEN go back and check the keyboard again. A slightly more elegant way of writing it would be:

```
250 PRINT "PRESS SPACE-BAR WHEN READY"
260 FOR X = 0 TO 1 STEP 0
270 IF INKEY$ = "   " THEN LET X = 2
280 NEXT X
290 GOSUB *START*
```

In this program fragment the loop (to scan the keyboard) is executed only if the space-bar has not been pressed. If the space-bar has been pressed (i.e. INKEY$ = "   ") then the program exits from the FOR . . . NEXT loop to line 290, which is the call to the START subroutine. (NB. We are using 'labels' or names for subroutines. Many versions of BASIC cannot call subroutines by name and you will have to use line numbers instead of labels.)

We haven't encountered STEP before, and this is perhaps an unusual application for it. When using a FOR . . . NEXT loop, STEP allows the 'index' to be incremented in units other than one. FOR I = 1 TO 10 STEP 2 will cause I to have the value 1 on the first pass of the loop, followed by 3,5,7 and 9. The next increment (to 11) will exceed the limit of 10 so the loop will be finished. It is even possible to have the index counting backwards. For I = 10 TO 1 STEP −1 will cause I to count from 10 down to 1. Using STEP 0 is really a clever trick that ensures that the loop

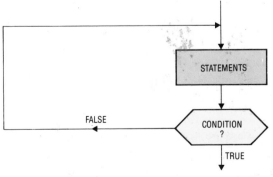

The REPEAT . . . UNTIL Control Structure
The loop is repeated until the condition becomes True. The statements will always be executed at least once

will never finish unless X is 'artificially increased' — as in the case of our IF . . . THEN statement.

Another useful control structure, again not directly available in BASIC but easily simulated, is REPEAT . . . UNTIL. Here the condition test comes after the main body of the loop, so the statement or statements in the main body will always be repeated at least once. Look at this 'random number generator':

```
10 PRINT "HIT THE SPACE-BAR"
20 FOR X = 0 TO 1 STEP 0
30 LET R = R + 1
40 IF R > 9 THEN LET R = 1
50 IF INKEY$ = "   " THEN LET X = 2
60 NEXT X
70 PRINT "THE VALUE OF R IS   ";R
```

Here, the main body (incrementing the value of R) is always executed at least once since the test to branch out of the loop (IF INKEY$ = "   ") does not come until after the increment statement (LET R = R + 1).

Yet another non-essential but useful control structure is that usually called CASE. In BASIC, the CASE structure is implemented using either ON . . . GOTO or ON . . . GOSUB. This is how it works. ON . . . GOTO is a multiple-branching statement that incorporates several IF . . . THEN conditional tests into a single statement. Consider a program fragment that converts the numbers 1 to 7 into the words for the seven days of the week:

```
1050 IF D = 1 THEN GOTO 2020
1060 IF D = 2 THEN GOTO 2040
1070 IF D = 3 THEN GOTO 2060
1080 IF D = 4 THEN GOTO 2080
1090 IF D = 5 THEN GOTO 3000
2000 IF D = 6 THEN GOTO 3020
2010 IF D = 7 THEN GOTO 3040
2020 PRINT "MONDAY"
2030 GOTO *END*
2040 PRINT "TUESDAY"
2050 GOTO *END*
2060 PRINT "WEDNESDAY"
2070 GOTO *END*
2080 PRINT "THURSDAY"
2090 GOTO *END*
3000 PRINT "FRIDAY"
3010 GOTO *END*
3020 PRINT "SATURDAY"
3030 GOTO *END*
3040 PRINT "SUNDAY"
3050 GOTO *END*
```

A more compact way of achieving the same object in BASIC is to use ON . . . GOTO like this:

```
1050 ON D GOTO 2020,2040,2060,2080,
          3000,3020,3040
```

ON . . . GOSUB works the same way, except that the value of the variable determines which subroutine is branched to. Here is a slight modification of the dice program (see page 194) using ON . . . GOSUB to select the appropriate graphics for the dice selected by the RND function:

DECIMAL	BINARY	CHARACTER
32	0 0 1 0 0 0 0 0	= (space)
33	0 0 1 0 0 0 0 1	= !
34	0 0 1 0 0 0 1 0	= "
35	0 0 1 0 0 0 1 1	= #
36	0 0 1 0 0 1 0 0	= $
37	0 0 1 0 0 1 0 1	= %
38	0 0 1 0 0 1 1 0	= &
39	0 0 1 0 0 1 1 1	= '
40	0 0 1 0 1 0 0 0	= (
41	0 0 1 0 1 0 0 1	=)
42	0 0 1 0 1 0 1 0	= *
43	0 0 1 0 1 0 1 1	= +
44	0 0 1 0 1 1 0 0	= ,
45	0 0 1 0 1 1 0 1	= -
46	0 0 1 0 1 1 1 0	= .
47	0 0 1 0 1 1 1 1	= /
48	0 0 1 1 0 0 0 0	= 0
49	0 0 1 1 0 0 0 1	= 1
50	0 0 1 1 0 0 1 0	= 2
51	0 0 1 1 0 0 1 1	= 3
52	0 0 1 1 0 1 0 0	= 4
53	0 0 1 1 0 1 0 1	= 5
54	0 0 1 1 0 1 1 0	= 6
55	0 0 1 1 0 1 1 1	= 7
56	0 0 1 1 1 0 0 0	= 8
57	0 0 1 1 1 0 0 1	= 9
58	0 0 1 1 1 0 1 0	= :
59	0 0 1 1 1 0 1 1	= ;
60	0 0 1 1 1 1 0 0	= <
61	0 0 1 1 1 1 0 1	= =
62	0 0 1 1 1 1 1 0	= >
63	0 0 1 1 1 1 1 1	= ?
64	0 1 0 0 0 0 0 0	= @
65	0 1 0 0 0 0 0 1	= A
66	0 1 0 0 0 0 1 0	= B
67	0 1 0 0 0 0 1 1	= C
68	0 1 0 0 0 1 0 0	= D
69	0 1 0 0 0 1 0 1	= E
70	0 1 0 0 0 1 1 0	= F
71	0 1 0 0 0 1 1 1	= G
72	0 1 0 0 1 0 0 0	= H
73	0 1 0 0 1 0 0 1	= I
74	0 1 0 0 1 0 1 0	= J
75	0 1 0 0 1 0 1 1	= K
76	0 1 0 0 1 1 0 0	= L
77	0 1 0 0 1 1 0 1	= M
78	0 1 0 0 1 1 1 0	= N
79	0 1 0 0 1 1 1 1	= O
80	0 1 0 1 0 0 0 0	= P
81	0 1 0 1 0 0 0 1	= Q
82	0 1 0 1 0 0 1 0	= R
83	0 1 0 1 0 0 1 1	= S
84	0 1 0 1 0 1 0 0	= T
85	0 1 0 1 0 1 0 1	= U
86	0 1 0 1 0 1 1 0	= V
87	0 1 0 1 0 1 1 1	= W
88	0 1 0 1 1 0 0 0	= X
89	0 1 0 1 1 0 0 1	= Y
90	0 1 0 1 1 0 1 0	= Z
91	0 1 0 1 1 0 1 1	= [
92	0 1 0 1 1 1 0 0	= \
93	0 1 0 1 1 1 0 1	=]
94	0 1 0 1 1 1 1 0	= ^
95	0 1 0 1 1 1 1 1	= _
96	0 1 1 0 0 0 0 0	= `
97	0 1 1 0 0 0 0 1	= a
98	0 1 1 0 0 0 1 0	= b
99	0 1 1 0 0 0 1 1	= c
100	0 1 1 0 0 1 0 0	= d
101	0 1 1 0 0 1 0 1	= e
102	0 1 1 0 0 1 1 0	= f
103	0 1 1 0 0 1 1 1	= g
104	0 1 1 0 1 0 0 0	= h
105	0 1 1 0 1 0 0 1	= i
106	0 1 1 0 1 0 1 0	= j
107	0 1 1 0 1 0 1 1	= k
108	0 1 1 0 1 1 0 0	= l
109	0 1 1 0 1 1 0 1	= m
110	0 1 1 0 1 1 1 0	= n
111	0 1 1 0 1 1 1 1	= o
112	0 1 1 1 0 0 0 0	= p
113	0 1 1 1 0 0 0 1	= q
114	0 1 1 1 0 0 1 0	= r
115	0 1 1 1 0 0 1 1	= s
116	0 1 1 1 0 1 0 0	= t
117	0 1 1 1 0 1 0 1	= u
118	0 1 1 1 0 1 1 0	= v
119	0 1 1 1 0 1 1 1	= w
120	0 1 1 1 1 0 0 0	= x
121	0 1 1 1 1 0 0 1	= y
122	0 1 1 1 1 0 1 0	= z
123	0 1 1 1 1 0 1 1	= {
124	0 1 1 1 1 1 0 0	=	
125	0 1 1 1 1 1 0 1	= }
126	0 1 1 1 1 1 1 0	= ~

ASCII
Here is a complete list of the ASCII values between 32 and 126, their binary equivalents, and the characters they represent. The meaning attached to values outside this range varies considerably from machine to machine

```
390 REM SELECT SUBROUTINE
400 REM USING ON...GOSUB
410 ON D GOSUB 530,600,670,740,810,880
470 RETURN
```

Although your version of BASIC probably contains many statements and functions we have not covered, most will be extensions to the 'basic' BASIC designed to take advantage of particular features of your machine. Many of these will relate to graphics features built into the hardware — instructions such as PAINT, PAPER, INK, BEEP and CIRCLE. These tend to be 'machine specific' and so we have not included them in this chapter, though we will be giving you more details later.

Before ending the basic part of our BASIC course, however, there are some loose ends to tie up — a discussion of the ASCII character set, together with a couple of functions for helping manipulate characters, and a way of defining new functions (or functions not included in your version of BASIC).

Several methods of representing letters of the alphabet and other characters such as numbers and punctuation marks in digital form have been devised over the years. One of the first was Morse code, which uses combinations of dots and dashes to represent characters. From the computer's point of view, Morse code suffers from the disadvantage of using different numbers of bits for different letters — between one and six dots and dashes for each character. Other attempts at making a more regular and systematic character code (e.g. the Baudot code, which uses five bits to represent up to 32 characters) have fallen by the wayside and the almost universal system now in use is the ASCII code (American Standard Code for Information Interchange).

The ASCII code uses one byte to represent the 94 printable characters, the 'space' and a number of control 'characters'. Eight bits could give 256 unique combinations (2^8), but this is far more than is needed to represent the characters of a standard typewriter or computer keyboard, so only seven are used, allowing for 128 unique combinations. (The eighth bit is usually wasted but is sometimes used to specify an alternative set of foreign language or graphics characters.) The binary and decimal ASCII codes for the standard range of characters are given in the table on page 201.

As you can see from the table, the ASCII code for the letter A is 65 and for B is 66. The codes for the lower case letters a and b are 97 and 98. Every lower case letter has an ASCII code value larger by 32 than its upper case equivalent. This constant 'offset' makes it easy to convert lower case letters in character strings into upper case letters, and vice-versa. To do this we will need two further functions not used so far in the Basic Programming course — ASC and CHR$.

The ASC function takes a printable character and returns its ASCII code equivalent, so PRINT ASC("A") would print the number 65 on the screen; PRINT ASC("b") would print 98.

The CHR$ function does the opposite; it takes a number, assumes it is an ASCII code and returns the character it represents. Thus PRINT CHR$(65) would print A, while PRINT CHR$(98) would print b. The CHR$ and ASC functions are widely used, along with LEFT$, RIGHT$ and MID$ in programs making heavy use of character strings. Here's a short program that accepts a character from the keyboard, checks to see if it is upper case and converts it to upper case if it is not:

```
10 REM LOWER TO UPPER CASE CONVERTER
20 PRINT "INPUT A CHARACTER"
30 INPUT C$
40 LET C = ASC(C$)
50 IF C > 90 THEN LET C = C −32
60 PRINT CHR$(C)
```

We shall see more of this type of string manipulation later in this section.

Finally, in this round-up, a look at functions you may not have in your version of BASIC. Almost all versions of the language allow the programmer to create new functions, and these are almost as easy to use as built-in functions. The DEF statement signals to BASIC that a new function is being defined. Here's how to define a function to calculate the volume of a sphere (the formula is $V = \frac{4}{3}\pi r^3$, where r is the radius of the sphere and π (pi) is the constant approximately equal to 3.14159):

```
10 REM FUNCTION TO CALCULATE VOLUME OF A
   SPHERE
20 DEF FNV(X) = 4 * 3.14159 * X * X * X/3
30 PRINT "INPUT RADIUS OF SPHERE"
40 INPUT R
50 PRINT "THE VOLUME OF A SPHERE OF RADIUS
   ";R;" IS"
60 PRINT FNV(R)
70 END
```

This way of defining a function is fairly straightforward, but let's look at the line in detail:

```
DEFines   function identifier
    ↓         ↓
20 DEF FNV(X) = 4* 3.14159 * X * X * X/3
       ↑    ↑
FuNction  dummy variable
```

When the function is defined, the letters FN are followed by an identifying letter — V in the case of the function above — and this must then be followed by a 'dummy variable'. This dummy variable must also be used in the function definition on the right of the equals sign. When the function is used in a program, any numeric variable can be used in place of the dummy variable in the definition.

At a further point in the program above it would be equally possible to use the 'volume of a sphere' function like this:

```
999 LET A = 66
1000 LET B = FNV(A)
1010 PRINT B
```

```
1020 LET C = 5
1030 LET D = B + FNV(C)
1040 PRINT D
1050 LET G = FNV(16)
1060 PRINT G
```

Some BASICS allow multiple variables to be used in the defined function. Thus, a function to find the average of two numbers could be written:

```
110 DEF FNA(B,C) = (B + C )/ 2
110 INPUT "ENTER TWO NUMBERS";B,C
120 LET A = FNA(B,C): REM THE 'AVERAGE'
    FUNCTION
130 PRINT "THE AVERAGE OF ";B;" AND ";C;" IS ";A
```

Notice that line 110 above combines the equivalent of two separate statements in one. Most BASICS will automatically print words appearing in double quotation marks following the INPUT statement, so this line is equivalent to:

```
110 PRINT "ENTER TWO NUMBERS"
115 INPUT A,B
```

Line 120 also manages to get the equivalent of two statements in one line by using the colon (:) separator. Statements that would normally belong on separate lines may be written on one line

provided each 'stand-alone' statement is separated from the preceding one by a colon. This can help to save space in long programs, but its use is not to be encouraged as it makes programs less readable and mistakes more likely.

We have now covered all the main points of the BASIC language. In later parts of the Basic Programming course we shall look at program development and program design, rather than at the details of BASIC.

Answers To Exercises On Page 199
Bugs
An 'OUT OF DATA ERROR' will result, because there should be a total of 12 values in the DATA statement in line 130. Secondly, an error will arise in line 100 when it tries to address an element A(4,1). Line 100 should read:

```
100 PRINT A(X,Y)
```

Assigning Values
Below is one version of a program that will perform the required functions. Your own program may look different

```
10 DIM A(8,13)
20 FOR R=1 TO 7
30 FOR C=1 TO 12
40 READ A(R,C)
50 NEXT C
60 NEXT R
70 REM ADD TOTALS
80 GOSUB 300
90 REM PRINT REQUESTED DATA
100 GOSUB 200
110 PRINT "MORE DATA?"
120 PRINT "Y OR N"
130 INPUT A$
140 IF A$="N" THEN GOTO 160
150 GOTO 100
160 END
200 PRINT "WHICH MONTH?"
210 PRINT "1-FOR JANUARY,"
220 PRINT "13 FOR TOTAL, ETC"
230 INPUT M
240 PRINT "WHICH EXPENSE?"
250 PRINT "1-FOR PETROL"
260 PRINT "8-FOR TOTAL, ETC"
270 INPUT X
280 PRINT "VALUE IS ";A(X,M)
290 RETURN
300 FOR R=1 TO 7
310 LET T=0
320 FOR C=1 TO 12
330 LET T=T+A(R,C)
340 NEXT C
350 LET A(R,13)=T
360 NEXT R
370 FOR C=1 TO 13
380 LET T=0
390 FOR R=1 TO 7
400 LET T=T+A(R,C)
410 NEXT R
420 LET A(8,C)=T
430 NEXT C
440 RETURN
500 REM YOUR DATA FOLLOWS HERE
510 REM EIGHTY-FOUR VALUES
520 REM 'DATA 11.35, 9.87' ETC
```

Basic Flavours

The Dragon 32 has a non-standard version of ASCII, which does not permit lower case characters, so the lower to upper case converter program will not convert lower case to upper case; try it anyway, and read your manual for more information about the Dragon 32 character set.

On the Oric-1, the Vic-20, the Dragon 32 and the Commodore 64 you cannot write more than one variable inside the brackets.

On the Spectrum and the ZX81, replace:

ASC(A$) by CODE A$

and replace:

CHR$(65) by CHR$ 65

If the argument is an expression, it must be put in brackets. Simple arguments — like A$ and 65 — do not need brackets, however.

These statements are not available on the ZX81, Spectrum or Lynx. All these machines allow GOTO and GOSUB to take an arithmetic expression rather than a simple line number as their argument. So replace line 410 by:

410 GOSUB (460 + 70*D)

On the BBC Micro replace

INPUT "ANY MESSAGE";M$$

by

INPUT "ANY MESSAGE",M$$

On the BBC Micro you must define functions at the end of the program after the word END or STOP, not at the beginning as in the example given. In this case, as in many others, BBC BASIC is more powerful than standard BASIC, so consult your manual for more information.

On the Oric-1 in the two program fragments that demonstrate a good loop structure, replace:

IF INKEY$ = "   " THEN LET X = 2

by

IF KEY$ = "   " THEN LET X = 1

On the Dragon 32 replace it by:

IF INKEY$ = "   " THEN LET X = 1

On the Vic-20 and the Commodore 64 replace:

IF INKEY$ = "   " THEN LET X = 2

by

GET A$:IF A$ = "   " THEN LET X = 1

Directory Enquiry

Using all the techniques of Basic programming that we have learnt so far, we now take the first steps towards developing a database program

Now that many of the fundamentals of BASIC have been covered, it is time to put what we have learned to good use by developing a real program. Of course, all the programs we have encountered so far have been 'real' programs in the sense that they performed a specific task, but they were illustrations of how various parts of the BASIC language work rather than the kind of program you might want to use every day. They illustrated how the 'cogs' of BASIC could be put together to make a simple mechanism. Now let's build a whole clock!

One of the most common questions put to computer users by non-users is: 'What can the computer actually be used for?' The question is not as simplistic as it seems. The usual responses tend to go along the lines of: 'Well, you can computerise your recipes' or 'You can create a computerised telephone or address book.' This tactic seldom works because the questioner usually responds with remarks like: 'I can look at my recipe book when I want to cook something and I can look through my address book when I want to find somebody's address, without the trouble of spending hours writing a program to do it.' At what point does a problem become worthy of a computer solution rather than a conventional solution? We'll answer this by working through the specific example of a computerised address book.

An ordinary address book commonly features an alphabetical finger index designed to enable the user to locate, very approximately, the location of any particular name. Names are usually added as and when needed, and not in strict alphabetical order. Your first entry under P might be David Peterson. Later, you might add Brian Peters or Shashi Patel. Although these are not in alphabetical order, they are all grouped together under P so the task of finding any particular surname beginning with P will not be too great. On the other hand, if you did not use any kind of index finding a name would be a nightmare.

The other entries usual in an address book are the person's address and telephone number together, perhaps, with more personal information. A conventional address book, however, couldn't give you a separate list of all the people who live in Birmingham, or who corresponds to the telephone number 258 1194.

Now this may not represent a serious shortcoming, but if you were the owner of a small mail order company it could be a valuable asset if you could obtain specific information about the people on your mailing list. For example, if you had a new line of children's nightwear you could anticipate new orders by informing your clients, but to save on postage it would probably not be worth sending 'mail shots' to customers without children. This is the sort of consideration that must be evaluated before deciding if a problem is worthy of a computer solution or a conventional solution.

If the computer solution is suitable, then the next consideration must be whether to buy commercially available software or not. A glance through the advertisements in the computer magazines would suggest that every possible eventuality has already been thought of by computer programmers. Closer examination, however, may show that a commercially available program may not do exactly what you want, or it may not be available for your model of computer, or it may be too expensive. The cost of a program generally reflects the development costs. A word processor package might cost £350, but writing your own could cost you far more if it takes you six months of dedicated work.

On the positive side, software you write yourself can be made to do exactly what you want it to. The other factor is the sheer satisfaction of successfully writing a major program for yourself and by yourself.

Designing a program involves several stages. The first is a thorough understanding of the problem. This involves a Clear Statement of the Problem — the CSP stage.

The second is to find an approach to the solution of the problem. This involves a description of the expected form of the input and output as a 'first level description' of the problem. The problems and the solutions should be stated in the broadest terms and these should be gradually refined until we are at the stage where we can code into a particular language.

The third stage is the coding itself. We will use BASIC as our high level language, but it could just as well be any other language. Up to the final stage of coding into BASIC, we will use a pseudo-language intermediate between the freedom and flexibility of English and the rigid structures of an actual computer language such as BASIC.

The approach to programming just described is usually called 'top-down' programming. It works from the topmost level — a general statement of the overall objectives, through various levels of refinement, down to the fine details of the program needed to start coding into the chosen high level language. We shall also try to adhere to the principles of so-called 'structured programming'. These principles will become clear during the course of developing this project.

The steps in the development of the program can be summarised like this:

1. A clear statement of the problem
2. The form of the input and output (first level description)
2.1 Refinement (second level description)
2.2 Further refinement (third to nth level description)
3. Coding into high level language

Before embarking on a major software project, it is essential to state the problem clearly. This is a far from trivial exercise. Let's try a few ideas for our computerised address book.

First we'll start with a list of desirable features — later we can decide which of these can be implemented with a reasonable amount of programming effort. We want to be able to:

1. Look up an address, telephone number and notes by entering a name at the keyboard
2. Get a list of names, addresses and telephone numbers by entering only part of a name (perhaps just the surname or first name)
3. Get a list of names, addresses and telephone numbers for a particular town or area
4. Get a listing of all names starting with a particular initial
5. Get a full listing of all names in the address book, sorted alphabetically
6. Add new entries at will
7. Change entries at will
8. Delete entries at will

Assume that the address book program has been written. What form should the input and output take? How would you like the program to work from the user's point of view? Broadly speaking, programs can be 'menu-driven', 'command-driven' or a combination of both. In a menu-driven program, at every point where a decision has to be taken the user is prompted with a list (menu) of options. The selection can usually be made by pressing just one key. With command-driven programs the user types in specific command words or phrases, usually without prompting. Some programs combine both techniques. The advantage of a menu-driven program is that it should be easy for a newcomer to use, making the program more 'user friendly'. A command-driven program should be faster for an experienced user to use. We will opt for a menu-driven approach, though you might decide to implement this program using command routines instead — the choice is yours.

Given that the program will be centred on a list of names, the first thing we must consider is what form those names should take. Will the computer understand all of the following formats, for example?

> A. J. P. Taylor
> Leonardo da Vinci
> Glenda JACKSON
> Liz T.
> P. O'Toole
> e. e. cummings
> P Jackson
> Twiggy
> GROUCHO MARX
> Sir Freddie Laker

This may seem like splitting hairs, but consider what would happen if you had entered P Jackson and then you asked the program to search for P. Jackson. Unless you had anticipated the problem, the computer would probably respond with NAME NOT FOUND.

There are two ways the problem could be tackled: we can either have 'fuzzy' input, allowing names to be input in any form, together with clever routines to allow for this when searches are made; or we can insist on names being input in a strictly defined form. Any name that did not conform to the convention would result in an error message such as NAME FORMAT UNACCEPTABLE. The choice is an arbitrary one, but we shall opt for very 'fuzzy' input and let the program worry about converting names to a standard form.

From the point of view of an alphabetic search, names can be thought of as having two parts — surnames and the rest. A surname is relatively easy to define: any string of upper or lower case alphabetic characters terminated by a Carriage Return and preceded by a space (ASCII 32). A problem immediately presents itself: what would happen if the name 'Twiggy' were entered without a space at the front? Presumably the program would reject it as an unacceptable format. We'd better change our definition.

A name comprises one or more parts: a surname or a surname and forename. The name may consist of either upper or lower case characters, full stops, apostrophes and hyphens. It will always start with an alphabetic character and be terminated with a Carriage Return (terminal full stops will not be allowed). If there is a space, the last group of characters — including apostrophes and hyphens — will be counted as a surname and other parts, including the space, will be counted as the forename. If there is no space, the whole name will be counted as the surname.

The surname needs special consideration because in any alphabetic search, it always takes precedence over forenames. Thus Albert Peterson would come after Zoltan Patel. If a name consists of only one group of characters, such as Trevanian, Twiggy or a nickname like Baldy, it can be considered as a surname for the purposes of our program.

In an alphabetic search, which name would come first — A. J. P. Taylor or Alfred Taylor? The decision is arbitrary, but the simplest solution would be to ignore the full stops and spaces before the final space and to make the names equivalent to AJP TAYLOR and ALFRED TAYLOR. If we were to do this, both AJP and ALFRED could be considered as forenames, and so AJP would come first.

Part of our program would accept as an input a name and produce as an output a name, address and telephone number (note that we have not even begun to consider the meanings of 'address' and 'telephone number'). If we were to accept names with a 'fuzzy' format as input, with internal conversion to a standardised format, would we expect the output to be in the 'standardised' form, or in the same form as the original entry? The most 'user friendly' output would be for the name to be in the original form, but, as we shall see, this will complicate the programming.

As an initial programming task, let's suppose that a name has been assigned to the string variable NAME$ and that we have two other variables, FORENAME$ and SURNAME$. How will we assign the appropriate parts of NAME$ to FORENAME$ and SURNAME$? Ignoring, for the moment, the problem of keeping a record of the original form in which the name was entered (so that it can be retrieved when needed later), a simple statement of the program could be:

Convert all characters to upper case
Eliminate all non-alphabetic characters except the final space
Assign all characters following a final space to SURNAME$
Assign all characters preceding a final space to FORENAME$

Before considering how this problem could be coded into BASIC, we'll see how the process of 'top down programming' can take us from a very broad statement of our objective to the point where coding into a particular programming language becomes possible. You will notice that we are using not only long variable names like SURNAME$, but command words like BEGIN, LOOP and ENDLOOP. These are constructions that we have invented to help us describe our program. At the final stage of development, they will be replaced with equivalent commands from BASIC. We'll explain more about these commands, and why we have indented some of the lines in the next part of the exercise.

1ST STATEMENT OF OBJECTIVES
INPUT
A name (in any format)
OUTPUT
1. A forename
2. A surname

1ST REFINEMENT
1. Read NAME$
2. Convert all letters to upper case
3. Find last space
4. Read SURNAME$
5. Read FORENAME$
6. Discard non-alphabetics from FORENAME$

2ND REFINEMENT
1. Read NAME$
2. (Convert all letters to upper case)
   BEGIN
   LOOP while unscanned characters remain in NAME$
      Read out characters from NAME$ in turn
      IF character is lower case
         THEN convert to upper case
         ELSE do nothing
      ENDIF
      Assign character to temporary string variable
   ENDLOOP
   LET NAME$ = temporary string variable
   END
3. (Find last space)
   BEGIN
   LOOP while unscanned characters remain in NAME$
      IF Character = "   "
         THEN note position in a variable
         ELSE do nothing
      ENDIF
   ENDLOOP
   END
4. (Read SURNAME$)
   BEGIN
   Assign characters to right of last space in NAME$ to SURNAME$
   END
5. (Read FORENAME$)
   BEGIN
   LOOP while unscanned characters remain in NAME$ up to last space
      SCAN characters
      IF character is not a letter of the alphabet
         THEN do nothing
         ELSE assign character to FORENAME$
      ENDIF
   ENDLOOP
   END
6. (Discard non-alphabetics from FORENAME$)
   (This has been handled in 5 above)

This second level refinement is now very near the stage where it could be coded into a programming language. Let's develop 2 (Convert letters to upper case) to a third level of refinement and then code it into BASIC. We've encountered an algorithm for doing this before (see page 200).

3RD REFINEMENT
2. (Convert all letters to upper case)
   BEGIN
   READ NAME$
   LOOP
   FOR L = 1 TO length of string
      READ character L
      IF character is lower case
         THEN subtract 32 from ASCII value of character
         ELSE do nothing
      ENDIF
      LET TEMPSTRING$ = TEMPSTRING$ + character
   ENDLOOP
   LET NAME$ = TEMPSTRING$
   END

This program fragment in pseudo-language is now close enough to a programming language to be coded. Our version of Microsoft BASIC does not allow the names of string variables to be full words, so single letters will be used instead. Thus NAME$ becomes N$.

```
1000 REM UPPER CASE CONVERSION SUBROUTINE
1010 INPUT "INPUT NAME"; N$: REM FOR TESTING
     ONLY
1020 LET P$ = "": REM ENSURE STRING IS EMPTY
1030 FOR L = 1 TO LEN(N$): REM INDEX OF LOOP
1040 LET T$ = MID$(N$,L,1): REM EXTRACTS
     CHARACTER
1050 LET T = ASC(T$): REM FINDS ASCII VALUE OF
     CH.
1060 IF T >= 97 THEN LET T = T – 32: REM U/C
     CONV.
1070 LET T$ = CHR$(T)
1080 LET P$ = P$ + T$: REM P$ IS TEMPSTRING
1090 NEXT L: REM END OF LOOP
1100 LET N$ = P$: REM N$ IS NOW ALL UPPER CASE
2000 PRINT N$: REM FOR TESTING ONLY
2010 END: REM FOR TESTING ONLY. SUBSTITUTE
2020 REM 'RETURN' IN ACTUAL PROGRAM
```

This program fragment would normally be used as a subroutine to be called from a main program. We have written it for testing purposes with an INPUT statement, a PRINT statement, lots of REM statements, and an END. These would be removed before the subroutine was incorporated into a full program.

Basic Flavours

The Lynx has a function, UPC$(A$), that converts the letters in A$ to upper case, so the program reduces to:
```
1010 INPUT "input name";N$
1020 LET N$=UPC$(N$)
2000 PRINT N$
2010 REM "RETURN" HERE IN ACTUAL
     PROGRAM
```

The Spectrum program in full is:
```
1010 INPUT "INPUT NAME";N$
1020 LET P$=""
1030 FOR L=1 TO LEN N$
1040 LET T$=N$(L)
1050 LET T=CODE T$
1060 IF T>=97 THEN LET T=T—32
1070 LET T$=CHR$ T
1080 LET P$=P$+T$
1090 NEXT L
2000 LET N$=P$
2010 PRINT N$
2020 REM "RETURN" HERE
     IN ACTUAL PROGRAM
```

This program will run on the Dragon, but lower case characters are reserved for the printer, so the problem doesn't really arise

Replace line 1010 with:
1010 INPUT "input name", N$

Exercises

■ Refine all the stages above to the point where they could be turned into a BASIC program. The 'pseudo-language' you use does not need to be the same as ours, but it is a good idea to follow the convention of using upper case letters for keywords that will probably correspond to statement words in the target language (e.g. LOOP, IF, LET etc.). Use small letters for operations that will need to be stated more explicitly when finally coded. These can be in ordinary English.

■ Having developed the programs to a satisfactory level of refinement, convert them into program modules (subroutines) in BASIC. Test them individually using dummy inputs and print statements that can be removed later if they work properly.

Revision Exercises

These exercises demonstrate most of the commonly used statements and functions in BASIC. There are no 'trick' questions and nothing new is being introduced. If you can do all or most of these exercises without difficulty you may consider yourself on the way to becoming a fully fledged BASIC programmer. Answers on page 256.

■ Write a program to accept two numbers input from the keyboard, to add them and to print out the result.

■ Assign two words (character strings) to two string variables and then create a third string variable that concatenates (joins together) the two original words. Print the third variable.

■ Write a program that allows you to type in any word on the keyboard and then prints the length of the string in the message THE WORD YOU TYPED HAS * CHARACTERS (* stands for a number).

■ Write a program that accepts a single character typed in at the keyboard and then tells you what the ASCII value of the character (in decimal) is.

■ Write a program that prompts you with the message TYPE IN A WORD and then answers with the message THE LAST LETTER OF THE WORD WAS *(* stands for a letter).

■ Write a program that prompts you to TYPE IN A PERSON'S NAME and then responds with THE SPACE WAS THE *TH CHARACTER.

■ How would you modify the program above to print 2ND instead of 2TH if the space was in the second position?

■ Write a program that prompts you to TYPE IN A SENTENCE and then responds with the message THE SENTENCE YOU TYPED HAS * WORDS (assume that there will be one word more than there are spaces in the sentence).

■ Test your computer to see if characters (or special graphics) have been assigned to ASCII values from 128 to 255 (use a loop and the CHR$(X) function).

Rank And File

Continuing our programming project to develop a computerised address book, we now look at how our file of data will need to be split up into records and fields

We ended the previous instalment of the Basic Programming course by setting the task of refining the elements of the programming exercise through one or more layers of 'pseudo-language', up to the point where the examples could be coded into BASIC. We will start by revising this exercise and giving some possible solutions. The first 'Statement of Objectives' for the exercise was:

INPUT
A name (in any format)
OUTPUT
1. A forename
2. A surname

In our first level refinement we found that this could be broken down into six steps (later we found that the last step could be dispensed with). These were:

1. Read the name (★ READ ★)
2. Convert all the letters to upper case (★ CONVERT ★)
3. Find the last space (★ SPACE ★)
4. Read the surname (★ READSURNAME ★)
5. Read the forename (★ READFORENAME ★)
6. Discard the non-alphabetics from the forename

We are treating all of these activities as subroutines and the name we have assigned to each subroutine is given in brackets. Unfortunately, most versions of BASIC are unable to call subroutines by name and it will be necessary when writing the final program to insert line numbers after the respective GOSUBs. During the development phase, however, it is much easier to refer to subroutines by name. These names can then later be incorporated in REM statements. We are indicating this use of named subroutines by putting the names within asterisks. In languages that can call subroutines by name (such as PASCAL), subroutines like these are usually referred to as 'procedures'.

Even though your BASIC may not be able to handle procedures, it is recommended that you pretend it can while programming at the pseudo-language stage. Similarly, your version of BASIC may not be able to handle long variable names such as COUNT or STREETNAMES, but at the pseudo-language level it is easier and clearer to assume that it can. Try to make them descriptive. It is much clearer to call a temporary variable for a string TEMPSTRING$ than to call it XV$. Fortunately, many versions of BASIC now allow longer variable names.

We have already developed the second of the steps (Convert all the letters to upper case) through a second and third level of refinement and created a short program in BASIC to do this task. We will now attempt this for the other steps:

2ND REFINEMENT
3. (Find last space)
BEGIN
LOOP while unscanned characters remain in NAME$
  IF Character = " "
    THEN note position in a variable
    ELSE do nothing
  ENDIF
ENDLOOP
END

3RD REFINEMENT
3. (Find last space)
BEGIN
READ FULLNAME$
LOOP (while unscanned characters remain)
  FOR L = 1 to length of FULLNAME$
  READ character from FULLNAME$
  IF character = " "
    THEN LET COUNT = position of character
    ELSE do nothing
  ENDIF
ENDLOOP
END

We are now in a position to code from pseudo-language into programming language:

```
10 INPUT "INPUT FULL NAME "; FULLNAME$
20 FOR L = 1 TO LEN (FULLNAME$)
30 LET CHAR$ = MID$ (FULLNAME$,L,1)
40 IF CHAR$ = " " THEN LET COUNT = L
50 NEXT L
60 PRINT "LAST SPACE IS IN POSITION ";COUNT
70 END
```

Note that line 10 is a dummy input for testing the routine; line 60 is a dummy output, also for testing; and line 70 will have to be changed to RETURN when the routine is used as a subroutine.

Now let's try the same process for step four:

2ND REFINEMENT
4. (Read surname)
BEGIN
Assign characters to right of last space to SURNAME$
END

3RD REFINEMENT
4. (Read surname)
BEGIN
  READ FULLNAME$

```
        Locate last space (call ★ SPACE ★ subroutine)
    LOOP while characters remain in string after space
        READ characters and add to SURNAME$
    ENDLOOP
END
```

Before going on to code this into BASIC, you should note some potential pitfalls. In locating the last space in the final refinement above, the pseudo-language calls for the use of the ★SPACE★ subroutine, but it would not be possible to write this out in BASIC and test it if the ★SPACE★ subroutine had not already been written. As a general rule, it is not worth coding each module into BASIC (or any other high level language) until the whole program has been developed in pseudo-language. However, if you do wish to test a module, you may need to write some dummy variable values as well as dummy inputs and outputs. In the example above, COUNT is the variable that holds the value of the position of the last space in FULLNAME$. In testing, we can cheat a little by assuming that the routine to do this works properly:

```
10 LET FULLNAME$ = "TOM BROWN"
20 LET COUNT = 4
30 FOR L = COUNT + 1 TO LEN (FULLNAME$)
40 LET SURNAME$ = SURNAME$ + MID$
   (FULLNAME$,L,1)
50 NEXT L
60 PRINT "SURNAME IS "; SURNAME$
70 END
```

Here is the process for finding the forename (step five). Remember, we decided that a forename is a concatenation of all the alphabetic characters up to the last space in the name. Full stops, apostrophes, spaces and so on were to be discarded.

2ND REFINEMENT

```
5. (Read forename)
BEGIN
LOOP while characters remain in FULLNAME$ up to
    last space
    Scan characters
    IF character is not a letter
        THEN do nothing
        ELSE add character to FORENAME$
    ENDIF
ENDLOOP
END
```

3RD REFINEMENT

```
5. (Read forename)
BEGIN
LOOP while characters remain up to COUNT
    LET TEMPCHAR$ = Lth character in string
    IF TEMPCHAR$ is not a letter
        THEN do nothing
        ELSE LET FORENAME$ = FORENAME$ +
            TEMPCHAR$
    ENDIF
ENDLOOP
END
```

Now we are ready to code into BASIC, but as an intermediate stage, we are going to use un-numbered BASIC statements in a structured format so that you can compare the structure with the stage above:

CODING

```
5. (Read forename)
REM BEGIN
REM LOOP
    FOR L = 1 TO COUNT − 1
        LET TEMPCHAR$ = MID$ (FULLNAME$,L,1)
        LET CHAR = ASC(TEMPCHAR$)
        IF CHAR > 64 THEN FORENAME$ =
            FORENAME$ + CHR$(CHAR)
    REM ENDIF
    NEXT L: REM ENDLOOP
REM END
```

In ordinary BASIC this would be:

```
10 FOR L = 1 TO COUNT − 1
20 LET TEMPCHAR$ = MID$(FULLNAME$,L,1)
30 LET CHAR = ASC(TEMPCHAR$)
40 IF CHAR > 64 THEN FORENAME$ = FORENAME$
   + CHR$(CHAR)
50 NEXT L
60 END
```

As it stands, however, this program would not work. There are three problems with it: COUNT needs to be assigned a value; there is no provision for inputing a name (assigning a string to FULLNAME$); and there is no 'output' in the form of a print statement for us to check if it has worked properly.

If this routine were part of a subroutine, the parameters passed to it (the input) and the parameters passed from it (the output) would have to be handled elsewhere in the program. This is a very important consideration: the flow of information within a program should always be carefully thought through before we begin to code into BASIC. This is particularly important when we are using variables (COUNT, for example) and the same variable name is used in different parts of the program. There is no point in calling a subroutine that uses a variable such as COUNT if the subroutine has no way of knowing what its value is supposed to be. If a subroutine initialises the value of COUNT, that value will remain the same unless a new value is assigned later — perhaps in another subroutine. This is one reason why it is not good programming practice to jump out from the middle of a loop, since the value of the loop variable will be unknown. Consider the consequences of having these two program fragments as parts of different subroutines in a program:

Part of subroutine X

```
FOR L = 1 TO LEN(WORD$)
LET CHAR$ = MID$(WORD$,L,1)
IF CHAR$ = " . " THEN GOTO 1550
NEXT L
```

Part of subroutine Y

```
FOR Q = 1 TO LIMIT
LET A(L) = P(Q)
NEXT Q
```

This part of subroutine Y is reading values into a subscripted array, where the subscript is denoted by the variable L. If subroutine Y is called after subroutine X, and if the test condition in subroutine X has been met (that one of the characters is a " . "), the value of L would be completely unpredictable and so we would not know which element of the array values were being assigned to in subroutine Y. Apart from the error of branching out of a loop, this subroutine also uses a GOTO, and this practice should also be avoided. GOTOs lead to confusion and they should be avoided wherever possible.

To avoid confusion when using variables, it is good practice to make a list of them at the pseudo-language stages of program development, together with notes saying what they are being used for. Some languages (but not BASIC) allow variables to be declared as 'local' or 'global' — that is, they have values that apply either in only part of a program (local) or throughout the whole program (global). Many variables, such as those used in loops (for example, the L in LET L = 1 TO 10), are almost always local, so it is often wise to initialise the value of the variable before it is used (for example, LET L = 0). Some languages, such as PASCAL, insist on this; and although BASIC always assumes the initial value of a variable is 0 (unless otherwise stated), initialising is still recommended.

So far we have formulated a reasonable definition of a name for the purposes of our computerised address book, and developed some routines that can handle names in various ways that we shall use in our complete program. Now let's once again distance ourselves from the details of program coding and consider the structure of the 'records' in our address book 'file'

The terms 'record', 'file' and 'field' have fairly specific meanings in the computer world. A *file* is a whole set of related information. In a computer system it would be an identifiable item stored on a floppy disk or on a cassette tape and it would have its own name, usually referred to as a filename. We can consider our entire address book as a file, and we shall call it ADBOOK.

Within a file we have *records*. These are also sets of related information. If we think of our address book as a card index box, the file would be the whole box full of cards and the records would be the individual cards — each one with its own name, address and telephone number.

Within each record we have *fields*. The fields can be considered as one or more rows of related information within the record. Each of the records in our ADBOOK file will have the following fields: NAME, ADDRESS and PHONENUMBER. A typical record would look like this:

Peter Edvadsen
16A Holford Drive
Worsley
Manchester
061-540 2588

In this record there are three fields: the name field, which comprises alphabetic letters (and, possibly, the apostrophe in names such as Peter O'Toole); the address field, which comprises a few numbers and many letters; and the telephone number field, which comprises only numbers (ignoring the problem of whether or not to allow hyphens in numbers like 01-258 1191). Before we can begin to write a program to handle complex information such as this with flexibility, we must decide how to represent the data within the computer. One way might be to consider all the information within a record to be just one long character string. The problem with this approach is that extracting specific information is extremely difficult. Let's assume that the following entry is just one long character string:

PERCIVAL R. BURTON
1056 AVENUE OF THE AMERICAS
RIO DEL MONTENEGRO
CALIFORNIA
U.S.A.
(415) 884 5100

If we were searching the records to find the telephone number of PERCIVAL R. BURTON, would it be safe to assume that the last 14 characters in the record represented the number? What if we had included the international dialling code, like this: 0101 (415) 884 5100? Then the number would have had a total of 19 characters. To overcome this difficulty, the telephone number is assigned a separate field, and the program will give us all the characters (or numbers) in that field when requested.

The difficulty with this approach is that there has to be some way of relating the various separate fields, so that referring to one field (the name field, for example) can give us the other fields on the record, as well. One way this could be tackled is to have a further field associated with the record just for indexing purposes. If a record was, for example, the 15th record in the file, its index field would contain the number 15. This could then be used to point to the elements in a number of arrays. To illustrate this, let us suppose one record looked like this:

Jamie Appleton	NAME field
15 Pantbach Road	STREET field
Llandogo	TOWN field
Gwent	COUNTY field
0594 552303	PHONE NUMBER field
015	INDEX field

If we knew the name of this person and wanted his telephone number, all we would have to do would be to search through the elements of the array holding the names until a match was found. We would then find which element of the array the name was in — in this case, number 15. Then all we would need to do would be to find the 15th element in the PHONE NUMBER array to get the right telephone number.

If we had a number of friends in the Forest of

Dean area, we might want the program to search for every occurrence of 'Cinderford' in the TOWN field. The program could search through the TOWN fields and note the location of each occurrence of Cinderford. All that would then be necessary, to print the names and addresses of all these friends, would be to retrieve all the elements having the same number from all the arrays for each 'Cinderford' record. Using this approach, there would be no need to inspect the INDEX field, and the technique has the merit of being a relatively simple operation.

In the next part we will look at some of the problems involved in searching through lists to find specific items.

Exercise

■ Assume that records with the following fields will be adequate for our computerised address book:

NAME field
STREET field
TOWN field
COUNTY field
PHONE NUMBER field

Suppose that one of the options offered by a menu in the computerised address book is:

5. CREATE A NEW ENTRY

You type 5 and the program branches to the part where new records are created (you may assume that there are no entries in the address book yet). Since the program is to be fully menu-driven, you will always be prompted for the entries expected — with prompts such as ENTER THE NAME, ENTER THE STREET and so on. Here is a list of the expected results:

1. An element in an array for the name
2. An element in an array for the street
3. An element in an array for the town
4. An element in an array for the county
5. An element in an array for the phone number

Your task is to develop this, through a process of top-down programming using a pseudo-language, to a point where direct conversion into BASIC becomes possible. The pseudo-language can follow your own rules; we only suggest that you use capital letters for keywords such as IF, LOOP and so on, and small letters for descriptions in ordinary English of the operations to take place.

Basic Flavours

Step 3

```
10 INPUT "INPUT FULL NAME";F$
15 LET COUNT=0
20 FOR L=1 TO LEN F$
30 LET C$=F$(L)
40 IF C$=" " THEN LET COUNT = L
50 NEXT L
60 PRINT"LAST SPACE IS IN
    POSITION";COUNT
70 STOP
9990 DEF FN M$(X$,P,N)=X$(P TO
    P+N-1)
9991 DEF FN L$=X$(    TO N)
9992 DEF FN R$=X$(LEN X$-N+1 TO    )
```

In this programming project, the string functions MID$, LEFT$, RIGHT$ will be much used. Their equivalents in Sinclair BASIC are:

LEFT$(F$,N)	replace by F$(TO N)
RIGHT$(F$,N)	replace by F$(LEN(F$)-N+1 TO)
MID$(F$,P,N)	replace by F$(P TO P+N-1)
MID$(F$,P,1)	replace by F$(P)

Note that string variable names on the Spectrum cannot be more than one letter long (plus the "$").

Step 4

```
 5 LET S$=""
10 LET F$="TOM BROWN"
20 LET COUNT=4
30 FOR L=COUNT+1 TO LEN F$
40 LET S$=S$+F$(L)
50 NEXT L
60 PRINT "SURNAME IS  ";S$
70 STOP
```

Step 5

```
 5 LET C$=""
10 FOR L=1 TO COUNT -1
20 LET T$=F$(L)
```

```
30 LET CHAR=CODE T$
40 IF CHAR>64 THEN LET C$=C$+CHR$
    CHAR
50 NEXT L
60 STOP
```

In this fragment, the problem of single letter string variable names has arisen: F$ is the Spectrum equivalent of the variable FULLNAME$, so C$ has to stand in for the variable FORENAME$.

Part of subroutine X

```
FOR L=1 TO LEN W$
LET C$=W$(L)
IF C$=" . " THEN GOTO 1550
NEXT L
```

Part of subroutine Y

```
FOR Q=1 TO LIMIT
LET A(L)=P(Q)
NEXT Q
```

Of the most popular home computers, only the BBC Micro supports long variable names such as FULLNAME$. The Spectrum allows long numeric variable names, but only single letter string variable names. The Dragon 32, Vic–20, and Commodore 64 support long variable names, but only the first two characters are significant, so that FULLNAME$ is valid, but refers to the same memory location as FUJIYAMA$: both have the same first two characters.

On the Oric-1 variable names cannot be more than two characters (first a letter then a number or a letter), while the Lynx allows only single letter variable names, though both lower- and upper-case letters are valid and distinct.

New Entries

In order to insert a new entry in an array, it is first necessary to find a blank space. The binary search is an efficient way of achieving this

We saw in the previous instalment how a file of data is made up of records, which are divided into fields, each of which can be given access to the other fields through an indexing field. Now we will consider some of the techniques of searching through these lists.

Creating records for our address book is not difficult. Assume that a separate string array exists for each of the fields in the record. These can be called FLNAMES (for full name), STREETS, TOWNS and PHONES (we'll talk later about our use here of a string variable rather than a numeric variable for the phone number field). In the list of eight desirable functions of the address book program, number six was the facility to add new entries. If these eight choices were presented on the screen at the beginning when the program was run, selecting 6 would take you to an input routine of the type presented as an exercise.

Assume there are already a number of entries in the address book, but you can't remember how many. It is essential that new entries are not written over existing entries, so one of the tasks of the program might be to search through the elements in one of the arrays to find the first one containing no data.

Searching through an array to see whether an element is 'occupied' is not difficult. String variables can be compared in BASIC just as numeric variables can. IF A$="HOME" THEN... is just as valid as IF A=61 THEN..., at least in most versions of BASIC. If any of the arrays in our address book has an entry already, this will consist of at least one alphanumeric character. An 'empty' element will contain no alphanumeric characters, so all we need to do is search through the elements, starting at the beginning, until we find one containing no characters.

If there are arrays for the name, the street, the town and the phone number, we will have four arrays with one element in each for each field in the record. Since all these fields 'go together', the 15th record will have its name data in the 15th element of the name array, its street data in the 15th element of the street array, the town data in the 15th element of the town array, and the phone number data in the 15th element of the phone number array. We therefore need only to search through one of these arrays to find an empty element; we don't need to check all the arrays.

If the variable POSITION represents the number of the first free element in any one of the arrays, a program to locate POSITION (assuming it is not already known) could be as simple as this:

PROCEDURE (find free element)
```
BEGIN
  LOOP
    REPEAT UNTIL free element is located
    READ Array (POSITION)
    POSITION = POSITION + 1
    IF Array(POSITION) = "  "
      THEN note POSITION
      ELSE do nothing
    ENDIF
  ENDLOOP
END
```

In BASIC, this could be as simple as:

```
1000 FOR L = 0 TO 1 STEP 0
1010 LET POSITION = POSITION + 1
1020 IF FLNAMES(POSITION) = "  " THEN LET
     L = X
1030 NEXT L
1040 REM rest of program
```

Note that the value of X in line 1020 is the value required to terminate the FOR...NEXT loop and this value varies from machine to machine (see Basic Flavours). It is also important to note that this is a program fragment, and it is assumed that FLNAMES() is DIMensioned and that POSITION has been initialised. To run this fragment as a program on its own, you must DIMension FLNAMES() and initialise POSITION and X, at some point before line 1000.

Although we have used the FOR X = 0 TO 1 STEP 0 technique before, this is a good place to examine in more detail how it works. Usually, a FOR...NEXT loop in BASIC 'knows' beforehand how many times the program fragment is expected to repeat. If you want to repeat something 30 times, FOR X = 1 TO 30 will do admirably. This time, however, we are simulating a REPEAT...UNTIL loop. Although ordinary versions of BASIC do not have REPEAT...UNTIL on offer, it is easy enough to simulate using FOR...NEXT. As long as the test in line 1020 fails, L (the FOR...NEXT loop counter) remains at the value 0, with 0 added to it at every iteration (repetition of the loop); while line 1010 causes POSITION to be increased by 1 every iteration. When the test in line 1020 is true (that is, when an empty element of FLNAMES() is found), L is set to the value X, and the FOR...NEXT loop is terminated at line 1030. This leaves POSITION pointing to the first free element of FLNAMES().

POSITION is a value we are likely to need to

establish early, each time the address book program is used, and one that is likely to need updating several times during the use of the program. It is therefore going to be one of our 'global' variables, and establishing its value will need to be part of an 'initialisation' routine. This can be done every time the program is run, or a 'flag' can be created which indicates whether or not the value of POSITION has changed since the program was last run. The latter approach is not difficult, but at this stage it creates an unnecessary complication. We'll keep things simple and find the value of POSITION as one of the early tasks whenever the program is run.

Let's revise the activities we want the computerised address book to do and see if we can move towards an overall program strategy. This time we'll be slightly more rigorous and assume that each of the activities will be dealt with as a separate subroutine (the name of which will be indicated by being enclosed in asterisks).

1. Find record (from name)	*FINDREC*
2. Find names (from incomplete name)	*FINDNAMES*
3. Find record (from town)	*FINDNMTWN*
4. Find records (from initial)	*FINDINIT*
5. List records (all)	*LISTRECS*
6. Add record	*ADDREC*
7. Change record	*MODREC*
8. Delete record	*DELREC*
9. Exit program (save)	*EXPROG*

We now know, in broad terms, what the desired 'inputs' and 'outputs' of the program are, so we can already start thinking in terms of a main program. All the detailing can be done through the process of top-down programming and coded in the various subroutines. We know that several things will need to be initialised, including the value of POSITION. We know that, as the program is to be menu-driven, we will be presented with a set of choices whenever the program is run. We also know that, whatever our response to the choices presented, we will want one of them at least to be executed.

So the body of the main program can already take shape:

MAIN PROGRAM
```
BEGIN
    INITIALISE (procedure)
    GREET (procedure)
    CHOOSE (procedure)
    EXECUTE (procedure)
END
```

In BASIC it would look like this (with line numbers substituted for the subroutine names):

```
10 REM H.C.C. ADDRESS BOOK PROGRAM
20 GOSUB *INITIALISE*
30 GOSUB *GREET*
40 GOSUB *CHOOSE*
50 GOSUB *EXECUTE*
60 END
```

The *GREET* subroutine or procedure would display a greeting on the screen for a few seconds, followed by the menu. The greeting could, perhaps, look like this:

WELCOME TO THE
BASIC PROGRAMMING COURSE
COMPUTERISED ADDRESS BOOK
(PRESS THE SPACE-BAR WHEN READY TO CONTINUE)

In response to the request to press the space bar, the program will branch to the *CHOOSE* subroutine and the user will be presented with a screen like this:

DO YOU WISH TO
1. FIND A RECORD (from a name)
2. FIND NAMES (from part of a name)
3. FIND RECORDS (from a town)
4. FIND RECORDS (from an initial)
5. LIST ALL RECORDS
6. ADD A RECORD
7. CHANGE A RECORD
8. DELETE A RECORD
9. EXIT AND SAVE
CHOOSE 1 TO 9
FOLLOWED BY RETURN

At this point, the program will branch to the appropriate subroutine depending on the number entered. The structure of the program is now beginning to take shape. All options except number 9 (to EXIT and SAVE) will need to end with an instruction to return to the *CHOOSE* subroutine. But there are many details of the internal organisation of the data that we have not considered. We will come to these later.

Let's assume that we are running the program, that it already has all the records in it that we need, and that we want to search for a full record by inputting a name only. This calls for option 1 — FIND A RECORD (*FINDREC*). Before we attempt to design this part of the program, let's consider some of the problems involved in computerised search routines.

Searching

Textbooks on programming techniques tend to deal with searching and sorting together. Readers may recall that we have already touched on sorting in a program designed to sort names into alphabetical order (see page 184). Both sorting and searching raise interesting points about how data is organised — in a computer or any other information system.

If a 'manual' address book comprised a note-book without a thumb index, and if entries were added when new names and addresses were thought of, without being sorted into alphabetical order, we would have a data structure known as a 'pile'. A pile is a set of data collected in the order in which it arrives. It is obvious that a pile is the least effective way of organising data. Every time you want to find someone's address and telephone number you have to look through the whole address book. The same is usually true of computer systems, though there are occasions when the criteria by which data is accessed are so unpredictable that a pile is as good a data structure as any.

A more organised data structure, and one much easier for both people and computers to use, is achieved when the data is organised according to a recognised and simple system. A telephone directory is a good example of a set of information (names, addresses and telephone numbers) where the name field is ordered according to simple rules of alphabetic sequencing. The numbers themselves are, to all intents and purposes, randomly ordered, but the names — which are more 'meaningful' — are organised according to easy-to-follow rules.

Inasmuch as we have thought about the internal organisation of the data in our computerised address book, the data is organised as a pile, with one record being stored in name array element ×, street array element × and so on, and the next record being stored in name array element ×+1, street array element ×+1 and so on. Finding a particular item of data — BILL SMITH, for example — would therefore involve looking at the first element in the name array and seeing if it was BILL SMITH, looking at the second element and seeing if it was BILL SMITH and so on until we had either located the field or discovered that there was no entry for BILL SMITH.

If the data we want to search for has already been ordered into a recognisable structure, we can see how it will simplify the search. Suppose you have a database on football teams, and one of the fields in the records is the score for a particular week. A powerful database might allow you to find which team or teams had scored 11 goals in that week. Here is the array holding team scores for the week in question:

1,6,2,2,1,9,0,0,2,1,4,11,4,2,12,5,2,1,0,1

It should be obvious that the scores are in team order and not in score order. Twenty teams are involved and only one team actually managed to score 11 goals that week. This was the 12th team entered in the array. With unstructured data like this, the only way to find the information you want is to look at the first element and see whether it was 11; if it was not, look at the next element to see whether it was 11, and so on until either an 11 was located or no element equal in value to 11 was found.

If we analyse this data, we will see that there was a total of 20 scores, ranging in value from 0 to 12. This example is relatively trivial, and even if we had to search through every item it would not take long to discover that 11 was in the 12th element of the array. But what if there were thousands of elements in a large array? Searching through numerous unstructured data items could slow down a program to an undesirable extent.

The solution is to order the data first, so that searches can take place far more quickly. Here is the array of scores again, arranged in numerical order:

0,0,0,1,1,1,1,1,2,2,2,2,4,4,5,6,9,11,12

If we know the number of teams is 20, then the quickest way to find the position of the score we want is to split the array into two parts and search only the part likely to contain the number we want. Remember that sifting through large quantities of data is likely to take far more time than simple arithmetic operations such as dividing a number by two. The algorithm for locating the score would now look like this:

Find the array containing the scores
Read the number we want to search for
Find the length of the array
Find the midpoint of the array
Loop until the number is located
    If the item at the midpoint is equal to the number we are searching for, then the number has been located
    If not, see if the number sought is larger or smaller than the number at the midpoint
    If the number sought is larger than the number at the midpoint, then find the midpoint of the upper part of the array
    If the required number is smaller than the number at the midpoint, then find the midpoint of the lower part of the array
    (Repeat this until the number is located)

This can be formalised to:

```
BEGIN
    Find the array of scores
    INPUT NUMBER (to be searched for)
    LOOP until the number is located
        IF NUMBER = (midpoint)
            THEN note position of midpoint
            ELSE
                IF NUMBER > (midpoint)
                    THEN find midpoint of upper half
                    ELSE find midpoint of lower half
                ENDIF
        ENDIF
    ENDLOOP
    IF NUMBER is located
        THEN PRINT position of midpoint
        ELSE PRINT "NUMBER NOT FOUND"
    ENDIF
END
```

If you think through this program in pseudo-language you will see that it cannot fail eventually to locate the number being searched for if it exists in the array. Let's develop this pseudo-language until we can arrive at a working program. This process of searching by repeated subdivision is called a 'binary search'.

A program in BASIC based on the pseudo-language above is presented for you to try. It creates an array and reads in the scores from a data statement. It then prompts for the score to be searched. If it finds the score, it prints the element of the array the number was found in.

```
10 REM A PROGRAM TO LOCATE A NUMBER IN AN
   ARRAY
20 DIM SCORES(20)
30 FOR Z = 1 TO 20
40 READ SCORES(Z)
50 NEXT Z
60 DATA 0,0,0,1,1,1,1,1,2,2,2,2,2,4,4,5,6,9,11,12
70 LET L = 20
80 LET BTM = 1
90 LET TP = L
100 INPUT"INPUT SCORE ";N
110 FOR Z = 0 TO 1 STEP 0
120 LET L = TP — BTM
130 LET MD = BTM + INT(L/2)
140 IF N = SCORES(MD) THEN LET Z = X
150 IF N > SCORES(MD) THEN LET BTM = MD
160 IF N < SCORES(MD) THEN LET TP = MD
170 NEXT Z
180 PRINT "THE SCORE WAS IN ELEMENT NO.
    ";MD
190 END
```

Again, note that X will need to be initialised according to your machine's requirements (see Basic Flavours).

If the data held in a file or array is fairly regular, as in the case of a telephone directory, where names are distributed reasonably evenly across the alphabet, then the binary search is an efficient way of finding a particular entry. However, it is by no means the most efficient, and there are alternative algorithms that can find the data using fewer iterations. One such is the technique of 'hashing', where the program makes an educated guess at the approximate location of the entry, refining the guess until it is found. Such methods, however, are beyond the scope of this book, and the binary search method is sufficient for our needs.

Exercises

If you run this program, you will see that it works provided you enter a score that exists in the array. If you enter a score such as 3, which is not in the array, the program fails to terminate and no error message appears. If you type in 12, which exists in the array, the program fails to locate it. The program also assumes that every number in the sorted array will be different but, as you can see from the data statement, several numbers occur more than once. The program neither detects this nor reports all the locations where the number occurs.

Your task is to:

1. Analyse the program and find out why it cannot locate a score of 12
2. Modify one line of the program to rectify this defect
3. Establish why the program is unable to handle numbers that do not exist in the string and devise a strategy to overcome this defect.

Basic Flavours

SPECTRUM

The following is the Spectrum listing for the first BASIC program fragment:

```
100 DIM F$(6,4)
110 LET POSITION = 0
120 LET F$(1) = "MIKE"
130 LET F$(2) = "KATE"
140 LET F$(4) = "MARY"
1000 FOR L = 0 TO 1 STEP 0
1010 LET POSITION = POSITION + 1
1020 IF CODE (F$(POSITION)) = 32 THEN
     LET L = 2
1030 NEXT L
1040 PRINT "NO. OF 1st FREE ELEMENT
     IS ";POSITION
1050 STOP
```

Notice that lines 100 to 140, as well as line 1040, transform the program fragment (lines 1000 to 1030) into a working demonstration program. The values and format of these extra lines can be changed to investigate the working of the program fragment.

The second program for the Spectrum is:

```
10 REM A PROGRAM TO LOCATE A
   NUMBER IN AN ARRAY
20 DIM S(20)
30 FOR Z = 1 TO 20
40 READ S(Z)
50 NEXT Z
60 DATA 0,0,0,1,1,1,1,1,2,2,2,2,2,4,4,5,6,
   9,11,12
70 LET L = 20
80 LET BTM = 1
90 LET TP = L
100 INPUT"INPUT SCORE";N
110 FOR Z = 0 TO 1 STEP 0
120 LET L = TP—BTM
130 LET MD = BTM + INT(L/2)
140 IF N = S(MD) THEN LET Z = 2
150 IF N>S(MD) THEN LET BTM = MD
160 IF N<S(MD) THEN LET TP = MD
170 NEXT Z
180 PRINT"THE SCORE WAS IN ELEMENT
    NO. ";MD
190 STOP
```

For variations in variable names, see previous 'Basic Flavours' (page 211).

VARIABLES

STEP 0

In both programs in the main text there is a reference to ". . . THEN LET Z = X". The values for the variable X are:

Oric-1	replace X by 1
Dragon 32	replace X by 1
Lynx	replace X by 2
BBC Micro	replace X by 2
Commodore 64 and Vic-20	replace X by 1

LYNX

Both programs in the main text will run on the BBC, the Dragon 32, the Lynx, the Oric-1, the Commodore 64 and Vic-20 provided that the Basic Flavours concerning variable names and Step 0 are implemented. The Spectrum listings differ from the norm in the DIM statement in line 100 above, and in the test in line 1020 above, otherwise they may be used as a guide to implementation on the other machines. The Lynx version of line 100 above is:

```
100 DIM F$(4)(6)
```

TONY LODGE

F
G
H
I
J
K
L
M
N
O
P
Q
R
S
T
U
V

Branching Out

As a long program is developed, its structure takes on the appearance of a tree, with more branches at each successive stage of refinement

In the previous part of the Basic Programming course, we took a look at some of the problems involved in searching through a list to find a specific item — assuming that the list had already been sorted into order. This is a topic to which we will return in more detail when the time comes to start writing search routines. In the meantime, however, we will develop the theme of top-down programming to produce code for the second two parts of the main program. This contains four calls to subroutines or procedures:

```
MAIN PROGRAM
BEGIN
    INITIALISE (procedure)
    GREET (procedure)
    CHOOSE (procedure)
    EXECUTE (procedure
END
```

The first procedure, *INITIALISE*, will involve numerous fairly complex activities — setting up arrays, reading data into them, performing various checks and so on — and we will leave the details of this procedure until later. The next two parts of the main program comprise the GREET and CHOOSE procedures. In developing these procedures, we will suggest a methodology that helps prevent the many layers involved in top-down program development from becoming disorganised and confusing.

The problem with the top-down refinement approach to program development is that the number of steps needed before we are ready to start coding into a high level language is indeterminate. Two or three steps may be enough for simple procedures, but more difficult procedures may require many steps before the problem has been sufficiently analysed to allow 'source code' (as the high level language program is called) to be written. This means that writing a program using this method is similar to drawing a tree lying on its side. As the 'branches' proliferate (that is, as the refinements become more detailed) they take up more space on the page. Eventually, it becomes impossible to fit everything onto a single sheet, and that is the point where it becomes easy to lose track of what's going on.

One very effective way to organise the documentation of the program is to number the stages of its development systematically. We have used Roman numerals to indicate the level of refinement and Arabic numerals to indicate the subsection of the program. A separate sheet of loose-leaf paper is then used for each level of refinement and the pages for each program block or module can be easily kept together. Here is the numbering system for our program:

```
I MAIN PROGRAM
BEGIN
    1. INITIALISE
    2. GREET
    3. CHOOSE
    4. EXECUTE
END
```

As mentioned above, we are leaving the development of INITIALISE for the moment, and concentrating on developing the GREET and CHOOSE procedures.

```
II 2 (GREET)
BEGIN
    1. Display greeting message
    2. LOOP (until space bar is pressed)
       ENDLOOP
    3. Call *CHOOSE*
END
```

```
III 2 (GREET) 1 (display message)
BEGIN
    1. Clear screen
    2. PRINT greeting message
END
```

```
III 2 (GREET) 2 (LOOP wait for space bar)
BEGIN
    1. LOOP (until space bar is pressed)
        IF space bar is pressed
        THEN
        ENDLOOP
END
```

```
III 2 (GREET) 3 (call *CHOOSE*)
BEGIN
    1. GOSUB *CHOOSE*
END
```

At this point it should be clear that **III-2-1** and **III-2-3** are ready to be coded directly into BASIC, but that **III-2-2** needs another stage of refinement:

```
IV 2 (GREET) 2 (LOOP)
BEGIN
    1. LOOP (until space bar is pressed)
        IF INKEY$ is not space THEN continue
        ENDLOOP
END
```

We are now at the point where all the coding into

BASIC for GREET can be tackled with little further refinement:

IV 2 (GREET) 1 (display message) BASIC CODE

```
REM *GREET* SUBROUTINE
PRINT
PRINT
PRINT
PRINT
PRINT TAB(12);"*WELCOME TO THE*"
PRINT TAB(9);"*HOME COMPUTER COURSE*"
PRINT TAB(6);"*COMPUTERISED ADDRESS
    BOOK*"
PRINT
PRINT TAB(5);"(PRESS SPACE BAR TO CONTINUE)"
```

V 2 (GREET) 2 (LOOP wait for space bar) BASIC CODE

```
LET L = 0
FOR L = 1 TO 1
IF INKEY$ <> "    " THEN LET L = 0
NEXT L
```

IV 2 (GREET) 3 (call *CHOOSE*) BASIC CODE

```
GOSUB *CHOOSE*
RETURN
```

Notice that we have now started to initialise variables in the various routines that we write, by using statements of the form LET I = 0. Strictly speaking, this is unnecessary in some of the circumstances in which we have used it. Nevertheless, it is a good habit to get into if you can remember, and if you have enough RAM space available. There are three reasons: first because having a list of LET statements at the start of any routine serves as a useful reminder of what local variables that routine uses. Secondly, because you cannot be sure of what was left in a variable from the last time it was used in a routine (though this does not always matter). Thirdly, as we shall be explaining later in the chapter, putting in statements of the form LET I = 0 in the right order can speed up the execution of a program.

We have changed the way in which we use a FOR...NEXT loop to simulate a DO...WHILE or REPEAT...UNTIL structure from previous parts of the chapter. Instead of using FOR I = 0 TO 1 or FOR I = 0 to 1 STEP 0, we are now using FOR I = 1 to 1. This should run correctly on the vast majority of all the home computers, where the other methods required 'Basic Flavours' for various machines. FOR I = 1 TO 1...NEXT I will execute the loop just once. However, if anywhere in the body of the loop I is set to 0 then the loop will execute again, and so on. We can either insert a LET I = 0 statement as the result of an exit condition failing or we can set I to 0 immediately after the FOR statement and set it to 1 if the exit condition succeeds. Thus, both the following loops achieve the same objective.

```
FOR I = 1 TO 1
IF INKEY$ <> "    " THEN LET I = 0
NEXT I
    or
```

```
FOR I = 1 TO 1
LET I = 0
IF INKEY$ = "    " THEN LET I = 1
NEXT I
```

The BASIC code we have just produced is all that is needed for the complete GREET block in the main program. We haven't put in line numbers because we can't really do that until all the program modules are ready for final coding. For instance, we do not know at this stage what the appropriate line numbers are for the GOSUB commands. If you want to test the module at this stage, it will be necessary to create some dummy inputs and dummy subroutines. Some points to note about this program fragment are the use of the TAB function and the 'clear screen' statements. TAB moves the cursor along the line by the number (the 'argument') specified in the brackets. The numbers we have given will print the message neatly centred in a screen 40 characters wide. If your display has less than this (for example, the Spectrum displays 32 characters per line) or more (larger computers usually display 80 characters), these TAB arguments will need to be altered accordingly. The instruction to clear the screen in many versions of BASIC is CLS, but the version of Microsoft BASIC used to develop this program does not support this. Instead, we have used PRINT CHR$(12), since our machine uses ASCII 12 as its 'clear screen' non-printable character — others commonly use ASCII 24 for the same function.

```
10 REM DUMMY MAIN PROGRAM
20 PRINT CHR$(12)
30 GOSUB 100
40 END
100 REM *GREET* SUBROUTINE
110 PRINT
120 PRINT
130 PRINT
140 PRINT
150 PRINT TAB(12);"*WELCOME TO THE*"
160 PRINT TAB(9);"*HOME COMPUTER COURSE*"
170 PRINT TAB(6);"*COMPUTERISED ADDRESS
    BOOK*"
180 PRINT
190 PRINT TAB(5);"(PRESS SPACE BAR TO
    CONTINUE)"
195 LET L = 0
200 FOR L = 1 TO 1
210 IF INKEY$ <> "    " THEN LET L = 0
220 NEXT L
230 PRINT CHR$(12)
240 GOSUB 1000
250 RETURN
1000 REM DUMMY SUBROUTINE
1010 PRINT "DUMMY SUBROUTINE"
1020 RETURN
```

We will now use exactly the same approach to refine the CHOOSE procedure.

II 3 (CHOOSE)

```
BEGIN
    1. PRINT menu
```

```
    2. INPUT CHOICE
    3. Call CHOICE subroutine
END
```

III 3 (CHOOSE)1 (PRINT menu)

```
BEGIN
    1. Clear screen
    2. PRINT menu and prompt
END
```

III 3 (CHOOSE) 2 (INPUT CHOICE)

```
BEGIN
    1. INPUT CHOICE
    2. Check that CHOICE is within range
END
```

III 3 (CHOOSE) 3 (call CHOICE)

```
BEGIN
    1. CASE OF CHOICE
        ENDCASE
END
```

III-3-1 (PRINT menu) can now be coded into BASIC:

IV 3 (CHOOSE) 1 (PRINT menu) BASIC CODE

```
REM CLEAR SCREEN
PRINT CHR$(12): REM OR 'CLS'
PRINT
PRINT
PRINT
PRINT
PRINT "1. FIND RECORD (FROM NAME)"
PRINT "2. FIND RECORD (FROM INCOMPLETE
    NAME)"
PRINT "3. FIND RECORD (FROM TOWN)"
PRINT "4. FIND RECORD (FROM INITIALS)"
PRINT "5. LIST ALL RECORDS"
PRINT "6. ADD NEW RECORD"
PRINT "7. CHANGE RECORD"
PRINT "8. DELETE RECORD"
PRINT "9. EXIT & SAVE"
```

III-3-2 (INPUT CHOICE) and **III-3-3 (call CHOICE)**, however, need further refinement. Let's look first at the next level of development of **III-3-2**.

Assigning a numeric value to the variable CHOICE is perfectly simple: after the prompt, an INPUT CHOICE command will do this. However, there are only nine possible choices. What would happen if we mistakenly entered a 0, or 99? Since the CHOICE we make will determine which part of the program is called next, we want to be sure that unwanted errors are not caused, so we need to perform a 'range checking' procedure. This is a small routine that checks to see if the number input is within the acceptable range before allowing the program to continue. Here is a sample routine designed to trap an erroneous input.

RANGE CHECKING ROUTINE

```
1 REM ROUTINE
10 LET L = 0
20 FOR L = 1 TO 1
30 INPUT "ENTER 1-9"; CHOICE
40 IF CHOICE <1 THEN LET L = 0
50 IF CHOICE >9 THEN LET L = 0
60 NEXT L
```

```
70 PRINT "CHOICE WAS ";CHOICE
80 END
```

Many versions of BASIC can make this routine simpler by including a boolean operator in the test like this:

```
10 LET L = 0
20 FOR L = 1 TO 1
30 INPUT "ENTER 1-9";CHOICE
40 IF CHOICE < 1 OR CHOICE > 9 THEN LET L = 0
50 NEXT L
60 PRINT "CHOICE WAS ";CHOICE
70 END
```

These routines also illustrate another point about the INPUT statement. INPUT causes the program to stop and wait for an input from the keyboard. BASIC does not know when the whole number has been entered until the RETURN key has been pressed, so you will also have to remember to press RETURN after entering the number.

A more 'user friendly' approach would be to have the program continue as soon as a valid number had been entered. This is possible using the INKEY$ function. Here, BASIC reads a character from the keyboard whenever INKEY$ is encountered. The program does not stop, however, and will proceed to the next part of the program without pausing. It is usual, therefore, for INKEY$ to be used within loops. The loop to check for a key being pressed can be IF INKEY$ = "" THEN... — in other words, if the key being pressed is 'nothing' (that is, no key is being pressed), go back and check again. A suitable loop for our purposes would be:

```
LET I = 0
FOR I = 1 TO 1
LET A$ = INKEY$
IF A$ = "" THEN LET I = 0
NEXT I
```

The only disadvantage of using INKEY$ is that it returns a character from the keyboard, rather than a numeric. When there is a CASE OF construct, where one out of several choices are made (a multi-conditional branch), it is easier in BASIC to use numbers rather than characters. This is where BASIC's NUM or VAL functions come in. They convert numbers in character strings into 'real' numbers (that is, numeric values, not ASCII codes representing numerals). They are used like this:

```
LET N = VAL(A$) or LET N = NUM(A$)
```

By using the NUM or VAL functions, we can have the program convert inputs, using INKEY$, into numeric variables. This removes the need to use the RETURN key after the number key has been pressed. Out-of-range checking is still advisable, however.

The following program fragment involves two loops, one nested within the other. The inner loop waits for a key to be pressed; the outer loop converts the string to a number and checks that it is within range:

```
FOR L = 1 TO 1
   PRINT "ENTER CHOICE (1-9)"
      FOR I = 1 TO 1
         LET A$ = INKEY$
         IF A$ = "" THEN LET I = 0
      NEXT I
   LET CHOICE = VAL(A$)
      IF CHOICE < 1 THEN LET L = 0
      IF CHOICE > 9 THEN LET L = 0
NEXT L
```

Finally, we reproduce a complete program in BASIC for the *CHOICE* module, including dummy input and subroutines for testing purposes. We should stress again that the line numbers are for testing purposes only, and will need to be replaced when the final program is put together.

```
10 PRINT CHR$(12)
20 PRINT "SELECT ONE OF THE FOLLOWING"
30 PRINT
40 PRINT
50 PRINT
60 PRINT "1. FIND RECORD (FROM NAME)"
70 PRINT "2. FIND NAMES (FROM INCOMPLETE
   NAME)"
80 PRINT "3. FIND RECORDS (FROM TOWN)"
90 PRINT "4. FIND RECORD (FROM INITIALS)"
100 PRINT "5. LIST ALL RECORDS"
110 PRINT "6. ADD NEW RECORD"
120 PRINT "7. CHANGE RECORD"
130 PRINT "8. DELETE RECORD"
140 PRINT "9. EXIT & SAVE"
150 PRINT
160 PRINT
170 LET L = 0
180 LET I = 0
190 FOR L = 1 TO 1
200 PRINT "ENTER CHOICE (1-9)"
210 FOR I = 1 TO 1
220 LET A$ = INKEY$
230 IF A$ = "" THEN LET I = 0
240 NEXT I
250 LET CHOICE = VAL(A$)
260 IF CHOICE < 1 THEN LET L = 0
270 IF CHOICE > 9 THEN LET L = 0
280 NEXT L
290 ON CHOICE GOSUB 310,330,350,370,390,410,
   430,450,470
300 END
310 PRINT "DUMMY SUBROUTINE 1"
320 RETURN
330 PRINT "DUMMY SUBROUTINE 2"
340 RETURN
350 PRINT "DUMMY SUBROUTINE 3"
360 RETURN
370 PRINT "DUMMY SUBROUTINE 4"
380 RETURN
390 PRINT "DUMMY SUBROUTINE 5"
400 RETURN
410 PRINT "DUMMY SUBROUTINE 6"
420 RETURN
430 PRINT "DUMMY SUBROUTINE 7"
440 RETURN
450 PRINT "DUMMY SUBROUTINE 8"
460 RETURN
470 PRINT "DUMMY SUBROUTINE 9"
480 RETURN
```

At the next stage of development, we will look at file structures and begin refining the INITIALISE procedure.

Basic Flavours

SPECTRUM

In the dummy main program, and throughout, replace PRINT CHR$(12) by CLS, and END by STOP.

RANGE CHECKING ROUTINE
```
1 REM ROUTINE
10 LET L = 0
20 FOR L = 1 TO 1
30 INPUT"ENTER 1-9 ";CHOICE
40 IF CHOICE < 1 THEN LET L = 0
50 IF CHOICE > 9 THEN LET L = 0
60 NEXT L
70 PRINT"CHOICE WAS ";CHOICE
80 STOP
```

FINAL LISTING
```
10 CLS
```
then copy the list in the main text until:
```
240 NEXT I
250 LET CHOICE = CODE A$ - 48
260 IF CHOICE < 1 THEN LET L=0
270 IF CHOICE > 9 THEN LET L=0
280 NEXT L
290 GOSUB (CHOICE*20 + 290)
300 STOP
```
then copy the main list from line 310 to line 480.

TAB

Some versions of the Oric-1 do not obey the TAB command, even though it is part of Oric-1 BASIC: in this case, insert this line at the start of the program:

```
5 LET S$="
```

Between the quotes in this line there should be as many spaces as there are characters on a complete screen line — 40 for an Oric-1. Then whenever the program says TAB(12) replace it by LEFT$(S$,12), copying the number in the TAB statement into the LEFT$( ) function.

CHR$(12)

On the Oric-1, the Dragon 32, the Lynx and the BBC Micro, replace PRINT CHR$(12) by CLS. On the Commodore 64 and the Vic-20 replace CHR$(12) by PRINT"shiftkey+CLR/HOME key": this should result in a 'reverse field heart' being printed. See the manual if you're puzzled.

ON.. GOSUB

This is not available on the Lynx, but can be replaced by line 290 in the final Spectrum listing above.

VARIABLES

See 'Basic Flavours' page 211.

INKEY$

See 'Basic Flavours' page 195, and Commodore owners replace LET A$=INKEY$ by GET A$, and replace IF INKEY$="" THEN by:
GET A$:IF A$="" THEN

Expanding Files

Having established an overall structure, we now continue our programming project with a look at file handling

The address book program that we have been developing in these instalments of the Basic Programming course is actually a type of simple database, and as such involves the concept of 'files'. The word is used in a number of related, but slightly different, ways. We shall start by discussing these in a little more detail so that we can subsequently use the word with more precision.

In computer programming, a 'file' can be thought of in much the same way as a file in a filing cabinet. It is a collection of related pieces of information stored together. Computers store files on magnetic tapes or disks. Each 'file' of information is given a unique name so that the computer can gain access to it whenever necessary. The information on a cassette tape or a floppy disk may be a program, or it may be 'data' used by a program. Taking the computerised address book as an example, the information needed consists of two separate parts: the program itself, and the data that the program works on. The program is the set of instructions that allows the computer (and the user) to manipulate and work on the data.

The data used by the program is the set of records containing the information you would expect to find in an address book — names, addresses and so on. It also includes certain types of data not normally available to the user. This is the 'housekeeping' data used by the program to help it work. Examples of this type of data might include: 'flags'; information relating to the current size of the database (i.e. the number of records in it); whether or not a sort has been conducted since a new record was last inserted; or possibly an indication of how many times a particular record has been accessed or printed out. The reason why data such as this — and the data comprising the records — needs to be treated separately from the program will become apparent as soon as we try to implement the program.

In earlier parts of the Basic Programming course we have used the READ and DATA statements as ways of putting data to work within a program. This is suitable only if the data is not subject to change, such as the number of days in a month. If the data is liable to change, the program can prompt for it on the screen, and INPUT, INKEY$ or other methods can be used to convey the data to the program. An example of the appropriate use of this form of data input might be a numbers guessing game, in which part of the program might take the form of:

```
PRINT "GUESS THE NUMBER"
INPUT N
IF N < > COMPNUM THEN ...
```

The data in the address book program, however, is subject to considerable modification. In theory, all the records could be stored within the program and read into appropriate arrays using READ and DATA statements. But then all the data comprising the records would have to be entered as part of the program. Whenever changes were made — names and addresses added or removed, for example — considerable alterations would need to be made to the program itself. At the very least, this would involve printing out the program, checking to see where the changes were needed, writing new segments of the program and then typing them in. The biggest problem, however, would be that the new program segments would not be complete program modules that could be independently tested — the changes would be scattered haphazardly throughout the program. The only way of knowing that the modified program worked properly would be to run it and see.

Fortunately, none of this is necessary because data can be stored independently of the program. This is done by creating data files on the cassette or disk. These files are collections of records treated in much the same way as the data in a DATA statement. The program is able to 'open' one or more of these files, read the data from it (usually into an array) and then 'close' the file. If an alteration to the data is needed, the program opens the appropriate file, reads in the data, modifies it, and then writes the modified data back to the file.

With disk-based computer systems, locating a particular file and reading from it or writing to it is quite fast — the location of the file takes only a fraction of a second and the read or write operations usually take a few seconds at most. A cassette-based computer system, on the other hand, may be quite a lot slower and may involve the user in rewinding the tape and waiting for the tape to play through until the right file has been found. Another advantage of using disks is that it is possible to have more than one file 'open' at a time, whereas this is not practical with cassette-based systems.

Files, then, are collections of data stored on a bulk storage medium that are available to be used by one or more programs. A word processing program, for example, might want access to the same set of names and addresses for 'personalised' automatic letter writing.

Files are handled in different ways according to the version of BASIC used. The best way to find out how your computer deals with them is to see what the manual has to say about the OPEN and CLOSE statements and try out a few examples. The description we are presenting here is very generalised and is designed to give an overall impression of using files.

Files may be either sequential or random. In a serial file, the information is stored with the first piece of information first, followed by the next piece, followed by the third and so on. A random file is organised so that the computer can go directly to the piece of data required, without having to start at the beginning and go through the data until the required piece has been located. Watching a film is more like a serial file; you start at the beginning and watch it all the way through to the end. Watching a film on a video recorder at home is a little bit like a random file; you can wind the tape back and forth and watch any part you choose. We shall consider only sequential files, because they're more appropriate to cassette systems.

Suppose you want to keep a record of average daily temperatures for a week. These might be:

MONDAY	13.6
TUESDAY	9.6
WEDNESDAY	11.4
THURSDAY	10.6
FRIDAY	11.5
SATURDAY	11.1
SUNDAY	10.9

To keep things simple, all this data will be treated as numeric data, with Monday being Day 1 and Sunday being Day 7. The data can then be represented like this:

1,13.6,2,9.6,3,11.4,4,10.6,5,11.5,6,11.1,7,10.9

To store this data in a sequential file, the following steps will be needed in the program:

OPEN the file
Write the data to the file
CLOSE the file

Whenever the OPEN statement is used it is necessary to state whether we are writing data from the computer to the file (an output) or reading data from the file into the computer (an input). In the BBC Micro, this is done using the OPENOUT and OPENIN statements. The equivalent in Microsoft BASIC is OPEN "O" and OPEN "I". A short program fragment to write the data above into a file (in Microsoft BASIC) would be:

```
100 OPEN "O", #1, "TEMP.DAT"
110 PRINT #1,1,13.6,2,9.6,3,11.4,4,10.6,5,
    11.5,6,11.1,7,10.9
120 CLOSE #1
```

The word OPEN in line 100 makes the file available to the program. OPEN is followed by "O" to indicate that data will go out from the program to be stored in the file. This is followed by #1, which tells the computer that we'll be referring to this as file number 1 in our program. Each file is given an arbitrary number that will subsequently be used with the INPUT# or PRINT# statements when we want to read or write data to that file. Finally, we have the filename in double quotation marks. We've called our file TEMP.DAT to indicate that it contains temperature readings, and is a data file rather than a program.

A complete Microsoft BASIC program to enter the data into a file and subsequently read it out and print it is given below:

```
100 OPEN "O", #1, "TEMP.DAT"
110 PRINT # 1,1,13.6,2,9.6,3,11.4,4,10.6,5,11.5,6,
    11.1,7,10.9
120 CLOSE #1
130 REM LINES 130 & 140 ARE 'DUMMY' LINES TO
140 REM REPRESENT INTERVENING PROGRAM
150 OPEN "I", #1, "TEMP.DAT"
160 FOR X = 1 TO 7
170 INPUT #1, DAY, TEMP
180 PRINT "DAY ";DAY,TEMP
190 NEXT X
200 CLOSE #1
210 END
```

This opens a file, numbered #1 and named TEMP.DAT, writes data into it using the PRINT# statement and then CLOSEs the file. Later in the program the same file is opened using both the number and the filename (the number does not need to be the same as when the file was created, but the number used in the PRINT# or INPUT# statements must be the same as the one assigned to the filename when the file was opened). INPUT #1 in line 170 indicates that the input will come from a file numbered #1 (that is, the file TEMP. DAT) and not from the keyboard.

We shall leave this look at file handling for the moment and return to the address book program and some of the components involved in the INITIALISE subsection of the program. First, let's look at the amount of memory space required for a single record in the address book file (the word 'file' here is being used in the database sense of being the set of all related records, not in the operating system sense of being a named group of data stored on tape or disk).

The use of fixed-length fields is somewhat wasteful of memory space, but makes the programming a lot simpler. If we allow one whole line for each field, with 40 characters to a line, all of this will be saved in an array even if most of the line consists of blank spaces. In some versions of BASIC, however, when string arrays are DIMensioned, each element can be up to 256 characters long. The dimensioning merely sets the number of elements in the array, not the size of each element.

If you have a BASIC that can handle multi-dimensional arrays it would be possible to use a separate dimension for each of the fields, but many versions of BASIC cannot do this so we shall explore alternative approaches. The simplest method is to use a separate string array for each of the fields. But here's a way to 'cheat' if you want to use multi-dimensional arrays and your BASIC cannot handle them.

The trick is to treat all the elements that would be in the multi-dimensional array as though they were elements in a one-dimensional array. For example, a two-dimensional array with three rows and five columns would be dimensioned like this: DIM A(3,5) and would contain a total of 15 elements: A(1,1) to A(3,5). The same information could be held in an ordinary subscripted array like this: DIM A(15). Everywhere that a two-dimensional array referred to A(R,C), we would substitute A((R−1)*5+C).

If we use a separate string array for each field, we have to decide how to DIMension the arrays. The simplest way is to use a fixed array size, but this limits the total number of records we can store in the database. A better approach would be to set the array size according to how many records there are in use. Not all dialects of BASIC, however, allow string arrays to be as big as you would like. Even if they did, a large number of records in the database could soon use up all the available memory in the computer. Here is a program that will enable you to find out the maximum number of elements your computer will allow. Many versions of BASIC, however, will allow as many elements in an array as you want, right up to the point where all available memory is used up. Each time the program asks you 'WHAT ARRAY SIZE?' enter a larger value until you eventually get an error message. The CLEAR in line 100 has the effect of eliminating the array at the end of each pass. Without this statement, you would get an error message in line 30 through attempting to re-dimension an array.

```
10 READ D$
20 INPUT "WHAT ARRAY SIZE";A
30 DIM N$(A)
40 FOR L = 1 TO A
50 LET N$(L) = D$
60 NEXT L
70 FOR L = 1 TO A
80 PRINT L, N$(L)
90 NEXT L
100 CLEAR
110 GOTO 10
120 DATA "HOME COMPUTER COURSE"
130 END
```

Even if only 40 characters were allowed in each element, with five fields per record, and if there were 256 elements set aside for each array, the amount of memory required to hold all the data within the main memory becomes prodigious. If one byte is required for each character to be stored, we would need 51,200 bytes (5×40×256 bytes) for the data alone. It is obviously not practicable to use up so much main memory on the data, and that's why separate data files are used.

Unfortunately, as we have already suggested, file handling routines can be a little difficult to use. If we wish to avoid using external files, the only

alternative is to put the data in a DATA statement so that it is always present in the program. Apart from the strain this imposes on the computer's memory capacity, this technique makes modification to the data extremely tedious and prone to error. Therefore it is preferable to use external data files. Once you have tried a few short programs to write data to and from external files, however, the whole process will become much clearer and easier to understand. By way of illustration, we have chosen two very different machines and versions of BASIC to supplement our short daily temperature program given in Microsoft BASIC. These are for the Sinclair Spectrum and the BBC Micro. Both these versions of BASIC differ considerably from our usual Microsoft BASIC, and readers are referred back to the 'Basic Flavours' boxes in earlier parts of the Basic Programming course for details on some of these differences.

In Spectrum BASIC, OPEN# and CLOSE# are reserved for use with the Microdrive. When cassette storage is used, special versions of the SAVE and LOAD commands are needed. The ordinary SAVE command is used for storing programs and program variables on tape (and, of course, ordinary data in DATA statements). Arrays can be saved on tape using the SAVE-DATA statement. This takes the form:

```
SAVE filename DATA array name()
```

The filename is the name given to the file (TEMP.DAT in the Microsoft program). The array name is simply the name of the string array followed by a pair of closed and empty brackets. To SAVE the daily temperature results, we would first have to create a DIMensioned string array and write the data into it, perhaps using READ-DATA statements. To make the difference between the filename and array name more apparent, we will call the array c$ and the filename will be "TEMPDAT".

```
10 DIM c$(14,4)
20 FOR x = 1 TO 14
30 READ c$(x)
40 NEXT x
50 DATA "1", "13.6", "2", "9.6", "3", "11.4", "4", "4",
   "10.6", "5", "11.5", "6", "11.1", "7", "10.9"
60 SAVE "TEMPDAT" DATA c$()
70 STOP
80 LOAD "TEMPDAT" DATA c$()
90 FOR L = 1 TO 14 STEP 2
100 PRINT "DAY";c$(L),c$(L+1)
110 NEXT L
120 STOP
```

Line 60 saves all the data in the string array c$ in a data file with the filename TEMPDAT. The program will then stop at line 70, and you should rewind the tape. The keyword CONT will restart the program. Line 80 reverses the process and stores the data in TEMPDAT in the c$ array.

The BBC Micro has one of the most sophisticated dialects of BASIC available on home computers. It allows structured programming with such advanced features as a REPEAT-UNTIL construct and 'procedures'. Before a procedure can be used it must first be defined, and we will see how this is done in the version of the program for the BBC below. Notice that BBC BASIC defines the direction of data flow in the 'open' statement, using either OPENOUT or OPENIN:

```
10 DIM C$(2,7)
20 FOR R = 1 TO 7
30   FOR C = 1 TO 2
40     READ C$(C,R)
50   NEXT C
60 NEXT R
70 DATA 1,13.6,2,9.6,3,11.4,4,10.6,5,11.5,6,11.1,7,10.9
80 INPUT "TYPE S TO SAVE DATA",K$
90 IF K$ < > "S" THEN GOTO 80
100 PROCSAVE: CLEAR: DIM C$ (2,7)
110 INPUT "REWIND DATA TAPE THEN TYPE L", K$
120 IF K$ < > "L" THEN GOTO 110
130 PROCLOAD
140 PRINT "DAY    TEMP"
150 FOR R = 1 TO 7
160   FOR C = 1 TO 2
170     PRINT C$(C,R);"        "
180   NEXT C: PRINT
190 NEXT R
200 END
300 DEF PROCSAVE
310 X = OPENOUT ("TEMPDAT")
320 FOR R = 1 TO 7
330   FOR C = 1 TO 2
340     PRINT # X, C$(C,R)
350   NEXT C
360 NEXT R
370 CLOSE #X
380 ENDPROC
400 DEF PROCLOAD
410 X = OPENIN ("TEMPDAT")
420 FOR R = 1 TO 7
430   FOR C = 1 TO 2
440     INPUT # X, C$ (C,R)
450   NEXT C
460 NEXT R
470 CLOSE # X
480 ENDPROC
```

One of the advantages of BBC BASIC is that the file handling statements work equally well for cassette files or disk files, and programs written to run on a cassette can be used with no modification if a disk drive is added later.

So far we have seen how data can be transferred from DATA statements via arrays to data files on tape (or disk) and vice versa. The next step will be to look further at the INITIALISATION process to see exactly how many arrays will be needed, how many elements each will need and at what points in the program data will need to be transferred into and out of them.

Exercise

Write a program with the following components:

```
BEGIN
   INITIALISE
   ENTER DATA
   CHOOSE
      Save data
      Load data
      Exit program
END
```

INITIALISE will initialise any variables and arrays needed by the program. The data will comprise, say, 15 names, entered from the keyboard with prompts on the screen. CHOOSE will provide the user with a menu asking if you want to SAVE DATA?, LOAD DATA? or EXIT PROGRAM? See if you can create a flag in the EXIT PROGRAM? part that will automatically save the data if, and only if, a SAVE has not already been carried out.

Basic Flavours

VARIABLES

Of the most popular home computers, only the BBC Micro supports long variable names such as FULLNAME$. The Spectrum allows long numeric variable names, but only single letter string variable names. The Dragon 32, Vic-20, and Commodore 64 support long variable names, but only the first two characters are significant, so that FULLNAME$ is valid, but refers to the same memory location as FUJIYAMA$: both have the same first two characters.

On the Oric-1 variable names cannot be more than two characters (first a letter then a number or a letter), while the Lynx allows only single letter variable names, though both lower- and upper-case letters are valid and distinct.

OPEN

CLOSE

PRINT #

On the Dragon 32 you must use this format:

```
OPEN "O", #-1, "TEMPDAT"
PRINT #-1, 1,13.6,2,9.6,3,11.4, etc.
CLOSE #-1
```

and

```
OPEN "I", #-1, "TEMPDAT"
INPUT #-1,D,T
CLOSE #-1
```

On the Commodore 64 and the Vic-20 use this format:

```
OPEN 1,1,2,"TEMPDAT"
PRINT 1,1:PRINT #1,13.6: etc.
CLOSE 1
```

and

```
OPEN 1,1,0 "TEMPDAT"
INPUT # 1, D, T
CLOSE 1
```

LYNX

ORIC-1

The Lynx and the Oric-1, in their standard form, do not support cassette files. However, expansions to permit this will be available in the future.

TONY LODGE

J
K
L
M
N
O
P
Q
R
S
T
U
V
WX
YZ

Changing Places

After looking at how to insert new records, we move on to ways of retrieving them. As anticipated, we first encounter the problem of finding an exact match

We ended the last segment with an exercise for you to write a database-type program that allowed data to be entered into it. Let's look at some of the steps involved in entering a new record as a way of continuing our examination of what is involved in the INITIALISE stage of our main program. First, let's assume that there are the following fields and corresponding arrays:

FIELD	ARRAY
1 NAME field	NAMFLD$
2 MODIFIED NAME field	MODFLD$
3 STREET field	STRFLD$
4 TOWN field	TWNFLD$
5 COUNTY field	CNTFLD$
6 PHONE NUMBER field	TELFLD$
7 INDEX field	NDXFLD$

The meaning of most of these fields should be reasonably clear, with the possible exception of fields 2 and 7. Let's first consider the MODIFIED NAME field. When we initially looked at the problem of the data format for the name, we debated whether to have the name format tightly specified (rigid) or loosely specified (fuzzy) and we opted for the latter. Since the way a name can be entered is extremely variable, a rigid format would have made search and sort routines very difficult. To solve this we decided that all names would be converted to a standardised format: all letters converted to upper case, all non-alphabetic characters (such as spaces, full stops, apostrophes, etc.) removed and that there would be only a single space between the forename (if any) and the surname.

The need to standardise names like this arises because the sort and search routines have to have some way of comparing like with like. On the other hand, when we retrieve a name and address from the database, we want to have the data presented in the form it was originally entered. There are two ways of handling this problem: either each name filed is converted into standard form only when sorts and searches are taking place, or the name field can be converted into standard form and stored as a separate field so that sort and search routines can have instant access to standardised names.

There are advantages and disadvantages in both approaches. Converting the name fields temporarily when they are wanted by other routines saves memory space, since less data needs to be stored in the file. On the other hand, this procedure is extremely time-consuming.

However, if a separate field is reserved for the standardised form of the name, the conversion will need to be performed only once for each record. And although extra memory is consumed, searches and sorts will be executed quicker.

The other field that may cause confusion is the INDEX field. This is really included as a spare field to allow for future expansion or modification of the database without the need for major rewriting of the program. Its inclusion introduces the topic of 'binding' — a term that means the fixing of data and processing relationships. All the fields or elements in each of the records are bound because they have the same index (the same element number or subscript in their respective arrays), and because all the fields in a record will be stored in a file together. This can make the addition of new data types or relationships at a later stage a difficult task, possibly involving the complete reorganisation of the file structure and a major rewriting of the program. The incorporation of the INDEX field at this stage will make future changes to the program much simpler.

Before attempting to add a new record to the database, we will make a few assumptions about the structure of the files. First, we will limit the number of records to 50 (even though this is really too small for a useful address book — we'll find out how to handle large amounts of data later). We will also assume that all the data has already been transferred — as part of the INITIALISE procedure — into arrays.

When a new record is added, it is simplest to add it to the end of the file (that is, to the first empty element in each array). There is a good chance that the new record will be out of order with the others, but that is a problem we can investigate later. The first thing to do, therefore, will be to find out how big the array is. Since this is a piece of information likely to be useful in many parts of the program, the best place to do it is in INITIALISE. This is a clear case of the need for a global variable (that is, a variable that can be used in any part of the program). We will call it SIZE. Another global variable likely to be useful is the index of the current record. Since no record will be current when the program is first run, assigning an initial value to CURR will have to wait until the program does something to the data. CURR can, however, be initialised to zero in the INITIALISATION procedure. Initialising a variable to zero is not strictly necessary in BASIC as this is done automatically. It is, however, good practice and

TONY LODGE

should always be done for local variables to prevent 'side effects' from the use of the same variable elsewhere in the program.

When the program is first run, various types of initialisation will take place and data will be loaded from disk or tape and transferred to string variables. The CHOOSE menu will then be presented. If the user chooses option 6 (to add a record to the file), the value of variable CHOICE returned will be 6, and this will call the sub-program ADDREC. ADDREC will assume that SIZE has already had a value assigned to it and so it can start prompting for inputs (note: this also assumes that INITIALISE has already correctly DIMensioned the necessary arrays).

Adding a new record also means that the file is now, potentially at least, out of order. Since a sort may take some time, it may not be necessary to sort the records after each addition has been made — that is a decision we shall defer for the moment. Instead, we will set a flag to indicate that a new record has been added.

We are now in a position to start making a tentative list of possible arrays, variables and flags that may be needed by the program.

ARRAYS

NAMFLD$	(name field)
MODFLD$	(modified name field)
TWNFLD$	(town field)
CNTFLD$	(county field)
TELFLD$	(telephone number field)
NDXFLD$	(index field)

VARIABLES

SIZE	(current size of file)
CURR	(index of current record)

FLAGS

RADD	(new record added)
SORT	(sorted since record modification)
SAVE	(save executed since record modification)
RMOD	(modification made since last save)

It is likely that in the course of developing the program a few more arrays will be needed. Certainly more variables will be needed. As for the flags, it is apparent that although others will be necessary, the four given above may not all be required. There will be no need either to save or sort the file (assuming it is already saved and sorted) unless a modification has taken place, so RMOD is possibly the only flag really needed. But if we do decide to use all four flags, the INITIALISATION sub-program should set them all to their appropriate values. As further practice in top-down program refinement, let's see how easy it is to code *ADDREC*.

I 4 (EXECUTE) 6 (ADDREC)
```
BEGIN
    Locate current size of file
    Prompt for inputs
    Assign inputs to ends of arrays
    Set RMOD flag
END
```

II 4 (EXECUTE) 6 (ADDREC)
```
BEGIN
    (size of file is SIZE)
    (prompt for inputs)
    Clear screen
    Print prompt message for first array(SIZE)
    Input data to array(SIZE)
    (prompt and input for all arrays)
    Set RMOD to 1
END
```

All this is straightforward and does not involve loops or other complicated structures. The next step can be direct coding into BASIC. The only points to note are that SIZE is a variable set during the execution of INITIALISE and does not need to be coded as part of this section.

III 4 (EXECUTE) 6 (ADDREC) BASIC CODE
```
CLS: REM OR USE PRINT CHRS(24) ETC TO CLEAR
    SCREEN
INPUT "ENTER NAME";NAMFLD$(SIZE)
INPUT "ENTER STREET";STRFLD$(SIZE)
INPUT "ENTER TOWN";TWNFLD$(SIZE)
INPUT "ENTER COUNTY";CNTFLD$(SIZE)
INPUT "ENTER TELEPHONE NUMBER";
    TELFLD$(SIZE)
LET RMOD=1
LET NDXFLD$=STR$(SIZE)
GOSUB *MODNAME*
RETURN
```

The third to last line sets the NDXFLD$ field to the value of SIZE (converted into a string by STR$), so that it can act as an index at a later stage. The subroutine *MODNAME*, called just before the end of the program, is none other than the program described in detail on page 208. A few slight changes will be needed to that program, but these are just details. This subroutine has the function of taking the ordinary (fuzzy) name input and converting it into a standard form. The output from this subroutine will be an element (SIZE) in an array called MODFLD$. All name searches and sorts can now be conducted on the elements in MODFLD$, and since the element will have the same index as the other fields in the record, it will be easy to display the name and address as they were originally entered. In other words, the search will be made on MODFLD$ but the display will come from NAMFLD$.

That's about all that's involved in adding a new record to the file, although we have not made allowances for any error checking, or provision for what would happen if there is no more space left in the array. Since all our programs are being written in modular form, modifications and improvements such as these can easily be made later without having to rewrite the whole program.

The sub-programs MODREC and DELREC (to modify and delete records respectively) are fairly similar to ADDREC, except that before they can be executed we have to locate the record we want to change. Consequently, both of these sub-

K
L
M
N
O
P
Q
R
S
T
U
WX

programs will start by calling FINDREC. This sub-program is based on a search routine similar to the one described on page 213. The chief difference this time is that (in all probability) no two data items will be identical, since few people have completely identical names.

There are two ways a search can be conducted. One is to search through an unordered pile. This makes the searches slower than they need to be. In the worst case, the routine might have to search through all of the data items before locating the item being searched for. Searching through an unordered pile does have the advantage, however, that sort routines are not required every time a record is added, deleted or modified.

If the data is ordered in some way — either numerically or alphabetically, for example — the program will have to search through only a small fraction of the items in the list. The longer the list is, the more efficient a binary search becomes compared with searching through an unordered pile. In fact, if there is enough data in the file to warrant it, the sorting of the records after a modification can be speeded up by conducting a preliminary search to locate the first and last occurrence in the array of the initial letter of the surname in the record involved.

Another way to speed up the sort routine might be to maintain a look-up table of the locations in the array of the first occurrence of each letter of the alphabet. This table, however, would need to be carefully maintained (updated) whenever any changes were made to the data.

The subject of searching and sorting is one of the largest areas in programming, and books have been devoted to it. We will not attempt to find the optimal solution for our address book program since this depends on a large number of factors, including the number of records in the file and whether or not disk drives are available.

A program in pseudo-language for a search through the elements in the MODFLD$ array is now given. The string variable KEY$ is the key for the search. The term 'key' here means the identifying group of characters used to specify which record (or records) is required.

```
Prompt for name to be searched
LET KEY$ = name (to be searched)
LET BTM = 1
LET SEARCHING = 0
LET TOP = SIZE
LOOP while (BTM < = TOP) AND (SEARCHING = 0)
    LET MID = INT ((BTM + TOP)/2)
    IF KEY$ = MODFLD$(MID)
        THEN
            PRINT NAMFLD$(MID)
            PRINT STRFLD$(MID)
            PRINT TWNFLD$(MID)
            PRINT CNTFLD$(MID)
            PRINT TELFLD$(MID)
            LET SEARCHING = 1
        ELSE
            IF KEY$ > MODFLD$(MID)
                THEN LET BTM = MID+1
                ELSE LET TOP = MID−1
            ENDIF
    ENDIF
ENDLOOP
IF SEARCHING = 0 THEN PRINT "RECORD NOT
    FOUND"
END
```

This piece of pseudo-language is closely based on the program used for searching football scores on page 215, but you will see that it does have a suitable output if the record cannot be found (the last PRINT statement), which will be executed only if the loop fails to locate an exact match between KEY$ and MODFLD$(MID).

Unfortunately, an exact match is rather unlikely, even if the name and telephone number you want is in the database. This is because the IF KEY$ = MODFLD$ statement is totally inflexible; it does not allow for the slightest difference between the character string input by the user in response to the prompt and the character string stored in MODFLD$(MID). In an ordinary address book, the eye scans down the page and is able to allow for all sorts of small differences in the actual representation of the record and what you are looking for. The computer cannot do this.

There are, however, ways of avoiding this, although they all involve extra programming effort and will take a little more time to run. The first improvement would be to check only the surname first, and for this reason it makes sense for the name stored in MODFLD$ to be in the form SURNAME (space) FORENAME. We developed a routine for reversing the order of a name earlier in the Basic Programming course (see 'Basic Flavours') and this can be incorporated as a subroutine within the ADDREC routine when the MODFLD$ field is created.

Having successfully located the first occurrence of the required surname, the FINDREC routine should then check the forename part of that element to see if it is identical to the name input (KEY$). If it is, there is no problem — the record has been located. If it is not, however, the problem starts to get complicated, and we have to plan our strategy carefully. We could, for example, search through all the forenames, and if an exact match is not found, start looking for an approximate match. The difficulty here is: what exactly constitutes an approximate match?

Instead of the "RECORD NOT FOUND" message in the program above, it might be better to give a message like "EXACT MATCH NOT FOUND, TRY FOR A CLOSE MATCH? (Y/N)?" What do the words 'close match' mean? Is Bobby a close match to Robert? How about Robrt? Both of these represent possible inputs in the FINDREC program. Let's try to define what we mean by a close match and then start to develop a program in BASIC to find the closest match to an input string.

Suppose the string in memory was ROBERT. Which of the following is the closer match: ROB or RBRT? The second gets four letters right out of six, while the first gets only three out of six. On the other hand, the first has three letters in correct sequence, while the second has only two.

The choice is largely arbitrary. We will opt for giving priority to an exact match between KEY$ and a substring of the name in memory. If no exact match with a substring can be found, the program will try to get the largest number of common letters. Here's the program stated in terms of input and output:

INPUT
A character string
OUTPUT
The closest match to the input string

The following program, in a pseudo-language close to BASIC, will search through the strings in an array and examine the first 'n' letters in each, where 'n' is the number of letters in the key (KEY$). If there is no match, a message to that effect will be printed:

```
DIM ARRAY$(4)
FOR L = 1 TO 4
READ ARRAY$(L)
NEXT L
DATA "ROBERT", "RICHARD", "ROBIANA",
    "ROBERTA"
LET KEY$ = "RON"
LET LKEY = LEN(KEY$)
LET SEARCHING = 0
LOOP FOR INDEX = 1 TO 4
    IF KEY$ = LEFT$(ARRAY$(INDEX),LKEY)
        THEN PRINT "MATCH IS ";ARRAY$(INDEX)
            LET SEARCHING = INDEX
    ENDIF
ENDLOOP
IF SEARCHING = 0
    THEN PRINT KEY$; "IS NOT AN EXACT MATCH
        OF ANY"
        PRINT "FIRST ";LKEY; "CHARACTERS"
```

After this, the program could go on to look at groups of characters LKEY long, starting with the second character in each string. If none of these matches, groups starting with the third character could be searched, and so on. Finally, if none of the triplets of characters in the strings matches, the program could try to find which string had the largest number of letters in common with KEY$. This is left as an exercise for the reader.

We could in fact write pages on the subject of 'fuzzy' matching, and the different techniques employed in commercial database packages. Most offer the ability to search on the first few characters in the field, like the code we have just been developing. Others will retrieve a record if the specified sequence of characters appears anywhere in the field, or indeed anywhere in the record. A 'wildcard' facility is particularly useful, so that specifying: J?N would find JONES, or JANE but not JOHN. The most sophisticated form of fuzzy matching works phonetically, so that entering SMITH would also find SMYTHE.

Basic Flavours

SPECTRUM

This is the listing of that part of the program which reverses the order of Firstname and Surname, first presented on page 186:

```
100 CLS
200 PRINT "ENTER NAME IN THE FORM"
300 PRINT "FIRSTNAME SURNAME"
400 PRINT "E.G. JILL THOMPSON"
500 INPUT "ENTER NAME";N$
600 GOSUB 9500
700 PRINT "NAME IN STANDARD FORM IS"
800 PRINT N$
1000 STOP
9500 REM S/R TO REVERSE NAME ORDER
9520 GOSUB 9600
9540 IF P=0 THEN RETURN
9560 LET N$=S$+",  "+F$
9580 RETURN
9600 REM S/R TO SLICE N$ AT A SPACE
9620 LET N=LEN (N$)
9630 LET P=0
9640 FOR K=1 TO N
9650 IF N$ (K)=" " THEN LET P=K
9655 IF N$ (K)=" " THEN LET K=N
9660 NEXT K
9670 IF P=0 THEN RETURN
9680 LET F$=N$( TO P-1)
9700 LET S$=N$(P+1 TO )
9720 RETURN
```

LEFT$

RIGHT$

MID$

On the Commodore 64, Vic-20, Oric-1, and Lynx, replace lines 9600 to 9720 of the Spectrum listing by these lines:

```
9600 REM S/R TO SLICE N$ AT A SPACE
9620 LET N=LEN (N$)
9630 LET P=0
9640 FOR K=1 TO N
9650 IF MID$(N$,K,1)="    " THEN LET P=K:
    LET K=N
9660 NEXT K
9670 IF P=0 THEN RETURN
9680 LET F$=LEFT$(N$,P-1)
9700 LET S$=RIGHT$(N$,N-P)
9720 RETURN
```

INSTR

On the Dragon 32 and the BBC Micro, replace lines 9600 to 9720 of the Spectrum listing by these lines:

```
9600 REM S/R TO SLICE N$ AT A SPACE
9620 LET N=LEN (N$)
9640 LET P=INSTR(N$, " ")
9670 IF P=0 THEN RETURN
9680 LET F$=LEFT$(N$,P-1)
9700 LET S$=RIGHT$(N$,N-P)
9720 RETURN
```

As we have mentioned before, INSTR is a useful function, particularly when dealing with database-type applications such as this. If your machine has INSTR, then you may like to attempt a more sophisticated form of 'fuzzy' matching.

INPUT

On the BBC Micro, replace line 500 of the Spectrum listing by:

```
500 INPUT "ENTER NAME", N$
```

L
M
N
O
P
Q
R
S
T
U
V
WX
YZ

Assembly Lines

We can now bring together the sub-programs that will process our computerised address book, and examine ways of making the program more user-friendly

Although many details of the address book program have yet to be finalised, the overall structure should now be becoming clear. At this point in the development of a program of any size it is as well to draw a block diagram of the program and to think through the flow of activities in the program.

This is also the point at which the program writer should think about the 'human interface' and 'user image' aspects of the program. These important concepts and practices are often not given the attention they deserve, even in commercial software.

'Human interface', simply defined, means the 'ergonomics' of the software, or how easy it is to use. 'User image' is concerned with how the user perceives the program being used. We shall examine these concepts with regard to our program as developed so far, and determine to what extent we will be able to implement them.

The table shows the main blocks of the program that have been considered so far. As a convention, and simply to keep things tidy, we have used names with six characters for procedures or subroutines, seven characters (including $) for string arrays, four characters for simple numeric variables and five characters (including $) for simple string variables that are global. Local variables (in loops, for example) will usually be single letters.

Each of the major program blocks in the second column needs to be further broken down into sub-units, and the sub-units will need to be further refined until we have enough detail to write the actual code in BASIC. The processes involved in this form of 'stepwise refinement' have been illustrated for many of the blocks in earlier parts of the Basic Programming course.

Assuming that all or most of the program modules have been worked out, coded into BASIC, and individually tested, how can they be linked together to form a complete program? The best way to tackle this problem is to save each module on tape or disk, giving it the same filename used in the program development notes. Thus ADDREC can be written and tested as far as possible, and then saved under the filename ADDREC. Normally, when a program is loaded from tape or disk, we use the LOAD command, followed by the filename, as in LOAD "ADDREC". This has the effect, however, of clearing everything in memory, so if we load ADDREC and then subsequently load MODREC, the whole of the ADDREC program will disappear.

Fortunately, there is a partial solution. The MERGE command loads a program from tape or disk without erasing any program already in memory. But there is one important proviso. If any of the program line numbers in the MERGEd program are the same as line numbers in the program already in memory, the new line numbers will overwrite the old line numbers and cause chaos. Versions of BASIC with the RENUM command can get round this by renumbering the lines in a program module before they are saved, so that when they are merged there will be no conflict.

Unfortunately, many versions of BASIC on home computers do not have the RENUM command, and therefore careful planning of the line numbers from the beginning will be necessary. When a full chart of all the major program modules has been worked out (as we have partially done in the table), starting line numbers for each block can be assigned. Parts of the program likely to have extensive modifications or changes, such as the main program or file-handling parts of the program, should have increments of 50 or even 100 in order to leave plenty of room for additions. Program modules less liable to modification, such as the GREETS routine, can have line number increments of 10. Putting lots of blank REMs in the program not only makes the program easier to read, but also allows additional statements or calls

MAIN PROGRAM BLOCKS

	CREARR	(creates arrays and initialises variables)
INITIL	RDINFL	(reads in file from tape or disk)
	SETFLG	(sets flags and modifies variables)
GREETS		(prints greeting message)
CHOOSE	CHMENU	(prints options menu)
	INCHOI	(assigns option to CHCE)
	FNDREC	(locates and prints a record)
	FNDNMS	(locates names from partial input)
	FNDTWN	(locates records for specific town)
	FNDINT	(locates names from initials)
EXECUT	LSTREC	(lists all records)
	ADDREC	(adds a new record)
	MODREC	(modifies existing record)
	DELREC	(deletes a record)
	EXPROG	(saves file and exits program)

to subroutines to be added later. If your BASIC doesn't feature MERGE either, then you will have to type in the various modules as they are written, and save them together.

The program blocks in the table have been merged as a 'trial run' in the listing printed here, to illustrate the pitfalls of the 'try it and see' approach encouraged by languages such as BASIC. Our program would not run properly because the flow of control through it has not yet been thought through carefully enough. There is no point in typing in the whole of this program just to find out that it will not work, but if you have saved all the routines from earlier parts of the course, and if your BASIC has the RENUM command, you can try renumbering and then MERGEing to produce a similar listing.

The first block in the main program is INITIL, which is supposed to initialise variables, dimension arrays, read in files, assign the data to the arrays, set flags and so on.

The *INITIL* subroutine is broken down into *CREARR* (to create the arrays), *RDINFL* (to read in files and assign the data to the appropriate arrays) and *SETFLG* (to set flags etc.).

When all this has been done, the program moves on to *GREETS*, a subroutine to print a greeting message on the screen. The last part of this routine waits for the user to press the space bar for the program to continue.

The program then goes on to *CHOOSE*. This comprises two parts: the first presents a menu of the options offered by the address book program; the second accepts the choice input from the keyboard and assigns the (numeric) value to a variable called CHOI.

The value of this variable is used by the next program block, EXECUT, to select one of nine further program blocks. All of these, except EXPROG, will need to return to *CHOOSE* after they have been executed so that the user has the opportunity of selecting another option. This will not be required if 9 (EXPROG) has been selected because this option is supposed to terminate the operation of the program.

The chief problem with this program as it stands is that the control flow is not correct. INITIL insists that we read in a file from mass storage whether a file exists or not. If the program is being run for the first time, no records will have been entered and there will be no data files on the tape or disk. Any attempt to open and read a non-existent file will result in an error message and the program will not work.

What is required is to have the *RDINFL* routine called only by one of the EXECUT modules, and then only once each time the program is run. This suggests that there should be an INFL flag, originally set to 0, that will be set to 1 once the file has been read in. If it has been set to 1, it will inhibit further attempts to read in. ADDREC will then always search through the arrays to locate the first empty element and will write the information there. This record will almost certainly not be in the proper sort sequence, so there should be a RMOD flag which will be set to 1 when executing The RMOD flag should also be set to 1 if MODREC or DELREC are executed. You can try writing the relevant code to achieve this, or if you simply want to run the program change line 1310 to RETURN.

Adding a record, deleting one or modifying one all mean that the sequence of records is likely to be out of order, so any module (FNDREC, for example) should first check RMOD to see if any changes have been made. If they have, we could either insist on a sort before a search is made, or put up with an inefficient search through a pile. EXPROG will automatically check RMOD and call the sort routine if it is set (to 1) before saving the data in the file on tape or disk.

The 'human interface' aspects of the program, which we mentioned earlier, can be broken down into the following categories:

User interface
User image
Error recovery
Security
Adaptability

User interface refers to the way the user of the program communicates with the program. We have opted for the use of menus throughout (rather than commands). Many people prefer commands, but the important point is that, whatever form of intercommunication is used, it should be consistent. Similar commands should not do different things in different parts of the program. If they do, the user has to read each menu carefully before each choice is made and 'reflexes' cannot be built up.

As our program stands, it is poor in this respect: the greeting message is terminated by hitting the space bar; the options menu is terminated automatically by hitting any of the number keys from 1 to 9; and the data entry in ADDREC is terminated (for each field) by hitting the RETURN key. This kind of inconsistency may be acceptable in a 'home-brew' program, but should be considered unacceptable in commercial software.

User image refers to the way the user perceives the operation of the program. It is considerably influenced by the quality of the user interface. Most of the operations going on inside the computer are completely hidden from the computer operator. The only way the operator can form an idea of what's going on in the program is from the visual input he receives from the screen in response to the inputs from the keyboard. The user image we would want from our address book program would be that of an actual, physical address book. Similarly, the user image desirable from a word processing program would be that of a piece of 'paper' (on the screen) upon which we type. In this case, ideally, bold type would appear bold on the screen, underlined type would be underlined, and justified type (type with a straight right margin) would be justified on the screen.

A perfect user image is seldom possible — no

real address book expects you to 'PRESS 1' to find a name. Nevertheless, a good user image involves well designed screen layouts and a consistent pattern to the operations. Prompts should always appear in the same position on the screen (some well known word processors, for example, display some prompts on the top line of the screen and some on the bottom line, apparently at random). A program with a good user image will also inform the user at any time where he is in the program. If you are in the ADDREC mode, there should be a message always visible to tell you this. If you have just entered a field (to add to a new record), there should be a message to say, for example, HIT RETURN IF ENTRY IS CORRECT, ELSE HIT ESCAPE (which brings us to the important subject of error recovery and reporting, which we will come to later).

Ideally, all formatting should appear on the screen, so that, for example, the record displayed on the screen will be of the same format as a record printed out by the printer. Many commercially available pieces of software incorporate 'help menus' which will tell you what to do next if you're not sure.

The user image of a program is best when it is concrete — a piece of typing paper or an index card — rather than abstract with 'sub-files', 'buffers' and so on. Many commercial database programs suffer in this respect; the user has constantly to keep in mind that certain pieces of information are in sub-files or temporary, hidden fields. These factors tend to make the use of such a program more of an intellectual burden.

Error recovery is also an important subject. What happens, for example, if you have just entered someone's name but realise that you made a typing error? Will you have to go ahead and then call MODREC to correct it, or will the program give you the option to 'quit' before you go any further? Most versions of BASIC will report errors in the entering of a program, either when the erroneous line is entered, or when the program is run. However, this is not part of the 'user interface'. BASIC does include a number of messages that re-prompt the user for a correct entry if an incorrect one is made (for example, the REDO prompt if an unsuitable entry is made in response to an INPUT statement).

Handling errors has two facets — error reporting and error recovery. One well known word processing program, for example, has good error reporting but poor error recovery; if you create a long document and try to save it on a disk that is already nearly full, the program gives you the helpful message DISK SPACE EXHAUSTED. It does not, unfortunately, allow the user to recover from this error — a new disk cannot be formatted without first destroying the text that you may have spent hours typing in!

Any operation performed by the user that could result in the loss of data (MODREC, for example) should always be queried before execution. Messages such as THIS WILL DESTROY THE RECORD. ARE YOU SURE? (Y/N) should always be provided. In a word processor, a similar message would be: THE 'SAVE' COMMAND WILL NOT KEEP A BACKUP OF THE OLD DOCUMENT. IS THIS OK? (Y/N).

Error handling (trapping and reporting) should be considered in the design of a program wherever there is a possibility of wrong data input, wrong menu choice, wrong commands and whenever data is to be modified or saved, especially if the save involves writing over old data.

You must pay attention to security — what happens to the program or data if there is a fatal error (such as a power failure). The program designer should consider how much data it is possible to lose and devise methods of recovering as much as possible or making the remaining data usable. One rather sophisticated word processor incorporates a program called RECOVER so that if there is a catastrophic error (a power failure, for example, or switching off the computer before saving the document), almost nothing is lost. Such advanced programming techniques, sadly, are beyond the scope of this course. The point is, though, to make your programs as secure as possible by anticipating all possible fatal errors beforehand (that can be reasonably dealt with), and writing routines designed to cope with them.

Adaptability, the ease with which the program can be customised, is also important. We have touched on this topic a number of times already. At the simplest level, always leave plenty of room between line numbers (in BASIC) and incorporate plenty of empty REMs that can be filled later with statements and GOSUBs if necessary. When creating arrays, at least one redundant array should be built in to allow for future expansion. It is a cardinal rule of program writing that future requirements cannot be anticipated. The only thing certain is that a good program can always be made better, and making it better is likely to mean writing more code.

Basic Flavours

SPECTRUM

See the program on page 222 for the Spectrum version of lines 1300 to 1370. The loop in the main program between lines 3750 and 3780 will work on the Spectrum, but may cause problems because Spectrum keys repeat if held down for more than a fraction of a second. The Spectrum handbook recommends that this type of INKEY$ loop contain an extra line to avoid this:

3755 IF INKEY$ <> "" THEN GOTO 3755

The Spectrum supports the VAL(A$) function, but will crash the program if the first character of A$ is non-numeric; in this program the problem can be avoided by:

3790 LET CHOI=CODE A$-48

but this is not a complete solution — it works only when A$ is a single character (as it must be in the program). The Spectrum does not support ON...GOSUB, but it does allow you to write GOSUB (numeric expression) as well as simply GOSUB (line number); line 4010, therefore, may be replaced by

MERGE

4010 GOSUB (290+CHOI*20)

The Spectrum does not support RENUMBER.

This is not supported by the Oric-1, the Commodore 64 and Vic-20, the Lynx, the Dragon 32, and the BBC Micro. Often, however, there will be a way of simulating the MERGE command that a user group or specialist publication may reveal. The Lynx has the command APPEND, which allows you to LOAD one program onto the end of the program in memory: this can replace MERGE provided that the first line number of the progam on tape is higher than the last line number of the program in memory.

RENUMBER

This is not supported by the Spectrum, the Commodores, and the Oric-1: on these machines, renumbering can be done line-by-line using the EDIT facilities.

See 'Basic Flavours' page 195.

INKEY$

See 'Basic Flavours' page 223.

OPEN CLOSE

PRINT CHR$(12)

Replace this by CLS, except on the Commodore 64 and Vic-20 — on these machines type PRINT"shiftkey+CLRkey", which should cause a reverse-field heart or capital S to appear between the quotes.

ON... GOSUB

In line 4010, ON...GOSUB will cause control to pass to non-existent lines — 310, 330, 350, etc. — which will cause the program to crash. These lines will later be expanded to contain the menu execution subroutines; in the meantime, enter these lines to your program as 'dummies', like this:

310 RETURN
330 RETURN

and so on.

STR$

The Lynx does not support this command, so replace line 9080 by:

9075 N=SIZE
9077 GOSUB 9500
9080 NDXFLD$(SIZE)=N$

and insert this subroutine:

9500 REM To convert N into N$ where N is an integer
9510 LET N$=" "
9520 IF N<0 THEN LET N$=""
9530 N=ABS(N)
9540 X=10
9550 I=1
9560 FOR K=1 TO 8
9570 I=I*X
9580 R=K
9590 IF I>N THEN K=8
9600 NEXT K
9610 FOR K=1 TO R
9620 I=I/X
9630 Z=INT(N/I)
9640 LET N=N-Z*I
9650 N$=N$+CHR$(48+INT(Z))
9660 NEXT K
9670 RETURN

```
10 REM  'MAINPG'
20 REM  *INITIL*
30 GOSUB 1000
40 REM  *GREETS*
50 GOSUB 3000
60 REM  *CHOOSE*
70 GOSUB 3500
80 REM  *EXECUT*
90 GOSUB 4000
100 END
1000 REM  *INIT* SUBROUTINE
1010 GOSUB 1100: REM  *CREARR* (CREATE ARRAYS) SUBROUTINE
1020 GOSUB 1300: REM  *RDINFL* (READ IN FILES) SUBROUTINE
1030 GOSUB 1320: REM  *SETFLG* (SET FLAGS) SUBROUTINE
1040 REM
1050 REM
1060 REM
1070 REM
1080 REM
1090 RETURN
1100 REM *CREARR* (CREATE ARRAYS) SUBROUTINE
1110 DIM NAMFLD$(50)
1120 DIM MODFLD$(50)
1130 DIM TWNFLD$(50)
1140 DIM CNTFLD$(50)
1150 DIM TELFLD$(50)
1160 DIM NDXFLD$(50)
1170 REM
1180 REM
1190 REM
1200 REM
1210 LET SIZE = 0
1220 LET RMOD = 0
1230 LET SVED = 0
1240 LET CURR = 0
1250 REM
1260 REM
1270 REM
1280 REM
1290 RETURN
1300 REM *RDINFL* SUBROUTINE -- SEE 'FLAVOURS' BOX
1310 ON ERROR GOTO 1370
1320 OPEN "I",#1,"ADBK.DAT"
1330 FOR L = 1 TO 50
1340 INPUT #1 NAMFLD$(L),STRFLD$(L),TWNFLD$(L),CNTFLD$(L),TELFLD$(L)
1350 NEXT L
1360 CLOSE #1
1370 RETURN
1380 REM  DUMMY *SETFLG* ROUTINE
1390 RETURN
3000 REM  *GREET* SUBROUTINE
3010 PRINT
3020 PRINT
3030 PRINT
3040 PRINT
3050 PRINT TAB(12);"*WELCOME TO THE*"
3060 PRINT TAB(9);"*HOME COMPUTER COURSE*"
3070 PRINT TAB(6);"*COMPUTERISED ADDRESS BOOK*"
3080 PRINT
3090 PRINT TAB(5);"(PRESS SPACE-BAR TO CONTINUE)"
3100 FOR L = 1 TO 1
3110 IF INKEY$ <> " " THEN L = 0
3120 NEXT L
3130 PRINT CHR$(12)
3140 RETURN
3500 REM  *CHOOSE* SUBROUTINE
3510 REM
3520 REM  'CHMENU'
3530 PRINT CHR$(12)
3540 PRINT "SELECT ONE OF THE FOLLOWING
3550 PRINT
3560 PRINT
3570 PRINT
3580 PRINT "1. FIND RECORD (FROM NAME)"
3590 PRINT "2. FIND NAMES (FROM INCOMPLETE NAME)"
3600 PRINT "3. FIND RECORDS (FROM TOWN)"
3610 PRINT "4. FIND RECORD (FROM INITIAL)"
3620 PRINT "5. LIST ALL RECORDS"
3630 PRINT "6. ADD NEW RECORD"
3640 PRINT "7. CHANGE RECORD"
3650 PRINT "8. DELETE RECORD"
3660 PRINT "9. EXIT & SAVE"
3670 PRINT
3680 PRINT
3690 REM  'INCHOI'
3700 REM
3710 LET L = 0
3720 LET I = 0
3730 FOR L = 1 TO 1
3740 PRINT "ENTER CHOICE (1 - 9)"
3750 FOR I = 1 TO 1
3760 LET A$ = INKEY$
3770 IF A$ = "" THEN I = 0
3780 NEXT I
3790 LET CHOI = VAL(A$)
3800 IF CHOI <1 THEN L = 0
3810 IF CHOI >9 THEN L = 0
3820 NEXT L
3830 RETURN
4000 REM  *EXECUT* SUBROUTINE -- SEE 'FLAVOURS' BOX
4010 ON CHOI GOSUB 310,330,350,370,390,410,430,450,470
4020 RETURN
9000 REM *ADDREC* SUBROUTINE
9010 PRINT CHR$(12)
9020 INPUT "ENTER NAME";NAMFLD$(SIZE)
9030 INPUT "ENTER STREET";STRFLD$(SIZE)
9040 INPUT "ENTER TOWN";TWNFLD$(SIZE)
9050 INPUT "ENTER COUNTY";CNTFLD$(SIZE)
9060 INPUT "ENTER TELEPHONE NUMBER";TELFLD$(SIZE)
9070 LET RMOD = 1
9080 LET NDXFLD$(SIZE) = STR$(SIZE)
9090 GOSUB *MODNAM*
9100 RETURN
```

N
O
P
Q
R
S
T
U
V
W X
Y Z

TONY LODGE

Dummy Run

In order to use data files it is first necessary to create them in skeleton form, and then fill them with information

At the end of the last segment of the course, readers were left with the problem of solving this apparent dilemma: how can we make a program read in a file that does not exist (on tape or disk) when the program is first run? The initial activity we are likely to want the program to perform will be to read in the data file and assign this data to arrays or variables. Yet, if we insist on writing to the file first, whenever the program is run, we will have to be very careful in the programming not to lose all the data in the file. As we discovered last time, attempting to open a non-existent file will either simply not work, or else cause the program to 'crash' (stop functioning).

Fortunately, there's a very simple solution. Many commercial software packages include an 'install' or 'set-up' program that has to be run before the program proper can be used, and this is the approach that we shall adopt. Such programs typically allow the user to do a small amount of 'customising' (such as selecting whether the printer to be used will be an Epson or a Brother, parallel or serial, and so on), but they also create data files that will later be used by the main program. Remember, unlike program files, data files can be accessed by any program (see page 220).

To solve our problem and allow *RDINFL* (the routine that reads in the file and assigns the data to the arrays) to be performed, we can write a very simple set-up program that does nothing more than open a file and write a dummy value into it. We will choose a value that can be subsequently recognised by the program proper as not being a valid address book record. A suitable value would be the character string @FIRST, because no name or address, no matter how obscure its origin, is likely to start with this particular string. *RDINFL* will have to be slightly modified so that when it opens and reads in from the file, it tests for this value before going any further. If your computer doesn't have the @ symbol, then you will have to replace it with '!' or another character — as long as this is a string that won't occur naturally in your address book. First, however, here is the set-up program:

```
10 REM THIS PROGRAM CREATES A DATA FILE
20 REM FOR USE BY THE ADDRESS BOOK
   PROGRAM
30 REM IT WRITES A DUMMY RECORD THAT CAN
40 REM BE USED BY *RDINFL*
50 REM
60 REM
70 OPEN "O", #1, "ADBK.DAT"
80 PRINT #1, "@FIRST"
90 CLOSE #1
100 END
```

As mentioned previously in the Basic Programming course, the details of reading and writing files differ considerably from one version of BASIC to another, but the principle is almost always the same. First, the file must be declared OPEN before it can be used for either input or output. Then the direction of data flow is declared, either IN or OUT. Next a 'channel' number is assigned to the file. This allows more than one file to be open and in use at the same time (for the time being, however, we will use only one file). Finally, the name of the file we wish to use must be declared.

Line 70 in the program (left) is in Microsoft BASIC and is similar in principle to the OPEN statements used by most BASICS (BBC BASIC is somewhat different — see page 223). OPEN, of course, declares that a file is to be OPENed and 'O' says that data will be output. #1 is the number we are assigning to the file for this operation; a different file number could be used later if needed. 'ADBK.DAT' is the name we have given to the file.

Line 80 simply writes a single record to the file. The syntax of writing data to a file is usually (in most BASICS) exactly the same as the syntax used for PRINTing, except that the PRINT statement must be followed by the file number — #1 in this case.

Line 90 CLOSEs the file. Files may be left open for as long as needed in the program, but 'open' files are very vulnerable and should be CLOSEd as soon as possible within the program in order to protect the data in them. If, for example, you were to switch off the computer accidentally while the file was open, you could find that data has been lost when you next read the file.

There is some confusion over the way the terms record and file are used in computers, and this confusion is worst when we are talking about databases, on the one hand, and data files on the other. In a database, the file is a whole set of related information. Using the analogy of an office filing cabinet, the file could be a drawer labelled PERSONNEL. This file could comprise one record (a card in a folder) on each person in the company. Each record (card) would contain a number of fields, identical for each record, containing such information as NAME, SEX, AGE, SALARY, YEARS OF SERVICE etc.

If the PERSONNEL file were computerised, all the information would be treated in exactly the same way conceptually — one file containing many records, each record containing many fields — just like our computerised address book.

A sequential file on a disk or cassette tape, however, doesn't care how the information in it is used or organised by the program. Data files just contain a series of data items, and each individual item of data is called a record. A single record in a data file wouldn't, therefore, normally correspond to a record in the database sense of the word.

It's up to the program to read in records from the data file and assign them to variables or arrays. These variables and arrays need to be organised to form a 'conceptual' record containing a limited set of related information. There is no one-to-one relationship between the records in a data file and the records comprising a database.

Once the set-up program has been run it should never be needed again. In fact, if it ever were run again it would destroy any 'legitimate' data you might have entered in the address book database. We will see why this would happen when we look at the modified *RDINFL* program.

When the program is run it does not 'know' if there is legitimate data in the data file or not. The first thing *RDINFL* does is to OPEN the 'ADBK.DAT' file and read in the first record (or data item). This is not read into an element in an array, as you might expect, but into a special string variable we have called TEST$. Before any other records are read in, TEST$ is checked to see if it contains the string @FIRST. If TEST$ does contain @FIRST, the program knows there is no valid data in the file and so there is no point in trying to read in any more data and assign it to arrays. Consequently, the file can be closed and the rest of the program can continue. Since there is no valid data in the file, the user can do nothing useful until at least one record has been entered and so the value of TEST$ can also be used to force the program to go to the *ADDREC* subroutine so that at least one valid record will be added before anything else can be done.

If, on the other hand, the value of TEST$ is not @FIRST, the program can assume that there is valid data in the file and can start assigning the data to the appropriate arrays. The modified *RDINFL* subroutine follows:

```
1400 REM *RDINFL* SUBROUTINE
1410 OPEN "I",#1,"ADBK.DAT"
1420 INPUT #1,TEST$
1430 IF TEST$ = "@FIRST" THEN GOTO 1530: REM
     CLOSE AND RETURN
1440 LET NAMFLD$(1) = TEST$
1450 INPUT #1,MODFLD$(1),STRFLD$(1),TWNFLD$
     (1),CNTFLD$(1),TELFLD$(1)
1460 INPUT #1,NDXFLD$(1)
1470 LET SIZE = 2
1480 FOR L = 2 TO 50
1490 INPUT #1,NAMFLD$(L),MODFLD$(L),STRFLD$
     (L),TWNFLD$(L),CNTFLD$(L)
1500 INPUT #1,TELFLD$(L),NDXFLD$(L)
1510 REM  SPACE FOR CALL TO 'SIZE'
     SUBROUTINE
1520 NEXT L
1530 CLOSE #1
1540 RETURN
```

Line 1420 assigns a single record from the ADBK.DAT file to the variable TEST$. The next line then checks this to see if its value is @FIRST. If it is, a

GOTO is used to jump to the line that closes the file (line 1530) and then the subroutine RETURNs to the calling program. No further attempts are made to read in data. Assuming that there is no valid data in the file, program control will be returned to *INITIL*, which then calls *SETFLG*. All this routine does at the moment is to set the value of SIZE to 1 if TEST$ = @FIRST. The code for *SETFLG* is given below. Note that there are several REMs to allow space for further flag setting should we want to do this later.

```
1600 REM  *SETFLG*
1610 REM  SETS FLAGS AFTER *RDINFL*
1620 REM
1630 REM
1640 IF TEST$ = "@FIRST" THEN LET SIZE = 0
1650 REM
1660 REM
1670 REM
1680 REM
1690 RETURN
```

SETFLG then RETURNs to *INITIL*, which in turn RETURNs to the main program. *MAINPG* then calls *GREETS*, which displays the greeting message. *GREETS* does not need any modification from the version already given.

The next routine called by the main program is *CHOOSE*. A very small modification to the *CHOOSE* subroutine on page 231 will establish a way of forcing the user to add a record if the program is being run for the first time.

```
3500 REM  *CHOOSE* SUBROUTINE
3510 REM
3520 IF TEST$ = "@FIRST" THEN GOSUB 3860
3530 IF TEST$ = "@FIRST" THEN RETURN
3540 REM  'CHMENU'
3550 PRINT CHR$(12)
3560 PRINT "SELECT ONE OF THE FOLLOWING
3570 PRINT
3580 PRINT
3590 PRINT
3600 PRINT "1. FIND RECORD (FROM NAME)"
3610 PRINT "2. FIND NAMES (FROM INCOMPLETE
     NAME)"
3620 PRINT "3. FIND RECORDS (FROM TOWN)"
3630 PRINT "4. FIND RECORD (FROM INITIAL)"
3640 PRINT "5. LIST ALL RECORDS"
3650 PRINT "6. ADD NEW RECORD"
3660 PRINT "7. CHANGE RECORD"
3670 PRINT "8. DELETE RECORD"
3680 PRINT "9. EXIT & SAVE"
3690 PRINT
3700 PRINT
3710 REM  'INCHOI'
3720 REM
3730 LET L = 0
3740 LET I = 0
3750 FOR L = 0 TO 1
3760 PRINT "ENTER CHOICE (1 - 9)"
3770 FOR I = 1 TO 1
3780 LET A$ = INKEY$
3790 IF A$ = "" THEN I = 0
3800 NEXT I
3810 LET CHOI = VAL(A$)
3820 IF CHOI <1 THEN L = 0 ELSE L = 1
3830 IF CHOI >9 THEN L = 0
3840 NEXT L
3850 RETURN
```

Two lines have been added. The first tests TEST$. This variable still contains the value read into it in the *RDINFL* routine. If it is @FIRST we know that there is no valid data in the file and so the only appropriate option is ADDREC, which is number 6. If the test is passed, control is passed to *FIRSTM*, a routine that displays an appropriate message and sets the CHOI variable to 6. When the subroutine returns to line 3530, TEST$ is tested again (it is bound to pass) and the subroutine RETURNs to the main program skipping the rest of the *CHOOSE* subroutine since it is inappropriate.

You may have wondered why TEST$ is tested twice. This is to prevent the subroutine RETURNing to the wrong point in the program. Without line 3530, the program would continue on down the rest of *CHOOSE*, presenting the choice menu even though it is not needed. It also avoids the use of GOTOs, though IF TEST$ = "@FIRST" THEN GOTO 3850 would work just as well. GOTOs make the program messy and difficult to follow (programs making excessive use of GOTOs are referred to as 'spaghetti coding').

Before going on to look at *FIRSTM*, readers are referred back to *RDINFL* and the GOTO in line 1430. Since we have consistently argued against using GOTO, why has one been used here? It would have been perfectly easy to CLOSE the file and RETURN by simply testing the value of TEST$ in two separate lines. We used a GOTO here instead to illustrate one of the few instances where its use is excusable. This is within a very short and identifiable program segment, and its function is obvious (and made more so by the REM comment). GOTOs should never be used to jump out of a loop (this can leave the value of variables in an unpredictable state), never used to jump out of a subroutine (this will confuse the RETURN instruction unless a matching jump back into the subroutine is used), and never used to jump to remote regions of the program (this makes the program all but impossible to follow).

The *FIRSTM* subroutine is simple and straightforward: the screen is cleared and a message is displayed informing the user that a record will have to be entered. Line 3870 sets CHOI to 6 so that when control is passed back to *EXECUT* the *ADDREC* routine will be executed automatically. The code for *FIRSTM* follows:

```
3860 REM  *FIRSTM* SUBROUTINE (DISPLAY
     MESSAGE)
3870 LET CHOI = 6
3880 PRINT CHR$(12): REM  CLEAR SCREEN
3890 PRINT
3900 PRINT TAB(8);"THERE ARE NO RECORDS IN"
3910 PRINT TAB(8);"THE FILE. YOU WILL HAVE"
3920 PRINT TAB(6);"TO START BY ADDING A
     RECORD"
3930 PRINT
3940 PRINT TAB(5);"(PRESS SPACE-BAR TO
     CONTINUE)"
3950 FOR B = 1 TO 1
3960 IF INKEY$ <> " " THEN B = 0
3970 NEXT B
3980 PRINT CHR$(12): REM  CLEAR SCREEN
3990 RETURN
```

The *ADDREC* subroutine, given on page 235, has two small but important changes from the version we encountered before. After the fields have been entered as elements in the various string arrays, the variable SIZE is incremented and TEST$ is set to a null string (see lines 10090 and 10100). SIZE is an important variable used in various parts of the program so that it knows which records are being operated on. SIZE was originally set to 0 as part of the *CREARR* subroutine. Later, in *SETFLG*, it is set to 1 if TEST$ = "@FIRST". This is done so that

when *ADDREC* is first executed, the INPUT statements will put the data into the first element of each array. In other words, INPUT "ENTER NAME";NAMFLD$(SIZE) is equivalent to INPUT "ENTER NAME";NAMFLD$(1).

Line 10090 increments SIZE, so that it now becomes 2. If *ADDREC* is executed again, data will be entered into the second element of each array. Finally, *ADDREC* sets TEST$ to " " in line 10100. This is done because a record has now been entered (though not yet stored in the tape or disk data file). If *CHOOSE* is executed again, as it must be to save the data and exit the program, we will not want to be forced to add a new record again. If TEST$ were not cleared, the program would get stuck in an endless loop, and the only way to get out of it would be to reset or unplug the computer, and all the data would be lost.

By setting TEST$ to a null string, the tests in lines 3520 and 3530 of *CHOOSE* will fail and allow the options menu to be displayed. What then happens to SIZE will depend on which routine is executed. So far we have only ensured that SIZE = 1 if there is no valid data in the file, and that this is incremented by 1 each time a record is added. But what would happen if there had been a number of valid records in the file? To answer this we'll have to look at *RDINFL* again.

Line 1420 reads the first data item into TEST$. If it is not @FIRST, it is assumed to be a valid data item. The records in the file are always in the same order, namely: NAMFLD, MODFLD, STRFLD, TWNFLD, CNTFLD, TELFLD, NDXFLD, NAMFLD, MODFLD, etc. If the first record read out is valid data, it must belong in the first element of the NAMFLD$ array, so line 1440 transfers this data from TEST$ to NAMFLD$(1). The next two lines fill up the first elements in the other five arrays. We now know that we have at least one complete (database) record, so SIZE is set to 2. This value must be one greater than the number of valid records read into the arrays, otherwise *ADDREC* would write new data into elements already containing valid data.

Then a loop from 2 to 50 reads the records into all six arrays, incrementing the index L each time round. We have already made the decision to restrict our program to dealing with files of 50 names and addresses, and the DIM statements in the *CREARR* subroutine allocated space for this. However, when you first start using the program, you are unlikely to have a complete file of 50 entries, so we will need a routine in the program that can detect when this is the case, set the variable SIZE accordingly, and abort the reading-in loop.

Consequently, we have included line 1510 to provide a call to a 'SIZE' subroutine, which we will be developing later in the course. There are three ways in which this problem could be handled. First, when we write the data to tape, we could arrange that the first record to be written is the variable SIZE. The *RDINFL* subroutine could then be modified to read in SIZE first and then set up a loop of the form FOR L=1 TO SIZE to read in the records. The second, and preferable, method (since it doesn't clash with our earlier test for @FIRST in line 1430) is to set up a procedure to be executed after all the records have been written, in which a special flag (of the form @END, perhaps) can be written at the end. A test can then be inserted into *RDINFL* to abort the loop when @END is encountered.

The third method is to make use of the EOF (End Of File) function offered on some computers, which is really an automated version of the second method. These computers have an EOF flag, which is normally set to 0 that is, FALSE but takes on another value (typically 1 to represent TRUE) when the end of file has been reached. Some BASICS allow the EOF flag to be tested as a BASIC variable; in which case, a construct of the form:

```
WHILE NOT EOF(N) (N is the file number)
  DO
      INPUT #N, data to read in)
ENDWHILE
```

will handle the problem. On other machines, the EOF flag is represented as a single bit that must be accessed using the PEEK statement. To find out if your machine has an EOF function, you will need to consult the instruction manual. Because it differs so greatly between machines, we will not be using EOF in our program. But as an exercise, readers might like to attempt to modify the *RDINFL* subroutine for all three possible methods of dealing with files of less than 50 entries.

Generally, it is always a great deal easier to write programs that deal with files of fixed length, but tackling the problem of 'dynamic length' files at this early stage will enable us to modify the program later to cope with files with more than 50 entries.

```
4000 REM  *EXECUT* SUBROUTINE
4010 REM
4019 IF CHOI = 6 THEN GOSUB 10000: REM  SEE
     FOOTNOTE
4020 REM  NORMALLY 'ON CHOI GOSUB etc' --
     SEE FOOTNOTE
4030 REM
4040 REM  1 IS *FNDREC*
4050 REM  2 IS *FNDNMS*
4060 REM  3 IS *FNDTWN*
4070 REM  4 IS *FNDINT*
4080 REM  5 IS *MODREC*
4090 REM  6 IS *ADDREC*
4100 REM  7 IS *MODREC*
4110 REM  8 IS *DELREC*
4120 REM  9 IS *EXPROG*
4130 REM
4140 RETURN
```

The *EXECUT* routine would not normally have line 4019 (hence the odd line number), and line 4020 would normally be either:

    ON CHOI GOSUB number,number,number etc

or a series of:

    IF CHOI = 1 THEN GOSUB number
    IF CHOI = 2 THEN GOSUB number etc

Line 4019 is included so that the program will work even though the other *EXECUT* subroutines have not yet been coded .

```
10 REM  'MAINPG'
20 REM  *INITIL*
30 GOSUB 1000
40 REM  *GREETS*
50 GOSUB 3000
60 REM  *CHOOSE*
70 GOSUB 3500
80 REM  *EXECUT*
90 GOSUB 4000
100 END

1000 REM  *INITIL* SUBROUTINE
1010 GOSUB 1100: REM  *CREARR* (CREATE ARRAYS) SUBROUTINE
1020 GOSUB 1400: REM  *RDINFL* (READ IN FILE) SUBROUTINE
1030 GOSUB 1600: REM  *SETFLG* (SET FLAGS) SUBROUTINE
1040 REM
1050 REM
1060 REM
1070 REM
1080 REM
1090 RETURN

1100 REM  *CREARR* (CREATE ARRAYS) SUBROUTINE
1110 DIM NAMFLD$(50)
1120 DIM MODFLD$(50)
1130 DIM TWNFLD$(50)
1140 DIM CNTFLD$(50)
1150 DIM TELFLD$(50)
1160 DIM NDXFLD$(50)
1170 REM
1180 REM
1190 REM
1200 REM
1210 LET SIZE = 0
1220 LET RMOD = 0
1230 LET SVED = 0
1240 LET CURR = 0
1250 REM
1260 REM
1270 REM
1280 REM
1290 REM
1300 RETURN

10000 REM *ADDREC* SUBROUTINE
10010 PRINT CHR$(12): REM  CLEAR SCREEN
10020 INPUT "ENTER NAME";NAMFLD$(SIZE)
10030 INPUT "ENTER STREET";STRFLD$(SIZE)
10040 INPUT "ENTER TOWN";TWNFLD$(SIZE)
10050 INPUT "ENTER COUNTY";CNTFLD$(SIZE)
10060 INPUT "ENTER TELEPHONE NUMBER";TELFLD$(SIZE)
10070 LET RMOD = 1: REM  'RECORD MODIFIED' FLAG SET
10080 LET NDXFLD$(SIZE) = STR$(SIZE)
10090 LET SIZE = SIZE + 1
10100 LET TEST$ = ""
10110 REM  INSERT CALL TO *MODNAM* HERE
10120 REM
10130 REM
10140 REM
10150 RETURN
```

Basic Flavours

SPECTRUM

Because the Spectrum has the facility for saving or loading whole arrays using the command SAVE-DATA, as explained on page 222, the *RDINFL* subroutine will be completely different — reading in each of the arrays (NAMFLD$, MODFLD$ etc.) in succession. When we begin writing the data in the next segment, we will include a complete version of the relevant subroutines for this machine. In the meantime, as an exercise, Spectrum owners can tackle the problem of how to create the dummy file containing @FIRST, as well as determining how many valid entries there are in the array, when reading the file in.

BBC Micro

The BBC Micro will not accept MODFLD$ as a variable name because MOD is a BBC BASIC command, so replace MODFLD$ by MDFLD$ throughout

See 'Basic Flavours' page 223

OPEN CLOSE

P
Q
R
S
T
U
V
X
Z

Time And Motion

Sorting an array in Basic can be a time-consuming operation, but will ultimately speed up our searches for specific records

So far we have developed most of the code needed to create entries in the address book 'database', but have not yet tackled the necessary programming for saving the entries on tape or disk. The only major omission has been a suitable routine for the creation of the MODFLD$ field, as specified earlier in the series.

The complete program to do this is given in this segment of the course. First, all characters are converted to upper case (capital letters) in lines 10250 to 10330. Lines 10350 to 10370 then count through the characters in the string and check each one to see whether it is a space. The last space encountered leaves the variable S set to the value corresponding to its position in the string.

Lines 10400 to 10420 transfer characters, one at a time, from the string of upper case characters to CNAM$. Characters are transferred, until we get to the last space, if they have an ASCII value of more than 64. Any characters that fail this test are ignored, so this process eliminates full stops (ASCII 46), apostrophes (ASCII 39), spaces (ASCII 32) and all other punctuation marks. Lines 10450 to 10470 do the same for the characters after the final space, transferring them to SNAM$.

If N$ contains only a single word, TREVANIAN, for example, variable S will be 0 and all the characters will be transferred to SNAM$. The variable used for the forename has been called CNAM$ rather than FNAM$. CNAM$ is used to remind us of 'Christian name', as variables starting with the letters 'FN' will confuse many BASICS into thinking that a call to a user-defined function has been made.

Lines 10490 and 10500 are needed to set the string variables used in this routine to nulls before they are used again. This is a point to watch out for whenever structures of the type LET X$ = X$ + Y$ are used. Failure to 'clear' the variables will result in more and more unwanted characters accumulating in them each time they are used. Notice that CHOI is set to 0 in the ADDREC routine, since we only want to make sure that the user adds a record if there are none in the file (that is, the first time the program is used).

Now that we have a way of adding as many new records to the file as we want, we need a way of saving the file on tape or disk. The simplest way would be to write all the records to the data file (ADBK.DAT in this version of the program) in the order they happen to be in. The chief disadvantage of this approach is seen when we need to search the

file for a particular record. if we cannot be sure that all records in the file are sorted in some way, the only way to search for a record would be to start at the beginning and examine each record in turn to see if it matches the 'key' of the search. If the record you were searching for happened to be the last one entered, every record in the database would need to be examined before the one you wanted was located. If the last record entered was for a William Brown (i.e. MODFLD$(SIZE-1)="BROWN WILLIAM"), a search routine should anticipate the record to be somewhere near the beginning of the file — if the records had been sorted. Unfortunately, both sorting and searching are very time-consuming activities; so it is a question of determining your priority. We have adopted the principle that an address book is consulted far more often than it is added to (or modified in some other way). This being so, it is better to assume that searches will be far more frequent than sorts, so we will always ensure that the records are sorted before they are stored in the data file after the program has been used.

With this in mind, a variable called RMOD is created to use as a flag. It can have one of two values: 0 or 1. It is initially set to 0 to indicate that no record has been modified during the current execution of the program. Any operation that does modify the file in any way — such as adding a new record — sets RMOD to 1. Operations that 'need to know' if the file has been modified will check the value of RMOD before proceeding. For example, EXPROG, the routine that saves the file and exits from the program, checks RMOD in line 11050. If RMOD=0, no sorting and saving is needed as the data file on tape or disk is assumed to be in a fully sorted and unmodified form. Other routines, such as those that search through the file for a particular record, will also need to check RMOD. If RMOD is 0, the search (or other operation) can proceed. If RMOD is 1, the routine will first have to call the sort routine. After the whole file has been sorted, the sort routine will then reset RMOD to 0.

Our sorting routine, called *SRTREC* in the program listing, resets RMOD to 0 in line 11320 after all the records have been sorted. Before going on to look at *EXPROG* (the routine that saves the file on tape or disk and then ENDs), a few words about *SRTREC* are called for. *SRTREC* is a form of a simple sorting technique called a 'bubble sort' (see page 148). There are many ways of sorting data and the bubble sort is one of the simplest and slowest. A good case could be made for a more efficient sorting routine, but more sophisticated sorts are much harder to understand than the one we have used. Whether or not you should consider a better sort routine depends on the number of items to be sorted. The 'time complexity' of a bubble sort such as ours is n^2. In other words, the time taken for the data to be sorted increases as the square of the number of items being sorted. If two items took four milliseconds to sort, four items would take 16 milliseconds, 50 items would take two and a half seconds and 1,000 items would take more than 16 minutes. A wait of two or three seconds might be perfectly acceptable during the use of a program like ours, but a wait of a quarter of an hour certainly wouldn't be.

The way this program has been written allows a maximum of only 50 records, so unacceptable delays during sorts should not be a problem. Later in the course, however, we shall outline some of the techniques that can be used to create dynamic files that can grow to almost any size. If you do attempt such a modification to the program, a more advanced sort routine would be one of the first problems to be tackled.

The data items being sorted are the character strings in MODFLD$(L) and MODFLD$(L+1). Records are swapped only if MODFLD$(L) is greater than MODFLD$(L+1), and the index field (which is not being used at present) is updated in lines 11490 and 11570. Every time two records have been swapped, the variable S (to indicate that a swap has taken place) is set to 1. When the sorting routine reaches line 11290 it checks the value of S and branches back to compare all the records again. When all the records are in order, the value of S will be left at 0 and the routine will be terminated after the value of RMOD has been reset to 0.

The EXPROG routine (referred to as *EXPROG* in the program listing) begins at line 11000. It starts by checking to see if any record has been modified during the current execution of the program (line 11050: IF RMOD=0 THEN RETURN). If there has been no modification of the file, there will be no need to save again, so the routine RETURNs to the main program. This will take us back to line 100, which checks the value of CHOI. If CHOI has a value of 9 (as it would if *EXPROG* is being executed) the main program simply goes on to the END statement in line 110.

If the program finds that RMOD is 1 in line 11050 it means that one or more records have been modified in some way and that there is a chance that they are no longer in order. This being so, the *EXPROG* routine calls the sort routine (line 11070) and then, after all the records have been sorted, saves them onto tape or disk.

The save routine (*SAVREC*) is called in line 11090 and the routine starts at line 12000. *SAVREC*, in the main listing, is written in Microsoft BASIC, so it is important to bear in mind that the details of file-handling vary from one version of BASIC to another (see 'Basic Flavours'). Line 12030 opens the ADBK.DAT data file and

assigns the channel number #1 for the operation. Line 12050 sets the limits for the loop that counts through all the records in the file. The upper limit is SIZE−1, not SIZE, because the SIZE variable always has a value one greater than the number of valid records in the file (so that if a new record is added, it will not be written over an existing record).

The format of lines 12060 and 12070 is particularly noteworthy. Each field is separated by a ",", which is also sent to the file. This comma is required by most versions of BASIC because INPUT# and PRINT# work in the same way as the ordinary INPUT and PRINT statements. Consider the statement INPUT X,Y,Z. This would expect an input from the keyboard such as 10,12,15<CR>, which would assign 10, 12 and 15 to X, Y and Z respectively. Without the commas, the INPUT statement would not be able to tell where each data item ended and would assign all the data to the first variable. Similarly, the INPUT# statement (in most BASICS) would not be able to tell where each data file record ended and would try to fill each string variable with as much data as could be fitted in. Since in most BASICS string variables can hold up to 255 characters, the data in the data file would soon all be assigned long before the FOR L = 1 TO SIZE−1 loop had terminated. This would result in an INPUT PAST END error message (which indicates that an INPUT statement was issued after all the data has been exhausted) and the string variables (such as NAMFLD$(x)) containing far more data than they should.

Once all the records have been stored in the data file, from L=1 TO SIZE−1, *SAVREC* RETURNs to line 90 in the main program. Line 100 checks the value of CHOI to see if the last operation was *EXPROG* or not. If it was 9 (save and exit), the program goes on to the END statement in line 110. If CHOI has any other value, the program jumps back to *CHOOSE* and allows the user to select another option again.

As a final footnote, we should mention the *FLSIZE* routine that starts at line 12500. This is offered as a possible alternative to the statement in line 1510. As presented, the program depends on the presence of an end-of-file function: IF EOF(1) = −1 THEN LET L = 50. All BASICS have some way of indicating that the end of a file has been reached, either with a special function such as EOF(x) or a PEEK to a special memory location. The *FLSIZE* routine at line 12500 is offered as a suggestion if an EOF function is not available, in which case line 1510 would need to be replaced by GOSUB 12500.

Basic Flavours

SPECTRUM Before running the address book program you must create on tape the name-field file. The following program will achieve this.

```
10 REM PROGRAM TO CREATE NFLD FILE ON
   TAPE
20 DIM Z$(1,30)
30 LET Z$(1)="@FIRST"
40 SAVE "NFLD" DATA Z$( )
50 STOP
```

SPECTRUM

The Spectrum does not allow line numbers greater than 9999. The final Spectrum version (see page 250) has all relevant changes and correct line numbers. Basic Flavours continues to refer to the MicroSoft version line numbers
The following are the Spectrum versions of lines and subroutines in the main listing:

```
1100 REM *CREARR*
1110 DIM N$(50,30)
1120 DIM M$(50,30)
1130 DIM S$(50,30)
1140 DIM T$(50,15)
1150 DIM C$(50,15)
1160 DIM R$(50,15)
1170 DIM X$(50,30)
1180 DIM B$(30)
1190 DIM Z$(30)
1250 LET Z$="@FIRST"

1400 REM *RDINFL* SR
1410 LOAD "NFLD" DATA N$( )
1420 IF N$(1)=Z$ THEN LET Q$=Z$:RETURN
1430 LOAD "MFLD" DATA M$( )
1440 LOAD "SFLD" DATA S$( )
1450 LOAD "TFLD" DATA T$( )
1460 LOAD "CFLD" DATA C$( )
1470 LOAD "TELFLD" DATA R$( )
1480 LOAD "NDXFLD" DATA X$( )
1490 REM *FLSIZE*
1500 GOSUB 12500

1540 RETURN

1640 IF Q$=Z$ THEN LET SIZE=1

3520 IF Q$=Z$THEN GOSUB 3860:RETURN

3810 LET CHOI=CODE A$-48

10090 LET Q$=" "

10200 REM *MODNAM* SR

10250 LET D$=N$(SIZE):LET P$=" "
10260 FOR L=1 TO LEN (D$)
10270 LET A$=D$(L)
10280 LET T=CODE A$
10290 IF T>=97 THEN LET T=T-32
10300 LET A$=CHR$ T
10310 LET P$=P$+A$
10320 NEXT L
10330 LET D$=P$:LET P$="":LET A$="":LET
     T=LEN(D$)
10340 REM LOCATE LAST SPACE
10350 FOR L=1 TO T
10360 IF D$(L)=" " THEN LET S=L:LET L=T
10370 NEXT L
10380 REM REMOVE RUBBISH
10390 REM STORE FORENAME IN P$
10400 FOR L=1 TO S-1
10410 IF CODE (D$(L))>64 THEN LET
     P$=P$+D$(L)
10420 NEXT L
10430 REM REMOVE RUBBISH
10440 REM STORE SURNAME IN A$
10450 FOR L=S+1 TO LEN (D$)
10460 IF CODE(D$(L))>64 THEN LET
     A$=A$+D$(L)
10470 NEXT L
10480 LET M$(SIZE)=A$+" "+P$
10490 LET P$="":LET A$=""
10510 RETURN
```

N.B. Because of the way that the Spectrum handles strings, the routine above splits the name at the first, not the last, space.

```
12000 REM *SAVREC* SR
```

```
12030 SAVE "NFLD" DATA N$( )
12040 SAVE "MFLD" DATA M$( )
12050 SAVE "SFLD" DATA S$( )
12060 SAVE "TFLD" DATA T$( )
12070 SAVE "CFLD" DATA C$( )
12080 SAVE "TELFLD" DATA R$( )
12090 SAVE "NDXFLD" DATA X$( )

12150 RETURN

12500 REM *FLSIZE* SR
12510 LET SIZE=50
12520 FOR L=1 TO 50
12530 IF N$(L)=B$ THEN LET SIZE=L:LET
     L=50
12540 NEXT L
12560 RETURN
```

LYNX

The Lynx does not support the command STR$. See 'Basic Flavours', page 231. For DIMensioning string arrays see 'Basic Flavours', page 215

EOF

On the Commodore 64 and Vic-20 replace line 1520 by:

1520 IF ST AND 64 THEN LET L=50

On the Dragon 32 delete line 1520 and replace it by:

1485 IF EOF(-1) THEN GOTO 1510

On the BBC Micro replace it by:

1520 IF EOF# X THEN LET L=50

where X is the numerical variable used in the OPENOUT statement (see page 223)

OPEN CLOSE

See Basic Flavours and adjacent BBC program on page 223

```
10 REM  'MAINPG'
20 REM  *INITIL*
30 GOSUB 1000
40 REM  *GREETS*
50 GOSUB 3000
60 REM  *CHOOSE*
70 GOSUB 3500
80 REM  *EXECUT*
90 GOSUB 4000
100 IF CHOI <> 9 THEN 60
110 END
1000 REM  *INITIL* SUBROUTINE
1010 GOSUB 1100: REM  *CREARR* (CREATE ARRAYS)
     SUBROUTINE
1020 GOSUB 1400: REM  *RDINFL* (READ IN FILE) SUBROUTINE
1030 GOSUB 1600: REM  *SETFLG* (SET FLAGS) SUBROUTINE
1040 REM
1050 REM
1060 REM
1070 REM
1080 REM
1090 RETURN
1100 REM *CREARR* (CREATE ARRAYS) SUBROUTINE
1110 DIM NAMFLD$(50)
1120 DIM MODFLD$(50)
1130 DIM STRFLD$(50)
1140 DIM TWNFLD$(50)
1150 DIM CNTFLD$(50)
1160 DIM TELFLD$(50)
1170 DIM NDXFLD$(50)
1180 REM
1190 REM
1200 REM
1210 LET SIZE = 0
1220 LET RMOD = 0
1230 LET SVED = 0
1240 LET CURR = 0
1250 REM
1260 REM
1270 REM
1280 REM
1290 REM
1300 RETURN
1400 REM *RDINFL* SUBROUTINE
1410 OPEN "I",#1,"ADBK.DAT"
1420 INPUT #1,TEST$
1430 IF TEST$ = "@FIRST" THEN GOTO 1540: REM  CLOSE AND
     RETURN
1440 LET NAMFLD$(1) = TEST$
1450 INPUT #1,MODFLD$(1),STRFLD$(1),TWNFLD$(1),CNTFLD$
     (1),TELFLD$(1)
1460 INPUT #1,NDXFLD$(1)
1470 LET SIZE = 2
```

```
1480 FOR L = 2 TO 50
1490 INPUT #1,NAMFLD$(L),MODFLD$(L),STRFLD$(L),TWNFLD$
     (L),CNTFLD$(L)
1500 INPUT #1,TELFLD$(L),NDXFLD$(L)
1510 LET SIZE = SIZE + 1
1520 IF EOF(1) = -1 THEN LET L = 50
1530 NEXT L
1540 CLOSE #1
1550 RETURN
1600 REM  *SETFLG* SUBROUTINE
1610 REM   SETS FLAGS AFTER *RDINFL*
1620 REM
1630 REM
1640 IF TEST$ = "@FIRST" THEN LET SIZE = 1
1650 REM
1660 REM
1670 REM
1680 REM
1690 RETURN
3000 REM  *GREETS* SUBROUTINE
3010 PRINT CHR$(12):REM  CLEAR SCREEN
3020 PRINT
3030 PRINT
3040 PRINT
3050 PRINT
3060 PRINT TAB(12);"*WELCOME TO THE*"
3070 PRINT TAB(9);"*HOME COMPUTER COURSE*"
3080 PRINT TAB(6);"*COMPUTERISED ADDRESS BOOK*"
3090 PRINT
3100 PRINT TAB(5);"(PRESS SPACE-BAR TO CONTINUE)"
3110 FOR L = 1 TO 1
3120 IF INKEY$ <> " " THEN L = 0
3130 NEXT L
3140 PRINT CHR$(12)
3150 RETURN
3500 REM  *CHOOSE* SUBROUTINE
3510 REM
3520 IF TEST$ = "@FIRST" THEN GOSUB 3860: REM *FIRSTM*
     SUBROUTINE
3530 IF TEST$ = "@FIRST" THEN RETURN
3540 REM  'CHMENU'
3550 PRINT CHR$(12)
3560 PRINT "SELECT ONE OF THE FOLLOWING"
3570 PRINT
3580 PRINT
3590 PRINT
3600 PRINT "1. FIND RECORD (FROM NAME)"
3610 PRINT "2. FIND NAMES (FROM INCOMPLETE NAME)"
3620 PRINT "3. FIND RECORDS (FROM TOWN)"
3630 PRINT "4. FIND RECORD (FROM INITIAL)"
3640 PRINT "5. LIST ALL RECORDS"
3650 PRINT "6. ADD NEW RECORD"
3660 PRINT "7. CHANGE RECORD"
3670 PRINT "8. DELETE RECORD"
3680 PRINT "9. EXIT & SAVE"
3690 PRINT
3700 PRINT
3710 REM  'INCHOI'
3720 REM
3730 LET L = 0
3740 LET I = 0
3750 FOR L = 1 TO 1
3760 PRINT "ENTER CHOICE (1 - 9)"
3770 FOR I = 1 TO 1
3780 LET A$ = INKEY$
3790 IF A$ = "" THEN I = 0
3800 NEXT I
3810 LET CHOI = VAL(A$)
3820 IF CHOI <1 THEN L = 0
3830 IF CHOI >9 THEN L = 0
3840 NEXT L
3850 RETURN
3860 REM *FIRSTM* SUBROUTINE (DISPLAY MESSAGE)
3870 LET CHOI = 6
3880 PRINT CHR$(12): REM  CLEAR SCREEN
3890 PRINT
3900 PRINT TAB(8);"THERE ARE NO RECORDS IN"
3910 PRINT TAB(8);"THE FILE. YOU WILL HAVE"
3920 PRINT TAB(6);"TO START BY ADDING A RECORD"
3930 PRINT
3940 PRINT TAB(5);"(PRESS SPACE-BAR TO CONTINUE)"
3950 FOR B = 1 TO 1
3960 IF INKEY$ <> " " THEN B = 0
3970 NEXT B
3980 PRINT CHR$(12): REM CLEAR SCREEN
3990 RETURN
4000 REM  *EXECUT* SUBROUTINE
4010 REM
4020 IF CHOI = 6 THEN GOSUB 10000
4030 REM
4040 REM  1 IS *FNDREC*
4050 REM  2 IS *FNDNMS*
4060 REM  3 IS *FNDTWN*
4070 REM  4 IS *FNDINT*
4080 REM  5 IS *LSTREC*
4090 IF CHOI = 6 THEN GOSUB 10000
4100 REM  7 IS *MODREC*
4110 REM. 8 IS *DELREC*
4120 IF CHOI = 9 THEN GOSUB 11000
4130 REM
4140 RETURN
10000 REM *ADDREC* SUBROUTINE
10010 PRINT CHR$(12): REM  CLEAR SCREEN
10020 INPUT "ENTER NAME";NAMFLD$(SIZE)
10030 INPUT "ENTER STREET";STRFLD$(SIZE)
10040 INPUT "ENTER TOWN";TWNFLD$(SIZE)
10050 INPUT "ENTER COUNTY";CNTFLD$(SIZE)
10060 INPUT "ENTER TELEPHONE NUMBER";TELFLD$(SIZE)
10070 LET RMOD = 1: REM  'RECORD MODIFIED' FLAG SET
10080 LET NDXFLD$(SIZE) = STR$(SIZE)
10090 LET TEST$ = ""
10100 GOSUB 10200: REM  *MODNAM*
10110 LET CHOI = 0
10120 LET SIZE = SIZE + 1
10130 REM
```

```
10140 REM
10150 RETURN
10200 REM  *MODNAM*  ROUTINE
10210 REM   CONVERTS CONTENTS OF NAMFLD$ TO UPPER CASE,
10220 REM   REMOVES RUBBISH, AND STORES IN THE ORDER:
10230 REM   SURNAME+SPACE+FORENAME IN MODFLD$
10240 REM
10250 LET N$ = NAMFLD$(SIZE)
10260 FOR L = 1 TO LEN(N$)
10270 LET TEMP$ = MID$(N$,L,1)
10280 LET T = ASC(TEMP$)
10290 IF T >= 97 THEN LET T = T - 32
10300 LET TEMP$ = CHR$(T)
10310 LET P$ = P$ + TEMP$
10320 NEXT L
10330 LET N$ = P$
10340 REM  LOCATE LAST SPACE
10350 FOR L = 1 TO LEN(N$)
10360 IF MID$(N$,L,1) = " " THEN S = L
10370 NEXT L
10380 REM  REMOVE RUBBISH AND STORE FORENAME
10390 REM   IN CNAM$
10400 FOR L = 1 TO S - 1
10410 IF ASC(MID$(N$,L,1)) > 64 THEN CNAM$ = CNAM$ +
      MID$(N$,L,1)
10420 NEXT L
10430 REM  REMOVE RUBBISH AND STORE SURNAME
10440 REM  IN SNAM$
10450 FOR L = S + 1 TO LEN(N$)
10460 IF ASC(MID$(N$,L,1)) > 64 THEN SNAM$ = SNAM$ +
      MID$(N$,L,1)
10470 NEXT L
10480 LET MODFLD$(SIZE) = SNAM$ + " " + CNAM$
10490 LET P$ = "": LET N$ = "": LET SNAM$ = "": LET
      CNAM$ = ""
10500 LET P$ = "": LET N$ = "": LET SNAM$ = "": LET
      CNAM$ = ""
10510 RETURN
11000 REM  *EXPROG* SUBROUTINE
11010 REM   SORTS AND SAVES FILE
11020 REM   IF ANY RECORD HAS BEEN
11030 REM   MODIFIED (RMOD = 1)
11040 REM
11050 IF RMOD = 0 THEN RETURN
11060 REM
11070 GOSUB 11200: REM  *SRTREC*
11080 REM
11090 GOSUB 12000: REM  *SAVREC*
11100 RETURN
11200 REM  *SRTREC* SUBROUTINE
11210 REM   SORTS ALL RECORDS BY MODFLD$ INTO
11220 REM   ALPHABETICAL ORDER AND UPDATES NDXFLD
11230 REM
11240 REM
11250 LET S = 0
11260 FOR L = 1 TO SIZE - 2
11270 IF MODFLD$(L) > MODFLD$(L + 1) THEN GOSUB 11350.
11280 NEXT L
11290 IF S = 1 THEN 11250
11300 REM
11310 REM
11320 LET RMOD = 0: REM  CLEARS 'RECORD MODIFIED' FLAG
11330 REM
11340 REM
11350 REM  *SWPREC* SUBROUTINE
11360 LET TNAMFDS = NAMFLD$(L)
11370 LET TMODFDS = MODFLD$(L)
11380 LET TSTRFDS = STRFLD$(L)
11390 LET TTWNFDS = TWNFLD$(L)
11400 LET TCNTFDS = CNTFLD$(L)
11410 LET TTELFDS = TELFLD$(L)
11420 REM
11430 LET NAMFLD$(L) = NAMFLD$(L + 1)
11440 LET MODFLD$(L) = MODFLD$(L + 1)
11450 LET STRFLD$(L) = STRFLD$(L + 1)
11460 LET TWNFLD$(L) = TWNFLD$(L + 1)
11470 LET CNTFLD$(L) = CNTFLD$(L + 1)
11480 LET TELFLD$(L) = TELFLD$(L + 1)
11490 LET NDXFLD$(L) = STR$(L)
11500 REM
11510 LET NAMFLD$(L + 1) = TNAMFDS
11520 LET MODFLD$(L + 1) = TMODFDS
11530 LET STRFLD$(L + 1) = TSTRFDS
11540 LET TWNFLD$(L + 1) = TTWNFDS
11550 LET CNTFLD$(L + 1) = TCNTFDS
11560 LET TELFLD$(L + 1) = TTELFDS
11570 LET NDXFLD$(L + 1) = STR$(L + 1)
11580 LET S = 1
11590 REM
11600 RETURN
12000 REM  *SAVREC* SUBROUTINE
12010 REM
12020 REM
12030 OPEN "O",#1,"ADBK.DAT"
12040 REM
12050 FOR L = 1 TO SIZE - 1
12060 PRINT #1,NAMFLD$(L);",";MODFLD$(L);",";STRFLD$
      (L);",";TWNFLD$(L)
12070 PRINT #1,CNTFLD$(L);",";TELFLD$(L);",";NDXFLD$(L)
12080 NEXT L
12090 REM
12100 REM
12110 REM
12120 REM
12130 CLOSE #1
12140 REM
12150 REM
12500 REM  *FLSIZE* SUBROUTINE
12510 IF NAMFLD$(L) = "" THEN LET L = 50
12520 IF NAMFLD$(L) = "" THEN RETURN
12530 LET SIZE = SIZE + 1
12540 REM
12550 REM
12560 RETURN
```

Search Warrant

The time taken to locate a particular record can be greatly reduced using the 'binary search' — provided that the file has already been sorted into an appropriate order

The three most important activities in the address book program — adding new records, saving the file on tape or disk, and reading in the file from mass storage when the program is first run — have now been developed. But an address book is no use if you can only add information and cannot extract any. What is needed next is a routine to find a record.

Finding a complete record from a name is likely to be the most frequent activity, and that's why the first option on the choice menu (*CHOOSE*) is FIND RECORD (FROM NAME). Searching is a highly important activity in many computer programs, especially in database programs where specific items of data often need to be retrieved from a file. Broadly speaking, there are two search methods — linear and binary. A linear search looks at each element in an array, starting at the beginning, and carries on until the particular item is located. If the data items in the array are in an unsorted state, a linear search is the only type that can be guaranteed to work. The time to locate the item using a linear search in an array of N items has an average value proportional to N/2. If there are few items to be searched through, N/2 may be perfectly acceptable, but as the number of items increases, the time taken to perform the search may become excessive.

If the data in the file is known to be in a sorted state, however, there's a far more efficient searching method, known as the 'binary search', which works in the following way. Suppose you want to find the definition of the word 'leptodactylous' in a dictionary. You don't start at the first page and see if it's there, and go on to the second page if it's not, working your way through the dictionary until you find it. Instead, you put your thumb roughly in the middle of the book, open the page and see what's there. If the page you open happens to start with 'metatarsal', you know you've gone too far, so the second half of the book is irrelevant and the word you want will be somewhere in the first half of the book. You then repeat the process, treating the page you originally opened as though it were the end of the dictionary. Again you split the first part of the dictionary in two and open the page to find 'dolabriform'. This time you know that the page selected is too 'low' and (for the purposes of our search for 'leptodactylous') can be considered as though it were the first page — all earlier pages are irrelevant as they are known to be too 'low' in the sense that

'l' is 'higher' than 'd'. The 'first' and 'last' pages of the dictionary can now be considered as the ones starting with 'dolabriform' and 'metatarsal' respectively. Again you put your thumb in the middle of the 'relevant' section and open up at 'ketogenesis'. Again this is too 'low' so the word we are looking for must lie between this page and the 'metatarsal' page. Repeating this process often enough is guaranteed to locate the word we are looking for — as long as it is in the dictionary!

In the example we have just considered, 'leptodactylous' was the 'search key'. The search key is the entry we are trying to find. Each time we examine a record, we will compare the search key against the 'record key' to locate the 'target' or 'victim'. Together with the record key we can expect to find what is called 'additional information', logically enough. The additional information for the record key 'leptodactylous' would be the dictionary definition of the word — in this case, slender–toed.

The analogy with searching through a file in a database for a target record is a close one, provided that the records have been previously sorted as the entries in a dictionary have. Think how difficult a dictionary would be to use if the entries were in the order the lexicographer first thought of them!

The search routine required for our address book will need to be more complicated than we might first appreciate for reasons that will become apparent. The first thing the search routine — let's call it *SCHREC* for the time being — will do is request the name to be searched for. This is called the search key. Suppose that somewhere in the file there is a record for a person called Peter Jones. The record for this person will have a field (with the name in standardised form) containing JONES PETER. The search routine might prompt us with a message such as WHO ARE YOU LOOKING FOR?, and we would respond with PETER JONES, or perhaps P. JONES or Pete Jones. Before this gets too complicated, let's assume that we respond with the full name, Peter Jones. The first thing the search routine will do will be to convert this response to the standardised form, JONES PETER. Next, it will compare our input, the search key, with the various contents of the MODNAM$ fields. If the program were using a linear search, the search key would be compared with each MODNAM$ field in sequence until a match was found or until it was discovered that an exact match did not exist.

As we have already noted, however, a linear search is not efficient compared with a binary search if the data is already sorted. The search routine can ensure that the records are sorted by starting with an IF RMOD = 1 THEN GOSUB *SRTREC*. The program knows that the lowest element in the array to be searched will be MODFLD$(1) and the highest will be MODFLD$(SIZE – 1). To conduct the search, we will need three variables: BTM for the bottom of the array (MODFLD$(1) at the beginning); TOP for the top of the array (MODFLD$(SIZE – 1) at the beginning); and MID for the value corresponding to the middle element.

Using the dictionary analogy, we can assume that BTM = ARRAY(1) and TOP = ARRAY(SIZE – 1). In other words, the array we have to consider for the search starts with the 'smallest' element and ends with the 'largest' element. We can therefore LET

BTM = 1 and LET TOP = SIZE – 1 (remember that SIZE is always one larger than the number of records currently in the address book).

Suppose that there are 21 valid entries in the address book. SIZE will have a value of 22. BTM will have a value of 1. TOP will have a value of 21. The value of MID, the position of the middle element, can be derived in BASIC from INT((BTM + TOP)/2). If the BTM value is 1, and the TOP value is 21, the MID value will be 11.

To conduct a binary search, we first assume that the whole file is valid and find the mid point INT((BTM + TOP)/2) inside a loop that is terminated either if the target is found or if there is no match. Then we check to see if the search key (SCHKEY$) happens to be equal to the MID value of the array. If the MID value of the array is too small, we know that ARRAY(MID) is the lowest part of the array we

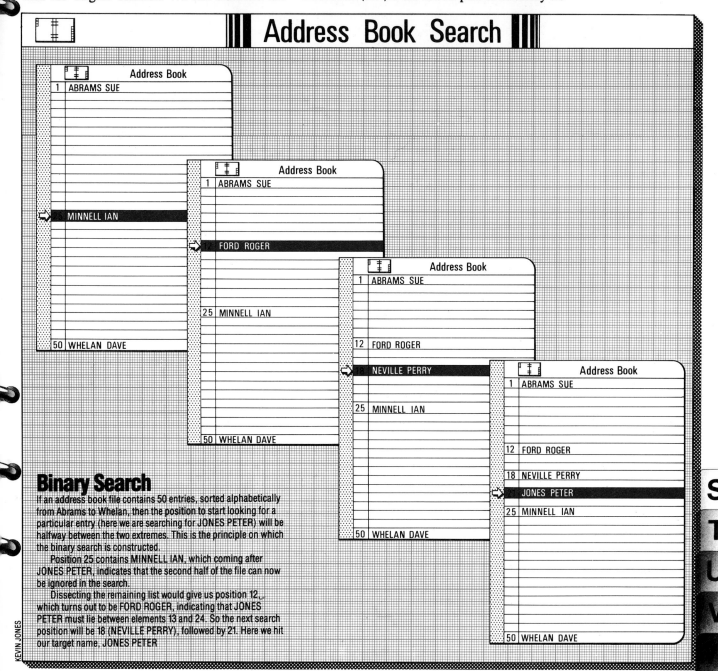

Binary Search

If an address book file contains 50 entries, sorted alphabetically from Abrams to Whelan, then the position to start looking for a particular entry (here we are searching for JONES PETER) will be halfway between the two extremes. This is the principle on which the binary search is constructed.

Position 25 contains MINNELL IAN, which coming after JONES PETER, indicates that the second half of the file can now be ignored in the search.

Dissecting the remaining list would give us position 12, which turns out to be FORD ROGER, indicating that JONES PETER must lie between elements 13 and 24. So the next search position will be 18 (NEVILLE PERRY), followed by 21. Here we hit our target name, JONES PETER

KEVIN JONES

S
T
U
V
X

need to consider, so BTM could be set to MID. Slightly more efficient, however, is to set BTM to MID + 1, since we already know that ARRAY(MID) is not equal to the search key. Similarly, IF ARRAY(MID) > SCHKEY$, TOP may be set to MID - 1.

As an interim step towards developing a fully working routine, the program shown can take a dummy input (which needs to be in exactly the same format as the MODFLD$ fields) and will either print RECORD NOT FOUND if there is no match, or RECORD IS NO (MID) if there is a match. As the routine starts with line number 13000, it can be added on to the end of the program as presented on page 239, and will work as long as line 4040 is changed to IF CHOI = 1 THEN GOSUB 13000.

Line 13240 contains the STOP statement. This will stop the program temporarily as soon as the RECORD NOT FOUND or RECORD IS NO (MID) messages are displayed. The program can be restarted at the same line number, without losing data, by typing CONT. Without STOP, the program would rush on to the RETURN statement in line 13250 and the message would appear too briefly to be legible.

Let's consider this program fragment in more detail. Line 13100 sets BTM to 1, the position of the lowest element in the MODFLD$ array. TOP is set to SIZE-1 in line 13110. This is the position in the MODFLD$ arrays where the highest element is located. Line 13120 initialises a loop that will only be terminated when either a match is found or no match is known to exist.

Line 13130 finds the mid point of the array by halving the sum of the bottom and top index of the array (INT is used to round off the division, so that MID cannot assume a value such as 1.5). There's a chance that the contents of MODFLD$(MID) will be the same as the search key (SCHKEY$), but if they are not the same, as is likely, L will be set to 0, ensuring that the loop will be repeated. If the test in line 13140 fails, MODFLD$(MID) will either be lower or higher in value than SCHKEY$. The value of BTM will then be set to one more than the old value of MID (line 13150), or the value of TOP will be set to one less than the old value of MID. The reason the value of MID itself is not used is that the failure of the test in line 13140 has already demonstrated that MODFLD$(MID) is not the target we are searching for and there is no point in looking at that element of the array next time round the loop.

If no match is found, the value of BTM will eventually exceed the value of TOP. The loop can be terminated (line 13170) and a RECORD NOT FOUND message printed (line 13200).

This program fragment is presented for demonstration purposes and to enable the search routine to be tested. As it stands, its use is rather limited. Without the STOP in line 13240 we wouldn't even have time to see the message flashed on the screen. What is required is a display of the full record, as it was originally typed in. Once the record number is known, it is a simple matter to retrieve any of the additional information required — NAMFLD$, STRFLD$ etc.

Below the display of the record, we would probably want a message such as PRESS SPACE BAR TO CONTINUE (back to the main menu) and perhaps further options such as PRESS "P" TO PRINT.

Not so easy, unfortunately, is deciding how to handle the input of *FNDREC*. In the program fragment, the input expected (in line 13020) must be in the standardised form — JONES PETER, for example. This is clearly not good enough. People don't think of names in inverse order, and it's an unreasonable burden on the user to have to enter the name in upper case letters. Additionally, the slightest deviation between the name input originally would result in a RECORD NOT FOUND. The first two problems could, one would expect, be handled by *MODNAM*. The third problem of how to cope with an approximate match is far more interesting, but very much harder to solve.

Before considering this problem, let us see why *MODNAM* will not solve the first two problems. If you go back and look at *MODNAM*, which starts at line 10200, you will discover a good illustration of one of the commonest traps into which programmers fall — lack of generality. This subroutine ought to be able to handle conversions from 'normal' names to 'standardised' names whenever this operation was needed. Even though it was written as a separate subroutine, it was clearly written with *ADDREC* in mind. It assumes that the name to be converted will always reside in NAMFLD$(SIZE) and that after conversion the modified name will always be stored in MODFLD$(SIZE). Faced with this situation, the programmer has three choices: either completely rewrite *MODNAM* to make it general, which would in turn involve further changes in other parts of the program. Or write an almost identical routine just to handle the input for *FNDREC*, which represents wasted effort and takes up more space in memory. Or resort to some bad programming technique to allow the unmodified *MODNAM* routine to be used. This last alternative is in some ways the least attractive. It will solve the problem, but the actual working of the part of the program that has been modified is likely to be unclear, even to the writer of the program, and a nightmare to anyone else trying to use the program.

The moral of the story is: make subroutines as general as possible, so that they can be called by any part of the program.

To illustrate bad programming technique, or 'dirty' programming as it is often called, and to show how unclear it can make the program, consider line 13020 of the program fragment, INPUT "INPUT KEY ";SCHKEY$ and then look at the modification or 'fix' that would allow *MODNAM* to be used:

```
13020 INPUT "INPUT KEY";NAMFLD$(SIZE)
13030 GOSUB 10200: REM *MODNAM*
     SUBROUTINE
13040 LET SCHKEY$ = MODFLD$(SIZE)
13050...
```

Luckily, SIZE is always one bigger in value than the highest valid record. In other words, there is no record at position SIZE in the arrays, so this fix will not modify any existing record. But without some extensive REMs explaining what's going on, think how confusing these three lines would be to someone who had not been involved in the development of the program!

Back to the more interesting problem of dealing with 'near misses'. Suppose we had entered someone's name as Pete Jones during an *ADDREC* operation, but as Peter Jones during *FNDREC*. These would be converted to the standardised forms JONES PETE and JONES PETER respectively, and no match would be found during the search, even though the record we wanted was there. We will not attempt to solve this problem, because a satisfactory solution would represent a major programming task. For readers interested in experimenting, however, here are some pointers:

```
BEGIN {search array for exact match}
   IF exact match found
      THEN PRINT full record
      ELSE search array for close-match
         IF close-match found
            THEN PRINT record for close-match
            ELSE PRINT "NO RECORD FOUND"
         ENDIF
   ENDIF
END
```

The procedure for close-match could be something along the lines of:

```
BEGIN {close-match}
   Search array for exact surname match
   IF exact surname match
      THEN search forenames for max-match
      PRINT record for max-match
      ELSE search surnames for max-match
         IF surname max-match found
            THEN PRINT record for max-match
         ENDIF
   ENDIF
END
```

The procedure for max-match could be roughly defined as finding the target string with the maximum number of characters in common with those in the key string. Or it could accept a situation in which the key string was wholly contained within the target string, or vice versa. There are no simple solutions, but plenty of scope for enterprising programming.

There is one 'side effect' of the program fragment presented. Suppose the following sequence of events takes place. There are ten records in the data file. You run the program and then use *ADDREC* to add a new record, followed by *FNDREC* to locate a record. When *EXPROG* is finally run, to save the file and terminate the program, the record you added will not be saved (although all the other records will be). This is a direct result of something that happened in the execution of *FNDREC*. Can you see why the

record added will not be saved?

In the next segment of the course we will explain how to prevent this loss of data; show what the CURR variable is used for, and describe how to delete or modify a record. Other options on the main menu (*FNDTWN* etc.) are closely similar to routines we have already worked out. Readers will be left to implement them for themselves if they are required.

Finally, consider what would happen if there were exactly 50 records in the data file and the modified *FNDREC* routine (that calls *MODNAM*) were used. (Hint: SIZE will have the value 51.)

Basic Flavours

SPECTRUM

For the Spectrum, the following modifications are required:

```
13000 REM *FNDREC* TEST VERSION
13010 IF RMOD = 1 THEN GOSUB 11200
13020 PRINT "INPUT KEY"
13030 IINPUT SS
13100 LET BTM = 1
13110 LET TP = SIZE - 1
13120 FOR L = 1 TO 1
13130 LET MD = INT((BTM+TP)/2)
13140 IF M$(MD) < > S$ THEN LET L=0
13150 IF M$(MD) < S$ THEN LET BTM=
      MD+1
13160 IF M$(MD) > S$ THEN LET TP=MD
      - 1
13170 IF BTM > TP THEN LET L=1
13180 NEXT L
13200 IF BTM > TP THEN PRINT "RECORD
      NOT FOUND"
13210 IF BTM <= TP THEN PRINT "RECORD
      IS NO";MD
13240 STOP
13250 RETURN
```

The variable names TOP and MID may correspond to BASIC commands on some machines, so change to TP and MD

```
13000 REM VERSION OF *FNDREC* FOR TESTING
13010 IF RMOD = 1 THEN GOSUB 11200
13020 INPUT "INPUT KEY ";SCHKEY$
13030 REM
13040 REM
13050 REM
13060 REM
13070 REM
13080 REM
13090 REM
13100 LET BTM = 1
13110 LET TOP = SIZE - 1
13120 FOR L = 1 TO 1
13130 LET MID = INT((BTM + TOP)/2)
13140 IF MODFLD$(MID) <> SCHKEY$ THEN L = 0
13150 IF MODFLD$(MID) < SCHKEY$ THEN BTM = MID + 1
13160 IF MODFLD$(MID) > SCHKEY$ THEN TOP = MID - 1
13170 IF BTM > TOP THEN L = 1
13180 NEXT L
13190 REM
13200 IF BTM > TOP THEN PRINT "RECORD NOT FOUND"
13210 IF BTM <= TOP THEN PRINT "RECORD IS NO ";MID
13220 REM
13230 REM
13240 STOP
13250 RETURN
```

TONY LODGE

Finishing Touches

By removing the anomalies caused by stringing together the modules, and adding a few more facilities, our address book program is now complete

In the last instalment of the course, readers were left with the problem of working out why running the address book program, then adding a record (using *ADDREC*), then locating a record (using *FINDREC*), and then exiting from the program (using *EXPROG*) would result in the added record not being saved. The problem arose through the use of the variable RMOD as a flag to indicate that a record had been modified (implying that the file might be out of order). The *SRTREC* subroutine would sort the file into alphabetical order, and then set RMOD to 0 on the assumption that the file is in order. Executing *EXPROG* checked to see if the file was in order (RMOD = 0) and didn't bother to save the file if it was in a sorted condition.

Adding a record (using *ADDREC*) would set RMOD to 1 (since a record had been modified, i.e. a new record had been added), but *SRTREC* would set RMOD to 0, indicating that the file had been sorted. What is really needed, however, irrespective of whether the file has been sorted or not, is a flag that signals that a record has been modified and a separate flag to show if the file is in a sorted condition or not. Then, subroutines that need to know that the file is sorted can check the 'sorted' flag, and subroutines that need to know if any record has been modified can check the 'modified' flag.

Suitable names for the two flags would be RMOD, to show if a record has been modified, and SRTD, to show if the file has been sorted.

When the program was presented on page 239, line 1230 contained the statement LET SVED = 0. The SVED variable has not been used so far, but when the line was included, it was realised that RMOD alone would not be enough. The variable name SVED was chosen with the idea that certain conditions would have to be true before a save (to tape or disk) would be necessary.

A more appropriate name for this flag would be SRTD (to indicate that the file is in a sorted condition). The original line 1230 has been changed to:

1230 LET SRTD = 1

There are now four possible states regarding the condition of the data file. These are:

RMOD	SRTD	
0	0	Not modified, not sorted (illegal)
1	0	Modified, not sorted
0	1	Not modified, sorted
1	1	Modified, sorted

RMOD=0 and SRTD=0 is illegal because the program ensures that the data file is always sorted before it is saved. When the program is run, RMOD is set to 0 (line 1220) to indicate that no modifications have taken place, and SRTD is set to 1 (line 1230) to indicate that the file is sorted.

Any operation that modifies a record (such as *ADDREC*, *DELREC* or *MODREC*) sets RMOD to 1 and this flag is not reset by any subsequent operation. SRTD, which is initially set to 1, is reset to 0 by any activity that might mean the data has become out of order (such as in *MODREC* if the name field is altered). Any activity that needs to assume the data is sorted (such as *FINDREC*) always checks SRTD and calls the sort routine if SRTD = 0. By using these two flags, instead of just RMOD, the program is able to terminate without saving the data file if no modifications have taken place during the current run of the program. It will not be 'tricked into' terminating without saving if a sort takes place after a record modification.

The other variable not used so far is CURR. This variable is used to save the 'current' position in the array of a record after one has been located by the search routine. CURR is not cleared after a value has been assigned to it; it is used to carry information about the target record to other routines in the program. The end of the *FINDREC* (search) routine has been modified in lines 3320 and 3330 to set the value of CURR: to 0 if the search failed to find the target record; and to MID if the search was successful.

Line 13340 branches to the *NOTREC* subroutine if CURR is 0. This displays a message saying that the record has not been found and displays the search key ,NAMFLD$(SIZE). *NOTREC* returns to the main menu after the space bar has been pressed. *NOTREC* could be modified quite easily to give the user the opportunity to:

PRESS RETURN TO TRY AGAIN OR
SPACE BAR TO CONTINUE

It might appear that the easiest way to achieve this would be to call *FINDREC* again if RETURN were pressed. However, calling a subroutine from within itself, whilst not illegal in BASIC, 'confuses' the return address and will cause the subroutine to be repeated again even when you don't want it to. There are ways of getting round this problem, but the programming starts to get a bit tricky!

An easier way would be to have used a flag (such as NREC for not record) and reset it in *NOTREC*, allow the subroutine to return in the normal way, and force a jump back to *EXECUT* in the main program, for example: 95 IF NREC=0 THEN 80. This approach was tried, and worked. But the coding started to look untidy. In accordance with our principle of avoiding GOTOs, we decided to keep things simple and just return to the main menu if a record is not found by *FNDREC*.

A small addition to the line 10490 in *MODNAM* should be noted. Numeric variable S should also be reset (LET S=0). Failure to do so can, under certain unusual circumstances, cause *MODNAM* to malfunction.

The other routine implemented in this final version of the program is *MODREC*. This routine first locates the record to be modified by calling *FNDREC* (line 14120). This line calls line 13030, not 13000, in order to suppress *FNDREC*'s clear screen statement. If the record cannot be located, the program will return to the main menu in the usual way (in line 14130). If the record is located, the target record is left displayed on the screen and users are instructed to:

MODIFY NAME?
PRESS RETURN TO ENTER NEW NAME
OR SPACE BAR FOR NEXT FIELD

The routine that finds out which of the two options is required can be found in lines 14190 to 14280.

Lines 14190 to 14220 constitute a simple loop that terminates only if either the space bar or RETURN is pressed. If A$ is NOT CHR$(13) (the ASCII value for a carriage return) AND NOT a space (you could also use CHR$(32) instead of " ") I will be reset and the loop will repeat. If the key pressed was RETURN (i.e. the name field is to be changed) the next few lines will fill the NAMFLD$(CURR) with the new name, set RMOD, reset SRTD, call *MODNAM* and fill MODFLD$(CURR) with the standardised name created by *MODNAM* and located in MODFLD$(SIZE).

The rest of *MODNAM* works in exactly the same way. Note, however, that modifying the other fields does set RMOD but does not reset SRTD (see line 14490, for example). The reason for this is that only changing the name field implies that the data file may be out of order, since the file is ordered by name. Changing any other field merely indicates that a record has been changed (RMOD = 1) and that the file must be saved when the program is terminated.

The other routine implemented is *DELREC* — to delete a record. This is very straightforward. First it clears the screen (line 15020) and displays a message explaining what's going on. It then calls *FNDREC* to locate the record to be deleted. A choice is then offered: to press RETURN to delete the record or the SPACE BAR to return to the main menu. A warning message is also displayed (line 15160). An even better approach might be to respond with an ARE YOU SURE? message if RETURN is pressed and then only delete the record if the Y key is pressed (i.e. IF INKEY$ = "Y" THEN ...).

DELREC does not reset the SRTD flag. Since the file is already in alphabetical order by name,

deleting a complete record will not upset this order. It does, however, mean that the file has been modified and so RMOD is reset in line 15340 and SIZE is reduced by one in line 13550 to take account of the fact that the file now has one fewer valid records. All the records are moved 'down one' in lines 15260 to 15320.

You may also have noticed that *FNDREC* includes a conditional call to a subroutine called *LSTCUR* to print out the CURRent record located by *FNDREC*. If you don't have a printer, simply replace line 13540 with a REM for future implementation and omit lines 13600 to 13690.

This completes the address book program. We have carried out all the major options presented in the main menu: finding a record, adding a record, changing a record, deleting a record, and exiting from the program. The purpose of the computerised address book has been to illustrate how a programmer should set about specifying, designing and implementing a program. An essential modification by anyone who intends the program as a piece of application software will be to check for — and trap — the problem that would arise if SIZE were ever to equal 51. This would happen as soon as there were 50 records in the file.

In the next instalment of the Basic Programming course we will discuss programming style and cover a few of the more advanced aspects of the BASIC language.

Basic Flavours

LPRINT

This command is not available on the Commodore 64, Vic-20, BBC Micro, or Dragon 32.

On the BBC Micro with a parallel printer insert the following lines:

13605 VDU 2
13680 VDU 3

These enable and disable the printer in turn. Substitute PRINT for LPRINT in lines 13610 to 13670. For more information see the user manual.

On the Commodores insert these lines:

13605 OPEN 4,4:CMD 4
13680 PRINT # 4: CLOSE 4

These enable and disable the printer in turn. Substitute PRINT for LPRINT in lines 13610 to 13670.

On the Dragon 32 insert these lines:

13605 OPEN"O", −2
13680 CLOSE −2

These enable and disable the printer in turn. Substitute PRINT −2, (the comma here is part of the command) for LPRINT in lines 13610 to 13670.

SPECTRUM

You will find the address book program in full for the Spectrum on page 250.

Address Book Program

```
10 REM 'MAINPG'
20 REM *INITIL*
30 GOSUB 1000
40 REM *GREETS*
50 GOSUB 3000
60 REM *CHOOSE*
70 GOSUB 3500
80 REM *EXECUT*
90 GOSUB 4000
100 IF CHOI <> 9 THEN 60
110 END
1000 REM *INITIL* SUBROUTINE
1010 GOSUB 1100: REM *CREARR* (CREATE ARRAYS) SUBROUTINE
1020 GOSUB 1400: REM *RDINFL* (READ IN FILE) SUBROUTINE
1030 GOSUB 1600: REM *SETFLG* (SET FLAGS) SUBROUTINE
1040 REM
1050 REM
1060 REM
1070 REM
1080 REM
1090 RETURN
1100 REM *CREARR* (CREATE ARRAYS) SUBROUTINE
1110 DIM NAMFLD$(50)
1120 DIM MODFLD$(50)
1130 DIM STRFLD$(50)
1140 DIM TWNFLD$(50)
1150 DIM CNTFLD$(50)
1160 DIM TELFLD$(50)
1170 DIM NDXFLD$(50)
1180 REM
1190 REM
1200 REM
1210 LET SIZE = 0
1220 LET RMOD = 0
1230 LET SRTD = 1
1240 LET CURR = 0
1250 REM
1260 REM
1270 REM
1280 REM
1290 REM
1300 RETURN
1400 REM *RDINFL* SUBROUTINE
1410 OPEN "I",#1,"ADBK.DAT"
1420 INPUT #1,TEST$
1430 IF TEST$ = "@FIRST" THEN GOTO 1540: REM CLOSE AND RETURN
1440 LET NAMFLD$(1) = TEST$
1450 INPUT #1,MODFLD$(1),STRFLD$(1),TWNFLD$(1),CNTFLD$(1),TELFLD$(1)
1460 INPUT #1,NDXFLD$(1)
1470 LET SIZE = 2
1480 FOR L = 2 TO 50
1490 INPUT #1,NAMFLD$(L),MODFLD$(L),STRFLD$(L),TWNFLD$(L),CNTFLD$(L)
1500 INPUT #1,TELFLD$(L),NDXFLD$(L)
1510 LET SIZE = SIZE + 1
1520 IF EOF(1) = -1 THEN LET L = 50
1530 NEXT L
1540 CLOSE #1
1550 RETURN
1600 REM *SETFLG* SUBROUTINE
1610 REM SETS FLAGS AFTER *RDINFL*
1620 REM
1630 REM
1640 IF TEST$ = "@FIRST" THEN LET SIZE = 1
1650 REM
1660 REM
1670 REM
1680 REM
1690 RETURN
3000 REM *GREETS* SUBROUTINE
3010 PRINT CHR$(12):REM CLEAR SCREEN
3020 PRINT
3030 PRINT
3040 PRINT
3050 PRINT
3060 PRINT TAB(12);"*WELCOME TO THE*"
3070 PRINT TAB(9);"*HOME COMPUTER COURSE*"
3080 PRINT TAB(6);"*COMPUTERISED ADDRESS BOOK*"
3090 PRINT
3100 PRINT TAB(5);"(PRESS SPACE-BAR TO CONTINUE)"
3110 FOR L = 1 TO 1
3120 IF INKEY$ <> " " THEN L = 0
3130 NEXT L
3140 PRINT CHR$(12)
3150 RETURN
3500 REM *CHOOSE* SUBROUTINE
3510 REM
3520 IF TEST$ = "@FIRST" THEN GOSUB 3860: REM *FIRSTM* SUBROUTINE
3530 IF TEST$ = "@FIRST" THEN RETURN
3540 REM 'CHMENU'
3550 PRINT CHR$(12)
3560 PRINT "SELECT ONE OF THE FOLLOWING"
3570 PRINT
3580 PRINT
3590 PRINT
3600 PRINT "1. FIND RECORD (FROM NAME)"
3610 PRINT "2. FIND NAMES (FROM INCOMPLETE NAME)"
3620 PRINT "3. FIND RECORDS (FROM TOWN)"
3630 PRINT "4. FIND RECORD (FROM INITIAL)"
3640 PRINT "5. LIST ALL RECORDS"
3650 PRINT "6. ADD NEW RECORD"
3660 PRINT "7. CHANGE RECORD"
3670 PRINT "8. DELETE RECORD"
3680 PRINT "9. EXIT & SAVE"
3690 PRINT
3700 PRINT
3710 REM 'INCHOI'
3720 REM
3730 LET L = 0
3740 LET I = 0
3750 FOR L = 1 TO 1
3760 PRINT "ENTER CHOICE (1 - 9)"
3770 FOR I = 1 TO 1
```

```
3780 LET A$ = INKEY$
3790 IF A$ = "" THEN I = 0
3800 NEXT I
3810 LET CHOI = VAL(A$)
3820 IF CHOI <1 THEN L = 0
3830 IF CHOI >9 THEN L = 0
3840 NEXT L
3850 RETURN
3860 REM *FIRSTM* SUBROUTINE (DISPLAY MESSAGE)
3870 LET CHOI = 6
3880 PRINT CHR$(12): REM CLEAR SCREEN
3890 PRINT
3900 PRINT TAB(8);"THERE ARE NO RECORDS IN"
3910 PRINT TAB(8);"THE FILE. YOU WILL HAVE"
3920 PRINT TAB(6);"TO START BY ADDING A RECORD"
3930 PRINT
3940 PRINT TAB(5);"(PRESS SPACE-BAR TO CONTINUE)"
3950 FOR B = 1 TO 1
3960 IF INKEY$ <> " " THEN B = 0
3970 NEXT B
3980 PRINT CHR$(12): REM CLEAR SCREEN
3990 RETURN
4000 REM *EXECUT* SUBROUTINE
4010 REM
4020 REM
4030 REM
4040 IF CHOI = 1 THEN GOSUB 13000: REM *FNDREC*
4050 REM 2 IS *FNDNMS*
4060 REM 3 IS *FNDTWN*
4070 REM 4 IS *FNDINT*
4080 REM 5 IS *LSTREC*
4090 IF CHOI = 6 THEN GOSUB 10000: REM *ADDREC*
4100 IF CHOI = 7 THEN GOSUB 14000: REM *MODREC*
4110 IF CHOI = 8 THEN GOSUB 15000: REM *DELREC*
4120 IF CHOI = 9 THEN GOSUB 11000: REM *EXPROG*
4130 REM
4140 RETURN
10000 REM *ADDREC* SUBROUTINE
10010 PRINT CHR$(12): REM CLEAR SCREEN
10020 INPUT "ENTER NAME";NAMFLD$(SIZE)
10030 INPUT "ENTER STREET";STRFLD$(SIZE)
10040 INPUT "ENTER TOWN";TWNFLD$(SIZE)
10050 INPUT "ENTER COUNTY";CNTFLD$(SIZE)
10060 INPUT "ENTER TELEPHONE NUMBER";TELFLD$(SIZE)
10070 LET RMOD = 1: LET SRTD = 0: REM MODIFIED & NOT SORTED
10080 LET NDXFLD$(SIZE) = STR$(SIZE)
10090 LET TEST$ = ""
10100 GOSUB 10200: REM *MODNAM*
10110 LET CHOI = 0
10120 LET SIZE = SIZE + 1
10130 REM
10140 REM
10150 RETURN
10200 REM *MODNAM* ROUTINE
10210 REM CONVERTS CONTENTS OF NAMFLD$ TO UPPER CASE,
10220 REM REMOVES RUBBISH, AND STORES IN THE ORDER:
10230 REM SURNAME+SPACE+FORENAME IN MODFLD$
10240 REM
10250 LET N$ = NAMFLD$(SIZE)
10260 FOR L = 1 TO LEN(N$)
10270 LET TEMP$ = MID$(N$,L,1)
10280 LET T = ASC(TEMP$)
10290 IF T >= 97 THEN T = T - 32
10300 LET TEMP$ = CHR$(T)
10310 LET P$ = P$ + TEMP$
10320 NEXT L
10330 LET N$ = P$
10340 REM LOCATE LAST SPACE
10350 FOR L = 1 TO LEN(N$)
10360 IF MID$(N$,L,1) = " " THEN S = L
10370 NEXT L
10380 REM REMOVE RUBBISH AND STORE FORENAME
10390 REM IN CNAM$
10400 FOR L = 1 TO S - 1
10410 IF ASC(MID$(N$,L,1)) > 64 THEN CNAM$ = CNAM$ + MID$(N$,L,1)
10420 NEXT L
10430 REM REMOVE RUBBISH AND STORE SURNAME
10440 REM IN SNAM$
10450 FOR L = S + 1 TO LEN(N$)
10460 IF ASC(MID$(N$,L,1)) > 64 THEN SNAM$ = SNAM$ + MID$(N$,L,1)
10470 NEXT L
10480 LET MODFLD$(SIZE) = SNAM$ + " " + CNAM$
10490 LET P$ = "": LET N$ = "": LET SNAM$ = "": LET CNAM$ = "":
        LET S = 0
10500 RETURN
11000 REM *EXPROG* SUBROUTINE
11010 REM SORTS AND SAVES FILE
11020 REM IF ANY RECORD HAS BEEN
11030 REM MODIFIED (RMOD = 1)
11040 REM OR NOT SORTED (SRTD = 0)
11050 REM RMOD = 0 AND SRTD = 0 IS ILLEGAL
11060 REM
11070 IF RMOD = 0 AND SRTD = 1 THEN RETURN
11080 IF RMOD = 1 AND SRTD = 0 THEN GOSUB 11200: REM *SRTREC*
11090 GOSUB 12000: REM *SAVREC*
11100 RETURN
11200 REM *SRTREC* SUBROUTINE
11210 REM SORTS ALL RECORDS BY MODFLD$ INTO
11220 REM ALPHABETICAL ORDER AND UPDATES NDXFLD
11230 REM
11240 REM
11250 LET S = 0
11260 FOR L = 1 TO SIZE - 2
11270 IF MODFLD$(L) > MODFLD$(L + 1) THEN GOSUB 11350
11280 NEXT L
11290 IF S = 1 THEN 11250
11300 REM
11310 REM
11320 LET SRTD = 1: REM SETS 'FILE SORTED' FLAG
11330 REM
11340 RETURN
11350 REM *SWPREC* SUBROUTINE
11360 LET TNAMFD$ = NAMFLD$(L)
11370 LET TMODFD$ = MODFLD$(L)
11380 LET TSTRFD$ = STRFLD$(L)
```

```
11390 LET TTWNFD$ = TWNFLD$(L)
11400 LET TCNTFD$ = CNTFLD$(L)
11410 LET TTELFD$ = TELFLD$(L)
11420 REM
11430 LET NAMFLD$(L) = NAMFLD$(L + 1)
11440 LET MODFLD$(L) = MODFLD$(L + 1)
11450 LET STRFLD$(L) = STRFLD$(L + 1)
11460 LET TWNFLD$(L) = TWNFLD$(L + 1)
11470 LET CNTFLD$(L) = CNTFLD$(L + 1)
11480 LET TELFLD$(L) = TELFLD$(L + 1)
11490 LET NDXFLD$(L) = STR$(L)
11500 REM
11510 LET NAMFLD$(L + 1) = TNAMFD$
11520 LET MODFLD$(L + 1) = TMODFD$
11530 LET STRFLD$(L + 1) = TSTRFD$
11540 LET TWNFLD$(L + 1) = TTWNFD$
11550 LET CNTFLD$(L + 1) = TCNTFD$
11560 LET TELFLD$(L + 1) = TTELFD$
11570 LET NDXFLD$(L + 1) = STR$(L + 1)
11580 LET S = 1
11590 REM
11600 RETURN
12000 REM  *SAVREC* SUBROUTINE
12010 REM
12020 REM
12030 OPEN "O",#1,"ADBK.DAT"
12040 REM
12050 FOR L = 1 TO SIZE - 1
12060 PRINT #1,NAMFLD$(L);",";MODFLD$(L);",";STRFLD$(L);",";TWNFLD$(L)
12070 PRINT #1,CNTFLD$(L);",";TELFLD$(L);",";NDXFLD$(L)
12080 NEXT L
12090 REM
12100 REM
12110 REM
12120 REM
12130 CLOSE #1
12140 REM
12150 RETURN
13000 REM  *FNDREC* (FIND RECORD) SUBROUTINE
13010 PRINT CHR$(12): REM  CLEAR SCREEN
13020 REM
13030 IF SRTD = 0 THEN GOSUB 11200: REM  *SRTREC*
13040 PRINT
13050 PRINT
13060 PRINT TAB(9);"SEARCHING FOR A RECORD"
13070 PRINT TAB(16);"BY NAME"
13080 PRINT
13090 PRINT TAB(9);"TYPE IN THE FULL NAME"
13100 PRINT TAB(7);"IN FIRSTNAME SURNAME ORDER"
13110 PRINT
13120 PRINT
13130 REM
13140 INPUT "NAME IS ";NAMFLD$(SIZE)
13150 GOSUB 10200: REM  *MODNAM* SUBROUTINE
13160 LET SCHKEY$ = MODFLD$(SIZE)
13170 REM
13180 REM
13190 REM
13200 REM
13210 REM
13220 LET BTM = 1
13230 LET TOP = SIZE - 1
13240 FOR L = 1 TO 1
13250 LET MID = INT((BTM + TOP)/2)
13260 IF MODFLD$(MID) <> SCHKEY$ THEN L = 0
13270 IF MODFLD$(MID) < SCHKEY$ THEN BTM = MID + 1
13280 IF MODFLD$(MID) > SCHKEY$ THEN TOP = MID - 1
13290 IF BTM > TOP THEN L = 1
13300 NEXT L
13310 REM
13320 IF BTM > TOP THEN LET CURR = 0
13330 IF BTM <= TOP THEN LET CURR = MID
13340 IF CURR = 0 THEN GOSUB 13700: REM  *NOTREC*
13350 IF CURR = 0 THEN RETURN
13360 REM
13370 REM
13380 PRINT CHR$(12)
13390 PRINT
13400 PRINT TAB(13);"*RECORD FOUND*"
13410 PRINT
13420 PRINT "NAME:",NAMFLD$(CURR)
13430 PRINT "STREET:",STRFLD$(CURR)
13440 PRINT "TOWN:",TWNFLD$(CURR)
13450 PRINT "COUNTY:",CNTFLD$(CURR)
13460 PRINT "PHONE:",TELFLD$(CURR)
13470 PRINT
13480 PRINT TAB(7);"PRESS ANY LETTER TO PRINT"
13490 PRINT TAB(7);"OR SPACE-BAR TO CONTINUE"
13500 FOR I = 1 TO 1
13510 LET A$ = INKEY$
13520 IF A$ = "" THEN I = 0
13530 NEXT I
13540 IF A$ <> " " THEN GOSUB 13600: REM  *LSTCUR*
13550 RETURN
13600 REM  *LSTCUR* (LIST CURRENT RECORD) SUBROUTINE
13610 LPRINT
13620 LPRINT "NAME:",NAMFLD$(CURR)
13630 LPRINT "STREET:",STRFLD$(CURR)
13640 LPRINT "TOWN:",TWNFLD$(CURR)
13650 LPRINT "COUNTY:",CNTFLD$(CURR)
13660 LPRINT "PHONE:",TELFLD$(CURR)
13670 LPRINT
13680 LPRINT
13690 RETURN
13700 REM  *NOTREC* (RECORD NOT FOUND) SUBROUTINE
13710 PRINT CHR$(12): REM CLEAR SCREEN
13720 PRINT TAB(11);"*RECORD NOT FOUND*"
13730 PRINT TAB(4);"IN THE FORM: ";NAMFLD$(SIZE);" *"
13740 PRINT
13750 PRINT TAB(5);"(PRESS SPACE-BAR TO CONTINUE)"
13760 FOR I = 1 TO 1
13770 IF INKEY$ <> " " THEN I = 0
13780 NEXT I
13790 REM  *MODREC* (MODIFY RECORD) SUBROUTINE
14000 REM
```

```
14010 REM
14020 PRINT CHR$(12): REM  CLEAR SCREEN
14030 PRINT
14040 PRINT
14050 PRINT
14060 PRINT
14070 PRINT TAB(10);"*TO MODIFY A RECORD*"
14080 PRINT TAB(3);"*FIRST LOCATE THE DESIRED RECORD*"
14090 REM
14100 REM
14110 REM
14120 GOSUB 13030: REM  *FNDREC* SUBROUTINE WITHOUT CLS
14130 IF CURR = 0 THEN RETURN: REM  RECORD NOT FOUND
14140 PRINT
14150 PRINT TAB(14);"MODIFY NAME?"
14160 PRINT
14170 PRINT TAB(5);"PRESS RETURN TO ENTER NEW NAME"
14180 PRINT TAB(6);"OR SPACE-BAR FOR NEXT FIELD"
14190 FOR I = 1 TO 1
14200 LET A$ = INKEY$
14210 IF A$ <> CHR$(13) AND A$ <> " " THEN I = 0
14220 NEXT I
14230 IF A$ = CHR$(13) THEN INPUT "NEW NAME";NAMFLD$(CURR)
14240 IF A$ = CHR$(13) THEN RMOD = 1
14250 IF A$ = CHR$(13) THEN SRTD = 0
14260 IF A$ = CHR$(13) THEN NAMFLD$(SIZE) = NAMFLD$(CURR)
14270 IF A$ = CHR$(13) THEN GOSUB 10200: REM  *MODNAM* SUBROUTINE
14280 IF A$ = CHR$(13) THEN LET MODFLD$(CURR) = MODFLD$(SIZE)
14290 PRINT
14300 PRINT TAB(13);"MODIFY STREET?"
14310 PRINT
14320 PRINT TAB(5);"PRESS RETURN TO ENTER NEW STREET"
14330 PRINT TAB(6);"OR SPACE-BAR FOR NEXT FIELD"
14340 FOR I = 1 TO 1
14350 LET A$ = INKEY$
14360 IF A$ <> CHR$(13) AND A$ <> " " THEN I = 0
14370 NEXT I
14380 IF A$ = CHR$(13) THEN RMOD = 1
14390 IF A$ = CHR$(13) THEN INPUT "NEW STREET";STRFLD$(CURR)
14400 PRINT
14410 PRINT TAB(13);"MODIFY TOWN?"
14420 PRINT
14430 PRINT TAB(5);"PRESS RETURN TO ENTER NEW TOWN"
14440 PRINT TAB(6);"OR SPACE-BAR FOR NEXT FIELD"
14450 FOR I = 1 TO 1
14460 LET A$ = INKEY$
14470 IF A$ <> CHR$(13) AND A$ <> " " THEN I = 0
14480 NEXT I
14490 IF A$ = CHR$(13) THEN RMOD = 1
14500 IF A$ = CHR$(13) THEN INPUT "NEW TOWN";TWNFLD$(CURR)
14510 PRINT
14520 PRINT TAB(12);"MODIFY COUNTY?"
14530 PRINT
14540 PRINT TAB(4);"PRESS RETURN TO ENTER NEW COUNTY"
14550 PRINT TAB(6);"OR SPACE-BAR FOR NEXT FIELD"
14560 FOR I = 1 TO 1
14570 LET A$ = INKEY$
14580 IF A$ <> CHR$(13) AND A$ <> " " THEN I = 0
14590 NEXT I
14600 IF A$ = CHR$(13) THEN RMOD = 1
14610 IF A$ = CHR$(13) THEN INPUT "NEW COUNTY";CNTFLD$(CURR)
14620 PRINT
14630 PRINT TAB(8);"MODIFY TELEPHONE NUMBER?"
14640 PRINT
14650 PRINT "PRESS RETURN TO ENTER NEW TELEPHONE NUMBER"
14660 PRINT TAB(8);"OR SPACE-BAR TO CONTINUE"
14670 FOR I = 1 TO 1
14680 LET A$ = INKEY$
14690 IF A$ <> CHR$(13) AND A$ <> " " THEN I = 0
14700 NEXT I
14710 IF A$ = CHR$(13) THEN RMOD = 1
14720 IF A$ = CHR$(13) THEN INPUT "NEW NUMBER";TELFLD$(CURR)
14730 REM
14740 REM
14750 RETURN
15000 REM  *DELREC* (DELETE RECORD) SUBROUTINE
15010 REM
15020 PRINT CHR$(12): REM  CLEAR SCREEN
15030 PRINT
15040 PRINT
15050 PRINT
15060 PRINT
15070 PRINT TAB(10);"*TO DELETE A RECORD*"
15080 PRINT TAB(3);"*FIRST LOCATE THE DESIRED RECORD*"
15090 REM
15100 REM
15110 REM
15120 GOSUB 13030: REM  *FNDREC* SUBROUTINE WITHOUT CLS
15130 IF CURR = 0 THEN RETURN: REM  RECORD NOT FOUND
15140 PRINT
15150 PRINT TAB(3);"DO YOU WANT TO DELETE THIS RECORD?"
15160 PRINT TAB(5);"*WARNING -- NO SECOND CHANCES"
15170 PRINT
15180 PRINT TAB(9);"PRESS RETURN TO DELETE"
15190 PRINT TAB(8);"OR SPACE-BAR TO CONTINUE"
15200 FOR I = 1 TO 1
15210 LET A$ = INKEY$
15220 IF A$ <> CHR$(13) AND A$ <> " " THEN I = 0
15230 NEXT I
15240 IF A$ = " " THEN RETURN
15250 FOR L = CURR TO SIZE - 2
15260 LET NAMFLD$(L) = NAMFLD$(L + 1)
15270 LET MODFLD$(L) = MODFLD$(L + 1)
15280 LET STRFLD$(L) = STRFLD$(L + 1)
15290 LET TWNFLD$(L) = TWNFLD$(L + 1)
15300 LET CNTFLD$(L) = CNTFLD$(L + 1)
15310 LET TELFLD$(L) = TELFLD$(L + 1)
15320 LET NDXFLD$(L) = STR$(L)
15330 NEXT L
15340 LET RMOD = 1
15350 LET SIZE = SIZE - 1
15360 REM
15370 REM
15380 REM
15390 RETURN
```

A Matter Of Style

Now that we have covered the fundamental rules of Basic, we can concentrate on important aspects of programming style and some new commands to perfect programming technique

The computerised address book program we have developed during the course of this chapter uses many of the more important features of the BASIC language, but certainly not all of them. In the concluding parts of the Basic Programming course we will look at where BASIC can take you next if you wish to become an advanced programmer. Unfortunately, this cannot be exhaustive, and readers are advised to refer to the owner's manual, or one of the many supplementary books that have been published for most of the popular home computers, for more extensive analysis of their machine's version of BASIC.

Machine Language Programs

Most versions of BASIC allow routines written in machine language to be included as part of the program. Broadly, there are two ways of doing this. The simplest is to use PEEK and POKE. PEEK is a statement used to examine specific memory addresses. For example, LET X = PEEK(1000) will get the value stored in address location 1000 and assign it to the variable X. Executing PRINT X will then print the value that was (and still is) in location 1000. Here is a short program that will PEEK at the contents of 16 memory locations and print them out on the screen:

```
10 INPUT "ENTER 'PEEK' START ADDRESS";S
20 PRINT
30 FOR L = 1 TO 16
40 LET A = PEEK(S)
50 PRINT "LOCATION ";S;" CONTAINS: ";A
60 LET S = S + 1
70 NEXT L
80 PRINT "PRESS SPACE BAR TO EXAMINE NEXT 16
   LOCATIONS"
90 PRINT "OR RETURN TO END"
100 FOR I = 1 TO 1
110 LET C$ = INKEY$
120 IF C$ < > CHR$(13) AND C$ < > " " THEN
    I = 0
130 NEXT I
140 IF C$ = CHR$(13) THEN GOTO 160
150 GOTO 30
160 END
```

The loop in lines 100 to 130 checks the input from the keyboard and then either goes to the end of the program, if the character typed was a RETURN (13 in ASCII), or back to the beginning, skipping the INPUT statement.

If desired, the ASCII character of the memory location can also be printed by using PRINT CHR$(A). But be careful, as ASCII values lower than decimal 32 (ASCII for the 'space' character) are not uniformly defined. All ASCII values from 0 to 31 represent non-printable characters or special functions, such as cursor controls. About the only agreement between different computer manufacturers is that ASCII 13 is usually the carriage return and ASCII 7 sounds the internal speaker or produces a 'beep'.

POKE is the converse of PEEK. It allows you to write any value from 0 up to 255 in any RAM memory location. This facility must be used with extreme caution, however, as writing to a part of memory that is already being used by the program can cause unexpected or catastrophic results. Routines written in machine code can be POKEd to the appropriate addresses and invoked when the program is run by the CALL statement. How to write programs in machine code is beyond the scope of a course on BASIC. Suffice it to say that machine code runs very much more quickly than even the best BASIC dialects. In situations where speed of execution is essential, or where great precision is required, machine code is by far the better alternative.

Moving The Cursor

Many home computers now allow locations on the screen to be addressed directly, but even if your machine does not support this, it is possible to move the cursor to the left, right, up and down the screen relatively easily. First you need to know what ASCII codes are used to represent the cursor control keys. The following short program will ask you to type a key and will then report the ASCII value corresponding to that key:

```
1 REM FINDING THE ASCII CODES FOR THE CURSOR
  KEYS
10 PRINT "PRESS A KEY";
20 FOR I = 1 TO 1
30 LET K$ = INKEY$
40 IF K$ = "" THEN I = 0
50 NEXT I
60 PRINT ASC(K$)
70 GOTO 10
80 END
```

This routine will also allow you to find the code for the RETURN key (usually 13), ESCape (usually 27) and the space key (usually 32), in addition to the codes for the cursor control keys. The Sord M23 computer, on which the programs in the Basic Programming course were developed, uses the values 8 for cursor left, 28 for cursor right, 29 for cursor up and 30 for cursor down. Your computer will probably use different values. Substituting the values you have found for your computer's cursor control codes in the program above, try the following program:

```
10 PRINT CHR$(12): REM USE CLS OR
   APPROPRIATE CODE
20 FOR L = 1 TO 39
30 PRINT "*";
40 NEXT L
50 FOR L = 1 TO 22
60 PRINT CHR$(8); :REM USE 'CURSOR LEFT' CODE
70 NEXT L
80 FOR L = 1 TO 4
90 PRINT "@";
100 NEXT L
110 END
```

This should print a line on the screen looking like:

```
*****************@@@@*****************
```

Lines 20 to 40 would simply have printed a line of 39 stars. However, lines 50 to 70 'printed' the cursor left 'character' 22 times, so the cursor moved back along the line 22 places. Lines 80 to 100 then printed @ four times and the program then ended. Programming techniques such as this allow the programmer to move the cursor around the screen to print new characters in new positions that may not be known until the values are calculated in the program. This technique has the advantage of enabling ordinary screen characters to be used to plot simple graphs, without resorting to the computer's special graphics facilities (if it has any).

To see how this kind of cursor control can be used to produce graphs as an output from your programs, try the following short program:

```
10 PRINT "THIS PROGRAM PRINTS A BAR GRAPH OF
   3 VARIABLES"
20 INPUT "INPUT THE THREE VALUES "; X,Y,Z
30 PRINT
40 FOR L = 1 TO 2
50 FOR A = 1 TO X
60 PRINT "*";
70 NEXT A
80 PRINT CHR$(13)
90 NEXT L
100 FOR L = 1 TO 2
110 FOR A = 1 TO Y
120 PRINT "+";
130 NEXT A
140 PRINT CHR$(13)
150 NEXT L
160 FOR L = 1 TO 2
170 FOR A = 1 TO Z
180 PRINT "#";
190 NEXT A
200 PRINT CHR$(13)
210 NEXT L
220 PRINT
230 END
```

The program prints out a bar graph of the three variables. The bars are printed in horizontal rows, starting from the left and following the 'natural' cursor movement. Notice that a PRINT CHR$(13) is needed in lines 80, 140 and 200. They are needed because semi-colons at the end of PRINT statements suppress carriage returns (13 is the ASCII code for <CR>).

More About Variables

So far we have treated variables as though there were only two kinds (numeric and string). In fact, there are several types of numeric variables recognised by BASIC, and a good programmer will always specify the right type to economise on memory and ensure correctness.

When a variable is declared in a programming language, a certain amount of memory space will be automatically allocated to store that variable. If the program knows that the variable will always be an integer, (e.g. LET SCORE = TOTAL + BONUS — PENALTY) less memory needs to be set aside for the variable. If we have a variable that can take an infinite number of different values (e.g. LET AREA = PI * RADIUS * RADIUS), more memory space will have to be allocated.

In the development of our computerised address book, we became familiar with the convention of specifying string variables by using the $ sign after the variable name (e.g. LET SCHKEY$ = MODFLD$(SIZE)). Variables without the 'dollar' sign were assumed to be ordinary numeric variables. However, similar conventions can be used after variable names to specify the type of numeric variable. A variable name with no specifier is assumed to be a real numeric variable of single precision. Other signs recognised by most BASICs include: % to specify an integer variable, ! to specify a single precision variable, and # to specify a double precision variable (i.e. the variable can store twice as many significant digits). Here is a fragment of a hypothetical program that uses these signs:

```
70 LET PLAYER$ = "JOHN": REM A STRING
   VARIABLE
80 LET SCORE% = 0: REM AN INTEGER VARIABLE
90 LET PI! = 3.1416: REM A SINGLE PRECISION
   VARIABLE
100 LET AREA# = PI*R*R: REM DOUBLE PRECISION
   VARIABLE
110 LET GOES = 6: REM ASSUMED TO BE SINGLE
   PRECISION REAL
```

Having said that, it must be pointed out that not all BASICs support all these variable types. The Spectrum, for example, does not have integer variables. Integers are simply stored as single precision real numbers. Neither does it support double precision numbers. However, single precision numbers in Spectrum BASIC are calculated to nine significant figures, against only seven significant figures in Microsoft BASIC. The BBC Micro does support variables of the integer type and single precision reals calculated to nine significant figures. Microsoft BASIC supports double precision variables to 16 significant places.

Computers that do accept integer variables usually allocate two bytes to store the number, which can be in the range −32,768 to 32,767. This range is usually perfectly adequate for such variables as scores, numbers of employees, FOR ... NEXT loop counts and other numbers likely to have only integer values. Since only two bytes are used to store the number, using integer variables if they are available will save on memory, although in many BASICs this is true only for integer arrays, and not for individual variables.

The final part of the Basic Programming course considers the advantages and disadvantages of BASIC as a language.

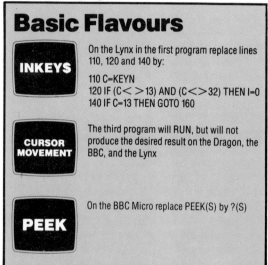

Basic Flavours

INKEY$

On the Lynx in the first program replace lines 110, 120 and 140 by:

```
110 C=KEYN
120 IF (C<>13) AND (C<>32) THEN I=0
140 IF C=13 THEN GOTO 160
```

CURSOR MOVEMENT

The third program will RUN, but will not produce the desired result on the Dragon, the BBC, and the Lynx

PEEK

On the BBC Micro replace PEEK(S) by ?(S)

Spectrum Address Book

This is the full Spectrum version of the Address Book program. Basic Flavours for the Lynx, Dragon 32, BBC Micro, Commodore 64 and Vic-20 can be found on page 254, and refer to this listing.

```
1 REM *CREATE DATA FILE*
2 DIM N$(50,30)
3 LET N$(1)="?FIRST"
4 INPUT"INSERT DATA TAPE, HIT
  'ENTER'";A$
5 SAVE "NFLD" DATA N$()
6 INPUT"REWIND TAPE, PRESS PLAY, HIT 'ENTER'";A$
7 VERIFY "NFLD" DATA N$()
8 STOP
```

This is the initialising program that creates the array on tape for the first time. When you have run this program, rewind the Data Tape, LOAD the Main Program (listing below) and RUN. You will not need the initialising program again unless you want to create a new address book file.

```
10 REM 'MAINPG'
20 REM *INITIL*
30 GOSUB 1000
40 REM *GREETS*
50 GOSUB 3000
60 FOR M=1 TO 1
70 LET M=0
80 REM *CHOOSE*
90 GOSUB 3500
100 REM *EXECUT*
110 GOSUB 4000
120 IF CHOI=9 THEN LET M=1
130 NEXT M
140 STOP

1000 REM *INITIL* S/R
1010 GOSUB 1100
1020 GOSUB 1400
1030 GOSUB 1600
1090 RETURN

1100 REM *CREARR* S/R
1110 DIM N$(50,30)
1120 DIM M$(50,30)
1130 DIM S$(50,30)
1140 DIM T$(50,15)
1150 DIM C$(50,15)
1160 DIM R$(50,15)
1170 DIM X$(50,30)
1180 DIM B$(30):DIM Z$(30)
1190 DIM U$(30):DIM W$(15)
1210 LET SIZE=0
```

```
1220 LET RMOD=0
1230 LET SRTD=1
1240 LET CURR=0
1250 LET Z$="?FIRST"
1260 LET Q$=B$
1300 RETURN

1400 REM *RDINFL* S/R
1405 INPUT"INSERT DATA TAPE, PRESS PLAY, & HIT
     'ENTER'";A$
1410 LOAD "NFLD" DATA N$()
1420 IF N$(1)=Z$ THEN LET Q$=Z$:RETURN
1430 LOAD "MFLD" DATA M$()
1440 LOAD "SFLD" DATA S$()
1450 LOAD "TFLD" DATA T$()
1460 LOAD "CFLD" DATA C$()
1470 LOAD "TELFLD" DATA R$()
1480 LOAD "NDXFLD" DATA X$()
1485 INPUT"STOP THE TAPE, & HIT 'ENTER'";A$
1490 REM 'FLSIZE'
1500 LET SIZE=51
1510 FOR L=1 TO 50
1520 IF N$(L)=B$ THEN LET SIZE=L:LET L=50
1530 NEXT L
1540 RETURN

1600 REM *SETFLG* S/R
1640 IF Q$=Z$ THEN LET SIZE=1
1690 RETURN

3000 REM *GREETS*
3010 CLS
3020 PRINT:PRINT:PRINT:PRINT
3060 PRINT TAB(8);"*WELCOME TO THE*"
3070 PRINT TAB(5);"HOME COMPUTER COURSE*"
3080 PRINT TAB(2);"*COMPUTERISED ADDRESS BOOK*"
3090 PRINT
3100 PRINT TAB(1);"(PRESS SPACE-BAR TO CONTINUE)"
3110 FOR L=1 TO 1
3120 IF INKEY$<>" " THEN LET L=0
3130 NEXT L
3140 CLS
3150 RETURN

3500 REM *CHOOSE* S/R
3520 IF Q$=Z$ THEN GOSUB 3860:RETURN
3540 REM 'CHMENU'
3550 CLS
3560 PRINT"SELECT ONE OF THE FOLLOWING"
3570 PRINT:PRINT:PRINT
3600 PRINT"1. FIND RECORD (FROM NAME)"
3610 PRINT"2. FIND NAMES (FROM INCOMPLETE NAME)"
3620 PRINT"3. FIND RECORDS (FROM TOWN)"
3630 PRINT"4. FIND RECORD (FROM INITIAL)"
3640 PRINT"5. LIST ALL RECORDS"
3650 PRINT"6. ADD NEW RECORD"
3660 PRINT"7. CHANGE RECORD"
3670 PRINT"8. DELETE RECORD"
3680 PRINT"9. EXIT AND SAVE"
3690 PRINT:PRINT
3710 REM 'INCHOI'
3750 PRINT"ENTER CHOICE (1-9)"
3760 FOR L=1 TO 1
3770 FOR I=1 TO 1
3780 LET A$=INKEY$
3790 IF A$="" THEN LET I=0
3800 NEXT I
3810 LET CHOI=CODE(A$)-48
3820 IF (CHOI<1) OR (CHOI>9) THEN LET L=0
3840 NEXT L
3850 RETURN

3860 REM *FIRSTM* S/R
3870 LET CHOI=6
3880 CLS
3890 PRINT
3900 PRINT TAB(4);"THERE ARE NO RECORDS IN"
3910 PRINT TAB(2);"THE FILE.  YOU WILL HAVE"
3920 PRINT TAB(2);"TO START BY ADDING A RECORD"
3930 PRINT
3940 REM *CONTINUE*
3950 GOSUB 3100
3990 RETURN

4000 REM *EXECUT* S/R
4040 IF CHOI=1 THEN GOSUB 5700
4050 REM 2 IS *FNDNMS*
4060 REM 3 IS *FNDTWN*
4070 REM 4 IS *FNDINT*
4080 REM 5 IS *LSTREC*
4090 IF CHOI=6 THEN GOSUB 4200
4100 IF CHOI=7 THEN GOSUB 6600
4110 IF CHOI=8 THEN GOSUB 7500
4120 IF CHOI=9 THEN GOSUB 5000
4140 RETURN

4200 REM *ADDREC* S/R
4210 CLS
4220 INPUT "ENTER NAME";N$(SIZE)
4230 INPUT "ENTER STREET";S$(SIZE)
4240 INPUT "ENTER TOWN";T$(SIZE)
4250 INPUT "ENTER COUNTY";C$(SIZE)
4260 INPUT "ENTER PHONE NUMBER";R$(SIZE)
4270 LET RMOD=1:LET SRTD=0
4280 LET X$(SIZE)=STR$(SIZE)
4290 LET Q$=""
4300 GOSUB 4500
4310 LET CHOI=0
4320 LET SIZE=SIZE+1
4350 RETURN

4500 REM *MODNAM* S/R
4510 REM CONVERT TO U/CASE
4520 LET D$=N$(SIZE):LET P$=""
4530 FOR L=1 TO LEN(D$)
```

```
4540 LET A$=D$(L)
4550 LET T=CODE A$
4560 IF T>=97 THEN LET T=T-32
4570 LET A$=CHR$ T
4580 LET P$=P$+A$
4590 NEXT L
4600 LET D$=P$:LET P$="":LET A$="":LET T=LEN(D$)
     :LET S=0
4610 REM LOCATE FIRST SPACE
4620 FOR L=1 TO T
4630 IF D$(L)=" " THEN LET S=L:LET L=T
4640 NEXT L
4650 REM REMOVE RUBBISH, PUT FORENAME IN P$
4660 FOR L=1 TO S-1
4670 IF CODE(D$(L))>64 THEN LET P$=P$+D$(L)
4680 NEXT L
4690 REM REMOVE RUBBISH, PUT SURNAME IN A$
4700 FOR L=S+1 TO LEN(D$)
4710 IF CODE(D$(L))>64 THEN LET A$=A$+D$(L)
4720 NEXT L
4730 LET M$(SIZE)=A$+" "+P$
4740 LET P$="":LET A$="":LET S=0
4750 RETURN

5000 REM *EXPROG* S/R
5010 IF (RMOD=0) AND (SRTD=1) THEN RETURN
5020 IF (RMOD=1) AND (SRTD=0) THEN GOSUB 5200
5030 GOSUB 5600
5040 RETURN

5200 REM *SRTREC* S/R
5210 FOR K=1 TO 1
5220 LET S=0
5230 FOR L=1 TO SIZE-2
5240 LET T=L+1
5250 IF M$(L)>M$(T) THEN GOSUB 5400
5260 NEXT L
5270 IF S=1 THEN LET K=0
5280 NEXT K
5290 LET SRTD=1
5300 RETURN

5400 REM *SWPREC*
5410 LET U$=N$(L):LET N$(L)=N$(T):LET N$(T)=U$
5420 LET U$=M$(L):LET M$(L)=M$(T):LET M$(T)=U$
5430 LET U$=S$(L):LET S$(L)=S$(T):LET S$(T)=U$
5440 LET W$=T$(L):LET T$(L)=T$(T):LET T$(T)=W$
5450 LET W$=C$(L):LET C$(L)=C$(T):LET C$(T)=W$
5460 LET W$=R$(L):LET R$(L)=R$(T):LET R$(T)=W$
5470 LET X$(L)=STR$(L)
5480 LET X$(T)=STR$(T)
5490 LET S=1
5500 RETURN

5600 REM *SAVREC* S/R
5605 INPUT"INSERT RECORDING TAPE & HiT 'ENTER'";A$
5610 SAVE "NFLD" DATA N$()
5620 SAVE "MFLD" DATA M$()
5630 SAVE "SFLD" DATA S$()
5640 SAVE "TFLD" DATA T$()
5650 SAVE "CFLD" DATA C$()
5660 SAVE "TELFLD" DATA R$()
5670 SAVE "NDXFLD" DATA X$()
5680 INPUT"STOP THE TAPE & HIT 'ENTER'";A$
5690 RETURN

5700 REM *FNDREC* S/R
5710 CLS
5720 IF SRTD=0 THEN GOSUB 5200
5730 PRINT:PRINT
5740 PRINT TAB(5);"SEARCHING FOR A RECORD"
5750 PRINT TAB(12);"BY NAME"
5760 PRINT
5770 PRINT TAB(5);"TYPE IN THE FULL NAME"
5780 PRINT TAB(3);"IN FIRSTNAME SURNAME ORDER"
5790 PRINT:PRINT
5800 INPUT"NAME IS";N$(SIZE)
5810 GOSUB 4500
5820 LET U$=M$(SIZE)
5830 LET BTM=1
5840 LET TP=SIZE-1
5850 FOR X=1 TO 1
5860 LET MD=INT((BTM+TP)/2)
5870 IF M$(MD)<>U$ THEN LET X=0
5880 IF M$(MD)< U$ THEN LET BTM=MD+1
5890 IF M$(MD)> U$ THEN LET TP=MD-1
5900 IF BTM>TP THEN LET X=1
5910 NEXT X
5920 IF BTM>TP THEN LET CURR=0
5930 IF BTM<= TP THEN LET CURR=MD
5940 IF CURR=0 THEN GOSUB 6400:RETURN
5950 CLS
5960 PRINT
5970 PRINT TAB(9);"*RECORD FOUND*"
5980 PRINT
5990 PRINT"NAME:",N$(CURR)
6000 PRINT"STREET:",S$(CURR)
6010 PRINT"TOWN:",T$(CURR)
6020 PRINT"COUNTY:",C$(CURR)
6030 PRINT"PHONE:",R$(CURR)
6040 PRINT
6050 PRINT TAB(3);"PRESS ANY LETTER TO PRINT"
6060 PRINT TAB(3);"OR SPACE-BAR TO CONTINUE"
6070 FOR I=1 TO 1
6080 LET A$=INKEY$
6090 IF A$="" THEN LET I=0
6100 NEXT I
6110 IF A$<>" " THEN GOSUB 6200
6120 RETURN

6200 REM *LSTCUR* S/R
6210 LPRINT
6220 LPRINT"NAME",N$(CURR)
6230 LPRINT"STREET",S$(CURR)
6240 LPRINT"TOWN",T$(CURR)
```

```
6250 LPRINT"COUNTY",C$(CURR)
6260 LPRINT"PHONE",R$(CURR)
6270 LPRINT:LPRINT
6280 RETURN

6400 REM *NOTREC* S/R
6410 CLS
6420 PRINT TAB(7);"*RECORD NOT FOUND*"
6430 PRINT TAB(4);"*IN FORM ";N$(SIZE);" *"
6440 PRINT
6450 REM 'CONTINUE'
6460 GOSUB 3100
6470 RETURN

6600 REM *MODREC* S/R
6610 CLS
6620 PRINT:PRINT:PRINT
6630 LET E$=CHR$ 13
6640 PRINT TAB(6);"*TO MODIFY A RECORD*"
6650 PRINT TAB(3);"*FIRST LOCATE THAT RECORD*"
6660 GOSUB 5720
6670 IF CURR=0 THEN RETURN
6680 PRINT
6690 PRINT TAB(10);"MODIFY NAME ?"
6700 PRINT
6710 PRINT TAB(1);"PRESS 'ENTER' TO ENTER NEW NAME"
6720 PRINT TAB(2);"OR SPACE-BAR FOR NEXT FIELD"
6730 FOR I=1 TO 1
6740 LET A$=INKEY$
6750 IF (A$<>E$) AND (A$<>" ") THEN LET I=0
6760 NEXT I
6770 IF A$=E$ THEN INPUT"NEW NAME";N$(CURR)
6780 IF A$=E$ THEN LET RMOD=1
6790 IF A$=E$ THEN LET SRTD=0
6800 IF A$=E$ THEN LET N$(SIZE)=N$(CURR)
6810 IF A$=E$ THEN GOSUB 4500
6820 IF A$=E$ THEN LET M$(CURR)=M$(SIZE)
6830 PRINT
6840 PRINT TAB(8);"MODIFY STREET ?"
6850 PRINT
6860 PRINT TAB(1);"PRESS 'ENTER' TO ENTER NEW STREET"
6870 PRINT TAB(2);"OR SPACE-BAR FOR NEXT FIELD"
6880 FOR I=1 TO 1
6890 LET A$=INKEY$
6900 IF (A$<>E$) AND (A$<>" ") THEN LET I=0
6910 NEXT I
6920 IF A$=E$ THEN LET RMOD=1
6930 IF A$=E$ THEN INPUT"NEW STREET:";S$(CURR)
6940 PRINT
6950 PRINT TAB(10);"MODIFY TOWN ?"
6960 PRINT
6970 PRINT TAB(1);"PRESS 'ENTER' TO ENTER NEW TOWN"
6980 PRINT TAB(2);"OR SPACE-BAR FOR NEXT FIELD"
6990 FOR I=1 TO 1
7000 LET A$=INKEY$
7020 IF (A$<>E$) AND (A$<>" ") THEN LET I=0
7030 NEXT I
7040 IF A$=E$ THEN LET RMOD=1
7050 IF A$=E$ THEN INPUT"NEW TOWN";T$(CURR)
7060 PRINT
7070 PRINT TAB(9);"MODIFY COUNTY ?"
7080 PRINT
7090 PRINT TAB(2);"PRESS 'ENTER' FOR NEW COUNTY"
7100 PRINT TAB(2);"OR SPACE-BAR FOR NEXT FIELD"
7110 FOR I=1 TO 1
7120 LET A$=INKEY$
7130 IF (A$<>E$) AND (A$<>" ") THEN LET I=0
7140 NEXT I
7150 IF A$=E$ THEN LET RMOD=1
7160 IF A$=E$ THEN INPUT"NEW COUNTY";C$(CURR)
7170 PRINT
7180 PRINT TAB(4);"MODIFY PHONE NO. ?"
7190 PRINT
7200 PRINT TAB(1);"PRESS 'ENTER' FOR NEW PHONE NO"
7210 PRINT TAB(2);"OR SPACE-BAR FOR NEXT FIELD"
7220 FOR I=1 TO 1
7230 LET A$=INKEY$
7240 IF (A$<>E$) AND (A$<>" ") THEN LET I=0
7250 NEXT I
7260 IF A$=E$ THEN LET RMOD=1
7270 IF A$=E$ THEN INPUT"NEW NUMBER";R$(CURR)
7280 RETURN

7500 REM *DELREC* S/R
7510 CLS
7520 PRINT:PRINT:PRINT:PRINT
7530 LET E$=CHR$ 13
7540 PRINT TAB(6);"*TO DELETE A RECORD*"
7550 PRINT TAB(3);"*FIRST LOCATE THE DESIRED RECORD*"
7560 GOSUB 5720
7570 IF CURR=0 THEN RETURN
7580 PRINT
7590 PRINT "DO YOU WANT TO DELETE THIS RECORD ?"
7600 PRINT " *WARNING* - NO SECOND CHANCES !"
7610 PRINT
7620 PRINT TAB(5);"PRESS 'ENTER' TO DELETE"
7630 PRINT TAB(4);"OR SPACE-BAR TO CONTINUE"
7640 FOR I=1 TO 1
7650 LET A$=INKEY$
7660 IF (A$<>E$) AND (A$<>" ") THEN LET I=0
7670 NEXT I
7680 IF A$=" " THEN RETURN
7690 FOR L=CURR TO SIZE-2
7700 LET T=L+1
7710 LET N$(L)=N$(T)
7720 LET M$(L)=M$(T)
7730 LET S$(L)=S$(T)
7740 LET T$(L)=T$(T)
7750 LET C$(L)=C$(T)
7760 LET R$(L)=R$(T)
7770 LET X$(L)=X$(T)
7780 NEXT L
7790 LET RMOD=1
7800 LET SIZE=SIZE-1
7810 RETURN
```

TONY LODGE

Language Lab

To conclude our course, we take a critical look at the Basic language, and at some of the alternatives to it

As a postscript to our Basic Programming course, we would like to discuss briefly some of the strengths and weaknesses of BASIC compared with other programming languages.

BASIC is an off-shoot of FORTRAN, one of the earliest programming languages. Unlike most other languages, BASIC is interpreted. This means that when a BASIC program is executed, a special program elsewhere in the computer's memory interprets the code line by line and converts the BASIC statements into machine code. Here's what would happen in a short BASIC program like this:

```
10 CLS
20 PRINT "TYPE IN A NUMBER"
30 INPUT X
40 PRINT "TYPE IN A SECOND NUMBER"
50 INPUT Y
60 "PRINT "THE PRODUCT OF THE TWO NUMBERS
   IS: ";
70 PRINT X*Y
80 PRINT
90 PRINT "DO YOU WANT ANOTHER GO?"
100 PRINT "PRESS 'Y' TO TRY AGAIN"
110 PRINT "OR 'N' TO END"
120 FOR X = 1 TO 1
130 LET A$ = INKEY$
140 IF A$ < > "Y" AND A$ < >"N" THEN X = 0
150 NEXT X
160 IF A$ = "Y" THEN GOTO 10
170 END
```

When the BASIC interpreter encountered line 10 it would work out the machine code needed to clear the screen. For line 20 it would work out the machine code instructions necessary for sending the TYPE IN A NUMBER message to the screen. For line 30 it would set up the memory space needed to store a real number, wait for input from the keyboard and then convert the number typed in into binary and store it in the space allocated to variable X. All this would be repeated for lines 40 to 60. If the user wanted to repeat the program by typing Y, the interpreter would branch back to line 10 and repeat all the calculations and computations again.

Most languages other than BASIC are 'compiled'. This means that after the program has been written it is processed by a 'compiler' before it can be run. The compiler is a separate program that goes through the 'source code' (the original program) and produces a second version of it in machine code. When the compiled program is run, it is likely to work very much faster than an

interpreted program because all the time-consuming translations into machine code have already been done.

If compiled programs work so much faster than interpreted programs, you might wonder why all programming languages don't use compilers. There are several advantages to using interpreted programs, such as BASIC. Most of these stem from the fact that it is an interactive language, which is one that can be tested and de-bugged 'at the keyboard' while the program is being developed. BASIC, for example, allows the STOP command to be inserted at any point in the program. When the interpreter encounters a STOP statement, it stops interpreting the program and allows 'commands' to be issued from the keyboard.

Commands are instructions that can be directly executed by the interpreter when the program is not running. BASIC is provided with a large number of these and they can be invaluable in de-bugging. After a BASIC program has been executed (i.e. the interpreter has encountered the END statement) or when the interpreter encounters a STOP statement, it is possible to PRINT the values of all the variables. Try running the address book program, for example. Run the program and type 9 to exit from the program. If it runs all the way through without any error messages appearing, it should end with the BASIC prompt (this is usually an OK, > or *). Then type PRINT RMOD<CR>. The interpreter should print a 0 on the screen (provided you have not added any records!). Then try PRINT SIZE<CR>. The interpreter will print a number on the screen one larger than the number of records you have in the data file.

Basic's Advantages

BASIC is often called the ideal language for the inexperienced programmer because it allows bugs to be removed at the keyboard. It has another great advantage: it is comparatively easy to learn. For example, in the Basic Programming course, we have covered all the fundamentals and many of the advanced aspects of BASIC in just 86 pages. Syntax errors such as 40 PRNT A(12) will usually result in easily understandable error messages when the program is executed, such as SYNTAX ERROR IN 40. A glance at the line number referred to usually makes it clear where the error lies, and rectifying the error is usually no more difficult than typing EDIT 40<CR> (followed by a few editing commands) or re-typing the correct line. Whenever the BASIC interpreter encounters an error in syntax or logic it stops the execution of the program and reports the error. Fixing the bugs is as simple as trying a new line in place of the erroneous line, and typing RUN<CR> again.

Basic's Disadvantages

The BASIC programming language has a number of disadvantages, however, some of which are subtle and some glaring. Because it is interpreted (although a few compiled versions of BASIC do exist) it runs very slowly. If speed is not very critical (as in a program to calculate your current bank balance, for example) the slowness of interpreted BASIC will be of no consequence. If, on the other hand, speed is of the essence (as in a screen animation program using graphics, or a 'clock' used to time reactions in a laboratory experiment) interpreted BASIC is likely to be far too slow.

If you need speed in your programs, there are two routes to follow: programming in either machine code or Assembly language (see page 162) — a difficult and time consuming process — or programming in a compiled language such as PASCAL or FORTH. Compiled languages are not difficult to learn, but the source code (the original program) is almost sure to contain bugs, which the compiler will find when it tries to compile the program. These are difficult to rectify, compared with bugs in BASIC. After corrections have been made to the source code, the program will have to be compiled all over again. Most compilers take two or three 'passes' through the source code, and each pass is likely to result in error messages, each of which will have to be corrected before the program can be re-compiled.

Producing a correctly compiled program is likely to be a far more time consuming processs than achieving a working program in interpreted BASIC. On the other hand, BASIC is likely to lead the novice programmer from the 'straight and narrow' by allowing bad programming techniques that highly structured languages such as PASCAL would reject. BASIC allows the programmer to write very careless programs, full of GOTOs for example, and these bad habits can make the transition to more advanced languages difficult.

What Next After Basic?

BASIC is a flexible language, and one that is not difficult to learn. It has excellent string handling facilities, but is slow and fails to take full advantage of the power of a home computer. On the other hand, more modern languages, such as PASCAL and FORTH, offer programming facilities either difficult or impossible in BASIC.

PASCAL was also devised as a teaching language, and specifically designed to encourage the development of well constructed, 'structured' programs. PASCAL is a compiled language, which

means that users encounter numerous errors picked up by the compiler (after the source code has been written and before the compiled 'object code' can be run), and this can be very frustrating. Novice PASCAL programmers also tend to find the restraints of the language, such as the need to declare all variables at the beginning of the program (and to state what type they are — real, integer, etc.), to be an impediment to free and flexible programming.

On the other hand, PASCAL demands that the programmer thinks through the logic of the program properly before writing. Programs in PASCAL are likely to throw up numerous syntactical errors in the source code. But they are also more likely to be well designed and less likely to contain fundamental logical errors.

FORTH has recently become a very popular alternative to BASIC as a programming language on home micros. Although FORTH is not as difficult to learn as Assembly or machine code language, it must be said that it is far less 'intuitive' than either BASIC or PASCAL. Even so, FORTH has many unique merits that make it a contender as the programmer's second language.

Although FORTH is a high level language, it runs nearly as fast as machine code, owing to the unique way it works. Whereas languages such as BASIC have a fixed number of statements and commands, FORTH users can define their own vocabulary.

The keyword PRINT in BASIC means that any character following it enclosed in double quotes will be printed on the screen. Nothing the programmer does can alter this. In FORTH, PRINT could be defined to produce, say, a listing on the screen of the hexadecimal equivalents of the ASCII codes, printed in a vertical column, of the characters in a string.

FORTH gives the programmer the power to define any word to mean whatever is wanted and to produce the desired results whenever it is used from then on. Not only is FORTH extremely flexible in this way, but it also produces programs that can be compiled to object code (see page 70) which are nearly as compact and fast running as machine language programs.

Although there are many programming languages available, most hobbyists moving on from BASIC will be inclined to choose from Assembly language, PASCAL and FORTH. Very briefly, the advantages and disadvantages of each can be summarised thus:

BASIC
Easy to learn
Easy to remember
Easy to de-bug
Slow in execution
Uses lots of memory
Does not encourage structured programming

Assembly Language:
Not very easy to learn
Not very easy to remember

Difficult to de-bug

Very fast in execution

Gives complete control over the microprocessor

PASCAL

Moderately easy to learn

Moderately easy to remember

De-bugging more difficult than in BASIC

Encourages better programming techniques

Execution faster than BASIC but slower than Assembly

Needs to be compiled, which takes time; once correctly compiled, runs nearly as fast as Assembly

Gives fair control over the microprocessor, but less than Assembly; string handling not as easy as in BASIC

FORTH

Not very easy to learn; easier for complete beginners, not so easy for BASIC programmers

Moderately easy to remember

De-bugging in interpreter mode very easy

Can be compiled; executes almost as quickly as Assembly language

Gives complete control over the microprocessor

Very economical on memory

Easier to learn than Assembly language, though less 'intuitive' than BASIC

Basic Flavours

```
1  REM *CREATE DATA FILE*
2  DIM N$(30)
3  LET N$="@FIRST"
4  DIM F$(15)
5  LET F$="DUMMY"
6  LET Z=2
7  EXTBACK 1
8  EXTSTORE 1,Z,N$,N$,N$
9  EXTSTORE 1,F$,F$,F$,F$
10 INPUT "INSERT DATA TAPE, PRESS
      RECORD, & TYPE 'Y'";A$
11 SSAVE 1, "ADDBKDAT"
12 PRINT "STOP THE TAPE, AND REWIND"
13 END
```

NB This is the initialising program for the 96K Lynx; we have no information on cassette file handling for the other models.

Main Program Variables

Copy the Spectrum list with these substitutions for the numeric variables:

Replace: SIZE by Z

RMOD by R

SRTD by D

CURR by C

CHOI by H

BTM by b

MD by m

TP by t

and make the following line changes, substitutions, and deletions:

```
1100 REM *CREARR* S/R
1110 DIM N$(30)(50)
1120 DIM M$(30)(50)
1130 DIM S$(30)(50)
1140 DIM T$(15)(50)
1150 DIM C$(15)(50)
1160 DIM R$(15)(50)
1170 DIM X$(15)(50)
1180 DIM Z$(30)
```

```
1210 LET Z=0
1220 LET R=0
1230 LET D=1
1240 LET C=0
1250 LET Z$="@FIRST"
1260 LET Q$=""
1300 RETURN
.
1400 REM *RDINFL* S/R
1405 PRINT "INSERT DATA TAPE AND PRESS
      PLAY"
1410 GOSUB 3100
1420 SLOAD 1, "ADDBKDAT"
1430 PRINT "STOP THE TAPE"
1440 GOSUB 3100
1450 EXTBACK 1
1460 EXTFETCH 1,Z
1470 FOR K=1 TO Z-1
1480 EXTFETCH 1,
      N$(K),M$(K),S$(K),T$(K),C$(K),R$(K)-
      ,X$(K)
1490 NEXT K
1500 LET Q$=N$(1)
1510 RETURN
.
3120 IF KEYN<>32 THEN LET L=0
.
3780 LET A$=KEY$
.
3810 LET H=VAL(A$)
3820 IF (H<1) OR (H>9) THEN LET L=0
.
4500 REM *MODNAM* S/R
4510 REM CONVERT TO U/CASE
4520 LET D$=UPC$(N$(Z))
      (delete lines 4530-4590)
.
4600 LET P$=""
4601 LET A$=""
4602 LET T=LEN(D$)
4603 LET S=0
.
4610 REM LOCATE LAST SPACE
.
4630 IF MID$(D$,L,1)=" " THEN LET S=L
.
4670 IF MID$(D$,L,1)>"@" THEN LET
      P$=P$+MID$(D$,L,1)
.
4710 IF MID$(D$,L,1)>"@" THEN LET
      A$=A$+MID$(D$,L,1)
```

Lines 5410 to 5460 must be reduced to single statements, for example:

```
5410 LET U$=N$(L):LET N$(L)=N$(T): LET
      N$(T)=U$      becomes
5410 LET U$=N$(L)
5411 LET N$(L)=N$(T)
5412 LET N$(T)=U$
```

and so on, no changes otherwise.

```
5600 REM *SAVREC* S/R
5605 PRINT "INSERT DATA TAPE AND PRESS
      RECORD"
5610 GOSUB 3100
5620 EXTBACK 1
5630 EXTSTORE 1,Z
5640 FOR K=1 TO Z-1
5650 EXTSTORE 1,
      N$(K),M$(K),S$(K),T$(K),C$(K),R$(K)-
      ,X$(K)
5660 SSAVE 1, "ADDBKDAT"
5670 PRINT "STOP THE TAPE"
5680 GOSUB 3100
5690 RETURN
.
5855 LET X=0
```

```
5860 LET m=INT((b+t)/2)
5870 IF M$(m)=U$ THEN LET X=1
5880 IF U$>M$(m) THEN LET b=m+1
    .
6080 LET A$=KEY$
    .
6110 IF A$=" " THEN RETURN
6120 GOSUB 6200
6130 RETURN
    .
6730 FOR I=1 TO 1
6735 LET I=0
6740 LET A$=KEY$
6750 IF (A$=E$) OR (A$=" ") THEN LET I=1
6760 NEXT I
```

This fragment must be reproduced at lines 6880-6910, 6990-7030, 7110-7140, 7220-7250, 7640-7670

Initialising Program
This is the initialising program for the Dragon 32.

```
1 REM *CREATE DATA FILE*
2 LET Z=2
3 LET N$="@FIRST"
4 OPEN "O", #-1, "ADBKDAT"
5 INPUT "INSERT DATA TAPE, PRESS
    RECORD, & TYPE 'Y'";A$
6 PRINT # - 1, Z: FOR I = 1 TO 7: PRINT # 1,
    N$: NEXT
7 CLOSE #-1
8 PRINT "STOP THE TAPE, AND REWIND"
9 STOP
```

On the BBC Micro replace lines 4, 6 and 7 by:

```
4 F1=OPENOUT("ADBKDAT")
6 PRINT #F1,Z,N$,N$,N$,N$,N$,N$,N$
7 CLOSE#F1
```

On the Commodore 64 and Vic-20 replace lines 4, 6 and 7 by:

```
4 OPEN 1,1,2,"ADBKDAT"
6 PRINT # 1, Z: FOR I = 1 TO 7: PRINT # 1,
    N$: NEXT
7 CLOSE 1
```

Main Program Variables
On the Dragon, the Commodores, and the BBC Micro copy the Spectrum list (published in full on page 250) with these substitutions for the numeric variables.

```
Replace: SIZE   by Z
         RMOD   by R
         SRTD   by D
         CURR   by C
         CHOI   by H
         BTM    by BT
         MD     by MD
         TP     by TP
```

and make the following line changes, substitutions, and deletions:

```
1100 REM *CREARR* S/R
1110 DIM N$(50)
1120 DIM M$(50)
1130 DIM S$(50)
1140 DIM T$(50)
1150 DIM C$(50)
1160 DIM R$(50)
1170 DIM X$(50)
```

Delete lines 1180-1190

```
1210 LET Z=0
1220 LET R=0
1230 LET D=1
1240 LET C=0
1250 LET Z$="@FIRST"
1260 LET Q$=""
```

```
1300 RETURN
```

This is the Dragon 32 version of subroutine 1400:

```
1400 REM *RDINFL* S/R
1410 OPEN "I", #-1, "ADBKDAT"
1420 PRINT "INSERT DATA TAPE AND PRESS
    PLAY"
1430 GOSUB 3100
1440 INPUT#-1,Z
1450 FOR K=1 TO Z-1
1460 INPUT#-1,N$(K),M$(K),S$(K),T$(K),-
    C$(K),R$(K),X$(K)
1470 NEXT K
1480 Q$=N$(1)
1490 CLOSE#-1
1500 PRINT "STOP THE TAPE"
1510 GOSUB 3100
1520 RETURN
```

In the preceding list, on the BBC Micro replace line 1410 by:

```
1410 F1=OPENIN("ADBKDAT")
```

and replace #-1 by #F1 in lines 1440, 1460, 1490
In the preceding list, on the Commodore 64 and Vic-20 replace line 1410 by:

```
1410 OPEN 1,1,0,"ADBKDAT"
```

Replace #-1 by #1 in lines 1440 and 1460, and replace 1490 by:

```
1490 CLOSE 1
```

On the BBC Micro replace INKEY$ by INKEY$(0) throughout; and replace INPUT"..message..";A$ by INPUT"..message..",A$. On the Commodores replace LET A$=INKEY$ by GET A$ throughout; and replace IF INKEY$... by GET GT$: IF GT$...

On the BBC Micro, the Dragon, and the Commodores in subroutine 4500 replace all references to D$(L) by MID$(D$,L,1). Replace CODE... by ASC(...). Replace FIRST by LAST in line 4610.
Delete : LET L=T from the end of line 4630.

This is the Dragon version of subroutine 5600; for BBC and Commodore variations see the Initialising Program notes above.

```
5600 REM *SAVREC* S/R
5610 OPEN "O", #-1, "ADBKDAT"
5620 PRINT "INSERT DATA TAPE AND PRESS
    RECORD"
5630 GOSUB 3100
5640 PRINT#-1,Z
5650 FOR K=1 TO Z-1
5660 PRINT#-1,N$(K),M$(K),S$(K),T$(K)-
    ,C$(K),R$(K),X$(K)
5670 NEXT K
5680 CLOSE #-1
5690 PRINT "STOP THE TAPE"
5693 GOSUB 3100
5695 RETURN
```

In subroutine 6200 on the BBC Micro insert:

```
6205 VDU 2
6275 VDU 3
```
and replace LPRINT by PRINT.

On the Commodores insert:

```
6205 OPEN 4,4:CMD 4
6275 PRINT#4:CLOSE 4
```

and replace LPRINT by PRINT.

On the Dragon replace LPRINT by PRINT #-2.

Answers To Exercises

How did you get on with the revision exercises on page 207? Here are some model solutions, though you may have found alternative methods that also work

On page 207 we posed nine problems, designed to test your skills at using the statements and functions commonly encountered in BASIC. Here are our suggested solutions.

If you've been following the Basic Programming course so far, you may have recognised the exercises as problems that have already been met and solved. Your solutions may be different from those we have suggested here. There is seldom only one way of solving a problem; your way may be as good as, or better than, ours.

If you find the solutions as puzzling as the questions, read pages 191 onwards again and study the solutions as you progress. If you did well on exercises 2, 4, 6 and 8 you have understood most of the lessons of these articles.

```
100 REM REVISION EXERCISE 1
200 INPUT "TYPE IN ANY NUMBER";A
300 INPUT "TYPE IN ANOTHER NUMBER";B
400 LET C = A + B
500 PRINT "THEIR SUM IS ";C
```

```
100 REM REVISION EXERCISE 2
200 LET A$ = "FIRSTWORD,"
300 LET B$ = "SECONDWORD"
400 LET C$ = A$ + B$
500 PRINT C$
```

```
100 REM REVISION EXERCISE 3
200 INPUT "TYPE IN ANY WORD";W$
300 LET L = LEN(W$)
400 PRINT "THE WORD YOU TYPED HAS ";L;"
    CHARACTERS"
```

```
100 REM REVISION EXERCISE 4
200 PRINT "HIT ANY KEY"
300 FOR C = 0 TO 1 STEP 0
400 LET A$ = INKEY$
500 IF A$ < > "" THEN LET C = 2
600 NEXT C
700 PRINT "ASCII VALUE OF ";A$;" IS ";ASC(A$)
```

See 'Basic Flavours', pages 195 and 203. On the Spectrum, replace line 700 with:

```
700 PRINT "ASCII VALUE OF ";A$;" IS ";CODE(A$)
```

```
100 REM REVISION EXERCISE 5
200 INPUT "TYPE IN ANY WORD";W$
300 LET L$ = RIGHT$(W$,1)
400 PRINT "THE LAST CHARACTER OF THE WORD
    IS ";L$
```

See 'Basic Flavours', page 191. This exercise on the Spectrum reads:

```
100 REM REVISION EXERCISE 5
200 INPUT "TYPE IN ANY WORD";W$
250 LET N = LEN(W$)
300 LET L$ = W$(N)
400 PRINT "THE LAST CHARACTER OF THE WORD
    IS ";L$
```

```
100 REM REVISION EXERCISE 6
200 PRINT "TYPE IN A NAME IN THE FORM:"
300 PRINT "FIRSTNAME SECONDNAME"
400 PRINT "E.G. JILL THOMPSON"
500 INPUT "NAME ";N$
600 LET S = 0:LET L = LEN(N$)
700 FOR P = 1 TO L
800 IF MID$(N$,P,1) = "    " THEN LET S = P
900 NEXT P
950 PRINT "SPACE WAS THE ";S;"TH CHARACTER"
```

See 'Basic Flavours', page 191. On the Spectrum, replace line 800 above with:

```
800 IF N$(P) = "    " THEN LET S = P
```

```
100 REM REVISION EXERCISE 7
150 LET X$ = "TH"
200 PRINT "TYPE IN A NAME IN THE FORM:"
300 PRINT "FIRSTNAME SECONDNAME"
400 PRINT "E.G.JILL THOMPSON"
500 INPUT "NAME ";N$
600 LET S = 0:LET L = LEN(N$)
700 FOR P = 1 TO L
800 IF MID$(N$,P,1) = "    " THEN LET S = P
900 NEXT P
925 IF S = 2 THEN LET X$ = "ND"
950 PRINT "THE SPACE WAS THE ";S;X$;"
    CHARACTER"
```

```
100 REM REVISION EXERCISE 8
200 INPUT "TYPE IN A SENTENCE ";S$
300 LET C = 1
400 FOR P = 1 TO LEN(S$)
500 IF MID$(S$,P,1) = "    " THEN LET C = C + 1
600 NEXT P
700 PRINT "THE SENTENCE HAS ";C;" WORDS"
```

See 'Basic Flavours', page 191. On the Spectrum, replace line 500 above with:

```
500 IF S$(P) = "    " THEN LET C = C + 1
```

```
100 REM REVISION EXERCISE 9
200 FOR C = 128 TO 255
300 PRINT "CHARACTER NO. ";C;" = ";CHR$(C)
400 REM A SHORT DELAY HERE
500 FOR D = 1 TO 500
600 NEXT D
700 REM END OF DELAY
800 NEXT C
```

Section 8

Sound
And Light

Modern microcomputers vary greatly in their
ability to handle sound and display graphics.
With the right information, though, you can
coax the very best out of your machine.

Introducing Sound

This is the first article in a series that will teach you how to get the most from the sound and graphics facilities on your computer

As home computers have developed over the last few years the features provided have become more comprehensive. Games facilities have been of vital importance to the popularity of each new computer and much time and effort has gone into developing sophisticated colour graphics capabilities. Though not so obvious in importance, sound and music-making features have been developed to a similar degree. If you asked successful games writers how important sound routines were in their programs they would probably place them a close third behind the game concept and graphics. Intelligent use of sound effects and music add considerably to the excitement and entertainment value of all arcade-type games.

In addition to games applications it is possible to further your knowledge of music by using the sound capabilities provided by your home computer. In many cases special music commands are provided in BASIC to enable you to write short programs to play quite complex tunes that even include chords. Some computers also provide ways to change the nature of the sound to make it more pleasing to the ear or approximate the sounds of conventional musical instruments. In all cases the computer keyboard can be configured, by means of a suitable program, to act in a similar manner to a piano keyboard, enabling you to play music in 'real time'.

Even if you have little knowledge of programming it is possible to write short and simple programs that make reasonably sophisticated musical sounds. If you wish to use the sound facilities to their best advantage, most software houses produce comprehensive music programs that enable you to write and play tunes immediately. Whichever approach you take, it is useful to understand how your computer generates, shapes and controls its sound output.

...And Light

Low and High Resolution

Graphics on microcomputers can be divided into two categories: low resolution and high resolution. The difference between low and high resolution is best described by considering how a character (a letter, number or shape) is made up.

If you take a close look at a standard character printed on a television screen you can see that its shape is made up of a group of small squares. These squares are called picture elements, or 'pixels', and every character or shape that appears on the screen is an arrangement of these in a pattern. On most home computers the characters are formed from a square of 64 pixels, grouped into eight rows of eight. The letter 'A' can be made up of a pixel pattern like this:

Each illuminated pixel on the grid can be represented in the computer's memory by a '1' and each dark pixel by a '0'. Eight bits make a byte, so each row of the character grid may be stored in one single location of the computer's memory. Thus it takes eight memory locations to hold a single character.

Graphic displays are sometimes made up of blocks the size of whole, half, or quarter character grids. Graphics designed using these large, simple building blocks are said to be of low resolution. On many home computers it is now possible to design graphic displays that are built up from single pixels. These are high resolution displays. A good way to demonstrate the difference between the two types is to look at a plot of a sine curve, as illustrated, using both kinds of resolution.

BIT PATTERN

PIXEL PATTERN

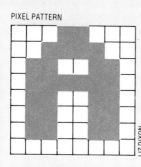

LIZ DIXON

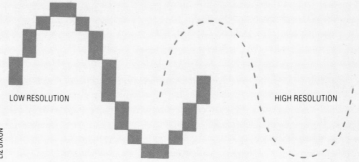

LOW RESOLUTION

HIGH RESOLUTION

Oscillators

Oscillators are electronic circuits that produce repetitive signals. When these signals are amplified and fed to a speaker they make sounds of a given pitch. The number of oscillators provided by home computers varies between one and four — the more oscillators you have the more notes you can play at once.

Three characteristics describe the sound created: frequency, envelope (which includes volume) and waveform. Frequency will be introduced here and envelope generators and waveform dealt with on page 260.

Frequency

This is the most important characteristic that we need to control, as it determines the pitch of the sound. Frequency is the number of times a signal repeats itself every second and is measured in hertz (Hz, cycles per second). Sounds that can be heard by the human ear have frequencies greater than 20Hz but less than about 20,000Hz. Although we cannot hear frequencies below 20Hz

they can be used to modify the characteristics of an audible sound. This technique is called modulation and at present can be applied only on the Commodore 64 among home computers.

However, it is not necessary to delve deeply into frequencies. What you really need to know is how to play musical notes. The ease with which you can do this varies enormously from one machine to another. Some have BASIC commands that work out the frequencies for you so that you need only specify a pitch number or even a musical letter symbol — A, A#, B, and so on. Others make it much more difficult by providing only a table in the user manual where you look up the frequency corresponding to the required note and POKE the frequency value into a memory location. The table shows accurate conversions for the scale of middle C. It will also be useful for those wishing to program music in machine code, where BASIC is unable to help you calculate the frequencies.

Music Notes To Frequencies
You can work out the frequency of each note in the scale by multiplying the frequency of the note one semitone below it by 1.0594631. This may appear a little baffling but if the multiplication is carried out 12 times the original frequency is doubled. There are 12 semitones in an octave (the difference between two notes with the same letter) so doubling the frequency moves the sound up one octave. This table provides accurate conversions from music note symbols (for the scale of middle C) to frequencies

User-Defined Characters

To create unusual and attractive screen displays it is often useful to have characters available that are different from the normal alphanumeric character set. The Vic-20 and Commodore 64 have a special set of graphic characters that can be used directly from the keyboard, but even these do not cover every eventuality. On most home computers it is possible to create new characters. This is usually achieved by redefining the binary patterns of the eight locations of memory in which a character is stored. In the process the old set of binary patterns is often lost, or 'overwritten', and the 'user-defined' character takes on some of the properties of the one it has replaced in memory. Thus the new character can be used in PRINT statements by simply pressing the key of the character it has replaced. Here is an example of a user-defined character, together with its associated binary codes:

The ease with which user-defined characters can be set up varies greatly according to the computer being used. For example, with the Sinclair Spectrum's USR command, all that is required is to enter the appropriate binary patterns; whereas on the Commodore 64 the user first has to move the complete character set from ROM to RAM before POKEing in to memory the eight decimal equivalents of the bit patterns that make up the shape. However, several character-designing utility programs, available from independent suppliers, make life easier for the Commodore 64 owner.

To create larger figures it is possible to group two or more user-defined characters together. The alien figures shown (right) were constructed from four user-defined characters. The program, which runs on the Commodore 64, PRINTs the character groups on the screen in three different colours. The characters were created by using a short routine to move the normal character set from ROM to RAM and replace the graphics characters ▟ , ▢ , ◣ , and ' ' by reading in decimal numbers from DATA statements and using POKE commands to place them in the appropriate locations. (See Peek And Poke on page 72 and page 260).

Even when sprites (see page 128) are available there is often a limit to the number that can be displayed at any one time on the screen, so user-defined graphics come in useful where many similar shapes need to be displayed at the same time.

Extra Terrestrial
These alien creatures were created from four characters, each defined by the programmer. This method can be used on many machines that don't have sprites

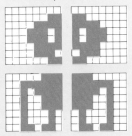

PIXEL PATTERN

BIT PATTERN

128	64	32	16	8	4	2	1
1	0	0	1	1	0	0	1
0	1	0	1	1	0	1	0
0	0	1	0	0	1	0	0
0	0	0	1	1	0	0	0
0	0	0	1	1	0	0	0
0	0	1	0	0	1	0	0
0	0	1	0	0	1	0	0
0	1	1	0	0	1	1	0

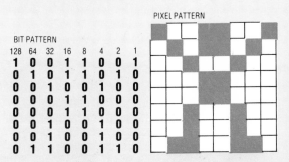

IAN McKINNELL

Sound Advice

Continuing our explanation of computer music jargon

As part of the series on generating sound on a microcomputer we now look at some of the most advanced features on home computers.

Envelope Generators

The envelope of a sound is the pattern of its volume changes, from the instant it is played until it dies away. Envelopes similar to those of a piano note and other instruments are shown in the diagram. Envelopes are commonly divided into four parts, usually called Attack, Decay, Sustain and Release (ADSR). In the case of the piano, volume rises rapidly to its highest level after the piano key is pressed (attack), then settles down more slowly (decay) to the roughly constant volume (sustain level) while the key is held down, and finally falls rapidly to zero (release) when the key is let go. Notice that sustain is a volume level, whereas attack, decay and release are intervals of time. A device that can control all four aspects of an envelope is called an ADSR generator.

Any device that can turn a sound on and off is an envelope generator of sorts.

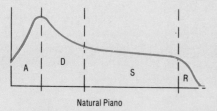
Natural Piano

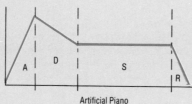
Artificial Piano

Most computers have nothing more sophisticated than a 'beep' generator, which is just a switch to turn on the sound at a constant volume for a specific time. In this case the A, D and R elements are equal to zero.

The Oric-1 provides some envelope control, but the most versatile home computers in this respect are the BBC Micro and the Commodore 64, both of which have ADSR generators that can imitate the envelopes of most common instruments, as well as some 'unnatural' ones.

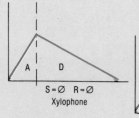
S=∅ R=∅
Xylophone

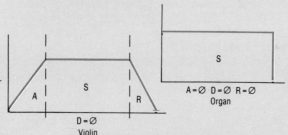
A=∅ D=∅ R=∅
Organ

D=∅
Violin

...Light Reading

Simple animation using the POKE and PRINT commands

Having looked at the basic principles of computer graphics, we're now going to see how some simple animation can be achieved. First, however, it will be necessary to detail the ways in which characters can be made to appear on the screen and how their positioning can be controlled using a BASIC program. Two main methods are available to the programmer: the POKE command, and the PRINT command with its associated functions.

The POKE command places a number in any specified memory location. There is a special series of memory locations inside every computer, each relating to a specific character position on the screen. On a standard 25-row by 40-column screen, 1,000 locations are set aside for this purpose. Each location holds a number that corresponds to a particular character in that machine's character set. This may be the standard ASCII code of the character (see page 202) or a code designated by the machine's manufacturer. In addition to these character code locations there is usually another set of locations that hold information about the colour of a character displayed in any screen position

On the Commodore 64, for example, there are very few graphics commands in BASIC to help the programmer, and the POKE command is often used to create screen displays. The addresses of the locations that hold character codes run from 1024 to 2023, and the locations that hold the colour information have addresses from 55296 to 56295. For the Commodore, the character A has a screen code 1 and the colour black is represented by a colour code of 0; thus the commands required to place a black letter A in the top left-hand corner of the screen are:

```
10 POKE 1024,1
20 POKE 55296,0
30 END
```

Simple modifications can be made to display a row of black A's on the top line of the screen:

```
10 FOR X = 0 TO 39
20 POKE 1024+X,1
30 POKE 55296+X,0
40 NEXT X
50 END
```

The A's are produced by the FOR...NEXT loop, which increases the character and colour location addresses by one each time. If we incorporate a command to rub out an old A every time a new one is created then the A will appear to move across the screen: a crude form of animation!

The Commodore character code for a space is 32. All that is necessary is for the program to place this in the appropriate location, one place behind where the new A is about to be displayed. Insert this line into the above program:

```
35 POKE 1024+X,32
```

Alternatively,

```
15 POKE 1024+(X- 1),32
```

Having to POKE locations with numbers to produce graphics is a laborious process. The method is probably best used to create static background displays using READ and DATA statements to enter the character codes before POKEing them to the correct location.

Most home computers have many graphics commands as part of the standard BASIC instruction set, allowing the user to create impressive and colourful displays using only a few simple statements. Commands to construct geometric patterns in high resolution are often included. With these instructions the user can plot points on the screen and connect them with straight lines; draw squares, arcs and circles; and colour the interiors of the shapes drawn.

It is often a straightforward matter to replot old shapes with the same colour as the background, which has the effect of rubbing them out. Rapid plotting, rubbing out and replotting at a new position is, in fact, the basis of simple graphic animation. The realism of the action largely depends on the speed at which the process can be achieved. Sprites are much more effective because they do not require unplotting as they move to a new position, and this greatly improves the speed at which they appear to move. Indeed, the development of sprites means that for the first time it is possible to write arcade-style games in BASIC, where previously machine code was essential.

The principles of moving graphics can be used in conjunction with simple BASIC programs. Many home computers have commands that allow the user to PRINT at specific positions on the screen, such as PRINT AT on the Spectrum and PRINT@ on the Dragon.

Star Formation
Here is a short program for the Dragon using PRINT. In this the variable X is the screen location where the star is to be printed. Notice that line 40 rubs out the old star as the new one is PRINTed.

```
10 CLS: REM CLEAR
SCREEN
20 FOR X = 160 TO 191
30 PRINT@X,"*";
40 PRINT@X-1," ";
50 NEXT X
60 END
```

Waveform

The waveform is the repetitive 'shape' of the signal produced by an oscillator (see page 259) and gives the sound its character. Two different instruments playing notes of the same pitch do not sound the same, and this is partly because the waveforms are different. The most common waveforms are square (or pulse), triangle and sawtooth — as shown below.

Most home computers provide only one waveform, usually of the pulse type. This is why many have that unmistakable harsh synthetic sound.

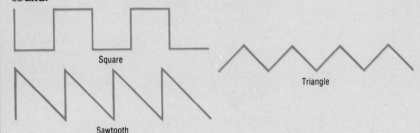

Square

Triangle

Sawtooth

The Commodore 64 is currently the most interesting computer musically, mainly because you can select any of the three basic waveforms on each of three oscillators. The waveforms can be modified by the use of filters, which alter the tone in much the same manner as the bass/treble controls on a hi-fi and have the effect of mellowing the sound. Even more useful is the ability to change these filter settings throughout the duration of a note. This enables you to simulate natural sounds more closely and produce more exciting unnatural sounds.

Noise

Noise is a complex type of sound made by random vibrations. The ear cannot pick out a repetitive pattern, so it does not hear any specific pitch. Imagine some everyday sounds like rain, wind and thunder. These noises do not sound the same because they are a combination of pure (unpredictable) noise with some dominant tones. Most microcomputers with a noise facility therefore allow you to modulate the noise in some way, or to mix it with pure notes. The possible effects range from 'whistling wind' to violent explosions.

Output

Output is usually through the television speaker. If this is the case you can connect the television set to your hi-fi via a video recorder. Some computers, however, can output sound only through a small built-in speaker. For these it is impossible to obtain good quality sound without modifying the hardware of the computer or buying an external add-on. Your computer may have an output suitable for connection directly to your hi-fi, making the effort involved in producing complex sound shapes worthwhile.

Sounding Out Vic

A close look at sound generation on the Vic-20...

The Vic-20 was one of the first home computers to appear in the UK. As a consequence, its facilities may appear to be a little lacking in comparison with more recent computers. Additionally, Commodore don't make it particularly easy to construct sound or music programs as Vic-20 BASIC, in common with Commodore 64 BASIC, has no commands that relate specifically to sound. All sound control is achieved by a series of POKEs into memory locations. This principle also applies to the Commodore 64 and the techniques outlined here for the Vic-20 would be useful to the Commodore 64 user. The degree of sound control available is limited to volume (equivalent to envelope with $A = D = R = 0$), frequency on three oscillators and a noise generator. Output is available via the television speaker alone. In addition, due to inaccuracies in the way the Vic–20 selects frequencies it is impossible to obtain the correct pitch for all notes on the musical scale.

With only these capabilities the Vic-20 has little value for music making; although with thought, patience and a little knowledge of BASIC programming these limited features can be used to create 'tunes' of two and three note chords.

Sound Control

The Vic-20 is supplied with three square wave oscillators and a noise generator. Each oscillator covers approximately three octaves of sound, offset in frequency as follows:

Osc.1	Osc.2	Osc.3	Freq. Range (Hz)	Octave
●			(65.41-123.47)	1
●	●		(130.81-246.94)	2
●	●	●	(261.63–493.88)	3
	●	●	(523.25-987.77)	4
		●	(1046.5-1975.53)	5

This arrangement allows the user to cover five octaves in total with at least one oscillator available in each octave. Octave 3, which starts at middle C and contains the standard reference A at 440Hz, is available to all three oscillators.

Control of the oscillators is exercised by changing the contents of five memory locations as follows:

Memory Location	Oscillator
POKE 36874,X	1
POKE 36875,X	2
POKE 36876,X	3
POKE 36877,X	noise

In each case X is a whole number between 135 and 241 (0 switches that oscillator off), which refers to a table of equivalent note values on page 73 of the booklet supplied with each Vic-20. Before the selected frequency can be heard the volume level must be set, as follows:

POKE 36878,V

where V can be set between 0(off) and 15(loud) affecting all oscillators and noise. For example:

POKE 36874,219:POKE 36875,219:POKE 36876,219:POKE 36878,7

This plays reference A at 440Hz on oscillator 1, A an octave higher on oscillator 2 and A an octave higher still on oscillator 3, all at a mid-range volume of 7. Don't forget to POKE each location to 0 to turn them off!

Notes And Pauses

Without a duration for each note and the correct pauses between them, a sequence of notes blurs one into another. To facilitate these 'wait' periods, one of two methods can be used to make the computer 'mark time' between POKEs. The first method is FOR...NEXT loops where the pause is timed by a long empty loop such as:

```
10 POKE 36878,7
20 POKE 36876,203
30 FOR P=1 TO 200
40 NEXT P
50 POKE 36878,0
60 POKE 36876,0
```

This sequence of commands plays the note D# for 200 FOR...NEXT steps. However, this method depends on careful external timing of the loop for accuracy. An easier and more elegant way to set durations and pauses is by using the Vic-20's built-in clock, which counts in 60ths of a second (jiffys) and can be referenced within a program using the variable TI. This is extremely useful, as a command can be constructed to 'wait' for an accurately measured period of time, as follows:

```
10 POKE 36878,7
20 POKE 36876,203:D=TI
30 IF TI-D<15 THEN 30
40 POKE 36878,0
50 POKE 36876,0
```

These commands play the same note as before but for a period of 15 jiffys (a quarter of a second). D is set at the value of TI when the sound is switched on. Line 30 counts off 15 jiffys before proceeding to line 40. Tunes can be constructed by using the same principle to pause before playing a different note, and so on. Next time we look at the Vic-20 in the Sound And Light chapter, we'll investigate how to play tunes.

Lighting Up Dragon

...and graphics capabilities of the Dragon 32

The Dragon 32 computer features a particular dialect of BASIC known as 'Microsoft Extended Colour Basic'. Several other computers on the market are also based on this version of BASIC, most notably the Tandy range of colour computers. Microsoft BASIC is easy to use and has a good range of commands to draw lines, circles, and other geometric shapes. Once drawn, these shapes may be coloured in to give impressive screen displays for little programming effort.

The Dragon 32 has seven levels of resolution, giving the user the ability to work with the screen divided into 512 individual points at the lowest level, and up to 49,152 points at the highest. There are eight colours available, but the choice may be limited to four or even two colours when working in high resolution.

Modes Of Resolution

The normal 16 rows by 32 columns character screen forms the lowest level of resolution and the PRINT@ command enables a character to be placed in any one of the 512 screen locations. As well as the normal character set there are also 16 low resolution graphics characters available in eight colours.

The next mode of resolution divides the screen into 32 rows and 64 columns. The size of each square in this mode is therefore a quarter of that of a normal character. Points of this size can be plotted on the screen by the SET command and may be rubbed out by the RESET command.

Both of the above modes can be displayed at the same time and are termed the low resolution text screens. There are also five levels of high resolution screens, but these cannot be displayed simultaneously or with the low level screens. The five high resolution modes offer choices based on the standard of resolution and the number of colours available and are selected using the PMODE command.

PMODE	Resolution	Colours Available
0	128*96	2
1	128*96	4
2	128*192	2
3	128*192	4
4	256*192	2

There is, of course, a trade-off between resolution, colour and the amount of memory needed to store the screen information and this must be taken into

account when writing large BASIC programs that also use high resolution displays.

Although there are only a limited number of colours available in high resolution, the Dragon does have a facility for selecting one of two colour sets. This is accomplished by the SCREEN command. For example, SCREEN 1,0 selects a high resolution screen and colour set 0. SCREEN 1,1 again selects a high resolution screen but this time an alternative colour set is used.

PAINT
This command is very useful in assisting the programmer to produce interesting pictures. Using PAINT causes the computer to start colouring in the screen from a given point until a boundary line is reached. This means that circles, triangles and any other closed shape can be filled in simply.

DRAW
DRAW mimics the movement of the pencil on the screen, allowing the user to draw lines in any one of four directions. The DRAW command will also allow the completed picture to be rotated or enlarged.

GET and PUT
GET instructs the computer to store a screen display in its memory and PUT causes such a display to be reprinted on the screen.

PSET and PRESET
These commands are the high resolution equivalents of SET and RESET discussed earlier and switch a particular point on the screen either on or off. The colour of the point can also be determined.

LINE
The LINE command joins two specified points together with a straight line in high resolution.

CIRCLE
CIRCLE allows the user to draw high resolution circles with a given centre and radius. Fractions of a whole circle may also be drawn to form arcs and the circular shape may be condensed to produce ellipses.

The Dragon 32 is a reasonably priced computer with many advanced commands to aid graphics programming. It is more suited to uses that involve static displays rather than those that require fast-moving action. The high resolution mode commands, in particular, make this an ideal computer for the adventurous-minded child. The Dragon's main drawback is its inability to display both text and high resolution graphics on the screen simultaneously. This means that it cannot be used to display statistical data in the form of bar charts or pie charts.

IAN McKINNELL

Colour Command
This display is typical of the effects that can be achieved on a Dragon using just a few of its high level commands

High Resolution
Here is a short program for the Dragon 32 to demonstrate some of its high resolution capabilities. The program uses PMODE 3; this is not the highest mode but it does allow some use of colour.

```
10 PCLS:PMODE3,1
20 SCREEN1,0
30 COLOR 0, 1
40 FOR X=0 TO 127 STEP 10
50 LINE(X,85)−(127,85−X/3),
   PSET
60 LINE(X,85)−(127,85+X/3),
   PSET
70 LINE(255−X,85)−(127,85−
   X/3),PSET
80 LINE(255−X,85)−(127,85+
   X/3),PSET
90 NEXT X
100 CIRCLE(127,85),128,4,0.3
110 CIRCLE(127,85),30,4,3
120 PAINT(130,30),3,4
130 PAINT(130,130),3,4
140 GOTO 140
150 END
```

Simple Sounds

Sound generation on the Sinclair Spectrum

The Spectrum is rapidly becoming the most popular home computer. It features excellent colour graphics facilities and useful memory options at a low price. Unfortunately, some facilities have been sacrificed in order to keep the price down. Most complaints concern the keyboard and the use of a non-standard BASIC, but it can be argued that its minimal sound capabilities are its weakest feature. The Spectrum provides the barest essentials for sound generation and produces unrewarding 'music' from a single 'pulse'-type oscillator. It is possible to control the duration of a note and its pitch, but there is no way to alter the tone of a note or change its envelope (see page 260). Another handicap is the standard output, which is through a very small internal piezo-electric speaker that makes the sound of a harsh 'beep'. However, Sinclair have provided alternative signal outputs from the 'mic' or 'ear' cassette ports, suitable for external amplification via a hi-fi system, but because of the lack of sound quality this is a dubious benefit. The Spectrum's sound capabilities do have the advantage of the simplicity of the associated BASIC commands of

BEEP and PAUSE, which enable the user to understand the principles of computer-generated sound more easily. And the machine does have a very impressive frequency range of 10 octaves.

Before any sound can be produced on the Spectrum, it is first necessary to either connect it to a hi-fi or make the internal 'beeper' audible by entering the following direct command before RUNning a sound program:

POKE 23609,100

This also increases the volume of the 'click' feedback that occurs as a key is pressed on the keyboard.

Sound Control

To instruct the computer to output a particular note the BEEP command is used like this:

BEEP d,n

where 'd' represents the duration of a note, and 'n' represents the pitch of the note. The duration value can be set between 0.00125 and 10 seconds; and the pitch is expressed as the number of semitones from middle C (given a value of 0) in the range from −60 to 69. For example, the following statement plays the note 'A' at 440Hz, which is nine semitones from middle C, for a duration of half a second:

BEEP .5,9

To play a whole string of notes with an accurately timed space between each one, we can use the PAUSE command:

PAUSE ms

Primary Pictures

The graphics capabilities of the Commodore Vic-20

Like Commodore's other home computers, the Commodore 64 and the PET, the Vic-20 is a well-constructed machine, but its makers do not give much away in the machine's BASIC instruction set. No special graphics commands are available to the Vic-20 user, who has to have either a very good knowledge of the machine's internal workings or buy one of the accessories designed to make graphics programming easier. However, Commodore provide an extensive set of special characters that can, with a little ingenuity, be put

together to produce interesting results.

Sixteen colours are available on the Vic-20 and each character square can contain four colours. The screen display is made up of 23 rows and 22 columns of eight by eight pixel character cells, but characters can also be displayed in a 16 by 8 rectangular format. High resolution graphics are possible on the standard Vic-20 but this is rather difficult for the average user to program.

Low Resolution Capabilities

Upper and lower case alphabetic characters are available, as well as more than 60 special PET graphics characters. Two small squares are marked on the front of many of the Vic-20's keys each displaying a particular pattern. In addition to half- and quarter-character squares there are playing card symbols, chequerboard designs, where 'ms' represents the time in units of 0.001 second (milliseconds). To play an octave in a key of C major (C, D, E, F, G, A, B, C) from middle C, with each note lasting half a second and a PAUSE of a quarter second between notes, the following format can be used:

```
10 FOR I = 1 TO 8
20 READ N
30 BEEP .5,N
40 PAUSE 250
50 NEXT I
60 DATA 0,2,4,5
70 DATA 7,9,11,12
```

This program is a good illustration of the format of a scale. An octave extends from the root note (in this case middle C) to the next note with the same name (the next C above) and spans 12 semitones. It is called an octave because it consists of eight notes in a major scale.

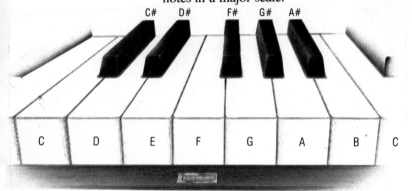

C major

Scales And Pianos

By using the INKEY$ command, the Spectrum keyboard can be used to approximate the keyboard of a piano:

```
10 REM *************
20 REM *OCTAVE PIANO*
30 REM *************
40 IF INKEY$="Q" THEN BEEP1,0
50 IF INKEY$="2" THEN BEEP1,1
60 IF INKEY$="W" THEN BEEP1,2
70 IF INKEY$="3" THEN BEEP1,3
80 IF INKEY$="E" THEN BEEP1,4
90 IF INKEY$="R" THEN BEEP1,5
100 IF INKEY$="5" THEN BEEP1,6
110 IF INKEY$="T" THEN BEEP1,7
120 IF INKEY$="6" THEN BEEP1,8
130 IF INKEY$="Y" THEN BEEP1,9
140 IF INKEY$="7" THEN BEEP1,10
150 IF INKEY$="U" THEN BEEP1,11
160 IF INKEY$="I" THEN BEEP1,12
170 GOTO 40
```

Many improvements can be made to a program like this in order to create a more efficient keyboard 'instrument'. Generally, the Spectrum is of little use as a sound source because of its lack of facilities for reasonable sound generation. It does, however, make a very useful aid to teaching music. The only way that acceptable sound can be obtained is by purchasing additional sound generating hardware that is compatible with the machine.

circles, and numerous other symbols that can be put together on the screen to draw graphs, make up tables, produce large lettering and create other effects. Each character can be displayed inverted (black on white instead of white on black), further increasing the possibilities. With patience and imagination, high-quality displays can be produced.

Characters can be made to appear on the screen either by use of the PRINT statement or by POKEing the required codes into the Vic-20's screen and colour memories. Commodore's version of the PRINT statement is extremely powerful, allowing the user to define the colour of each character individually. Cursor movement can also be controlled from within the PRINT statement to produce moving displays with ease. POKEing characters to the screen is not as fast as PRINTing them but this method can be useful in certain circumstances.

High Resolution Capabilities

High resolution graphics are possible on an unexpanded Vic-20, but there is enough memory available to utilise only about half the screen. The process by which high resolution can be achieved is known as 'bit-mapping', a technique that enables the programmer to control each individual pixel within a given area of the screen. Each character cell on the grid of 23 rows by 22 columns consists of 64 pixels arranged as eight rows of eight. There is a mathematical relationship between the given co-ordinates of a pixel dot (x,y) and the corresponding bit in the character matrix. This may be used, together with a combination of POKE commands, to produce displays made up of individual pixels.

Super Expander Cartridge

Producing high resolution graphics by bit-mapping can be a long and difficult process. An alternative approach is to buy Commodore's Super Expander cartridge, which gives the user high resolution, colour and music commands in BASIC. High resolution commands include GRAPHIC to set the display mode, POINT to plot a pixel dot on the screen, and PAINT.

There are two main drawbacks to using the cartridge: there is no UNPOINT command to rub out the pixel dot, and it is not possible to PAINT both sides of a diagonal line without disturbing the line itself.

The Vic-20's low resolution graphics are well designed and very flexible, but high resolution graphics are difficult to use without incurring the expense of a plug-in cartridge.

Run Rabbit
This program listing for the Vic-20 demonstrates the versatility of the special set of Commodore characters. The rabbit figure created is constructed entirely from this predefined character set. It is easier to see exactly how it is made up by moving the cursor over the screen display when the program has been typed in and run

Sound Systems

A second look at the Vic-20's sound capabilities

Last time we looked at the Vic-20 in this section (see page 262) we learnt how the machine's three oscillators can be controlled by POKEing memory locations; how to set the volume levels; and how to control the duration of a note. We investigated how the duration of the notes and the pauses between them can be determined by the use of FOR...NEXT loops or, more efficiently, by using the Vic-20's clock to count in jiffys (60ths of a second). Management of these three musical elements — frequency, volume and timing — enables you to build simple tunes on the Vic-20 and produce useful sound effects.

The Light Program

First steps with the BBC's sophisticated graphics

The BBC Micro is one of the most popular home computers in Britain. Truly stunning graphics effects can be simply achieved in a few lines of BASIC, and the speed at which displays are produced on the screen using BASIC is also impressive.

There are several high resolution commands in BBC BASIC, including instructions to draw straight lines, plot points, and plot and fill triangles. This last function is used to colour in shapes as a series of small triangles as there is no PAINT-type command available. The BBC Micro also lacks a BASIC command to draw circles and ellipses, and has no sprite programming capability. However, it does have several unusual and interesting features that the majority of its rivals do not possess. These include the ability to mix text and graphics on the screen, separately controllable text and graphics cursors, and access to the part of the machine operating system that controls screen display, from within a BASIC program. This is accomplished by the set of VDU or screen commands. Text and graphics 'windows' can also be defined on the screen, enabling the user to divide up the display into separate sections for graphics and text.

Playing Tunes

To construct a tune you must first assemble the required notes. These could be, for example, the notes of the first line of 'Oh, I do like to be beside the seaside'. In the correct order these can be selected as:

D# E F D# C A# G# G G# D# D#

Using the techniques described on page 262, the duration of the notes and pauses can be set by using the TI facility. Our tune can therefore be played by RUNning the following program (notice the use of variables to simplify the selection of POKEs):

```
10 V = 36878
20 FOR I = 1 TO 11
30 READ N: REM *NOTE*
40 POKE V,7:P=TI: REM *VOL ON*
50 IF TI-P < 15 THEN 50: REM *PAUSE*
60 POKE V-3,N:D=TI: REM *PLAY NOTE*
70 IF TI-D < 20 THEN 70: REM *DURATION*
80 POKE V-3,0: REM *STOP NOTE*
90 NEXT I
100 DATA 203, 207, 209, 203: REM *NOTE VALUES*
110 DATA 195, 187, 179, 175
120 DATA 179, 203, 203
130 POKE V,0: REM *VOL OFF*
140 END
```

Different colours can be defined for each window and each may also be cleared independently.

Display Modes

The BBC Micro has eight graphics modes, three of which support text displays only. There is a choice of 20, 40, or 80 characters across the screen, depending on which mode has been selected. Two, four or 16 colours are available, again depending on the mode selected, but a pleasing feature of the limited colour modes is that two or four colours to be used in that mode are not fixed and can be selected by the programmer from the 16 generally available.

MODE 7 is different from all the others in that the standard set of ASCII characters and associated codes are not used. Instead, the display is made up of Teletext characters. Normal graphics commands, such as PLOT and DRAW, do not work in MODE 7.

The following table shows the resolution and colour choices specified by selection of any mode:

Mode	Text	Graphics	Colours
0	80 × 32	640 × 256	2
1	40 × 32	320 × 256	4
2	20 × 32	160 × 256	16
3	80 × 25		2 (black & white)
4	40 × 32	320 × 256	2
5	20 × 32	160 × 256	4
6	40 × 25		2 (black & white)
7	40 × 25		Teletext

This program simply plays the notes in the correct sequence with equal durations and pauses. Consequently, the resulting tune is somewhat stilted. With experimentation you can construct more complex programs that provide different intervals and durations for individual notes.

Sound Effects

By using two or three oscillators it is possible to play simple chords. The program below plays the chord of D major (F#, A and D) starting with the F# on its own, and adding the A and D after set delays of one second each. The chord then continues for a further two seconds.

```
10 POKE 36878,7
20 POKE 36874,233:D=TI
30 IF TI-D < 60 THEN 30
40 POKE 36875,219:D=TI
50 IF TI-D < 60 THEN 50
60 POKE 36875,147:D=TI
70 IF TI-D < 120 THEN 70
80 POKE 36878,0: POKE 36874,0
90 POKE 36875,0: POKE 36876,0
100 END
```

A lot can be done, however, to make the tone of these sounds more interesting. For instance, the volume can be varied over the duration of a note — rising and falling according to a variable. For example:

```
100 V = 36878
110 FOR I= 1 TO 12
120 POKE V,I
```

```
130 NEXT I
140 POKE V,0
```

This causes the volume to rise in steps of 1 to a peak of 12, where the total range is from 0 (off) to 15 (loud). Volume can be 'pulsed' by alternating a high and low volume setting, as well. The frequency can be similarly varied to 'bend' a note by changing line 120 above to:

```
POKE V-3,203+I
```

It is also worth trying different combinations of noise, oscillator frequencies and volumes. This can often result in a more pleasing tone. Whether making music or adding sound effects to games, the aim in computing is to reduce boredom by avoiding the constant repetition of monotonous notes.

We have shown how the simple sound facilities on the Vic-20 can be manipulated to produce interesting tones and note sequences. The main problem is the lack of sound commands, which involves the use of complex BASIC statements to carry out relatively simple tasks. This results in long program routines that prevent the BASIC interpreter from processing the code in between notes quickly enough. The only simple way to avoid this problem is to invest in one of the many commercial software packages that supply extra commands for music programming. Commodore's Super Expander cartridge provides a useful range of sound commands, as well as a facility for storing tunes written with the aid of the cartridge. However, if you require more than rudimentary sound or music facilities from a home computer it would be necessary to investigate other models, such as the BBC Micro, the Commodore 64, the Dragon 32 or the Oric-1.

The high resolution screen is defined with its origin in the bottom left-hand corner of the screen, regardless of the mode selected. Vertical values range from 0 to 1023, and horizontal values range from 0 to 1279. This consistent method of mapping the screen becomes very convenient when you decide to change the display from one mode to another. Incidentally, if the mode of display is changed during the course of a program then the screen is automatically cleared.

Background, text and graphics colours are set using the COLOUR and GCOL commands. The BBC Micro uses the interesting idea of logical and actual colours to allow the user to select a limited set of colours from the 16 allowed. To illustrate this it is best to use the example of using colour in MODE 0 where only two colours can be specified. Two possible foreground colours are given the logical colour numbers 0 and 1, and unless the computer is instructed to do otherwise, it takes 0 as black and 1 as white. The COLOUR command selects the text foreground colour. COLOUR 1 would select logical colour number 1 as the text colour, but it is possible to reset the logical text colour using one of the VDU commands. VDU19

defines the logical colour. To set logical colour 1 to green (actual colour number 2) the following command is needed:

```
VDU19, 1, 2, 0, 0, 0,
```

The three noughts on the end have no significance and are there for future expansion of the system.

The GCOL command has two numbers associated with it. The second number is the logical colour number for graphics display, the first relates to the way in which that colour is used on the screen. For the command GCOL a,b values of a can range from 0 to 4 allowing the user to specify whether the point or line should be displayed in the logical foreground colour, whether it should be ANDed, ORed or exclusive ORed with the colour already present, or whether the original colour should be inverted.

In another part of the Sound And Light chapter we will return to the BBC Micro and explain high resolution capabilities, defining characters, and look more closely at the set of VDU commands.

Sound Qualities

Sound generation on the BBC Model B

Exceptional sound facilities and comprehensive BASIC commands to control them place the BBC Micro among the best computers available for the home user who is particularly interested in sound. Three independent square wave oscillators, eight types of noise and four independent ADSR (Attack, Decay, Sustain and Release) and pitch envelopes are supplied as standard. This means that music sequences can be constructed consisting of up to three voices in harmony and special commands ensure that notes selected to form a chord are played at exactly the same time.

Sound Creation

In its simplest form, sound can be created by the use of the SOUND command:

    SOUND C,V,P,D

In this case:

    C=Channel or oscillator number (0-3)
    V=Volume
    P=Pitch of note
    D=Duration or length of note

Any one of three oscillators (1, 2 and 3) may be selected to play a note and 0 selects noise. Volume takes a value between 0 (off) and −15 (loud). Pitch is defined in steps, of a quarter of a semitone between 0 (A# at 116.5Hz) and 253 (D at 4698.64Hz) giving a range of five and a half octaves. Middle C is set by the value of 53. If the noise channel has been specified, there are eight types available, which set up the following pitch numbers:

Number	Noise Type
0	High pitch 'tremolo'
1	Medium pitch 'tremolo'
2	Low pitch 'tremolo'
3	'Tremolo'. Pitch varies with the pitch of channel 1
4	High pitch
5	Medium pitch
6	Low pitch
7	Pitch varies with the pitch of channel 1

Finally, duration of note is controlled in steps of 20th of a second between 1 and 255, which give a maximum note length of 12.75 seconds. A command to play A above middle C on channel 1 at a medium volume of −7 for half a second is constructed as:

    SOUND 1, −7, 89, 10

If the computer receives a second SOUND command before the first is completed the note is placed in the channel queue.

Light Construction

Commodore 64 graphics capabilities

BACKGROUND COLOUR

MULTI-COLOUR 1

MULTI-COLOUR 2

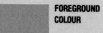
FOREGROUND COLOUR

The Commodore 64 computer has a great number of possibilities for the graphics programmer. The main drawback is that, in common with the Vic-20, there is only an extremely limited set of BASIC commands provided as standard. POKEing and PEEKing inside the computer's memory allow the programmer access to all the machine's features but some of the procedures required can be quite confusing. Again, as with the Vic-20, there are several ways out of this maze. These take the form of a number of independently produced software packages that make the creation of sprites or user-defined characters much simpler. In addition to these, Commodore produce their own plug-in cartridge, called 'Simon's BASIC'.

The Commodore 64 has the standard upper and lower case character sets available in normal or inverse display modes. Also available are the special graphics characters that were first developed for the PET and which are also used on the Vic-20. The screen display consists of 40 columns and 25 rows and characters are positioned on it either by PRINTing them to the screen in any chosen colour or by POKEing the relevant codes into the screen and colour memories detailed in the user manual. The special Commodore graphics characters form an extremely flexible medium in which to put together attractive displays in low resolution. More than 60 special characters may be used in this way. Again, each of these special characters may be displayed in normal or inverse mode, giving the user well over 120 options from which to choose when designing a figure.

If the exact character cannot be found then it is possible to define new characters for use in the display. This is, unfortunately, not very easy to do. To define a character the programmer must first copy all the normal characters that will be required from ROM memory to RAM, before POKEing the necessary numbers into the series of locations that are to hold the new character.

In addition to the simple functions outlined, the capabilities of the SOUND command can be extended by changing its format to:

SOUND &HSFC,V,P,D

In this case the ampersand sign & instructs the computer to treat HSFC as a four digit hexadecimal number (base 16). However, to understand how to use the modified command it is only necessary to analyse the function of each digit. Only three of these are significant as C is merely the usual channel number described in SOUND.

H can either be unspecified (0) or set at 1. H = 1 allows the previous note on the same channel to continue to completion. Otherwise, if a note has been constructed with a long release phase (dying away slowly) the computer will mistakenly assume the note is complete while it is still sounding and start the next note abruptly in the middle of it. H set at 1 forces the computer to wait for completion. If the H parameter is used the remaining parts of the SOUND & command, apart from the channel number, are ignored.

S allows the user to specify a number of notes to be played at the same time on different channels, creating a chord. S = 0 leaves the command in its normal state. S is set to 1 if it is required that a note on one other channel is played at the same time. If set to 2, notes on both the other channels will play. In effect, when the computer encounters an S value it holds the relevant note back until it can account for the associated one or two other notes in the chord that are indicated by the same S number on the remaining channels. It then plays all the specified notes together.

F is set to either 0 or 1. Zero has no effect but 1 causes the computer to discard all notes that are waiting in the channel queue to be played, stops the current note playing and plays the note contained in its own command immediately.

SOUND & is best illustrated with an example. This program plays the first line of 'Happy birthday to you' in the key G# (below middle C) as:

G#G#A#G#C#D#

It also includes a three part major chord for the final D#

```
10 SOUND 1,-7,37,10:REM *1ST G#*
20 SOUND 1,-7, 37,10:REM *2ND SHORT G#*
30 FOR I=1 TO 3: READ N
40 SOUND 1,-7, N,10: NEXT I: REM *A#,G#,C#*
50 SOUND &201, -7,37,15: REM *G#*
60 SOUND &202, -7,53,15: REM *C*
70 SOUND &203,-7,65,15: REM *D#*
80 DATA 45,37,57
90 END
```

The sound capabilities given by the command ENVELOPE will be discussed later.

Each character cell is made up of eight by eight rows of pixel dots that are represented in binary form as groups of 1s and 0s. Normally 1 is interpreted as a pixel set to the foreground or character colour, and 0 interpreted as a pixel set to the background or screen colour. There is a facility on the Commodore 64 to allow up to four colours to be represented within any character cell. This is known as multi-colour mode. When the computer is switched into multi-colour mode it uses two bits to represent the colour of each pixel.

There are four possible combinations for any pair of bits and this fact is used to represent four different colours inside the character cell. Each character cell on the screen can be set either to be interpreted in the normal way or as a multi-colour character, but in the latter case the choice of colours available is reduced from 16 to 8. Further drawbacks are that the two multi-colours must be the same for all the characters on the screen, and that when in multi-colour mode the horizontal resolution is reduced by a factor of two.

There are no high resolution graphics commands in Commodore BASIC. However, it is possible to create high resolution displays by using the technique known as 'bit-mapping'. The Commodore 64's screen display is made up of 64,000 pixels. Bit-mapping works by allowing the programmer to turn each pixel on or off individually. This is a fairly complex procedure for the average user to undertake and the use of BASIC in this way makes for an extremely slow build-up of the high resolution picture. In practice, there are two alternatives open to those who wish to exploit high resolution graphics: the first is to purchase the Simon's BASIC cartridge from Commodore and the second is to learn to program in machine code. Standard high resolution mode on the Commodore 64 divides the screen into 200 rows of 320 pixels. Multi-colour mode is also available in high resolution, allowing up to four different colours within any eight by eight block.

Here is a short program that uses the Commodore character set to create a supermarket scene. Later in the Sound and Light chapter we will discuss sprites and Simon's BASIC in more detail.

Step One
This static supermarket scene was created using low resolution graphics. In a future instalment of the Sound And Light course we'll add a moving shopper with a trolley, using sprite graphics

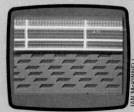

IAN McKINNELL

```
3000 REM ** SUPERMARKET **
3010 PRINT "⊐"
3020 POKE53280,6:POKE53281,12
3030 PRINT"▓▓████▓  ▓▓██████████▓  ▓▓██████████"
3040 PRINT"▓▓OOO▓  ▓▓OOOOOOOOOOO▓  ▓▓OOOOOOOOOOO"
3050 PRINT"▓                                  ▓"
3060 PRINT"▓●●●●▓  ▓▓●●●●●●●●●●●▓  ▓▓●●●●●●●●●"
3070 PRINT"▓●●●●▓  ▓▓●●●●●●●●●●●▓  ▓▓●●●●●●●●●"
3080 PRINT"▓●●●●▓  ▓▓●●●●●●●●●●●▓  ▓▓●●●●●●●●●"
3090 PRINT"▓                                  ▓"
3100 PRINT"▓▼▼▼▼▓  ▓▓▼▼▼▼▼▼▼▼▼▼▼▓  ▓▓▼▼▼▼▼▼▼▼▼"
3110 PRINT"▓▼▼▼▼▓  ▓▓▼▼▼▼▼▼▼▼▼▼▼▓  ▓▓▼▼▼▼▼▼▼▼▼"
3120 PRINT"▓                                  ▓"
3130 PRINT"▓                                  ▓"
3140 PRINT"▓▓   ▼   ▼   ▼   ▼   ▼   ▼   ▼   ▼   ▼"
3150 PRINT
3160 PRINT"  ▼   ▼   ▼   ▼   ▼   ▼   ▼   ▼   ▼"
3170 PRINT
3180 PRINT"▼   ▼   ▼   ▼   ▼   ▼   ▼   ▼   ▼"
3190 PRINT
3200 PRINT"▓   ▼   ▼   ▼   ▼   ▼   ▼   ▼   ▼"
3210 PRINT
3220 PRINT"▓   ▼   ▼   ▼   ▼   ▼   ▼   ▼   ▼"
3230 PRINT
3240 PRINT"  ▼   ▼   ▼   ▼   ▼   ▼   ▼   ▼   ▼"
3250 FORI=1063T02023STEP40
3260 POKEI,160:POKE54272+I,6:NEXT
3270 GOTO3270
```

Sound Proof

Sound synthesis using the Dragon 32

The Dragon 32 is supplied with only a single square wave oscillator for programming sound, but the wonderfully simple sound commands allowed by Microsoft Extended Colour BASIC enable the construction of music strings that play a passable tune with one command. Unfortunately, there is no means of generating noise. This is very strange as it is difficult to imagine an arcade-type game that does not require noise at some point to make the sound effects interesting.

The SOUND command is useful for sound effects only and the format is as follows:

    SOUND P,D

where: P = Pitch (1-255) and D = Duration (1-255). Pitch is highly inaccurate and bears little relation to a standard musical scale, though middle C can be approximated with the value 89 and reference A at 440Hz is about 159. Duration is similarly inexact but 16 is near to one second, 32 roughly equivalent to two seconds and so on.

This program shows how SOUND can be used for a special effect; in this case, with a little imagination, a UFO taking off:

    10 FOR P=10 TO 170 STEP 10
    20 FOR D=16 TO 1 STEP −1
    30 SOUND P,D
    40 NEXT D
    50 NEXT P

PLAY can set an exact pitch, duration and volume for a note. It can also specify a string of such notes to be PLAYed with a selected pause between them at a variable tempo. This makes the construction of tunes with different note lengths and pauses very easy — all PLAYed with this single command:

    PLAY "T;O;V;L;N;P"

where: T = Tempo (T1−T255); O = Octave (O1−O5); V = Volume (V0−V15); L = Length of note (L1−L255); N = Note value (1−12 or note letter); and P = Pause before next note (P1−P255).

It isn't strictly necessary to use the semi-colons between parameters but it would be wise to include them for clarity. The example is very much an arbitrary representation as the parameters can be set in any order. T, O, V, and L retain their values until specified otherwise. In fact, T, O, V, L, and P default to T2, O2, W15, L4 and P0 respectively, unless otherwise specified, so it isn't always necessary to include them in the PLAY statement.

Where timing is involved, as in L and P, the values specified can be thought of as 'notes', and fractions of 'notes' where L1 or P1 is a whole note, L2 or P2 a half note and so on. The actual timing of these is selected by the tempo parameter T, where T1 is slow (a note has a long duration) and T255 is

Light Entertainment

The second instalment of the graphics capabilities of the BBC Model B

BBC BASIC does not provide the full range of high resolution commands that are available on some microcomputers. For example, there are no CIRCLE or PAINT commands. However, it is possible to simulate most facilities using a few lines of BBC BASIC.

The graphics screen has the same co-ordinates regardless of the level of resolution selected, and the axes have their origin in the bottom left-hand corner. The following commands provide control over the graphics screen:

    MOVEx,y

This command moves the graphics cursor to the point with (x,y) co-ordinates, but does not draw a line. Note that the graphics cursor can move completely independently of the text cursor.

    DRAWx,y

As the name suggests, DRAW draws a line from the current graphics cursor position to the point on the screen with the (x,y) co-ordinates.

    PLOTk,x,y

PLOT is a multi-purpose command; its function is governed by the value given to the variable k:

Value of k	Function
0	move relative to last point
1	draw line from origin in foreground colour
2	draw line from origin in inverse colour
3	draw line from origin in background colour
4	same as MOVE
5	same as DRAW
6	same as DRAW but in inverse colour
7	same as DRAW but in background colour

very fast (a note has a short duration). In addition, note lengths can be more flexibly defined by the addition of dots such as L1...or L5. where each dot increases the note length by half its normal value. Therefore L1... $= 1 + \frac{1}{2} + \frac{1}{2} + \frac{1}{2} = 2\frac{1}{2}$ notes and L5. $= \frac{1}{5} + \frac{1}{10} = \frac{3}{10}$ note.

There is no absolute way in which the relationship between note and tempo can be represented. The values required can vary for each tune and are best selected by trial and error. This may be a little time consuming but it makes the command very flexible.

The parameter O specifies the octave in which the next note is to be played. O1 starts with C at 131Hz and O5 ends with B at 2093Hz. Middle C begins O2 which is the default octave. Within an octave, notes can be specified in two ways. In the first case a number can be used that corresponds to a musical note as follows:

1	2	3	4	5	6
C	C#	D	D#	E	F
7	8	9	10	11	12
F#	G	G#	A	A#	B

This makes it possible to specify a note as a variable within a selected octave. Alternatively, the required note letter can be used directly to make the statement easier to understand in a listing.

The above explanations are best illustrated with an example. The following command plays F (6) in the default octave O2, for half a note length (L2) at default volume V15. It then pauses for a quarter

note length (L1) at volume V20. Tempo is set at T3:

PLAY "T3;L2;6;P4;O3;V20;L1;A#"
       〈 F 〉 〈   A#   〉
               pause

In addition, the T, O, V, and L parameters can be varied by preset amounts from within the command by the addition of a suffix:

Suffix	Effect
+	Adds one to current value
–	Subtracts one from current value
>	Multiples current value by two
<	Divides current value by two

The format is: T+, T–, T > or T< for each parameter.

The most useful Dragon facility is the ability to PLAY tunes using substrings. These are first defined, and then PLAYed in any order or repeated:

```
10 A$="F;A#;G"
20 B$="C;D#;F;P4;XA$;"
30 PLAY B$
```

This defines A$ and then includes it in B$ as substring XA$. The resulting tune is C—D#—F—P4—F—A#—G. This technique can be continued as necessary where sequences of notes are repeated a number of times within a piece of music. In all cases the semi-colon following a substring must be included, as in XA$, above.

Higher numbers repeat these eight functions but with extra effects, such as dotted lines instead of solid lines. Values of k between 80 and 87 fulfil a particularly useful function. PLOT80,x,y joins the point (x,y) to the two previously plotted points to form a triangle. The triangle is then filled in with the current foreground colour. This provides the only simple means of PAINTing graphic shapes.

VDU x is equivalent to the more usual BASIC command PRINT CHR$(x). We saw in the introduction to graphics on the BBC Micro that VDU can be followed by a series of numbers. VDU v,w,x,y,z is equivalent to:

```
PRINT CHR$(v);CHR$(w);CHR$(x);CHR$(y);
    CHR$(z)
```

The VDU commands allow the user access to the part of the BBC's operating system that controls graphics and screen display. Although VDU commands may be used within BASIC programs they actually work independently of the language employed. Thus the same VDU commands could be used for a graphics display in PASCAL or any other language offered for the BBC. Each of the BASIC graphics facilities so far discussed can also be implemented by the appropriate VDU command.

Defining characters is very easy on the BBC

Micro. VDU 23 controls this function. In the section on user-defined graphics (see page 259) we learned that normal ASCII codes are constructed from a block of eight by eight pixels. The pixels that are visible can be represented by a 1 in binary and those not visible by a 0. Each row of eight bits can then be converted to its decimal equivalent, giving a total of eight decimal numbers to define a character. VDU 23 allows the user to redefine the character with an ASCII code between 224 and 255. For example:

```
10 REM DEFINE A CHARACTER
20 MODE 2
30 VDU 23,240,16,56,124,146,16,16,16,0
40 PRINT CHR$(240)
50 END
```

This short piece of program redefines the character with ASCII code 240 to create an arrow shape. The last eight numbers define this new shape, and line 40 PRINTs the character on the screen.

VDU 24 and VDU 28 respectively control the creation of graphics and text 'windows' on the screen. Using these functions, graphics and text output to the screen can be limited to definable areas. This can be particularly useful when designing interactive programs where a split screen is desirable. All that is required to define a graphics window is to specify the co-ordinates of the bottom left- and top right-hand corners.

MODE 1
This short program listing draws a colourful spiral flower on the screen using MODE 1 resolution. Note the use of filled in triangles to produce the flower petals.

```
10 REM FLOWER
20 CLS
30 MODE 1
40 FOR D=1 TO 3
50 A=600 : B=500
60 MOVEA,B
70 FOR C=1 TO 550 STEP3
80 GCOL0,RND(3)
90 S=(C/(RND(5)+10))
100 X=S*5*SIN(C/16)+A
110 Y=S*5*COS(C/16)+B
120 PLOT85,X,Y
130 NEXT C
140 NEXT D
150 END
```

The spiral pattern is produced by the combination of sine and cosine in lines 100 and 110. Normally this relationship between the x and y co-ordinates produces a circle but the FOR...NEXT loop gradually increases the radius C producing the spiral effect. The co-ordinates of the centre of the spiral, A and B, may be altered to re-position the flower

271

Sound Spectacular

The Oric-1 permits sophisticated sound control on a budget

MUSIC And PLAY

The following program uses the MUSIC and PLAY commands to play the chord of C major (C,G, & E) using each envelope in turn:

```
10 REM ********
20 REM *CHORD*
30 REM ********
40 MUSIC 1,4,1,0:REM
   *C*
50 MUSIC 2,3,8,0:REM
   *G*
60 MUSIC 3,3,5,0:REM
   *E*
70 FOR E = 1TO7:REM
   *SELECT ENV*
80 PLAY 7,0,E,750:REM
   *PLAY CHORD*
90 PLAY 0,0,0,0:REM
   *STOP CHORD*
100 WAIT 50:REM
   *PAUSE*
110 NEXT E:REM *NEXT
   ENV*
```

The Oric-1 is supplied with an extensive range of facilities, and among the more impressive of these are its sound capabilities. It has a range of seven octaves and standard features include three oscillators, a noise generator and seven preset envelopes (see page 260) that can be selected to shape the sounds produced. Sound out is via the built-in speaker.

The Oric-1's BASIC defines a set of sound commands — ZAP, PING, SHOOT and EXPLODE — that describe themselves very well. The following program shows how they are used, as well as demonstrating the useful WAIT command, which causes the computer to pause for the time stated in hundredths of a second (in this case two seconds):

```
10 ZAP:WAIT 200
20 EXPLODE
30 GOTO 10
```

The SOUND command is best used for your own special effects, and is constructed like this:

SOUND C,P,V

where C=Channel or oscillator number (1–6); P=Pitch (10–5000); and V=Volume (0–15). Channel, set at 1, 2 or 3, selects any one of the three oscillators (4, 5 or 6 are equivalent but select noise as well). Pitch is a little inaccurate, but 10 is the highest note (at approximately 10KHz), and 5000 the lowest (at 100Hz). Volume is highest at

15, but 6 is a comfortable level. If V is set at 0, control is taken by a volume envelope selected by the PLAY command.

The biggest drawback to the SOUND command is that there is no way to set a note duration. This also means that SOUND cannot turn itself off! The only way to stop a note sounding is by using the PLAY command and then stopping PLAY by specifying all zeros.

The MUSIC command is ideal for specifying notes accurately. Its simple construction makes it easy to understand a quite complex music program. The format is as follows:

MUSIC C,O,N,V

where C= Channel (1, 2 or 3); O= Octave (0-6); N= Note (1-12); and V= Volume (0-15). This command works in a similar way to SOUND. Channel selects oscillators 1, 2 or 3 (although noise cannot be set in MUSIC) and Volume ranges from 0 (where control is taken by the PLAY command) to 15. Octave allows the selection of a specific octave in which the note (N) will be part of the commands, played. Octave set at 0 gives the lowest notes starting at 32.7Hz. Octave 6 extends to 3951.07KHz. For the note (N) part of the command, the numbers 1 to 12 correspond to the standard musical notes in this way:

1	2	3	4	5	6
C	C#	D	D#	E	F

7	8	9	10	11	12
F#	G	G#	A	A#	B

Light Show

The Spectrum's graphics, though limited, are easy to use

The Spectrum makes an excellent starting point for those who are interested in high resolution graphics and colour. The simplicity of use makes graphics design easily accessible, even for those with limited programming experience.

The normal upper and lower case character sets are available, together with several of Sinclair's

own characters. These may be PRINTed in any one of eight colours. Colours for the character, screen and border are set by the appropriately named INK, PAPER and BORDER commands. In addition to the standard character set, up to 21 graphics characters can be defined by the user.

The screen display consists of 24 rows of 32 character spaces. The bottom two rows are, however, reserved for messages from the computer or for keyboard entries. This means that the useable screen is 22 × 32 characters. In high resolution, this converts to 176 × 256 pixels. One extremely useful feature of the Spectrum is that it has the ability to mix high resolution displays with text on the screen, allowing the creation of labelled diagrams, bar charts and so on. Once a screen display has been designed it is then possible to SAVE the display onto tape to be reloaded when required. The SCREEN$ command is responsible for this and can also be used to transfer the contents of the screen to a printer.

Low resolution output may be positioned on the screen using the PRINT AT command, which

To play note A at 440Hz on channel 1 at a volume of 6, the command would be:

MUSIC 1,3,10,6

However, to achieve the full range of the Oric-1's capabilities, it is best to use MUSIC in conjunction with PLAY. The PLAY command is made up like this:

PLAY C,N,E,P

where C=Channel (0-7); N=Noise (0-7); E= Envelope (1-7); and P=Envelope Period (0-32767). Channel and Noise select more complex options than the previous commands, in the following ways:

Number	Channel	Noise
0	All Oscs. off	off
1	Osc. 1	+ Osc. 1
2	Osc. 2	+ Osc. 2
3	Oscs. 1 & 2	+ Oscs. 1 or 2
4	Osc. 3	+ Osc. 3
5	Oscs. 1 & 3	+ Oscs. 1 or 3
6	Oscs. 2 & 3	+ Oscs. 2 or 3
7	Oscs. 1, 2 & 3	+ Oscs. 1, 2 or 3

Previously defined MUSIC (or SOUND) commands with volume set at 0 can be PLAYed together, according to the channel number selected, to produce chords of up to three notes. The Noise

part of the command selects which oscillators, if any, are to have noise mixed with them. Envelope selects one of seven preset volume envelopes for the specified note or notes. These options are given in the Oric User Manual.

The only variable control over the Envelope is given by the Envelope Period part of the command. This allows the programmer to specify the full duration of an envelope (from 0 to 32767). This varies with each envelope, but as a guide an envelope of 5000 lasts approximately 2 seconds.

The Oric-1's sound commands are easy to use, and show that much thought has gone into providing sensible built-in facilities. The only other home computer that offers helpful BASIC and control over envelope is the BBC Micro, which goes a lot further in the ways it can create a sound. Even so, the low cost of the Oric-1 makes it marvellous value for anyone who wants to make computer music on a small budget.

SOUND
This little program uses SOUND to make a noise like a landing space ship:

```
10 REM **********
20 REM *LANDING*
30 REM **********
40 FOR P=10 TO 3000
   STEP 10
50 SOUND 2,P,6
60 PLAY 2,0,1,1
70 NEXT P
80 WAIT 75
90 PLAY 0,0,0,0
100 END
```

allows vertical as well as horizontal character positioning. There are a number of special effects available also. As well as the usual inverse display, characters can be FLASHing or BRIGHT. A further useful low resolution facility is the OVER command, which allows a second character to be merged with the original in any one character position. This is particularly effective when merging text and a high resolution display, as it is possible to write over diagrams without rubbing them out. This effect must, however, be used with some caution because whenever the INK colour is reset in a particular square the original display also changes to the new colour.

The screen display is governed by two areas of memory: one that displays the characters, and another that holds information about the attributes of any particular character position. The list of attributes includes such information as: the INK and PAPER colours, whether the character is FLASHing, and so on. These attributes are represented by a single byte and the state of any screen position can be interrogated from a BASIC program using the ATTR command.

High resolution displays are easily achieved on the Spectrum using BASIC commands. This is largely due to the fact that there is no separate high resolution screen, making it simple to mix graphics and text into a single display.

BASIC commands include:

PLOTx,y

This sets the pixel with co-ordinates (x,y) to the current INK colour.

DRAWx,y,p

As the name suggests, DRAW creates a line between the current cursor position and a point specified by the command co-ordinates relative to the current cursor position. If a third number is added then the line changes to a circular arc. This number is normally a fraction of PI (3.14159...). Making the number PI would cause a semicircle to be drawn; PI/2 would cause a shallower arc to be drawn. Arcs can bend to either side of the straight line between the points by making the third number positive or negative.

CIRCLEx,y,r

The CIRCLE command causes a circle, with centre (x,y) and radius r, to be drawn. With most CIRCLE commands in BASIC it is possible to squash the circular shape to form ellipses, but unfortunately the Spectrum does not provide this facility.

There is one main drawback to using colour in high resolution displays. As a consequence of being able to mix text and graphics, only one INK colour may be specified within any one square of eight by eight pixels. Thus, if two lines of different colours cross then, inside the character square where they meet, all set pixels will take on the last INK colour.

Smile Please
This program demonstrates the use of the high resolution commands PLOT, CIRCLE, and DRAW to create a 'smiley' face.

```
10 REM * SMILEY FACE *
20 CLS
30 BORDER 6
40 PAPER 6
50 INK 2
60 CIRCLE 122,88,50
70 CIRCLE 97,108,5
80 CIRCLE 147,108,5
90 PLOT 92,68
100 DRAW 60,0,PI/3
110 STOP
```

Sounds Incredible

The BBC Model B's ENVELOPE command gives almost unlimited control

In an earlier part of the chapter, the format of the BBC Micro's SOUND command was discussed. However, it is only when it is used in conjunction with the versatile ENVELOPE command that the sound capabilities of the BBC are fully explored. ENVELOPE enables the user to shape up to four sounds to the extent that quite passable emulations of conventional instruments can be programmed. In addition, sound effects for games can be refined to sound much more like the explosions or gunfire that they represent.

ENVELOPE is constructed as follows:

ENVELOPE N,T,PS1,PS2,PS3,NS1,NS2,NS3,
AR,DR,SR,RR,FAL,FDL

The first parameter, N, sets the envelope number and serves to identify the envelope to the related SOUND or SOUND & commands. One of up to four envelopes can be substituted for the fixed volume (V) set with a negative number (0 to −15, see page 268) by SOUND.

T (0 to 127) & (128 to 255)

This is the master timing control for the command. It sets the duration of each 'step' in the construction of the envelope in hundredths of a second. Therefore, T=5 means that each envelope step lasts for five hundredths of a second (0.05 seconds). By adding 128 to the step duration

required, the auto-repeat of the pitch envelope will be suppressed, so that T set to 5 + 128 = 133 gives a step duration of five hundredths of a second in a pitch envelope that occurs once within the note.

Pitch Envelope

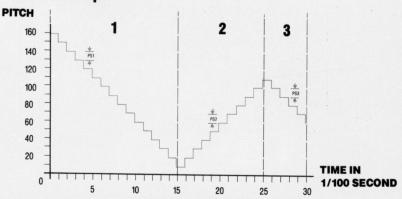

The use of the term 'pitch envelope' may seem a little confusing as envelope has previously been used in terms of volume, but in this case it refers to the variation of pitch over the duration of a note. This facility has little value in musical terms unless a 'vibrato' is required, but it can be useful to give sound effects interesting 'warbles'. As shown in the diagram, the pitch envelope is divided into three sections. The response of each section can be set by the associated PS and NS number as follows:

Light Relief

Using sprites on the Commodore 64

One of the most exciting features of the Commodore 64 is its ability to use sprites. Sprites are built up in the same way as a user-defined graphic character, but are much larger, consisting of 21 rows of 24 pixels. Sprites are not displayed in the normal character screen matrix and this allows them to be moved a single pixel at a time, rather

than requiring eight pixels to move a character from one cell to the next. Up to eight sprites can be displayed at any one time on the screen and each sprite has the following individually programmable characteristics:

Shape And Colour

A sprite is defined in much the same way as an eight by eight pixel character, but 63 bytes are needed to hold the patterns encoded in binary form. Once the shape has been defined in this way, it is held in a block of 63 consecutive locations. Each sprite has a data pointer that points to the area from which the sprite derives its shape. This means that more than one sprite can 'look' at the same area of memory; i.e. sprites can be identical. Also, a sprite can change its shape by switching its pointer to look at a different area of memory.

Each sprite may be coloured in any one of the 16 colours given. Sprites can also be multi-coloured with the usual penalty of halving horizontal resolution.

Size And Movement

Sprites can be expanded horizontally or vertically, or in both directions, to double the original size. A fully expanded sprite is 42 × 48 pixels. Again there

PS1, PS2 & PS3 (−128 to 127)

PS refers to Pitch Step. At the start of the associated note, pitch is set by the SOUND command. PS1 sets the positive or negative change of pitch per step in the first section, PS2 for the second section, and PS3 for the third section. In a similar manner to SOUND, PS is set in quarter semitones.

NS1, NS2 & NS3 (0 to 255)

NS refers to Number of Steps per section; and in conjunction with PS selects the rate at which pitch changes in a section and also the duration of the whole pitch envelope. The PS and NS values for the above example are as follows:

```
T=1   PS1 = −10   NS1 = 15
      PS2 = +10   NS2 = 10
      PS3 = −10   NS3 = 5
```

In this case, pitch is set by SOUND = 160. This results in:

ENVELOPE 1,1,−10,10,−10,15,10,5,0,0,0,0,0,0

The duration of the envelope is given as (NS1+NS2+NS3)×T, which in this case is (15+10+5)×1 = 0.3 seconds. Normally, the pitch envelope will automatically repeat over the duration of a note unless disabled by the timing parameter, T.

On page 276 of the Sound And Light chapter we will return to the sound features of the BBC Microcomputer and explain the operation of the volume envelope.

is a price to be paid, in that resolution is halved in the direction of expansion.

A sprite can move one pixel at a time and the old position is automatically erased. Sprites can also move in and out of the normal viewing area of the screen.

Priority And Collision

When two sprites cross each other's path, one appears to pass in front of the other. If there are any holes in the sprite that is passing in front, the sprite behind will show through. Priority can be used to achieve some interesting three-dimensional effects. Each sprite is given a number from 0 to 7 and the simple rule governing priority is that lower-numbered sprites appear to move in front of higher-numbered ones. Usually, sprites appear to move in front of any normal characters on the screen, but they can be programmed to move behind as well. Again this feature can be used to give the impression of depth on the screen.

When two sprites cross each other this is signalled in a collision register. PEEKing this register can give the programmer details of which sprites have been involved. There is another similar register that signals when a sprite has been in collision with any background characters.

As a consequence of the availability of these features, writing programs to control fast-moving games in BASIC is now possible. Unfortunately, there are no special BASIC commands to control sprite features; everything has to be done by a succession of POKEs into the Commodore 64's memory. An alternative and easier method of creating sprites is to invest in a Simon's BASIC cartridge.

Simon's Basic

For approximately £50, it is possible to purchase a plug-in cartridge to extend the high resolution and sprite handling capabilities available to the BASIC programmer. The cartridge comes complete with a weighty manual detailing the 114 extra commands. These include commands to turn on high resolution mode, select background and foreground colours, and to draw circles, ellipses, rectangles and straight lines. Sprite handling instructions include: assistance with sprite design and creation, commands to switch sprites on and off, and ways of positioning them on the screen

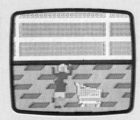

Step Two

These lines may be added to the Supermarket program listing given on page 269. This section of the program uses two expanded, multi-coloured sprites to make up the human figure and a further expanded sprite to make up the shopping trolley. The sprite data pointers are manipulated so that the woman changes shape. This gives the effect of the figure dancing as it crosses the screen. To use the supermarket program, as a subroutine in this program, change line 3270 to read: 3270 RETURN

```
90 REM ** SPRITES 64 **
100 PRINT""
110 V=53248
120 REM----READ SPRITE DATA----
130 FORI=12288TO12350:READA:POKEI,A:NEXT
140 FORI=12352TO12414:READA:POKEI,A:NEXT
150 FORI=832TO894:READA:POKEI,A:NEXT
160 FORI=896TO958:READA:POKEI,A:NEXT
170 FORI=12416TO12478:READA:POKEI,A:NEXT
180 REM----EXPAND SPRITES----
190 POKEV+23,7:POKEV+29,7
200 REM----COLOR SPRITES----
210 POKEV+39,10:POKEV+40,10
220 POKEV+41,1
230 REM--MULTI COLOR--
240 POKEV+28,3:POKEV+37,7:POKEV+38,9
300 REM----MEMORY POINTERS----
310 POKE2040,192:POKE2041,193:POKE2042,194
320 REM----SET Y COORDS----
330 Y0=150:Y1=Y0+42:Y2=Y0+34
340 POKEV+1,Y0:POKEV+3,Y1:POKEV+5,Y2
400 REM----TURN ON SPRITES----
410 POKEV+21,7
500 GOSUB3000:REM OMIT IF NO SUBROUTINE
1000 X0=20
1010 POKE2040,13:POKE2041,14
1020 POKEV,X0:POKEV+2,X0:POKEV+4,X0+48
1030 FORI=1TO500:NEXT
1040 POKE2040,192:POKE2041,193
1050 X0=X0+5
1060 POKEV,X0:POKEV+2,X0:POKEV+4,X0+48
1070 FORI=1TO500:NEXT
1080 X0=X0+5
1090 IFX0>200THEN1110
1100 GOTO1010
1110 FORJ=1TO10
1120 POKE2040,13:POKE2041,14
1130 FORI=1TO50:NEXT
1140 POKE2040,192:POKE2041,193
1150 FORI=1TO50:NEXT
1160 NEXT
1170 GOTO1170
9000 REM----DATA WOMAN TOP----
9010 DATA0,0,0,0,21,0,0,21,0,0,22,0,0,86,0
9020 DATA0,86,0,0,86,0,0,40,0,0,252,0
9030 DATA15,255,0,255,255,0,255,255,0
9040 DATA195,255,0,195,255,0,195,243,254
9050 DATA207,243,254
9060 DATA143,240,0,143,252,0,15,252,0
9070 DATA15,252,0,15,252,0
9100 REM----DATA WOMAN BOTTOM----
9110 DATA15,252,0,15,252,0,15,252,0
9120 DATA15,252,0,5,84,0,5,84,0,5,84,0
9130 DATA5,84,0,10,40,0,234,40,0,234,40,0
9140 DATA234,40,0,192,40,0,63,40,0,63,40,0
9150 DATA0,40,0,0,63,0,0,63,0,0,0,0,0,0,0
9160 DATA0,0,0
9200 REM----DATA WOMAN TOP #2----
9210 DATA0,0,0,20,32,32,85,32,32,105,48,48,105,48
9220 DATA48,105,48,48,105,48,48,40,48,48,252,48
9230 DATA63,255,240,63,255,240,63,255,0
9240 DATA3,255,0,3,255,0,3,240,0
9250 DATA15,240,0
9260 DATA15,240,0,15,252,0,15,252,0
9270 DATA15,252,0,15,252,0
9300 REM----DATA WOMAN BOTTOM #2----
9310 DATA15,252,0,15,252,0,15,252,0
9320 DATA15,252,0,5,84,0,5,84,0,5,84,0
9330 DATA5,84,0,10,40,0,58,168,0,58,168,0
9340 DATA58,0,0,58,0,0,10,0,0,10,0,0
9350 DATA10,0,0,15,192,0,15,192,0,0,0,0,0,0,0
9360 DATA0,0,0
9400 REM----TROLLEY DATA----
9410 DATA192,0,0,224,0,0,118,0
9420 DATA0,55,192,0,32,60,0,53
9430 DATA87,240,32,0,15,53,85,85
9440 DATA32,0,3,53,85,85,0,0,3
9450 DATA21,85,85,31,255,255,24,0
9460 DATA0,12,0,0,12,0,0,31,255
9470 DATA240,31,255,255,1,0,2,7
9480 DATA0,14,7,0,14
```

Sound Ideas

Continuing our look at the BBC Micro's sophisticated ENVELOPE command

In the previous two pages of the Sound And Light chapter we introduced the BBC Micro's ENVELOPE command. This is one of the most powerful commands available to the BASIC programmer when used with the SOUND command, discussed on page 268. We now continue our explanation of ENVELOPE by looking at 'volume envelope'.

In the following line of programming parameters, N to NS3 are concerned with the pitch envelope, and these were dealt with on page 274.

ENVELOPE N,T,PS1,PS2,PS3,NS1,NS2,NS3,AR,DR, SR, RR,FAL,FDL

The remaining parameters are all concerned with the volume envelope, between them setting peak volumes and rate of change of volume over the duration of the note set by the associated SOUND command.

AR & DR (−127 to 127) + FAL & FDL (0 to 126)

AR sets the Attack Rate of the note. Although the software allows a negative value, in practical terms the range is 1 to 127. This relates to the number of volume changes per time step and continues to rise until the Final Attack Level (FAL) of volume is reached, which indicates the beginning of the decay phase. Decay Rate is controlled in a similar manner by DR, usually a negative value, causing volume to fall until it reaches the Final Decay Level (FDL). Although software allows a range of 0 to 126 for final volume levels, current hardware only allows 0 to 16, so a FAL value of 50 would be automatically scaled down and rounded off to a volume of 6.

SR & RR (−127 to 0)

The Sustain Rate (SR) and Release Rate (RR) also refer to volume changes per time step although both must take negative values. Sustain continues until the duration set by the SOUND command is complete. This means that if the Attack time and Decay time together are greater than or equal to the set Duration time, there will be no Sustain

Light Waves

Atari's graphics set a trend that other manufacturers have followed

The Atari 400 and 800 home computers are well known for their plug-in cartridge systems, but the machines themselves also have fairly sophisticated graphics facilities available in BASIC. These facilities, common to both machines, support nine levels of screen display — three text modes (offering different character sizes) and six graphics modes. The maximum resolution obtainable is 320 x 192 dots.

There are 16 colours to choose from on the Atari computers, but the maximum number that can be displayed at any one time is five. The standard ASCII upper and lower character sets are available, as well as 37 special Atari graphics characters. These characters may be used in PRINT statements to build up low resolution displays and tables. The Ataris also allow cursor movement to be controlled from a BASIC program. This is done using cursor control characters within PRINT statements to position the text that follows on the screen. The cursor control characters allow up/down or backwards/forwards movement of the cursor.

One of the most attractive features of the Ataris is their ability to use sprite-style graphics, known as 'Player-Missile' (PM) graphics, which allow the user to write fast-moving arcade games in BASIC. There are, however, no special BASIC commands to use PM graphics, and all the necessary work has to be done by manipulating the memory locations in RAM, using PEEK and POKE. Player-Missile graphics will be discussed in more detail later (see page 280).

Display Modes

Modes 0, 1 and 2 are for text display. When the machine is switched on, the display is set to mode 0 and the screen is formatted into 24 rows, each containing 40 character spaces. In this mode the display characters are based on the standard eight by eight ASCII format. Characters PRINTed in mode 1 are twice the width of mode 0 characters, but are still the same height; whilst mode 2 characters are twice the height and width of those in mode 0.

With the exception of mode 0, all graphics modes have a split screen, the bottom few lines being reserved for miscellaneous data such as error messages. To PRINT to the main body of the screen in modes 1 and 2, a device number must be specified. PRINT #6 allows text to be PRINTed to the phase, even if it has been programmed in. Release begins when Duration is complete. Volume falls to zero at the set rate unless a new note is started on the same oscillator, which means that Release is cut off unless 'H' has been set to '1' by means of a new SOUND & command.

Volume Envelope

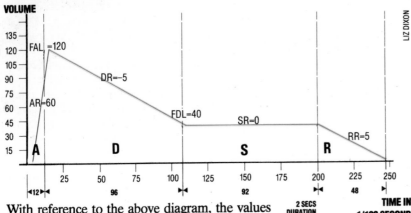

With reference to the above diagram, the values required to give the piano-like envelope would be as follows:

T=6	AR=60	SR=0	FAL=120
	DR=–5	RR=–5	FDL=40

SOUND duration =40 (two seconds)

Resulting in:

ENVELOPE 1,6,0,0,0,0,0,0,60,–5,0,–5,120,40

The following program employs all the sound associated BBC BASIC commands to play a well known sequence of notes with the piano volume envelope, and a short triangular repeated pitch envelope on the final chord.

```
10 REM**COSMIC**
20 ENVELOPE 1,6,0,0,0,0,0,0,60,–5,0,–5,120,40
30 ENVELOPE 2,6,1,–1,1,1,2,1,60,–5,0,–5,120,40
40 FOR I=1TO4:READ N
50 SOUND 1,1,N,20:REM**PLAY A B G G**
60 SOUND &1001,0,0,5:NEXT I
70 SOUND &201,2,77,40:REM**FINAL**
80 SOUND &202,2,89,40:REM**D MAJOR**
90 SOUND &203,2,109,40:REM**CHORD**
100 DATA 137,145,129,85:REM**A B G G**
```

graphics part of the screen. Modes 3 to 8 are graphics modes and allow points and lines to be plotted on the screen with varying degrees of resolution and a choice of colours. This table shows the complete range of options available to the user:

MODE	TYPE	ROWS	COLS	COLOURS
0	text	24	40	2
1	text	20	20	5
2	text	10	20	5
3	graphics	20	40	4
4	graphics	40	80	2
5	graphics	40	80	4
6	graphics	80	160	2
7	graphics	80	160	4
8	graphics	160	320	1

The choice of mode will depend on how much memory there is available for screen display. Mode 5, for example, requires almost twice as much memory to support four colours as mode 4 needs to support two.

Basic Commands

There are a number of commands in Atari BASIC to help with graphics. These commands also work in modified form in the three text modes.

SETCOLOR a,b,c

There are five colour registers to control the use of colour on the screen, but not all of them are used in every mode. SETCOLOR is used to select the colours used by these five registers. In this command a is the colour register number, 0-4; b is the colour number to be used, 0-15; and c enables each colour to be displayed in one of eight levels of brightness, by choosing an even number between 0 and 14.

COLOR n

This command works in two ways, depending on whether a text or a graphics mode has been selected. In modes 0, 1, and 2, n is a number in the range 0 to 255. In its binary form this number is made up of eight bits: the first six bits relate to the ASCII code of the character being PLOTted, and the other two bits are reserved for the colour information about the character.

In the graphics modes, n takes on a value between 0 and 3, and is used to select a particular colour control register when PLOTting a point.

PLOT x,y

The origin of the Atari screen is placed in the top left-hand corner of the screen. PLOT illuminates the graphics point with co-ordinates (x,y). Similarly, the POSITION command:

POSITION x,y

places an invisible cursor at the point (x,y) on the screen.

DRAWTO x,y

draws a straight (or as straight as is possible in the lower resolution modes) line from the old cursor position to the point (x,y). Finally the line:

X10 18,#6,0,0,"S:"

employs the Atari input/output command X10, which allows the user to fill or paint a shape drawn on the screen. It is rather complicated, but can produce some good results if used carefully. Once a closed shape has been drawn on the screen, then the cursor should be set to the bottom left-hand corner of the area that is to be coloured in. The colouring will start from the top of the shape and will fill it in, between the boundaries, until the cursor position is reached at the bottom. The colour is set by POKE 765,C where C is 1, 2, or 3, as used in the COLOR command.

XL Size

Atari graphics can be quite interesting but are not particularly easy to use. Limited colour choice and the lack of many of the 'standard' high resolution commands, such as CIRCLE, mean that the programmer has to work fairly hard to achieve good results. Atari does have the advantage, however, of a large range of text modes. The following program demonstrates the use of double size characters, in conjunction with the POSITION command, to PRINT a message on the screen:

```
10 REM* BIG LETTERS *
20 GRAPHICS 2+16
30 SETCOLOR0,3,6
40 FOR X=19TO8 STEP-1
50 POSITION X,1
60 FOR J=1TO100: NEXT J
70 PRINT#6; "HOME "
80 NEXT X
90 FOR X=19TO6 STEP-1
100 POSITION X,3
100 FOR J=1TO100: NEXT J
120 PRINT#6;
      "COMPUTER "
130 NEXT X
140 FOR X=13TO7 STEP-1
150 POSITION X,9
160 FOR J=1TO100: NEXTJ
170 PRINT#6; "COURSE "
180 NEXT X
190 SETCOLOR 0,5,5
200 FOR Y=9TO5 STEP-1
210 POSITION 7,Y
220 PRINT#6; "COURSE "
230 NEXT Y
240 GOTO240
```

Note that when a mode is selected, the split screen effect can be overridden by adding 16 to the mode number

Sound Principles

The sound functions of the Atari models include four independent voices

The Atari sound facilities are good — as can be heard in many of the cartridge games — though the means of controlling them are a little idiosyncratic. Four independent square wave oscillators are provided, each with a range of three octaves. As a bonus, the oscillator output can be distorted in seven ways to colour the sound. These facilities are easily accessible from BASIC via the SOUND command provided, but this doesn't make full use of the extra features of the Atari sound chip POKEY, which with high-pass filters and special modes of operation can extensively modify the sound produced. As a consequence, the full range of sound control can be fully exploited only by using complex POKEs or machine code, which is beyond the scope of this part of the book. Output is via the television speaker only.

SOUND

This is a very simple command with the following format:

```
SOUND O,P,D,V
```

O = Oscillator (0-3)
P = Pitch (0-255)
D = Distortion (even numbers 0-14)
V = Volume (1-15)

Each SOUND command can select only one oscillator, so it is impossible to start more than one oscillator at a time. This is not normally a problem, but if music is programmed using all oscillators for four-part harmonies the delay is noticeable.

Pitch is calculated a little strangely and as a consequence some frequencies are inaccurate. Frequency decreases as the pitch number increases, giving an effective range from 'C' at 29 (1046.5Hz) to 'C' at 243 (130.81Hz). The following table indicates some of the pitch numbers for music note symbols. A full list is given in the Atari BASIC reference manual.

Octave-1	Octave-3
(Mid) C — 121	C — 29
B — 128	B — 31
A — 144	A — 35
G — 162	G — 40
F — 182	F — 45
E — 193	E — 47
D — 217	D — 53
C — 243	C — 60

The distortion parameter 'P' is equivalent to the noise channel on most computers but it is far more versatile. Each even number causes a different arrangement of random pulses to be mixed with the standard oscillator output. Curiously, 10 gives

Light Refreshment

A quick look at the Oric's graphics shows many similarities with the Spectrum

The Oric-1 home computer was released in the middle of 1983 and is designed as an obvious rival to Sinclair's ZX Spectrum. The Oric offers four modes of display. Only one mode, however, enables the use of high resolution graphics. There are eight colours available; foreground and background colours respectively being set by the commands INK and PAPER. Oric BASIC includes several special high resolution commands to aid the graphics programmer.

The screen is made up of 28 lines, each containing 40 character spaces. The Oric's characters are not designed using the usual eight by eight pixel grid, but are constructed on an eight by six grid. In high resolution mode the screen has 240×200 pixel resolution, the bottom three lines being reserved for information such as error messages. There is no PAINT-type command, but with a little thought it is possible to accomplish the function using the FILL command. As with the Spectrum (see page 272) it is possible to mix high resolution graphics and text together on the same screen, but the Oric allows each line inside a character square to be coloured individually, whereas the Spectrum allows only one colour to be specified within any one character square.

Now let us look in more detail at the low resolution modes offered by the Oric-1. The Oric has three low resolution modes: TEXT, LORES0, and LORES1. The only difference between LORES0 and LORES1 is that they use different character sets. In the TEXT mode, letters can be positioned horizontally by the TAB command. In the two LORES modes, however, this facility is improved to a distortion-free signal, not 0, as might be expected. With experimentation the careful use of distorted sounds can provide interesting tones and is particularly useful for special effects.

Volume 'V' can be set between 1 and 15 and a reasonable average level would be 7 or 8. Note that there is no convenient way of timing the duration of notes or the pauses between them. The usual method under these circumstances is to use carefully timed FOR...TO...NEXT loops.

To illustrate the use of SOUND, the following commands play an undistorted 'G' in octave 3 on oscillator 1 at a volume of 8 for 50 FOR...TO...NEXT steps:

```
10 SOUND 1,40,10,8
20 FOR N=1TO50:NEXT N
30 END
```

The END in line 30 turns all oscillators off. Alternatively, a new SOUND command for the same oscillator stops the old note and immediately plays the new one. A program to play a simple tune could be constructed like this:

```
10 REM*DIXIE*
20 FOR I=1TO7
30 READ N:REM*NOTE*
40 SOUND 3,N,10,7:REM*PLAY NOTE*
50 FOR P=1TO400:NEXT P:REM*PAUSE*
60 NEXT I
70 DATA 219,162,128,144
80 DATA 162,193,162
90 END
```

It is possible to access the sound capabilities of the Atari's POKEY chip from BASIC by POKEing numbers into memory locations 53760 to 53763. With this method, sound routines run faster and all oscillators can be started at one time. All information necessary to accomplish this, plus more adventurous machine code techniques, are contained in *De Re Atari*, available from the Atari Program Exchange (APX), and also the excellent *Atari Sound And Graphics,* published by John Wiley & Son.

allow the user to specify vertical as well as horizontal positions using the PLOTx,y,A$ command, where x and y are the co-ordinates of a particular character position and A$ is the word or phrase to be PRINTed. The following short program demonstrates how this facility may be used to write a name vertically.

```
10 REM VERTICAL LETTERS
20 CLS
30 LORES0
40 A$="STEVE"
50 FOR X=1TO5
60 B$=MID$(A$,X,1)
70 PLOT16,11+X,B$
80 NEXT X
90 END
```

The command HIRES allows the user to enter the Oric's high resolution mode. In HIRES mode the screen has its origin in the top left-hand corner of the screen.

There are several commands in Oric BASIC to help specifically with graphics: CURSETx,y,k positions the cursor at the point with co-ordinates (x,y). The third number 'k' allows different functions to be employed with CURSET.

Value Of k	Function
0	plots pixel in background colour
1	plots pixel in foreground colour
2	inverts colours
3	does nothing

CURMOVx,y,k is similar to CURSET, except that the cursor movement is relative to its previous position. DRAWx,y,k draws a straight line from the current cursor position to a point x units across and y units up. CIRCLEr,k is a command that will draw a circle of radius 'r' on the screen. PATTERNn is an unusual and interesting command. PATTERN breaks up lines or circles drawn into a series of dots or dashes. The exact pattern is defined by the number 'n', which lies in the range 0 to 255. The Oric takes this number and uses the bit pattern of its binary equivalent to produce a repeating pattern of dots, dashes or spaces. Here are two examples to illustrate its use:

Value Of n	Binary Equivalent	Pattern Produced
170	10101010	- - - - - - - -
15	00001111	— —

Finally, there is the command FILLa,b,n. Each row of every character space on the Oric screen has a number associated with it that relates to the foreground and background colours, the character present and whether the character is flashing or not. This number is known as the 'attribute' of that row. FILLa,b,n fills 'b' character cells by 'a' rows with the attributes represented by the number 'n'.

```
10 REM CONE
20 HIRES
30 CURSET120,0,3
40 PAPER3 : INK4
50 FOR R=1TO65
60 PATTERN 200-R
70 CURMOV0,2,3
80 CIRCLE R,1
90 NEXT R
100 END
```

Cone PATTERN
This program demonstrates some of the high resolution capabilities of the Oric-1. A cone shape is drawn using a set of circles of increasing radius. Note also the use of the PATTERN command to break up the circumference of the circles as they are drawn

Sounds Ideal

The Commodore 64's Basic doesn't match up to its remarkable sound facilities

Among the current range of home computers, the Commodore 64 is supplied with the most sophisticated sound-making facilities. These are attributable to a specialised chip called the Sound Interface Device — or SID, as it is better known.

SID provides capabilities similar to that of a commercial monophonic synthesiser. There are three oscillators with an eight-octave range (0-3900Hz in 65,536 steps); a master volume control, from 0 to 15; four waveforms for each oscillator (triangle, sawtooth, variable pulse and noise); oscillator synchronisation; and envelope generators allowing ADSR control for each oscillator. Further features include: ring modulation; programmable filter with low pass, band pass, high pass, notch output (which blocks out a narrow band of frequencies) and variable resonance; envelope filtering; two analogue-to-digital potentiometer interfaces that can be used to control SID facilities; and an external audio input, which enables additional SID chips to be linked together. Other audio signals can be input, filtered and mixed with the standard SID outputs.

It would be impossible to detail the operation of each of these features here (several good books are available), but we can explain what all these phrases mean. First of all, oscillator synchronisation causes two signals (in this case two specified voices) to be harmonically locked together, making a single, more complex tone out of the two separate signals.

Modulation is the modification of one signal by another, affecting either the frequency or amplitude (volume) of the sound. Ring modulation is the amplitude modulation of one voice by another. This results in a tone that is clear but has a jarring, discordant effect and can be used to produce bell-like sounds similar to those of steel drums. Such sounds are said to have inharmonic overtones.

Filters enable specified frequency ranges to be eliminated from a signal. The different types of filtering possible on the Commodore 64 have effects that are suggested by their names: low pass filters cut out frequencies higher than a specified frequency; band pass filters eliminate frequencies above and below a specified 'band' of frequencies; notch filters are the inverse of band pass filters — they cut out a specified band; high pass filters cut

Guiding Light

Player-Missile graphics are one of the strong points of the Atari machines

Player-Missile Graphics

Player-Missile or 'PM' graphics form an important part of the Atari's graphics capabilities. They are similar in nature to the sprite graphics available on the Commodore 64 (see page 274) and the Sord M5, allowing the programmer to design and control up to eight different high resolution shapes. These movable shapes operate independently of any background display and may be programmed to move either in front of or behind any other shapes drawn on the screen. This allows the programmer to add a third dimension to the screen effects. PM graphics can be moved smoothly, at speed, across the screen and so are ideal for fast-moving arcade games. They can also be used to create more colourful static displays than are possible using the normal graphics modes, as PM objects can be coloured independently of each other and of the background display.

As with all sprite graphics, the secret of PM graphics' facilities lies in dedicated hardware. Special registers are designed to control the movement, colour and screen display of the PM objects. All the programmer has to do is place certain values in these registers to manipulate the objects. In BASIC this is done using the POKE command. Once a number is POKEd into the relevant register then the Atari's own hardware takes over the rest of the work. This is done at machine code speed and is therefore much faster than if the process was controlled from BASIC.

Let us now look at the creation of PM objects and the registers that control them. Players are designed from a vertical strip, eight pixels wide and 128 or 256 pixels high. Each row across the strip is represented as a single byte in the computer's memory. By POKEing suitable binary codes it is possible to define the shape of a player using a similar method to that used to create user-defined characters (see page 259). Up to four players may be defined in this way, each taking up

```
10 SID=54272
20 POKESID+23,0
30 POKESID+24,15
40 POKESID+5,40
50 POKESID+6,201
60 FOR N=1TO5
70 READ FH,FL,D
80 POKESID+1,FH:
   POKESID,FL:
   REM*PLAY
   NOTE*
90 POKESID+4,33
100 FORI=1TO300*
    D:NEXT I
110 POKESID+4,32
120 FORI=1TO100:
    NEXT I
130 NEXT N
140 FORI=1TO2000:
    NEXT I
150 POKESID+24,0
160 REM**FH FL D**
170 DATA 57,172,1
180 DATA 64,188,1
190 DATA 51,97,1
200 DATA 25,177,1
210 DATA 38,126,2
220 END
```

out frequencies lower than a specified one; and variable resonance can be applied to all the above filters to emphasise the frequencies around the cut-off points. Envelope filtering is a special case: it has a different effect from the others in that digitised ADSR values set for envelope 3 can be read from the SID chip and applied to a signal in such a way that the harmonic structure changes throughout the course of a note. It works like a variable filter.

These sophisticated features enable you to build highly complex sounds into interesting effects and convincing emulations of conventional instruments. The daunting aspect of SID is that CBM BASIC V2, the dialect supplied with the 64, provides no commands dedicated to sound at all. Control is exercised by PEEKing from and POKEing into the 29 SID control registers. A lot of BASIC code is therefore needed to generate even simple effects, and in some cases BASIC isn't fast enough to do full justice to the full range of SID's possibilities.

A full description of the SID control registers would require more space than this complete chapter of Choosing And Using Your Computers, but it is possible to play notes with pleasing tones as shown in the program on the left.

Although the program is 22 lines long, it plays merely five notes of a simple tune on one oscillator. Line 20 disconnects the filter from the oscillators; line 30 sets the master volume at its maximum; and lines 40 and 50 specify a piano-like envelope. Line 80 sets the note frequency; 90 and 100 start and stop the ADSR cycle and select a sawtooth wave for voice 1; and timing is achieved with FOR . . . NEXT loops in lines 100, 120 and 140.

Programming sound on the Commodore 64 in BASIC is a major effort in terms of both learning and writing code. Moreover, it can be a very frustrating exercise, as the only way to discover if a more complex set of BASIC statements will run in an acceptable time is by trial and error. If you want simpler methods of sound generation it is worth investigating the many sound editing programs that are commercially available. These are usually written in machine code and make the most of the marvellous features of the Commodore 64.

its own 256 or 128 bytes of memory.

Each of the four players has a missile figure associated with it that is two bits wide. To create players and missiles it is necessary to POKE the bit patterns that define their shape into a certain area of memory. The area of RAM used can be chosen by the programmer but the computer must be informed by setting a pointer to the beginning of the area.

If the programmer elects to use single-pixel vertical resolution then twice as much memory is required than for two-pixel vertical resolution. The following program designs player 0 in two-pixel vertical resolution as a space ship:

```
10 REM *** DEFINE A PLAYER ***
20 P=PEEK(106) -8:REM SETS P TO 2K BELOW
   TOP OF RAM
30 POKE 54279,P:REM SETS POINTER TO PM
   AREA
40 BASE = 256*P:REM SETS PM AREA BASE
   ADDRESS
50 FOR I = BASE+512 TO BASE+640
60 POKE I,0:REM CLEAR PLAYER 0 AREA
70 NEXT I
80 FOR I = BASE+512+50 TO BASE+530+50
90 READ A:POKE I,A:REM DEFINE FIGURE
100 NEXT I
110 DATA 16,16,16,56,40,56,40,56,40
120 DATA 56,56,186,186,146,186,254,186,146
```

Each player figure has several registers associated with it. These registers control colour, horizontal position and size. The last of these enables the

programmer to increase the width of a player by a factor of two or four. Further registers control player-to-background priority. Missiles take on the colour of their parent player but missile size can be changed independently. For games applications a series of registers is set aside to detect on-screen collisions between players, missiles and background. However, there is no vertical position register for missiles or players. Vertical movement must be achieved by moving the contents of each location that holds the bit patterns for the figure up through the area of memory set aside for that player. This is a fairly straightforward task in Assembly language but would be relatively slow in BASIC. It is a good idea to try to make characters that move vertically as short and stubby as possible.

Player-Missile graphics considerably extend the Atari's graphics potential, although they are not as versatile or as easy to use as the Commodore 64's sprites. Here is a continuation of the program started earlier, to colour the space ship and move it from left to right across the screen.

```
130 POKE 559,46:REM ENABLE PM 2 LINE
    DISPLAY
140 POKE 53277,3:REM ENABLE PM DISPLAY
150 POKE 704,88:REM COLOUR PLAYER 0 PINK
160 GRAPHICS 0
170 SETCOLOUR 2,8,2:REM SET BACKGROUND TO
    DARK BLUE
180 FOR I = 0 TO 320
190 POKE 53248,I:REM SET HORIZONTAL
    POSITION
200 NEXT I
210 END
```

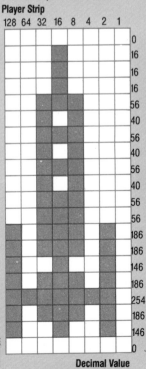

Rocket PM
Before a player object can be defined, it must first be drawn out and the decimal values for each row of pixels calculated

Player Strip

128	64	32	16	8	4	2	1		Decimal Value
									0
									16
									16
									16
									56
									40
									56
									40
									56
									40
									56
									56
									186
									186
									146
									186
									254
									186
									146
									0

LIZ DIXON

281

Glossary

A

Accumulator. A special memory location in the microprocessor that stores data temporarily while it is being processed.

Acoustic coupler. A device that connects a telephone handset to the computer and enables the latter to communicate over the telephone network. With its aid, a computer can communicate with other home computers, exchange messages with them and retrieve information stored in large computers.

Address. The number in an instruction that identifies the location of a 'cell' in a computer's memory. By means of its address, a particular memory location can be selected so that its contents can be examined or, in the case of RAM, both examined and altered.

Adventure game. A game in which the user plays one role while the computer takes other parts. Typically, it involves a series of rooms or caves to accumulate treasure while avoiding traps.

Algorithm. A set of logical steps that describe how a particular problem may be solved or how a task may be accomplished.

Alphanumeric. A character that is either a letter or a number.

ALU. Arithmetic Logic Unit. The part of a microprocessor that carries out arithmetical and logical operations.

Analogue. Describes the expression of a quantity in terms of continuous change rather than by numbered stages (contrast with *Digital*). For example, a mercury thermometer rises and falls continuously, and is thus an analogue device.

Analogue-to-digital converter. A device for converting analogue signals into a digital form that can be processed by a digital computer.

Animation. The creation with a computer of moving images for display on a screen.

Applications program. A program that instructs the computer to perform a specific task — as opposed, for example, to an *Operating system* program, which tells the computer *how* to do it.

Architecture. The arrangement and interconnection of the various parts of a microprocessor and computer system.

Array. An arrangement of rows and columns in which numbers can be stored for easy access by the computer.

Artificial intelligence. The ability of certain specially developed computer programs to 'learn' and incorporate their own 'experience' into their operation.

ASCII. American Standard Code for Information Interchange. A commonly used way of representing the numbers, letters and other symbols that can be entered from the computer's keyboard.

Assembly code. A programming language in which *Machine code* commands have particular names that suggest their purposes. An assembly code program must be translated into machine code (by an assembler) before it can be executed by a microprocessor.

B

Bar code. Information represented as a pattern of thick and thin printed lines. The information is fed into the computer through an intermediary device — either a *Light pen* or a bar code reader.

Base. Also known as *Radix*. The basis of any positional system of number representation. The binary system has base 2; the decimal system has base 10.

BASIC. Beginners' All-purpose Symbolic Instruction Code. The programming language used in almost all home computers, BASIC was specifically designed to be easy to learn and simple to use.

Baud. The unit for measuring the rate at which digital data are transmitted over a telegraph or telephone channel.

BCD. Binary Coded Decimal. A coding system for decimal numbers in which each digit is represented by a group of four binary digits.

Benchmark. A standard task that can be given to different computers to compare their speed, efficiency and accuracy.

Binary notation. The number system with base 2, in which all numbers are made up from the two binary digits 0 and 1. A typical four-digit number is 1001. In such a number, the digits are weighted according to their positions, with the least significant digit on the right and the most significant on the left. The weighting factor for the least significant digit is 1, and the weighting factor increases by a factor of 2 for each digit position to the left. In this way, the weighting factors are (from right to left) 1, 2, 4, 8 and so on for numbers having more digits. Thus, the binary number 1001 is equivalent to the decimal number given by: $(1x8) + (0x4) + (0x2) + (1x1)$ equals 9.

Binary number. A number represented in binary notation.

Bit. Contraction of **B**inary dig**it**. A binary digit is one of the two digits, represented by 0 and 1, that are used in the binary number system.

Booting or **Bootstrapping.** Using certain preliminary instructions to load a program into a computer.

Breakpoint. A point at which a program stops automatically to check that it is operating correctly.

Buffer. A temporary storage area to hold information during transfers from one part of the system to another, for example from the keyboard to the computer's central processing unit (CPU). A buffer can be used to regulate the way data are passed between devices operating at different speeds, such as a computer and a much slower printer, thus making more efficient use of each.

Bug. An error or fault in either a program or the computer itself.

Bus. A path or channel through which data and signals can be transferred.

Byte. A group of eight bits, which forms the smallest portion of memory that the CPU can recall from, or store in memory. Its contents can be any binary number from 00000000 to 11111111.

C

CAD. Computer Aided Design. The use of computers in design. They can help in a wide variety of projects, from the design of cars and electronic circuits to the creation of home interiors.

CAE. Computer-Aided Education. The use of the computer to help with education. CAI (Computer-Aided Instruction) and CAL (Computer-Aided Learning) are two aspects of CAE.

Cartridge. A specially packaged memory chip containing software which can be plugged directly into a special socket that appears on the computer.

Cassette. Ordinary audio cassettes are used to store programs and data for home computers.

Character. Any symbol that can be represented in a computer and displayed by it, including letters, numbers and graphics symbols.

Character block. The group of dots on a display screen by means of which a single character may be displayed by selective illumination of some of the dots.

Character set. The set of all the letters, numbers and symbols available on a computer.

Character string. A sequence of characters that can be stored or manipulated as a single unit, e.g. a word or collection of words.

Chip. The tiny slice of silicon on which an integrated electronic circuit is fabricated. The term is also used to refer to the integrated circuit itself.

Clock. The master electronic timer that produces a signal to time and synchronise all the activities of a computer.

Code. 1. The commands and instructions that go to make up a program. 2. Unique patterns of binary digits, representing characters or instructions, that can be stored in the computer's memory.

Command. Any programming instruction that is expressed in a computer language.

Compiler. A program that converts complete programs written in a language like BASIC (which we can understand) into a language called *Machine code* (which devices inside the computer can understand).

Computer generations. The past technological and historical development of computer hardware is described in terms of four different stages or 'generations'. First generation computers used valves, the second generation used individual transistors, the third generation uses integrated circuits and the fourth generation uses **L**arge **S**cale **I**ntegration (LSI) circuits. (See *Fifth generation*.)

Computer literacy. Being aware of computers: what they are, how they work and what they do.

CP/M. **C**ontrol **P**rogram for **M**icroprocessors. A standard *Operating system* found on many microcomputers.

CPU. **C**entral **P**rocessing **U**nit. The component at the heart of any computer system that interprets instructions to the computer and causes them to be obeyed.

Cursor. A movable marker, usually a flashing square, indicating where the next character is to appear on the screen.

Cursor control keys. Keys that move the *Cursor* around the screen.

D

Daisy-wheel printer. A printer that can produce high quality or 'typewriter quality' documents. Its characters are created by the impact of letters positioned at the end of a series of 'petals' arranged in a circle.

Database. A collection of data stored in a systematic way so that it is simple to retrieve or update any item or items.

Data Capture. The term which describes the collection of data from any outside sources that are linked in some way to a central computer.

Debugging. Correcting the errors (bugs) in a program or in the computer itself.

Decimal notation. The familiar number system with base 10, using the digits 0 to 9, representing numbers of units, tens, hundreds, thousands and so on.

Diagnostic. A message automatically produced by a computer to indicate and identify an error in a program.

Digital. Describes the expression of a changing quantity in terms of discrete steps rather than by a continuous process (contrast with *Analogue*).

Digitiser. See *Graphics tablet*.

Disk. A flat, circular piece of plastic coated on one or both sides with a magnetisable surface and used as a medium for storing data. The disk is housed at all times in a square protective envelope or plastic box. See *Floppy disk* and *Winchester*.

Disk drive. The unit that records information on the magnetisable surface of a spinning disk and 'reads' (recovers) information recorded on it.

Documentation. The manuals that are supplied with computers or software to explain how they are operated.

Download. The transfer of information from one computer to another.

DOS. **D**isk **O**perating **S**ystem. The software that controls all the operations of a disk drive.

Dot matrix. A rectangular array of dots, commonly eight rows of eight dots, on which a character can be displayed by the selection of certain of the dots.

E

Editing. Correcting or making changes to data, a program or text.

EPROM. **E**rasable **P**rogrammable **R**ead-**O**nly **Me**mory. Similar to the PROM, except that the memory contained in the chip can be erased using ultra-violet light and new programming recorded.

Expert system. A system that stores facts about a particular subject according to the rules laid down by human experts. The system is capable of answering questions on its subject to the level of human expertise.

Expression. A simple or complex formula used within a program to perform a calculation on some data.

F

Fifth generation computers. The next *Computer generation*. These machines will use **V**ery **L**arge **S**cale **I**ntegration (VLSI) circuits and will be much easier to operate than present day computers. They will provide input devices less cumbersome and more direct than the keyboard (for example some will be able to recognise speech), and run software that incorporates developments from artificial intelligence. See *LSI*.

File. A collection of information stored outside the computer on cassette or disk.

Firmware. Software stored on a chip; for example, a program stored in ROM.

Fixed-point number. A number represented, manipulated and stored with the radix point in a specified, consistent position. (The radix point or 'decimal point', separates the digits that represent a whole number (integer) from those representing a fraction.)

Floating-point number. A number represented, manipulated and stored with a movable radix point (see *Fixed-point number*). The method is particularly useful when dealing with large numbers.

Floppy disk. A flexible *Disk*, usually 5¼ inches in diameter, that is used to store computer data in recorded magnetic form. Housed inside a protective square envelope, it offers less storage and is less reliable than the more expensive *Winchester* (hard) disk.

Flowchart. A diagram representing the steps of a computer program and thus the progress of a sequence of events.

Forth. A programming language intermediate between a *High-level language* and *Machine code*. By comparison with BASIC it is difficult to learn, but programs run much faster.

G

Gate. One of the most elementary building blocks from which computers are constructed. The gate performs a single logical operation on several inputs to produce one output. For example, it may give an output when, and only when, all the inputs are activated; or it may do so when, and only when, none of them is activated.

Graphics. The generation and display of pictures and images by a computer. The images are usually displayed on the computer's screen, although a permanent 'hard' copy can be obtained by using a special graphic printer attached to the computer.

Graphics character. A shape or pattern specially designed to be useful in creating images. Some computers provide them, and on others they can be created.

Graphics mode. The mode to which some computers must be set to display graphics (rather than text). When there is more than one graphics mode available, they will offer varying degrees of picture clarity.

Graphics tablet. Also known as a Digitiser. A device with which pictures can be turned into a sequence of digits and put into a computer.

H

Handshaking. A sequence of electronic signals which allows and synchronises the exchange of data between a computer and a peripheral, or between two computers.

Hard copy. Paper printout of a program listing or other text or a graphics display.

Hardware. The electronic and mechanical parts of a computer system.

Heuristic. A trial and error method of getting closer to the solution of a problem. It does not guarantee to provide the solution, but it may speed up the process of finding one.

Hexadecimal notation. The number system that employs 16 digits represented by 0 to 9 and A, B, C, D, E and F. In each number the places or 'columns' have weighting factors of 1, 16, 16^2, etc. In this system the three-digit hexadecimal number 23A is equivalent to: $(2 \times 16^2) + (3 \times 16) + (10 \times 1)$, which equals 570. Similarly, B4D represents $(11 \times 16^2) + (4 \times 16) + (13 \times 1)$, which is 2893.

High-level language. A 'user-orientated' language like BASIC, which programmers can easily understand and learn. A device called a *Compiler* translates this into *Machine code*, which the computer can understand.

I

Icon. A visual representation on a TV screen of the action that a piece of software can carry out — for instance, a jar of money for a budgeting program.

IEEE-488. One of the standard *Interfaces* for connecting devices to a microcomputer.

Information. The meaning that is conveyed by, and can be extracted from, data.

Information technology. Describes new facilities for the processing and distribution of information, resulting from the convergence of technical developments in computing and communications that in turn have been made possible by advances in microelectronics.

Initialise. To attribute specific values to variables before beginning a computation.

Input. Data and information supplied to the computer from its keyboard, cassette unit, disk unit or other input source.

Instruction. A single directive to a computer to perform a particular operation. A collection or sequence of instructions form a program.

Integrated circuit. An electronic circuit that can consist of a large number of components and is formed in miniature on a silicon chip, typically a few millimetres square.

Intelligent peripheral. A device that is linked to a computer and has its own computing ability.

Interactive. Permitting a continuous exchange of communication between user and computer.

Interface. A circuit or socket that makes signals between two items of hardware compatible and allows their interconnection.

Interpreter. A piece of software that translates one *high-level language* statement at a time into *machine code,* for execution by the computer.

I/O. Input/Output. Equipment enabling communication of data to and from a computer. Also, the data involved in these communications.

Iteration. The repeated execution of a series of instructions until some condition is satisfied.

J

Joystick. A device consisting of a shaft that swivels on a base. When manipulated by its user it transmits signals to the computer, thus enabling it to control the movement of an object on the screen. Often used in computer games, the joystick sometimes has a 'fire' button.

K

k. In the metric system, this represents $1000 (10^3)$, as, for instance, in kilometre (km) which is 1000 metres. However, since computers use the binary system (with base 2), K (written as a capital letter in this context) is taken as 1024, which is 2 raised to the tenth power (2^{10}).

Kbyte. The unit of measure for memory size, being 1024 bytes (see *k*). Typical memory sizes for microcomputers are 16 Kbytes, 32 Kbytes and 64 Kbytes.

Keyboard. An arrangement of marked pads that the user presses to enter characters. The arrangement of keys usually follows the layout of a standard typewriter.

L

LCD. Liquid Crystal Display. A display used on digital watches and calculators — and now several portable microcomputers — that is flat and consumes little power.

Light pen. A device, shaped like a pen and sensitive to light, that, when moved over a display screen, allows the user to feed information to the computer. It works like a pointer and allows the computer to know which part of the screen is being pointed to.

Line number. The number at the beginning of each line in a BASIC program — used purely to identify that line.

Lisp. List Processor Language. A high-level language much used in the world of artificial intelligence research.

Logic. The electronic components that carry out the elementary logical operations and functions, from which every operation of a computer is ultimately built up.

Logo. A high-level computer language. It is highly regarded as an educational aid, since it is simple enough to be learned even by very young children.

Loop. A sequence of instructions in a program that is executed repeatedly by the computer until a certain condition is satisfied.

Low-level language. A programming language in which each instruction corresponds to the computer's *machine code* instruction.

LSI. Large Scale Integration. The technology of packing large numbers of electronic components and circuits on a single silicon chip. Future generations of computers will use VLSI technology (Very Large Scale Integration).

M

Machine code. The programming language that is directly understood by a microprocessor, since all its commands are represented by patterns of binary digits.

Mainframe. A large computer.

Man-machine interface. The 'area' where the user and computer are exchanging information. At present this usually involves the use of a screen and keyboard. In the future, these may be replaced by, for instance, an input device which recognises the user's spoken commands, and *Speech synthesis.*

Matrix. An arrangement of data in the form of a grid or a table, technically termed a two-dimensional, rectangular array.

Memory. The internal store of the computer where programs and data are kept. The memory is divided into sections, each of which can be identified and accessed individually.

Memory map. A table showing how the various areas of memory (e.g. memory available to the user, screen memory, operating system, and so on) have been allocated in any particular machine and software configuration. As a general rule, these areas are defined by the manufacturer/s of the combined system.

Menu. A set list of choices given by a program. When many options are available the user may first be presented with a main menu from which other menus can be selected. A well-designed menu system can make a complex program simple to use.

Microprocessor. A complex integrated circuit that can be programmed to perform different tasks.

Modem. A contraction of Modulator-Demodulator. A device that allows a computer to transmit and receive data via a communications network, such as the telephone system.

Monitor. 1. A high quality visual display unit. 2. Software providing the fundamental set of commands needed to operate a computer system.

Mouse. A hand-operated device, connected electronically to the computer, that can be rolled across the surface of a desktop, causing a corresponding arrow or cursor to move on the screen.

N

Network. A system of communication channels connecting various units, such as computers, and that allows them to exchange data.

Noise. Random fluctuations in an electrical system, which distort or corrupt signals. Noise can be deliberately generated by some computers for use as sound effects, such as explosions, in games.

Non-numeric computation. Computing by the manipulation of symbols rather than numbers only. This is useful for areas such as *Expert systems* where facts and knowledge are being manipulated as opposed to just words and numbers.

Number system. Any system for representing numeric values and quantities.

Numeric keypad. A section of the keyboard in which the number keys are grouped together as on a calculator, to facilitate entry of numeric data.

O

OCR. Optical Character Recognition. A means of reading printed or written characters with an optical scanning device and suitably coding them so that they can be input automatically to a computer.

Operating system. The software that controls and supervises all the internal operations of a computer.

Output. Data and information leaving the computer; for example, the results of a program to be displayed on the screen, sent to a printer, stored, or sent to some other device.

Overwrite. To write data to a part of the memory where information is already stored, thereby replacing the original contents.

P

Paddle. A rigid, hand-held controller with a 'trigger' button, mainly for use with games (see *Joystick*).

Parallel interface. A data transmission device in which each bit in a byte has its own wire, allowing them to be transmitted simultaneously. (See *Serial interface*.)

Pascal. A high-level programming language that encourages *Structured programming*.

PEEK. The function in BASIC that is used to examine the contents of a specific memory location.

Peripheral. An accessory that, once connected, will increase the capabilities of a computer.

Piracy. The unauthorised copying of software (and hardware) for financial gain.

Pixel. Contraction of **picture cell**. The smallest pattern of dots on the display screen that can be accessed individually by a graphics programmer; hence it is the building block of images.

Plotter. A computer-controlled device that moves one pen or more across a sheet of paper to draw pictures or 'write' characters.

POKE. The statement in BASIC that is used to place a value in a specific memory location.

Port. A socket through which signals bearing data can enter or leave a computer; the visible part of an *Interface*.

Portability. 1. Relating to computers that are small and light enough to be carried easily and used at different locations, often using batteries as a source of power. 2. Property of software that can be run on more than one kind of computer.

Printed circuit board. A sheet of plastic with metallic connectors formed in strips on it that link together the electronic components.

Printer. A device for printing out text, results and program listings under the control of a computer. Some printers can also produce graphs and diagrams.

Program. A sequence of instructions written in a computer language that, when executed, causes the computer to perform a required task.

Program development. The analysis of an intended computer application and the program writing and editing that results.

Programming language. A set of special command words and rules designed to describe to a computer how it should carry out a computation.

Prolog. A programming language that describes what a computer should do rather than how it should do it.

PROM. **P**rogrammable **R**ead-**O**nly **M**emory. A chip that is programmable with the use of a special device, and then becomes a read-only chip, or *ROM*.

Prompt. A visible indication from a computer that it requires a response from the operator.

PSU. **P**ower **S**upply **U**nit. A device that converts the household electricity supply into the form needed by a computer.

Q

QWERTY keyboard. A computer keyboard with its keys arranged in the same way as those of a standard typewriter keyboard. The name derives from the sequence of the first six letters of the top row of alphabetical characters.

R

Radix. See *Base*.

RAM. **R**andom **A**ccess **M**emory. Memory in which stored information can be altered by the user. Its contents can be examined, or read, and also overwritten — that is, replaced by other information. This type of memory is known more accurately as read-write memory. The amount of RAM available determines how much memory the programmer can use to store programs and data. Dynamic RAM needs to be refreshed every few milliseconds to retain its contents. When the computer is switched off, the contents are lost. Static RAM retains its information.

Random number. A number generated in such a way that its value cannot be predicted. Random numbers are used in games, simulation and mathematical operations.

Raster. The patterns of horizontal rows in which *pixels* are displayed on a screen.

Real-time operation. The mode of operating a computer where it controls some activity — for example, an industrial process — as it happens.

Recursion. A series of repeated routines within a program in which the result of each repetition depends on the outcome of the previous one. The routine recalls itself until the task is completed.

Refresh. 1. To recreate the display on a screen as new pictures arrive. 2. To renew the information in *RAM*, without changing it, by passing an electric current.

Register. A special memory location (often within the micro-processor itself) that is used for temporary storage.

Remark. A statement included in a program, usually in the form of a comment written in plain English, that is not executed by the computer but which is included to provide assistance to the user.

Reserved word. A command word forming part of a computer language which, therefore, cannot be used, for example, as a name for a *Variable*.

Resolution. The amount of detail in which images can be displayed, determined by the number of squares into which the display grid is divided. High-resolution graphics give a lot of detail, while low-resolution graphics are 'chunky' and less detailed, the component parts of the image being more in evidence.

Reverse Polish notation. A notation for writing arithmetic expressions in which operators (plus, minus, multiply and divide signs) follow the values to which they apply. For example, A + B is entered A B +.

RF Modulator. A device that converts the video output from a computer into a form suitable for feeding into the aerial socket of a TV.

ROM. **R**ead-**O**nly **M**emory. Memory in which information is stored permanently. Its content can only be examined, or read; it cannot be altered. ROM is used typically to provide facilities that are always needed by the computer. The BASIC ROMs that are found in many microcomputers, for example, enable them to 'understand' BASIC.

Routine. A sequence of instructions for carrying out a well-defined and frequently encountered task.

RS232C. One of the standard *Interfaces* used in the transfer of data between a computer and a peripheral device.

RUN. The command in BASIC that instructs the computer to begin executing a program.

S

Screen editor. Software that permits editing of text displayed on the screen.

Scrolling. The automatic upward movement of the information on a screen to allow new information to be displayed at the bottom of the screen. Sideways scrolling is used in some graphics so that a scene can be 'scanned'.

Serial interface. A data transmission device through which bits are sent sequentially.

Simulation. Representation by means of a computer program of a physical system or process, e.g. flight simulation.

Soft key. A key on the keyboard that, by use of software, can be made to perform a specific function, defined by the user, each time it is pressed.

Software. The programs run by or associated with the operation of a computer.

Software engineering. The disciplines involved in writing software.

Sound generator. The facilities possessed by many home computers for producing sounds.

Speech recognition. The identification of commands and other messages by a computer from an operator's spoken words.

Speech synthesis. The production of simulated speech by a device under the control of a computer.

Spreadsheet. A program intended primarily for forecasting and financial planning. It provides an electronic representation of a large table of numbers, entered by the user, that show, say, financial results and projections. The screen becomes a 'window' through which any part of the sheet may be viewed.

Sprite. A character, or group of characters, that can be displayed and kept moving at a specified speed by the computer.

Stack. A part of memory where data can be stored continually, but where only the last item stored can be retrieved at any one time.

Statement. An instruction, or sequence of instructions, in a computer program.

String. See *Character string*.

String handling. The manipulation of character strings.

Structured language. A computer language that, if used properly, constructs programs that are easily understood and modified.

Structured programming. The discipline of writing computer programs that are compact, efficient and easy to understand and thus easy to modify and correct.

Subroutine. A self-contained part of a program that can be called up and run by other parts of the program. It is usually written to perform a task that is needed frequently by the main program.

Syntax error. An error that occurs when a program statement has

been incorrectly written.

T

Terminal. An *I/O* device, generally a display screen plus keyboard, connected to a central computer.

Text. The alphanumeric characters making up a document or conveying a message.

Truth table. A table that specifies the operation of a *Gate* by showing its output for all possible combinations of inputs.

Turtle. A wheeled mechanical robot (floor turtle) or a (usually triangular) shape on the screen (screen turtle), the movements of which can be controlled by commands from a computer.

Turtle trail. A floor *Turtle* can draw a line with a pen to mark the path it has been programmed to describe, while

a screen turtle can leave a trace showing the line it has been made to take on the video display unit. Both of these may be called a turtle trail.

U

ULA. Uncommitted Logic Array. A type of integrated circuit suitable for many different applications, the actual functions of which can be specified comparatively late in the design of the device.

Utility. Any complete program used to perform a common operation, such as sorting data or copying files.

V

Variable. An item included in a computer program that can be identified by name, but whose actual value may be made to vary during the execution of a program.

VDU. Visual Display Unit. The piece of equipment that provides the screen display for a computer. It is usually any ordinary television set or a specially designed unit called a monitor. The latter, though more expensive, will offer greater clarity and definition of picture.

Video. The electronic signals and circuitry producing the display on a *VDU*.

W

Winchester. A rigid magnetic *Disk* that is housed in a hermetically sealed container for greater protection of data.

Word. A collection of binary units treated as one unit that can be stored in a single memory location.

Word processor. A combination of software and hardware for writing, editing and printing out letters and documents.

Index